THE ORGANIZATIONAL CONTEXT OF MANAGEMENT ACCOUNTING

THE ORGANIZATIONAL CONTEXT OF MANAGEMENT ACCOUNTING

Robert H. Chenhall,

Senior Lecturer in Accounting,
Macquairie University, Sidney

Graeme L. Harrison,

Senior Lecturer in Accounting and
Financial Management,
Macquairie University, Sidney

David J. H. Watson,

Professor of Commerce,
University of Queensland, Australia

Pitman

Boston • London • Melbourne • Toronto

PITMAN PUBLISHING INC.
1020 Plain Street, Marshfield, Massachusetts 02050

Pitman Books Limited
39 Parker Street, London WC2B5PB

Associated Companies
Pitman Publishing Pty Ltd., Melbourne
Pitman Publishing New Zealand Ltd., Wellington
Copp Clark Pitman, Toronto

Library of Congress Cataloging in Publication Data
Main entry under title:
The Organizational context of management accounting.
1. Managerial accounting—Addresses, essays, lectures.
2. Cost accounting—Addresses, essays, lectures.
3. Management—Addresses, essays, lectures.
I. Chenhall, R.H. II. Harrison, Graeme L. III. Watson, David J.H.
HF5635.O74 658.1'511 81–844
ISBN 0–273–01644–X (pbk.) AACR2

Manufactured in the U.S.A.

10 9 8 7 6 5 4 3 2 1

Table of Contents

Foreword

It is well recognized that accounting has played a crucial role in the development of modern society. At a fundamental level, the existence of double entry bookkeeping is a necessary condition for the collection, processing, and transmission of financial data concerning the performance of large-scale economic entities. This, in turn, is a prerequisite for decision making and control of these entities. At a higher level, the existence of financial statements is a requirement for the development of widespread ownership of corporate securities, and, in turn, for the accumulation of the vast pools of assets which are held by some modern industrial and commercial organizations.

During the past decade, our concept of the field of accounting as well as the nature of accounting education and research has undergone significant change. Scholars, managers, accounting practitioners, and students have come to recognize that it is necessary to view accounting as more than merely a technology for recording, summarizing, and presenting economic transactions in financial terms; rather, we must understand and appreciate the broader role of accounting in organizations and society as well. We have come to realize that the *medium of accounting* itself impacts human thought and action; that the boundries of accounting are not static and may be redefined; and that accounting, though very much a measurement system, is not free from issues of social values. New dimensions of accounting have been recognized, and the very terminology of accounting has changed to bring forth "Social Accounting," "Human Resource Accounting," and "Behavioral Accounting."

After more than a decade of change, the field of accounting is still in transition. Yet the new perspectives have begun to mature. The *raison d'etre* of the Pitman series on the Role of Accounting in Organizations and Society is to present a set of books and monographs by leading scholars and educators which deal with accounting from this new perspective. Our interest is in presenting a series of books which deal with major aspects of accounting with an appreciation for the organizational, institutional, and societal implications of accounting, as well as its technological dimensions.

The Organizational Context of Management Accounting by Chenhall, Harrison, and Watson is the first book in this new Pitman series. The book focuses upon contemporary management accounting and control problems from the perspective of modern organizations. The authors' basic premise is that accounting and control issues must be viewed in the broader context of the organizational and external environments in which the management accounting system operates.

The authors have drawn upon the contingency theory of organizations as the basis for their own conceptual framework for organizing this book. The book itself is a skillful intergration of readings and text.

The textual material represents a substantive contribution in itself. The authors have developed frameworks for each part of the book; these frameworks present their own approaches as well as a synthesis of the major research themes in organizational and accounting literature. The readings comprise a rich set of ideas, and have been selected to complement the textual material.

In my view, the book provides sophisticated and penetrating analysis of a set of major issues involved in the design and use of accounting information and control systems. As such, it makes a contribution to the continuing development of management accounting, as well as to accounting education.

Eric G. Flamholtz
Series Editor

Preface

Traditionally the design of management accounting systems (MAS) has involved consideration of technical issues of systems design, and behavioural issues of implementation. However, it has only been in recent years that MAS design has been extended to recognise formally broader issues from modern organizational research.

The purpose of this book is to provide an analysis of contemporary management accounting informational and control systems issues, drawing on developments in organizational theory. The introduction to the book provides a way of thinking about these developments and concludes that a contingency type approach forms a useful basis for examining management accounting systems.

The readings in the book are organized using such a contingency theme and emphasise that MAS design should consider the contextual setting within which the system operates. This setting is described by constructs that increase in their level of specificity.

At the broadest level we are concerned with the importance of interrelationships between the organization and the external environment. At the next level, aspects of the organization's internal characteristics relevant to MAS design are considered; and finally we consider the importance of interactions between the individual and the management accounting system.

These levels of specificity provide the framework for organization of the book into its four parts. The readings in each part are preceded by textual material which has a dual purpose. One is to present foundational material from organizational and behavioural theory relevant to MAS design, the other and primary purpose is to allow examination of the interactions between management accounting and organizational and behavioural theory. Because the emphasis in the textual material is on the links between MAS and organizational theory, we do not attempt to provide foundational organizational or management accounting material in depth. Traditional textbooks in each of these areas may be used to obtain additional detail.

We wish to acknowledge the cooperation of the authors of articles included in this book and the assistance of publishers of the journals from which the articles have been reprinted. In particular, we recognise the importance of the journal *Accounting, Organizations and Society* which has provided a valuable forum for the generation and communication of research in this area.

Introduction

An essential aspect of the study of organizations is the consideration of their managerial decision making and control processes. Management accounting systems are an integral part of these processes because their role is to provide information to managers.

Due to the dynamic nature of the environment of contemporary organizations, these decision making and control processes have become increasingly complex. Management accounting information systems need to recognize this, and need to be sufficiently elaborate and flexible so that managers can adapt their organizations to the environmental complexity. However, textbook approaches to management accounting systems (MAS) design have traditionally given little explicit consideration to the varied informational requirements of decision making in these situations.

The approach presented in this book is that MAS design should recognize the organizational context within which decisions are made; this context incorporates both internal and external dimensions which operate in dynamic and complicated ways. An important aspect of this which is stressed in many readings in this book is the two-way nature of this interaction. In one direction, the organizational setting influences MAS design; in the other direction, the accounting system may affect aspects of the decision and control setting.

The purpose of this introduction is to briefly trace the development of organization theory during the last century. Although the theoretical analysis of organizations considerably pre-dates this period, approaches during this century have concentrated on the administrative, rather than the political, aspects of organizations (Pugh, 1971, p. 9), and have had considerable impact on the development of management accounting. An extended discussion of current thinking in both organizational analysis and management accounting is contained in the textual material that introduces each of the individual parts of the book. This material provides a basis for evaluating the readings.

The primary purpose of this book is to examine the interaction of management accounting and organizational theory; consequently, we cannot provide the details which are necessary to consider each of these disciplines in depth. For in-depth study, readers must turn to the traditional textbooks in each of these areas. Suggested references to these texts are given where appropriate.

HISTORICAL DEVELOPMENT OF ORGANIZATION THEORY

This section traces the evolution of the theory of organizational behaviour during the last century. Our perspective concentrates on shifts in the way that organization theorists have taken account of the organization's environment, and the quickening rate of change which has been experienced in recent years.

Increases in the rate of social change have been traced back 5000 years (Huxley, 1942, pp. viii–ix). In modern history, the Industrial Revolution marked one period of very rapid change in industrial techniques, technical inventions, and innovations (Pollard, 1965, p.124). Similarly, the phenomenon of the "accelerative thrust" in the rate of environmental change has been observed by several social commentators (Toffler, 1970; Boulding, 1964; Snow, 1959), as being particularly pronounced in the current century, and has become an explicit construct of modern organization theory (Bennis, Benne and Chin, 1969). The orientation of current organization theory is that an organization interacts with, reacts to, and attempts to shape a changing, sometimes turbulent environment. Technical ways of describing an organization's environment will be examined later in this introduction, and in relevant sections of the book.

Developments in Organization Theory

The starting point for our analysis of organization theory is the scientific management movement. The central theme of scientific management was that work—particularly tasks performed by production workers—could be studied systematically, with the objective being the development of the "one best way" of performing those tasks.

Some principles of scientific management, formulated by Taylor (1911) and summarised in most organizational texts (Dessler, 1976, p. 26; Khandwalla, 1977, p. 146) include:

1. observation and analysis through time study to set the optimal production rate;
2. scientific selection of the best person for the job, and training in the procedures he is expected to follow;
3. payment on an incentive basis using a differential piece rate system; and
4. division of work between managers and workers with managers having the responsibility for work planning and preparation.

Scientific management theorists attempted to formulate organizational analyses which conceptually closed off the organization from its environment, and consequently did not accommodate differential rates of environmental change. Some commentators have suggested that this closure was a result of a relatively stable environment (Dessler, 1976, p. 28).

Scientific management was concerned mainly with analysis of production and did not address broader administrative issues. Administrative theorists sought to develop prescriptions related to broader issues, such as planning, organizing, leadership, coordination and control. Fayol (1916) and Gulick and Urwick (1937) formulated principles of management such as unity of command, distinctions between line and staff, departmentalization by purpose, process, person and place, authority and responsibility, and span of control.

The management functions addressed by administrative theorists included considerations that involved the firm's interaction with its environment. This was a considerable broadening of analysis from the issues of production studied by scientific management theorists. The founders of administrative theory, however, still tended to close the organization off from its environment. It was implicitly assumed that production tasks, the availability of inputs, and the disposal of outputs were not highly problematic.

Weber (1946), a theorist researching organizational issues at the same time as the early administrative theorists, did recognize the environmental context of organizations. Weber's central consideration was the design of an organizational form which was capable of administering increasingly dynamic environments. He described the ideal form of organization as "bureaucracy". This ideal form involved the following:

1. dividing tasks according to function;
2. possessing a well-defined system of procedures for dealing with tasks;
3. possessing a well-defined hierarchy of authority to coordinate and handle exceptions;
4. possessing a system of rules which defined the rights and duties of position encumbents;
5. using technical competence as the only criterion for selection and promotion; and
6. maintaining an impersonal (i.e. unbiased) approach to interpersonal relationships.

The word "bureaucracy" has a layman's connotation of inefficiency. It is important to note that Weber's concept was a strictly technical description of an ideal form which was appropriate for the demands placed on the administrators of large organizations. While Weber's theory was a response to the need for organizations to react quickly to environmental change, it still involved a single "best" organizational form.

While there is some evidence that large organizations were developing innovative management and organizational processes in response to environmental changes which were occurring over the period from 1920–1960 (Chandler, 1962), it was not until the 1960s that the effect of environmental situations was examined by organizational theorists. Research by authors such as Chandler (1962), Burns and Stalker (1961), Emery and Trist (1960), and Lawrence and Lorsch (1967) recognized the potential effect of the environmental context on the administrative processes. This research, along with other works, formed the basis for a contingency framework for examining organizations. Before considering the contingency approach, however, several important developments over the first few decades of this century will be reviewed.

As we have seen, scientific management and administrative theories provided a framework for guiding organizational design and for conducting applied research on improving the efficiency of organizations. The environmental context was not explicitly considered in these approaches. Further, the behavioural element, at least at the worker and administrator levels, was addressed through implicit assumptions, which were subsequently challenged as being insufficiently complex and comprehensive. Studies carried out by Roethlisberger and Mayo demonstrated the importance of an alternative, fuller perspective on the role of human behaviour in organizational performance. They showed the significance for individual performance of such factors as the social (as well as the physical) environment of the work setting, and the group norms that developed among workers.

The pioneering work of Mayo was extended in the human relations and human resources schools of organizational theorists. Researchers including Lewin (1951), Homans (1950), Likert (1961), McGregor (1960), Argyris (1964), and Maslow (1954) sought to incorporate an explicit consideration of the needs and aspirations of individual workers and work groups in organizational analysis. Their research led to attempts to improve the decision making process in organizations (particularly the decisions that affect the work environment of workers and middle management), and to describe better ways of structuring and leading work groups.

While the broader aspects of management and the organization's environment were not completely ignored by these researchers, they were not central features of their theories. In addition, like scientific management and administrative theorists, they tended to suggest that there was a "best way" to administer the organization. Aspects such as participatory management, democratic leadership and a pleasant work environment were seen to be invariably preferable to, for example, an autocratic leadership and more hierarchically structured decision making. The variables of interest had shifted from the scientific management and administrative theories, but not the underlying drive to establish a universal "best way" of designing an organization.

The contributions of several other writers were important to the development of organization theory during this time. Theorists such as Follett (1924) and Barnard (1938) recognized the importance of some of the concepts which were developed within the human relations and human resources schools. However, Barnard particularly extended approaches beyond a human relations orientation, and sought to incorporate the organization's internal system and its interaction with its environment in the analysis. Barnard viewed the organization as a cooperative system, and proposed that organizational analysis be approached through the study of the decision making information flows.

The approach to organizational analysis through its decision processes formed a basis for the Carnegie-Mellon school of thought. Before the Carnegie research, the dominant concept of man's decision making process came from economic theory—that of the rational man striving to maximize his satisfaction or his expected utility. Simon (1957), by contrast, viewed man as being intentionally rational, adaptive and concerned with satisfying rather than maximizing. He saw man as possessing a limited capacity to perceive information, processing information sequentially rather than simultaneously, perceiving reality selectively rather than totally, being goal directed, and having a limited capability to endure cognitive strain (uncertainty).

On the basis of these assumptions about individual behaviour, the Carnegie theorists considered the decision making process to be a search for simple or proximate solutions. This is the concept of "bounded rationality" (Simon, 1957). The satisficing principle proposes that a decision maker stops searching for a solution once a "satisfactory" solution, rather than an optimal solution, is found. The description of the decision making process by March and Simon (1958) was one of an individual applying heuristics to a decision problem. This implies sequential attention to multiple, conflicting goals, limited planning, and in terms of traditional economic theory, suboptimal decision making.

The Carnegie research represented a major step in understanding administrative man, and in developing explanations of how individuals react to uncertainty and to the decision demands placed upon them. Examples of later approaches developed from foundations similar to the Carnegie school include Lindblom's (1959) concept of "muddling through," and Cohen, March and Olsen's (1972) "garbage-can" model of decision making.

THE CONTINGENCY THEORY FRAMEWORK

The theories which have been cited so far do not explicitly examine how organizations react to differential environments. This aspect was approached by systems and contingency theorists.

The depression of the 1930s forced many companies to develop new products and technological processes to counteract the decline in demand for existing products. The Second World War also required and produced a significant degree of technological advance. The post-war period witnessed a tremendous economic expansion which was fueled, in part, by the technological progress of the 1930s and the war period. The rate of change quickened substantially, and the environment faced by many organizations became increasingly uncertain and diverse. The pace of change has become even more critical during the 1960s and 1970s (Toffler, 1970); consequently, the need to respond to change has become an increasingly important organizational requirement.

As organizational theorists recognized the complex and varied nature of an organization's environment and the diversity of possible adaptive responses, their analyses developed to explicitly incorporate the context of organizational decision making, and the possibility for situation specific responses rather than universalist prescriptions.

Systems analysis provided an orientation that focused on the need for organizations to develop adaptive decision responses with sufficient variety to counter environmental variety. Ashby (1960) refers to this as the generation of "requisite variety". A similar concept was developed by contingency theorists, who attempted to identify the aspects of the organization's environment that influence managers' adaptive responses. The particular response that concerned early contingency theorists was the formal organization structure appropriate to the context of the manager's decision situation. However, in more recent years, the general orientation of contingency theory has been applied to other aspects of management.

Several texts have applied contingency theory to organizational design (Dessler, 1976; Khandwalla, 1977); useful collections of works on systems research are found in Baker (1973) and Emery (1969), and on contingency theory in Kast and Rosenzweig (1973). Part 1 of this book explores the significance and limitations of these approaches to MAS design. At this stage, however, we will briefly review a few contingency studies to indicate the ways in which organizational context may be described.

Several early works that drew attention to environmental influence were built on the notion that organizations are open systems interacting with their environment. The model of environment developed by Emery and Trist (1963) is an example of this approach. Emery and Trist describe various critical linkages among organizations and the environment. These are illustrated in Figure 1.

In Figure 1, the L_{11} cell represents activities (such as information flows, interpersonal relations, product movements) that occur solely within an organization. Cost accounting data for evaluating the efficiency of workers on a production line is an example of information flows occurring totally within an organization. These flows are controlled completely within the organization, and when examining or using them in decision making, one can safely ignore any environmental impacts.

The L_{22} cell represents activities or interactions that take place immedi-

L_{11}	L_{12}
L_{21}	L_{22}

L indicates some potentially "lawful connection" between organization and environment.

Suffix 1 refers to the organization

Suffix 2 refers to the environment

FIGURE 1. Connections between Organizations and Environment (Emery & Trist, 1963)

ately within the environment which have no obvious connection to the organization. In essence, these environmental activities do not directly relate to the activities of organizations.

It is cells L_{12} and L_{21} which are of particular interest. Here the environment can impact organization decisions and vice versa. Organizations are concerned with those aspects of the environment that impact on them because these determine what the firm has to anticipate, and the way in which it has to adapt. Organizations are also concerned with the way in which they may influence the environment, because this provides them with the potential to control their operating situation, rather than merely react to it.

It is these aspects of environment that have concerned contingency theorists. Some contingency theorists have separated a "task", or "specific" environment from a more "general" environment. The task environment refers to those factors which affect the on-going operations of the organization, while the general environment includes broad social and economic factors affecting all organizations.

The interdependencies between the organization and the environment, as depicted in cells L_{12} and L_{21} in Figure 1, can be seen as arising from three major choices made by organizations. The first choice is the area of competence; that is, the organization's product and market areas. The second choice is the technology. A distinction which can be made here is between capital intensive and labour technologies; for example, while one may lead to greater interdependencies between the organization and labour groups, the other may lead to greater interdependencies between the organization and financial intermediaries. Finally, the choice of where to locate influences the immediate environmental interdependencies; for example, which particular individuals and organizations interact with the enterprise.

Having identified parts of the environment in which managers of organizations are interested, we need to characterize the way in which environment influences the manager's decision making tasks. Various researchers have developed ways of thinking about environmental pressure and its resulting influence on decision styles and processes. One of the first aspects of environment which was identified by contingency theorists was its uncertain and unpredictable nature. In 1961, Burns and Stalker conducted an empirical investigation that identified environmental uncertainty as a key variable. These researchers identified two styles of management that were seen to be appropriate to different levels of uncertainty. These styles were distinguished in terms of their level of formality and flexibility. The highly formal or mechanistic style involved reliance on formal structuring of authority and communications. The alternative style was termed organic, and involved highly flexible communications and authority based on situational expertise rather than the formal structure. The authors identified environmental uncertainty in terms of the levels of market and technological change faced by firms. Firms facing rapid change could best adapt by employing an organic style, while the mechanistic form was the most appropriate style for firms facing more stable conditions.

The notion that different management processes are contingent upon the levels of environmental uncertainty was strikingly demonstrated in a U.S. study undertaken in the mid-1960s by Lawrence and Lorsch (1967). They observed that different parts of a firm face different levels of uncertainty in their task environments. The way in which the different parts of a firm develop effective administrative structural arrangements is strongly influenced by the levels of uncertainty. Lawrence and Lorsch argued that organizational success is influenced by the application of structural arrangements appropriate to the environmental conditions. The nature of these structural arrangements is further discussed in Part 2.

Since these studies, several other research efforts have examined the notion of environmental uncertainty together with other dimensions of environment. Perhaps the most important study is the theoretical work by Thompson (1967). Thompson described two aspects of environment: a "stable-dynamic" dimension and a "homogeneous-heterogeneous" dimension. The stable-dynamic dimension is concerned with how quickly elements in the task environment are changing. If the critical elements stay relatively the same over a reasonable period of time, the environment is termed "stable"; if the elements change quickly, the environment is characterized as "dynamic". The homogeneous-heterogeneous dimension is concerned with the diversity of elements facing the organization, i.e., the similarity or dissimilarity between elements. Several approaches to developing contingency models for MAS design have applied environmental classification schemes based on Thompson's work (Hayes, 1977; Watson, 1975). The article by Hayes (1977) is included in Part 2 of this book.

During the 1970s contingency theorists developed schemes that identified additional dimensions of environment. One of the difficulties in interpreting this research is a lack of consistency in the specification of these constructs and their measurement. The following example illustrates some of these dimensions. An increase in complexity caused by firms' diversification into a variety of activities was studied by Chandler (1962), Channon (1973), and Rumelt (1974). The writings of these authors have been referred to as the "strategy and structure" studies and are discussed as a contingency model in an organizational behaviour text by Dessler (1976). Khandwalla (1977) also references the "diverse" nature of the firm's market. These notions of complexity and diversity are similar to Thompson's homogeneous-heterogeneous dimensions.

Environmental "hostility", "stress", "restrictiveness" or "aggressiveness" have also been referenced. These aspects of environment involve factors such as the availability of opportunities, and the extent to which the firm is manipulated or controlled by other organizations, including competitors, suppliers, customers, social and government bodies. A useful discussion of these more recent environmental classification schemes may be found in Khandwalla (1977, Ch. 9).

Contingency theorists have argued that, in addition to the external environment, organization design (including MAS design) should be consistent with the internal characteristics of the organization. The most important studies of internal context have been developed by authors who considered the design of organizational structure. Two dimensions that have been widely examined by these researchers are size and technology (Blau & Schoenherr, 1971; Child & Mansfield, 1972; Harvey, 1968; Perrow, 1967; Pugh et al, 1969[a], 1969[b]). The studies by Pugh et al provide a comprehensive array of internal contextual variables which include, in addition to size and technology, factors such as origins and history, ownership and control, location, resources, dependence of sub-units on a parent body and charter (goals or organizational purpose).

The discussion above has briefly reviewed several works that have used contingency theory with the purpose of demonstrating the way in which environmental context may be characterized. To gain a greater appreciation of the nature of these dimensions and the problems of measuring them, it is recommended that the reader consult textbooks on organizational design that review these works in detail. See for example, Jackson and Morgan (1978), Khandwalla (1977), Dessler (1976), Hall (1977), Mintzberg (1979), Hellriegel and Slocum (1978), and O'Shaughnessy (1976).

The textual material in Parts 1 and 2 considers systems and contingency approaches to organizational design in more detail, and discusses their implications for management accounting.

ORGANIZATION THEORY AND MANAGEMENT ACCOUNTING

In this section we will consider the issues arising from organization theory which have been recognized as influencing MAS design. These have, in the main, concerned "structure" problems and "people" problems.

Structure Problems

Management accounting has been closely linked with the questions of organizational structure. Organizational theorists have studied aspects of structure that formally allocate work tasks to different groups of individuals throughout the organization, and provide a means of directing and controlling the implementation of these tasks. Several early accounting studies sought to examine how accounting systems might vary between different types of structural arrangements.

The first study which focused clearly on both organizational behaviour and accounting concerns was the seminal work of Simon, Guetzkow, Kozmetsky and Tyndall (1954). These researchers studied seven organizations, seeking insight into the question, "What makes a controller's department effective?" They were particularly interested in how effectiveness varied with the centralized or decentralized nature of the organization. By centralization and decentralization the authors meant, ". . . centralized to the extent that decisions are made at relatively high levels in the organization; decentralized to the extent that discretion and authority to make important decisions are delegated by top management to lower levels of executive authority". The study examined the degree of centralization and decentralization of some of the broad accounting functions of controllership in relation to the degree of centralization or decentralization within operating units.

The researchers concentrated on three internal accounting functions that relate to how accounting data are used, namely:

1. score card questions, "Am I doing well or badly?";
2. attention-directing questions, "What problems should I look into?"; and
3. problem-solving questions, "Of several ways of doing the job, which is best?" (Simon et al, 1954, p.3).

A fourth fairly routine function, record-keeping, was also examined. What is particularly impressive about this research is the fact that even today, leading managerial accounting textbooks, such as Horngren (1977), still explain the controllership function based on these four functions and utilize the viewpoint and data base established by Simon et al.

As indicated earlier, contingency theory research on organizations suggests that the collection, provision and determination of requisite decision information will be affected by a wide variety of situational and behavioural factors. The contingent nature of the results of the Simon et al study can be seen in the following significant conclusions:

1. for the attention directing function, it is essential for the controller's department to develop direct and active channels of communication with operating executives at those points in the organization where operations are being measured;
2. for the score card function, there needs to be a close and direct relationship between accounting and operating personnel;
3. for the problem solving function, the capability for conducting special studies is emphasized by, for example, interdisciplinary teams that include members of the controller's staff; and
4. for the record-keeping function, the accessibility of documents and reliability of source records are the important aspects when considering centralization versus decentralization of the records function. (At the time of the study this result pointed to geographical decentralization of the source records. However, today, with the advent of sophisticated computers and time sharing facilities, this implication is somewhat questionable. It may have a greater implication for data bank structure rather than location. Record-keeping is particularly important because the other three functions require accurate, reliable and accessible data.)

A second significant paper, which related accounting information to issues of structure, was that of Golembiewski (1964). Golembiewski examined the role of an accounting department in firms that have traditional organizational structures which specify functions and processes, centralize authority and provide the means for detailed supervision. Accounting was seen as providing information to chief executives for the purposes of "scorekeeping", "problem solving" and "attention directing". Golembiewski demonstrated how the identification of accounting as a "staff" function which served chief executives rather than operating line managers limits its usefulness. He argued that structural innovations which involve the establishment of fully autonomous, decentralized sub-units, together with the location of the accounting department within these decentralized entities, provide a structure whereby accounting can still generate information necessary for scorekeeping, and be particularly effective in providing relevant data for attention directing and problem solving. Questions of the location of accounting departments are still addressed in many management accounting textbooks and in practice.

A conclusion that may be drawn from the two studies reviewed above is that the design of information systems and the design of entities that control or operate these systems must take account of contingencies operating on the total organization, in order that there can be a matching of the information system with the organization. For example, failure to recognize the nature of certain interdependent relationships may lead to the collection, analysis and consideration of cost data based on inappropriate structural assumptions, and the consequent invalid assignment of responsibility.

The first function researched by Simon et al (1954) provides another example. The question "Am I doing well or badly?" implies measurable, specific, meaningful and attainable goals, ends that are organizationally important, understood by all parties, viewed as achievable by all parties and which can be translated into specific actions. Many behavioural problems arise from this analysis. How standards are to be established, who should participate in their establishment, what elements of performance are important, and how they should be measured are some of the more apparent ones. These types of questions, which have been researched by organization theorists, are part of the larger set of problems addressed by accountants in their attempt to understand and implement information systems.

In Part 2, the meaning of organizational structure, and its implications for management accounting systems design, are further explored.

People Problems

Caplan (1971) argued that management accounting, a product of the interactions among engineering, management theory and economic theory, began with no explicit concepts of human behaviour and no definitive basis for examining how "people problems" were linked to the management accounting system. Rather, management accounting implicitly absorbed the behavioural assumptions underlying the disciplines from which it developed.

The scientific management theorists referred to earlier were concerned with establishing engineering standards of efficiency for jobs, based on the assumptions that each job could be analyzed into its fundamental parts, and the most efficient method of performing these parts could then be devised. It was a short step to the application of costs to these engineering standards, beginning with labour costs, then material costs, until the present situation where cost standards can be developed for a wide range of manufacturing, marketing and distribution activities. There are many similarities between cost standards and other rules and routines in organizations. They are used as coordinating and control devices in most organizations, and measure the efficiency of individuals and groups through the comparison of actual performance with pre-determined standards.

From this development came some of the implicit assumptions of what Caplan called a "traditional management accounting model of the firm" (Caplan, 1971, p. 17). For example, the accounting system is often viewed as a control device which is aimed at allowing management to identify and correct undesirable performance.

Other behavioural assumptions of the traditional management accounting model were derived from economic theory. These assumptions were based on the concepts of rationality and maximization in decision making, and did not allow for perceptual and other human information processing limitations. In addition, management accounting implicitly accepted a particular model of individual motivation which was based on monetary rewards and penalties.

Contributions of the human relations, human resources, and Carnegie-Mellon schools directed attention to the greater complexity of human behaviour, and to specific study of the interactions of the organization and its systems with the individuals. For management accounting, this development led to considerable research into questions of the behavioural and motivational impact of budgetary planning and control systems, standard cost systems, and the processes of establishing budgets and standards.

One question which was related to individual motivation was if economic incentives did not sufficiently encapsulate motivational forces, what additional factors were necessary for a fuller understanding of motivation? This question was significant in that it carried implications for the organization's incentive system, and also for the accounting based performance evaluation system which needed to recognize and reflect the important factors.

Another question concerned the use of budgetary and standard cost systems as coordination and communication mechanisms, as well as control mechanisms. If human perceptual and information processing activities were complex, how could the MAS designer ensure that managers' objectives would be effectively communicated through the budget and standard cost systems, and that organizational members would accept and attempt to achieve those objectives?

Examination of these and related behavioural questions over the last two decades has led to acceptance of an important relationship between the management accounting information and control system, and the decision making behaviour of managers and employees at all levels in the organization. Hopwood (1974, pp. xi–xii) has noted that "it is impossible to deal adequately with accounting problems without also considering the motivations, values and behaviours of the human members of the enterprise".

Because of the importance of the behavioural implications of management accounting systems, recent accounting research has formally examined theories and concepts relevant to individual and group behaviour and motivation in the basic behavioural disciplines of psychology, social psychology and sociology. The third part of this book is concerned with the behavioural dimensions of MAS design. It develops the contingency framework first by demonstrating that MAS design is dependent upon individual and group variables, and second by examining how the effect of these variables on the management accounting system may, in turn, depend upon organizational contextual factors.

CONCLUSION

Much of the empirical work which has examined modern contingency theories of organizations in recent years emphasizes the environment, which has been defined in various ways, as the major problem facing complex organizations. The environment, along with other internal contingencies such as technology, size and structure, appears to have considerable influence on internal organizational processes and decision making.

The readings in this book are organized along a contingency theme. That is, it is suggested that analysis of MAS design should take into account the organizational context. This context is approached through constructs that use different levels of analysis.

At the broadest level, readings are considered that stress the importance of the organization's interrelationships with the external environment. These are considered in two parts of the book. The main concern of Part 1 is the application of systems and contingency approaches to highlight the organization's interactions with the task environment. It is the task environment that is viewed as the most important aspect of the external environment. However, it is recognized that social factors which are related to a more general environment may influence MAS design. Readings that relate the importance of this aspect of the external environment to management accounting are considered in Part 4. The location of this material at the end of the book enables a logical connection to be made between the task environment (Part 1), and aspects of the internal context (Parts 2 and 3). The aspects of internal context that are of particular concern to the design of MAS, as developed in this book, are the formal administrative arrangements and the organizational members. Part 2 develops the meaning of formal structure and its implications for management accounting. Part 3 stresses that accounting information ultimately affects the behaviour of individuals.

THE ORGANIZATIONAL CONTEXT OF MANAGEMENT ACCOUNTING

PART 1

Organizational Environment—Systems and Contingency Approaches to Management Accounting

Much of the research on organizations has been directed at developing ways of improving their efficiency and productivity. This research sought to aid managers' comprehension of their decision tasks by developing simplified ways of approaching their decision problems. Many approaches assumed that managers had control of, or could readily predict, outcomes and relationships related to organizational problems. These approaches may be referred to as "rational" models of the organization, and as employing a closed systems approach to organizational analysis (Thompson, 1967). In this approach, the organization is considered apart from its external environment, and it is assumed that decision making can be undertaken within this closed system. Approaches to organizational theory, such as scientific management (Taylor, 1911), administrative theories (Fayol, 1949; Gulick and Urwick, 1937) and to some extent bureaucratic theories (Weber, 1947), are examples of closed systems approaches to organizational design. Many of the traditional approaches to economic and financial analysis of management decision making and control activities may be regarded as closed systems approaches.

Because many textbook approaches to management accounting systems (MAS) design have often been based on the generation of information for the purposes of economic and financial decision making and control, they have also tended to follow a closed system logic. In these approaches, the MAS design process assumes that information requirements are clearly determined by the underlying financial decision and control models. For example, it is implicit in most textbooks that standard costing and budgetary control systems generally provide information to control situations where the input-output relationships are clearly articulated. These approaches may be considered to be appropriate for controlling more routinized or programmable decision processes. Their adequacy as control tools may be questioned in decision situations which are characterized by non-routine or non-programmable decisions. Similarly, in the case of responsibility accounting, the textbook approaches generally presume the existence of a highly formalized organizational structure, and assume that economic factors are readily distinguishable into controllable and non-controllable activities for which managers may be held accountable.

In general, closed system approaches are appropriate in directing attention to the search for "rational" decision behaviour within the organization (Thompson, 1967). However, they often tend to be inaccurate representations of reality, because they exclude many complex interactions between sub-parts of the organization, and isolate the organization from problems of change and uncertainty in the external environment.

An alternative approach for organizational analysis that directs attention at the complex interactions between parts of the organization and between the organization and its external environment has been derived from general systems research and, in more recent years, from contingency theories of organizational processes. In these approaches the various organizational activities are not considered as isolated elements, but as a number of interdependent parts, which contribute to and receive something from the whole. In turn, the whole is perceived as taking in from the environment various forms of input and information, transforming or changing these inputs into outputs by productive processes, and exchanging outputs with the environment in return for additional resources. System theorists, Katz and Kahn (1966, Ch. 2), referred to this exchange process as "the energic input into the system, the transformation of energies within the system, and the resulting product or energic output". From an accounting or information systems outlook, a general systems view focuses attention on the organization as a network of decision centers, which are linked together and to the outside world by communication channels that carry information relevant to decision making.

The articles included in this section represent examples of recent attempts to apply general systems research and contingency theory to MAS design. Before considering these articles, though, some relevant principles from systems research and contingency theory will be discussed.

GENERAL PROPERTIES OF OPEN SYSTEMS

The application of a systems approach draws attention to certain properties that aid the understanding of organizational functioning. These properties may be grouped into two categories. The first is concerned with an organization's interaction with its external environment, while the second is concerned with the way in which the internal characteristics of the organization are interrelated. Properties of relevance to the environmental association include the problem of identifying and maintaining the boundaries between the system and its external environment, the question of an organization's purpose, the tendency for a system to be subject to entropy (the process of decay), and properties that sustain the organization's activity. The second group of properties relates to the interaction between internal sub-systems.

The External Environment

An important aspect of systems research is the identification of the elements that make up the system and its environment. The system is comprised of a set of elements which are actively interrelated and which operate in some sense as a bounded unit. This may not be static as the boundaries between the system and environment may change. The system's environment is seen as a set of elements that interact with the system. Environmental elements are usually separated into general and specific categories. The general environment refers to the factors that affect most organizations, such as the overall state of the economy, and community, social and political values. The specific environment, which is sometimes called the task or substantial environment, includes those elements that directly relate to the organization in the normal course of its business.

The first task in applying a systems approach is to define the boundaries between the organization and its environment. Katz and Kahn (1966, pp. 60–61) define boundaries as the demarcation lines or regions for the definition of appropriate systems activity, admission of members into the system, and other imports into the system. However, in some cases it may be difficult to define boundaries. For example, are shareholders a part of the firm or are they part of its environment? There is rarely any absolute way of defining systems boundaries and the final distinction will depend on the purpose of the analysis. In the shareholders example, if the analysis is concerned with the acquisition of capital funds for a publicly owned firm, then shareholders might be included in the external environment as part of the capital market. On the other hand, in a family owned firm, shareholders might be more appropriately considered as part of the system. Baker (1973, p. 6) provides a useful discussion of systems boundaries. He indicates the difficulty of using physical factors to determine boundaries and suggests that a more appropriate basis is the discontinuity in patterns and clustering of human interactions.

The identification of the system and its relevant environment is important to the design of accounting for management decision making and control. Usually the boundaries of management accounting systems are co-extensive with the boundaries of the organization. Systems relying on standard costing are often closed to the environment, being concerned only with the control of events internal to the organization. However, in situations where the information relates to unpredictable aspects of the external operating situation, an open systems approach is appropriate. This point is developed in many of the readings included in this section.

Accounting systems that do provide information on the external environment often identify the relevant environment as those aspects that directly affect decision and organizational processes, and over which managers have a degree of control. It is important, however, for information systems to reflect elements that influence decisions but over which managers have no direct control. Obvious examples of this are the actions of competitors, such as advertising, pricing, personnel changes; changes in government or social attitudes; overseas trends; and many other factors which are typically regarded as non-controllable. An example of the dangers of inadequately defining the relevant environment is reported by Roberts (1964). A summary of this example is found in Amey and Eggington (1973, pp. 555–557).

It may be concluded that the factors which are relevant to the design of accounting systems should be broadly based and sensitive to the complex underlying interaction between the organization and its environment. An open systems approach provides a way of thinking that directs attention to this process. Good examples of applications of a systems approach to management are found in Kast and Rosenzwieg (1974), and Murdick and Ross (1971), and to accounting systems, in Lowe and McInnes (1971) and, more recently, Amey (1979). Three articles that have applied systems notions to MAS design are included in this section (Ansari, 1979; Lowe and Tinker, 1977; Nelson and Machin, 1976).

Organizational Purpose

The existence of an organizational system raises the question of its purpose. Management accounting has typically provided information for decision making and control based on the traditional view that ultimately the organization seeks to be effective in achieving some organizational goal. In business enterprise this goal has been profit. The open systems approach to organizational purpose does not consider traditional goals. Rather, the appropriate concern is successful adaption by means of the continued transformation of inputs into outputs. Open systems approaches are concerned with the dynamics of adaption, rather than prescriptions, for arriving at predetermined end results. This process includes the achievement of a dynamic state of equilibrium, organizational learning which enables managers to anticipate environmental disturbance, and the storing of resources to meet future difficulties.

While systems approaches do draw attention to the fundamental concern of organizations with their own survival, there are several criticisms that may be leveled at the systems view of organizational purpose. First, without some specific statement of goals, it is difficult to evaluate the effectiveness of organizational activity. This is of particular relevance to the management accounting function of control, through comparisons of actual with expected outcomes. A second criticism of systems approaches (and of goal models that treat the organizations as possessing goals) is that they isolate the system from its members. Gouldner (1959, p. 412) argues that systems approaches lack a systematic concern with the way in which the diverse social activities that people bring to the organization may affect organizational behaviour. This separation of the system from its members has been referred to as "reification" and is discussed by Silverman (1970, pp. 64–65).

In recent years, various approaches have been suggested which seek to identify the way in which goals and organizational activity interact. This has involved studying the ends that organizations appear to be seeking, as opposed to the formally stated pronouncements. These are sometimes called operational or operative goals (Perrow, 1970). These goals may be conflicting and may change, depending on the relative balance of power of those who can influence the direction of organizational activity (both within and outside the firm). Goal formulation may also reflect prior commitments to particular courses of action (Cyert and March, 1963).

A further development which is related to the issue of goals has been an attempt to identify factors within and outside the organization that influence the achievement of goals. A useful framework for this analysis is provided by Steers (1977). He categorizes factors as contributing to achievement of goals as related to: external environment, internal organizational climate, organizational characteristics—structure and technology, managerial policies and practices, and employee characteristics—attachment to the organization and job performance (Steers, 1970, p. 8).

While some management accounting texts have recognized the existence of multiple goals (the General Electric scheme is often quoted—profitability, market position, productivity, product leadership, personnel development, employee attitudes, public responsibility, balance between long and short range goals), there tends to be an emphasis on traditional economic goals.

Some recent work has drawn attention to the way in which accounting can provide information related to the broadly based adaptive needs of organizations, such as environmental monitoring, forecasting, uncertainty avoidance, creation of organizational reserves and many others (Amey, 1979; Amey and Eggington, 1973, Ch. 3). The article by Amey (1979), is one example of an attempt to relate accounting to goals associated with adaptation.

The development of accounting to provide information on goals related to organizational members (for example human resource accounting), has received some attention and is reviewed in Part 4 of this book. It appears that the development of MAS to provide information relevant to "operative goals" and "factors contributing to their achievement" will continue to be a fruitful area for research.

Entropy, Transformation and Feedback

Open systems approaches stress that the purpose of organizational activity is to assure adaptation. The essential difficulty in achieving adaptation is the tendency for a system to be subject to the natural process of entropy. This means that there is a natural tendency for systems to move to a situation of disorder, decay and finally disintegration. Organizations can combat entropy only by the input of information, materials and energy from the environment and the transformation of these elements into outputs. Entropy is offset by building up a surfeit of resources, when possible, that may be used in times of crisis when the pressure for entropy increases.

The analysis of organizations in terms of the transformation of inputs into outputs can be used to draw attention to the cyclical nature of activity. That is, the export of energy or output from the organization to the environment makes possible the input of resources. This enables the organization to process the inputs into outputs, which are then exported to the environment, thus renewing the cycle. This process demonstrates the vital role of environment as the means for adaptation. Lowe and McInnes (1971, p. 221) stress this point:

> Once one accepts a view of the enterprise process as a purposeful collection of individuals having vital transactions with its environment it is then essential to analyse it as an open system. Moreover, it is important to understand the vital sense in which an enterprise exists by means of its environment and not simply within its environment. Initially the system is determined and created by the needs which come from a general environment and clearly its success depends upon the degree to which it satisfies those needs; in a real sense by the degree to which it, as it were, "integrates" with and relates to the environment.

In this section, readings by Lowe and Tinker (1977), Lorange and Scott Morton (1974) and Amigoni (1978) are examples of approaches that have stressed the importance of environmental context.

Given a goal orientation and a transformation process, feedback mechanisms enable managers to determine the extent to which progress is being made toward goals. Feedback may be negative, which involves comparison between current and expected outcomes, or positive, which adjusts required standards to suit changing circumstances. It is in the area of feedback mechanisms that management accounting is particularly relevant. Traditional standard costing and budget control techniques are examples of feedback. However, too often these control mechanisms assume the existence of well-defined, highly structured decision processes and do not represent the complex realities of the situation to be controlled. Attempts to improve control based on feedback have employed techniques from disciplines of operations research (Ackoff, 1966), industrial dynamics (Forrester, 1961) and cybernetics (Ashby, 1964; Beer, 1964, 1966).

These techniques have attempted to develop control mechanisms that accurately reflect both internal and external elements of the organization. A challenge for management accounting systems design is to incorporate insights from these disciplines. For discussion of the association between accounting and cybernetics and operations research see AAA, Report on the Committee on Information Systems (1971) and Chenhall (1974).

Internal Characteristics

The second set of properties which is derived from open systems research relates to characteristics within the firm. An important principle of open systems research is that organizations seek improved efficiency through movement towards more complex forms of specialization in the functions performed. The way in which these specialized tasks are grouped into sub-units and the way in which such units' activities are coordinated form the basis for examining organizational structure. This topic and its association with accounting are discussed in Part 2 of this book.

Identification of the sub-parts of organizations may follow many approaches; however, a useful systems approach was developed by Parsons (1960). This scheme separates sub-systems into technical, which are concerned with the actual production aspect of the transformation process; organizational, which are concerned with the scheduling, coordination and control of the activities in the technical sub-system; and finally institutional sub-systems, that deal with individuals and entities in the organization's external environment which provide the resources or consume outputs. Figure 1.1 represents an elaboration of this model as developed by Katz and Kahn (1966).

It is important that management accounting systems designers recognize the different decision needs of sub-systems managers. For example, if productive processes in the technical sub-system are well defined, accounting may adopt a "closed systems" logic that is concerned with well defined productive processes. This occurs because the technical sub-system tends to be protected from disturbance by the smoothing and buffering actions of other "boundary spanning" parts of the organization (Thompson, 1967). Traditional standard costing and static budgeting are examples of tools which are appropriate to control technical sub-systems facing relatively certain environments.

However, the information needs for decision making and control in the institutional sub-systems may be quite different. Because of the lower degree of influence that managers have over factors affecting decisions, a highly flexible open systems approach to MAS design would be appropriate. This type of accounting system should be consistent with broad goals which are related to ways of adapting to a changing and unpredictable environment. For example, accounting may focus on providing information to indicate the degree of technological and marketing superiority, trends in industry productivity and levels of research and development. Further, in unpredictable environments, accounting may have to service the information needs of novel decision problems which may involve non-routine decision processes.

A further aspect of the internal characteristics of systems which is relevant to organizational control is the way in which the separate activities of sub-systems are coordinated. Systems theorists have pointed out that activities in different sub-systems are often interrelated in complex ways. For example, changes in the technical system, such as an increase in the diversity of

TECHNICAL	OPERATIONAL	INSTITUTIONAL
Production (e.g. technical)	Maintenance (e.g. personnel, rewards and sanctions, production maintenance crews)	Production support (e.g. purchasing, sales)
	Managerial (coordinates internal and external activities, resolves conflict)	Adaptive (research and development, market research, operations research)
		Institutional (obtains social support and legitimacy for organization)

FIGURE 1.1

outputs, may increase the complexity of administering tasks, and as a consequence outputs. This could trigger a change in the formal structuring of activities within the organizational sub-system, which might affect the incentive to work of those individuals who are working in the technical and institutional sub-systems. This type of consideration was first developed in an approach referred to as a "socio-technical analysis" (Emery and Trist, 1969).

As interdependencies become more complex, the task of coordinating separate activities becomes more difficult. To aid in this coordination, management accounting should accurately reflect, or map, these interdependencies. The importance of interdependence on choice of structure and accounting systems is explored further in Part 2.

In conclusion, identification of sub-systems and the way in which they interrelate is an important criterion for analysis of management accounting systems. Identification of the different sub-systems may reveal the different information needs of managers' decision making and control tasks. Further, as the interaction between sub-systems becomes more complex, the need for accounting to reflect these interdependencies becomes an important aspect of design.

Equifinality

The final property drawn from open-systems research is the notion of equifinality. Equifinality means that systems may reach the same desired state from different initial situations and in different ways. This implies that several satisfactory solutions may exist to some problems, and that organizations which are faced with the same problem may resolve it by using different strategies.

CONTINGENCY THEORY

Contingency theorists have argued that no universal solution exists to resolve organizational problems; rather, effective problem solving depends on the character of the organization and the environmental situation within which it operates. Systems and contingency approaches have many similarities and the latter may be considered to be an extension of the former. Both approaches stress the important role of environment in influencing managers' decision making. However, there are certain differences between the approaches. Systems research is concerned with the dynamics of organizational processes and focuses on a wide range of elements to explain these processes. On the other hand, contingency theory has tended to concentrate on identifying which organizational and environmental characteristics and relationships are associated with the outcome of various aspects of organizational activity. Most of the early contingency research was concerned only with the organizational sub-system, and the form of organizational settings in particular (Burns and Stalker, 1961; Lawrence and Lorsch, 1967; Pugh et al, 1969; Woodward, 1965).

In recent years there has been some interest in applying contingency theory to the analysis of effective design of management control and accounting systems. Thus far, several approaches have been developed to establish the relevant variables that describe the contextual setting of control and information systems. Articles by Ein-Dor and Segev (1978), Lorange and Scott Morton (1974), and Amigoni (1978), which are included in this section, are examples of this approach. It is noteworthy that few researchers have subjected their models to empirical testing. Notable works that have involved empirical validation are by Hayes (1977) and Bruns and Waterhouse (1975). These articles are included in Part 2 of this book.

A fundamental difficulty which is associated with contingency approaches to management accounting is the lack of consistent classification of variables that describe the contextual setting (the independent variables) and the purpose of the accounting system (the dependent variable). A variety of factors have been identified by different authors as being representative of independent and dependent variables. The dependent variable is often constructed in terms that reflect the effectiveness of the management control system to the organization, or the characteristics of the system itself. However, effectiveness has been defined in many ways. The definitions range from general managerial use of the control system as identified by Ein-Dor and Segev (1978) (included in Part 2), to meanings that focus on particular aspects of the decision or control situation. Hopwood (1974) and Hayes (1977) are examples that focus on performance evaluation of sub-units, while Amigoni (1978) and Ansari (1977) stress desired features of the system. It is useful when evaluating contingency research to establish quite clearly what are the ends that are sought by the information and control system.

A similar problem exists in contingency research with the identification of independent variables. Researchers have attempted to identify the contextual variables which have a significant influence on management accounting and control systems. Studies may be grouped into those that use constructs that aggregate factors into broad dimensions such as the "stable-dynamic" and "homogeneous-heterogeneous" nature of the environment (see, for example, Hayes, 1977, in Part 2 and Watson, 1975); those that identify particular elements of context such as organization size, structure and technology among others; and specific external environmental characteristics like uncertainty, hostility, diversity, and dependence between organizations. The article by Bruns and Waterhouse (1975), which is included in Part 2, is an example of the approach that uses more specific notions of context.

There are advantages to both approaches. The use of aggregate dimensions captures the overall effects of context. The more specific measures of context provide a richer description of the setting of the accounting system.

However, the problem of consistent identification and measurement of elements of the context hinders the development of knowledge, as different studies are not accurate replications of each other. At this stage in the development of contingency approaches to accounting, research is still establishing exactly what are the dependent and independent variables.

There are several additional problems associated with contingency approaches. First, the theory stresses "ends" rather than "means". Understanding the decision processes or the means by which managers take decisions may be neglected. A particularly important aspect of this criticism is the tendency for contingency approaches to ignore the human element. It is argued in this book that the human element can be included in contingency theories. There have been some attempts in the accounting literature to include the human component in the design process. These approaches draw on the concept of organizational climate or the organization's "interaction-influence" system (Likert, 1961). This approach is implicit in the articles by Ansari (1977) and Hopwood (1974) which are included in Part 2.

THE READINGS

The purpose of management accounting systems is to provide information relevant to organizations' decision and control processes. As suggested earlier, general systems research and contingency theory provide an analytical framework whereby the MAS designer may attempt to match the system with the needs of organizations as they attempt to adapt to external environmental situations. These approaches seek to identify the external and internal characteristics that may affect the design of information and control systems including MAS.

The first work by Lowe and Tinker (1977) provides an introductory overview of a systems approach to organizational management which describes accounting as a sub-system of a broader organizational control system. Their approach classifies organizational variables into three sub-systems—decision and control, financial funds, and operating (physical transformation)—and uses these to demonstrate both the interdependencies that may exist within the management control situation, and the importance of interactions between sub-systems and the environment. The research does not develop a specific scheme for a particular organization; rather it represents a first step in the task of systems design. The authors suggest that their approach is "a model to classify and order ideas about ideas for managing an enterprise in a coherent manner".

Nelson and Machin (1976) also apply systems thinking to the development of a framework for designing management control systems. The article defines management activity in terms of the degree of constraint or the specificity of the task, with the more closely specified activities approximating a closed system, and those where the purpose is diffuse and the outcomes unpredictable, as open systems. The activity constraint is described in terms of the utilization of resources, commitment to specified outputs or outcomes, and human and organizational relationships. These categories are associated with three purposes of management control: assuring effective interactions between the manager's center of responsibility and others in the organization, assuring coordinated functioning between interdependent units, and assuring effective operations within centers of responsibility. The combination of specificity of activity with purpose of control provides a matrix, in which each cell represents a variable in the process of management. The authors' model enables control systems to be designed for different situations by means of determining the appropriate degree of "openness" of the system. As the need for a more open approach to control becomes evident, the system design "falls back" from a closed state to a contingent state, and finally to an open state. The article includes a field study of the control of absenteeism in a large hospital, and describes a move from a closed to open systems control perspective.

The article by Ansari (1979) provides an example of an application of systems thinking to the design of a budgetary system. It is argued that existing budgetary control typically reflects a closed systems view of the organization. The author notes the significant difficulty of operationalizing the concept of "controllability". An open systems approach is suggested as a means of recognizing the dynamic interacting nature of organizational units, and of orientating budgeting to problem solving and control of the organizational whole. A scheme is provided for classifying variances in a way which highlights the nature and origin of disturbance, and the form of interdependence between sub-units and their internal and external environment.

The reading by Lorange and Scott Morton (1974) is a further attempt to develop a framework to aid design of control systems. They argue that control systems can aid managers' decision making by providing a formal framework for identifying pertinent control variables, the development of good short-term plans, recording the degree of fulfillment of short-term plans along the set of controls, and the diagnosis of deviations. The independent variables affecting the choice of control variables are identified as formal organizational structure, organizational members, the technological processes and the external environment. The authors also discuss the implications for management control systems design of the development of multi-dimensional structures such as matrix forms, the importance of non-monetary control variables, and the linkage between planning and management control due to increasingly unstable environmental conditions.

The article by Ein-Dor and Segev (1978) adopts a contingency approach to management information systems design. The work seeks to identify a broad range of internal organizational contextual factors that may influence information systems. A noteworthy aspect of the research is the use of a propositional approach to develop relationships between contextual factors and information systems. The dependent variable is identified as managers' use of the information system, while ten independent variables are grouped into categories of uncontrollable, partially controllable and fully controllable. On the basis of a comprehensive survey of literature concerned with construction and use of management information systems, the authors construct twenty-two propositions. While the research does not apply any empirical tests, the developed propositions provide a useful base for such investigation.

The final reading by Amigoni (1978) is a further application of contingency theory. In this example the author directs attention specifically at management accounting as an aspect of information systems. The dependent variable is defined in terms of several features of accounting control tools. These features are degree of detail, relevance, selectivity, formal responsibility, procedural rigidity; style of control; quickness or timeliness; and orientation towards such events as outputs or inputs, particular managerial activities, past and future events. The independent variables are the degree of structural complexity within the company and the degree of turbulence in the external environment. Accounting tools are shown to contribute in varying degrees to the different features of the control system, and conversely the features are established by appropriate combinations of accounting tools. The accounting tools are identified as financial accounting, ratio analysis, cost accounting, responsibility accounting, investment budgeting.

The articles included in this section apply general systems research and contingency theory to the design of management control and information systems. These works provide a valuable basis for future research into the role of accounting systems as an aspect of the "organizational subsystem", and for considering the most appropriate design for particular contextual settings.

DISCUSSION QUESTIONS

1. An important aspect of systems and contingency approaches to MAS design is the interaction between the organization and the external environment. Define organizations and external environment.
2. Discuss the similarities and differences between systems and contingency approaches to organizational analysis.
3. Describe how managers' choices concerning the markets and technologies could influence the development of their organization.
4. How do varying rates of change in the environment affect an organization?
5. Briefly define the following: closed and open systems, entropy, equifinality, socio-technical analysis, operative goals.
6. A useful way of appreciating contingency approaches to MAS design is to identify the purpose of the MAS (the dependent variables) and factors that describe the organizational and environmental context (the independent variables). Identify both dependent and independent variables of the proposed models in the readings included in this section. To what extent do these various approaches represent a comprehensive view of the context of an MAS? What additional factors may be helpful in describing context?
7. To what extent are open systems approaches to concepts such as external environment, organizational purpose, entropy, feedback, organizational interactions helpful in the design of:
   (i) standard costing systems
   (ii) responsibility accounting systems
   (iii) budgetary planning systems.

New Directions for Management Accounting

E. A. Lowe

A. M. Tinker
University of Sheffield

Using a general systems rationale, this paper develops a theoretical structure for approaching the problem of management accounting. The management control problem is explicated in terms of maintaining a relationship between the enterprise's structure and its environment. An enterprise's structure is composed of three elements (and their inter-relations): a decision and control subsystem; a financial funds subsystem and an operating (physical transforms) subsystem. Portrayed in these terms, the problem of management accounting is shown to require a methodology which is able to take cognizance of economic, sociological, psychological and other aspects of the enterprise system. The model described here provides a general intellectual frame of reference for ordering the problem.

INTRODUCTION

The real tragedy of the Titanic was that the whole episode was avoidable! The unsinkable embodiment of engineering excellence sank for lack of a careful analysis of the ship's prospective environmental conditions in relation to her capabilities for remaining afloat.

Has the accountancy profession anything to learn from the loss of the Titanic in relation to the design of their education system? The career period of a newly qualified accountant is approximately 40 years. Although post-qualifying education and experience sometimes play an important role in an accountant's development, it is the expected demand conditions for 'accounting services' expected to prevail over this 40 year time horizon rather than current or past circumstances that define the accountancy education problem. Yet do we ever see an assessment of such expected demand conditions used to derive proposals for professional accountancy training? We think not. The rapid expansion of consultancy divisions of audit firms; the increasing importance of the industrial and commercial employment sector; greater competition from university graduates in economics, behavioural science, operations research, etc.; all such trends in the accountancy profession's environment emphasise this change in longer-term demand for accounting skills. Fortunately some recent events suggest that the UK profession acknowledges educational change as a necessary first step in

From *Omega*, Vol. 5, No. 2 (1977), pp. 173–183.

inducing revisions in accountancy 'technology' and practice. In particular, there is now evidence that the professional accounting bodies are making painstaking and deliberate progress towards proposals for changing accountancy practice [1, 11].

This paper is intended to contribute to the debate by describing a conceptual scheme of the management process that would not only enable the student to relate his accounting expertise to other views of management, but also provide a frame of reference for relating to more detailed proposals for accountancy training. This formulation is developed from a general systems perspective of the management process.

Thus our proposals here are directly relevant to the problems of training management accountants (or 'accountants in management'). Only partly do they apply to the problems of training accountants for professional practice since the latter also requires a training which fully recognises *the socio-economic responsibilities of accountancy practice.*

A GENERAL SYSTEMS ANALYSIS

We can begin by recognising that management scientists (including management accountants), like any other (social) scientists, are not concerned with objects or entities in their entirety. Rather they abstract a particular viewpoint which depends upon the kinds of problems they are most immediately concerned about. A general systems viewpoint is concerned with identifying the whole of the system to which the problem relates and thus seeks to avoid taking that system apart in a manner which results in the loss of essential characteristics of the problem. The problem in this instance may be said to be the survival of a particular enterprise at a specified level of 'welfare'. This requires an understanding of those fundamental traits which contribute to its viability and adaptivity as a financial entity. In this respect accountancy practice and textbooks are grievously at fault, emphasising, as they do, the mechanistic and routine aspects of management processes at the expense of the fundamental innovative and imaginative aspects on which longer term financial viability and adaptivity depend.

The firm's behaviour may be described in terms of, for example:

- An accounting viewpoint, e.g. different accounting profits associated with different budgets for the firm.
- A moral or social viewpoint, e.g. number of employees satisfied with career prospects; improvements in the firm's avoidance of polluting the environment.
- A Government viewpoint: numbers of employees; taxes paid; accident rates; contribution to exports, etc.
- An economic viewpoint: product prices; factors influencing cost levels; output level decisions, etc.

Many management theorists have argued that certain 'ideal-type' organisational structures exist that would serve all firms in all circumstances [7]. These 'ideal-types' often approximate to Weber's bureaucratic form of organisation. According to this thesis the entire problem of management resides in the organisation's arrangement within its 'own boundary'.

We argue precisely to the contrary: the appropriate form of organisation for realizing a firm's objectives is contingent upon its environmental conditions. From both a cybernetic and information systems viewpoint a formal matching between the firm's 'substantial' environment and its internal organisation can be shown to be a requirement for a 'successful' organisation. (Remember the Titanic!)

The impact of environmental conditions (represented by vector A in Fig. 1), the behavi-

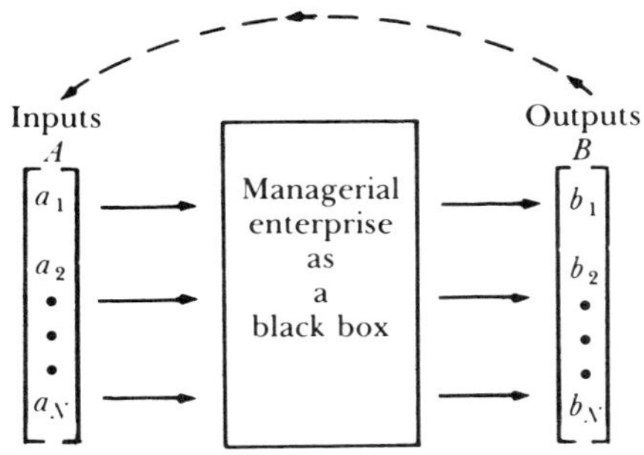

FIGURE 1. Matching the environment and organisation of an enterprise.

our of the firm (represented by vector B), has been recognised in part by management accountants in, for instance, the distinction between controllable factors and uncontrollable factors as determinants of organisational performance. But to take such a specific instance for illustrative purposes this cost classification for control purposes can be said to have led accountants sadly astray since it results in a failure to understand the decision consequences of such a classification in the light of general systems theory. The pertinent message is that 'uncontrollable' factors are often critical because of their influence on the firm's well-being. Consequently the message implies that the firm's management should not assume that because some factor is uncontrollable, no action is required on their part. Clearly if the firm's objectives imply its survival, the uncontrollable factor requires to be 'controlled' by appropriate adaptation of the organisation. In many cases the 'control' of uncontrollable factors (sic) requires that other information relating to that factor is necessary for the firm's related decision-making processes. In practice, one often finds that the required information demands an improved ability to predict the changes in that environmental factor; often an improvement in the firm's forecasting faculty is called for.

Thus, at this general level of analysis, the behaviour under consideration (vector B), is a product of environmental conditions (vector A) and the organisation of the firm. That is: $B = T(A)$ where T is the transformation or organisation of the firm that relates environmental inputs to the behaviour of the whole organisation, in terms of its outputs.

At this level of analysis, the firm is regarded as a black box: the precise form of the transformation remains unspecified. Such a specification, in terms of a firm's technology, the deployment of resources through possible management policies, search rules, decision procedures, etc. requires further elaboration of the conceptual framework that is our concern here.

Given that aspects of the environment, relevant to explaining and predicting the behaviour of the organisation, have been identified, closure (in systems analysis terms) may be effected thereby, thus circumscribing the firm's 'substantial' (or relevant) environment.[1] These ideas are portrayed in Fig. 2.

In Fig. 2 the closure represented by the boundary is intended to signify that all (perceived) organisational and environmental factors involved in explaining and predicting the behaviour of interest have been so included in the systems analysis. Prediction is thus a neces-

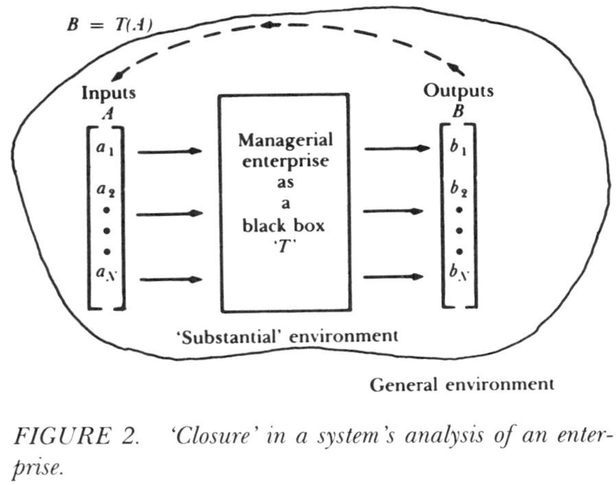

FIGURE 2. 'Closure' in a system's analysis of an enterprise.

[1]For discussions of the concept of closure in cybernetic modelling see Ashby [2] and Klir [6].

sary condition for all management control processes although of course, it is not a sufficient condition.

In any particular systems analysis, the boundary is subject to a time horizon or a 'time resolution level' relating to the period of analysis. Clearly the longer the period of analysis, then the more likely the environment is to 'make its presence felt'. Consequently the more untenable may become many existing assumptions and the greater is the need to incorporate additional factors (and changes therein) explicitly into that analysis; such factors as the state of technology, political forecasts, changes in consumption patterns, etc. That is to say in Fig. 2 we draw the boundary correspondingly wider. Economic models have always attempted to recognise this aspect of management by a clear distinction, for instance, between short-term and long-term economic analysis. Unfortunately whilst the distinction is clear, the economic analysis of the short-term and long-run has not yet been made helpful to firms in an operational sense. Discounted cash flow methods probably represent our best attempt to do so, so far. But it is still quite evident that budgetary control methods, as presently generally practised and taught, have no formal means for including these notions in financial plans and budgets. This paper suggests that an operational distinction should be based on a specification of the whole causal mechanism intervening between various sets of inputs and outputs at a given time-accuracy resolution level. Fig. 3 provides a general portrayal of this idea.

In an analysis of the behaviour of a firm through time, a feedback relation links behaviour (outputs) to environmental inputs. In these circumstances, the conventional accountancy distinction between controllable and uncontrollable influences becomes a most unhelpful one. For example, the price of capital to a firm may be determined by a market mechanism that is itself affected by information about and from that firm over a sufficiently longer time period.

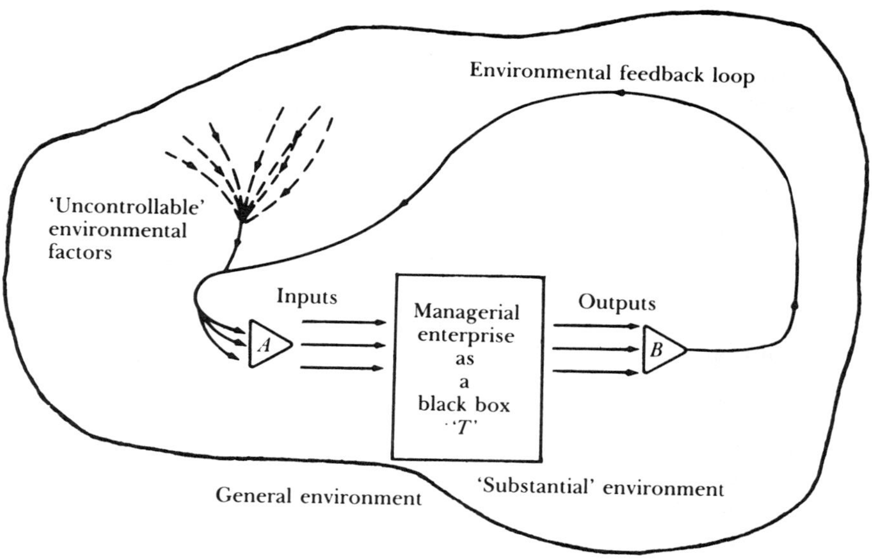

FIGURE 3. The 'casual' mechanism of enterprise stability.

In such vital matters it is extremely difficult to determine the precise impact of a decision by the firm with current analytical financial techniques. But general systems theory, for instance, enables us to state clearly the relevant interdependencies and relationships.

A CONCEPTUAL DESIGN FOR ACCOUNTING FOR MANAGEMENT CONTROL

The general approach previously outlined can be formulated in terms of the conception of a 'managerial enterprise' shown in Fig. 4.

There it is suggested that the financial management problem may be investigated by focusing on the significant attributes of inputs, outputs, the internal structure of the system, and the relations between them. Thus inputs, defined as human needs, are represented as information, financial funds and physical resources. Similarly, information, financial funds and product flows are characteristic descriptions of the enterprise's output of satisfactions of human needs.[2]

The internal structure of the enterprise in the illustration is portrayed as consisting of three interrelated principal elements, namely, the decision and control sub-system, the financial funds sub-system and the operating sub-system. These three elements are interrelated in that they are partial images of each other. In other words, input may be described by a vector with three components each of which describes the impact of that input upon each of the three sub-systems: the decision and control sub-system: the flow of funds sub-system: and the operating (physical transforms) sub-system. Conceptually the first is the most difficult to identify since it attempts to describe the 'informative' content of the input for the enterprise. It may be identified by its two principal component parts: a predictive model of the future possible (interdependent) states of the other two sub-systems; and, secondly, a model of choice that relates the feasible alternatives generated to the organisation's objective function.

Outputs in this model are the enterprise's responses to the stimuli (or inputs). They constitute the enterprise's attempts to influence the substantial environment and thus, in a cyclical sense, the next set of inputs to the enterprise. For instance, in our cost of capital example, it might be the capital market's revised view of the cost of capital to that firm, consequential upon the firm's changed policy with regard to matters such as the scope of its business or its means of raising capital or its dividend payments. Such changed policies might themselves be changed outputs (responses) in relation to previous inputs (stimuli) emanating from external, consumer and financial markets.

The decision and control sub-system, consisting of the 'brain' (the top managers) and the executive arm (those who execute formal policies, procedures and accounting control devices laid down by top management), is linked to the other two sub-systems. It is linked, firstly, to the financial funds element, thereby resulting in changes in the structure of funds according to criteria intended to achieve specific objectives; secondly, to the operating sub-system through a further two-way flow information-for-control linkage, thereby causing changes in production and production technology. In addition, the decision and control system contains management's 'imaginative faculty', for speculation and anticipation, involving both search for new opportunities and the reduction of hypothetical states to the consequences for the three sub-systems.

The financial aspects of the model, as a

[2]This argument is developed by Lowe [8, 9], and Lowe and McInnes [10].

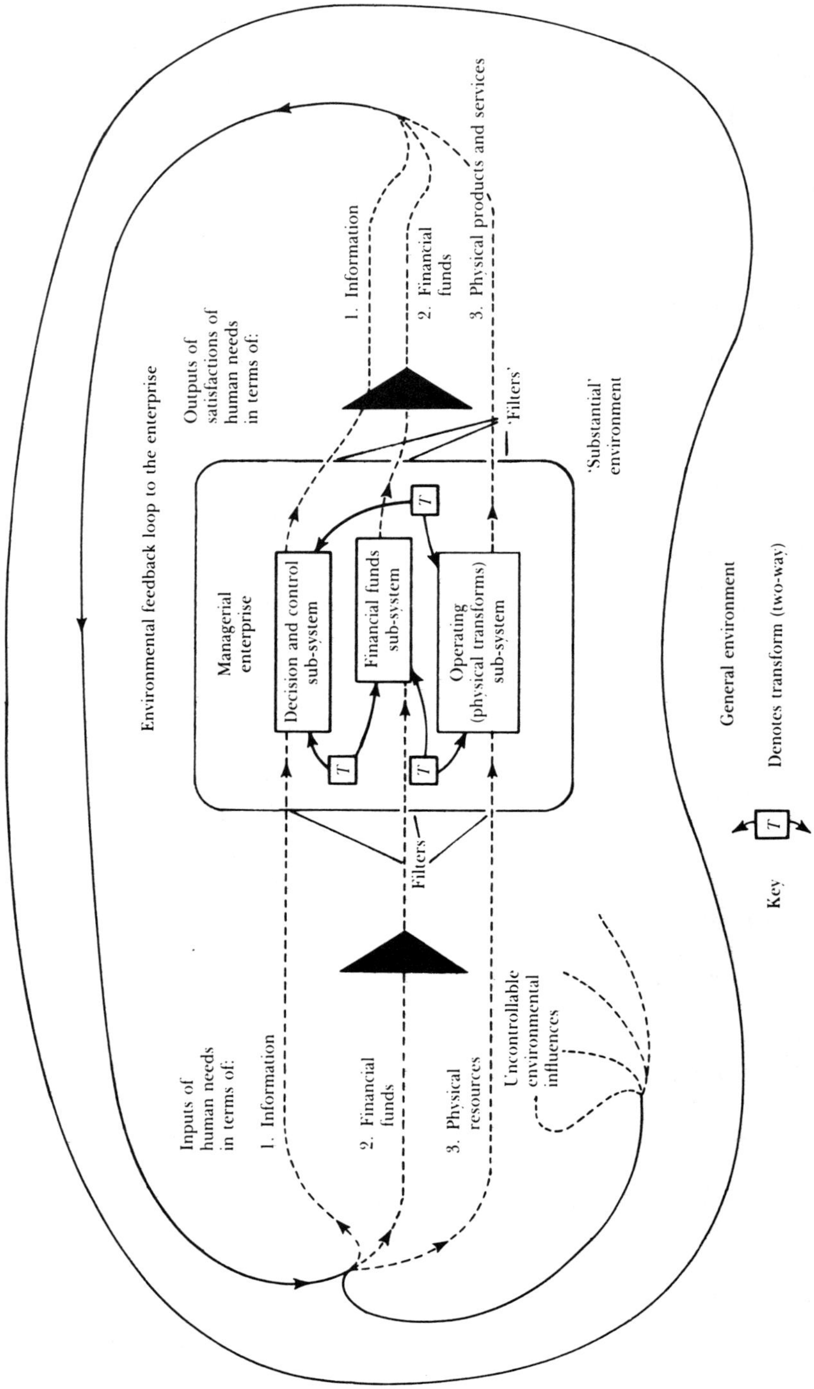
Environmental feedback loop to the enterprise
Inputs of human needs in terms of:
1. Information
2. Financial funds
3. Physical resources
Uncontrollable environmental influences
Filters
Managerial enterprise
Decision and control sub-system
Financial funds sub-system
Operating (physical transforms) sub-system
T
Outputs of satisfactions of human needs in terms of:
1. Information
2. Financial funds
3. Physical products and services
'Filters'
'Substantial' environment
General environment
Key
T
Denotes transform (two-way)

FIGURE 4.

characteristic (or attribute) of the whole system, may be emphasized through the financial funds stock sub-system. Thus the behaviour of this sub-system might, for instance, feature a present value measure of plans in the form of a discount rate reflecting an opportunity cost of funds to organisational participants [8]. Recognition of this relationship, between the attribute and the whole system has of course important implications for management research and thus for company policy (see [12] and [4]).

Alternatively a behavioural science emphasis would involve focusing on the internal structure of the decision and control sub-system. This could be related to the financial funds sub-system through the monetary returns to conflicting participants whose interests are represented by constraints and goals in the organisational decision system [4, 5].

The three sub-systems are circumscribed by an inner boundary which is permeable but monitored, and which contains the set of influence relations emanating from the co-operative character of the organisation (for example the set of role relations, and authority and power relations). These directed social influences are thus reinforced by the tendency to resolve internal conflict by seeking a partial consensus; by resorting to persuasion and legitimization to effect organisational change.

The use of this model can be briefly illustrated in relation to two fundamental kinds of management problems: problems of analysis and problems of synthesis [6]. Problems of analysis and synthesis may be defined with reference to this simple illustration.

AN ILLUSTRATION

A manager is interested in explaining the relationship between two input variables and one output variable of his firm *M*. Each of the input and output variables may take on only two states, (0,1) where

Input Variable	State	Meaning of State
A	0,	High unemployment in the locality
	1	Low unemployment in the locality
B	0,	Competitors, prices below those of firm *A*
	1	Competitors, prices above those of firm *A*
Output Variable	**State**	**Meaning of State**
W	0,	loss
	1	profit
A	(0,1), ⟶	Firm *M* ⟶ *A* (0,1)
B	(0,1), ⟶	

The systemic variety is $2^{2^2} = 16$.[3] The sixteen possible configurations of inputs and outputs (systemic or logical variety) are as follows:

A	B	W 1	2	3	4	5	6	7	8	9	10	11	12	13	14	15	16
0	0	0	0	0	0	0	0	0	0	1	1	1	1	1	1	1	1
0	1	0	0	0	0	1	1	1	1	0	0	0	0	1	1	1	1
1	0	0	0	1	1	0	0	1	1	0	0	1	1	0	0	1	1
1	1	0	1	0	1	0	1	0	1	0	1	0	1	0	1	0	1

From a large number of observations the manager notes from his empirical analysis that the firm behaves regularly according to transformation $W = 4$ above.

i.e.

A	B	W
0	0	0
0	1	0
1	0	1
1	1	1

To explain this regular pattern of relations between variables *A, B* and *W,* the manager needs to examine the internal structure of Firm *A.* The approach would be analogous to the procedure previously outlined: by defining different sets of elements of Firm *A* (e.g. departments, social groups, etc. representing the three sub-systems previously described) and examining the relations between characteristics of the elements and the inputs *A* and *B* and output *W,* the manager thus seeks a regular pattern that provides an explanation. For instance after examining the internal structure of Firm *A,* the manager may discover that in times of high unemployment in the locality, output may be restricted by informal agreement to avoid competition for jobs. This explanation is consistent with the relations between *A, B* and *W* in transformation 4. Thus problems of analysis involve determining an explanation of the relations between inputs and outputs (e.g. transformation 4) with reference to a given structure.

In certain respects problems of synthesis are the converse of problems of analysis. Given a desired or prescribed behaviour (for example, $W = 1$ = profit in the illustration), the problem is to synthesize that organisational form that will realise the desired behaviour. Further analysis of the internal structure may reveal that certain arrangements of the decision and control sub-system (e.g. employee payment schemes, redeployment programmes, etc.) affect the operating sub-system in a manner that realizes a satisfactory state of the financial funds sub-system for the firm in conditions of high unemployment. In this sense it may be possible to synthesise an internal structure, according to environmental conditions, that produces a profit.

This simple example perhaps serves to illustrate an approach to synthesizing an organisation in relation to a particular environment, and thereby changing output behaviour in accordance with the firm's objectives. It is important to note that, as in most management situations, the problems cannot be adequately resolved by a pre-occupation with the financial, personnel, marketing or production aspects

[3]For a discussion of systemic variety see [3].

alone. Such an approach would only do violence to a complex system of interrelated variables. Rather this total system must be respected, preserved as an entity and studied as a complete set of working relations through a general systems approach. The three sub-systems discussed previously provide a general method of classifying and relating these organizational variables.

CONCLUSIONS

The conceptual framework outlined in this paper may be regarded as an educational model for developing specific schemes for managing particular enterprises. It is not our purpose here to specify a way of programming the activity of a particular enterprise; rather we are concerned with the problem that is logically prior to this i.e. proposing a model to classify and order *ideas about ideas* for managing an enterprise in a coherent manner. This, we suggest, is the accounting educationalist's design problem. Thus it would be possible for an accounting student to enrich his view by considering, for instance, sociological, social psychological, quantitative, economic and other aspects of management problems, using such a model as the one presented here, as his 'intellectual framework for analysis'.

The meta-theoretic character of the model is particularly important from an educational viewpoint. The model is not a precise empirical theory, addressed directly to the workings of managerial problems; rather it provides a cognitive bridge for beginning to integrate ostensibly diverse theories and associated evidence and relating them to the problems of interest to us.

REFERENCES

1. Accounting Standards Steering Committee (1975) *The Corporate Report.* The Institute of Chartered Accountants in England and Wales.
2. Ashby R (1964) *Introduction to Cybernetics.* Methuen, London.
3. Beer S (1966) *Decision and Control: The Meaning of Operational Research and Managerial Cybernetics.* John Wiley, London.
4. Bonini CP (1967) *A Simulation of the Information and Decision Systems in the Firm.* Markham, London.
5. Cyert R & March J (1963) *A Behavioural Theory of the Firm.* Prentice-Hall, Englewood Cliffs, N.J.
6. Klir G (1969) *An Approach to General Systems Theory.* Van Nostrand, New York.
7. Koontz HD & O'Donnell CJ (1964) *Principles of Management.* McGraw-Hill, New York.
8. Lowe EA (1970) The information content of financial statements, financial planning and management control: towards an integration. *J. Bus. Fin.* 2(2), 3–11.
9. Lowe EA (1972) The finance director's role in the formulation and implementation of strategy: a framework for financial strategy. *J. Bus. Fin.* 4(4), 58–70.
10. Lowe EA & McInnes JM (1971) Control of socio-economic organisations: a rationale for the design of management control systems (Part 1). *J. Mgmt Studies* 8(2), 213–227.
11. Solomons D & Berridge T (1974) *Long Range Enquiry into Education and Training for the Accountancy Profession.* Gee, London.
12. Williamson O (1964) *The Economics of Discretionary Behaviour: Managerial Objectives in the Theory of the Firm.* Prentice-Hall, Englewood Cliffs, NJ.

Management Control: Systems Thinking Applied to the Development of a Framework for Empirical Studies

Edwin G. Nelson

John L. J. Machin

INTRODUCTION

Since the development of Anthony's framework for analysing planning and control systems,[1] there have been a number of attempts (most notably that of Lowe and McInnes)[2] to produce frameworks using elements of systems thinking which will provide assistance with empirical studies in the field of management control systems. The need has been to develop a framework for the analysis and improvement of the level of effective managerial control in an organization, which is both justifiable theoretically, and can be seen to be practically viable and useful to managers wrestling with the problem of ensuring flexible and successful organizational adaptation in a period when change in the substantive environment of employing organizations is at an unprecedented level.

The authors believed that by bringing together a selected number of the developed threads within control theory and some of the elements of general systems theory, a framework could be developed which would go some way towards helping managers to analyse the complexity of the management control process in such a way that they could both determine the potential opportunities available to them for raising the level of control, or adjusting the balance of controls within the organization, and then, subsequently, explain and demonstrate the results of such decisions as they make.

It has long been recognized that the topic of management control systems covers an area which draws into its material for the study of integration, valuable understanding from a number of other more traditional schools of academic study. Equally, the acceptance of management control frameworks at a practical level has been bedevilled by the need for them to be applicable both to those systems of control which have been rigorously and systematically developed, and also to the range of informal, situational, systems of control (usually larger in number and more divergent in type and purpose than formal systems) which have developed organically within the organization.

In this article the authors outline the basis on which one such new framework has been developed, and then describe the application of that framework in connection with a recent study of a major, costly, and hitherto

From *Journal of Management Studies,* Vol. 4, No. 3 (October 1976), pp. 274–287.

[1]Anthony, R. N., *Planning and Control Systems—A Framework for Analysis,* Boston, Mass.: Graduate School of Business Administration, Harvard University, 1965.

[2]Lowe, E. A. and McInnes, J. M., 'Control in Socio-Economic Organizations: A Rationale for the Design of Management Control Systems,' *Journal of Management Studies,* Vol. 8, No. 2, May 1971, pp. 1–12.

somewhat intractable managerial problem in one of the largest employing organizations in the U.K.

Using the framework, it has been possible to demonstrate that the changes brought about by managers within that organization, changes involving both new and reconstructed formal systems as well as new and altered informal systems, have raised significantly the overall level of control within the organization in respect of this problem area without simultaneously raising the overall level of constraint.

THE DEVELOPMENT OF CONTROL THEORY

The recognition given to management control as a subject for academic study does not have a long history in the U.K. It appears to have emerged from an airing of views about the concepts which would be most suitable for the integration of the somewhat fragmented theories of management. One school[3] of thought gravitated towards business policy and planning as the subjects which will spawn integrative concepts. That view has the appeal that the subjects are closely linked with general systems concepts and the importance of boundary exchanges between an organization and its environment. The publication of these views, however, drew a reply from another subject area—management control:

> Persons interested primarily in planning do not penetrate far enough into the territory where the interdisciplinary thinking needs to be done. . . . The area of control would seem to be a more favourable one. . . . Control, I have found, predisposes a person to focus effort on the more truculent area of divergence in both concepts and interests . . . as mergers and technological ingenuity force the pace of organizational adjustment and change.

In the opinion of that author[4] one of the important advantages of control concepts was that the student was compelled to bridge the gap between the behavioural sciences and the more quantitative subjects.

This apparent divergence of views, at first sight clear cut, becomes less distinct when Mills refers back to one of his own previous publications[5] and states, 'Planning and control are closely related functions in today's dynamic environment: they may indeed be considered a single function'. The apparent confusion of terms may lie in the two possible meanings of the word control. It can be regarded as a *post-factum* exercise—monitoring the outcome of activity, reviewing feedback, and if necessary, taking corrective action; or it can be regarded as an *ante-factum* exercise to direct managerial activities in the light of pre-knowledge of, or in anticipation of, future circumstances.[6] Some limit themselves to the cyclical monitor-review-correct definition and there has been a good number of works which contribute to the associated theories.[7] Others prefer to extend the definition to include both types of activity:[8] and *ante-factum* activities involve some kind of planning.

---

[3]Denning, B. W., 'The Integration of Business Studies at the Conceptual Level', *Journal of Management Studies,* Vol. 5, No. 1, February 1968; Manchester Business School Graduate Students, 'Integrated Organizational Strategy', *Journal of Management Studies,* Vol. 6, No. 1, February 1969, pp. 96–111.

[4]Mills, A. E., 'Management Control and Integration at the Conceptual Level', *Journal of Management Studies,* Vol. 7, No. 3, October 1970, pp. 364–75.

[5]Mills, A. E., '*Dynamics of Management Control Systems*' London: Business Publications Limited, 1967.

[6]Reeves, T. K. and Woodward, J., 'The Study of Managerial Control', in Woodward, J. (Ed.), *Industrial Organization: Behaviour and Control,* London: Oxford University Press, 1970 p. 38.

[7]Giglioni, G. B. and Bedeian, A. G., 'A Conspectus of Management Control Theory: 1900–1972', *Academy of Management Journal,* Vol. 17, No. 2, 1974.

[8]Tannenbaum, A. S., *Control in Organizations,* New York: McGraw-Hill, 1968.

There is a definition that can be interpreted flexibly: 'Management control is the process by which managers assure that resources are obtained and used efficiently and effectively in the accomplishment of the organization's objectives'.[9]

The object of those who study the subject is generally to determine the design of formal management and administrative systems that will facilitate the process most effectively. Their deliberations, and those of others who implement and operate management control systems, are governed by their concepts of the process. In the past it has often been possible to rely on a model in which goals and objectives established by top management are broken down for specific contributions by subordinate managers, with appropriate monitoring arrangements to help assure that they are made. Also, very often, it was possible to assume exclusive financial objectives and there was a great concentration on budgetary control. Such a model was much too simplistic for the public services (especially the personal services) employing professional or semi-professional people and where cost inputs cannot be related quantitatively to measures of outcome, nor is it now the sole suitable model for private commercial organizations either. Increasingly, it is being realized that management processes are described by more than one model and particularly when some of the outcomes are determined not by top managers but by other employees, and in the case of the National Health Service, for example, by participating clients.

Since the process can be depicted by a number of different models that may be called into operation spontaneously, then the management control system that facilitates it will have to feature a variety of control types. This, in turn, establishes a requirement for students and designers to be able to appraise and categorize the components of the total system of controls. Amongst other things, we will need to determine what, in practice, is a control—is it any part of the formal arrangements that facilitate the management process, such as, for example, job descriptions and staff appraisal schemes, or is the idea of management control more restricted than that? Ideally, we should be able to study the total system empirically for its effect, and not just as an inventory of managerial practices and arrangements. The proceedings of a multidisciplinary seminar on management control systems were published in the U.S.A. in 1964,[10] and a number of internationally known persons contributed. Of the proceedings the editors wrote in their introduction, 'Most of the work reported is not concerned with immediate applications of techniques or theories to actually operating [firms]. Current practice receives relatively little attention'. This situation is being gradually corrected, but without frameworks for empirical studies there is a constant danger that intellectual modelling exercises may drift away from reality.

A SYSTEMS FRAMEWORK FOR MANAGEMENT CONTROL

Systems thinking directs one to consider any unit of organization or a responsibility centre, not in isolation, but in interaction with the larger organization or environment of which it is a part. The relevance to the job of management of this acknowledgment of boundary considerations is well established by Emery,[11] in the introduction to his collection of readings about systems thinking. Yet the way in which boundary considerations are incorporated in

[9]Anthony, R. N., op. cit., p. 17.

[10]Bonini, C. P., Jaedicke, R. K. and Wagner, H. M., *Management Controls: New Directions in Basic Research,* New York: McGraw-Hill, 1964.

[11]Emery, F. E., *Systems Thinking,* Harmondsworth: Penguin, 1969.

management controls varies from situation to situation; for example, from those in which a specifiable activity will produce a specifiable outcome that will have a specifiable value for some person's purpose, to those in which the purpose is diffuse and the fulfillment of it surrounded by unpredictable contingencies. In the first example, once the variables and their relations have been specified, the responsibility centre can be controlled as a closed system and executive actions taken without further regard for external factors. In the second example this can never be the case, the responsibility centre must always be prepared to adapt its internal processes to unpredictable external events. In the terms customarily used to catalogue management responsibilities there are implicit references to the openness or closedness of the situations in which they are to be discharged, *e.g.* strategic, administrative, operational decision-making, or policy, programming and executive responsibilities. Following these, and bearing in mind the definition of Anthony, we can formulate three statements of the object of management control in the order in which boundary considerations are to be regarded as influential variables:

1. Assuring effective interaction between the manager's centre of responsibility (whether it be a section, a department or a larger organization), and others so that it can benefit from transactions with them.
2. Assuring coordinated functioning between centres of responsibility on which outputs or outcomes depend in common.
3. Assuring efficient operations within centres of responsibility.

The activities of managers, and those in which their resources are engaged to discharge the responsibilities stated above, can be the subject of varying degrees of specification or constraint. When an activity can be specified it usually forms the basis of constraint through training and/or professionalization. Depending on whether the activity is mechanical or one that requires, say, intellectual ability, the learned constraints may be combined with various incentives to recognize them, such as monetary rewards, or the prestige and esteem implicit in promotion. Otherwise, as in Management by Objectives, it is sought to establish an outcome constraint which itself offers positive stimulation. In respect of any outcome that may be regarded as the object of organizational endeavour there will be a network of dependent and interdependent relations between managers—senior management is dependent upon the commitment of their subordinates, who in turn are dependent on information passed down to them to help them determine their best contributions. On a horizontal plane, for example, the industrial relations climate in an organization affects other outcomes and itself may be just as much a function of the way in which technology is applied to work processes as of personnel policies. Determining and structuring these dependency networks is another category of constraint, deriving its principles from the subject of human relations. When a manager is fully committed to an outcome the mere recognition of a dependency network may constitute a considerable constraint on the way he uses his discretion. Otherwise, when activities and outcomes cannot be specified, management structures are relied on; based on authority and accountability they are so designed as to enable senior management to impose their will on subordinates when it becomes clear as to what precisely is required of them. Implicit in these considerations is a dimension based on the specificity of constraint placed on resource utilization. Its extremes, too, are associated with the closedness and openness of organizational systems—the more specific a constraint is concerning the activities in which resources have to be engaged, the more closed is the system. Thus, appropriate to situations ranging from more closed to more open, three categories of constraint can be stated:

1. Activity specifications for resource utilization.
2. Commitment to specified outputs or outcomes as the objects of activity in which resources are utilized.
3. Human and organizational relationships that establish values for possible outcomes of activity.

Taken together, the two parameters of 'constraint' and the 'objects of control' can be imagined as forming the framework for a matrix. Each cell would represent a variable in the process of management. The full matrix is developed using what might be described as a 'fall-back exercise'. Assume a closed system and that we want to impose tightest possible constraint on resource utilization: we can do it if we can specify the activities or tasks that are to be undertaken and calculate the volume of resources engaged or consumed in them. When this is not possible we can fall back on a statement of the output we expect from someone else who may be better placed or equipped to specify activities and mobilize resources. If circumstances do not permit this either, then we can fall back on appointing another with authority to supervise and ensure that resources are used efficiently on activities likely to result in acceptable outcomes. Thus, we have fallen back from a form of control of operations that would characterize a closed system, not having the competence to adapt itself to circumstances, to one that is more open and relying on the structuring of human relations. However, it might not be possible to specify the extent of authority that a supervisor is to exercise, then we would fall back on establishing those issues that might be the basis of negotiations between managers and seek to establish them as issues of common interest and requiring a spirit of cooperation. Finally, if no continuing bases for cooperation can be identified then we fall back on the recognition of interdependencies amongst the network of responsibility centres for which supportive relations are critical. In this case we have fallen back from internal considerations concerning the efficiency with which resources are used, to external considerations concerning relations with others contributing to a common outcome.

Filled out in this way the matrix for classifying controls appears as in figure 1. Once the question of the definition of a management control has been settled, and that might vary according to who requires it and for what purpose, the matrix can be used in an audit to classify the controls identified. This allows comparisons between organizations distinguished by other characteristics such as output, size, productive process, entrepreneurial/public service, performance, *etc.*

In any given organization a balance or bias may be observed amongst the formal controls in use. Differences are to be expected where management processes have evolved under the influence of considerations such as whether the product is concrete or abstract (*e.g.* a manufactured unit or a personal service); whether the organization is large with centralized power or small and decentralized; or whether the environment is a stable one or fluid and changeable as political environments usually are. It may be found, for instance, that the system of controls tends to emphasize constraint through attempts to specify activity tightly as in some corporate planning and P.P.B.S. systems. Comprehensive and detailed planning of this kind is often not the most flexible of arrangements and is more appropriate when a reasonable degree of stability is assumed. In some industries, the health services is one, the demand for resources to be engaged in activities is difficult to predict exactly, yet is expected to be satisfied, and effective interaction has been sought through flexible policies adopted by medical staff and others. The more difficult it is to prescribe activity the more we might expect to see control relying on the 'or-

Objects of control	Categories of constraint: Resource utilization	Commitments	Relationships
Assuring effective interaction	Corporate planning Determining strategies and policies for future decisions on the basis of anticipated circumstances	Contribution Determining the expectations held by other interested parties, and the sanctions they might bring to bear	Policy for interaction Determining the network of responsibility centres amongst which supportive relations are critical
Assuring coordinated functioning	Programming Programming allocation of resources so that responsibility centres with common interests complement each other	Objectives Establishing agreements to aim for outcomes that will maximize the benefits to parties with common interests	Responsibility Establishing those issues in respect of which it will be the responsibility of managers to cooperate with each other
Assuring efficient operations	Prescription of activity Specifying the activities that the resources of responsibility centres are to be engaged in	Output Estimating the expected outputs given a volume of resources	Authority Delegating and distributing the authority required to manage resource utilization

FIGURE 1. A matrix for classifying controls on the management process

ganic' areas of the matrix, *i.e.* to the right and above.

Where there is a choice in the controls that might be employed then it may embody a trade-off between effectiveness and efficiency, or the capacity to feature open systems behaviour against closed systems behaviour. Governing activities with standing orders, for instance, will assure that matters arising will be dealt with efficiently in a predetermined way, it won't assure that a suitable outcome is obtained if the case turns out to be an unusual one. Conversely, an open policy by top management renders the objectives of subordinates vulnerable and reduces their commitment to them, which in turn jeopardizes the efficiency with which they are pursued. In view of the possible biases, three basic requirements are postulated if a system of controls is to facilitate the management process:

1. *Control in the open state:* effective interaction and the maintenance of a supportive environment are better assured when the policies of managers are sensitive to changing circumstances.
2. *Control in contingent states:* coordinated functioning can be more easily assured and congruence amongst the separate commitments of centres of responsibility contributing to common outcomes more easily preserved when managing systems do not assume constant states, say, of stability or change.
3. *Control in the closed state:* efficiency is assured when activity can be prescribed to consume a minimum of resources in relatively stable circumstances.

Given the basic requirements, a varying emphasis of control types would be expected to occur as a result of the particular circumstances or characteristics of individual centres of responsibility.

CHARTING CHANGES TO A SYSTEM OF CONTROLS

In management control constraint is a variable not an objective. The degree of constraint has to reconcile what can be the conflicting objects of minimizing the possibility of dysfunctional behaviour and taking maximum advantage of the resourcefulness and innovative potential of managers. Proposals for changes to systems of control should be examined with this in mind, and to ensure that managers will be suitably directed or motivated and assisted. The dynamics of organizations rarely permit effective change to be implemented solely on the basis of *a priori* consideration. Change has to be managed and controlled as events unfold. The use of the matrix to chart and assess changes is demonstrated below.

A STUDY IN THE MANAGEMENT OF ABSENCE IN A LARGE ORGANIZATION

The hospital service is organized on functional lines and the nursing function contains the largest number of employees. Nationally, the number of nurses in 1973 exceeded 250,000 persons, and successive reorganizations within the Health Service in general and the nursing function in particular have established a management hierarchy in which senior nursing managers are in some cases personally responsible for up to 4000 subordinates. One such role is that of Chief Nursing Officer in some Health Areas, and the responsibilities attached to the job can be briefly described as being to provide economical nursing services on a scale and of a quality determined by the needs of patients and some other specialist functions.

This study is concerned with the nursing services in a large group of hospitals which were made the responsibility of a single Chief Nursing Officer in 1972. His particular concern was to develop a mix of systems to control the management of human resources—his primary resource—in this case the whole-time equivalent of more than 3000 persons. Systematic management of these huge human resources was embryonic; absence was a problem experienced by nurse managers but the rudimentary data provided scant information to assist an analysis of it. Clearly two major alternatives were facing the chief officer. The first was to improve the accuracy of absenteeism forecasting and the planning systems necessary to cope with forecast levels through flexible staffing schedules and relatively large pools of mobile nurses able and prepared to move to positions temporarily understaffed through absence. The second was to analyse the causes of absence and see whether any of them were amenable to improvement through management activity. Acting on the belief that both the economy and the quality of services were linked to staff absence rates, the chief nursing officer adopted objectives of containing and reducing them.

Hitherto, the management of staff absence had been purely a procedural affair. If an employee did not inform his/her superiors of any illness by 12 noon on the day of his absence, or subsequently produce a sickness certificate, he/she was deemed to be voluntarily absent for that day and could not claim sickness benefit. If a person came to the notice of management as frequently having short spells of sickness or voluntary absence for vague reasons, that person was 'counselled' progressively by more senior managers depending on how long the behaviour persisted or how doubtful it appeared. Data about absence was recorded by the two lower grades in the management hierarchy, but it never went any higher, though it was, of course, passed to the treasurer's department for the purposes of calculating wages.

Part of the procedure for handling absence had been reduced to writing in a set of standing instructions that were being gradually developed as reference for managers. Objectives had never been formally stated, but there was no doubt that the critical preoccupation was to ensure that wards were adequately staffed. In spite of fairly tight establishments, day-to-day staff allocation was flexible and nurses could be moved at short notice to relieve temporary pressures due to shortages. Paradoxically, movements tended to reduce the commitment of some of them and resulted in more absence. The managerial approach here quite clearly assumed closed system characteristics; controls were aimed at reducing the management process to prescribed procedure and coping with the symptoms of the problem. Although nurse managers were aware that absence was due to the influence of a variety of factors, few felt it their responsibility to explore them in sufficient depth to be able to produce a comparable variety of managerial response.

The appraisal of existing management arrangements revealed them to be essentially procedural and concerned with prescribing managerial activity to control absence behaviour. They were becoming increasingly redundant in modern conditions which permit considerable latitude for legitimating absence. A review of the range of factors that could be associated with absence behaviour made it clear that management would have to adopt a much more flexible approach.

The chief nursing officer called a meeting of his subordinate managers and informed them that he was giving a greater priority in his own job to the management of staff absence.

In order to stimulate his subordinate managers to do the same of their own accord rather than as the result of direction from him the chief nursing officer introduced a much more sophisticated information system in which absence data was passed up through the hierarchy and a comparative table showing the monthly rates of each unit within the group of hospitals was then published to all middle and senior management.

Initially, although the subordinate managers were willing to recognize the reduction of staff absence as an organizational objective, they were reluctant to set targets for improvement in their own set of objectives. They maintained that they did not know enough about the means of achieving success and doubted whether they held the necessary authority to do anything about it. The view was expressed strongly that the management of staff absence was a subject for general responsibility requiring cooperation between grades of manager and between management and staff functions such as personnel and staff health services.

This discussion brought into focus the question of the distribution of authority and a consideration of whether any more authority could be delegated to increase the influence that subordinate managers could exercise. It also led to a greater exploration and use of the dependency networks between line management and staff functions in respect of staff absence and led to positive moves for involvement in mutually supportive arrangements—the personnel function, for example, responded willingly to management requests for assistance. The interdependency between line managers, too, was highlighted when first-line managers seized an opportunity to bargain with senior management for a more rational allocation of staff, arguing that this was one of the work situation factors affecting absence.

The stages in bringing about change may be summarized as follows:

1. The C.N.O., after a trial period with new data collecting, processing and feedback arrangements involving all his subordinate managers, obtained their formal recognition that the reduction of staff absence was a managerial objective and they should continue to monitor absence behaviour.
2. Steps were taken to increase managers' understanding of absence behaviour and to encourage the selection of approaches to problems from a wider range of alternatives.
3. Arrangements were set in motion to facilitate the assumption of new responsibilities and to delegate the authority required to handle the absence phenomenon.
4. Discussions began on the need to modify established arrangements that impinged on questions of absence management.

5. During the implementation of these changes new liaisons sprang up with medical staff and personnel staff concerning the question of staff absence.

Some of the changes outlined above were clearly designed to increase the intensity of management control, some, on the other hand, grew organically from the discussion generated by the other changes. Originally, the approach was to try to 'police' absence behaviour and the management arrangements were aimed at doing this efficiently. Yet it became apparent that many of the factors causing absence were external to the organization and situationally variable. To reduce absence managers needed to be able to identify the external factors affecting their unit and be sufficiently committed to respond to them. Formerly the systems of control and the managerial climate did little to facilitate let alone encourage these aspects of the management process.

There is an increased emphasis on formal arrangements and more data handling is required. This could easily have been misconstrued as merely another example of increasing bureaucracy in nursing, and initially some of the nurse managers involved believed that this was the case.

Gradually, as nurse managers' attitudes to absence became more objective and analytical, and as they began to face the 'open' aspects of situations, information was valued more highly and the spectre of 'more bureaucracy for the sake of bureaucracy' was seen in its true light.

CHARTING THE CHANGES

Even before managerial results could be demonstrated, it was possible to trace the implications of the new arrangements against the matrix as shown in figure 2. The train of separate events can be related as parts of a system of developments and changes in respect of both axes of the matrix. In this case the new arrangements constitute a move along the open-closed systems dimension from a position that would have been described as closed and rather mechanistic towards one that is more open and organic.

Equally, a significant move has been made along the other axis from a general view of absence as a phenomenon concerning which data were produced for the purpose of wages calculation, and whose impact on the organization was accepted as a given in resource planning and use, to a view of absence as a human phenomenon capable of being managed only if its causes were understood, and enough authority was delegated to, and understanding developed in, subordinate managers so that they could respond in an interactive way in connection with nursing relationships.

CONCLUSION

Management control as a subject for study has been claiming increasing attention in the U.K. during recent years. With the restructuring of public services and a greater emphasis on the management of them the subject is given additional spheres for application (see the *Management Arrangements for the Reorganized National Health Services,* H.M.S.O., 1972), even if not under the specific title of management control. It is practised in situations subject to socio-industrial change when the basic premises concerning human motivations and behaviour might alter the requirements of systems of control. For this reason it is essential that concepts remain fluid, promote and do not suppress development. Bearing this in mind, systems thinking is ideally suited as a background from which to develop a framework for empirical studies.

Objects of control	Categories of constraint: Resource utilization	Commitments	Relationships
Assuring effective interaction		Values of the social systems external to the hospital began to be regarded objectively in the light of hospital problems	The recognition of the new objective brought the interdependence network of staff, hospital departments and the social system into clearer focus
Assuring coordinated functioning	Discussions were begun with a view to improving resource allocation formulae	An information system and comparative feedback enabled managers to recognize new objectives and varying priorities	Staff absence began to be recognized as an issue requiring responsible cooperation between nursing, personnel and staff health functions
Assuring efficient operations	Standing instructions prescribing some activities were supplemented by encouragement to engage in additional activity appropriate to the circumstances		The recognition of objectives and of joint responsibility between superiors and subordinates led to a new look at the distribution of authority

FIGURE 2. Charting changes in control influence: an example drawn from an innovation in the management of hospital nursing staff.

The extent to which systems of control achieve a balance of open and closed systems characteristics will determine an organization's ability to adapt to, and function successfully in, its environment.

One often detects a reaction to the idea of control as involving constraint on individual managers, which is then condemned as being contrary to the spirit of currently evolving social values and to notions of self-realization and management motivation.

The interesting conclusion to the case mentioned above is that formal procedures can be introduced into an organization in such a way that they permit a greater degree of control to be exercised on the management process without raising the level of constraint.

At the same time, the part of the organization into which the formal procedures were introduced became more open to external sources of information and influence. Thus, increases in the total level of control are not inconsistent with open systems qualities.[12]

It is hoped that organizations contemplating changes in their patterns of management control will find the framework helpful in analysing the implications of the range of possible approaches to change which face them, and then charting the subsequent results and, perhaps, to go into a control cycle of continuous appraisal and development of the systems of controls.

[12]For extensive reporting on this issue see Tannenbaum, A.S., op. cit.

*Towards an Open Systems Approach to Budgeting**

Shahid L. Ansari
Graduate School of Management, University of California, Los Angeles

The theory of open systems has been increasingly applied to the study of organizational planning and control systems. This is also true for the area of budgetary control. At present, however, there is a tendency for writers to treat the design problems as an either/or choice between an open or a closed system. This paper argues that the critical decision problem is where in a system closure can be most beneficially applied. It will show that the open systems view, with its emphasis upon the horizontal dimension in an organization, is better suited for designing effective budgetary control systems. The computation of budget variances is chosen as the key step at which the usefulness of this view can be fully appreciated. An alternative budget variances measurement scheme, based upon similar perspectives in the area of job design, is proposed. It is shown that variances computed under the proposed system more fully reflect the interacting nature of most organizations and provide better control information.

One feature which characterizes the post–World War II period is the growth of new and more complex organizational forms. The growth in government, for instance, has given rise to giant bureaucracies such as the Department of Defense (DOD) and the Department of Health, Education and Welfare (HEW). Similarly, new technologies have created their own organizational forms as evidenced by the National Aeronautics and Space Administration in the U.S. and EURATOM (a grouping of European countries for co-operation on atomic energy) in Europe. These newer organizational forms have changed the practice and philosophy of management. New concepts, designs and techniques of organizations and management have replaced their earlier counterparts.

One area of organizational design in which more fundamental change has been absent is in the design of management information systems (MIS). While recent technological advances have changed the structure of most MIS, the new structures are not necessarily in harmony with changes in other organizational and managerial variables. Elsewhere, I have argued that effective organizational design requires information structures which are consistent with the human-social, task and reward subsystems in organizations (Ansari, 1977).

From *Accounting Organizations and Society*, Vol. 4, No. 3 (1979), pp. 149–161.

*I gratefully acknowledge the help of Jan Oliver and Jack McDonough for their helpful comments on an earlier draft of this paper.

These arguments provide the central theme of this paper; that is: new developments in organizational forms and management systems require changes in the design of many MIS to make the functioning of the overall control system more effective.

This paper deals with this theme in the context of budget variance information. Budgets are selected because they are one of the most important and pervasive organizational control systems. The paper has a two fold purpose. First, it will be argued that while an "open" systems philosophy more closely reflects the nature of organizational changes; budget variances, as presently computed, reflect "closed" systems thinking. Second, the necessary changes will be outlined to make variance information consistent with this newer reality of organizational design.

The discussion is divided into four parts. The first part deals with changes in organizations which have necessitated a move from a closed systems view toward an open systems view. The next part of the paper argues that budgetary control systems are currently designed as closed systems. An open systems framework which is more consistent with the newer reality of organizations is presented in the subsequent part. The final section is devoted to a consideration of the relevance of the arguments presented earlier to changes in accounting systems.

ORGANIZATIONAL CHANGES—SOME BACKGROUND

Budgets operate within the context of other organizational variables such as technology, rewards and social systems. When that organizational context changes, it is now recognized that the changes must be reflected in the design of budgetary control systems. As recent studies of the contingent nature of management accounting systems have emphasized (Bruns & Waterhouse, 1975; Sathe, 1975; Waterhouse & Tiessen, 1978; Watson, 1975), budgetary control systems cannot be designed and operated in isolation of their organizational context.

Some of the changes in organizations which have necessitated a re-evaluation of budgeting in general and budget variances in particular will be discussed in this section. In doing so, a systems view of organizations will be adopted. There are two reasons for this. First, systems theory provides a useful metaphor because a lot of recent research on organizations uses its concepts and terminology. Second, and more important, the systems framework provides a powerful analytical model for the analysis of organizations because it allows designers to integrate the technical and social sides of an organization within a unified whole. It thus avoids a fragmented treatment of organizational problems.

Two views or approaches have been used in studying a phenomenon as a system. The first is a closed systems view which has its origins in classical physics and thermodynamics. The other is the open systems view which was first used in biology. Both of these approaches have been used in characterizing and studying organizations as systems.

Closed systems are characterized by *certainty, a static equilibrium,* and *little or no import or export of energy* from and to the environment.[1] Closure is designed to create a system whose future states are determined by its existing states. This, as Thompson (1967) observes, can happen only if the relationships are few and predictable.[2] Consequently, closed system approaches focus more on the internal organization and less on the relationships between a system and its environment.

[1]For a detailed discussion, see Emery & Trist (1969).

[2]Asby (1956, p. 27) describes this as a one-to-one transformation in which fixing its (a determinate system's) "circumstances and the state it is at will determine i.e. make unique, the state it next moves to".

In contrast, an open system is characterized by growth and *survival.* It achieves a *dynamic equilibrium* instead of a static equilibrium. The process of achieving it is marked by a constant *exchange (import and export) of energy* with the environment. Three other properties that mark an open system are: (i) *self-regulation* or use of negative feedback to take corrective action; (ii) *equifinality* or the ability to achieve the same final goal from different initial conditions; and (iii) *negative entropy* or the ability to store excess energy for use in counteracting later disturbances.[3]

As strategies for studying organizations closed and open systems' models differ in what they consider as playing a leading or independent role in explaining a system's behavior. In the closed system's model internal organizational structure plays a leading role; the open system's model ascribes a leading role to the environment. These differences are perhaps best captured by Gouldner (1959). He identified two models of organizations. The first, so-called "rational model", is a "mechanical" view of an organization as a structure of manipulable parts, subject to planned modification with a view to enhancing "the efficiency of the whole". The other is the "natural-system" model which stresses the interdependence of the parts of an "organismic" whole, in which the focus is on disruption of a homeostatically maintained organizational equilibrium rather than on "deviations from rationality". Later writers, such as Thompson (1967), have interpreted Gouldner's "rational-model" as a closed system and his "natural-system" model as an open system. Using this analogy, their differences may be summarized as follows: the closed systems strategy is aimed more at the autonomous behavior of a system's components whereas the open systems strategy aims to study the ways in which these components are integrated and the behavior of the resulting whole.

The pyramid type of organization structure with its clear cut lines of authority and responsibility, best exemplifies the rational closed system's model. Here the design emphasizes vertical power and authority relationships that bind an organization together. Efficiency is achieved by successive factoring of organizational goals into compartmentalized subunits that are supposed to function more or less autonomously. As Sayles & Chandler (1971, p. 34) point out:

> In traditional management thinking there is a clear line separating that which is delegated and that which is not, that which is in the jurisdiction of one manager and that which falls into the jurisdiction of an adjacent manager.

Such an emphasis on the achievement of certainty and efficiency by the use of organizational designs based on the delegation of authority and responsibility has not given attention to different organizational environments and the complex ways in which organizations depend on their environments (Katz & Kahn, 1966). Most of the newer organizational forms which have emerged can be best understood as responses to increasing complexity in both the internal and external organizational environment. The volatility of demand, the need to implement advanced technologies (as in space exploration), the complexity of tasks (as in HEW programs) are some of the many changes which have made it impractical to draw clear cut lines of authority and responsibility. This is due to considerable overlaps in the scope of problems and the differential distribution of technical abilities within an organization.

For instance, in their analysis of the impact of new high technology on organizational design, Sayles & Chandler (1971) note two major changes. First, advanced technology organizations, such as NASA are marked by

[3] A good description of open system properties is contained in Katz & Kahn (1966) and Thompson (1967).

greater interdependence of parts and are tied together horizontally as well as vertically. Second, project management (e.g. the Apollo Program) is replacing line management since most resources lie outside the domain of individual departments and often even the organization.[4] Projects borrow these resources for finite time periods for accomplishing specific goals. A similar emphasis on programs and missions is also true of large bureaucracies such as the DOD, HEW, etc. Sayles & Chandler (1971) conclude that one of the legacies of the Apollo Program is the innovation in organizational design which can be successfully transplanted to other organizations.

The organic or open systems model, with its emphasis upon interdependence between autonomous parts, is thus a better model for these newer organizational forms. There are at least two important implications of this model for management and hence management information systems. First, the absence of clear cut allocations of tasks and resources within any single unit requires the development of joint or shared systems of responsibility. In such systems, the regulation of the whole takes precedence over and is not synonymous with the regulation of its parts. Second, since no manager controls all of the resources, co-operation rather than competition becomes important. To encourage such behaviors performance evaluation becomes more an exercise in problem solving and less a method of assigning responsibility.

It should be noted that the prior discussion is not designed to suggest that closed and open systems are either/or choices. As Kast & Rosensweig (1973, p. 44) point out, "most social organizations and their subsystems are 'partially open' and 'partially closed'. Open and closed are a matter of degree". What needs to be recognized is that both are appropriate under certain circumstances. Thompson (1967) noted that the use of closed systems concepts is particularly needed at the technical core of any organization to reduce uncertainty and to create more effective performance at this level. The challenge is to avoid what Kremyanskiy (1958, p. 141) calls "conditionalism" or the tendency to ascribe an exclusive leading role to either the "inside" or the "outside" in explaining a system's behavior:

> . . . it is profoundly mistaken to stress—only the augmentation of the organisms' "independence" from the environment. This occurs in association with a deepening and widening mediated dependence. But in the highest development of means of adaptation to the environment there also lay the need for the opposite process —the development of new ways and means for combating the environment.

The emphasis upon such a mediated-dependence means that the behavior of certain systems sometimes can be best studied by proceeding inside out or vice versa. Kremyanskiy illustrates this by using the brain as an example. As he points out, "The brain first developed as an organ of primarily internal interconnections, and then primarily as an organ of interconnections with the environment". The following sections will show that in the development and analysis of budget information it is time to move away from placing primary emphasis on the "internal" toward placing more emphasis on "external" relationships.

BUDGETARY CONTROL AS A CLOSED SYSTEM

This section will demonstrate that existing budgetary cost control systems reflect the

[4]For a discussion of the implications of this point see, S. Ansari & R. O. Mason, "Control System Design for Inter and Intra Organizational Performance", AIS Working Paper, Graduate School of Management, UCLA.

closed systems view of organizations and therefore create problems which make them unsuitable for the newer types of organizations. This conclusion can be supported by examining a typical budgeting system described in the cost accounting literature. Figure 1 describes such a system for an individual unit within an organization. The dynamics of this system can be described in six different stages.

1. *Specification of budget* represents the planning phase, in which the monitor is fed goals and other control instructions (e.g. measurement methods, frequency, etc.) agreed upon by managers and subordinates. The monitor may be a man or a machine or may have elements of both.
2. *Measurement of actual output* in which the monitor carries out the predesigned measurement instructions fed in step 1.
3. *Report on variances* involves the preparation of a variance report after comparing actual and budgeted outputs. The level of detail in the report will depend upon the level of management for whom the report is intended.[5]

[5]For instance Shillinglaw (1972) defines the so-called "basic plan" and "single plan" variance reporting systems. The former are less detailed and are designed for higher echelon managers, while the latter are more detailed and are intended for immediate superiors.

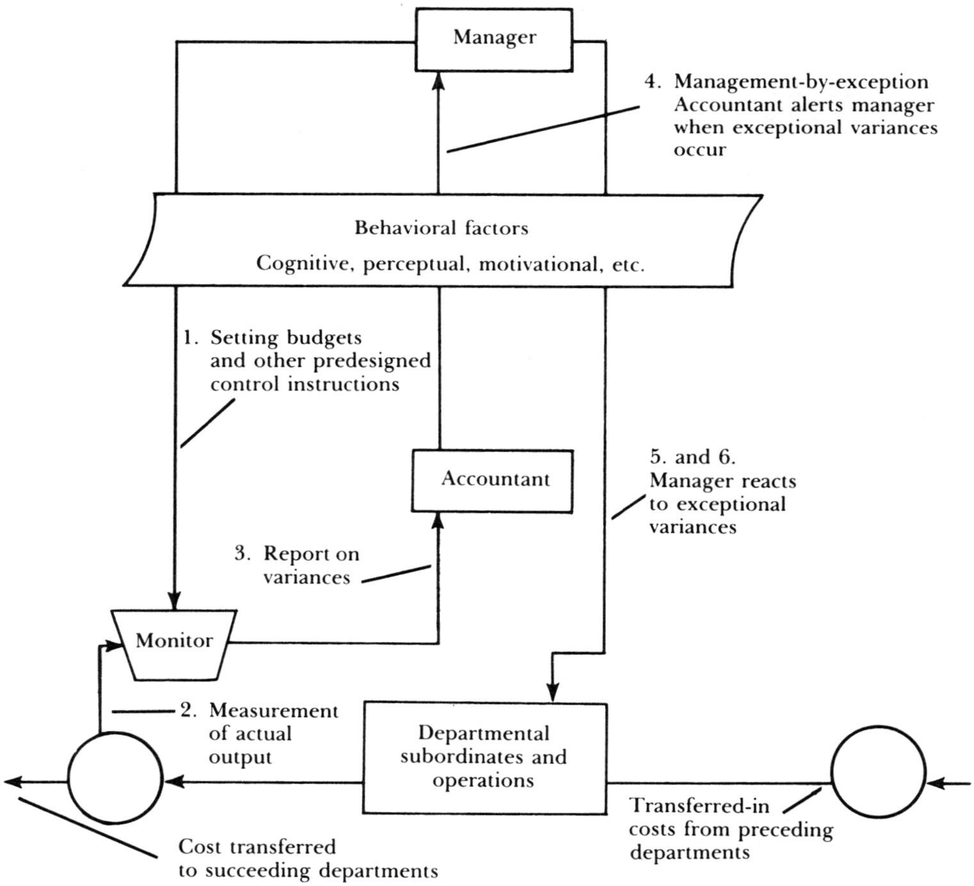

FIGURE 1. A typical budgetary cost control system for an organizational unit.

4. *Problem identification* requires a cost accountant to use the output of the monitor (the variance report) to decide if an exceptional situation requiring managerial attention has arisen. If so, he brings such deviations to the attention of the manager.
5. *Search for causes* is undertaken by managers for all deviations of exceptional nature. The search may involve dealing with both subordinates or other managers (if cause is of external origin).
6. *Response* or the taking of appropriate corrective measures if manager discovers an out-of-control situation. If, however, a cause is uncontrollable, then the budgets for the following periods are adjusted to account for it.

Two additional features of this system should also be noted. First, all information passes through cognitive or perceptual filters, representing the socio-psychological dimensions of this system. This aspect, though important, is not the central concern of this paper.[6] Second, a cost center is part of a dynamic system of work-flows. It receives inputs from preceding departments and transforms them into outputs for succeeding departments.

An analysis of the budgetary system outlined in Fig. 1 shows that both structurally and philosophically it reflects a closed systems view. Structurally, the system is analogous to a closed cybernetic control model known as the "error-controlled regulator".[7] This type of model works on the principle of feedback information on disturbances that affect a controlled variable. Regulatory action is taken only after some errors have occurred. That is, the system learns from small errors that it can tolerate and prevents more fatal errors.

This is precisely the principle on which budgetary control systems operate. Errors in this context are the budget variances. Two types of variances are computed from budgets. The first, which fall within some "normal" prespecified range, are called "nonsignificant" variances. The criterion for normality may be a rule of thumb, such as ± 10 per cent of the budget, or it may utilize more refined statistical methods. If the latter are used, then nonsignificant are usually defined as random variances. The second type represent the so-called "exceptional" or non-random variances, and are investigated by managers for underlying causes. A report "explaining" such variances to higher level management is then prepared. This type of feedback is what allows management to control such systems and is the key to successful regulation.

Philosophically, the central notion underlying budgetary control systems is that of "responsibility accounting". Horngren (1977, p. 156) describes responsibility accounting systems as systems which "recognize various decision centers throughout an organization and trace costs (and revenues, assets and liabilities, where pertinent) to the individual managers who are primarily responsible for making decisions about the costs in question". All costs traced to decision centers are separated into two categories: controllable and uncontrollable. Only controllable costs are used for managerial performance evaluation because these are costs "that are directly influenced by a *manager* within a *given time span*". (Horngren, 1977, p. 160.)

Operationally, budgets are prepared by cost centers which generally coincide with the major decision centers in an organization. For example, in a typical functionally organized manufacturing firm, cost centers generally will be the various functional units such as production, marketing, finance, etc. Each of these may be further subdivided into other cost centers along the lines of the vertical chain of command specified by a firm's organization charts. Thus,

[6]For a discussion of the interaction between information and human-social variables and its implications for design of control systems, see Ansari (1977).

[7]For a complete discussion of "error controlled" and other types of regulation in cybernetic models, see Ashby (1956, Chapter 11).

cost centers generally reflect the distribution of responsibility, authority and power in an organization. The assumption is that control will work by assigning managers precisely defined tasks and time-tables and matching these with an adequate allocation of resources and authority.[8]

The responsibility view, therefore, is a compartmentalized view of organizations which fails to consider the dynamic interactions and interdependencies between its parts. It focuses only on the vertical (chain of command) dimension and ignores the horizontal (work flow) dimension. This, in turn, leads to the use of variances for fixing blame (or discovering heroes) rather than on managing the entire system. The internal structure and efficiency of cost centers dominates over their external and environmental relationships and dependencies. These, of course, are the characteristics of a closed system approach described in the preceding section. They represent Gouldner's (1959) so-called "rational" model of organizations. Budgets based on this model, when applied to the newer types of interdependent organizations, can lead to at least three major problems.

First, as Shillinglaw (1972, p. 426) states: "No where does the responsibility accounting structure recognize organizational interdependence. It may even increase interdepartmental conflicts, as each manager seeks to improve his own record or protect himself from blame, without regard to what happens elsewhere". The accounting system is thus set up to reward *competition* and not *co-operation.* In many cases this leads to suboptimization.

Second, because the cost controllability criterion is interpreted in a jurisdictional sense, it ignores the fact that the underlying cause of a variance may be uncontrollable even though the cost itself is incurred within a cost center (e.g. a labor variance caused by improper workmanship in a prior department). That is, responsibility accounting defines controllability in terms of effects (outcomes) rather than causes. Much time and effort, therefore, is spent on unnecessary investigations on the part of higher managers, and defending, blame shifting, etc. on the part of lower managers. Given the fact that management-by-exception emphasizes negative performance more often than positive, these unnecessary investigations are likely to exacerbate a situation in which subordinates are conditioned to associate managers with a negative event. Lower morale and dysfunctional behavior aimed at "looking good" on measured variables thus are more likely to occur.[9]

Finally, the two-way variance classification places primary emphasis on performance evaluation and ignores the learning aspect of deviations. Managers do not have information about the underlying causes of system-wide variances. For example, a cause such as defective storage of raw materials may lead to cost variances in several departments, many of which are several stages away from the initial introduction of materials.[10] Its impact is not readily known to higher management since each department's variances are computed independent of others. Therefore, no system-wide learning takes place.

In this connection, it is interesting to note that a responsibility accounting system responds to the presence of interdependencies by attempting to create more artificial autonomy between parts and maintain the fiction of controllability. For example, it is not uncommon to

[8]For a more general discussion of the behavioral assumptions underlying management accounting see Caplan (1966).

[9]For a complete discussion of some of the dysfunctional behaviors which can result in control systems see Lawler & Rhode (1976, Chapter 6).

[10]An illustration of this is paper manufacturing. If timber is improperly stored and gets exposed to weather, problems are created several stages later in the production process.

charge inputs to departments at standard prices to protect them from cost fluctuations elsewhere. This only keeps management from focusing properly on the sources of disturbances because each manager pays attention to only those variances which have a sizeable impact in his department. Changing costs at standards thus ignores the larger problem of how problems in one area affect others.

To summarize, budgets, as part of responsibility accounting systems, are presently based upon a closed systems logic. One consequence of this is that the computation of budget variances fails to recognize the dynamic interacting nature of organizational units which may or may not correspond to established cost centers. Also, because the logic emphasizes rationality and efficiency, the existing two-way scheme of classifying variances is biased in favor of performance evaluation over learning. The system, therefore, reflects a "control over people" rather than a "control over system" view.

BUDGET VARIANCES—AN OPEN SYSTEMS APPROACH

The prior discussion shows that the deficiencies in budget information largely reflect the use of an organizational model which fails to capture the reality of many modern organizations. It also shows that for these organizations the open systems model is more suitable. This section explores the changes in budget variance information which are needed when organizations are viewed as open rather than closed systems.

The adoption of an open systems model requires a reorientation in the computation of variances along three dimensions.

First, in generating variances it should be recognized that a cost center does not exist in isolation. Rather it is characterized by an active exchange and adaptation to its environment. The impact of a cost center's environment on its performance needs to be recognized in generating variances. A recent empirical study by Hayes (1977) supports this conclusion. It shows that the performance of many organizational subunits is more contingent upon their interrelationships with other subunits (intra-organization environmental factors), and with environmental influences (inter-organizational environmental factors), than internal factors. Variances should inform managers about these interdependencies, and should also capture the likely system wide impacts of disturbances originating from any of these three contingencies.

Second, the open systems model views a manager as a "regulator" rather than as an authority figure. The concept of regulation, as used in the systems literature, accents the problem solving role of a manager over his evaluative role. This means that variances should aid managers in locating problems and bottlenecks and help them in neutralizing these sources of instability. It also means that the evaluative role of variances becomes less important.

Finally, since the management of the entire system takes precedence over the management of subunits, variances should help global problem solving rather than local problem solving. This is an important consideration since existing cost accounting literature either deals with standard costing for organizational subunits in which local optimization is emphasized, or with divisional performance measurement systems in which global optimization is more important. Currently, no systematic theory exists for the intermediate organizational level, which uses budget variance data as the primary control tool and requires both local and global optimization.

To implement this philosophy, two major changes must be made in the way in which variances are presently computed, reported and analysed. The first step is to develop a variance classification scheme which highlights the nature and origin of disturbances. Currently, as field studies done by the National Association of Accountants (NAA) (1974, p. 10) show, most companies compute variances by cost items (i.e. material, labor and overhead) for individual responsibility centers. That is, they use the same account classifications used for control and for inventory costing purposes. Control reports, therefore, provide little information to management on the underlying causes of these variances. The second step is to use this classification as a way of understanding the interaction between a cost center and its environment. This again is not available in current systems since they do not focus on the interdependencies within cost centers. Management can thus gain insights into the system wide impact of variances. These steps are described in more detail below.

Causal Classification of Variances

For purposes of control, management needs to know not only whether a variance is significant, but also the source or origin of the disturbances responsible for these variances. Without this knowledge, a lot of managerial effort may be expended in merely trying to discover where his efforts are most needed. The existing two-way classification of variances is not very informative in this regard. An alternative scheme, shown in Table 1, is suggested as a replacement.

There are two dimensions to the proposed scheme. The first one focuses on the nature or significance of the variances. However, instead of random-nonrandom it uses the terms *expected* and *unexpected* variances. This is because random is a statistical concept which is more suited for statistical variance investigation decision models.[11] It implies that a standard or budget represents the mean of a probability distribution of *chance* causes.[12] In practice, managers may choose to include within a standard causes which are technically nonchance and thus controllable. This may be either an economic

[11]The variance investigation decision is treated as a purely statistical problem in the literature. Hence the random-nonrandom scheme is used to decide which disturbances are worth investigating. For a review of these models see Kaplan (1975).

[12]An excellent example of this is the application of statistical quality control theory to investigation of cost variances. These models assume a constant cause system in which the standard is the expected value of a normal probability distribution. See Probst (1971).

TABLE 1. A Proposed Classification Scheme for Variances

Nature \ Environmental Origin	Internal (within a cost center)	External (from another cost center)	Exogenous (outside the organization)
Expected	11 e.g. Fluctuations in output caused by inexperienced workers	12 e.g. Defective raw materials purchased by stores agent	13 e.g. Change in prices of raw materials
Unexpected	21 e.g. Breakdown of machinery	22 e.g. Delay in receiving work from preceding department	23 e.g. Delay in shipment of materials due to strike

choice—because it is too costly to remove these causes—or a behavioral choice—it is desirable for motivational reasons to include some slack in budgets. In either case, expected variances are those that a manager judges to be insignificant.

The second dimension deals with the environmental source or origin of variances. Conceptually the environment of a cost center can be divided into three parts—*internal, external* and *exogenous.* Internal refers to those factors or disturbances which originate within a given cost or responsibility center. External highlights the interdependent nature of the cost centers and refers to those disturbances which originate in some other cost center. Exogenous disturbances are those which originate outside an organization's boundaries and are within the environment of the total organizational system.

Each cell in Table 1, therefore, represents a combination of judged significance and environmental origin of a variance. It also shows typical examples of variances which will fall within each cell. For effective control, all variances should be assigned to one of the six cells of Table 1. This will generate a list in which all variances will be identified by a digital code number referencing their cell classification. For example, a variance caused by "breakdown of machinery" will be given a number 21.1. The first two digits, 21, will tell a manager that this is an "internal" and "unexpected" variance (cell 21 of Table 1); the last digit is a sequential listing within this class—i.e. this is the first variance assigned to cell 21. To illustrate this process, a list of variances from an NAA study have been classified in Table 2 on the basis of the above scheme.

The proposed variance classification in Table 2 serves an important role in highlighting which disturbance sources or cell are most critical to a units' operations. This can help individual managers better focus their energies. For example, if most of the disturbances in a cost center originate in cells 12 and 22 that is, external to the cost center, then its manager should spend most of his time on managing external relationships. The scheme also serves a potentially greater and more valuable role in helping upper management understand a system's overall dynamics. That is, it can help management to better understand the interrelationships between the various responsibility units in an organization and the relationships between an organization and its environment. This, however, requires the second change proposed from the current usage of variances. Information on six-way variance analysis from individual cost centers now must be combined into a single organizational matrix to be used for inter cost center variance analysis.

Inter Cost Center Variance Analysis

The purpose of this step is to combine the causal information on variance (shown in Table 2) from individual cost centers into an overall organizational matrix. Such a matrix arranges all cost centers in a sequential order representing the organization's work flow. It then arrays all variance causes against their respective cost centers to isolate what are termed as "key causes".[13] These are defined as those causes which impact on several cost centers and thus may be causing bottlenecks within the overall work flow system. Table 3 shows such a matrix of key causes for a simple manufacturing organization in which work flows sequentially from *production* to *assembly* to *packaging*—the three cost centers in this organization.

The matrix in Table 3 is a partial representation of what is likely to be a large matrix

[13]The idea of a matrix of key causes is borrowed from the area of job design. In structuring and formulating jobs, designers use what is known as a matrix of "Key variances" (not accounting variances). These variances help them identify the *most important* technical requirements which impact upon the successful completion of a job. For details see Englestad (1972).

*TABLE 2. A Sample List of Departmental Variances Coded by the Proposed Scheme**

Dept. No. . . . .

Reason for Variance	Month of: Actual Hours	Month of: Variance Hours	Month of: Variance Cost	Year to Date: Actual Hours	Year to Date: Variance Hours	Year to Date: Variance Cost	Code†
No reason, variance less than 10 per cent							11.1
Estimated running time too high. Reported to Stds. Dept.							12.1
Estimated set-up time too high. Reported to Stds. Dept.							12.2
Men's effort and/or ability above average							21.1
New machine, standard has not been changed							21.2
Change in methods, standard has not been changed							21.3
New or improved tools, standard has not been changed							21.4
Used set-up from previous job							11.2
Time set for man operating one machine. Ran two							21.5
Time clock registers to 0.1 hours only							11.3
Work done under special supervision							21.6
Standard too low. Reported to Standards Dept.							22.1
First time job was made							11.4
Slow or obsolete machine used							21.7
Planning not correct. Was changed. Stds. Dept. notified							22.2
Could not follow oper. as planned, delivery requirements							23.1
Operations in previous departments not performed as planned							22.3
Time set for man operating two machines. One available							22.4
Quantity too small							13.1
Extra set-up result of machine breakdown							12.3
Extra work							13.2
Two men had to be assigned to jobs due to nature of job							21.8
Learner, apprentice, or student							11.5
Parts spoiled. Had to make additional parts							21.9
Tools not available at time job was started							23.2
Trying out new tools							13.3
Tools not correct when job was started. Had to be corrected							23.3

*TABLE 2. A Sample List of Departmental Variances Coded by the Proposed Scheme**

Dept. No. . . . .

Reason for Variance	Month of Hours	Month of Actual Variance Hours	Month of Actual Variance Cost	Year to Date Hours	Year to Date Actual Variance Hours	Year to Date Actual Variance Cost	Code†
Broke tool. Time lost redressing and sharpening							21.10
Oversized material used							23.4
Castings warped, but are within Foundry tolerances							12.4
Castings not to dimensions. Time lost waiting for instructions							22.5
Material too hard. Frequent sharpening of tools required							23.5
Improper supervision							21.11
Illegible blue prints							22.6
Blowholes and porous castings							22.7
Sheet stock, secondary material or scrap ends used							13.4

*This Table is adapted from Exhibit 1, Part II (NAA, 1974), pp. 12–13.

†See Table 1 for interpretation of first two digits of code numbers. The assignment here represents my guess of which category a cause should be assigned to.

TABLE 3. A Sample Matrix of Key Causes

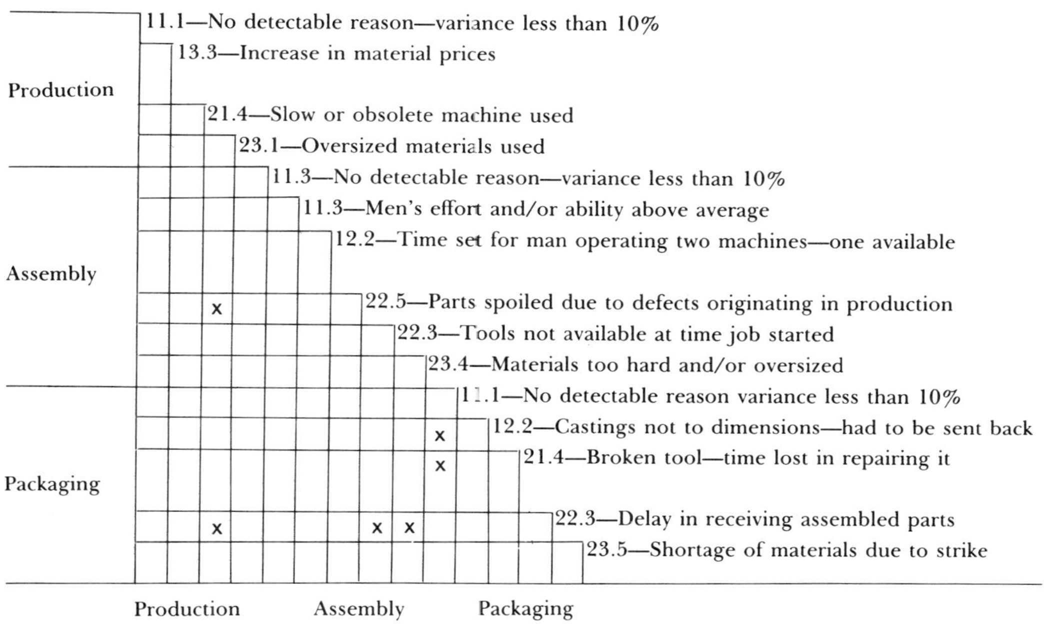

for most real situations. For illustrative purposes it is assumed that only 15 actual causes have been identified for the period under review. The first four (from top to bottom) of these causes resulted in variances in the production department; the next six caused variances in the assembly department; and the last four caused variances in the packaging department. Using the classification scheme of Table 1, all of these causes have been assigned to one of its six cells and sequentially numbered within each cell. It should be noted that the causes shown are not differentiated by traditional categories such as materials, labor or overhead. The emphasis at this stage is on the total performance of a cost center. However, if needed, the matrix and classification scheme can be easily expanded to include an identification of causes by cost elements.

To identify "key causes", a manager has to assess both the direct and indirect impact of a cause on costs. Direct impacts are measured by variances in the cost centers in which a cause is first isolated. Existing responsibility accounting reports currently provide such information and Table 3 incorporates it in the matrix. The indirect impact is assessed by analysing past data to see whether a cause resulted in variances in other cost centers. In Table 3, this is indicated by a cross (X) in an appropriate cell. For instance, under the column for the cause "slow or obsolete machine used", there are two crosses. The first cross is in the row "parts spoiled" in Assembly and the second is in "delay in receiving assembled parts" in Packaging. This means that the use of an obsolete machine causes spoiled parts in Assembly and causes delays in sending parts from Assembly to Packaging. Similarly, when the Assembly Department uses "hard materials" it causes Packaging to "send back castings" and "break tools". This information is obtained by reading those rows in Table 3 in which the crosses appear.

The total variance attributable to a cause can be computed by adding the crosses down the columns of Table 3. In the example cited above, the total variance attributable to the Production department cause "slow or obsolete machine used" is the sum of the variance resulting from this cause in Production and the variance in assembly and packaging due to "spoiled parts" and "delay in receiving parts" respectively. It shows that the total cost of an obsolete machine is larger than the amount shown in the Production Department. In fact, it is possible that the indirect costs may be much greater than the direct costs. Thus causes which might have been ignored in a typical responsibility accounting system may be key causes when both the costs are added. This type of information is not available in existing responsibility accounting structures and is extremely useful if budgetary control is to move toward the system regulation view discussed earlier. It helps to pinpoint those areas in which co-operation is needed more than competition. Also, for a designer this type of information is very useful. For instance, if most variances in packaging originate in assembly, then it may be useful to combine these two cost centers into one or to better co-ordinate their activities.

CONCLUDING REMARKS

The central theme of this paper is that the development of new and more complex organizational forms has led to a new view of organizations and management. This new view, which is best captured by an open systems model, emphasizes the vast commerce between an organization and its environment in explaining behavior. Most management and accounting information systems, however, continue to reflect a closed systems view of organizations. Thus, they currently constrain organizational development since the information provided fails to capture the impact of a system's environment on its performance.

The consequences of operating in a closed systems mode in a dynamic environment impacts on both the external and internal accounting functions. Externally, financial accounting systems have failed to meet the demands placed on them by a dynamically changed environment. Hence the frustration of the profession at being held accountable for things that the accounting system is ill equipped to handle. Internally, budgetary control reflects the same problem. Budgets are currently used for *ad hoc* problem solving rather than for developing systematic notions of accountability. A bottom line mentality prevails and budget variances are the key to this bottom line mentality. This is why the focus of this paper has been on budget variances. It shows that budget variances, as currently reported, lead to at least three major problems in organizations.

First, valuable managerial time and resources are expended on investigating causes that are not controllable within given cost centers. This is because current variance reporting does not recognize organizational interdependencies. Therefore, it also causes dysfunctional behaviors such as blame shifting, manipulation of data, etc. Second, managers are encouraged toward local rather than global problem solving. Again, this is due to lack of information on organizational interdependencies. Finally, variance information is designed to encourage competition rather than co-operation. This is inappropriate since a great deal of dependence between organizational parts exists. Knowing when to encourage co-operative behavior between parts is a major need of a manager.

To solve these problems, an alternative scheme for computing budget variances is proposed here. It supplements information from a traditional responsibility accounting system with information on variances in a cost center caused by its external interactions. The attempt is to discover and recognize those key causes whose impact extends well beyond the boundaries of a single cost center. These key causes can be instrumental in shifting management toward global system regulation. It can also replace the existing control over people with a control over system view.

In closing, it should be noted that what is proposed here is a change in *both* the philosophy and structure of computing budget variances. Thus, the new scheme for computing variances is good only if managers are willing to buy into the philosophy which underlies it. Managers who think in responsibility accounting terms rather than in terms of regulation or problem solving will not recognize the need for or use this type of information. Without expanding one's view of organization and management, information is unlikely to be very effective in controlling organizations.

BIBLIOGRAPHY

Ansari, S., An Integrated Approach to Control System Design, *Accounting Organization & Society* (1977), pp. 101–112.

Ashby, R., *An Introduction to Cybernetics* (London: Chapman & Hall, 1956).

Bruns, W. H. & J. H. Waterhouse, Budgetary Control and Organization Structure, *Journal of Accounting Research* (Autumn, 1975), pp. 177–203.

Caplan, E. H., Behavioral Assumptions of Management Accounting—Report of A Field Study, *Accounting Review* (April 1968), pp. 342–352.

Englestad, P. H., Socio-Technical Approach to Problems of Process Control in L. E. Davis and J. C. Taylor (eds.), *Design of Jobs* (Penguin Books, 1972).

Emery, F. E. & Trist, E. L., Socio-Technical Systems. In F. E. Emery (ed.) *Systems Thinking* (Harmondsworth, U.K.: Penguin Books, 1969).

Gouldner, A. W., Organizational Analysis. In Robert K. Merton, Leonard Broom, Leonard S. Cottrell, Jr. (eds.), *Sociology Today* (New York: Basic Books, 1959).

Hayes, D. C., The Contingency Theory of Managerial Accounting, *Accounting Review* (January 1977), pp. 22–39.

Horngren, C. T., *Cost Accounting: A Managerial Emphasis* (Englewood Cliffs, N.J.: Prentice-Hall, 1977).

Kaplan, R. S., The Significance and Investigation of Cost Variances, *Journal of Accounting Research* (Autumn 1975), pp. 311–337.

Kast, F. E. & Rosensweig, J. E., *Contingency Views of Organization and Management* (Palo Alto, CA: Scientific Research Associates, Inc., 1973).

Katz, D. & Kahn, R. L., *The Social Psychology of Organizations* (New York: John Wiley, 1966).

Kremyanskiy, V. I., Certain Peculiarities of Organisms As a System From the Point of View of Physics, Cybernetics and Biology. In F. E. Emery (ed.), *Systems Thinking.*

Lawler, E. E. & Rhode, J. P., *Information and Control in Organizations* (Pacific Palisades, CA: Goodyear Publishing Co., 1976).

National Association of Accountants, *Standard Costs and Variance Analysis* (New York: NAA, 1974).

Probst, F. R., Probabilistic Cost Controls: A Behavioral Dimension, *The Accounting Review* (January 1971), pp. 113–118.

Sathe, V., Contingency Theory of Organization Structure. In J. L. Livingstone (ed.), *Managerial Accounting: The Behavioural Foundations* (Grid, 1975).

Sayles, L. R. & Chandler, M. K., *Managing Large Systems: Organizations For The Future* (New York: Harper & Row, 1971).

Shillinglaw, G., *Cost Accounting: Analysis and Control* (Homewood, Illinois: Irwin-Dorsey, 1972).

Thompson, J. D., *Organizations In Action* (New York: McGraw Hill, 1967).

Waterhouse, J. H. & Tiessen, P., A Contingency Framework for Management Accounting Systems Research, *Accounting, Organizations and Society* (August, 1978), pp. 65–76.

Watson, D. J. H., Contingency Formulations of Organizational Structure: Implications for Managerial Accounting. In J. L. Livingstone (ed.), *Managerial Accounting: The Behavioural Foundations* (Grid, 1975).

A Framework for Management Control Systems

Peter Lorange
Massachusetts Institute of Technology

Michael S. Scott Morton
Massachusetts Institute of Technology

This article has two purposes. The first is to synthesize the current state-of-the-art of Management Control Systems, by pulling together some of the existing concepts into a framework which is useful in identifying gaps in the current understanding. The second is to use the framework to suggest directions in which control systems might be modified to increase their effectiveness. The discussion will be normative. Although the article is not based on a specific research project, the authors draw on pertinent research findings by others, as well as on their own recent field experience with planning and control systems. The authors have specified that all statements to be given are hypotheses and require testing.

INTRODUCTION

The process of control and the application of control system concepts to *management* control has been discussed at great length in the literature over the past twenty years. In its practical form control in organizations today is synonymous with financial control and, in particular, with budgets and the budgeting process. This will continue to be extremely important for all organizations. However, it is apparent from the recent increase in pressure from outside the organization that existing views of control systems will have to be modified if organizations are to continue to run effectively. There already is ample evidence of this shift in the control practices of many organizations, and these changes are taking place in three major areas:

1. The need for control systems to be modified to reflect the evolution from traditional organizational patterns (such as divisionalized organizations) to more complex patterns (such as multidimensional structures),
2. The use of non-dollar variables as a regular part of the formal control system,
3. The linkage between planning and control and between control and operations.

From *Sloan Management Review,* Vol. 16, No. 1 (Fall 1974), pp. 41–56.

MANAGEMENT CONTROL: PURPOSES AND STEPS IN THE PROCESS

Many reasonable definitions of management control systems have been suggested over the years.[1] Admittedly, some of these are so general that they yield less than desirable guidance for the researcher or the practitioner. Other definitions tend to be too partial by focusing on narrower aspects of what seems to be a broader management control process. Nevertheless, a number of useful definitions of management control exist. We propose that the *fundamental purpose* for management control systems is to help management accomplish an organization's objectives by providing a formalized framework for (1) the identification of pertinent control variables, (2) the development of good short-term plans, (3) the recording of the degree of actual fulfillment of short-term plans along the set of control variables, and (4) the diagnosis of deviations.

An overall illustration of the management control process model is given in Figure 1. The figure indicates the interrelationship between management control and the long-range planning process (A). The management control process is split into the control variable identification process (B), the short-term direction setting process (C), and the short-term plan accomplishment tracking process (D). The linkage between planning and control is illustrated by arrow (a). The relationship between the two control subprocesses is illustrated by arrows (b) and (d). The tracking of deviations between actual performance and budget may lead to a number of actions, arrows (c), (d), and (e).

[1]See, for instance, Anthony [3], Jerome [22], Anthony, Dearden and Vancil [4], Horngren [20] and [21], Welsch [33], Emery [14], and Dearden [11].

Identification of Control Variables

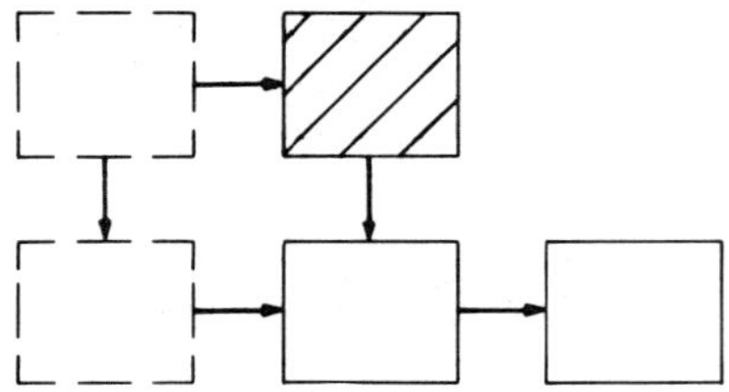

Control variables form the content of the short-term plan. They are the items that represent the goals of the organization, and they determine what is to be tracked. One of the central activities of management control is to identify what these control variables should be. In the following discussion it will be shown that control variables come from two major sources:

1. The goals and objectives
2. The situational setting, particularly the organization structure, the people in the organization, the technology available, and the external environment.

The choice of control variables is partially dependent on the choice of key variables in the long-range plans. This is indicated in Figure 1 by the arrow linking the key variable identification and the control variable identification processes. Key varibles are operational measures that reflect the goals of the organization. For example, change in market share might be a key variable used to reflect the organization's goal of growth. Some key variables cannot be used as control variables, because they are virtually uninfluenced by the organization. For instance, new product innovations by competitors could be a key variable but could not be a control variable. Nevertheless, the goals and objectives of the corporation, as represented by the key variables, are a major source for the determination of control variables.

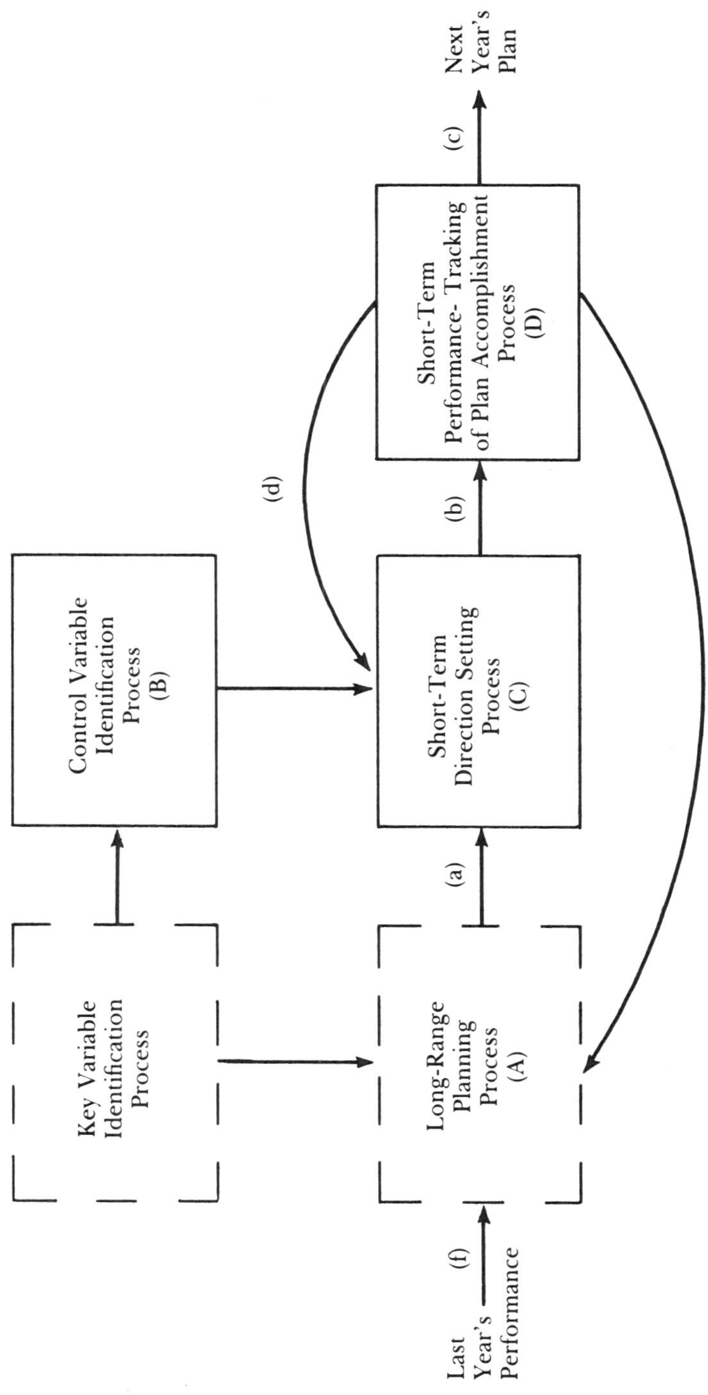

FIGURE 1. Interrelationship between the Components of the Long-Range Planning and Management Control Processes

The actual choice of control variables also will depend critically on each given corporate setting. Leavitt's work will be used to indicate the aspects of an organizational setting that should be considered in developing a situationally tailored set of control variables.[2] Leavitt argues that a particular task interacts strongly with three other sets of variables: the organizational structure in which the task is taking place, the people that are in the organization, and the technology that is available to support the task. He finds that these factors have to be in a state of dynamic equilibrium if an organization is to remain healthy. For the purposes of this article the external environment will be added as a fourth major independent variable. Each force will be discussed in detail in order to indicate the impact it has on the choice of control variables.

Organization Structure. The type of control system to be used is partially dependent on the organization structure that exists in the company. The generally accepted contingency theory of organizational design suggests that the choice of a structure depends on the company's situational setting. Since virtually all companies differ in this respect, there will be no one best way of designing the organization.[3]

Every corporation consists of a number of more or less autonomous decision-making units known as cost centers, investment centers, departments, divisions, areas, etc. Although there are many different types of responsibility center units, it will be claimed here that each center has several common features of the management control process. However, the control variables to be tracked through plans and budgets will differ, depending on the type of responsibility center that is involved. Further, an analysis of the common elements of management control with the responsibility center helps the exploration of management control for various combinations of centers, such as functional, divisional or matrix organizations. Thus, a management control problem is encountered at two levels: for individual responsibility centers and for combinations of centers.

People. The type of control variables and the nature of the control process may be significantly affected by several sets of variables that characterize people in organizations. The first of these might be labeled "style." The style of the managers and the style of the organization with respect to conflict resolution, attitudes toward risk, and the way decisions are made, often vary between organizations. Some organizations have a well-documented, bureaucratic approach toward each decision. Others tend to be more informal with largely verbal conversations and little or no documentation. The control system will obviously be different in these two types of organizations. The control system will also be affected by the educational levels and the degree of professionalism of the managers and by the history of the organization. These factors of style, education, and history are augmented by the "political science" of the organization. The importance of the informal power structure and the informal communication network of organizations has been well-documented elsewhere.[4] Although the control systems design cannot take all these factors into account explicitly, it is crucial for the designer to recognize that the people in the organization will determine in large measure what kind of control system is possible.

There is an important reverse effect of the control system on the people in the organi-

[2]See Leavitt [26].

[3]For a review of empirical studies on contingency theory, see Galbraith [15] and Lorsch and Allen [28]. For some viewpoints critical to the contingency theory school of thought, see Christenson [9].

[4]See Lorange [27] and Bower [6].

zation. Not only do the people affect the kind of control systems possible, but there often is a strong effect of the control system on the individuals involved. The question of the motivational impact of tight versus loose budgets is merely one example of this effect. The early work by Stedry and others attempted to illustrate some of the behavioral effects of the budgeting process.[5] Although this research focused largely on dollar budgets or on single dimensional budgets, it is clear that it had an impact.

Technology. There are at least three important aspects of technology with respect to control systems. The first and most prevalent is the management information system necessary to support the control system. A simple example of this is the computer-based information system which allows a much more elaborate and detailed budgeting system to be maintained than would be possible manually.

A second aspect is the problem of measurement techniques. In addition to the developments in cost measurement systems, there is a technology involved in tracking non-dollar key variables such as employee morale, market share, productivity, and product quality. If the measurement technology is not adequate to track these variables, it becomes impossible for them to form a robust part of the control system.

A third component of technology involves the mathematical techniques that allow us to make trade-offs between different objectives based on multi-attribute preference theory.[6] For instance, if the system requires tracking a series of control variables and each is measured on a different scale, it becomes necessary to find a way of assessing the status with respect to the combination of these objectives. Evaluating a division that is ahead on market share, behind in quality, and above inventory target levels is an example of such a problem. Further, a given course of action may have different effects on the various attributes and it may become difficult, or even impossible, to assess which action strategy would give the best results.

The reverse effect of the impact of the control system on technology probably is most significant in the information systems area. In many instances the information systems ought to be designed to support the control system and should not be built as ends in themselves. This view of subordinating information systems to the purposes of the control system is not widely shared by professionals in the field.[7]

Environmental Forces. The fourth set of forces that help determine the control system are those external to the organization. It might be more accurate to show a planning function between the environment and the control system since it is a purpose of the planning activity to assess the environment and its implications for the organization. As was argued at the beginning of the article, changes in the external environment may indicate that a shift in emphasis in the control system is appropriate. For example, the environment is exerting pressure for product quality or product safety. It is raising the costs of production due to energy shortages and is causing shifts in raw material supplies and their costs. The environment also is placing requirements on the organization from governmental authorities and is exerting competitive pressures due to shifting technology. It seems reasonable that the control system should change to include an expanded set of variables which will enable the organization to respond to these external forces.

[5]See Stedry [31] and Becker and Green [5].
[6]See Keeney [24] and [25].
[7]See Gorry and Scott Morton [19].

Setting Short-Term Direction

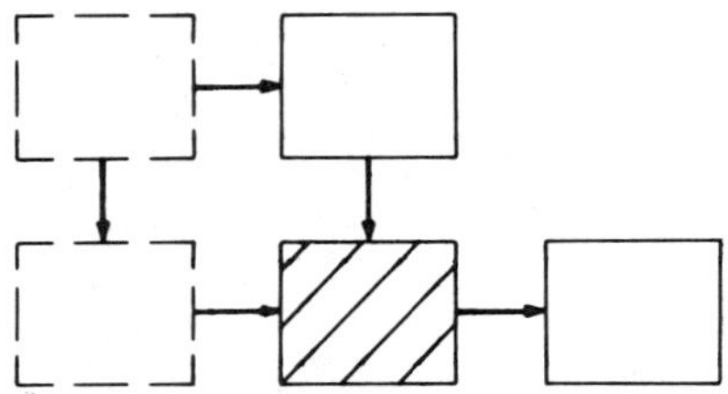

From Figure 1 it follows that the next step in the control process is to set short-term goals. A major objective of management control is to provide a vehicle for systematically narrowing down the wide number of business opportunities immediately facing the corporation into a single set of proposed business actions. Initially, the primary participants in the process will be top management, but as the control process proceeds, more of the organization's managers become involved. This procedure leads to the adoption of a course of action by a gradually increasing set of managers, and culminates in an agreement on a near-term plan to which all management should be committed.

One purpose of management control is to arrive at a "smart" set of short-term goals which may be specified in dollar numbers (as exemplified by the budget) or in non-monetary terms. Each responsibility center will attempt to develop its own short-term goals. There will be a number of inputs from the preceding planning, such as the responsibility center's charter, objectives, goals, and strategy. Also, a relatively broad and tentative resource allocation to the unit's overall programs typically will exist. The task of the short-term planning process is to further narrow down the span of immediate opportunities so that a good near-term plan will result. In case of little or no previous long-range planning or in case of loose linkage between the long-range and short-term planning parts of the process, much less narrowing down of strategic options will have taken place. Thus, at the short-term planning stage, more dramatic narrowing down will then be needed in order to arrive at the same near-term plan. In practice, this may jeopardize the quality of the short-term plan, since usually there is insufficient time to complete this more extensive procedure.

For a functionally organized combination of responsibility centers, the steps in the short-range, strategic goal-setting process may be that the corporate president's office states the overall corporate goals, based on a summary of the inputs from the preceding planning cycle. The departments then develop their short-range plans and submit them for coordination, review, and approval by the corporate headquarters. Approval implies allocation of funds to the short-range plans.

For a divisionalized organizational structure, each division proceeds in essentially the same way as a functionalized corporation. The most significant difference seems to be in the role of corporate headquarters which in this case requests each division to initiate the development of its short-term goals, operationalized by its short-term plans. Corporate headquarters and the division level responsibility centers will have agreed previously on both corporate and divisional long-range goals. This agreement, involving all three hierarchical levels of the divisionalized organization (corporate, divisional, and departmental), will be based on planning at earlier stages. Headquarters also will have made tentative allocations of available resources to the program "packages" of each division. In other words, it will have indicated how much will be allocated to each segment of the company so that the desired balance of profits, growth, and risk properties can be attained for the corporation overall.[8] Within the constraints imposed by this specification of linkage to long-range plans, the divisions will be asked to formulate their short-term plans.

[8] See Vancil and Lorange [32] and Carter and Cohen [8].

A number of characteristics of this process should be pointed out. First, close coordination often will be required between the functional departments; they are not developing their short-term plans in isolation. Second, the process is iterative. Typically, the short-term planning cycle will go through a number of "spins" before the budget is finalized. Third, the budgeting process is hierarchical. This implies that the higher organizational level will review the plans of the level underneath as a portfolio. Thus, each responsibility center plan at the lower level will be reviewed in terms of its effect on all the other responsibility center plans at that level.

The Performance Tracking and Diagnosis Steps

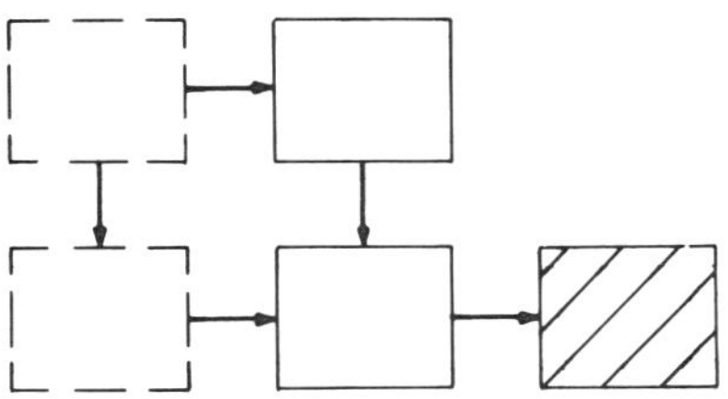

The third purpose of management control, as indicated by (D) in Figure 1, is to serve as a "tracking function" for measuring performance and as a basis for diagnosis of performance deviations. It provides a vehicle for systematically learning how to adjust to one's business environment by attempting *ex post facto* to determine why plans and budgets were not fulfilled. By making use of plans and budgets as benchmarks for reference in analyses of why the company did not realize its plans, important understanding about future direction-setting can be gained. In fact, since the management control process monitors both long-range and short-range plans, the tracking function will be essential for effective planning in both the long term and the short term.

The ability of an organizational unit to fulfill its short-term plans depends not only on its own performance but on the performance of other organizational units as well. For instance, a division's ability to realize its short-term plan depends considerably on how well its departments are attaining their short-term goals. Consequently, the tracking function must provide for signaling performance deviations to those organizational units for which such information is relevant. At this point, however, the tracking process will be discussed in terms of a single responsibility center. The tracking functions may be divided into two subfunctions: the recording of deviations from short-term plans and the diagnosis of deviations, hopefully leading to a determination of their causes.[9]

The first of the two subfunctions, the recording function, can in turn be separated into three components: the measurement of each control variable, the determination of the extent to which deviations are due to controllable factors and whose responsibility it is,[10] and the determination of the extent to which deviations are due to uncontrollable events in order to then initiate the proper adjustments. The control variable measurement function consists of measuring the progress over time of the short-term goal attainment. Since not all goals can be quantified in monetary terms, a measurement is needed for control variables that are expressed in non-dollar terms or in qualitative terms. A number of criteria have been proposed for judging the appropriateness of control measures; many of them originate from financial accounting.[11] The measures may have to satisfy criteria such as objectivity, reliability, and verifiability. But it is most important that the data being monitored are useful for decision making and management control.

[9]See Zannetos [34].

[10]See Kaplan [23], Dyckman [13], and Demski [12].

[11]See, in particular, American Accounting Association [1] and American Institute of Certified Public Accountants [2].

The second subtask of the tracking function is the diagnosis of variances which involves applying analytical tools to understand what caused the deviations. Since different types of variations are being analyzed for a variety of control variables, a number of analytical tools may have to be used. The diagnosis of a variance may lead to three different actions:

1. The performance deviation may trigger a corrective action process which could involve some alteration of the previous resource allocation. This is illustrated by arrow (d) in Figure 1.
2. In cases of serious deviations, corrective measures may be taken regarding the overall resource allocation pattern. This will be evidenced by a revision of the long-range plans and will be followed by a revision of the short-term goals. Arrow (e) illustrates this relatively rare effect.
3. In some cases no immediate corrective actions are taken, but the deviations may have an impact on next year's plan, as evidenced by arrow (c). (Of course, deviations in last year's performance similarly led to impacts on this year's plan, as illustrated by arrow [f].)

Complicating issues of tracking arise when working with hierarchical combinations of responsibility centers. In the case of a functionally organized company, performance measurements typically are for cost centers and/or discretionary expense centers. Diagnosis also focuses heavily on costs and expenses. These problems shall not be explored in detail, but reference is made to a relatively well-developed body of literature.[12] For the divisionalized corporation the performance tracking focuses not only on cost and expense centers, but also on profit and investment centers. Many difficult measurement problems arise when attempting to determine profits and even more arise when attempting to estimate an asset base. The various arguments within this field will not be discussed, but again reference is made to the literature.[13]

There is a danger that the performance tracking process will lead to decision-making behavior which violates the overall organizational goal congruence requirement. This is partly due to the "technical" measurement problems just referred to. These often stem from a desire to capture complex and multifaceted phenomena by means of a few variables, usually expressed in dollar terms. Oversimplification, leading to impossible measurement tasks, could be the result. Also, lack of goal congruence may arise due to inconsistencies between the time span used for control purposes and the time span that is appropriate for the business. For instance, a research laboratory organization would experience severe problems with a one-year time horizon for its control system when a five-year plan would be more appropriate.

The preceding discussion has attempted to synthesize the current view of management control systems. The literature contains a variety of views and most of them can be summarized by Figure 1. However, the literature does not emphasize three emerging areas of control which will be discussed in the next section.

EMERGING ISSUES

The three emerging areas of management control are linkage to planning, use of non-dollar control variables, and impacts from the added complexity of multidimensional organizational structures.

---

[12] See Horngren [20], Gordon and Shillinglaw [18], and Dearden [11].

[13] See, for instance, Solomons [30] and Dearden [10].

Control Implications of Multidimensional Organizational Structures

A result of the increasing complexity of today's technology is a greater interdependency between many intermediate production processes. This may lead to a considerable penalty in terms of diseconomies of scale in corporations that are divisionalized. Much duplication of effort may be taking place. Similarly, a company that is expanding multinationally may be too small to set up separate production facilities in each geographical area. In both instances, a matrix-type organizational structure may be adopted to achieve both production economies and business/area effectiveness. Given the trends toward increased complexity of technical processes and toward increased internationalization, multidimensional organizational structures probably will become more common.

For a company with a matrix structure key decision-making activities are carried out in committees made up of managers who represent diverse task backgrounds. Consequently, within part of such organizations, unidimensional hierarchical responsibility center patterns no longer exist. The managers on the matrix boards will represent one of the following three task types:[14]

1. *Business units:* These will have performance responsibility for a business family, similar to a divisional organization along business areas, and typically will be profit centers.
2. *Geographical units:* These will have performance responsibility for a geographical area, e.g. a country, and also will typically be profit centers.
3. *Functional units* (e.g., manufacturing, marketing, R & D): These will have performance responsibility for the functional services they render to each business or area unit, and typically will be cost centers.

Not all matrix organizations will have a three-dimensional structure; they may not have all three task types represented on the group decision-making matrix boards. For instance, a company that operates only on the domestic market may be matrix-organized only along the business and functional dimensions. A company which is manufacturing essentially one class of products world-wide may adopt a two-dimensional matrix with geographical and functional elements. Thus, only multinational, multiproduct corporations typically will adopt the more complex three-dimensional structure.

It should be stressed that a relatively small proportion of a company's decision makers will be directly involved in committee decision-making. The functional organizational hierarchies, such as marketing or production, will still exist, and unidimensional responsibility patterns will be evident within these hierarchies. However, at one level fairly high up in the organization each function will be coordinated with the other functions, and with the business and/or the area dimensions. A corporation may consist of a few or many matrix groups at this level.

Three distinctive types of control tasks emerge from such a matrix structure:

1. Control within each of the three task dimensions (i.e., the business, geographical and functional tasks). Particularly for the functional responsibility centers elaborate control similar to that found in unidimensional structures typically will be instituted.
2. Control of each matrix committee effort. The multidimensional responsibility and reporting patterns are a distinctive feature.
3. Control of the overall corporation. The major task is to control the overall portfolio of matrix team efforts.

[14]See Galbraith [15] and [16], and Goggin [17].

For a matrix structure the steps in the short-term planning process will be much more complicated. A high level of interaction among many executives and substantial interrelationships between sub-plans and sub-tasks will be necessary. The need for a formal system of management control becomes greater in such a setting in order to ensure proper timing, proper formats, and coordination of many diverse control activities.

One might speculate that in order to initiate the planning and control process, one of the three task dimensions should be given a more dominant role than the others. For instance, when developing the long-term plans, the business or geographic task units may be more involved than the functional dimensions. However, when options have been narrowed down and short-term budgeting is to take place, the functional units may play the more dominant role.

As a further illustration of the complexity of matrix structures, one can look at the measurement and diagnostic step. In multidimensional organizations the problem is compounded because of the multiple responsibility for tasks among decision makers. One implication is that costs and incomes must be tracked so they are assignable to matrix responsibility units as well as to functional, area, and/or business responsibility centers. A given income figure may be credited to two functional responsibility centers or to a functional unit and an area unit. Hence, income and cost figures normally will have to be divided and accounted for by more than one unit of the organization. Measuring costs and incomes so they can be divided in other than an arbitrary manner becomes a major task of performance tracking in matrix organizations.

A second implication of the complexity of matrix structures is the substantial increase in the volume of internal reporting that is needed. Because of the more complex patterns of interdependencies, the minimum time requirements for updating and revising plans must be expanded. A computer-based management information system could be cost-benefit advantageous for organizations of this type.

A third implication is the necessity to ensure consistency of formats for short-term plans and for procedures of calculating and reporting deviations.

The internal information-handling tasks become quite complex in a matrix organization. Consequently, the choice of a formal structure for the management control system becomes crucial, and the potential increases for utilization of advanced information-handling techniques.

Non-Dollar Variables

An emerging issue from the discussion of the identification of control variables was that many of the variables will not be measured in monetary terms. The inclusion of these control variables reflects the added importance of environmental pressures and suggests a fundamental shift from the traditional control systems.

It is implied here that the control systems design process should be adapted to reflect the need for an environmental diagnosis and to decide which control variables should be used. The shifting environment does not suggest that the fundamental nature of the control process should change. However, it does suggest that the kind of variables that are in the control system, the way they are derived, and the people, structure and technology that are employed may have to be changed. In particular, if the external environment is shifting as suggested, then the control system will require different control variables.

An example of this situation is the attempt by a furnace manufacturer to track dealer inventory levels in order to reduce hoarding. Dealer stockouts were occurring frequently because of a scarcity of parts at the factory which was caused by the energy shortage. Similar examples are easy to find. However, there does not exist a good statement of what such control variables should be or a well-understood methodology by which they can be derived. It is suggested that analysis of the five forces reflected in the list at the outset of the discussion on the identification of control variables is an effective first step which can be done readily by any organization.

Linkage of the Control System

The discussion outlining the steps in the management control process emphasized the linkage to planning. In addition, there are linkages between control and the action programs that are designed to correct the operations of the organization based on the diagnosis stage. A third linkage is caused by the need to connect control across the hierarchical levels of an organization.

The Linkage between Management Control and Planning. It has been indicated that the linkage between the long-range planning phase and the control phase is critical for the characterization of the control process. This is because the way and extent to which business opportunities have been previously narrowed down will largely dictate the activities of the control phase. Two aspects of this linkage, content and timing, will be discussed.[15] It has been suggested that content linkage between the long-range plan and the budget can be judged by comparing the two in terms of (1) comparability of the level of financial detail, (2) agreement between the plan and budget at a given time, (3) agreement of this year's budget with last year's plans and (4) the extent to which differences at a given time and over time are reconciled. Given the different purposes of planning and control, an alternative way to look at these linkages will be suggested. Although the key variables may be entirely compatible, the figures of the plan and budget need not coincide. Thus, situations with tight content linkage may exist despite this compatibility.

In cases with loose content linkage, little "narrowing down" of options occurs at the planning stage. This implies that most of the narrowing down is done at the short-term planning/budgeting stage. Consequently, heavier requirements will be placed on this process stage in order to arrive at a "smart" plan. It is important to realize that loose content linkage implies a shifting of the narrowing down from planning to control.

There may be several reasons for a rational choice of a specific degree of tightness or looseness of content linkage. During some stages of an organization's evolution, the linkage may be loose by default rather than by design. Typically, most companies have had much longer experience with budgeting than with long-range planning. When planning is initiated, it often will be difficult to integrate it with the mature control process. In effect, this means loose linkage, accompanied by the implications just discussed.

The time schedule for the completion of the planning and budgeting task also becomes important. If relatively little time elapses between the execution of the long-range planning tasks and the short-range planning (budgeting) tasks, a tighter *de facto* substance linking is indicated. However, because of the longer elapsed time between completion of the budget and the beginning of next year's planning, the outputs of this year's control process will have a looser impact on next year's plan. But the timing linkage question may be less significant than perceived by many because of the continuous nature of the processes and the necessity to perform them on a continual basis all year.

Linkage to Action Plans. The signals from the control system generate a diagnostic activity as part of the management control process. This diagnosis is used by the responsibility center manager to help establish an action plan to solve, or mitigate, the existing variances. Such

[15]See Shank *et al.* [29] and Camillus [7].

action plans may be more or less successful in curing the fundamental cause. The effectiveness of the existing signals in helping the manager to solve problems is an important consideration in redesigning the control system. This linkage between action and control has severe implementation problems and, judging from the existing literature, seems almost nonexistent. Measurement of cause and effect in these situations is difficult, but such a linkage is desirable if the control system is to be usefully modified over time.

Organizational Linkage. As many as three types of organizational levels must be considered. At the corporate level there is a linkage problem between the corporate long-term and short-term plans; at the division level there is a linkage problem between the division's business plan and its business budget. At the departmental level there is a linkage problem between the functional plan program and the functional budget. Further, there is the problem of linking each level's plans and budgets with those of the levels above and below. In dealing with a three-level interdependent linkage a number of issues are raised. Should the degree of content linkage be the same at the three levels? If corrective actions are taken at one organizational level, how are the other levels' long-range and/or short-range plans affected? Will the effect be the same under patterns of tight linkage and loose linkage?

This suggests that the planning/budgeting process model portrayed in Figure 1 should be expanded into a multi-level model in order to cope with these organizational linkage problems.

IMPLICATIONS

The above view of control systems has been designed to emphasize the implications of three emerging evolutionary trends for management control.

1. The increasingly unstable external environment necessitates a tighter linkage of the management control system to the formal planning system.
2. The instability of the external environment causes a need for a more robust set of control variables than exists with the current dollar-based budget.
3. The increasing diversification of large corporations often creates more complex organizational forms (at the extreme, the matrix structure) which operate in varying environments (the multidimensional corporation) and in different businesses (the conglomerate).

Even for small or medium-sized organizations these three factors are changing, and similar changes can be identified for public sector organizations. As a result, a clear view of control systems and their basic purposes is needed; without such a view it is difficult to build or run one effectively in an organization.

The framework suggested here is a first step in trying to build a structure which is useful for diagnosing existing control systems. Is there an agreement between this "normative" view and the descriptive model of the organization's existing control system? In particular, it would be argued that the framework presented here is useful for making changes in the management control system to reflect the continuing changes in the external environment, changes which exert considerable pressure on the corporation.

REFERENCES

1. American Accounting Association. *A Statement of Basic Accounting Theory.* Evanston, Ill.: Ameri-

can Accounting Association, 1966, chapter 4.
2. American Institute of Certified Public Accountants. *Objectives of Financial Statements.* (Trueblood Committee Report), New York: AICPA, 1973.
3. Anthony, R. N. *Planning and Control Systems: A Framework for Analysis.* Boston: Division of Research, Graduate School of Business Administration, Harvard University, 1965.
4. Anthony, R. N.; Dearden, J.; and Vancil, R. F. *Management Control Systems.* Homewood, Ill.: Irwin, 1972.
5. Becker, S., and Green, D., Jr. "Budgeting and Employee Behavior." *Journal of Business,* October 1962, pp. 392–402.
6. Bower, J. *The Resource Allocation Process.* Boston: Division of Research, Graduate School of Business Administration, Harvard University, 1970.
7. Camillus, J. C. *Formal Planning Systems: The Control Considerations in Design.* Unpublished D.B.A. Thesis, Graduate School of Business Administration, Harvard University, 1972.
8. Carter, E. E., and Cohen, C. "Portfolio Aspects of Strategic Planning." *Journal of Business Policy,* Summer 1972.
9. Christenson, C. "The Contingency Theory of Organization: A Methodological Analysis." Harvard Business School Working Paper, 1973.
10. Dearden, J. "The Case Against ROI Control." *Harvard Business Review,* September-October 1966.
11. ———. *Cost Accounting and Financial Control Systems.* Reading, Ma.: Addison-Wesley, 1973.
12. Demski, J. "Optimal Performance Measurement." *Journal of Accounting Research,* 1971.
13. Dyckman, T. R. "The Investigation of Cost Variances." *Journal of Accounting Research,* 1969.
14. Emery, J. C. *Organizational Planning and Control Systems.* New York: Macmillan, 1969.
15. Galbraith, J. *Organization Design: An Information Processing View.* Sloan School Working Paper, M.I.T., 1969, pp. 2–5.
16. ———. "Matrix Organization Design." *Business Horizons,* February 1971.
17. Goggin, W. C. "How the Multidimensional Structure Works at Dow Corning." *Harvard Business Review,* January–February 1974.
18. Gordon, M. S., and Shillinglaw, G. *Accounting: A Managerial Approach.* Homewood, Ill: Irwin, 1964.
19. Gorry, A., and Scott Morton, M. S. "A Framework for MIS." *Sloan Management Review,* Fall 1971.
20. Horngren, C. *Cost Accounting: A Managerial Emphasis.* Englewood Cliffs, N.J.: Prentice-Hall, 1972.
21. ———. *Accounting for Management Control.* Englewood Cliffs, N.J.: Prentice-Hall, 1974.
22. Jerome. W. T. III. *Executive Control—The Catalyst.* New York: Wiley, 1961.
23. Kaplan, R. S. "Optimal Investigation Strategies with Imperfect Information." *Journal of Accounting Research,* 1969.
24. Keeney, R. L. "An Illustrated Procedure for Assessing Multiattributed Utility Functions." *Sloan Management Review,* Fall 1972.
25. ———. "A Decision Analysis with Multiple Objectives: The Mexico City Airport." *Bell Journal of Economics and Management Science,* Spring 1973.
26. Leavitt, H. *Managerial Psychology.* Chicago: University of Chicago Press, 1972.
27. Lorange, P. *Behavioral Factors in Capital Budgeting.* Bergen, Norway: Universitetsforlaget, 1973.
28. Lorsch, J. W., and Allen, S. A. III. *Managing Diversity and Interdependence: An Organizational Study of Multidivisional Firms.* Boston: Division of Research, Graduate School of Business Administration, Harvard University, 1973.
29. Shank, J. K.; Niblock, E. G.; and Sandalls, W. T., Jr. "Formal Planning Systems: Getting Creativity and an Action Orientation." *Harvard Business Review,* November-December 1972.
30. Solomons, D. *Divisional Performance.* New York: Financial Executives Institute, 1965.
31. Stedry, A. C. *Budget Control and Cost Behavior.* Englewood Cliffs, N.J.: Prentice-Hall, 1960.
32. Vancil, R. F., and Lorange, P. *Steps in the Long-Range Planning Process.* Sloan School Working Paper, M.I.T., 1974.
33. Welsch, G. *Budgeting: Profit Planning and Control.* Englewood Cliffs, N.J.: Prentice-Hall, 1972.
34. Zannetos, Z. S. "On the Theory of Divisional Structures: Some Aspects of Centralization and Decentralization of Control and Decision-Making." *Management Science* 12 (1965).

*Organizational Context and the Success of Management Information Systems**

Phillip Ein-Dor†

Eli Segev†

This paper identifies the organizational context variables affecting the success and failure of MIS. The variables are categorized as uncontrollable, partially controllable and controlled, and a conceptual scheme is suggested. In addition, current information on these variables and the interactions between them is surveyed; propositions are stated concerning relationships between the variables and the success or failure of MIS.

INTRODUCTION

In their seminal paper "A Program for Research on Management Information Systems", Mason and Mitroff [37] proposed that "an information system consists of at least one PERSON of a certain PSYCHOLOGICAL TYPE who faces a PROBLEM within some ORGANIZATIONAL CONTEXT for which he needs some EVIDENCE to arrive at a solution and that the evidence is made available to him through some MODE OF PRESENTATION". It is the purpose of this paper to elaborate on one of the elements listed by Mason and Mitroff, namely the organizational context.

Under the heading of organizational context, Mason and Mitroff restrict their discussion to two of the "large, if not infinite, number of ways of discussing the influence of organizational *structure* on the design of MIS" (our emphasis). First they present Anthony's [3] hierarchy of strategic planning, management control and operational control and suggest that, from this point of view, "organizational structure is a reflection of the levels of problems the organization considers important to solve". Since most MIS to date have been implemented for operational control, they may play a dysfunctional role when a strategically oriented organizational structure is needed. Next Mason and Mitroff quote Wilensky's findings on the tendency of structural variables (hierarchy, specialization and centralization) to cause information pathologies (secrecy, blocking, leaks, etc.) [61]. Finally, they discuss the association between the "interdependency of the information systems and the organizational structure" and "its interdependency with the people who play organizational roles". They conclude that "the interactions of these aspects of the organiza-

From *Management Science,* Vol. 24, No. 10 (June 1978), pp. 1064–1077.

*Accepted by Arie Y. Lewin; received January 29, 1977. This paper has been with the authors 4 months, for 2 revisions.

†Tel-Aviv University.

tional context have not been systematically researched in conjunction with other aspects of MIS design".

Thus Mason and Mitroff identify two aspects of the organizational context, namely structure and people. The importance of the organizational context variable is underscored by the proceedings of a recent conference on Implementing Operations Research/Management Science [50]. The papers presented at this conference focussed on the issue of management science implementation from many different points of view and examined a large number of dependent variables. In spite of this variety of approaches, at least some of the aspects of organizational context appeared in the vast majority of the papers.

The rest of this paper is devoted to identifying all the aspects of organizational context and to their incorporation into a conceptual scheme based on their degree of controllability and the consequent amenity to change of the organizational context in conjunction with MIS design. In addition, current knowledge on each of the organizational context variables and on the interactions between them is surveyed and propositions are stated as a basis for research designed to formalize the currently intuitive approach to this area.

A rather complex model of information systems in organizations and a set of propositions concerning relationships between the variables have been proposed by Lucas, who has also studied some of the interrelationships empirically [29], [30], [31], [32]. Our own feeling is that the current state of knowledge is such that some preliminary work is necessary to establish a common framework for such research efforts. Thus, we have backed off somewhat from Lucas' all inclusive approach. Our intention is to focus only on the organizational context as it impacts on MIS, identifying the relevant variables as completely as possible, and to state a series of propositions about them based on their effects, direct or indirect, on one dependent variable, the success of MIS. The underlying assumption is that an understanding of the effects of each of Mason and Mitroff's elements individually will facilitate attempts to establish the network of interactions between them.

METHODOLOGY

The source of data for this paper is a survey of the scientific, managerial, professional and trade literature which has accumulated over the past decade on the construction and use of MIS. Since modern MIS are inevitably computer based, and often management science oriented (in fact many authors make no distinction between operations research application and MIS e.g. [50]), many of the problems of implementing MIS are the classical problems of computerization and management science in general. Our tendency, therefore, is to glean relevant knowledge wherever we find it in the entire field of computer and management science application.

Since new variables stopped turning up well before the end of the search, we are confident that the list obtained is quite complete. The final list contains about 120 variables which have been presented in a previous paper [13]. The current paper deals only with that specific subset of the total list of variables which relates specifically to the organizational context of MIS. Thus the presentation is a systematization of data currently scattered throughout the literature.

A rather exhaustive search of the relevant scientific literature yielded some 50 items of an empirical nature. A sampling of monographs, working papers and trade literature yielded a further 24 papers of this type. An additional 84 papers (53% of the 189 reviewed) are a sample of the abundance of position papers containing intuitive conceptualizations based on anything from one case to substantial practical experience. It is our position that, to the extent that the positions taken are based on experience, they are a source of data in an area where data are in scarce supply. It is symptomatic of the state of the art that even in the scientific literature, some 36% of the papers are conceptual rather than empirical. Thus the literature yielded not only a bare list of variables, but also a collection of opinions and empirical data on those variables. This collection of (mostly soft) data requires validation. We find it most useful, therefore, to present this information as a series of propositions which represent prevailing views on the issues examined.

In order to permit presentation of as much of the relevant material as possible, the presentation has been compressed. The propositions are general and are intended to indicate areas in which research is required rather than explicit hypotheses for specific research projects.

At the level of each individual variable, our propositions first regard the MIS as a black box; the organizational context variables are perturbed one at a time, assuming all other variables kept constant, and the effect on the success of the system is observed. Interactions between the variables are added to the analysis immediately after the discussion of the second of the interacting variables, thus rendering the black box a little less opaque.

DEFINITIONS

Definitions of MIS fall into two broad categories. Those in the first category are design oriented and place considerable emphasis on the physical realization of the system as one of the distinguishing features of an MIS, and refer to computer hardware and software, data bases and decision models (e.g. [9], [39], [53]). Definitions in the second category are user oriented and distinguish MIS entirely in terms of their function in the organization—support for management (e.g. [14], [26], [37]). We argue, in the spirit of the second group, that an information system becomes an MIS when it is used by a manager who finds it useful in the performance of his duties. Our definition of an MIS then:

> A management information system is a system for collecting, sorting, retrieving and processing information which is used, or desired, by one or more managers, in the performance of their duties.

As noted earlier, our dependent variable is the *success of MIS.* The literature suggests a number of criteria for success—profitability, application to major problems of the organization, quality of decisions or performance, user satisfaction and widespread use [6], [15], [32], [44], [56]. These criteria are clearly mutually dependent; profitability is correlated with performance, application to major problems and actual use. We claim that a manager will use a system intensively only if it meets at least some of the other criteria, and that use is highly correlated with them. Thus we choose use as a prime criterion of MIS success.[1] A better measure of MIS success would probably be some weighted average of the criteria mentioned above.

[1] A clear distinction should be made between the success of an MIS *project,* defined as completion on time and within budget, and the success of the MIS which is the end product of the project. A project may be successful and yet result in an unused and therefore unsuccessful system. A project may be plagued by cost overruns and schedule slippages and still result in a widely used system.

A CONCEPTUAL SCHEME

An examination of the variables suggests that they be categorized as uncontrollable, partially controllable and controlled. This categorization permits a stepwise scheme of analysis for the organizational context of MIS. The scheme is useful both for evaluating an MIS project before it is implemented and for analyzing problems or feasibility of change in functioning systems. Rules for the evaluation process are presented graphically in Diagram 1 and discussed below.

Uncontrollable variables are those whose status is given with respect to the MIS, first because the time required to change their values is well beyond the time frame of MIS implementation and second because there is

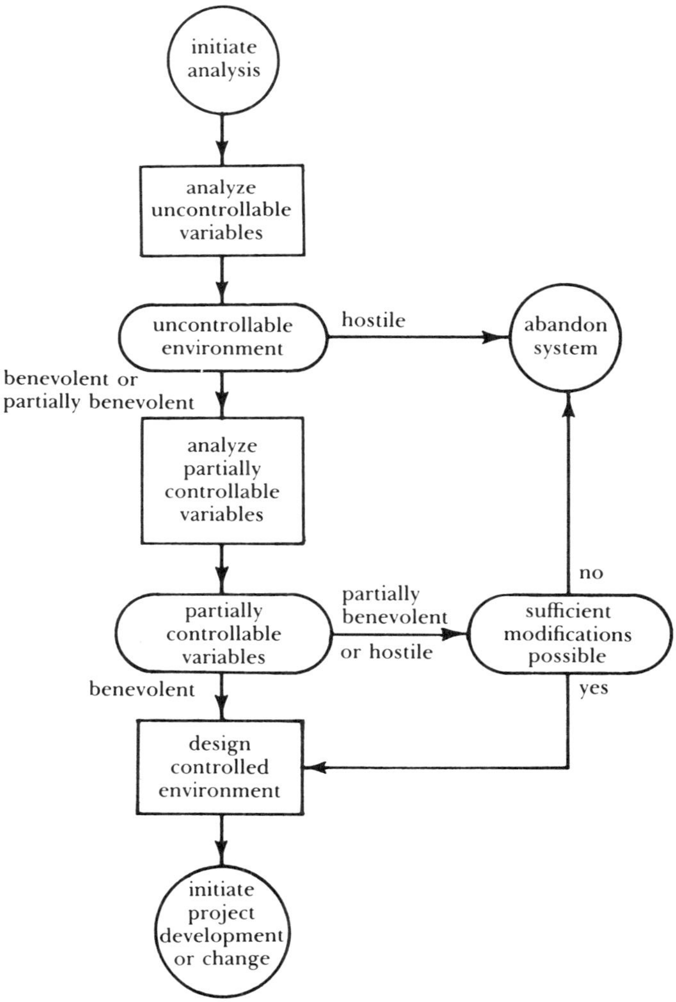

DIAGRAM 1. Conceptual Scheme for Evaluating Organizational Context Variables

very little the MIS unit can do to induce changes in these variables even in the long run; some of them are not under the control of the organization at all. The variables in this group are:

- organizational size,
- organizational structure,
- organizational time frame,
- the extra-organizational situation.

If analysis of the uncontrollable variables reveals a totally hostile front, there would seem to be little point in proceeding further. Any project or system would appear to be doomed to failure until such time as the uncontrollable part of the environment becomes more benevolent.

If the uncontrollable environment is considered sufficiently benevolent to vouchsafe a successful program of implementation or change, the partially controllable variables should then be analyzed. The partially controllable variables are those which are susceptible to change within a time frame compatible with that of the MIS; their exact values cannot be chosen at will, but changes in the desired direction can be induced. The variables describing the partially controlled sector of the environment are:

- organizational resources,
- organizational maturity,
- the psychological climate in the organization.

Even if the environment presented by the partially controllable variables is not benevolent, it may be possible, in many cases, to undertake programs to modify this sector of the environment in parallel with MIS development. As a matter of fact, the last two of these variables are affected, among other things, by the success of the MIS itself, thus heightening their controllability. This point is developed further below.

Having assessed the uncontrollable and partially controllable sectors of the environment, there remain those variables which are completely under the control of the top management of the organization. We define as such those variables whose exact values or states can be determined by the organization with precision and at any time desirable. The variables included in this category are:

- rank and location of the responsible executive,
- the steering committee.

In order to demonstrate the feasibility of using these variables, and as a supplement to the definitions in the text, operational measures are presented in Table 1. It should be noted that these operationalizations are offered as suggestions; the precise measure adopted would need to be fitted in each case to the specific research design. Thus the operationalization of a variable might be different in a laboratory experiment compared to a field survey, especially where behavioral variables are concerned.

There are also a number of interactions between variables. These are exhibited in Table 2. The interactions are indicated by a number in the appropriate matrix element. These numbers reference the comments on the interactions which follow the discussion of the second of the two interacting variables.

In addition to the organizational context variables discussed until now, the table contains one additional variable—MIS success. Since the individual variables were selected because of their effect on MIS success, all of them interact with this dependent variable (interactions 1); this is, in effect, the topic discussed under each of the individual variables. In some cases, however, there is a feedback relationship in which the degree of success in turn affects specific variables. In these cases, MIS success and the specific variable are mutually dependent (interactions 5, 7, 9).

The Variables: Areas for Research
Following is a discussion and presentation of propositions concerning each of the variables and the interactions between them.

UNCONTROLLABLE VARIABLES

Size of the Organization

PROPOSITION 1: *MIS projects are less likely to succeed in smaller organizations than in larger ones.*

A priori, it may not be evident that small companies should have more difficulties with MIS than do large organizations; in fact some authorities claim that they do not. But the types of problems faced by small organizations are certainly different to those confronting large ones. The differences find their expression in resource availability and in the degree of formalization of organizational systems, which in turn affect the lead times for MIS projects. Thus, indirectly at least, the size of the organization affects its prospects for success with MIS [11], [47], [58], [59]. Given the lack of concensus on the effect of size on MIS success, this is clearly an area in which research might improve our understanding.

Structure of the Organization

PROPOSITION 2: *The likelihood of success in building MIS, at the corporate level, is lower in decentralized than in centralized organizations.*

TABLE 1. Suggested Operational Measures for Organizational Context Variables

Variable	Operational Measures
Size of the organization	annual sales; work force; assets; market share.
Organizational structure	number of product-market units; number of profit centers; number of divisions; number of groups.
Organizational time frame	planning horizon; average length of strategic decision process; rate of technological change in industry.
Extra-organizational situation	availability of trained manpower; availability of hardware; availability of software; availability of decision techniques.
Organizational resources	size of budget; liquidity.
Organizational maturity	degree of system formalization; level of quantification; availability of decision-relevant data.
The psychological climate	attitudes to information systems; perceptions of information systems; expectations from information systems.
Rank of the responsible executive	number of levels below chief officer.
Location of the responsible executive	identification with specific functional area.
The steering committee	existence; organizational level.

TABLE 2. Interactions between Organizational Context Variables of MIS

	organizational size	organizational structure	organizational time frame	extra-organizational situation	organizational resources	organizational maturity	psychological climate	responsible executive	steering committee	MIS SUCCESS
UNCONTROLLABLE VARIABLES										
organizational size										1
organizational structure										1
organizational time frame	2									1
extra-organizational situation										1
PARTIALLY CONTROLLABLE										
organizational resources	3			4						5
organizational maturity	6							10		7
psychological climate				8						9
FULLY CONTROLLABLE										
responsible executive						10				1
steering committee							11			1
MIS SUCCESS						5	7	9		

One aspect of organizational structure whose impact on MIS has been documented is the degree of centralization of the organization. Some authors believe that, because of the nature of control in decentralized companies and the increasing complexity of the control problem in such organizations, the development of the new information technologies has been of little help in managing them.

Although this pessimistic point of view seems to us to be somewhat extreme, there are very definitely difficulties in developing MIS for decentralized companies. The major problem is to ensure that the systems built by different divisions can communicate with one another; if this is not done, the firm may find itself with a number of independent systems, which cannot be aggregated or compared. This would imply that the organization can then no longer produce a consolidated picture of itself as a whole, with consequent danger of loss of control [4], [11], [28], [42], [47]. As Mason and Mitroff [37] and Schultz and Slevin [50] indicated, the interaction of organizational structure and information systems is clearly an area requiring research.

Organizational Time Frame

PROPOSITION 3: *The shorter the organizational time frame, the greater the likelihood of MIS failure.*

The decision time frames of organizations differ. Among the factors which may affect the time frame are (1) the culture in which the organization is embedded, (2) the industry and (3) the size of the organization.

In some countries, since the environment is changing only slowly, firms do not need to react as quickly as those in more dynamic environments. But even in countries where the environment is dynamic, cultural factors may dictate styles of decision making with longer time frames. The technical characteristics of an industry and the nature of competition in it also have considerable influence on the company's time frame. Rapidly changing technologies or highly competitive environments can dictate a need for fast decisions. Finally, smaller companies are more likely to be pressed into short decision cycles than are larger ones.

The significance of the organizational time frame for MIS is that while organizational time frames are relatively short and tend to become ever shorter, the time frame for MIS development is quite long. The length of MIS lead times is caused partly by the length of time objectively required to implement information system projects and partly by the subjective inability of MIS staff to appreciate the exigencies of managerial decision making.

Thus there is a tendency to incongruence between organizational and MIS time frames. This tendency implies that it is much more difficult to mount a successful information systems effort when the organizational time frame is highly constrained than when it is relatively relaxed [11], [18], [22], [45], [58], [59].

Organizational Size and Time Frame (Interaction 2)

PROPOSITION 4: *Smaller organizations are more prone to MIS failures because of time frame problems.*

The need to systematize before developing systems and the relative scarcity of resources will generally result in longer lead times for MIS in small organizations than in large, thus exacerbating the natural tendency to incongruence of time frames between MIS and their users.

Thus small organizations tend to induce less favorable states of the resource, maturity and time frame variables than do larger organizations, and so are more prone to MIS failure [58].

The Extra-Organizational Situation

PROPOSITION 5: *The more plentiful the supply of requisite resources in the external environment, the greater the likelihood of MIS success.*

In addition to interacting with the internal features of the firm, the MIS also interacts directly with some features of its external environment. These interactions focus on the degree to which the environment offers those resources which are not immediately available within the firm itself. Specifically, the resources in question encompass decision techniques, software and hardware technology and data processing personnel. To the extent that resources required for implementing a project are unavailable inside the organization, success of the project will depend on their external availability [1], [2], [5], [24], [28], [34], [38], [40], [60].

PARTIALLY CONTROLLABLE VARIABLES

Organizational Resources

PROPOSITION 6: *The budgeting of sufficient resources increases the likelihood of MIS success.*

Resource availability problems are a frequent contributor to the failure of management information systems. First, the MIS function has to compete with other functions in the organization for whatever resources are available. A major difficulty for MIS projects in this regard is the fact that the normal method of justifying budgetary allocations is by cost-benefit analysis; in MIS, the benefits tend to be difficult to estimate in monetary terms.

The problem of obtaining budgetary allocations for MIS is further complicated by the fact that the information function is not generally perceived to be in the forefront of the organization's activities in the same way that production, marketing and finance are. Usually, only after the need for information systems has become self evident and the organization has become aware of their necessity do they achieve a position of significance in the organization's list of priorities.

The ability of the organization to translate its MIS budget into the physical resources required is dependent on the availability of such resources either internally or in the external environment, an issue dealt with above as the extra-organizational situation [4], [7], [34], [45], [59]. There has been some rather inconclusive research into the relationship between MIS budgets and the stages of MIS development in organizations [33], [42]. Here is another area in which systematic research is required.

Organizational Size and Resources (Interaction 3)

PROPOSITION 7: *Larger organizations tend to incur fewer MIS failures arising from insufficient resources.*

The amount of resources required by information systems poses a problem for small organizations, since there are considerable economies of scale in computer operations. Although this has become less pronounced since the advent of mini computers, there are still significant indivisibilities in programming and operations which make systems relatively greater burdens in small companies than in large.

The resource drain caused by information systems can seriously affect the financial situation of a small firm, whereas this is unlikely to be the case in larger organizations. As a result, small organizations may attempt to trim costs by acquiring underpowered hardware or by understaffing. The financial burden may also lead to pressures for quick results, which, combined with understaffing and insufficient hardware can quickly lead to failure [5], [59].

Extra-Organizational Situation and Resources (Interaction 4)

PROPOSITION 8: *The more benevolent the extra-organizational situation, the smaller the drain on organizational resources and the greater the likelihood of MIS success.*

The literature contains numerous reports on deficiencies in computer and management technology, as well as scarcities of data processing personnel, as constraints on the development of MIS. Such shortages affect the ability of organizations to translate budgetary allocations into physical resources, which in turn inhibits the successful development of MIS [1], [2], [5], [24], [28], [34], [38], [40], [60].

MIS Success and Organizational Resources (Interaction 5)

PROPOSITION 9: *MIS success and allocation of sufficient resources are mutually dependent.*

The allocation of sufficient resources has been posited as affecting MIS success. At the same time, the more successful the MIS, the greater the readiness to allocate resources to it, so enhancing the prospects for success. Conversely, MIS failure reduces readiness to allocate resources so increasing the likelihood of failure.

Organizational Maturity

PROPOSITION 10: *The more mature the organization, the greater the likelihood of successfully implementing MIS.*

We define mature organizations as those in which systems are formalized, quantified and produce data appropriate to their decision and control processes. Given this definition, old established organizations which are run informally and intuitively may be very immature, whereas a new, rationally structured and well planned organization may be very mature, in spite of its youth.

In order to construct a formal description of an organization it must be sufficiently well understood so that the relevant variables can be identified. If an analytic model is under consideration, understanding must be deepened to the point where relationships between the variables can be clearly stated.

The construction of formal information systems requires not only that processes be well understood, but that they also be presented in a form suitable for processing and analysis. This usually implies quantitative rather than qualitative description. Systems can be quantified only if data are both available and accessible. First, some of the data required for decision analysis may not have been collected in the past, or may be available only in a form unsuitable for use without considerable massaging. Second, the desired data may exist somewhere in the organization, but are of little use because of the difficulty entailed in actually putting them together [4], [20], [21], [22].

Another important aspect of organizational maturity is the degree to which the sociopolitical structure of the organization is rational and compatible with MIS development. While very little work has been done in this field, a research methodology has been proposed [17].

Organizational Size and Maturity (Interaction 6)

PROPOSITION 11: *Smaller organizations tend to be less mature, thus reducing the likelihood of MIS success.*

Smaller organizations tend to be less formal in structure and procedures. Since effective MIS entail the systematization of the relevant decision processes, considerable effort may need to be expended in formalizing and rationalizing the organization [58].

MIS Success and Organizational Maturity (Interaction 7)

PROPOSITION 12: *MIS success and organizational maturity are mutually dependent.*

We posited above that the degree of organizational maturity, defined in terms of systematization and data availability, promotes the success of MIS. At the same time, the success of an MIS effort increases systematization and enhances the availability of data, thus increasing the likelihood of future MIS success. Little work has been done yet on this seemingly critical interaction between organizational maturity and MIS success. Basic research is clearly needed in this area.

The Psychological Climate

PROPOSITION 13: *MIS projects will succeed to the extent that expectations are constrained from below by motivation and from above by reality.*

Every organization develops its own psychological climate with respect to MIS. This climate is set by the dominant view of MIS held by members of the organization. It finds its expression in the expectations, preconceptions and attitudes prevalent in the organization.

Excessive expectations can be both self-induced and fostered by experts, leading managers to expect much more of information systems than is reasonable. That this situation is widespread is revealed by most surveys of executives, which convey a feeling that computers have been oversold, or at least overbought.

On the other hand, the obverse error is sometimes made. This occurs when the experts, fearful of creating exaggerated expectations, play down the possibilities of MIS. The picture drawn may be so uninspiring as to dampen enthusiasm and to deter managers from making demands, or even from becoming involved. An additional source of low expectations is horror stories about MIS coming out of other organizations. People who have had bad experiences with MIS can be very effective in scaring off their acquaintances [1], [8], [11], [20], [23], [35], [43], [52], [57].

PROPOSITION 14: *Weak preconceptions facilitate the formation of realistic expectations.*

The task of creating realistic expectations regarding information systems can be affected by the state of preconceptions in the organization concerning such systems. In some cases, executives develop strong preconceptions about what the MIS should be like. The existence of such preconceptions can clearly distort the expectations held in the organization about information systems. The weaker the preconceptions held, the better the chances of creating realistic expectations [20].

PROPOSITION 15: *The generation of positive attitudes increases the likelihood of MIS success.*

Expectations and preconceptions play a predominant role in establishing the psychological climate in an organization before the installation of MIS. Once a system has been installed, the climate is also affected by the experience with it. It has been found that attitudes and perceptions of MIS are determined by the quality of the system. Good experience generates favorable attitudes and encourages widespread use of the system. Bad experience has the opposite effect. Since widespread use is one of our criteria for success, attitudes play an important role in determining success [32], [36]. The determinants of attitudes towards MIS clearly deserve extensive research.

Extra-Organizational Situation and Psychological Climate (Interaction 8)

PROPOSITION 16: *A generally favorable external environment fosters a benevolent psychological environment, thus enhancing MIS success.*

Attitudes to MIS are also affected by the extra organizational situation. When the general attitude towards MIS in the environment is favorable, this will tend to establish positive attitudes within the organization. A generally unfavorable external environment, on the other hand, will foster negative attitudes within the organization. Positive attitudes have been posited as one of the conditions for MIS success [23], [43].

MIS Success and Psychological Climate (Interaction 9)

PROPOSITION 17: *MIS success and psychological climate are mutually dependent.*

Expectations and preconceptions play a predominant role in establishing the psychological climate in an organization before the installation of an MIS. Once a system has been installed, the climate is also affected by the experience with it, which has considerable effect on attitudes. Thus Lucas found that the quality of the system determines attitudes towards it. Good experience with a successful system generates favorable attitudes and encourages continuing widespread use—a criterion of success [32].

The importance to successful MIS efforts of the psychological climate in the organization is brought to light by almost every survey in this area and has been recognized by many authorities. Little if any systematic study has been carried out in this field, however. Research in this field promises to contribute greatly to our understanding of the successes and failures of MIS and to the ability of management to establish an organizational environment benevolent to such systems.

FULLY CONTROLLABLE VARIABLES

Rank and Location of the Executive Responsible for MIS

PROPOSITION 18: *The likelihood of a successful MIS effort declines rapidly the lower the rank of the executive to whom the MIS chief reports and is virtually negligible if the executive responsible is more than two levels below the chief executive of the particular organization which the MIS serves.*

PROPOSITION 19: *The likelihood of success is increased if the responsible executive is not identified with any specific functional area.*

Experience, supported by the findings of several surveys, suggests that the likelihood of MIS success declines rapidly the lower the rank of the executive to whom the MIS chief reports, and is virtually negligible more than two levels below the chief officer of the particular organization which the MIS serves. Thus, in many corporations, the practice is that decisions on computers and information systems are kept at the highest level.

It is helpful to consider the problem of executive responsibility within the framework of the stages of system development defined by Nolan, namely initiation, expansion, formalization and maturity. Top management involvement is needed in all these stages, but the third stage, formalization, requires that the MIS department be autonomous and its head report to a vice-president or even to the president himself. This is confirmed by several field studies which have found that the rank of the executive responsible for information systems rises, as systems mature.

The assignment of responsibility for information systems is also dictated by the need, generally conceded, to elevate the level to which the MIS chief reports above any particular functional area. This assignment is necessary in order to liberate MIS from the constraints imposed by subordination to any one function in the organization [8], [10], [11], [15], [16], [19], [20], [21], [34], [35], [41], [57], [59].

Organizational Maturity and the Executive Responsible for MIS (Interaction 10)

PROPOSITION 20: *Organizational maturity is enhanced by the assumption of responsibility for MIS by executives at the highest levels.*

There is a reciprocal relationship between the maturity of the organization and the rank and location of the executive responsible. As information systems mature, the rank of the responsible executive has been found to rise, and his location tends to be independent of any particular function. On the other hand, the assignment of responsibility for MIS to the highest echelons in the organization facilitates system development and expedites the maturation of information systems and hence of the organization [41].

The Steering Committee

PROPOSITION 21: *The likelihood of MIS success is increased by the appointment of a high level steering committee.*

As organizations become aware of the importance of information systems, they tend to establish steering committees to guide the MIS effort. The functions of such committees are to establish policy on information systems, to identify potentially valuable projects and to recommend resource allocations. It has been suggested that companies with high level steering committees tend to be more successful with MIS than those with low level committees or without [7], [12], [16], [25], [30], [34], [41], [43].

The Steering Committee and the Psychological Climate (Interaction 11)

PROPOSITION 22: *Appointment of a steering committee promotes the establishment of a favorable psychological climate.*

The steering committee has been suggested as a means of exhibiting management support, thereby encouraging favorable attitudes towards MIS, which in turn promote success [30].

Research into the terms of reference and operating procedures of steering committees as well as into the structure of their relationships with MIS units could be valuable in promoting the effective incorporation of such committees into the organizational design of MIS.

CONCLUDING REMARKS

This paper is based on existing information and exhibits, therefore, many of the deficiencies of the state of the art, while attempting to rectify some of them. The deficiencies are in two areas. First, while we claim that the list of variables represents all current information, there is no guarantee that additional information will not be uncovered in the future. If it is, however, the framework is such that it should be possible to incorporate within it any new variables discovered.

Second, we have not attempted to establish the relative importance of the variables listed. We do not feel that sufficient evidence is yet available to permit even an ordering of the variables by degree of importance, let alone any kind of cardinal weighting.

The main contribution here is the attempt to establish a systematic conceptual scheme within which the issues of environmental context may be discussed and the suggestion of propositions for research consistent with the framework.

REFERENCES

1. Alexander, Tom, "Computers Can't Solve Everything," *Fortune,* Vol. 80, No. 5 (October 1969), p. 126 ff.
2. Ansoff, H. Igor, "Making Effective Use of Computers in Managerial Decision Making," *Automation* (October 1967), pp. 68–73.
3. Anthony, Robert, *Planning and Control Systems: A Framework for Analysis,* Harvard Univ. Press, Cambridge, Mass., 1965.
4. Bean, Alden S., Neal, Rodney D., Radnor, Mi-

chael and Tansik, David A., "Structural and Behavioral Correlates of Implementation in U.S. Business Organizations," Chapter 5 in Randall L. Schultz and Dennis P. Slevin (eds.), *Implementing Operations Research/Management Science,* American Elsevier, New York, 1975.

5. Brady, Rodney H., "Computers in Top-Level Decision Making," *Harvard Business Rev.* Vol. 45, No. 4 (July–August 1967), pp. 67–76.
6. Carlson, Walter M., "A Management Information System Designed by Managers," *Datamation,* Vol. 13, No. 5 (May 1967), pp. 37–43.
7. Coe, Ted L., "Allocating the Corporate Information Processing Resource," *J. Systems Management,* Vol. 25, No. 8 (August 1974), pp. 18–22.
8. Colton, Kent W., "Computers and Police: Patterns of Success and Failure," *Sloan Management Rev.,* Vol. 14, No. 2 (Winter 1972–3), pp. 75–97.
9. Davis, Gordon B., *Management Information Systems: Conceptual Foundations, Structure and Development,* McGraw-Hill, New York, 1974.
10. Dean, Neal J., "The Computer Comes of Age," *Harvard Business Rev.,* Vol. 46, No. 1 (January–February 1968), pp. 83–91.
11. Dearden, John, "MIS Is a Mirage," *Harvard Business Rev.,* Vol. 50, No. 1 (January–February 1972), pp. 90–99.
12. ——— and Nolan, Richard L., "How to Control the Computer Resource," *Harvard Business Rev.,* Vol. 51, No. 6 (November–December 1973), pp. 68–78.
13. Ein-Dor, Phillip and Segev, Eli, "A Paradigm for MIS," Tel-Aviv University, Faculty of Management, The Leon Recanati Graduate School of Business Administration, Working Paper 256/76 (May 1976).
14. Emery, J. C., "Management Information Systems" in Aronofsky, Julius (ed.), *Progress in Operations Research,* Vol. III, Wiley, New York, 1969.
15. Garrity, John T., "Top Management and Computer Profits," *Harvard Business Rev.,* Vol. 41, No. 4 (July–August 1963), pp. 6–12, 172–174.
16. Gibson, Cyrus F. and Nolan, Richard L., "Managing the Four Stages of EDP Growth," *Harvard Business Rev.,* Vol. 52, No. 1 (January–February 1974), pp. 76–88.
17. ———, "A Methodology for Implementation Research," Chapter 4 in Randall L. Schultz and Dennis P. Slevin (eds.), *Implementing Operations Research/Management Science,* American Elsevier, New York, 1975.
18. Grayson, C. Jackson, Jr. "Management Science and Business Practice", *Harvard Business Rev.,* (July–August 1973), pp. 41–48.
19. Gupta, Roger, "Information Manager: His Role in Corporate Management", *Data Management,* Vol. 12, No. 7 (July 1974), pp. 26–29.
20. Hammond, John, "The Roles of the Manager and Management Scientist in Successful Implementation", *Sloan Management Rev.,* Vol. 15, No. 2 (Winter 1974), pp. 1–24.
21. Hanold, Terrance, "An Executive View of MIS", *Datamation,* Vol. 18, No. 11 (November 1972), pp. 65–71.
22. Hayes, Robert H. and Nolan, Richard L., "What Kind of Corporate Modeling Functions Best", *Harvard Business Rev.,* Vol. 52, No. 3 (May–June 1974), pp. 102–112.
23. Heany, Donald F., "Education, the Critical Link in Getting Managers to Use Management Systems", *Interfaces,* Vol. 2, No. 3 (May 1972), pp. 1–7.
24. Jenkins, William E., "Airline Reservation Systems", *Datamation,* Vol. 15, No. 3 (March 1969), pp. 29–32.
25. Knutsen, H. Eric and Nolan, Richard L., "Assessing Computer Costs and Benefits", *J. Systems Management,* Vol. 25, No. 2 (February 1974), pp. 28–34.
26. Kriebel, C. H., "MIS Technology—A View of the Future", *Proc. Spring Joint Computer Conference* (1972), pp. 1173–1180.
27. ———, "Discussion Comments on Emery", *Data Base,* Vol. 5, Nos. 2, 3, 4 (Winter 1973), pp. 11–13.
28. Kronenberg, R. A., "Weyerhaueser's Management Information System", *Datamation,* Vol. 13, No. 5 (May 1967), pp. 28–30.
29. Lucas, Henry C., Jr., "A Descriptive Model of Information Systems in the Context of the Organization", *Data Base,* Vol. 5, Nos. 2, 3, 4 (Winter 1973), pp. 27–39.
30. ———, "Measuring Employee Reactions to Computer Operations", *Sloan Management Rev.,* Vol. 15, No. 3 (Spring 1974), pp. 59–67.

31. ———, "Systems Quality, User Reactions and the Use of Information Systems", *Management Informatics,* Vol. 3, No. 4 (August 1974), pp. 207–212.
32. ———, "Performance and the Use of an Information System", *Management Sci.,* Vol. 21, No. 8 (April 1975), pp. 908–919.
33. ——— and Sutton, Jimmy A., "The Stage Hypothesis and the S-Curve: Some Contradictory Evidence", *Comm. ACM,* Vol. 20, No. 4 (April 1977), pp. 254–259.
34. McFarlan, F. Warren, "Problems in Planning the Information System", *Harvard Business Rev.,* Vol. 49, No. 2 (March–April 1971), pp. 74–89.
35. McKinsey & Co., Inc., "Unlocking the Computer's Profit Potential: A Research Report to Management", *The McKinsey Quart.* (Fall 1968).
36. Manley, John H., "Implementation Attitudes: A Model and a Measurement Methodology", Chapter 8 in Randall L. Schultz and Dennis P. Slevin (eds.), *Implementing Operations Research/ Management Science,* American Elsevier, New York, 1975.
37. Mason, R. O. and Mitroff, I. I., "A Program for Research on Management Information Systems", *Management Sci.,* Vol. 19, No. 5 (January 1973), pp. 475–487.
38. Montijo, R. E., "California DMV Goes On-Line", *Datamation,* Vol. 13, No. 5 (May 1967), pp. 31–36.
39. Moravec, A. F., "Basic Concepts for Designing a Fundamental Information System," *Management Services,* Vol. 3, No. 4 (July–August 1965), pp. 37–45.
40. Murdick, Robert G. and Ross, Joel E., "Future Management Information Systems—Part I", *J. Systems Management,* Vol. 23, No. 4 (April 1972), pp. 22–25.
41. Nolan, Richard L., "Managing the Computer Resource: A Stage Hypothesis", *Comm. ACM,* Vol. 16, No. 7 (July 1973), pp. 399–405.
42. ———, "Computer Data Base: The Future Is Now", *Harvard Business Rev.,* Vol. 51, No. 5 (September–October 1973), pp. 98–114.
43. ——— and Knutsen, K. Eric, "The Computerization of the ABC Widget Co.", *Datamation,* Vol. 20, No. 4 (April 1974), pp. 71–76.
44. Powers, Richard F. and Dickson, Gary W., "MIS Project Management: Myths, Opinions and Reality", *California Management Rev.,* Vol. XV, No. 3 (Spring 1973), pp. 147–156.
45. Ramsgard, William L., "The Systems Analyst: Doctor of Business", *J. Systems Management,* Vol. 25, No. 7 (July 1974), pp. 8–13.
46. Reisman A. and De Kluyver, Cornelius A., "Strategies for Implementing Systems Studies", Chapter 14 in Randall L. Schultz and Dennis P. Slevin (eds.), *Implementing Operations Research/Management Science,* American Elsevier, New York, 1975.
47. Roark, Mayford L., "Centralization Versus Decentralization of the MIS Effort", *Proc. Second Annual Conference,* Society for Management Information Systems, Washington, D.C. (September 1970).
48. Sass, C. J., "MIS—Are You Missing the Plane?" *Infosystems,* Vol. 22, No. 3 (March 1975), pp. 50–51.
49. Schneidewind, Norman, Jr., "The Practice of Computer Selection", *Datamation,* Vol. 13, No. 2 (February 1967), pp. 22–25.
50. Schultz, Randall L. and Slevin, Dennis P. (eds.), *Implementing Operations Research/Management Science,* American Elsevier, New York, 1975.
51. ——— and ———, "Implementation and Management Innovation", Chapter 1 in Randall L. Schultz and Dennis P. Slevin (eds.), *Implementing Operations Research/Management Science,* American Elsevier, New York, 1975.
52. ——— and ———, "Implementation and Organizational Validity: An Empirical Investigation", Chapter 7 in Randall L. Schultz and Dennis P. Slevin (eds.), *Implementing Operations Research/Management Science,* American Elsevier, New York, 1975.
53. Schwartz, M. K., "Computer Project Selection in the Business Enterprise", *Datamation,* Vol. 15, No. 6 (June 1969), pp. 47–52.
54. ———, "MIS Planning", *Datamation,* Vol. 16, No. 10 (September 1970), pp. 28–31.
55. Singer, J. Peter, "Computer-Based Hospital Information Systems", *Datamation,* Vol. 15, No. 5 (May 1969), pp. 38–45.
56. Swanson, E. Burton, "Management Information Systems: Appreciation and Involvement", *Management Sci.,* Vol. 21, No. 2 (October 1974), pp. 178–188.

57. Townsend, Robert, *Up the Organization,* Alfred A. Knopf, New York, 1970.
58. West, G. M., "MIS in Small Companies", *J. Systems Management,* Vol. 26, No. 4 (April 1975), pp. 10–13.
59. Whisler, Thomas L., *The Impact of Computers on Organizations,* Praeger, New York, 1970.
60. Wimbrow, J. K., "A Large-Scale Interactive Administrative System", *IBM Systems J.,* Vol. 10, No. 4 (1971), pp. 260–282.
61. Wilensky, Harold D., *Organizational Intelligence,* Basic Books, New York, 1967.

Planning Management Control Systems

Franco Amigoni*

The Simon research team (1) found that there are three types of information needed for controlling any company, each serving a different purpose, depending on the answer to these questions:

1. Score-card questions: "Am I doing well or badly?"
2. Attention-directing questions: "What problems should I look into?"
3. Problem-solving questions: "Of the several ways of doing the job, which is the best?"

From the systems theorist's viewpoint we can find a tight relationship between these questions and some control mechanisms: score-card questions can be related to the feed-back loop, and problem-solving questions to the response function, i.e. "the function linking action variables with environmental variables" (2), while it is more difficult to find a precise cybernetics definition for the attention-directing questions.

These reference problems are a very useful starting point in designing and implementing a concrete management control system. Nevertheless the problems that controllers or consultants have to face in any specific company in order to provide managers at any level with appropriate control tools show that they need a more detailed framework. Unfortunately many of the attempts made to identify some kind of relation between company variables—i.e. dimension, turnover, number of workers, etc.—and control tools—i.e. financial and cost account responsibility accounting, budget, etc.—have failed. There are two likely explanations for this: a) the company variables identified were not the more relevant from a control point of view, and b) the description of a specific control system in terms of "tool" is incorrect, given the fact that each tool is multipurpose, and therefore can be used in any company in a very different way.

In order to propose a conceptual framework useful in designing and implementing a management control system in any specific company, we must proceed in various directions. First of all an effort must be made in defining the appropriate independent variables, i.e. the characteristics of the company and of its environment that actually influence the control process. Secondly, we should identify some distinctive features of management control systems, because, as we said above, these systems cannot be correctly analysed in terms of tools. Thirdly, significant relations have to be found between these features of control systems and the independent variables, between control tools and system features and hence between independent variables and control tools. (See Table 1)

From *Journal of Business Finance and Accounting,* Vol. 5, No. 3 (Autumn 1978), pp. 279–291.

*The author is Associate Professor of Accounting and Control, Scuola di Direzione Aziendale, Università "L. Bocconi", Milan. (Paper received September 1977, revised July 1978)

INDEPENDENT VARIABLES THAT ARE RELEVANT IN DESIGNING A MANAGEMENT CONTROL SYSTEM

The control system in any specific company must be tailored in relation to these company and environmental characteristics: a) the degree of structural complexity and b) the degree of discontinuity.

The Degree of Complexity

The structural complexity of the operations can be defined in relation to two dimensions, which, even though connected, must be considered separately. These are: i) number and degree of interdependence of business units and ii) number and type of organisational units.

The first dimension is related to the fact that the control process is simpler in a company, even given high turnover and a large work force, which produces and sells one or a few independent products in a single market than in another, even a small one, which operates in many different markets with joint products. Often the map of organisational units is closely linked with that of business units. However, we prefer to keep these two dimensions distinct, because their relationships are influenced by several factors, such as the size of the company, the values of

TABLE 1. Significant Conditions in the Design of a Management Control System

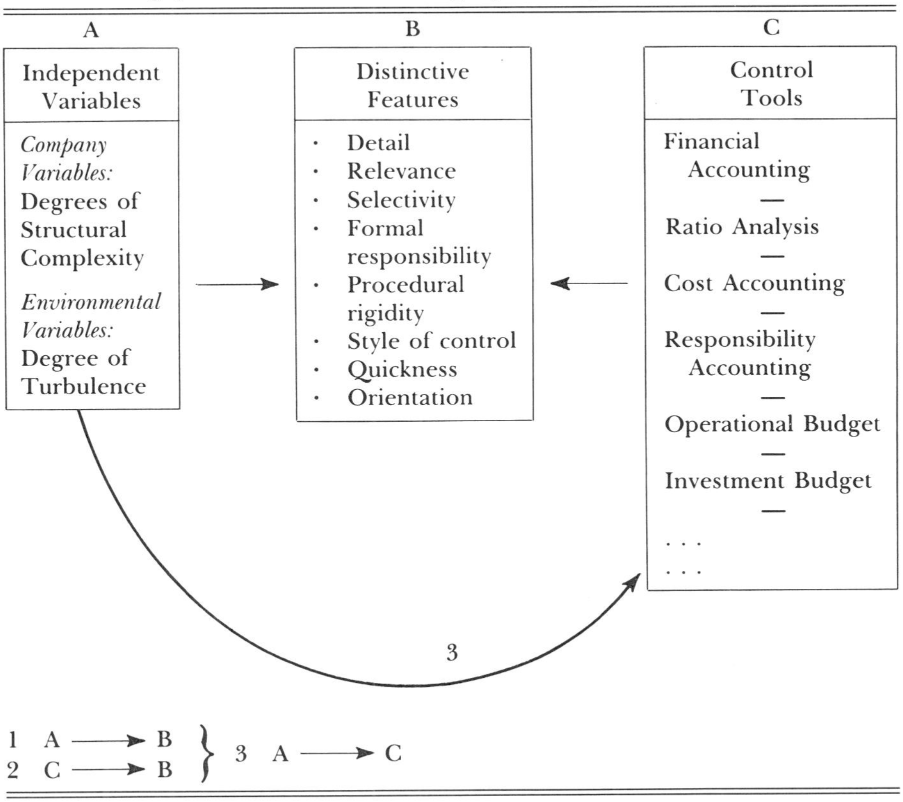

the managers, business turbulence, competitive pressure, etc.

With regard to the second dimension, there is a great distinction between two main organisational settings, with reference to the differentiation already achieved by the system. Any enterprise can be considered an "open system", when goal-directed behaviour results from the actions of its elements. In very simple systems, all the elements pursue the system's goals in an undifferentiated way, and their efforts are coordinated through the mechanism of "dynamic interaction" (3). In complex systems each element has a specialised function, and coordination is achieved through the process of factoring, that is through a hierarchic subdivision of the main system's goal into several coordinated sub-goals for every single organisational unit. At the unit level, the feedback loop and response function are the mechanisms for controlling the goal-directed behaviour.

Enterprises can be considered undifferentiated systems if operations are very simple, and the few men who manage them are owners, and therefore naturally interested in the success of the business. They are complex systems, if the process of differentiation is already well ahead. In this case we have three levels of goals: the system level, the organisational unit level, and the individual level.

The distinction between these two types of system is very important because in the first one the management control system's function is mainly information. To control his company the entrepreneur, who is also the owner and the only decision taker, needs only relevant information, readily and selectively. In complex systems the functions of the control process are far more complicated and range from providing each organisational unit with relevant information to structuring a well coordinated system of sub-goals, motivating managers to achieve their own sub-goals, evaluate their performances, etc. Hence the problems to be solved in designing and implementing management control systems in enterprises already "differentiated" are quantitatively and qualitatively far more complex than those of an "undifferentiated" company. In the first case, more than in the second, the success of the control process cannot be guaranteed without a close fit between all the managerial tools, such as organisation structure, managerial style, reward-punishment system, etc. (see Table 2).

The Degree of Discontinuity

The control process is simple if the company's operations are stable, which implies a stable environment. It becomes difficult if the environment is dynamic, i.e. a high but predictable rate of change, and very complex if the environment is discontinuous, i.e. a high but unpredictable rate of change. The degree of discontinuity is, in our opinion, the more relevant environmental variable, because control systems are systems of order. They are, in fact, projected and implemented with reference to certain assumptions about the economic scenario. If this changes it is difficult for the control system to adapt accordingly its signals to managers.

DISTINCTIVE FEATURES OF MANAGEMENT CONTROL SYSTEMS

To describe a specific control system we can observe certain distinctive features that each system, in differing degree, has. These are:

Degree of Detail

Control systems can be more or less detailed, in relation to the number of clusters (aggregations) in which raw financial data are collected and classified. The degree of detail is less if, for

TABLE 2. Factors Determining the Structural Complexity of the Enterprise and its Relations with the Environment

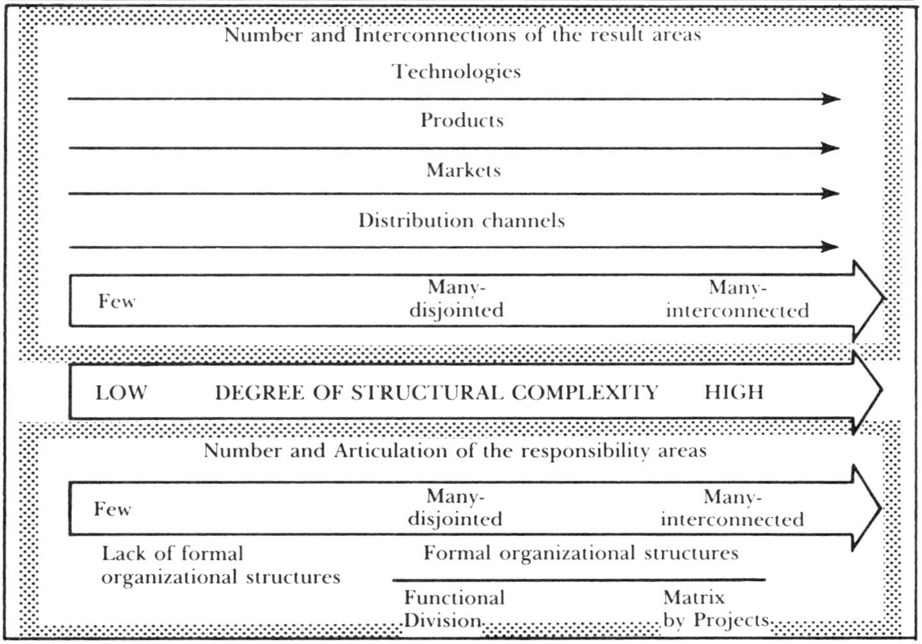

instance, the only control tool employed is the company financial accounting, where data are classified with reference to type of counterpart and nature of costs of revenues. The degree of detail is greater if data are classified also with reference to products, organisational units, variables, etc., as with cost accounting for example.

Degree of Relevance

As we know a datum is "relevant" in a specific situation if it is related to factors that can be influenced by the decision taken. A high degree of relevance means that each manager is provided with relevant information in direct correlation to his prevailing decisional activity. Direct cost accounting, for instance, increases the system's degree of relevance with respect to full cost accounting, because the distinction between variable and fixed costs is relevant in many decisions (4).

Degree of Selectivity

Often relevant information is confused with a lot of irrelevant information (5). The control system has a greater degree of selectivity the higher the ratio is between relevant and irrelevant information. This means also that the key economic variables greatly influencing the profitability of operations are clearly identified and the managers are aware of them. Hence the system operates as a filter for that information not actually useful in the managerial activity.

Degree of Formal Responsibility

We have said before that in complex systems control is based on a process of the hierarchic subdivision of the main company goal into many sub-goals, one for each organisational unit. So each responsibility centre has its own financial target, such as cost, revenue, profit, etc. A control system has a high degree of formal responsibility if the system of financial targets is very well developed. This means first of all that a very in-depth analysis has been made on the economic contribution of each organisational unit to the production process. And second, that these contributions—cost, revenue, profit, etc.—have been translated into a well articulated system of sub-goals. On the other hand, the degree of formal responsibility is low if the system of financial sub-goals is not very developed with respect to the business or organisational structure.

Degree of Procedural Rigidity

As far as procedural rigidity is concerned we can distinguish two types of control systems: standard control systems and contingency control systems. The former are made using formal tools and procedures that are projected in terms of regular and continuous employment. They are based on computerised information systems, are managed with well defined procedures and are supposed to be useful for solving the majority of problems that managers must face. Contingency control systems are "ad hoc" systems, created for the control—i.e. decision, evaluation, etc.—of certain problems that the management considers "unlikely" and, therefore, not worth constant attention in the control process. These systems are often managed without predefined procedures and are tailored to the specific problem to be solved at that specific moment. If we assume that any company has, in a defined period, its "problem fan", then we can say that the manager covers this fan in two ways: with standard and with contingency systems. The relationship between the two is a matter of judgment. The degree of procedural rigidity is higher the greater the standard system's predominance over the contingency system. (See Table 3)

Procedural rigidity is a distinctive feature of control systems that assume a high relevance in a discontinuous environment, when the "problem fan" is supposed to shift rapidly. Standard systems, because of their procedural rigidity, are difficult to shift accordingly. This means that the "problem fan" can remain uncovered, or, on the contrary, that procedures are implemented to no actual purpose. (See Table 4)

TABLE 3. Degree of Procedural Rigidity

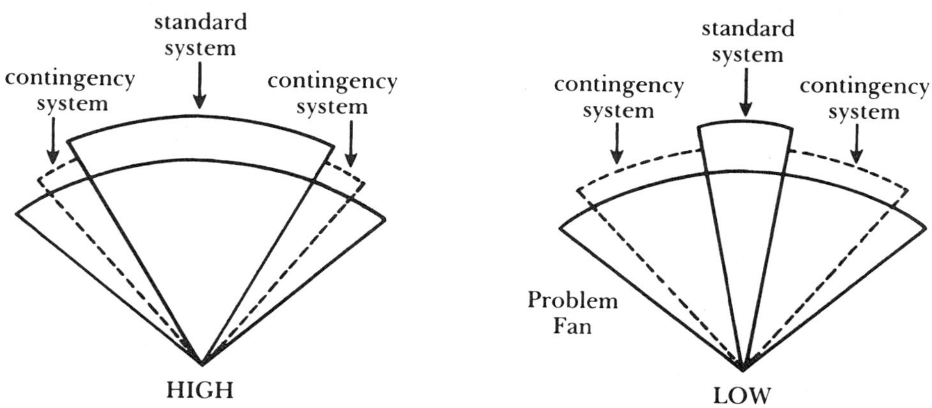

Style of Control

The behaviour of managers in implementing control systems has been defined as "style of control". This distinctive feature can be appreciated with regard to several factors. The more administrative control predominates over several and individual control, the more "tight" is this style (6). In the same way we can define as "tight" a control system when participation in setting objectives is low, targets are imposed and managers must consider them firm commitments, performance evaluation is oriented to accounting measures, etc. (7). On the other hand the style is "loose" if managers are conscious of the social and individual side of control, if participation is high, targets are negotiated and considered to be only reference points to be considered only in the context of actual environmental events and, finally, if managers are also evaluated on the basis of multiple, non qualitative, factors.

Quickness

One can evaluate the quickness of the control system by observing the period elapsing between the occurrence of an environmental event and its communication in an appropriate way to managers who must in turn react. The shorter this period is, the higher the degree of quickness. This feature of control systems must, of course, be judged with regard to the decisional activity of the managers.

Orientation

This feature of control systems describes their tendency to favour certain types of events, information or objectives with respect to others. Systems can be "productive factor oriented" if information is gathered mainly in accordance with production inputs, or "product oriented" if emphasis is given to production outputs. Other types of orientation are towards managerial activities vs. legal necessities, decisional rationality vs. controllability, etc. The main distinction in this case is between systems oriented towards the past and those oriented towards the future. Management control systems are oriented to the past if they focus on past events and on hypotheses and targets defined in advance. They are future oriented if they concentrate on future events which are explicitly considered in the system and towards which the entire system is geared (8).

TABLE 4. Degree of Procedural Rigidity and Environmental Discontinuity

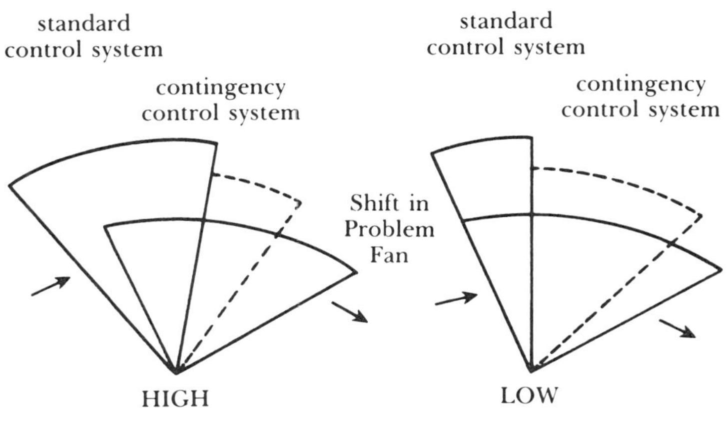

CONNECTIONS BETWEEN INDEPENDENT VARIABLES AND THE FEATURES OF MANAGEMENT CONTROL SYSTEMS

After having identified the independent companies and environmental variables and the distinctive features of management control systems, we can suggest some of the more important connections between the two (see Table 5).

Stable Environment

- The more numerous are the business units and the greater is the contact between them, the more detailed the systems must be with an orientation towards outputs—i.e. products and markets.
- The more complex the organisational structure is, the more relevant and selective it will be with regard to the decisional activity of each organisational unit. The degree of detail must be high at the lower levels and low at the top levels.
- The more complex the organisational structure is the higher the degree of formal responsibility and procedural rigidity and the tighter the style of control will be.

Turbulent Environment

The connections suggested for a stable environment are to be adjusted to the turbulence as follows:

TABLE 5. The Management Control: A Reference Plan

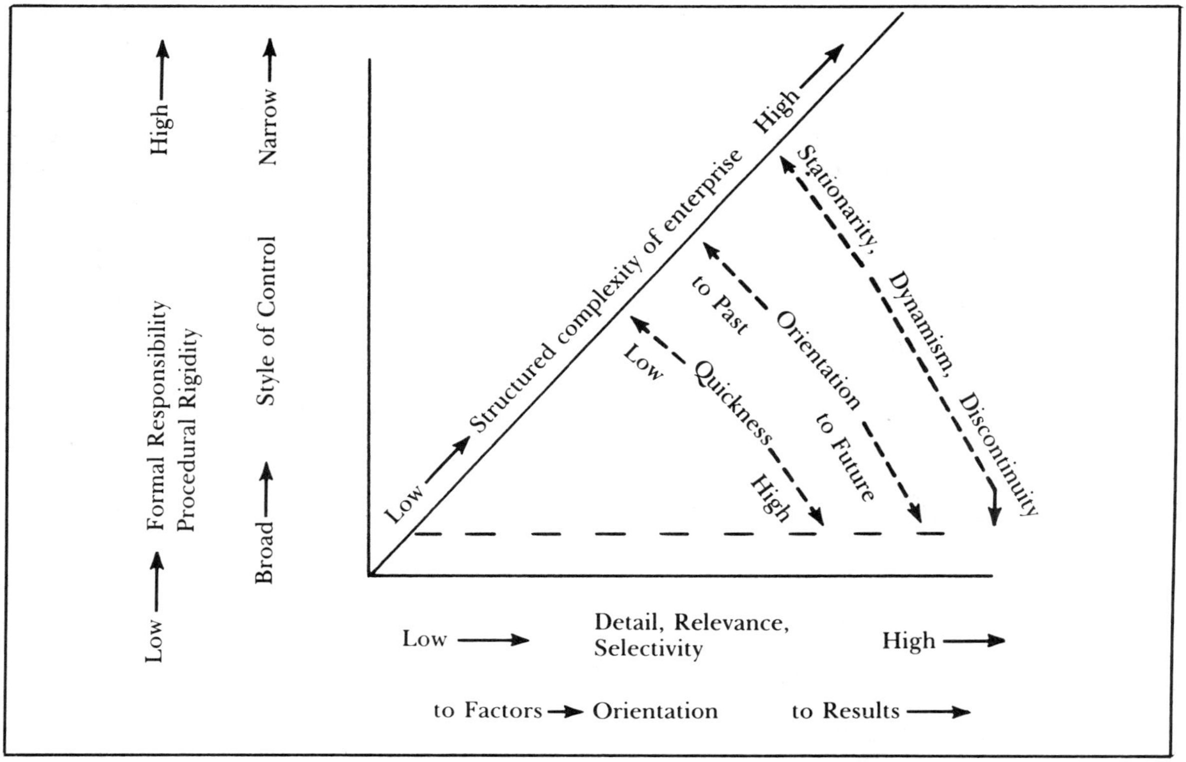

- The more discontinuous the environment is, the more the system must be oriented to the future and with a high degree of quickness
- The less discontinuous the environment is, the more procedural rigidity should decrease and the style of control change from tight to loose.

CONNECTIONS BETWEEN CONTROL TOOLS AND THE FEATURES OF MANAGEMENT CONTROL SYSTEMS

Management control systems assume a certain set of distinctive features in relation to: i) the tools from which they are composed, and ii) the way in which these tools are employed. In this sense it is very difficult, if not impossible, to identify the connection between tools and features without making a very deep analysis of the structure of each tool and the manner in which it is employed. For example, cost accounting can make very different contributions to the relevance and the formal responsibility of the system depending on the emphasis given to the variability or controllability criterion.

The budgeting process can be oriented to decisional rationality or motivational problems, and can be used with a tight or loose style. The same can be said for every control tool. Therefore, it becomes very difficult to fulfill the "control tool matrix" (see Table 6) where the connections between control tools and the features of the system are identified without reference to a specific company. Nevertheless we can try to give some guidelines. Financial accounting, the most common control tool, is oriented to the operational control of credits and debts. From a management control point of view, it contributes to the relevance and selectivity of the system mainly through Balance Sheets, where the profit and loss data constitute the main relevant information for managers. To increase the relevance of the system one must go more deeply, through ratio analysis, into the economic relations between the various items of the balance sheet. Financial models increase the future orientation, as well as the relevance, while, in our opinion, inflation accounting has a limited impact on the features of the system.

A great improvement is obtained by the use of cost accounting. This tool has a great impact on relevance, especially if it clearly shows direct costs, and on formal responsibility, if cost data are clustered according to responsibility centres and if a regular comparison between the standard and actual costs is made. Budgeting, together with responsibility accounting, contributes to all the features of the system, with special reference to formal responsibility and procedural rigidity; often it is used with tight style and has a limited orientation to the future. With capital budgeting and long range planning, formal responsibility and procedural rigidity usually remain unchanged or decrease, while orientation to the future, relevance, selectivity, etc. increase.

In conclusion we can say that each tool can contribute in varying degree to the different features of control systems and, conversely, that each feature is obtained from an appropriate combination of tools.

CONNECTIONS BETWEEN INDEPENDENT VARIABLES AND CONTROL TOOLS

Table 7 presents a very general framework for identifying the main connections between independent variables and control tools. It is important to point out that with increasing structural complexity, *any tool can be added to those previously in use,* which maintain their function within the system. On the other hand, with an increase in environmental discontinuity *new tools often substitute those previously in use,* which then lose their

TABLE 6. Control System Matrix

Control System Tools \ Control System Features	Detail	Relevance	Selectivity	Formal Responsibility	Procedural Rigidity	Style of Control	Quickness	Orientation
Financial Accounting								
Ratio Analysis								
Financial Models								
Inflation Accounting								
Actual Full Costing								
Actual Direct Costing								
Standard Costing								
Flexible Budgeting								
Operational Budgets								
Capital Budgets								
Long Range Plans								

TABLE 7. Connections between Independent Variables and Control Tools

Degree of Turbulence ↓ / Degree of structural complexity →	low						high
low	Financial Accounting		Yearly Balance Sheet	Actual Cost Accounting	Standard Cost Accounting	Responsibility Accounting	
		Ratio Analysis					
					Flexible Budgets	Operational Budgets	Capital Budgets
	Inflation Accounting						Long Range Plans
		Monthly Balance Sheet			Contingency Plans	Strategic Plans	
high	Financial Simulation Models						

function. This is because many control tools are projected for a stable environment and operate best under a certain set of environmental conditions. If these change rapidly, the tools lose their capacity to guide managers towards the goals of the company. An observance of Table 7 also reveals a shortage of tools for controlling very complex companies in a highly turbulent environment. This should probably be the main field of research on management control systems.

REFERENCES

1. Simon H.A., Guetzkow, H., Kozmetsky J. and Tyndal, J. *Centralisation Vs. Decentralisation in Organising the Controller's Department,* New York Controllership Foundation, Inc., 1954.
2. Sommerhoff, J. "The Abstract Characteristics of Living Systems" in *System Thinking,* edited by F.E. Emery, Harmondsworth, 1969, pp. 147–202.
3. Von Bertalanffy, L. *General System Theory,* New York, 1968.
4. American Accounting Association, "Report of Committee on Managerial Decision Models", *The Accounting Review,* Vol. XLIV, N. 1 (Supplement 1969), pp. 42–76.
5. Ackoff, R.L. "Management Misinformation Systems", *Management Science* Vol. 14, n.4, December 1967.
6. Dalton, G.W., Lawrence P.R., *Motivation and Control in Organisations,* Homewood, 1971, pp. 47–63; Dearden, J. "What's Wrong with your Financial Control System", *European Business,* Summer 1971.

7. Hopwood, A.G. *Accounting and Human Behaviour,* London 1974, p. 100.
8. Gilbert X.F. "A Framework for the Analysis of Management Planning and Control Systems", INSEAD, Fontainebleau, Unpublished Working Paper.

PART 2

Organizational Structure—Implications for Management Accounting

In this book an understanding of management accounting is sought by considering accounting as an integral part of managerial and organizational processes. In Part 1 it was argued that the design of management accounting systems (MAS) should be considered within the overall contextual setting of managers' decision and control situations. This broad concept of context may be distinguished from the notions of context which are often employed in traditional management accounting. These traditional approaches are often concerned with the provision of information for specific decision models such as capital budgeting evaluation, or control models such as short-term cash budgeting, which usually reflect only a limited appreciation of both external and internal circumstances. A broader approach considers aspects of both the external environmental setting and the internal organizational characteristics that affect managers' decision and control processes.

The importance of understanding external environmental context in analyzing organizational processes was considered in Part 1. The identification and measurement of the external environment form an important part of contingency research. Many different approaches to this problem may be found in the articles included in Parts 1 and 2. A particular aspect of the general environment, social issues, is considered in Part 4.

The internal context of management information systems examined in this book involves first the formal structuring of managers' activities and second the way in which individuals process and use accounting information. The articles included in this section are concerned with the formal structural context, while those in the next section relate to individual and group considerations. It is noteworthy that the majority of behavioural accounting research has traditionally been concerned with individual responses to accounting information. Only in recent years has the association between accounting and organizational variables been researched.

SEGMENTATION, DIFFERENTIATION AND INTEGRATION

Formal organizational structure is concerned with the specification of different roles for individual organizational members, or tasks for groups of individuals, to ensure that the activities of the organization are carried out. Formal structure is one of the most important aspects of internal context that influences the design of management accounting systems. The reason for this is that structure provides a framework within which decision making and control may be undertaken; management accounting forms an important part of the information and control systems that reinforce and support the basic intent of the formal structure. The central role of formal structure in controlling the activities of the firm is stressed by Hunt (1972, p. 13) and Thompson (1973), and the supportive nature of management accounting is discussed by Lorsch (1972) and Watson (1975).

An essential aspect of formal structure is the segmentation of organizational activities. This process seeks to identify particular tasks and to group these tasks into administrative units in such a way as to minimize the total cost of carrying out all the activities of the organization (March and Simon, 1958, p. 22; Thompson, 1967, p. 57). March and Simon (1958, pp. 22–23) refer to segmentation as departmentation, which they define as "a definite collection of tasks to be allocated among and performed by the employees of the department".

Segmentation can be considered as a means of enabling the organization's environment to be sub-divided into parts that are manageable by the organization's decision makers. Thompson (1967, p54) suggests that segmentation involves "delimiting responsibilities, control over resources, and other matters" and by this ". . . organisations provide their participating members with boundaries within which efficiency may be a reasonable expectation".

The notion of segmentation as a structural response to environmental circumstances has been developed through the concept of differentiation. This term was used by Lawrence and Lorsch (1967) to refer to the tendency for managers of organizational sub-units to develop their own ways of organizing work in order to cope with their part of the organization's total external environment. High levels of differentiation are a response to environmental uncertainty. In highly differentiated organizational sub-units, managers tend to develop their own orientation toward goals that they identify as appropriate in dealing with their sub-unit's environment, and their own interpersonal orientations and time horizons for decision making. In Lawrence and Lorsch's study, the more effective organizations in terms of financial performance, were those that had levels of differentiation appropriate to the degree of uncertainty that they faced in the external environment.

Formal structure involves more than segmentation and differentiation. Given that the organization is differentiated, it must seek to ensure that the separate sub-unit activities are coordinated and that they collectively aim to attain the overall goals of the firm. It is the purpose of structural integration to achieve this coordination. Lawrence and Lorsch (1967) refer to integration as the degree of collaboration and mutual understanding actually achieved among the various organizational sub-units. Again, the most successful organizations in their study achieved effective integration.

The notions of differentiation and integration seem particularly useful to the development of contingency approaches for the design of MAS. That is, these dimensions provide a useful means of considering structure in such a way that an association between structure and management accounting can be considered in the broader context of the influence of the external environment. Before these associations can be examined it is necessary to consider why formal structure is such an important aspect of the internal context of management accounting.

EFFECT OF STRUCTURE ON DECISION MAKING AND CONTROL

The way in which organizations differentiate and integrate their activities can affect managerial decision and control processes. For this reason, management accounting systems which are designed to provide information for decision making and control must be consistent with the broad intent of the structure. Several illustrations of the association between structure and decision making and control will be given.

For example, highly differentiated sub-units have been associated with high managerial motivation to engage in the sub-unit's activities (Burlingame, 1961; Heflebower, 1960), and the generation of innovative decisions (Hage and Aiken, 1970; Zaltman et al, 1973). A further line of research has shown that the analysis of resource allocation decisions should take into account structural arrangements (Berg, 1965; Bower, 1970; Kinnunen, 1976). Bower's (1970) research provides a particularly comprehensive approach to the influence of structural considerations on strategic resource allocation. He comments: "Management must recognize when it chooses a particular organizational form that not only is it providing the framework for current operations but also the channels along which information will flow in the future. These channels shape, or bias, the information which management will have available to it for planning in the future". (Bower, 1970, p. 287).

In regard to management control, structure provides mechanisms that facilitate the coordination of sub-unit activities. Differentiation and integration are associated in this respect. This is logical since the difficulties of integration are closely related to the extent to which the firm has differentiated. High differentiation generates a structural situation in which managers tend to follow their own ways of managing their part of the firm. Their orientation and actions may not be consistent with the needs of the organizational whole and integration may be needed to direct the efforts of managers toward organizational purposes. The preoccupation of managers of differentiated sub-units with their own units to the potential detriment of the organization as a whole has been observed by several researchers (Burns and Stalker, 1961; Lawrence and Lorsch, 1967; Selznick, 1969).

Differentiation is not the only factor that causes integration problems for the organization. Another important organizational characteristic that poses structural design problems is the type of interdependence between activities. Thompson (1967) argues that interdependence between an organization's activities may be classified as pooled, sequential or reciprocal. These represent increasing degrees of interdependence. Pooled interdependence is a situation in which each part of the organization renders a discrete contribution to the whole and each part is supported by the whole. The parts do not directly interact with one another on any continuous basis. An example of this is the conglomerate business enterprise where the only real intra-organization link among the separate companies is some scarce organizational resource such as capital. Sequential interdependence is a situation in which, in addition to the pooled aspect, direct interaction between the units can be pinpointed and the direction of that interdependence is one way. Examples of this include the typical assembly line in a manufacturing organization. Reciprocal interdependence refers to the situation in which the outputs of each unit become the inputs for other units. Pictorially, the various forms of interdependence are shown in Figure 2.1 where A, B and C represent organizational sub-units. The article by Hayes (1977) in this section uses Thompson's scheme to demonstrate problems of interdependence which are relevant to MAS design. Watson (1975) can also be read for further explanation of the implications of this typology for MAS design.

Thompson argues that the most effective structural response to interdependence is to locate interdependent activities within the one sub-unit. However, there are often limitations to this process, particularly in sequential and reciprocal situations. In these cases the problems of integration become highly complex.

A particular example of attempts to understand the association between the type of activities of the organization and its appropriate structure is the so called "Strategy and Structure" research (Chandler, 1962; Channon, 1973; Dyas and Thanheiser, 1976; Rumelt, 1974; among others). In this research the evolution of the divisionalized form of organizational structure is seen as a response to the development of highly diversified operations. In another study, Lorsch and Allen (1973) examined the problems of coordination within divisionalized firms. They found that complex problems of integration were caused by complex interdependence and great differentiation.

Accounting systems to support the divisional form of structure have been widely explored (Amey, 1969; Solomons, 1968; Tomkins, 1973; and many journal articles). Much of this research focuses on the design of a profit measure which is consistent with levels of individual differentiation, and with developing control mechanisms to assure optimal production when there are interdependencies between divisions (usually by means of a transfer pricing scheme). The need to examine accounting divisional controls by reference to broader structural issues is observed in an article by McNally (1973).

It may be concluded that differentiation and integration have a potential effect on the process of decision making and control. The problem of structural design is to achieve the requisite differentiation which enables decision makers to cope effectively with the level of environmental pressure related to their

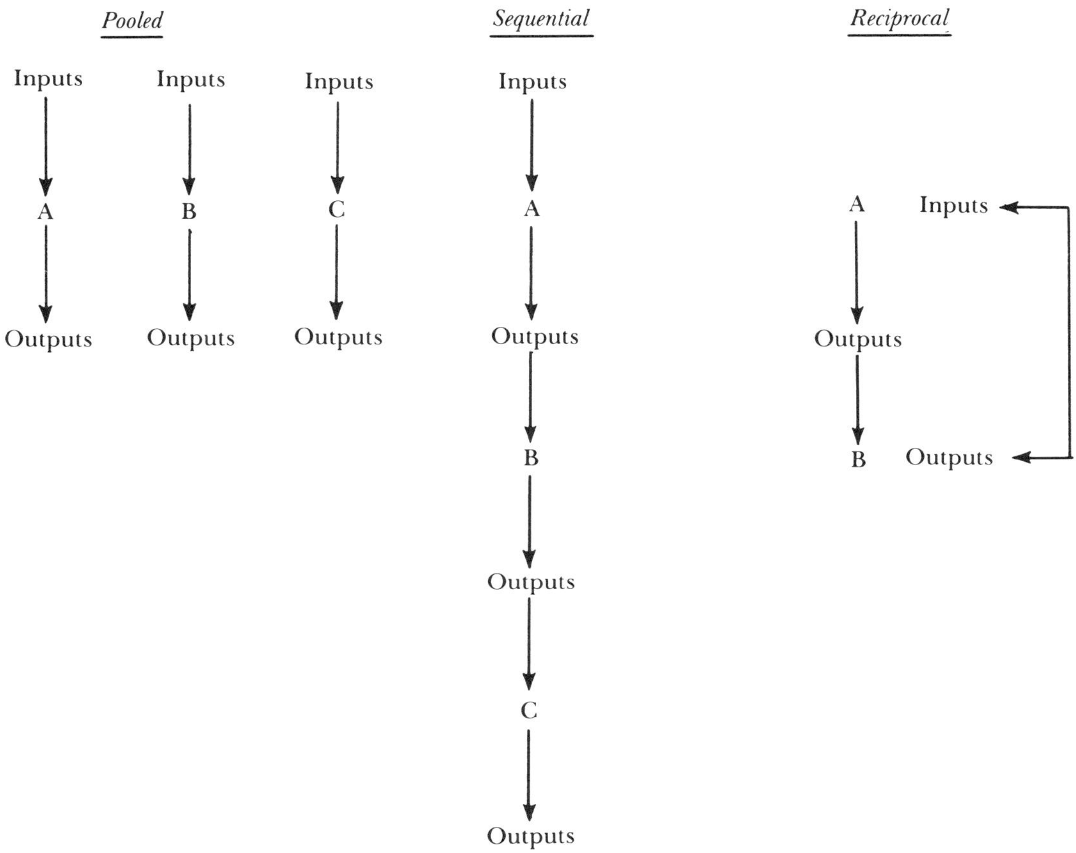

FIGURE 2.1

sub-units, while simultaneously achieving the required integration of the activities of sub-units.

It may be helpful to demonstrate how aspects of external environment and internal context can combine to form a picture of the processes involved in the design of organizations. First, we can represent the environment in terms of the dimension of uncertainty. We can state that the environment of an organization can vary from certain to uncertain. Second, we can reintroduce the concept of internal interdependence. If we combine interdependence with the environmental uncertainty we can picture the critical aspects of organizational design in Figure 2.2 (Watson, 1975).

The matrix suggests that any organization has more integration problems as the environment becomes more uncertain and as the internal relationships become more complex. This forces an organization to develop sophisticated structural design mechanisms if it is to effectively administer its activities. The reason these mechanisms are useful is that more information

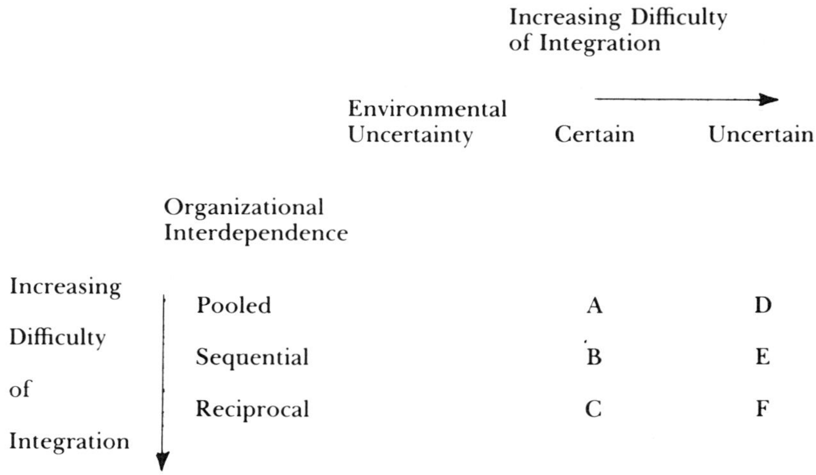

FIGURE 2.2

can be handled by the organization while it is carrying out its production tasks in situations where environments are uncertain and internal relationships are complex.

All organizations face the problems of differentiation and integration. These concepts represent aggregate notions of structure. The way in which these dimensions are realized involves the use of formal structural mechanisms. There are many descriptions of these structural mechanisms, the most important of which are reviewed below.

STRUCTURAL MECHANISMS

The level of differentiation is determined by the amount of freedom given to sub-unit managers to follow their own ways of managing. Structural mechanisms which are concerned with this are the extent to which managers have decision making autonomy and the degree to which their decisions are subjected to guidance and direction from above. The delegation of autonomy involves the decentralization of authority to make operating decisions, and in highly differentiated sub-units such as investment centers, a considerable sub-unit influence over capital investment decisions (Solomons, 1968, Ch. 1). The other aspect of structure that influences differentiation is the extent to which managers' actions are influenced by integrative mechanisms that direct decision making. In organizations with a low degree of sub-unit differentiation, managers' decisions can be guided or directed by rules and routines, by specifying through the formal hierarchy who is responsible for particular actions and by a degree of planned activity. These mechanisms may be considered to be relatively uncomplicated and appropriate where low differentiation does not cause integration problems. In more highly differentiated firms, authority is more decentralized and sub-unit managers are not as constrained, and integration must take place by means of more complex mechanisms. These may involve, in order of increasing complexity, direct contact between managers, integrating personnel such as temporary committees or task forces, individuals or departments that specialize in coordinating activities, and finally, the application of a matrix organizational form that involves joint decision making and shared responsibility.

This description of formal structural mechanisms follows from Lawrence and Lorsch (1967) and Galbraith (1974), and is consistent with the view suggested by March and Simon (1958) and Thompson (1967) that the more variable and unpredictable the context of operations, the greater the reliance on coordination by mutual adjustment rather than by plan or standardization. Similarly, Burns and Stalker (1961) suggest that structure in highly uncertain situations should follow an open, flexible, "organic" style rather than a highly bureaucratic, "mechanistic" structural form. (It is noteworthy that Burns and Stalker reject the notion that integrating personnel are appropriate integrators in highly uncertain situations. They argue that such personnel form bureaucracies that are inconsistent with a capacity for flexible decision responses).

Another important body of research that examined the meaning of structure and the association between structural mechanisms and aspects of organizational context has been developed by the "Aston" researchers (Pugh et al, 1969[a], 1969[b]). This research identified dimensions of "structuring of activities", "concentration of authority", "line control of workflow" (the degree to which control is exercised by line personnel instead of through impersonal procedures), and the "relative size of the support component" (non-workflow personnel). The contextual variables tended to be orientated to internal factors such as size, technology, origins and history, ownership, charter (ideology and type of outputs), location, resources, dependence (relations with other organizations). Replication studies have concluded that the main distinguishing dimensions of structure are "structuring of activities" and "concentration of authority" (Child, 1972; Inkson et al, 1970).

While the Aston studies reported the association between all structural and contextual factors, the most important elements of context that affected structure were size and to a lesser extent technology. Decentralization of authority and structuring of activities were associated with large size and technological complexity.

In terms of the structural dimensions of differentiation and integration, the Aston results identified an increase in differentiation by means of task specialization and decentralization of authority, with integration increasingly being achieved by standard routines and formalization. While these results provide support for the notion that organizations that are differentiated through high degrees of decentralization tend to seek integration through increased use of integrative mechanisms, the researchers did not investigate the use of the more complex mechanisms of integrative personnel in highly decentralized sub-units. The Aston approach has been widely applied to the study of organizational structure in its contextual setting. An example of the use of this approach in accounting research may be found in the article by Bruns and Waterhouse (1975) that is included in this section.

MANAGEMENT ACCOUNTING, STRUCTURE AND ENVIRONMENT

The basic theme of Part 2 is that MAS should be consistent with formal organizational structure, and that both structure and supporting accounting systems will best suit the decision and control needs of managers if they are appropriate for the environmental and internal context.

While the logic of the "environment–structure" effect on accounting systems has been developed only in recent years, the need for accounting systems to be consistent with structure is well accepted in some management accounting texts (Dopuch, Birnberg and Demski, 1974, Ch. 8; Horngren, 1977, Ch. 6). This point is developed in several works that attempt to show the limitations of responsibility accounting systems as they are traditionally described in management accounting (Pick, 1971; Gordon, 1963). The main point of these critiques is that responsibility accounting systems are typically designed to fit perfectly structured hierarchies of managerial authority. The systems achieve control by linking notions of controllability and traceability to the formal hierarchy. Pick (1971) and Gordon (1963) indicate that formal authority hierarchies may not accurately reflect who is accountable for a particular decision. Interdependence of activities, joint responsibilities and the action of those who implement integrative devices may cloud the precise determination of controllability and traceability. Problems like these seriously erode the usefulness of responsibility accounting systems. A review of the potential dysfunctional aspects of responsibility accounting which arise from problems of operationalizing the principle of controllability is provided in an article by McNally (1980).

While considerations of controllability and traceability are important, it may be argued that the task of achieving consistency between accounting systems and structure involves a consideration of the whole set of structural mechanisms rather than just the formal hierarchy of authority. Further, design of MAS may be most effective if consideration is given to the way in which the accounting systems and structure relate to contextual factors both within and outside the organization.

In situations where external environment does not present high levels of pressure or difficulty and internal technologies are not highly interdependent, an appropriate structure may involve considerable specialization of functions, possibly with the authority centralized in a top management decision making body. In terms of responsibility accounting schemes, sub-units may be expense centers concerned with production activities. Control may be sought through simple integrative mechanisms involving rules, routines and procedures. The form of accounting that may be most consistent with this situation is a standard costing system.

As environmental pressure increases, higher levels of differentiation may be expected, which in turn cause problems of integration. These difficulties will be further compounded if activities are sequentially or reciprocally interdependent and cannot be located within a single sub-unit. As a consequence of these factors, structure may typically involve delegation of authority to sub-unit managers, and the application of integrative mechanisms more complex than rules and standards. Clearly, rules and standards lose their effectiveness as control mechanisms in situations that are continually changing in unpredictable ways. Structural integration may be sought through the formal managerial hierarchy and the introduction of integrative personnel. This kind of arrangement is typical of the divisionalized organizational structure, and profit centers usually form the basis of the accounting system. Integration by means of integrative personnel often means the involvement in the affairs of divisions of corporate managers who are responsible to a centralized headquarters. It is important to remember that as the role of the integrative personnel increases, the motivational advantages associated with differentiated structure may be eroded. A careful balance between delegated decision authority and corporate involvement must be sought in divisionalized firms. As the role of the corporate body increases, problems of determining controllable and traceable costs and revenues increase, particularly where the technology of the organization involves complex interdependencies.

In situations where there are complex interdependencies, and the interdependent activities cannot be located in a single division, accounting systems can provide mechanisms to assure that the organization achieves an optimal flow of resources between sub-units. These mechanisms involve the determination of transfer prices for the interdependent activities. There has been a great interest in accounting to determine optimal transfer pricing schemes (Horngren, 1977, Ch. 22, and other texts have good summaries of this literature). The most common suggestions are to use market prices if available, various cost based prices such as marginal cost, or some variation of average cost plus. There have been several highly sophisticated schemes designed mathematically to resolve the problem of achieving optimal transfers in situations of complex interdependencies and resource constraints. (For a review see Abdel-Khalik and Lusk, 1974).

It is generally accepted that the use of market prices is consistent with structures which involve highly autonomous divisional operations. This scheme maintains the motivational advantages of differentiation while assuring optimal transfers from the viewpoint of the divisions and the firm as a whole. However, in situations where market prices are not available, alternative schemes must be adopted if the transfer pricing mechanism is to be maintained.

It is important to note that while the theoretical construction of these schemes provides an economic solution for optimal resource allocation, their implementation involves the application of a rule that specifies the appropriate transfer price. It was argued earlier that in situations of high differentiation and complex interdependence, rules may not be adequate as integrative mechanisms. It is possible that the motivational advantages of a high degree of differentiation may be lost by the application of rules determined by the corporate body such as the specification of transfer prices. It may be that transfer pricing should involve more complex integrative mechanisms such as interpersonal contact through a negotiation system, with integrating personnel possibly acting as arbitrators. This type of transfer pricing scheme is argued by Watson and Baumler (1975) in their article which is included in this section.

In situations of extreme environmental pressure, structuring by means of differentiation and integration may give way to more open, flexible arrangements that are consistent with joint decision making and shared responsibility. While it is unlikely that large formal organizations such as business enterprises or government departments could completely avoid all formal structuring, it is possible that those parts of the organization which face extreme environmental pressure may adopt matrix style arrangements, task forces, think-tanks and so forth.

In these circumstances the lack of formal lines of authority and communication channels make the task of designing accounting systems difficult. In terms of providing information for decision making, the accounting systems should be highly flexible and ideally should incorporate heuristic techniques to enable managers to anticipate outcomes under different probable circumstances. Decision making tools such as simulation and statistical analysis provide managers with helpful approaches in adapting their organizations to difficult environmental situations. Further, developments in electronic data processing technology have increased the capacity of accounting systems to develop large data bases that are readily accessible through real time computing and desk top input and output facilities. These facilities greatly improve the capacity of accounting to service the information needs of complex decision tasks.

With respect to control, in situations of high environmental pressure and open structural arrangements, accounting systems should enable assessment of the adaptability and responsiveness of managers' decision making. They should also be consistent with the development of cooperative contributions to a common collective outcome. The development of these measures is likely to involve factors other than traditional standards and budgetary control. Multiple measures, many of which might be non-quantitative, would be appropriate in these situations. The development of these measures remains a challenge for accounting systems designers.

THE INTERACTION–INFLUENCE SYSTEM

A further aspect of structure that is important in the design of accounting systems is the impact of structure on the psychological and social factors that influence the behaviour of individuals. The combining of technical factors such as structure and accounting systems with social considerations is sometimes referred to as a socio-technical approach to organizational design. The essence of this approach is the design of technical systems that are consistent with the organizational climate, where organizational climate refers to factors such as responsiveness, cohesiveness, flexibility, trust and so on. A useful description of the way structure and the factors influencing climate may be related is developed by Likert (1961). He refers to this combination as the "interaction–influence" system.

One aspect of the interaction–influence system that has been studied extensively by accounting researchers is the extent to which standard and budget setting should be participative. (Part 3 considers this line of research). However, little work has been done to relate the accounting system to the overall interaction–influence system. Good examples of approaches that have attempted this type of study are found in the works of Ansari (1977), Hopwood

(1974), Parker (1977) and Otley (1978). The first two of these are included in this part of the book.

THE READINGS

The first reading by Waterhouse and Tiessen (1978) develops the theme of the previous discussion by arguing that the design of accounting systems should largely depend on the structure of the organization, and that structure in turn depends on organizational context. The contextual variables considered are the internal technology and the predictability of the external environment. The authors note that organizational sub-units may be classified as either operating or managerial. They argue that the internal structure and processes of operating units can be best understood by considering technical variables while managerial units are more directly related to environmental factors. Aspects of organizational structure are identified as the delegation of authority and specialization of activity with the concept of social power serving to link external context to structure. Implications of structural context for the role of management accounting in aiding planning and resource allocation, and performance evaluation are examined.

The next two readings involve relatively complex statistical procedures which are used to test contingency models of accounting systems. They are included because of their valuable theoretical content and because they represent examples of empirical applications of the theory.

The article by Bruns and Waterhouse (1975) studies the interrelationships between organizational structure and the various forms of budget related behaviour. As in the previous reading, and the theme of this section, structure is viewed as being contingent upon external environment and internal organizational characteristics. The authors identify organizational context as the origins, size, technology and dependence. Structure is defined in terms of the "Aston" measures—structuring of activity and concentration of authority. Structure is seen as operating through intervening variables related to "control system complexity" and "perceived control" to influence budget related behaviour. This budget related behaviour is described as the "quality" of budget related behaviour, the "kind" of behaviour, and the "quality and satisfaction" in terms of the extent to which budgets are seen as being effective in achieving organizational goals. The authors tested the model on 25 organizations and reported associations between variables. On the basis of these associations, a series of possible contextual interactions are suggested.

In the reading by Hayes (1977), methods for evaluating sub-unit performance are seen to be contingent upon the internal structure and functions of the sub-unit (nature of tasks, type of people, interpersonal relationships, ability to measure and quantify functions), sub-unit interdependence (using Thompson (1967) typology), and the nature of the external environment (stability and homogeneity). Three propositions which relate explanators of performance for production, marketing, and research and development departments to context are developed. The research tested propositions by employing a questionnaire based survey of 103 firms and analyzed results by means of path analysis. A useful critique of this article was published by Tiessen & Waterhouse (1978).

The article by Watson and Baumler (1975) places the analysis of transfer pricing within an organization theory framework. The authors argue that transfer pricing systems can both enhance structural differentiation and facilitate integration. In situations where integration is not a great problem, transfer prices based on rules can enhance differentiation. If integration is more of a problem, transfer pricing may facilitate integration. The use of a negotiated transfer price system is suggested as being appropriate in this situation.

The second article by Ansari (1977) provides an example of an attempt to combine structural and behavioural (organizational climate) factors into a unified approach to management control system design. He argues that effective management control systems design requires a supportive combination of several structural and behavioural components. These components are structural information networks, a social component (leadership style and subordinate personalities), and a support component of extrinsic and intrinsic rewards. Effective combinations of these components lower the possibility of cognitive conflict between managers and subordinates, and encourage behaviour which can resolve such conflict with positive results for the organization's performance. The identification of these factors provides a criterion for evaluating the effectiveness of the system before the design is implemented.

The article by Hopwood (1974) also identifies variables that relate to both dimensions of the interaction–influence system. Organizational climate is viewed in terms of managers' willingness to develop supportive personal relations with subordinates, while the structural aspect is the specification of work roles. Accounting evaluation is categorized as being profit conscious, budget constrained (evaluation against short-term budget), and non-accounting style. A proposition is presented that relates the use of a budget constrained style of evaluation to leadership style (defined in terms of the interaction–influence system), and the extent to which the superior manager is also subject to a budget constrained evaluation style (a contagion effect). This proposition was tested by a field study in a division of a large manufacturing firm. Hopwood (1974) concludes that "the present findings suggest that the relationship between accounting data and decision behavior is moderated by the leadership style and social context of the decision maker".

DISCUSSION QUESTIONS

1. Discuss the relationship between organizational structure, environment and technological interdependence. In your answer indicate how an understanding of structural differentiation and integration can aid in examining the association between structure, environment and technological interdependence.
2. Describe the environment and tasks of your institution. Is the organiza-

tional structure of the institution appropriate for its tasks and environment? How might the required match be improved?

3. How do the demands for accounting information differ between sub-units engaged in advertising, research and development, specialized job order and continuous production lines?
4. It was argued in the reading by Ansari (1979) in Part 1 that one of the major problems of implementing responsibility accounting systems is the determination of which activities are under the control of particular managers. Discuss the implications of this problem of defining managerial controllability to the design of MAS.
5. Structural mechanisms may be highly formalized or more open and flexible. Discuss the implications for MAS design of both of these types of mechanisms.

A Contingency Framework for Management Accounting Systems Research

J. H. Waterhouse and P. Tiessen
The University of Alberta

This paper utilizes Contingency Theory to develop a model for the comparative analysis of organizations which permits us to identify possible control requirements of various organizational types and to address a number of related management accounting systems design issues. The model suggests that the structure of an organization is largely dependent on its context and that alternative structures create a need for different control mechanisms. By focusing on the control requirements of alternative structures, possible relationships between organizational structure and the efficient design of management accounting systems are then hypothesized.

The relevance of organizational variables to the design of management accounting systems (MAS) has long been recognized in the accounting literature. For example, Horngren (1972, p. 157) states "Ideally, the organization itself and its processes must be thoroughly appraised, understood, and altered, if necessary, before a (management accounting) system is constructed." Research by Simon *et al.* (1945), Anthony (1965), and Caplan (1971), among others, has recognized this need by focusing on the inter-relationships between MAS and organizational or behavioral variables. Organization theorists, too, have noted the relevance of MAS variables in understanding motivation, decision making, and control in organizations. Cyert & March (1963), Downs (1967) and Wildavsky (1964) have commented on the importance of MAS variables to organizational phenomena. In short, MAS are an integral part of an organization's fabric, interwoven with organizational structure and processes to enhance organizational control.

From an accounting perspective one of the most important aspects of organization structure and process is control. Indeed, the formal administrative structure of an organization may be viewed as a purposefully designed mechanism for exercising social control (V. Thompson, 1973). Budgeting, too, is chiefly concerned with planning and control as budgets are vehicles for formulating and conveying information on plans, establishing performance criteria, and allocating resources within organizations. Thus a substantial portion of research on the organizational, attitudinal and behavioral effects of MAS has focused on budgeting.

The behavioral research on budgeting has focused on two general areas. Following the pioneering study by Argyris (1952), studies by Stedry (1960), Stedry & Kay (1966), Hofstede (1967), DeCoster & Fertakis (1968), Swe-

From *Accounting, Organizations and Society,* Vol.3, No. 1 (1978), pp. 65–76.

ringa & Moncur (1972), Searfoss & Monczka (1973) and Hopwood (1974) have reported on the effects of budgeting on managerial attitudes and behavior. In general, this research has treated some aspect of budgeting such as the budget level (Stedry, 1960), budget pressure (DeCoster & Fertakis, 1968) or the method of budget formulation (Sweringa & Moncur, 1972) as the independent variable. Dependent variables have typically been either psychological (e.g. aspiration level) or interpersonal (e.g. leadership style). Thus the stated or assumed links in this approach are typically from a defined independent budgetary variable to the psychological or interpersonal effects of that variable which (presumably) increase job performance and/or satisfaction. In this approach, conclusions were drawn with respect to the efficient design of budgeting systems by focusing on the psychological or interpersonal effects of budgets within organizations. Inter-organizational differences in technology, environment and structure are a part of the unexplained variance in the model.

A second but less voluminous body of research on budgeting has focused at an organizational level of analysis. Several studies have been concerned with the element of slack in budgets (Williamson, 1964; Lowe & Shaw, 1968; Schiff & Lewin, 1968; and Onsi, 1973). Others, e.g. Khandwalla (1972), Watson & Baumler (1974), Bruns & Waterhouse (1975) and Hayes (1977), have suggested that the efficient design of budgets and MAS is contingent on certain characteristics of the organization and its environment. This comparative organizational approach to research on MAS requires that a model, capable of explaining the variance in organizational effectiveness, be constructed by forging a series of linkages leading from the context of organizations to the structural properties of the organization and finally to the efficiency of certain management and budgeting processes.

Adopting this latter posture to behavioral research on MAS has a number of potentially important conceptual and methodological implications. In comparison to the first body of research, budgeting and other MAS variables change in status from independent to instrumental or dependent variables. Further, by focusing on the variance in MAS variables between organizations it may be possible to pose certain questions which were raised only with difficulty by other approaches. For example; how important are MAS control systems relative to other means of exercising management control? What properties of the organization or its environment increase the reliance placed on formal MAS control systems? How does the distribution of power and authority within an organization affect the distribution of discretionary resources within the organization?

In this paper we develop a model for the comparative analysis of organizations which permits us to address a number of these MAS design issues. Our concern is with control in organizations and with the use of MAS for control. We argue that the structure of an organization is largely dependent upon its context and that alternative structures create a need for different control mechanisms. Thus by focusing on the control requirements of alternative organization structures we are able to hypothesize possible relationships between organizational structure and the efficient design of management accounting systems.

CONTEXTUAL VARIABLES AND ORGANIZATIONAL FUNCTIONS

Empirical research by Burns & Stalker (1961), Woodward (1965), Pugh *et al.* (1966), Hage & Aiken (1967), and Lawrence & Lorsch (1967) has demonstrated that technology and environment are important variables in understanding the structure and activity of complex organizations. This position is also supported by the conceptual work of Thompson (1967), Perrow (1972) and Hall (1972). Collectively this work has led to the development of the contingency theory of organizations. Contingency theory essentially states that efficient organization structures vary with organizational contextual factors such as technology and environment. It further implies that the efficacy of certain managerial techniques such as participative decision making or task directed leadership is contingent on the organization's context and structure. Thus the contingency theory literature provides a convenient point-of-departure for discussing the effects of organizational variables on MAS.

However, while contingency theory is supported by an impressive body of literatures, definitions and measures of variables have often lacked conceptual clarity. For example, the definitions of technology and environment have often varied and the distinction between the two has not been clearly established. As noted by Becker & Neuhauser (1975), Lawrence & Lorsch define environment to include the physical machinery and non-human aspect of production. Woodward, on the other hand, defines technology to include the physical flow of production. Because of these and other ambiguities in the contingency theory literature, we proceed in this section by defining the contextual variables in our model and by suggesting linkages between these variables and specific organizational functions. In the next section we suggest relationships between the contextual variables and organization structure.

Our model focuses on two contextual variables, technology and environment, which are treated as having separate and independent effects on organizations.[1] Other authors have alluded to the need to distinguish the organizational effects of environment from the effects of technology. For example, Perrow (1967) states that the impact of raw materials technology on structure is modified by the general environmental system in which the organization operates. Similarly, Thompson (1967) states that the technology employed by the organization will affect the design strategy utilized in buffering the organization against crucial environmental contingencies. Thus both Thompson and Perrow view technology and environment as separate variables having an interactive effect on organizational structure. Our preferences are to distinguish the effects of environment and technology more sharply, arguing as Becker & Neuhauser (1975) do that they will impact at different organizational levels.

Technology

Our definition of technology is similar to that of Perrow (1967). Perrow's framework centers on two variables: the number of exceptional cases encountered in the raw materials and the nature of the search process utilized when exceptional cases are found. The number of exceptional cases varies from few to many while search processes vary from logical, systematic, analytical, and possibly programmed to highly unstructured cases which may require the application of experience, intuition or guess work. A uni-dimensional representation of these variables may be presented ranging from routine where few exceptions which can be systematically analysed through to non-routine where many exceptions with less systematically analysable search processes would be encountered. Thus we think of technology in terms of the routineness or nonroutineness of the conversion processes for the organization's raw material. A concept of technology similar to

[1]It should be noted that research by Pugh *et al.* (1966), Hall, Haas & Johnson (1967), and Blau *et al.* (1966) has shown a correlation between organization structure and the size of organizations. We exclude size as a variable in our model because the direction of causation between this variable and structure is not clear. However, consistent observation of the relationship minimally requires that research in this area control for the effects of organizational size.

this has been suggested by Litwak (1968) and applied in the empirical work of Hage & Aiken (1969).

In conceptualizing technology as variable from routine to non-routine based on the nature of the raw materials and search processes, it should be noted that included in the technology variable is what others (e.g. Hall, 1972) term the technological condition of the firm's general environment. The actions or operations performed on raw materials are subject to search processes to determine the most suitable technology to be employed in their conversion. This search for new or different technologies may be centered inside or outside an organization. However, in spite of the fact that the technological search process takes place within an organization's environment (to be more fully discussed below) we believe that this search process is so central to the technology variable that it should not be included as part of an organization's general environmental condition. This is not to say that changes in the environment may not cause or initiate a search for new technologies. Indeed, we argue that environmental factors such as economic or political changes might force management to redefine or modify the organization's output which would result in exceptional cases for converting raw material and thus, by starting a search process, would impact the technological variable.

Environment

The other contextual variable in our model, environment, is conceptualized in a manner consistent with Duncan (1972) except that, as noted above, we do not include a technological component which he does. Duncan's conceptualization distinguishes an internal environment which consists of physical and social factors within the boundary of the organization from the organization's external environment. When focusing on organizational subunits this external environment can be further differentiated with regard to that environment external to the subunit but within the broader organization and that environment external to both the subunit and the broader organization. Each factor in the internal and external environment has a simple-complex and a static-dynamic dimension. The static-dynamic dimension, defined as the extent to which factors are subject to change over time, is an important contributor to uncertainty in decision making. Thus we suggest that factors in the organization's environment might be mapped on a certainty continuum ranging from highly predictable to highly unpredictable.

A major advantage of conceptualizing technology and environment as they have been above is that both may be related directly to subunits within an organization. An organizational subunit may be defined as a formally specified group with defined responsibilities under the direction of a superior. Focusing on narrowly defined organizational units has the advantage of decreasing intra-organizational variation in contingent (structural or behavioral) variables and hopefully of explicating relationships between these variables and contextual variables. Moreover by specifying our unit of analysis we hope to avoid some of the controversy associated with other related research on relationships between structure and context. (Donaldson, Child & Aldrich, 1975).

Managerial and Operations Functions of Organizations

Concentrating on organizational subunits as the unit of analysis has the further advantage of explicating a distinction that we wish to draw between managerial and operating functions. The operating decision function is viewed by us as the process of assuring that specific organizational tasks are accomplished as efficiently and effectively as possible. This function may be envisioned as focusing upon the problems involved in specifying, implementing, and coordinating procedures to be used in converting organizational inputs to outputs. The operations function therefore is concerned with the difficulties involved in the energy transformation of the through-put of an organizational unit. The managerial decision function is regarded as responsible for administering the operating functions of the organization by specifying the tasks to be performed, procuring the material and manpower resources to be used by organizational units (inputs), ensuring that the products produced by organizational units (outputs) are disposed of, coordinating and directing functional substructures, resolving conflicts between substructures, resolving conflicts between hierarchical levels, and coordinating boundary spanning activities.

Thus we suggest that particular organizational subunits within a broader organization may be predominantly operating units while others may be predominantly managerial units. It should be noted that managerial units are concerned with managing and coping with all facets of the environment including physical and social factors within the boundary of the organizational unit and the external environment. This leads us to conclude that the internal structure and processes of managerial functions can best be understood by focusing on environmental variables while the structure and process of operating units will be more directly related to the technological variable. Thus we suggest that technology and environment affect organizations at the operational and managerial levels respectively and independently.

ORGANIZATIONAL STRUCTURE AND CONTROL

As noted earlier, Contingency Theory suggests that efficient organization structures and processes are contingent on an organization's context. Having identified technology and environment as the major contextual variables in our model, we now indicate how these variables impact structure and examine the related organizational control processes. MAS are one type of control mechanism. Therefore, since our conceptual scheme suggests that the nature of organizational control is dependent on the type of organizational structure which, in turn, is contingent on technology and environment, the implication is that management accounting systems will need to be designed to meet the specific control requirements of specific organizational units. While attention to the need for different types of management accounting systems will be drawn during the discussion in this section, a detailed examination of the implications of this conceptual scheme for the design and use of management accounting systems will be provided in the next section.

Authority Structure and Control

The concept of social power provides an important link between the contextual variables of technology and environment, and organizational structural variables such as procedure specification and centralization of authority. Hickson *et al.* (1971) have proposed a strategic contingencies model of organizational power which states that power within an organization comes from the ability of individuals or organizational subunits to successfully cope with critical organizational uncertainties, the importance of the uncertainty, and the degree to which other individuals or subunits can provide substitute services. Similarly Crozier (1964) and Thompson (1967) have noted that power is related to uncertainties in the technology and environment faced by an organization. We therefore propose that the distribution of power within an organization is contingent on the context of the organizational subunit to the extent that environmental uncertainties or non-routine technologies form the bases from which individuals may realize power. Two additional variables, the individual's unique knowledge and skills, and his access to information pertinent to the uncertainty, are presumed to be critically related to the individual's ability to successfully cope and are therefore important factors in maintaining and exercising power.

Authority may be regarded as that part of power which is legitimate and normatively expected within an organization (Hickson *et al.*, 1971). Authority is granted to individuals and groups so that they may realize ownership goals.[2] The amount of authority distributed or realized by individuals within organizations does of course vary considerably and the form of authority distribution is one of the important elements of organization structure. The form of authority distribution is typically described in vertical terms, existing on a continuum ranging from centralized to decentralized.[3] For purposes of this discussion we define decentralization as the existence at lower levels within the organization of a broad scope or discretion over organizational activities. It should be emphasized that the types of activities over which a person has authority must be specified before the concept of decentralization can be adequately operationalized. Thus our model will predict that authority will be decentralized in response to environmental uncertainties, in the case of managerial subunits and in response to technological non-routineness in the case of operating subunits.[4]

The issue of authority and power distribution is crucial to an understanding of the control processes within an organization. Whenever an individual is granted authority the opportunity arises for that individual to exercise discretion in developing and implementing policies or procedures. If the goals of the individual diverge from those of the organization because of differential self interest, perceptions of reality, or access to information, authority delegation will be accompanied by a leakage of authority.[5] Since organizations exist to realize ownership rather than individual goals, compensatory mechanisms for coping with authority leakage, that is control mechanisms (such as management accounting systems), need to be developed if organizational goals are to be realized.

Centralized Authority

In general, the broader the decision making discretion permitted at lower levels within the organization (decentralized), the more authority leakage there will be and therefore the more difficult and costly it will be to exercise control at that level. Consequently we hypothesize that within the constraints of technology and environment organizations will prefer to centralize

---

[2]This concept of authority follows from the views of formal organizations proposed by V. Thompson (1973) and Perrow (1972, pp. 14–18) who view organizations as purposefully designed tools for accomplishing ownership goals. Formal organizations, or artificial systems, bring together human and financial resources to realize an externally defined (i.e. ownership) goal. As such, control is a central feature of organizations. The fact that organizations are composed of individuals gives rise to what Thompson terms the natural system which meets individual and group needs.

[3]A substantial body of research on organizations has treated decentralization of the authority structure as a major characteristic of organizations. See, e.g. Hage & Aiken (1967), Pugh *et al.* (1968), Hall (1962), and Blau & Schoenherr (1971). This research, however, has demonstrated a noticeable lack of consistency in operationalizing the concept of decentralization. Not surprisingly the results of the different approaches have not been coterminous.

[4]For research on organizations this suggests that measures of authority should be related to the domain of authority. This distinction has not always been made in the research to date. For example, the Pugh *et al.* (1966) research aggregated the centralization questionnaire responses to determine an overall organization score. Thus the research failed to recognize that authority may be centralized or decentralized along different dimensions. We have implicitly argued for two (at least) distinct authority domains in which authority may be independently centralized or decentralized.

[5]For an expansion of this point see Downs (1966, p. 134).

effective authority for reasons of efficiency. Centralization implies that the organizations must develop means for delegating activities to lower levels within the organization. This will be accomplished by unambiguously specifying the procedures to be followed in conducting either managerial or operating functions. Procedure specification for operating functions can best be accomplished when the task technology is known (that is when the through-put process is well specified) and relatively stable over time. Similarly at the managerial level procedures can be specified more readily when the environment of the organization is relatively predictable and stable over time. Indirect evidence in support of this position is provided by the Haas & Cullen (1963) study which demonstrated that the more frequently a task or event occurred the more likely there was to be a procedure developed to cover it.

Procedure specification has a number of important implications for the organization. First, since procedures which are formalized and standardized are not likely to be changed without considerable effort, rigidity is likely to increase and adaptability is likely to decrease. Secondly procedure specification is a relatively efficient means of organization with a stable environment and routine technology since procedures may be a convenient substitute for supervision (Gouldner, 1965). Perhaps the most important effect of specified procedures is that they tend to define and limit the authority of individuals within the organization. Crozier (1964), for example, noted that to the extent that role performance is governed by rules and is therefore predictable, role incumbents find it difficult to build power bases. Similar observations have been made by Mechanic (1962) and J. D. Thompson (1967). The existence of specified procedures defines and limits the power of individuals in an organization and facilitates the exercise of organizational control provided there are means for checking on compliance, for as noted by Mechanic procedures themselves may become a source of power for individuals.

Procedure specification is, thus, an important means of both defining and limiting the authority of organization members. The generation and use of data for planning and control purposes under conditions of specified procedures is relatively straightforward in that behavior is more easily predicted, observed and measured. Under these conditions one might predict that MAS performance measures will normally be based on criteria linked to through-put procedures rather than on measures of input, output or combinations of input and output measures. At the operational or technical level standard costing which predetermines prices and quantities of through-puts in the production process and compares actual prices and quantities to the standards is an example of an application of performance measures to a well specified process. The isolation of standard cost variances requires that procedures be well specified in advance of the act of production and variances serve the function of providing information on whether individuals complied with procedures. Similarly at the administrative or managerial level, certain procedures may be well specified and consequently well adapted to an application of routine cost reports. Examples of situations in this category include certain clerical functions.

Decentralized Authority

Fundamental to our framework is the notion that to the extent possible organizations will attempt to centralize authority and specify procedures. However, when the environment of the organization is uncertain or its technology is not routine, procedures become difficult if not impossible at the extreme to specify and document. In this type of situation knowledge and application of procedures lies primarily with individuals whose training and/or experience provides them with the ability to solve managerial or operational problems. Since, under these conditions, procedures are not documented, formalized, and standardized, individuals must exercise discretion in solving problems and performing tasks. This need to exercise discretion increases their power in the organization. The idea that increased task or environmental complexity results in a change in power distribution toward decentralization is implict in a number of works including that of Burns & Stalker (1961) and Thompson (1967). It should be noted, however, that decentralization may only occur as a response to environmental or technological demands within specific organizational subunits.

Under such conditions of environmental or technological uncertainty, direct control measures which specify procedures and then evaluate performance in terms of adherence to those procedures, as was the case with centralized organization structures, are not possible. Since the specific problem solving or decision processes now involve the organization members' discretion, control will focus to a large degree on planning and internal resource allocation, on monitoring outputs which result from organization members' actions, and on the selection, socialization, and professionalization of organization members.

Professionals have been defined by Etzioni (1964) as individuals who are formally trained to produce, preserve, communicate and apply specialized knowledge. Moreover, professionals are mandated to define or specify goals and to regulate the activities of their members. In this sense, professionals are individuals whose training uniquely equips them to apply knowledge to nonroutine technologies or uncertain environments. Moreover, the training of the professional acts as a form of control in that a level of technical competence can often be assumed.

The concept of professionalism is frequently applied to the technical or operational level of organizations. Clearly, elements of professionalism may exist at the managerial level also. For example, Taguiri (1965) has shown that managers may demonstrate the same kind of interest in social values as other professionals. Also, the growth in specialized knowledge and formal training in management, when applied to uncertain environments, will, we believe, increase the extent to which managers demonstrate characteristics similar to other professionals.

This should not imply that decentralized organizations with undefined or ambiguously specified procedures rely entirely (or even largely) on professionalism to achieve organizational control. Although the inherent values and training of the professional do provide the organization with some control, according to Ouchi (1977) organizations will, wherever possible, design control mechanisms to evaluate the outputs which result from members' actions. Heydebrand & Noell (1973), moreover, note that another way of limiting the autonomy of professionals is to shift control over resources to nonprofessional agents. The focus of control in these organizations, therefore, shifts from direct control of decision making to control over the premises of decision making (Perrow, 1976) and, to the extent possible, to control over the inputs and outputs of decision making. For example, the managerial subunit of a large company's manufacturing division might be controlled through a budgetary planning process which would indicate the resources available and specify the areas for which these resources could be used. Moreover, this process, in which divisional and corporate management jointly participate, serves the important function of establishing broad guidelines or premises for making a large number of the unspecified and undocumented divisional decisions during that budgetary period. This planning process also serves the purpose of defining mutually acceptable output measures such as divisional net income, return on investment, or residual income. Such controls over the amount of resources available and their use will ensure that resources are used in a manner consistent with overall company policy. The output controls then provide a check as to whether the available resources have generally been used efficiently by the division.

There are some types of organizations, however, where meaningful output measures may be impossible to develop. In such organizational units, effective control over subunit activities and its utilization of resources will rely heavily upon the selection and socialization of organization members. Ouchi (1977) cites the example of the U.S.A. foreign service officer corps which is charged with the goal of improving the foreign relations of the U.S.A. Here, in the absence of output measures, a rigorous selection process is used to ensure that personnel exceed generally accepted standards of training and ability. In an industrial organization, a basic research and development department may similarly rely on rigorous selection and training standards as a major means of control, since short-term output measures will be generally unavailable. Furthermore, Edström & Galbraith (1977) have noted that some personnel transfers at the managerial level in multinational corporations may be a means for specialization and for creating verbal information networks which facilitate control based on socialization. Thus, in both managerial and operational subunits, environmental and technological circumstances may be such that procedures cannot be specified and output measures cannot be developed and, therefore, selection and socialization become major means for exercising control.

MANAGEMENT ACCOUNTING SYSTEM IMPLICATIONS

Management accounting systems are an integral part of the formal control structure of organizations. Whether explicitly recognized or not the efficient design of the MAS must recognize the effects of organization variables. The model of organization suggested above hypothesizes that the distribution of organizational authority and the extent to which procedures can be specified are contingent on technology and environment. This section examines the implications of this model for research on MAS. We are specifically concerned with the manner in which an organization's structure may affect MAS processes such as planning, resource allocation, and performance measures.

Planning and Resource Allocation

As suggested above, centralization and procedure specification develop as efficient means of control in response to routine technologies and/or certain environments. Specified procedures have the effect of providing a program which predetermines the desirable through-put processes in the case of operational activities and the means for acquiring inputs and disposing of outputs in the case of managerial activities. This type of planning is efficient because once specified, procedures predetermine activities and sub-goals for relatively long time periods. We hypothesize that planning through procedure specification will decrease the reliance placed on planning through the budgeting process. Furthermore, since procedure specification implies that the knowledge base for operating or managing decisions is known to centralized decision makers, ownership goals will be factored into operational sub-goals with a minimum of conflict. Thus the planning process will exhibit a minimum input from lower organizational members—i.e. it will be nonparticipatory.

In contrast, control in decentralized organizations is more complex. We hypothesized that decentralization (that is, broad decision making discretion at lower levels) exists because managers and/or operators have access to information which is not available to the owner or his agents. Consequently procedures are difficult to specify and document. The implication of this is that the owner must rely on managers and operators for information on efficient means for coordinating and operating. In terms of the specific design and operation of the management accounting system this may mean that it is more difficult to establish non-conflicting and operational sub-goals. We hypothesize that the process of sub-goal formation will involve bargaining and conflict and that it will demonstrate characteristics of being participatory (i.e. jointly made) for this reason. In addition, we hypothesize that, as the budget document may be considered as an explicit surrogate statement of implied organizational goals, budgetary goals will now be broader and less clearly specified, than in organizations characterized by specified procedures.

One manifestation of bargaining over sub-goals may be the creation of budgetary slack, defined as the difference between the minimum necessary costs or maximum possible revenues and budgeted costs or revenues (Schiff & Lewin, 1968). Cyert & March (1963) have stated that slack arises unintentionally during the budgetary process and serves the purpose of stabilizing the firm's performance in spite of environmental fluctuations. A contrary opinion on the purpose of budgetary slack, proposed by Williamson (1964) and observed by Schiff & Lewin (1968), is that slack is consciously built into budgets by managers to serve their personal goals and establish "attainable" performance criteria. Moreover, Onsi (1973) states that budgetary slack is created as a result of pressure and the use of budgeted profit as a main criterion in evaluating managerial performance. Whichever of these views is accepted, a necessary condition for the creation of budget slack is the existence of power by managers or operators. This power presumably results from superior knowledge by operators and/or managers on optimum coordination and/or operating methods.

The concept of budgetary slack is closely related to Pondy's (1970) concept of discretionary resources, defined as the excess of revenues over all costs. Discretionary resources may be allocated to profit, that is to the owners of the firm as return on capital and risk, or to individuals within the organization in the form of increased salaries, extra staff, etc. The presence of positive information costs and goal incongruity raises questions about the internal allocation of discretionary resources. While the formal authority for allocating these resources within the firm may be centralized, information necessary for rational allocation decisions is distributed throughout the hierarchy because of technological and environmental uncertainties. Thus the centralized decision maker is faced with a dilemma. If he makes a unilateral decision on allocating resources to various activities, that decision may be sub-optimal for the organization because he does not have access to complete information. If the allocation decision is decentralized, inefficiencies still may result if lower level decision makers attempt to increase their own gain at the expense of the organization.

Watson & Baumler (1975) examined a similar issue to this, transfer pricing. They suggest that prices for input and output factors may be used as a means of communicating information within the organization. These artificial or market prices serve a control function to the extent that they provide information to decentralized decision makers on the optimum price and quantity of outputs. In the absence of competitively determined market based transfer prices, optimum transfer prices for the firm are related to the marginal cost of production at the subunit level. But the performance measurement system of the firm may cause decentralized decision makers to bias cost estimates so as to maximize their own performance criteria and sub-optimize the organization's performance. Necessary conditions for this behavior are subunit externalities and the existence of unique knowledge at the subunit level with regard to cost and revenue behavior. Watson and Baumler (1975) state that the organization's accounting system should play an important integration function in this type of situation. The specifics of how or when the MAS should or can achieve integration remain vague.

The issues of internal resource allocation (either in a transfer pricing or budgeting context) and the technology of information and information processing are closely related. A necessary condition for the existence of inefficiencies in internal resource allocation is that a centralized decision maker has incomplete information on production, cost or revenue functions. As knowledge of these factors becomes more rationalized and available to centralized decision makers, opportunities for inefficient allocations decrease. Analytical research on information production may be interpreted as attempting to rationalize the knowledge base available to centralized decision makers. However, to the extent that the application of information technologies requires professional judgment there may be a shift in organizational power from the operational and non-accounting managerial functions to the MAS department itself. Further rationalization of the MAS function may ultimately have the effect of decreasing the power of the MAS department and centralizing authority within the organization through routinization and procedure specification of the MAS. This train of thought leads us to conclude that the MAS plays an important role in the development of organizations and that empirical research on the MAS function has the potential for providing insight into the development of control processes within organizations including the process of bureaucratization.

Plans, stated either in the form of budgets or specified procedures, are a means of coordinating activities within organizations. Faced with a predictable environment managerial coordination rules may be formalized and documented in the form of a well defined and stable structure. However, faced with an unpredictable and changing environment focilized coordination rules are apt to decrease response times and ultimately lead to severe dysfunctions for the organization. We hypothesize that as environmental uncertainties increase the organization will increasingly rely on "time constrained coordination plans." We further propose that budgets may be viewed as time constrained coordination plans in the sense that they are developed for a specified period of time and for that time period prescribe desired levels of input and output for the organization and individual units within the organization. This may point to the importance of budget revision and budget flexibility as important organizational responses to unpredictable and changing environments.

Performance Measures

Planning is a form of *ex ante* control. The control process is incomplete in the absence of measures which provide feedback and compare actual results with plans. Performance measures, of which accounting measures of revenues, costs and other quantitative variables are a notable sub-set, are an important part of the organization's authority structure to the extent that they are used to apply sanctions or rewards.

Becker & Neuhauser (1975) developed a model of organizational effectiveness in which visibility of consequences, defined as "the degree to which the owner of an organization can and does evaluate the costs of obtaining a given level of goal attainment from a procedure-resource interaction" (p. 77), played a central role. According to Becker & Neuhauser procedures which increase visibility of consequences enhance organizational effectiveness by enabling the organization to deal constructively with usurpation, conflict, informal organization and change.

We concur that means for increasing visibility of consequences will increase organizational efficiency. However, from an MAS perspective, a number of issues remain to be explicated. MAS procedures to increase the visibility of consequences and appraise performance are a sub-set of the total number of procedures available to the organization. Other procedures for increasing the visibility of consequences which normally are not included in the formal MAS may include personnel appraisals and collegial or professional review. Recognizing the existence of different means for increasing the visibility of consequences raises questions about the characteristics of an organization or its environment which enhance the usefulness of MAS based procedures for performance evaluation.

Hayes (1977) examined the accuracy and importance of financial data in performance evaluation in production, research and development, and marketing subunits. He concluded that budgets may be relatively poor indicators of effectiveness, especially in marketing departments, because financial measures are poor surrogates for the entire set of factors which influence departmental performance. This suggests that the utility of traditional MAS based measures of performance may be related to underlying organizational processes such as procedure specification and centralization to the extent that well specified procedures may be surrogated by the MAS more readily. Indirect evidence in support of this contention is provided by Bruns & Waterhouse (1975) who concluded that budgets tend to be used as evaluative devices in centralized organizations.

While properties of organization structure may be important in explaining the relative utility and use of MAS based performance reports, important questions regarding the efficacy of alternative report designs may also be addressed within a contingency framework. Two examples of variables which may be included under the heading of report design are the frequency of reporting and the level of data aggregation in reports. While we know of no existing studies which have examined the relationships between properties of organizations and the technology of MAS design and implementation, the general thrust of the contingency approach to the study of organizations is such as to strongly suggest that organizational and MAS design variables are closely linked.

CONCLUSION

We have reviewed the literature on contingency theory and the behavioral aspects of MAS with the objective of presenting a framework for hypothesizing some relationships between organizational and MAS variables. In this section we will note a few of the more obvious implications of our review for possible empirical research on organizational and accounting variables.

The tenor of contingency theory suggests that efficient organizational design is contingent on technology and/or environment. Furthermore efficient management processes are contingent on some properties of organization structure such as centralization, procedure specification or autonomy. Although conceptually appealing, the evidence linking these contextual, organizational and managerial variables to effectiveness seems to us weak. A number of contingency like studies, for example, Pugh *et al.* (1969), Child (1973), and Hage & Aiken (1967) did not measure or attempt to measure organizational effectiveness. Others such as Burns & Stalker (1961) and Lawrence & Lorsch (1967) who related organizational variables to effectiveness did so with measures of effectiveness which are open to question and drew inferences from small sample sizes. Woodward's (1965) study seems to us to present some of the strongest empirical evidence linking technology, design and effectiveness in that it has withstood the test of replication (Zwerman, 1970). Nevertheless we cannot help but conclude that a substantial amount of research on the linkages between organizational and managerial variables and effectiveness remains to be done before policy prescriptions can be written with confidence.

We also cannot help but conclude that conceptual and methodological clarity in the contingency theory literature has been less than absolute. Our review noted that authors have often proposed different definitions for important terms such as technology, environment, centralization and other structural variables. As a consequence measures of variables and empirical relationships among variables are not clearly established. For example, Tossi, Aldig & Storey (1973) point to the methodological inadequacies of Lawrence and Lorch's environmental measures. We believe that validation studies such as reported by Pennings (1974) are sorely needed if contingency theory is to provide a sound theoretical foundation for the study of information issues. It should be noted that research on the behavioral and organizational implications of MAS has yet to confront many of those important problems partly because of a derth of activity in the area.

In spite of these limitations we do believe that the contingency approach to organizational research on MAS variables offers great potential for MAS and organizational researchers alike. In our opinion one of the most notable products of this research has been a realization of the importance of taxonomic schemes for theory development. This is not to say that adequate taxonomies have been developed; rather as important contextual, structural and processual factors are defined, and as the relatinships between these factors and behavioral variables are identified, useful taxonomies are evolving. Studies of MAS based processes have potential theoretical and practical implications because of their pervasiveness and their importance to organizational efficiency. Moreover many MAS activities are concrete and identifiable managerial processes with documented outputs (e.g. budgets). Therefore research on MAS variables may be a means of conceptualizing and observing more abstract processes such as goal formation, power attempts or conflict resolution.

BIBLIOGRAPHY

Anthony, R. N., *Planning and Control Systems: A Framework for Analysis* (Division of Research, Graduate School of Business Administration, Harvard University, 1965).

Argyris, C., *The Impact of Budgets on People* (The Controllership Foundation, 1952).

Becker, S. W. & Neuhauser, D., *The Efficient Organization* (Elsevier Scientific Publishing Co., Inc., 1975).

Blau, Peter M. *et al.,* The Structure of Small Bureaucracies, *American Sociological Review* (April 1966), pp. 179–191.

Blau, Peter M. & Schoenherr, R. M., *The Structure of Organizations* (Basic Books, 1971).

Bruns, W. J., Jr. & Waterhouse, J. H., Budgetary Control and Organization Structure, *Journal of Accounting Research* (Autumn 1975), pp. 177–203.

Burns, T. & Stalker, G. M., *The Management of Innovation* (Tavistock, 1961).

Caplan, E. H., *Management Accounting and Behavioral Science* (Addison-Wesley, 1971).

Child, J., Strategies of Control and Organizational Behavior, *Administrative Science Quarterly* (March 1973), pp. 1–17.

Crozier, M., *The Bureaucratic Phenomenon* (University of Chicago Press, 1964).

Cyert, R. M. & March, J. G., *A Behavioral Theory of the Firm* (Prentice-Hall, 1963).

Dahl, Robert A., The Concept of Power, *Behavioral Science* (July 1957), pp. 201–215.

DeCoster, D. T. & Fertakis, J. P., Budget-Induced Pressure and Its Relationship to Supervisory Behavior, *Journal of Accounting Research* (Autumn 1968), pp. 237–246.

Donaldson, L., Child, J. & Aldrich, H., The Aston Findings on Centralization: Further Discussion, *Administrative Science Quarterly* (September 1975), pp. 453–460.

Downs, Anthony, *Inside Bureaucracy* (Little, Brown and Company, 1967).

Duncan, Robert B., Characteristics of Organizational Environments and Perceived Environmental Uncertainty, *Administrative Science Quarterly* (September 1972), pp. 313–327.

Edström, A. & Galbraith, J. R., Transfer of Managers as a Coordination and Control Strategy in Multinational Organizations, *Administrative Science Quarterly* (June 1977), pp. 248–263.

Etzioni, A., *Modern Organizations* (Prentice-Hall, 1964).

Gouldner, A. W., *Patterns of Industrial Bureaucracy* (Free Press, 1954).

Haas, E. & Collen, L., Administrative Practices in University Departments, *Administrative Science Quarterly* (June 1963), pp. 44–60.

Hage, J. & Aiken, M., Relationship of Centralization to Other Structural Properties, *Administrative Science Quarterly* (June 1967), pp. 72–92.

Hage, J. & Aiken, M., Routine Technology, Social Structure and Organizational Goals, *Administrative Science Quarterly* (September 1969), pp. 366–376.

Hall, R. H., Intraorganizational Structural Variation: An Application of the Bureaucratic Model, *Administrative Science Quarterly* (December 1962), pp. 295–308.

Hall, R. H., The Concept of Bureaucracy: An Empirical Assessment, *American Journal of Sociology* (July 1963), pp. 32–40.

Hall, R. H., Professionalization and Bureaucratization, *American Journal of Sociology* (July 1963), pp. 32–40.

Hall, R. H., *Organizations: Structure and Process* Prentice-Hall, 1972).

Hall, R. H., Haas, J. E. & Johnson, N. J., Organizational Size, Complexity and Formalization, *American Sociological Review* (December 1967), pp. 903–911.

Hayes, D. C., The Contingency Theory of Managerial Accounting, *The Accounting Review* (January 1977), pp. 22–39.

Heydebrand, W. V. & Noell, J. J., Task Structure and Innovation in Professional Organizations, in Heydebrand, M. V. (ed.), *Comparative Organizations* (Prentice-Hall, 1973), pp. 294–322.

Hickson, D. J. *et al.*, A Strategic Contingencies' Theory of Intraorganizational Power, *Administrative Science Quarterly* (June 1971), pp. 216–229.

Hofstede, G. H., *The Game of Budget Control* (Van Gorcum, 1967).

Hopwood, A. G., Leadership Climate and the Use of Accounting Data in Performance Evaluation, *The Accounting Review* (July 1974), pp. 485–495.

Horngren, C. T., *Cost Accounting: A Managerial Emphasis* (Prentice-Hall, 1972).

Khandwalla, P. N., The Effect of Different Types of Competition on the Use of Management Controls, *Journal of Accounting Research* (Autumn 1972), pp. 275–285.

Lawrence, P. R. & Lorsch, J. W., *Organization and Environment* (Harvard University, 1967).

Litwak, E., Technological Innovation and Theoretical Functions of Primary Groups and Bureaucratic Structures, *American Journal of Sociology* (January 1968), pp. 468–481.

Lowe, A. E. & Shaw, R. W., An Analysis of Managerial Biasing: Evidence of a Company's Budgeting Process, *Journal of Management Studies* (October 1968), pp. 304–315.

Mechanic, D., Source of Power of Lower Participants in Complex Organizations, *Administrative Science Quarterly* (December 1962), pp. 349–364.

Onsi, M., Factor Analysis of Behavioral Variables Affecting Budgetary Slack, *The Accounting Review* (July 1973), pp. 535–548.

Ouchi, W. G., The Relationship Between Organizational Structure and Organizational Control, *Administrative Science Quarterly* (March 1977), pp. 95–113.

Pennings, J., Measures of Organizational Structure: A Methodological Note, *American Journal of Sociology* (May 1974), pp. 686–704.

Pennings, J., The Relevance of the Structural-Contingency Model for Organizational Effectiveness, *Administrative Science Quarterly* (September 1975), pp. 393–410.

Perrow, Charles, A Framework for the Comparative Analysis of Organizations, *American Sociological Review* (April 1967), pp. 194–208.

Perrow, Charles, *Complex Organizations* (Scott, Foresman and Co., 1972).

Perrow, Charles, Control in Organizations: The Centralized-Decentralized Bureaucracy, Paper Presented at 1976 Annual Meeting of the American Sociological Association.

Pondy, L. R., Toward a Theory of Internal Resource-Allocation, in Zald, M. N. (ed.), *Power in Organizations* (Vanderbilt University Press, 1970), pp. 270–311.

Pugh, D. S. *et al.,* Dimensions of Organization Structure, *Administrative Science Quarterly* (June 1968), pp. 65–105.

Pugh, D. S. *et al.,* The Context of Organization Structures, *Administrative Science Quarterly* (March 1969), pp. 91–114.

Schiff, M. & Lewin, A. Y., Where Traditional Budgeting Fails, *Financial Executive* (May 1968), pp. 57–62.

Searfoss, D. G. & Monczka, R. M., Perceived Participation in the Budget Process and Motivation to Achieve the Budget, *Academy of Management Journal* (December 1973), pp. 541–554.

Simon, H. A. *et al., Centralization vs Decentralization in Organizing the Controller's Department* (The Controllership Foundation, 1945).

Stedry, A. C., *Budget Control and Cost Behavior* (Prentice-Hall, 1960).

Stedry, A. C. & Kay, E., The Effect of Goal Difficulty on Performance: A Field Experiment, *Behavioral Science* (November 1966), pp. 451–470.

Swieringa, R. J. & Moncur, R. H., The Relationship Between Managers' Budget-Oriented Behavior and Selected Attitude, Position, Size, and Performance Measures, *Empirical Research in Accounting: Selected Studies, 1972.* Supplement to *Journal of Accounting Research* 10, pp. 194–209.

Tagiuri, R., Value Orientations and the Relationship of Managers and Scientists, *Administrative Science Quarterly* (June 1965), pp. 39–51.

Thompson, J. D., *Organizations in Action* (New York: McGraw-Hill, 1967).

Thompson, V. A., *Organizations as Systems* (General Learning Press, 1973).

Tossi, H., Aldag, R. & Storey, R., On the Measurement of the Environment: An Assessment of the Lawrence and Lorsch Environmental Uncertainty Subscale, *Administrative Science Quarterly* (March 1973), pp. 27–36.

Watson, D. J. H. & Baumler, J. V., Transfer Pricing: A Behavioral Context, *The Accounting Review* (July 1975), pp. 466–474.

Wildavsky, A., *The Politics of the Budgetary Process* (Little, Brown & Co., 1964).

Williamson, O. E., *The Economics of Discretionary Behavior: Managerial Objectives in a Theory of the Firm* (Prentice-Hall, 1964).

Woodward, J., *Industrial Organization: Theory and Practice* (Oxford University Press, 1965).

Zwerman, W. L., *New Perspectives in Organizational Theory* (Casebound, 1970).

Budgetary Control and Organization Structure

William J. Bruns, Jr.

John H. Waterhouse*

In spite of the widespread use of budgets for control of organization activities, relatively little is known about how budgets influence behavior. Furthermore, the interaction of budgets with other means of influencing human behavior has remained largely unexplored. This research explores the interaction and relationships of one source of control, organization structure, with another source of control, budgets. Data gathered from twenty-five organizations are analyzed to explore some of the interrelationships between organization structure and the use of budgets by managers. Data collected by mailed questionnaires were factor analyzed to provide measures of budget-related behavior that could be related to measures of organization structure and context that were collected in field interviews. The analysis of these data indicates clear relationships between organization structure and the use and effects of budgets and provides insight into several complex relationships suggested by other field and *a priori* research on control in organizations.

The findings of this study are consistent with those organizational studies which have concluded that the structure of organizations can be viewed as contingent upon environment and organization characteristics such as size, technology, and dependence (the extent to which an organization is autonomous in relationships with other organizations) (see Woodward [1965], Burns and Stalker [1961], Lawrence and Lorsch [1967], and Pugh, Hickson, Hinings, and Turner [1969]). Budget-related behavior is found to be contingent upon various aspects of organization structure such as centralization, autonomy, and the degree to which activities are structured. These findings lead to the conclusion that there must be alternative organizational control strategies in different kinds of organizations, and that prescriptions about how budgets should be used in organizational control should be written with care.

SOME THEORIES OF ORGANIZATION AND BUDGETARY CONTROL

Budgets are potential means of influencing behavior. Control is the successful exercise of power to influence behavior available to an organization. Two other primary means to influence behavior are interpersonal contact, i.e.,

From *Journal of Accounting Research*, Vol. 13, No. 2 (Autumn 1975), pp. 177–203.

*Professor, Harvard University and Assistant Professor, University of Alberta, respectively. Financial support for this research was provided by Associates of Harvard Business School and the Associates Workshop in Business Research, University of Alberta.

leadership, and organizational structure, i.e., the distribution of authority and work roles. This study focuses specifically on the relationship between formal properties of organizational structure and budgetary control. This is in contrast to other studies of budgeting which have examined the relationship between interpersonal variables and budgetary control (DeCoster and Fertakis [1968], Foran and DeCoster [1974], Hopwood [1974], Swieringa and Moncur [1972 and 1975]).

Organization Structure and Control

Structure refers to internal patterns of organization relationships (Thompson [1967], p. 51).[1] Organization implies some ordering of work roles whereby the authority and resources for making decisions and performing tasks are distributed to defined positions within the organization. Much of the administrative systems literature, being concerned with economic efficiency, has focused on the means whereby organization activities and tasks can be rationally grouped by specialized function and subjected to standardized operating procedures (Barnard [1938], Weber [1947], and Chandler [1962]). To the extent that activities are specialized, standardized, and formalized, decision-making authority and tasks can be controlled by decentralization and structuring of activities (the degree of formal regulation of intended activities of organization members). Child states the nature of control under decentralization with structuring in the following manner:

> . . . the locus of the decision-making authority on operational matters is decentralized down to the incumbents of official roles. These roles are structured by virtue of their specialized prescribed duties and particularly by a system of procedure and documentation designed to limit areas of discretion, as well as provide information on role performance (Child [1972b], p. 163).

This decentralized but structured approach comprises one strategy for organizational control.

An alternative strategy for control is to centralize decision-making authority at higher levels within the organization. Maintaining control by centralizing decision making reduces the need for organization, systems, procedures, and specialist personnel to operate administrative systems (Child [1973]). A number of empirical studies of organizations have found a negative correlation between centralization and the degree to which activities are structured (Blau and Schoenherr [1971], Inkson, Pugh and Hickson [1970], and Child [1972b]). Interpersonal relationships replace structured activities as primary means for maintaining control.

The choice between decentralization with structuring and centralization is limited to some extent by internal and external conditions faced by the organization. Several studies have shown that the size of the organization is positively associated with structuring of activities

---

[1]Research on organization structure is quite voluminous. A sample might include work cited below. Its diversity precludes more than recognition here that the structure of organizations has long fascinated many social scientists. The particular thread of research on organization structure to which our research most directly ties originates with Pugh, Hickson, Hinings, MacDonald, Turner, and Lupton (1963), who set out to devise measures of several dimensions of organization structures and to develop reresearch techniques which could be standardized and repeated in different settings. This research, which we will refer to as the Aston approach, has led to a substantial body of related work on organization structure. (A sample should include Hickson (1966), Pugh, Hickson, Hinings, and Turner (1968) and (1969), and Child (1972a) and (1972b). Research on organization structure has often been linked with research on behavior of organization members. The effects of structure and environment on organizational behavior have been explored in classic studies such as those of Woodward (1965), Burns and Stalker (1968), and Lawrence and Lorsch (1967). In addition, social psychologists have considered the role of organization structure as an influence on individual behavior (see, for a sampling, Vroom [1960], McGregor [1960], Argyris [1960 and 1964], Fiedler [1967] and Child [1972b and 1973]).

and negatively associated with centralization (see, for example, Pugh, Hickson, Hinings, and Turner [1969] and Child [1972b]). Technological sophistication may also be positively associated with structuring of activities (Child [1972a]). It appears that, as organizations become more closely tied to technology and means for standardized mass production, they formalize role definitions and decentralize decision-making authority (Perrow [1967]). Concurrently, these organizations develop means for maintaining control by utilizing procedures for defining and measuring role performance.

Organization Structure and Perceived Control

In a decentralized and structured organization, legitimate activities are clearly defined, areas of responsibility and authority are clearly delineated, and control is essentially impersonal. Since areas of authority are clearly defined, decision making can be delegated while organizational control is maintained. Individuals may feel they have a great degree of control within areas of defined authority. A decentralized and structured organization operating in a stable organizational environment seems particularly well suited to the use of budgetary control.

Centralization, where control of decisions is reserved to a small group at the top of an organization hierarchy, reduces perceived control by individuals at lower levels in the organization (Child [1973]). Whereas systems, procedures, and areas of authority are not or cannot be clearly defined, control by structuring may be replaced by interpersonal control. As a control strategy, centralization may allow control to be exerted and sanctioned not only from the organization *per se,* but also among individuals within the organization. Individuals can, and presumably do, build bases from which to exert influence and control within the organization. For example, Mechanic (1962) noted that, to the extent that subordinates can make supervisors dependent upon them, the subordinates have power. Crozier (1964) also has noted that when role performance is governed by rules and, therefore, is predictable, role incumbents find it difficult to build power bases. However, when organization structure does not clearly define areas of authority, a system of bargaining and power relationships may develop.

In those situations where work roles cannot be readily structured because either environment or technology is unstable, centralization may be adopted as a strategy for control. But these latter conditions may also create an opportunity for individuals to develop power bases, and a relatively high level of interpersonal bargaining and conflict might be expected. Budgets may be used as a means of control in either decentralized and structured or centralized organizations. However, the differences in structure may affect individual behavior in such a way that budget-related behavior will be different in organizations depending on the structural strategy an organization has adopted.

Budgetary Control

Control systems based upon financial measures are widely used in economic organizations. The principal designs for assigning financial responsibility in organizations can be classified as follows: standard cost centers, revenue centers, discretionary expense centers, profit centers, and investment centers (Vancil [1973]). The order of this classification is from narrowest to broadest in terms of the decision-making discretion permitted or required of the manager. The manager of a standard cost center has control over fewer financial variables than the manager of an investment center. Vancil (1973) concluded that the choice of a design for assigning financial responsibility should be a function of the organizational structure, which he defined in terms of the delegation of authority and the specialization of effort, and organizational strategy.

Budgets are financial plans and provide a basis for directing and evaluating the performance of individuals or segments of organizations. Through budgets, activities of different parts of an organization can be coordinated and controlled. A control system typically incorporates measures and techniques which conform to the responsibilities delegated to managers under the organization's structure. As decision-making authority is decentralized and parts of an organization become more autonomous, managers will be responsible for more financial variables, and financial control systems will be more complex in the sense that they will incorporate more variables.

Organization Structure and Budget-Related Behavior

The research domain in which this study is based is shown in figure 1. Organization structure is viewed as being contingent on the context in which the organization operates, including such characteristics as its size, technology, and dependence (the extent to which an organization is autonomous in relationship with other organizations). Two variables, control system complexity and perceived control, are seen as intervening to affect budget-related behavior including the quantity of such behavior, the kind of behavior, and the quality and satisfaction in terms of the extent to which the budget is seen as effective in accomplishing organizational goals.

In this study budget-related behavior is defined as the activities, actions, and interactions of managers with each other and their tasks that relate either directly or indirectly to budget systems. Budget-related attitudes are defined as affective feelings of managers toward budgets and budget-related behaviors of themselves and others. Budgets are plans against which performance may be compared. To a large extent, the use of budgets for control purposes is thought to be dependent upon the ability to plan with a fairly high degree of certainty and to measure output or role performance with a relatively high degree of accuracy. A budget not only specifies a goal (i.e., *X* units of production at an expected total cost), but it may also specify the means for accomplishing the goal (i.e., material, labor, and other inputs at standard costs). In decision-making terms, the budget specifies both an objective function and decision alternatives. The budget may be seen as a means for decentralizing certain types of operation decisions. However, since the objective function and decision alternatives are specified, the decisions faced by budgetees are really very structured.

Since budgets tend to structure the decision-making environment, budgets would appear to be particularly well-suited as control devices under the same types of operating circumstances that are also prevalent in decentralized but structured organizations. Moreover, the use of budgets for control purposes and the

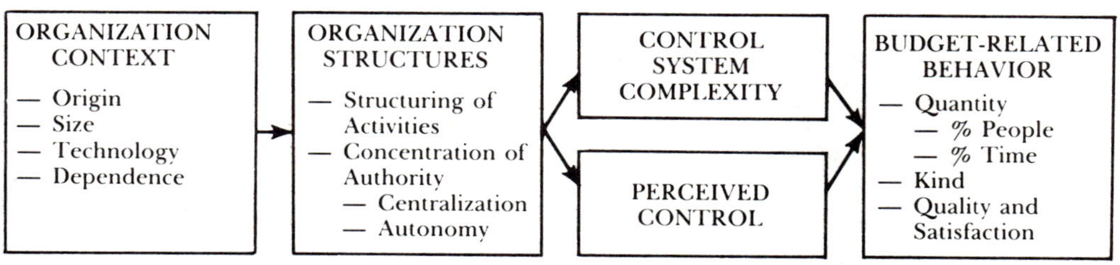

FIGURE 1. Research domain.

structuring of activities may be mutually reinforcing. A relatively stable and predictable environment which will allow decentralization with structuring of activities produces conditions amenable to the use of budgets, and budgets further structure activities. Therefore, we hypothesize that the quantity of budget-related behavior will be high in organizations which are decentralized and structured. Because roles and rules are clearly defined in a decentralized but structured organization, structuring of activities and perceived control are expected to be positively related. The individual in a structured situation may perceive himself and others as having greater control in their areas of defined responsibility. For these reasons we hypothesize that budget-related behavior will tend to be administrative in character rather than interpersonal. Since subordinate managers have less authority and may perceive themselves as having less control in centralized organizations, any attempt to hold individuals responsible for directly meeting a budget is less likely to meet with much success and is likely to produce negative attitudes toward budgets. To the extent that budgets are used as control devices in centralized organizations, we hypothesize that they will be used in a more interpersonal manner than in decentralized but structured organizations. The hypothesized relationships between organization context structure and budget-related behavior are illustrated in figure 2.

METHOD AND DATA

Twenty-seven organizations were contacted to seek their participation in the study. Two criteria were utilized in selecting organizations: first, because we hoped our sample would include organizations with a wide variety of different structures, organizations of different sizes, operating in different environments, and with diverse technologies were contacted; second, since each organization would be visited as part of the research, the sample was geographically limited to the U.S. Midwest and Eastern regions and to Ontario in Canada to minimize interviewing costs. Organizations were defined, for purposes of this study, so that

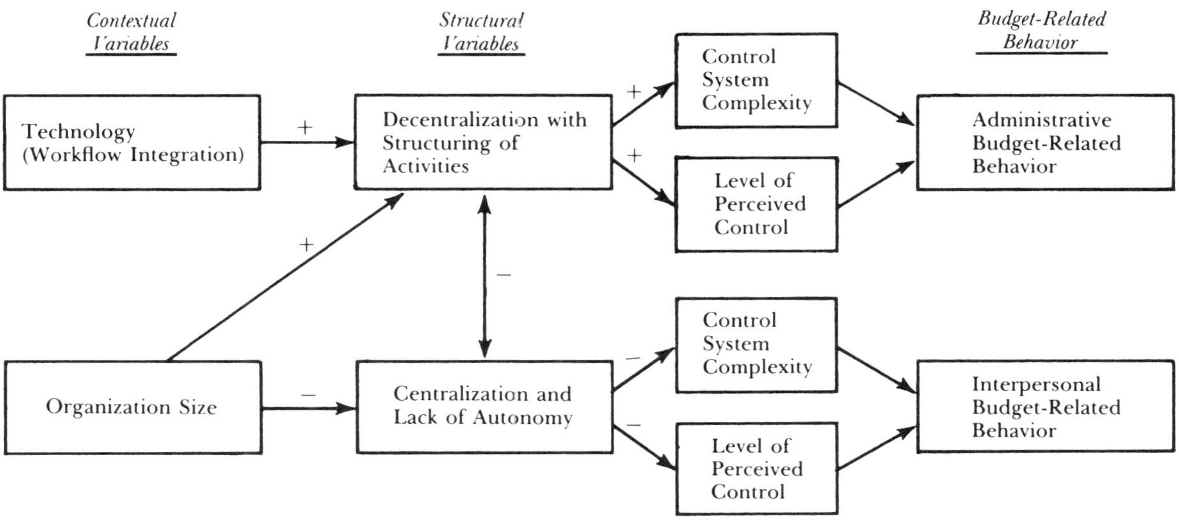

FIGURE 2. Expected relationships between organization context, structure, and budget-related behavior.

corporate divisions would comprise separate organizations. A letter was sent to the chief executive officer or another senior officer in each organization soliciting their cooperation in the project. The letter explained that we were engaged in a research project designed to learn something more about the effective use of budgets in organizations. Twenty-six organizations agreed to participate in the study. A profile of these organizations is provided in table 1. The research procedure included a two- to three-hour interview with the chief executive or a close associate in each organization. The interview time was spent in: (a) explaining the general nature of the study and why the cooperation of each executive was important; (b) administering questionnaires on organization structure and control systems according to the standard format of each (questionnaires will be described below) and in collecting necessary supporting documents (such as organization charts, etc.); and (c) identifying a sample of employees directly involved in preparing, using, or performing against a budget.

The identification of the employee sample usually occurred while the interviewee was explaining his organization chart. Our original plan to select a random sample from all employees in each organization proved unfeasible because organizations were reluctant or unable to make complete lists available to us. The number of employees identified varied from three to fifty depending on the size and nature of the organization. Budget-related behavior and perceived control questionnaires were mailed to each of the identified individuals, and their anonymous responses were returned by mail. Four hundred and twenty-nine questionnaires yielded two hundred and eighty-four usable responses for a response rate of sixty-six percent. The respondents had worked for their present employers an average of 14.8 years and in their current positions an average of 3.4 years. On the average they had worked for 22.3 years since leaving school. Respondents were experienced and held managerial positions.

TABLE 1. Organizations Sampled

Number of Employees	N	Organizations	
		Manufacturing	Service
0–249	7	Construction Products Building Materials	Research and Development Advertising Life Insurance (3)
250–999	6	Construction Products Utilities Vehicle Components Chemicals (2)	Sales
1,000–1,999	5	Food Products Newspaper Paper Products Electronic Equipment	Advertising
2,000 or greater	8	Paper Manufacturing Packaging Containers Vehicle Components (2) Steel	Life Insurance Facilities Maintenance

The Questionnaires

In total, four different questionnaires were administered. Wherever possible, questionnaires which had been validated through previous research were sought for reasons of practicality and to provide comparisons to prior research. A description of the questionnaires follows.

Organization Structure and Context. Instruments developed by the Aston Group were used to operationalize the concepts of organization structure and context (Pugh, Hickson, Hinings and Turner [1968 and 1969]). The Aston Group identified from a review of the literature six primary dimensions of organization structure: specialization, standardization, formalization, centralization, configuration, and flexibility. Sixty-four scales were constructed to measure the first five of these variables. A factor analysis of the data from forty-six organizations disclosed four independent dimensions of structure: structuring of activities; concentration of authority; line of control of workflow; and relative size of supportive components. Subsequent research (Hinings and Lee [1971], Inkson, Pugh and Hickson [1970], and Child [1972b]) utilizing the Aston methodology has concentrated on the first two dimensions of structure: structuring of activities and concentration of authority.[2]

The dimension called structuring of activities concerns the degree of formal regulation of the intended activities of employees. The scales used to measure this dimension are: specialization, the number and kinds of specialists; standardization, the extent to which activities are subject to standard operating rules and procedures; and formalization, the degree to which rules and procedures are committed to writing. Concentration of authority is defined as the extent to which authority for making decisions lies at higher levels within the organization or outside the organization. Concentration of authority is measured by two scales: centralization, the extent to which formal authority for making decisions rests at higher levels of an organization; and lack of autonomy, the extent to which decisions cannot be made in the organization but are reserved for managers who are not part of it.

The abbreviated Aston schedule, with minor modifications, was used to collect data on organization structure and context.[3] Structuring of activities was measured on two of the three scales previously discussed—specialization and formalization—both of which are combined to create a single intraorganization measure. Whereas the abbreviated schedule measures organization autonomy by asking only if the formal authority for making a number of decisions lies within or outside the organization, it was deemed desirable to also examine the degree to which these same decisions are centralized or decentralized within the organization. Consequently, the abbreviated schedule was modified to ask the respondent "which is the most junior level of job that has the authority to decide?" The resultant responses were scored according to the original unabbreviated Aston method. Three scales were used to measure organization context. Size of each organization was measured by the number of employees. Dependence was measured by scales which include relationships with owning or controlling organizations, if any, and other outside groups. Workflow integration was a measure of technology indicated by the degree of automated, continuous, fixed sequence operations.

The Aston questionnaire yielded data on

[2]The Aston research has not gone on without some criticism. Some of this has concerned the scales and methods used in the research while other criticism has focused on the analysis and interpretation of findings. See, for example, Aldrich (1972).

[3]An abbreviated schedule was found to achieve results very similar to the original Aston schedule and requires substantially less time to complete. See Inkson, *et al.*, (1970).

three organization context variables (size, dependence, and workflow integration) and three structural variables (centralization, lack of autonomy, and structuring of activities). Table 2 presents the means, standard deviation, observed ranges, and theoretical ranges of these variables. In general, the organizations appear to be relatively autonomous and structured. A direct comparison of structural data from this study with other similar studies is difficult. However, general comparisons indicate close similarities between this sample and other samples on all variables.[4]

Complexity of Control Systems. A short questionnaire to measure the breadth or complexity of control systems was developed for this research. Since the questionnaire was to be administered at the same time and to the same persons as the structure and organization context questions, a format similar to the Aston questionnaire was used. Questions such as, "Is your division an Investment Center, a Profit Center, a Discretionary Cost Center, a Revenue Center, or a Standard Cost Center?" and, "At what level in the organization are performance standards established?" were asked. An *a priori* numerical scoring method was devised for the questions, with the numerical values in descending order from most to least complex. Also, each chief executive was asked to estimate the approximate number of employees involved in either planning or evaluation aspects of budgeting so that this number could be related to the total number of employees in the organization. The theoretical range of data from the complexity of control systems questionnaire was from four (simple) to twenty-one (complex) with a theoretical mid-point of 12.5. The observed range of scores was five to eighteen with an observed mean of 12.43. The mean percentage of estimates of the proportion of employees involved in making or using budgets was 10.8 percent, and the mean percentage of time reportedly spent by these employees on budget-related activities was 18.5 percent.

Budget Behavior Questionnaire. The questionnaire used to collect data on budget-related behavior was originally developed by Fertakis (1967) and has been substantially modified by Swieringa and Moncur (1975). In its original form, the questionnaire was designed to measure budget-induced pressure. It incorporates descriptions of budget-related activities and relationships to which a manager could relate his own budget situation. The original ninety-seven item questionnaire was reduced through factor analysis by Swieringa and Moncur to

[4]For examples see Hickson, Hinings, McMillan, and Schwitter (1974) and Inkson, *et al.,* (1970). Table 2 shows our organization to be very similar to those reported in McMillan, Hickson, Hinings, and Schneck (1973).

TABLE 2. Summary of Measurements of Organization Context and Structure (N = 25)

	Means	Standard Deviation	Observed Range	Theoretical Range
Size	2660	7051	70–36,000	N.A.
Dependence	4.8	2.04	0–9	0–9
Workflow Integration	6.72	3.67	0–11	0–12
Structuring of Activities	25.72	5.18	14–32	0–36
Lack of Autonomy	5.56	4.22	0–13	0–23
Centralization*	36.95	12.23	19–62	0–115

*N = 20 (data needed to measure centralization could not be obtained from five organizations).

forty-four (shown in the Appendix). A continuous line response scale was used to measure frequency (how often does it take place?), normativeness (how often should it take place?), and the importance of each of the forty-four activities to the respondent. Each question was treated as a separate variable. The budget-related behavior data were reduced by factor analysis to uncover underlying patterns in the data. The factor analysis was conducted using the SPSS *(Special Programs for the Social Sciences)* statistical package (Nie, Bent, and Hull [1970]). A principal component analysis with iteration was conducted. The solution employed inferred factors, implying that any observed correlation between variables is due to common factors. Inferred factor techniques replace the main diagonal of the correlation matrix with communality estimates before factoring.[5] Thirteen factors were extracted with an eigenvalue greater than one. These thirteen factors accounted for 62.4 percent of the variance, with the first factor accounting for 20.8 percent of the variance. The thirteen factors were rotated using the orthogonal varimax criteria. Variables with a loading of .40 or greater on a factor were selected as the factor's domain. Variables loading on each factor and factor loading coefficients were used to develop descriptive factor names. The factors and the variables were factorally pure (in that they loaded on only one factor). Six variables, 1, 16, 17, 22, 29, and 40, did not load on any factor at greater than .40. Factor scores were computed for each individual respondent.

Satisfaction scores were computed for each individual by taking the absolute value of the differences between (a) how often does it take place? and (b) how often should it take place? multiplied by the value for (c) how important is it to me? This scoring procedure is similar to that developed by Porter (1961) to measure job satisfaction except for our inclusion of an importance weighting. The rationale for this procedure is that discrepancies between what is perceived to be and what should be (i.e., equity) produce feelings of satisfaction or dissatisfaction (Vroom [1969], p. 206), and in the present context we were attempting to measure attitudes toward specific aspects of budgeting. The resultant satisfaction scores have a theoretical range of zero to twenty. Responses to all forty-four variables were skewed to the left with an observed overall mean of 2.7 and standard deviation of 1.7. These data indicate a generally high level of satisfaction with budget-related activities within the organizations sampled. Since no statistical inferences were directly made from the raw satisfaction scores, this skewness was not felt to be a serious problem.

The satisfaction scores were factor analyzed using the same technique that was used for the descriptive variables. If a subject failed to answer either parts a, b, or c on a given question, his responses were omitted from further analysis. This procedure yielded between 275 and 281 usable scores for each variable from the 284 questionnaires which were returned. Fifteen factors were extracted with an eigenvalue greater than one. Satisfaction factors and the variables which load on each are presented in table 4. All variables were factorally pure. Fourteen variables did not load on any factors (> .40). No variable loaded on Sat-

[5]Swieringa and Moncur (1975) used a method of factor analysis which places unities in the diagonal of the correlation matrix. Only two of the factors in our analysis, FD_5 and FD_9 have an identical composition to factors reported by Swieringa and Moncur. Replacing the diagonal of our correlation matrix with unities did not change the composition of our factors substantially. Differences in factor composition may have arisen because of differences in sample size and/or sample composition. Swieringa and Moncur's sample size was 137 while ours was 284. Swieringa and Moncur sampled individuals from four companies which may have been selected because of similarities in industry, production methods, or markets. We purposely sampled from organizations from different industries, markets, and production methods. The fact that there are substantial differences between the factor results in the two studies lends support to the position that there are interorganizational differences in budget-related behavior.

TABLE 3. Analysis of Budget-Related Behavior
Descriptive Factor Loadings (>.40) After Orthogonal Rotation, and Percentage of Total Variance

Factor Number and Name	Variable Number	Loading	Percentage of Variance
FD_1	7	.700	20.8
Participation in planning	26	.633	
	8	.580	
	9	.560	
	5	.536	
	6	.483	
FD_2	24	.607	
Evaluation by the budget	25	.517	
	13	.417	5.9
	31	.416	
FD_3	41	.743	4.8
Enabling features of budgets	42	.643	
FD_4	38	.730	
Participation in budget systems	39	.648	4.1
	37	.476	
FD_5	34	.738	
Limiting features of budgets	35	.560	3.8
	33	.446	
FD_6	44	.760	3.4
Support from budget	43	.707	
FD_7	21	.596	3.3
Acceptance of methods	20	.573	
	23	.419	
FD_8	27	.637	
Required explanation of variances	19	.629	3.1
	32	.404	
FD_9	4	.651	2.9
Interaction with superior	18	.467	
FD_{10}	14	.544	
Difficulty in meeting budget	3	.451	2.8
	12	.422	
FD_{11}	15	.561	
Participation in feedback	36	.561	2.6
	16	.408	
FD_{12}	30	.600	2.5
	11	.417	
FD_{13}	2	.403	2.3

TABLE 4. Analysis of Budget-Related Behavior
Satisfaction Factor Loadings (>.40) After Orthogonal Rotation, and Percentage of Total Variance

Factor Number and Name	Variable Number	Loading	Percentage of Variance
FS_1	22	.726	14.9
Satisfaction with superior budget behavior	25	.461	
FS_2	9	.677	5.4
Satisfaction with participation in planning	8	.587	
	10	.548	
	6	.415	
	7	.408	
FS_3	43	.732	5.1
Satisfaction with usefulness of budgets	44	.698	
FS_4	42	.732	4.5
Satisfaction with flexibility permitted by budgets	41	.726	
FS_5	2	.519	3.6
Satisfaction with time-consuming aspect of budgets	3	.507	
FS_6	34	.633	3.5
Satisfaction with restrictive features of budgets	35	.571	
	33	.476	
FS_7	26	.732	3.4
Satisfaction with support from staff departments			
FS_8	40	.592	3.2
Satisfaction with outlets for discussing budget matters	23	.437	
FS_9	31	.673	3.1
Satisfaction with evaluative features of budgets	27	.406	
FS_{10}	37	.569	3.0
Satisfaction with participation in budget systems	38	.482	
FS_{11}	20	.523	2.6
Satisfaction with methods of reaching the budget	21	.452	
FS_{12}	30	.618	2.5
FS_{13}	16	.455	2.4
	18	.423	
FS_{14}	29	.455	2.3
	32	.423	

isfaction Factor 15 (FS_{15}) (> .40). Factor scores were computed for each individual in the same manner as for the descriptive factors.

The factor scores for the thirteen descriptive factors and the fifteen satisfaction factors were averaged across each organization. These means were computed on samples of between four and thirty-one questionnaires per organization. Justification for this procedure is found in the argument that the variables were being studied as features of organizations, not as individuals within organizations.

Perceived Control. Tannenbaum's control graph questionnaire (Tannenbaum [1968]), was administered without modification with the budget behavior questionnaire. The Tannenbaum questionnaire yields data on the degree of perceived influence at six levels within the organization. Respondents are asked to indicate the amount of influence on what goes on in their organization they feel is exerted by top management, location managers, line department managers, line foremen, workers, and staff departments. A five-point Likert Scale was used to measure responses. Plotting the mean perceived control against the organization level yields a control graph for each organization. Perceived control can be represented by the shape of the curve (distribution of control) or the average height of the curve (the total amount of control). In this study attention was focused on total amount of perceived control. The range of these scores was from 4.27 to 1.83 with an observed mean of 2.91.

RESULTS

Of the twenty-six organizations which agreed to participate in the study, one was excluded from the analysis because only one response to the budget behavior questionnaire was received. No imputation of causality should be made because our findings were derived through correlation analysis on cross-section data. In general our presentation of results is organized around the relationships specified in figures 1 and 2.

Organization Context and Organization Structure

Table 5 represents the product moment correlation coefficients between structural and contextual variables. These are quite similar to the results obtained by previous studies employing comparable measures (McMillan, *et al.* [1973]) with the exception of the low significance of the negative correlation between workflow integration and lack of autonomy. Size emerged as a strong predictor of organization structure. Size and structuring of activi-

TABLE 5. Product Moment Correlations Between Organization Structure and Context (N = 25)

Variable	Dependence	Workflow Integration	Concentration of Authority: Centralization*	Concentration of Authority: Lack of Autonomy	Structuring of Activities
Size**	−.02	.46****	−.39*****	−.03	.65***
Dependence		−.10	−.03	.35*****	.12
Workflow Integration			−.24	−.10	.41****
Concentration of Authority:					
Centralization				.76***	−.56****
Lack of Autonomy					−.12
Structuring of Activities					

*N = 20 (data needed to measure centralization could not be obtained from five organizations).
**Log of number of employees.
***Significant at $p < .001$.
****Significant at $p < .05$.
*****Significant at $p < .10$.

ties were strongly positively correlated (r = .65, $p < .001$), and there was a negative correlation ($r = -.39$, $p < .10$) between size and centralization. These results support the view that as organizations grow in size, economies of scale enable more specialists to fill role positions, and rules and procedures are developed to govern behavior. Also, size and workflow integration were correlated ($r = .46$, $p < .05$), and workflow integration was correlated with structuring of activities ($r = .41$, $p < .05$). These relationships imply that as organizations become more technologically sophisticated, they become larger and more structured.[6] Finally, structuring of activities was found to be negatively correlated with centralization ($r = -.56$, $p < .05$), supporting Child's (1972b) view that organizations exercise control either by centralizing decisions or by distributing decision-making authority but structuring roles and activities. The data appear consistent with classifying strategies for control into two extreme types: decentralized and structured organization as might be found in organizations with a more sophisticated technology, a larger number of employees, a larger number of functional specialists, and systems and procedures regulating performance; and centralization with responsibility centers dependent for decisions upon superiors and/or a parent organization.

[6]The causal relationships between size and technology, and structure are the subject of some debate. See for example Aldrich (1972) and Hilton (1972).

Organization Structure, Perceived Control, and Control System Complexity

Table 6 presents the product moment correlation coefficients between perceived control, control systems complexity, mean percentage of time spent on budget-related activities, and percentage of total employees affected by the budget. Perceived control was hypothesized to be positively correlated with structuring of activities and negatively correlated with centralization and lack of autonomy. While the signs of correlation coefficients relating these variables are as predicted (see table 6), only the correlation between structuring of activities and perceived control is statistically significant ($r = .39$, $p < .05$). This finding says, in effect, that as an organization specializes, standardizes, and formalizes, the managers in our sample felt they, and others, had more control. In addition, both variables were correlated with Descriptive Factor 1 (FD_1), participation in planning, as we will discuss below. Lack of autonomy was negatively correlated with control systems complexity ($r = -.64$, $p < .001$) as

TABLE 6. Product Moment Correlations Between Organization Structure Variables and Selected Accounting Control Variables (N = 25)

	Structuring of Activities	Concentration of Authority	
		Centralization*	Lack of Autonomy
Perceived Control	.39***	−.25	−.01
Control Systems Complexity	.04	−.70**	−.64**
Percentage of Employees Affected by the Budget****	.17	−.10	.16
Percentage of Time Spent on Budget Activities	.28	−.28	−.03

*N = 20 (data needed to measure centralization could not be obtained from five organizations).
**$p < .001$.
***$p < .05$.
****N = 22 (data needed to measure percentage of employees affected by the budget could not be obtained from three organizations).

was centralization ($r = -.70, p < .001$). This implies that, as organizations become more independent and less centralized in terms of decision-making authority on administrative matters, the accounting system is likely to be based on broader measurements, permitting managers more discretion on how to achieve financial results.

Budget-Related Behavior

Tables 7 and 8 present the product moment correlation coefficients between the structural variables, the descriptive factors, and the satisfaction factors, respectively. Three aspects of budget-related behavior were examined: quantity, mode, and quality. The quantity of budget-oriented behavior was operationalized by two

TABLE 7. Product Moment Correlations Between Selected Organizational Variables and Thirteen Descriptive Budget Behavior Factors ($N = 25$)

		Organization Variables				
			Concentration of Authority			
Descriptive Factors		Structuring of Activities	Centralization*	Lack of Autonomy	Perceived Control	Control Systems Complexity
FD_1	Participation in Planning	.44***	.03	.09	.64**	−.10
FD_2	Evaluation by Superiors	.32	−.14	−.02	.24	.06
FD_3	Support for Innovation and Flexibility	−.35****	.11	.03	−.17	−.04
FD_4	Participation in Budget Systems	.25	−.25	.00	.12	.19
FD_5	Limiting Features of Budgets	.08	−.24	−.15	−.35****	.42***
FD_6	Support for Successful Management	−.15	.26	.02	.14	−.10
FD_7	Acceptance of Methods	−.03	−.39****	−.38****	.34****	.29
FD_8	Required Explanation of Variance	.14	.34	.39****	.03	−.28
FD_9	Interaction with Superior	−.25	−.06	−.38****	.16	.38****
FD_{10}	Difficulty in Meeting Budget	.22	.05	.16	−.03	.09
FD_{11}	Participation in Feedback	.09	−.13	−.13	.13	−.08
FD_{12}	Detail in Budgets	−.28	.34	.09	−.24	−.34****
FD_{13}	Fac. 13	.19	−.16	−.10	.30	.26

*N = 20 (data to measure centralization could not be obtained from five organizations).
**$p < .001$.
***$p < .05$.
****$p < .10$.

TABLE 8. Product Moment Correlations Between Selected Organization Variables and Fifteen Budget Behavior Satisfaction Factors (N = 25)

	Organization Variables				
		Concentration of Authority			
Satisfaction Factors	Structuring of Activities	Centralization*	Lack of Autonomy	Perceived Control	Control System Complexity
FS_1 Satisfaction with Superior-Subordinate Relationship	−.01	−.30	−.57***	−.09	.30
FS_2 Satisfaction with Participation in Planning	−.20	.02	−.30	−.22	.02
FS_3 Satisfaction with Usefulness of Budgets	.06	.36	.45***	−.18	−.16
FS_4 Satisfaction with Flexibility Permitted by Budgets	.21	.15	.40***	.40***	−.23
FS_5 Satisfaction with Time-Consuming Aspects of Budget	−.16	.21	.10	.03	.02
FS_6 Satisfaction with Restrictive Features of Budget	.27	−.26	−.21	.14	.31
FS_7 Satisfaction with Support from Staff Departments	−.43***	.14	−.21	−.25	.02
FS_8 Satisfaction with Outlets for Discussing Budget Matters	.13	−.02	−.26	−.03	.09
FS_9 Satisfaction with Evaluative Features of Budget	−.31	.23	.02	−.09	−.08
FS_{10} Satisfaction with Participation in Budget Systems	.03	.00	.00	−.09	−.19
FS_{11} Satisfaction with Methods of Reaching the Budget	−.12	.14	.09	.31	−.25
FS_{12} Factor 12	.28	−.33	−.18	.30	.05
FS_{13} Satisfaction with Participation in Budget Achievement	.33****	−.03	−.11	−.15	.11
FS_{14} Factor 14	−.12	.24	−.12	−.06	−.31
FS_{15} Factor 15	.09	.08	−.15	.03	−.01

*N = 20 (data to measure centralization could not be obtained from five organizations).
**$p < .001$.
***$p < .05$.
****$p < .10$.

measures: the percentage of people in the organization involved in budget-related activities, and the percentage of a respondent's time spent on budget-related activities (involvement). Neither variable showed a significant ($p < .10$) relationship to the structure variables, although in each case the sign of the correlation was as predicted.

Structuring of Activities. Factor analysis of the budget-behavior questionnaire yielded thirteen descriptive factors which operationalized "kind of budget-related behavior." FD_1, participation in planning, was correlated with perceived control ($r = .64$, $p < .001$) and structuring of activities ($r = .44$, $p < .05$). We had hypothesized that structuring of activities would lead to higher levels of perceived control and more participation in budgeting. Holding the effects of perceived control constant yields a partial correlation of .26 between structuring of activities and participation. The reduction in the proportion of the common variance of structuring of activities and participation from 19.4% to 7.4% indicates that perceived control is an important intervening variable between structuring and participation. The argument that the direction of a causal link among these variables should be opposite, that is from participation to perceived control to structure, is not intuitively appealing. Therefore, it appears that a perceived participatory mode of budget administration is more typical of highly structured organizations partly because individuals within these organizations perceive themselves as exercising more control.

FD_3, support for innovation and flexibility, correlates negatively with structuring of activities, ($r = -.35$, $p < .10$). This is consistent with the idea that highly structured organizations are associated with routine, standardized activities. Controlling the effects of size yields a partial correlation between structuring of activities and FD_3 of $r = -.50$ ($p < .01$), which lends support to the argument that role formalization and specialization and not size decreases the extent to which the budget is seen as permitting flexibility and innovation. Contrary to expectations, there was no significant correlation between FD_6, support for successful management, and structuring of activities or any of the intervening variables.

Finally, additional evidence on the relationship between structuring of activities and budget-related behavior is found in the relationships between that variable and the satisfaction factors which were developed to operationalize "quality of budget-related behavior." Recall that the satisfaction scores were created by subtracting the normative value of a variable ("How often *should* I ask for assistance from staff departments. . . .?") from the descriptive value ("How often *do* I ask . . . ?"), and multiplying the absolute value of the differences by the importance ("How important is this to me?"). Thus, a high score indicates greater dissatisfaction.

Structuring of activities was negatively correlated ($r = -.43$, $p < .05$) with Satisfaction Factor 7 (FS_7), satisfaction with support from staff departments, which implies that greater structure is associated with greater satisfaction in asking for assistance from staff departments. The positive relation of FS_{13}, satisfaction with participation in budget achievement, with structuring of activities ($r = .33$, $p < .10$) implies that, as activities become more structured, satisfaction with participation in budget achievement is diminished.

However, we further investigated these relationships using partial correlation analysis which allowed us to control the effect of size (remember, size is highly correlated with structuring of activities). The results were that the new correlation of FS_7 and structuring of activities became statistically not significant ($r = -.26$, $p > .10$), and the correlation of FS_{13}, satisfaction with participation in budget achievement, with structuring of activities also became statistically not significant ($r = .21$, $p > .10$). Thus, both of these relationships appear to be influenced by the size of the organization.

Concentration of Authority. In this report we have separated the dimension of concentration of authority into two parts based on the scale used to measure it: centralization, or the extent to which decisions are reserved to high levels in the organization; and lack of autonomy, or the extent to which decisions are made outside the organization under study. Each of these scales was found to be negatively correlated with the complexity of control systems (see table 5). This implies that the more decisions are centralized or removed from the purview of an organization the less complex the organization's control system is likely to be. But concentration of authority is also linked to budget-related behavior in other important ways, for we found significant correlations between centralization and lack of autonomy and FD_7, acceptance of methods, FD_8, required explanation of variances, and FD_9, interaction with superior.

FD_7, FD_8, and FD_9 describe superior-subordinate relationships in budgeting. FD_7, acceptance of methods, correlates negatively with centralization ($r = -.39$, $p < .10$) and lack of autonomy ($r = -.38$ $p < .10$) and positively with perceived control ($r = .34, p < .10$), indicating that, as the organization becomes more centralized and less autonomous, individuals perceive having less independence and more interference from superiors and subordinates on budgeting matters. This is consistent with responses to FD_8, required explanation of variances, which was correlated with lack of autonomy ($r = .39, p < .10$). Further, the relationship between superiors and subordinates is not participative or advisory as revealed by the negative correlation of FD_9, interaction with superior, with lack of autonomy ($r = -.38$, $p < .10$). These relationships are interrelated with the effects of control system complexity. Holding the effects of control system complexity constant by calculating partial correlations decreases the common variance between FD_7, FD_8, and FD_9 with lack of autonomy and centralization more than one-half. Taken collectively these results support a conclusion that concentration of authority, complexity of control systems, and mode of budget administration are intertwined in organizations which lack autonomy or are centralized.

Analysis of the relationship between lack of autonomy and satisfaction factor FS_1, satisfaction with superior-subordinate relationship, may shed additional light on the nature and effects of the superior-subordinate relationship. FS_1 is negatively correlated with lack of autonomy ($r = -.57, p < .05$), which would seem to imply that as an organization becomes less autonomous and fewer decisions are required of managers, those managers find themselves more satisfied with superior-subordinate contacts about budget variances and their efficiency. One interpretation of these relationships would be that, as lack of autonomy increases, managers spend less time working with superiors on budget planning (FD_9), and they are more satisfied by their superior-subordinate contacts concerning comparisons of budgets and results.[7] But to further complicate these relationships, both FS_3, satisfaction with the usefulness of budgets, and FS_4, satisfaction with flexibility permitted by the budget, are positively correlated with lack of autonomy ($r = .45, p < .05$; $r = .40, p < .05$). This implies that lack of autonomy increases dissatisfaction with the usefulness of budgets and perceptions of the flexibility and innovation they encourage.

[7]DeCoster and Fertakis (1968) reported that budget-induced pressure was positively correlated with both initiating structure and consideration as measured by the Ohio State Leadership Questionnaire. If FD_7, FD_8, and FD_9 are representative of initiating structure and if FS_1 is reflecting consideration by the leader, these results would suggest that DeCoster and Fertakis sampled predominantly centralized organizations lacking in autonomy.

Perceived Control and Control Systems Complexity. The linkage we hypothesized between structure and budget-related behavior included linkages through the financial (accounting) control system and the control perceived by organization members. Where appropriate, the interrelationships between these intervening variables, organization structure, and budget-related behavior have been discussed above. Nevertheless, our analysis reveals additional relationships, apparently independent from structural variables, which are worthy of mention. Perceived control was found to be negatively correlated with FD_5, limiting features of budgets ($r = -.35$, $p < .10$) and positively correlated with FD_7, acceptance of methods ($r = .34$, $p < .10$). Recalling the statistically significant relationship between perceived control and FD_1, participation in planning, the degree of perceived control appears to be related in important ways to budget-related behavior.

Furthermore, involvement was correlated with perceived control, ($r = .43$, $p < .05$). It appears as if the order implied by structuring of activities reduces the uncertainties associated with centralized or external management, and people feel they are a part of their organization. This conclusion is consistent with our hypotheses.

Control system complexity was positively correlated with FD_5, limiting features of budgets ($r = .42$, $p < .05$), negatively correlated with FD_{12}, detail in budgets ($r = -.34$, $p < .10$), and, as was previously discussed, correlated with FD_9, interaction with superior ($r = .38$, $p < .10$). These relationships imply that complex control systems lead to perceptions that budgets limit activities, giving less attention to detail, and working more with superiors in preparing and achieving budgets. Other explanations of these interesting findings might be that complex systems are not as well understood and therefore are perceived as limiting activities, or are ignored, or require managers to seek help and approval from superiors.

DISCUSSION

In reviewing the relationships between organization structure and budget-related behavior several complex relationships appear. While in general the structural and intervening variables explained only a portion of the variance in budget-related behavior, there are definite and important relationships which appear worthy of future investigation. The existence of these relationships points to some limitations in existing research on budgetary behavior. Since a portion of budget-related behavior is explained by organization structure, inferences from studies based on limited samples drawn from organizations of unknown structural properties must be made carefully. Moreover, universal policy prescriptions about how budgets should be prepared would be unwise.

The relationships between organization context, organization structure, and budget-related behavior are consistent with the view that organization control strategies may be dichotomized into two general categories, decentralized but structured, and centralized. Further, these general forms of organization control tend to elicit particular types of budget-related behavior. For discussion purposes we chose to label the set of variables associated with decentralized but structured organizations as the Administrative Control Strategy, and those variables associated with centralized organizations as the Interpersonal Control Strategy.

Administrative Control

Figure 3 summarizes the observed relationships among the variables which appear to be typical of an Administrative Control Strategy. This control strategy predominates in larger, more technologically sophisticated organizations. Formalized and standardized operating procedures predominate, and there tend to be more specialists. Work-related behavior is gov-

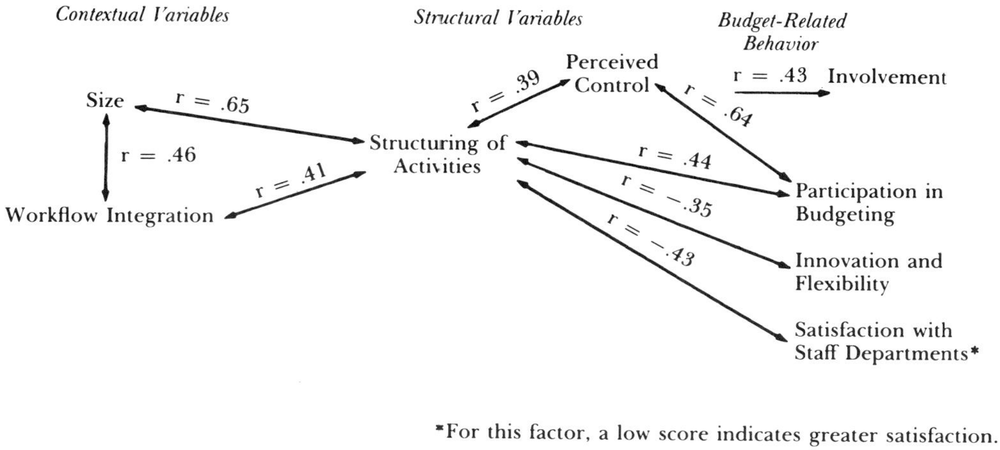

FIGURE 3. The administrative control strategy.

erned by rules, but managers tend to perceive themselves and others as having more control. Managers within these organizations perceive themselves as participating in setting budgetary goals and spend more time on budgetary activities. Managers tend to see the budget as limiting innovation and flexibility in structured organizations.

One of the more interesting aspects of this scenario is the relationship of participation in budget planning with structuring of activities and perceived control. The accounting and related behavioral science literature contains conflicting admonitions with respect to the value of participatory approaches to budgeting. Argyris (1952), Hofstede (1967) and Becker and Green (1962) have emphasized the potential positive effects of participatory budgeting. On the other hand, Stedry (1960) suggested that in some cases it may be more beneficial for management to set the budget. Morse and Reimer (1956) reported results showing that nonparticipatory groups outperformed participatory groups. The present study showed a strong relationship between participation and perceived control and between perceived control and structuring of activities. Assuming that organizations "learn" management techniques which are suited to their needs, these findings may indicate that participatory approaches to budgeting are more suited to, and perhaps more effective in, structured organizations.

Interpersonal Control

Figure 4 summarizes the observed relationships among the variables associated with an Interpersonal Control Strategy. This strategy predominates in organizations which are small or dependent on other organizations. Typically, important decisions are either centralized within the organization or referred to outside authority. Financial control systems tend to be based on simple or narrowly defined measures (i.e., variances from standard cost). Budget-related behavior factors which correlated with lack of autonomy and centralization centered mainly on the superior-subordinate relationship. Individuals perceive themselves as having more interaction with superiors and subordinates on budget-related matters, their methods of reaching the budget are not accepted, and they are required to explain budget variances. However, the individuals surveyed report being satisfied with their superior-subordinate relationship. These findings support the position

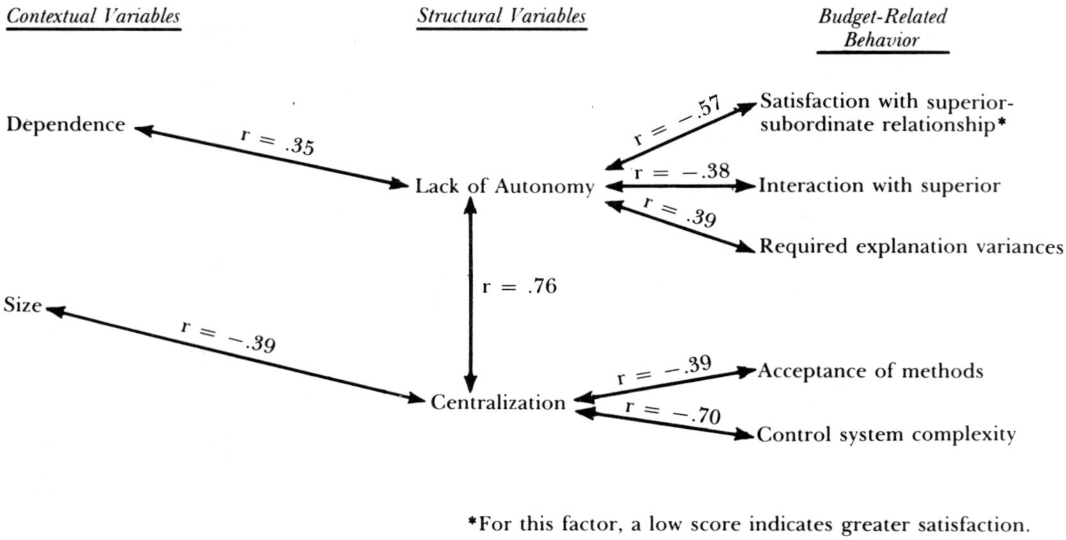

FIGURE 4. The interpersonal control strategy.

that interpersonal control may predominate in organizations that are centralized and lack autonomy. Lack of autonomy is associated with possible pressure-inducing actions by superiors who do not accept methods used to reach budgeted performance and require explanation of variances. Lack of autonomy seems to be related to a reduction in interaction between superiors and subordinates during budget preparation and about means to achieve the budget, but this does not seem to be linked with dissatisfaction about superior-subordinate behavior regarding variances or subordinate efficiency.

The results seem to support the findings of Argyris (1952) in part. Budgets do seem a potential source of budget-related pressure in organizations which are centralized or lack autonomy, but they do not seem to lead to perceptions of dissatisfaction about the relationships of the subordinate to the superior. On the contrary, subordinates report being satisfied with their superiors' demands regarding discussion of variances and subordinate efficiency as revealed through budgets. Whether this results from recognition that in a centralized organization "the boss is the boss, and therefore, what he does is right," or that satisfaction is induced through the interpersonal relationships developed in the centralized organization cannot be determined from our data.

SUMMARY AND CONCLUSIONS

This research sought to explore the extent to which budget-related behavior is dependent on the organization context and structure in which budgets are administered. A review of organization theory literature identified structuring of activities and concentration of authority as two important means of controlling behavior within organizations. A number of hypotheses relating the structural properties of organizations to budget-related behavior were developed and tested. The data showed that there are important interorganizational differences in budget-related behavior by managers. Those in highly structured organizations tend to perceive themselves as having more influence, they participate more in budget planning, and they appear to be satisfied with budget-related activities. Managers in organizations where authority is concentrated are generally held accountable for fewer financial variables, they experience superior-initiated pressure, they see budgets as being less useful and limiting their flexibility, but they appear to be satisfied with the use of budgets by their superiors.

By seeking to relate structural measures to budget-related behavior, we have not sought to link contextual variables to budget-related behavior directly. But we cannot conclude this discussion without some comments about the practical managerial implications of doing so. Where a choice or change in organizational control system is indicated, change in the organization structure might be a means of enhancing the effectiveness of budgetary control. This research shows high participation and perceived control are associated with structuring of activities. Two contextual variables, size of organization and technology, are significantly, positively correlated with structuring activities. One possible implication of this is that large, process dominated, technological organizations may be not as inhumane as they have been pictured in some places. For increased size and advanced process technology lead to or are at least correlated with structuring of activities, and structuring implies distribution of authority and an increase in perceived control as well as increased participation in planning and feelings of involvement on the part of managers. Those who speak against large organizational units may be ignoring the countervailing tendency of size to lead to structuring of activities and greater job involvement.

APPENDIX

Budget Behavior Questionnaire (Variables)

1. I start preparing the budget for my unit before I am asked to.
2. I spend time outside of normal working hours preparing the budget for my unit.
3. I am not able to spend as much time as I would like preparing the budget for my unit.
4. I work with my superior in preparing the budget for my unit.
5. I work with my subordinates in preparing the budget for my unit.
6. I work with other unit heads in preparing the budget for my unit.
7. I work with financial staff people in preparing the budget for my unit.
8. I am consulted about special factors I would like to have included in the budget being prepared.
9. New budgets include changes I have suggested.
10. The budget is not finalized until I am satisfied with it.
11. Preparing the budget for my unit requires my attention to a great number of details.
12. I am reminded of the importance of meeting the budget for my unit.
13. I am evaluated on my ability to meet the budget for my unit.
14. I have difficulty meeting the budget for my unit.
15. I am shown comparisons of actual and budgeted performance for other units.
16. My explanation of budget variances is included in performance reports.
17. I investigate favorable as well as unfavorable budget variances for my unit.
18. I go to my superior for advice on how to achieve my budget.

19. I am required to prepare reports comparing actual results with budget.
20. My methods of reaching budgeted performance are accepted without question by my subordinates.
21. My methods of reaching budgeted performance are not accepted without question by my subordinates.
22. My superior calls me in to discuss variations from the budget.
23. My superior accepts my explanation of budget variations in my unit.
24. My superior expresses dissatisfaction to me about results in my unit when the budget has not been met.
25. My superior mentions budgets when talking to me about my efficiency as a manager.
26. I ask for assistance from staff departments concerned with budgeting.
27. I am required to submit an explanation in writing about causes of large budget variances.
28. I use the budget to plan activities in my unit.
29. I am required to trace the cause of budget variances to groups or individuals within my unit.
30. I personally investigate budget variances in my unit.
31. I evaluate my subordinates by means of the budget.
32. I am required to report actions I take to correct causes of budget variances.
33. I find it necessary to stop some activities in my unit when budgeted funds are used up.
34. I find it necessary to charge some activities to other accounts when budgeted funds for these activities have been used up.
35. I have to shift figures relating to operations to reduce budget variances.
36. Budget matters are mentioned in informal conversations.
37. I express my opinions on budget matters.
38. I offer suggestions for the improvement of budget systems.
39. The budgeting system is changed in accordance with my suggestions.
40. I discuss budget items when problems occur.
41. The budget enables me to be more flexible.
42. The budget enables me to be more innovative.
43. The budget enables me to keep track of my success as a manager.
44. The budget enables me to be a better manager.

REFERENCES

Aldrich, H. E. "Technology and Organization Structure: A Re-examination of Findings of the Aston Group." *Administrative Science Quarterly* (March 1972):26–43.

Argyris, C. *The Impact of Budgets on People* (The Controllership Foundation, 1952).

———. *Personality and Organization; the Conflict Between Systems and the Individual* (Harper, 1957).

———. *Understanding Organizational Behavior* (Dorsey Press, 1960).

———. *Integrating the Individual and the Organization* (John Wiley and Sons, 1964).

Barnard, C. I. *The Function of the Executive* (Harvard University Press, 1938).

Becker, S. and D. Green, Jr. "Budgeting and Employee Behavior." *The Journal of Business* (October 1962):392–402.

Blau, P. M. and R. M. Schoenherr. *The Structure of Organizations* (Basic Books, 1971).

Burns, T. and G. M. Stalker. *The Management of Innovation* (Tavistock, 1968).

Chandler, A. D., Jr. *Strategy and Structure* (M.I.T. Press, 1962).

Child, J. "Organizational Structure, Environment and Performance—The Role of Strategic Choice." *Sociology* (January 1972a):1–22.

———. "Organization Structure and Strategies of

Control: A Replication of the Aston Study." *Administrative Science Quarterly* (June 1972b):163–77.

———. "Strategies of Control and Organizational Behavior." *Administrative Science Quarterly* (March 1973):1–17.

Crozier, M. *The Bureaucratic Phenomenon* (University of Chicago Press, 1964).

DeCoster, D. T. and J. P. Fertakis. "Budget-Induced Pressure and Its Relationship to Supervisory Behavior." *Journal of Accounting Research* 6 (Autumn 1968):237–46.

Fertakis, J. P. "Budget-Induced Pressure and Its Relationship to Supervisory Behavior in Selected Organizations." Doctoral dissertation. University of Washington, 1967.

Fiedler, F. W. *A Theory of Leadership Effectiveness* (McGraw-Hill, 1967).

Foran, M. F. and D. T. DeCoster. "An Experimental Study of the Effects of Participation, Authoritarianism, and Feedback on Cognitive Dissonance in a Standard Setting Situation." *The Accounting Review* (October 1974):751–63.

Gouldner, A. W. *Patterns of Industrial Bureaucracy* (Free Press, 1954).

Hickson, D. "A Convergence in Organization Theory." *Administrative Science Quarterly* (September 1966):244–37.

———, C. R. Hinings, C. J. McMillan, and J. P. Schwitter. "The Culture-Free Context of Organization Structure: A Tri-National Comparison." *Sociology* (January 1974):59–80.

Hilton, G. "Causal Inference Analysis:A Seductive Process." *Administrative Science Quarterly* (March 1972):44–57.

Hinings, C. R. and G. L. Lee. "Dimensions of Organization Structure and Their Context: A Replication." *Sociology* (January 1971):83–93.

Hofstede, G. H. *The Game of Budget Control* (Van Gorcum, 1967).

Hopwood, A. G. "An Empirical Study of the Role of Accounting Data in Performance Evaluation." *Empirical Research in Accounting: Selected Studies, 1972.* Supplement to *Journal of Accounting Research* 10:156–82.

———. "Leadership Climate and the Use of Accounting Data in Performance Evaluation." *The Accounting Review* (July 1974):485–95.

Inkson, J. H. K., D. S. Pugh, and D. J. Hickson. "Organization Context and Structure: An Abbreviated Replication." *Administrative Science Quarterly* (September 1970):318–29.

Lawrence, P. R. and J. W. Lorsch. *Organization and Environment* (Harvard University, 1967).

McGregor, D. *The Human Side of Enterprise* (McGraw-Hill, 1960).

McMillan, C. J., D. J. Hickson, C. R. Hinings, and R. E. Schneck. "The Structure of Work Organizations Across Societies." *Academy of Management Journal* (December 1973):555–69.

Mechanic, D. "Source of Power of Lower Participants in Complex Organizations." *Administrative Science Quarterly* (December 1962):349–64.

Morse, N. C. and E. Reimer. "Experimental Change of a Major Organizational Variable." *Journal of Abnormal and Social Psychology* (1956):120–29.

Nie, N., D. H. Bent, and C. H. Hull. *Statistical Package for the Social Sciences* (McGraw-Hill, 1970).

Perrow, C. "A Framework for the Comparative Analysis of Organizations." *American Sociological Review* (April 1967):194–208.

Porter, L. W. "A Study of Perceived Need Satisfaction in Bottom and Middle Management Jobs." *Journal of Applied Psychology* (1961):8–10.

Pugh, D. S., D. J. Hickson, and C. R. Hinings. "An Empirical Taxonomy of Structure of Work Organizations." *Administrative Science Quarterly* (March 1969):115–26.

———, D. J. Hickson, C. R. Hinings, K. M. MacDonald, C. Turner, and T. Lupton. "A Conceptual Scheme for Organizational Analysis." *Administrative Science Quarterly* (December 1963):289–315.

———, D. J. Hickson, C. R. Hinings, and C. Turner. "Dimensions of Organization Structure." *Administrative Science Quarterly* (June 1968):65–105.

———, D. J. Hickson, C. R. Hinings, and C. Turner. "The Context of Organization Structures." *Administrative Science Quarterly* (March 1969):91–114.

Searfoss, D. G. and R. M. Monczka. "Perceived Participation in the Budget Process and Motivation to Achieve the Budget." *Academy of Management Journal* (December 1973):541–54.

Stedry, A. C. *Budget Control and Cost Behavior* (Prentice-Hall, 1960).

———, and E. Kay. "The Effect of Goal Difficulty on

Performance: A Field Experiment." *Behavioral Science* (November 1966):451–70.

Swieringa, R. J. and R. H. Moncur. "The Relationship Between Managers' Budget-Oriented Behavior and Selected Attitude, Position, Size, and Performance Measures." *Empirical Research in Accounting: Selected Studies, 1972.* Supplement to *Journal of Accounting Research* 10:194–209.

———, and R. H. Moncur. *Some Effects of Participative Budgeting on Managerial Behavior* (New York: National Association of Accountants, 1975).

Tannenbaum, A. S. *Control in Organizations* (McGraw-Hill, 1968).

Thompson, J. D. *Organizations in Action* (McGraw-Hill, 1967).

Vancil, R. F. "What Kind of Management Control Do You Need?" *Harvard Business Review* (March-April 1973):75–86.

Vroom, V. H. "Industrial Social Psychology." *Handbook of Social Psychology,* Vol. 5. G. Lindsay and E. Aronson, Eds. (Addison-Wesley, 1969):196–268.

———. *Some Personality Determinants of the Effects of Participation* (Prentice-Hall, 1960).

Weber, M. *The Theory of Social and Economic Organizations* (Oxford University Press, 1947).

Woodward, J. *Industrial Organization: Theory and Practice* (Oxford University Press, 1965).

The Contingency Theory of Managerial Accounting

David C. Hayes

Working mainly from the literature of modern organization theory, it was possible to develop a model of organizational performance for internal subunits. The model hypothesizes three major contingencies which affect subunit performance: (1) factors internal to the subunit (internal factors); (2) interrelationships with other subunits (interdependency factors); and (3) interactions external to the firm (environmental factors). The contingencies operate differentially across organizational subunits. Three propositions derived from the model were examined empirically in a field study of large manufacturing organizations. Strong support for two of the propositions was found, along with indications of support for the third, by using the analytical methodology of path analysis. The final section of the paper explores the implications of the study approach and results for managerial accounting theory and practice.

The role of managerial accounting in business organizations generally is perceived to be the provision of information for decision making by various elements of the organization's hierarchy. The use of such information in the evaluation of performance is a critical aspect of the decision-making function. Despite the Demski paper [1972], the impact of analytical research in information economics has tended to divert attention from performance assessment,[1] one of the three managerial accounting functions discussed by Simon, et al. [1954] in their landmark study.

The managerial accounting tools of performance evaluation are restricted largely to financially quantifiable data. Although in textbook discussions such data are intended to serve a signal generating function, implicit within its use is the assumption that performance can be summarized and captured by a dollar number. The rationale for the research reported here is that this approach does not provide a sufficiently rich description of performance. On the other hand, organization theory provides a far more complete approach to organizational assessment, in general, and subunit evaluation, in particular.

The structure of the paper is as follows. Contingency theory research on assessment and a model derived from the literature are

From *The Accounting Review*, Vol. 52, No. 1 (January 1977), pp. 22–39.

This paper was a 1976 manuscript contest winner. David C. Hayes is Assistant Professor at the University of British Columbia.

Many helpful comments on an earlier draft of this paper were made by Philip Brown, Gerry Feltham and members of the UBC Accounting Workshop. Tom Burns and Jack Baumler provided a great deal of advice and assistance during the performance of the research.

[1]See, e.g., Feltham [1972], Horngren [1972] and Demski and Feltham [1976].

outlined. Three propositions implied by the model are suggested, followed by a description of the empirical research undertaken to test the model.

THE ASSESSMENT MODEL

Two major contributions to a contingency theory of organizations are provided by Thompson [1967] and Lawrence and Lorsch [1969]. Although conceptually abstract, Thompson deals more completely with the contingent aspects of performance than Lawrence and Lorsch, thus, the Thompson study serves as the basis for much of the proposed model development.

The essence of any evaluation task can be captured by two dimensions—performance criteria and the ability to discern cause-effect relationships. Thompson diagrams these via a 2 × 2 matrix as presented in Figure 1.

Situations posited by Cells I and II theoretically provide little challenge to the development of assessment devices and, consequently, encompass most of the currently employed managerial accounting assessment tools. However Cell II does involve uncertainty, typified by the allocation procedures

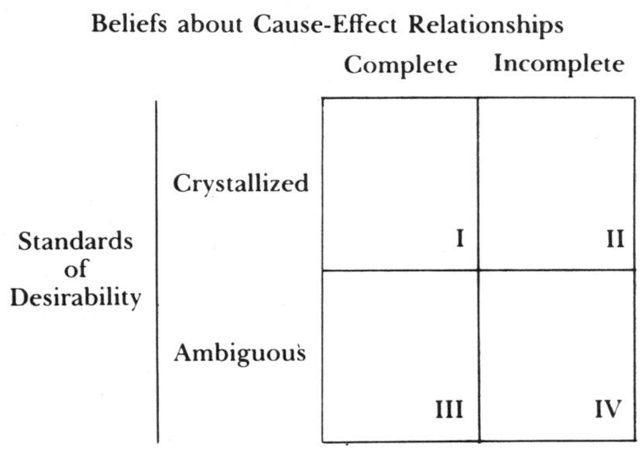

FIGURE 1. Potential Assessment Situations (From Thompson [1967, p. 86])

employed and proposed by accountants. Cells III and IV of the matrix suggest difficulties not generally addressed by managerial accounting. If standards are ambiguous (but not necessarily multiple and conflicting), the evaluation procedures employed by accountants may fail. These cells suggest assessment methods contingent on the particular situation faced by the organizational subunit of interest: the matrix as a whole implies combinations of contingent assessment procedures.

The contingency aspects explored within this study concern subunit interdependence, environmental relationships and factors internal to the particular subunit of interest.

Interdependence can be examined in the typology suggested by Thompson [1967, Ch. 7] following March and Simon [1958]. The interdependent relationships and the procedures for their coordination vary with organizational complexity. Stable, pooled interdependence occurs in those cases where the only connection between two subunits is that they belong to the same organization: No exchanges occur between them, and coordination involves the establishment of standardized procedures and rules.

Sequential interdependence occurs in cases where the outputs of one subunit are inputs to another, and thus a serial nonsymmetrical relationship exists between them. Careful planning of the interdependence is important because one unit cannot act prior to the actions of another. However, some degree of flexibility and buffering can be built into such an arrangement so that temporary failures by one subunit will not jeopardize substantively the operations of the other.

A reciprocal interdependence occurs in cases where there is a symmetrical flow between two subunits; that is, an input to one is an output of the other. Coordination in this complex situation may occur via a process of mutual adjustment, with no fixed plans or rules. If a continual consultative relationship occurs, the potential exists for new information and ideas to be introduced which may change the intended nature of the activities from those originally specified. Thus, depending on the type of interdependency existing between any two subunits, different methods of coordination and, consequently, assessment can be proposed.

The type of environment faced by an organization and its subunits can be viewed similarly on several dimensions. One typology suggested by Thompson is presented in Figure 2.

The two dimensions concern the relative stability and homogeneity of the environment faced by subunits. It is suggested that the uncertainty associated with dealing with elements of the environment is lowest in Cell I and greatest in Cell IV but that no ordering can be placed on the relationships of the other situations in such a typology.

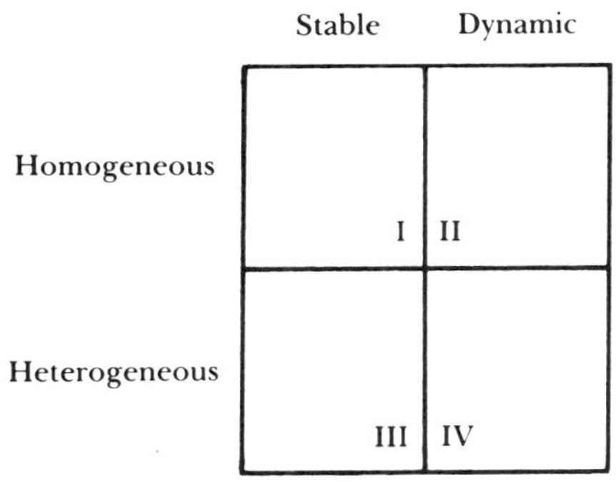

FIGURE 2. Environmental Representation (From Thompson [1967, p. 72])

The nature of the environment faced by a subunit will determine the relative difficulty such a unit will encounter in dealing with environmental elements. It would appear a priori that the more uncertain the environment, the more difficult will be the tasks of the subunit and the greater the extent of environmental influence on their functions. Thus, type of environment is another contingent aspect of performance, leading to contingent methods of assessment.

The other major contingency aspects of performance evaluation concern the internal structure and functions of a subunit. The nature of the tasks performed, types of people, interpersonal relationships and the ability to measure and quantify functions are all likely to vary with subunit type.

A three-dimensional model of the assessment function can be constructed on the basis of the three major contingencies associated with performance. This model is presented in Figure 3.

The model is not intended to suggest that all aspects of each dimension are appropriate for the evaluation of all subunits. Rather, only some aspects of each dimension would seem applicable for different types of subunits.

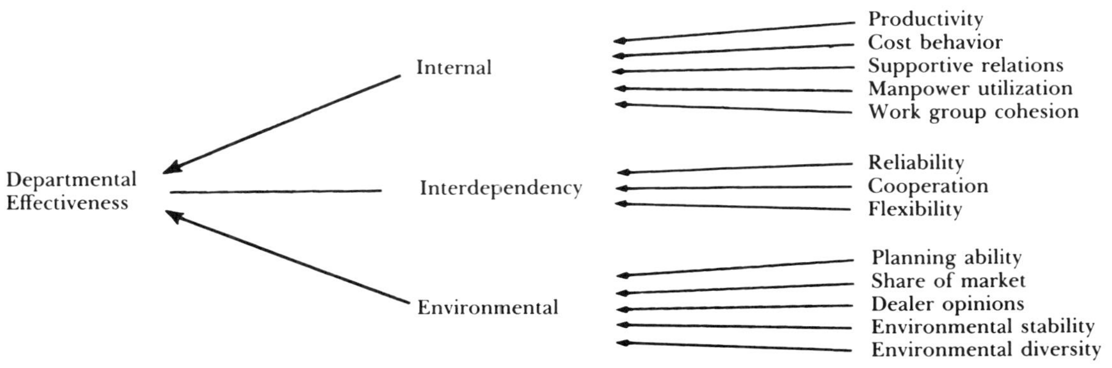

FIGURE 3. The Assessment Model

Some of these are outlined in the propositions presented.

Previous Research

Prior literature on contingent assessment is limited. Most organizational research in the area has been ad hoc in that the intent appears to have been data gathering and examination rather than exploration in the context of well-structured models and hypotheses. Despite this approach, the results are relatively uniform and tend to provide empirical support for the contingent model proposed previously.

The studies by Mahoney [1967], Mahoney and Weitzel [1969] and Mahoney and Frost [1974] represent several different examinations of the same data. Initially, the opinions of managers of different organizational subunits were solicited on variables a priori related to subunit effectiveness. The same managers also were requested to rate the overall effectiveness of the subunits. This rating was used as the dependent variable in the analyses of the latter two reports. In the first study, the variables were factor-analyzed; the four highest loading factors were interpreted to mesh neatly into the three dimensions of the model proposed in Figure 1. Two of the factors, planning and initiative, appear to be related to dealing with the task environment; the others, reliability and productivity, appear to be related to the interdependency and internal factors, respectively.

The second report utilized these factors in a regression analysis, and the third classified subunits on the basis of the dominant technology of the unit prior to performing a path analysis. In both these reports there were indications that assessment methods differed across subunits.

A study on production subunits of varying size by Wahba and Shapiro [1973] found results similar to the Mahoney studies. The three dimensions they posit with respect to effectiveness represent an expansion of the internal and interdependency dimensions proposed in this study.

Other studies by Georgopoulos and Tannenbaum [1957], Friedlander and Pickle [1968], and Seashore and Yuchtman [1967] highlighted major variables in the assessment of organizational subunits which can be categorized easily as corresponding to the three dimensions of the Figure 1 model. All of these studies were in a slightly different context than both the others cited and the research here.

Accounting-oriented studies on effectiveness are limited to those by Kinney [1969] and Solomons [1965]. Other approaches, such as the Hopwood [1974] and Klammer [1973] studies, are of only marginal relevance to this research. Kinney examined the effect on accounting performance measures of factors outside the control of the manager being assessed. The approach to assessment was narrow and only analyzed surrogate measures of management's ability to cope with the task environment faced. Although Solomons broadly addressed the assessment problem, its applicability is limited due to the primarily verbal analysis performed.

There is a limited amount of prior research in the area of concern to this study; it is apparent that the proposed model can satisfactorily explain such research. The following section outlines some propositions which may be drawn from the model, followed by the research design and discussion of results.

Propositions

Three propositions of interest can be derived with respect to the model just outlined.

PROPOSITION 1: Internal variables are the major explanators of performance for production departments, with a lesser contribution made by interdependency variables.

Within production departments, it is expected that variables classified as internal will best explain their effectiveness. Both cause-effect relations and standards or objectives are expected to be relatively well-established for these departments. Output and cost objectives of a production subunit can be evaluated readily by normal accounting techniques, such as standard cost variance analysis and rate of return. Thus, it is expected that internal variables will explain most of the effective performance herein. However, given the interrelationships with marketing, on the product output side, and R & D, on the technological input side, interdependency factors are expected to have some explanatory power.

PROPOSITION 2: Interdependency variables are the major explanators of performance for research and development departments.

Ambiguous desirability standards in research and development departments suggest that the use of internal variables in the evaluation of their effectiveness will have limited impact in explaining their performance. The extent to which they achieve budgeted cost levels in a given period gives little insight into their outputs or its value to the other subunits of the firm which it serves. This implies that the nature of the interdependent relationship it possesses with these units, and the degree to which it fulfills the expectations of other units via the cooperation achieved between them, would be the major evaluation factors employed.

PROPOSITION 3: Environmental and interdependency variables provide approximately equal contributions to the explanation of the performance of marketing departments.

A boundary-spanning unit such as marketing deals primarily with environmental constraints and contingencies operating on the firm. Thus, the nature of the environment faced would be of critical importance in defining the role of such a department. The role of a marketing unit is perceived to be two-fold, thus defining the important assessment variables. On the one hand, its relationships with production departments are critical in that there is a sequential relationship between them for products; the output of production is an input to marketing. Evaluation of this interdependence would seem relevant. On the other hand, its interrelationship with the environment to which it transfers this product represents its primary task for the firm. Thus, another element in the overall marketing assessment is expected to be the evaluation of this relationship.

RESEARCH DESIGN AND METHODOLOGY

Manufacturing firms in Ohio fitting two major characteristics were chosen for study. To overcome the problem of comparing the responses of individuals from very small with very large firms, an arbitrary size limit was selected as a cut-off rule for firm inclusion. Although different indicators of size can be used, such as total assets or sales, number of employees is a common measure in the literature.[2] Firms employing more than 500 persons were selected for inclusion in this study. The other major characteristic of the firms chosen was that each possessed research and development, marketing and production departments.

Two questionnaires sent to different individuals in each firm were prepared. The major questionnaire was sent to the marketing, production and research and development managers in each of the 109 firms which met the required characteristics. Two sets of responses were solicited from each manager; one set dealt with their perception of internal and

[2]See, e.g., Pugh, et al. [1968].

external factors that influence departmental performance, and the other dealt with their perceptions of the effectiveness of interdependent departments. The second questionnaire solicited from the controllers of the respective organizations a judgment on the effectiveness of the respective departments in the study. This judgment, independent from all of the departments, was used as the dependent variable in the path analysis.

Of the 430 questionnaires sent (4 to each of 103 firms, 3 to 6 others where one department or another had indicated an unwillingness to participate), an overall response of 274, or 63.7 percent, was achieved.[3] This overall response rate is broken down by departmental classification in Table 1. As the questionnaire sent to controllers was far shorter than that sent to the respective department managers, the same time commitment for completion was not required. Eliminating the responses of controllers from the total (274 less 84), the overall response rate decreased to 59.2 percent (190 replies received from 321 questionnaires sent). This still is a substantial rate for questionnaire studies.

Two further comments concerning Table 1 are necessary. First, it merely examines the total number of returns from each department group and does not indicate the number of firms from which more than one questionnaire was returned. This information is provided in Table 2. Second, the response rates differ markedly among departments, most noticeably between research and development (66.7 percent) and production (51.4 percent). This may be due to greater interest in general research by R & D managers and their greater familiarity with questionnaire surveys. The large controller difference is probably due to the shortness of the questionnaire and the inherent interest in an accounting study.

The nature of the research design necessitated returning an entire set of questionnaires (four) from each firm so that a complete analysis could be performed. As Table 2 shows, of the firms that received questionnaires, 24 (23 percent) responded. Only the analyses relating to the complete sets of returned questionnaires are reported here.[4]

A two-stage data analysis was undertaken on a departmental basis across firms. The data initially was factor-analyzed; then it was inputted to a path analysis as described below. Factor analysis was carried out for two reasons. The first reason was that it provided a statistically objective means of variable selection for the path analysis. Given the number of firms analyzed, it was apparent that a set smaller than the total number of variables (approximately 160) would have to be utilized in the path analysis. The highest loading variable on each factor in the three separate factor ana-

[3]Following Oppenheim [1966] as far as practicable given the nature of the questionnaire, examination for nonresponse bias was performed. There were no readily apparent differences between respondents and nonrespondents within the subunit categories.

[4]See Hayes [1975] for more extensive data analyses as well as for copies of the questionnaires utilized.

TABLE 1. Analysis of Questionnaire Returns

Questionnaires	Production Departments	Marketing Departments	R & D Departments	Controllers	Totals
Sent	107	109	105	109	430
Returned	55	65	70	84	274
Return percentages	51.4	59.6	66.7	77.1	63.7

TABLE 2. Questionnaire Returns for 109 Firms in Sample

Questionnaire	Complete Set of Returns	Three Returns	Two Returns	One or No Returns
Number	24	30	29	26

lyses was used as input to the path analyses to avoid the factor interpretation problem associated with using factor scores as secondary analysis input. Weighting and combining variables into a renamed combination usually lead to information loss and difficulty of understanding. It should be noted that the variables selected for inclusion in the path analyses by this approach conceptually represent the particular factors, not just themselves as separate entities.

The other reason for performing the factor analysis was that it provided a first crude picture of the pattern of results. As can be seen from the representations of the factors in Tables 3–5, the factors are quite "clean" in that high loading variables on each factor clearly relate to separate dimensions of the model in Figure 1, a first satisfactory result of the analysis.

Path analysis then was undertaken on the variables selected by the factor analysis. Stepwise regression was performed on this set of variables and a number of other variables—e.g., the independently obtained overall judgment on performance by controllers (the dependent variable) as well as summary overall performance judgments on each department made by the respective managers and their interdependent peers. The latter were added to the set of independent variables and interpreted as reflecting all aspects of departmental performance.

The path-analytic methodology is essentially similar to multiple regression, however, its advantages are numerous. As discussed by Duncan [1966], the method focuses heavily on variable interpretation, and its diagrammatic approach is a valuable tool in the search for alternative explanatory hypotheses. However, its greatest strength lies in the ability of the method to enable closure to be forced on a system of interrelated variables. This allows relative percentages of explanation to be associated with the independent variables by a partitioning of R^2, the coefficient of determination, which cannot be done with ordinary multiple regression.

RESULTS

The model and derived propositions refer to contingent assessment of organizational subunits. Subsequent to the discussion of the results for each department in the study, some general implications of the research are outlined which examine the results as a whole.

Production Departments

The proposition on production department assessment indicated that internal variables would be the major explanators of effectiveness, with interdependency variables of secondary importance. The buffering of production departments from the environment was expected to result in little or no explanatory power residing in the set of environmental variables.

It is apparent from examination of Figure 4 that this proposition is well-supported by the analysis. Although each of the three performance dimensions are present in this analysis, the relative sizes of the path and determination coefficients associated with the internal variables indicate their explanatory impact. The computation of the determination coefficients presented in the table accompanying the

TABLE 3. Production Department Factor Analysis: Highest Loading Variables

Factor 1	Factor 2*	Factor 3**	Factor 4	Factor 5	Factor 6	Factor 7	Factor 8	Factor 9	Factor 10
Price-F .75634	Extent of cooperation .82582	Extent of cooperation .72677	Superior/ subordinate relations .87118	Product quality-D .86001	Importance of budget .88200	Reliability of personnel .81004	Budget capturing of performance .82198	Delivery schedules-D .71081	Leadership ability .66984
Customer service-D .90141	Confidence expressed .89126	Task cooperation .66858	Skill utilization .76202	Product quality-F .74707		Performance pressure .66846	Financial data-capturing performance .83109	Delivery schedules-F .78016	
Customer service-F .88201	Task cooperation .92090	Productive conflict settlement .76062	Meeting of budget .65886	Company reputation-D .59351		Capturing of performance .83109			
Customer require-ments-D .91629	Productive conflict settlement .86747	Team feeling .84754							
Customer require-ments-F .90247	Team feeling .82021	Creative problem solutions .80435							
	Creative problem solutions .93583	Information exchange .84208							
	Information exchange .75786	Flexibility .67791							
	Flexibility .89668								

*Interdependency variables; as perceived by marketing departments.
**Interdependency variables; as perceived by research and development departments.
NOTE: All variables followed by D or F represnt the extent of influence of each on the performance of the department's daily or future planning tasks, respectively.

TABLE 4. Research and Development Department Factor Analysis: Highest Loading Variables

Factor 1*	Factor 2**	Factor 3	Factor 4	Factor 5	Factor 6	Factor 7	Factor 8	Factor 9	Factor 10
Extent of cooperation −.80188	Extent of cooperation .68762	Innovation-D −.58619	Reliability of personnel .70805	Skill utilization −.82457	Budget-capturing performance .75287	Product quality-D .75514	Superior/subordinate relations .89703	Leadership ability −.74834	Delivery schedules-D .71828
Confidence expressed −.88417	Confidence expressed .57247	Customer service-D −.93558	Price-F .83197		Financial data-capturing performance .85949	Product quality-F .84283		Delivery schedules-F .63185	
Performance pressure −.64060	Performance pressure .64712	Customer service-F −.78077				Company reputation-D .81213			
Task cooperation −.95992	Task cooperation .93685	Customer require-ments-D −.74815				Company reputation-F .82944			
Productive conflict settlement −.81206	Productive conflict settlement .83407	Customer require-ments-F −.74768							
Team feeling −.83261	Team feeling .85014								
Creative problem solutions −.91046	Creative problem solutions .83295								
Information exchange −.88354	Information exchange .91635								
Flexibility −.89618	Flexibility .81403								

*Interdependency variables as perceived by marketing departments.

**Interdependency variables as perceived by production departments.

NOTE: All variables followed by D or F represent the extent of influence of each on the performance of the department's daily or future planning.

TABLE 5. Marketing Department Factor Analysis: Highest Loading Variables

Factor 1*	Factor 2**	Factor 3	Factor 4	Factor 5	Factor 6	Factor 7	Factor 8	Factor 9	Factor 10	Factor 11
Extent of cooperation .62786	Confidence expressed .90771	Within-group work relations .85158	Customer service-D .62682	Innova-tion-D .72776	Budget-capturing performance −.74570	Product price-F −.94706	Product quality-D .66290	Price-D −.83286	Extent of cooperation .74215	Perfor-mance pressure .82156
Confidence expressed .84995	Task Cooperation .83195	Superior/subordinate relationships .86727	Customer service-F .84035	Company reputation-D .83393	Financial data-capturing performance −.79265		Delivery schedules-D .64272			
Performance pressure .74266	Productive conflict settlement .95920	Leadership .83871	Customer require-ments-F .89487	Company reputation-F .71002						
Task cooperation .91442	Team feeling .89592									
Productive conflict settlement .88451	Creative problem solutions .86215									
Team feeling .88160	Information exchange .88373									
Creative problem solutions .88118	Flexibility .80287									
Information exchange .93492										
Flexibility .90476										

*Interdependency variables, as perceived by research and development departments.
**Interdependency variables, as perceived by production departments.
NOTE: All variables followed by D or F represent the extent of influence of each on the performance of the department's daily or future planning.

figure is straightforward. Complete determination is given by

$$\sum_i P^2_{y \cdot i} + \sum_{i \neq j} P_{y \cdot i} P_{y \cdot j} r_{ij} = 1 \qquad (1)$$

where

$$\sum_i P^2_{y \cdot i} = \text{direct effects}$$

and

$$\sum_{i \neq j} P_{y \cdot i} P_{y \cdot j} r_{ij} = \text{indirect effects.}^5$$

In this case, suppressing the residual value,

$$\begin{aligned}
&\underset{P^2_{y\cdot 1}}{(.5471)^2} + \underset{P^2_{y\cdot 2}}{(.2415)^2} + \underset{P^2_{y\cdot 3}}{(.3039)^2} + \underset{P^2_{y\cdot 4}}{(-.2385)^2} \\
&\quad + [\underset{P_{y\cdot 1}}{(.5471)}\underset{P_{y\cdot 2}}{(.2415)}\underset{r_{12}}{(.2726)} \\
&\quad + \underset{P_{y\cdot 1}}{(.5471)}\underset{P_{y\cdot 3}}{(.3039)}\underset{r_{13}}{(-.2795)} + \cdots \\
&\quad + \underset{P_{y\cdot 4}}{(-.2385)}\underset{P_{y\cdot 3}}{(.3039)}\underset{r_{43}}{(-.3135)}] \\
&= .2993 + .0583 + .0923 + .0569 \\
&\quad + [(-.0427) + (.0050) - (.0392) \\
&\quad - (.0251)] = .4048 = R^2 \\
&\qquad \text{(with rounding errors).}
\end{aligned} \qquad (2)$$

The overall summary variable, production manager's own judgment on departmental performance, has both the largest path coefficient and provides the greatest explanation of variation in departmental effectiveness. As indicated earlier, this variable was interpreted as a summary combination of all elements relating to performance in the internal dimension of the model.

[5]The $P_{y \cdot i}$'s refer to the individual path coefficients, which can be shown to be equivalent to standardized regression beta weights. For an extensive discussion of the merits of the analysis and its utility, see Land [1969]. Further discussion of the methodology as utilized in the social sciences can be found in Aldrich [1972] and Boudon [1968] and in its original application in genetics in Wright [1921, 1934].

It is noteworthy that interdependence with marketing as summarized by the marketing manager judgment variable provides the second largest direct explanation after the internal variables, as hypothesized by the proposition. Although there is a positive association with effective performance ($P_{y \cdot 3} = .3039$), correlation with production manager judgment is negative ($r_{13} = -.2795$). A joint interpretation of this result suggests that while interdependence is an important element in explaining production department effectiveness ($P_{y \cdot 3} > 0$), interdependence and internal factors may be working against each other ($r_{13} < 0$). This highlights potential conflict and indicates the continual difficulty of successful differentiation and integration [Lawrence and Lorsch, 1969].

Limited association with effective performance was expected from variables on the environmental dimension. Both the direct (.0569) and net effects (.0318) computed for the coefficient of determination support this proposition. Further, assuming some consonance between future production and delivery schedules, the negative path coefficient ($P_{y \cdot 4} = -.2385$) suggests an inverse relationship with effectiveness. This implies that production departments are being buffered successfully from environmental influence by sufficient order lead times. Thus, the proposition concerning production department effectiveness is supported strongly by the analysis.

Research and Development Departments

The proposition advanced concerning research and development (R&D) departments stated that interdependency variables would be the main explanators of effectiveness. Internal and environmental variables were expected to have little or no influence.

Cursory examination of Figure 5 would lead to as ready a rejection of the proposition as acceptance in the case of production depart-

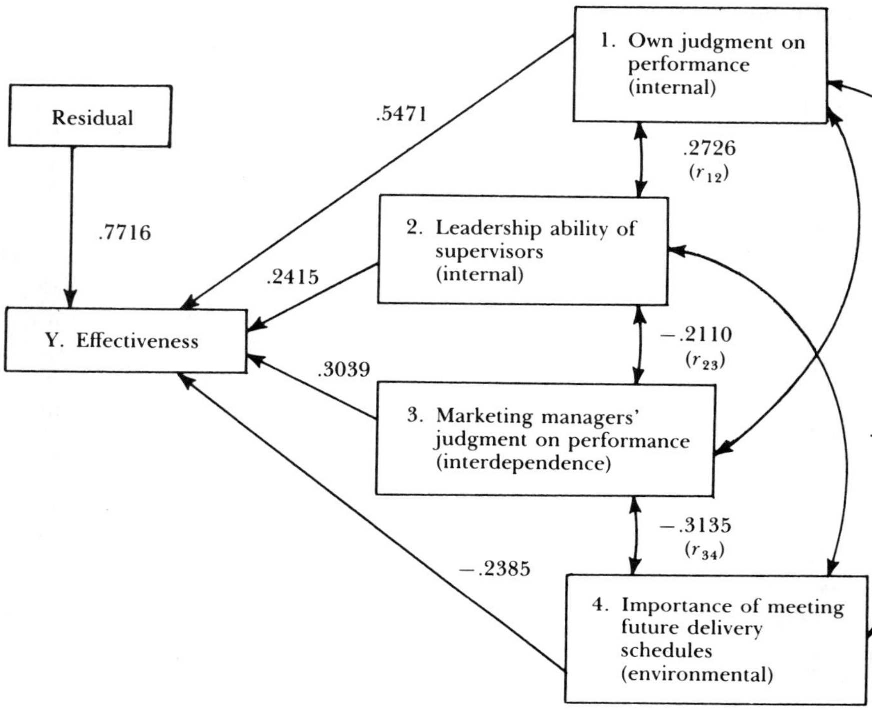

Coefficients of Determination

	1	2	3	4
Direct effect: $p^2_{y \cdot i}$	.2993	.0583	.0923	.0569
Indirect effect: $p_{y \cdot i} p_{y \cdot j} r_{ij}$	−.0427	.0050	−.0392	−.0251
Net effect:	.2565	.0633	.0531	.0318

FIGURE 4. Production Departments
Straight lines refer to paths of influence, in direction of arrow; respective path coefficients are indicated on each. Curved lines and associated numbers refer to correlations between variables. Size of respective coefficients of determination included in accompanying table.

ments. The size of the path and determination coefficients associated with the first variable, financial data, requires some explanation prior to hasty rejection of the proposition.

A *t*-test comparison of answers to selected questions was performed on the respective responses of all departmental managers. (See Table 1 for the numbers in each group.) On the question of how well they perceived financial data to measure their department's performance, the mean response of R&D managers was 2.62 on a scale of from 1–5. The R&D mean response was significantly lower ($P < .001$) in both instances than those of marketing managers (mean = 3.24) and production managers (mean = 3.64) to the same question. Clearly, R&D managers perceive financial measures of performance to be inappropriate for

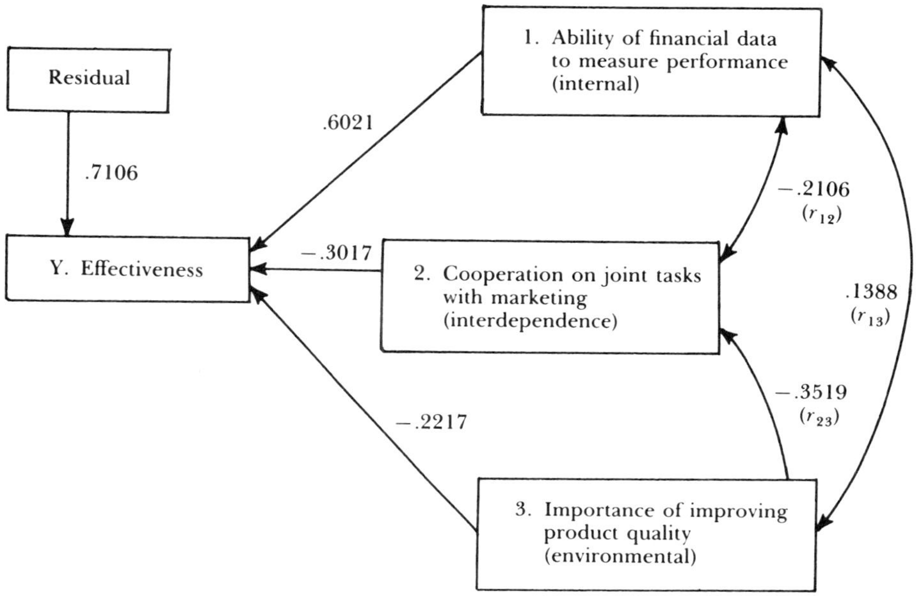

Coefficients of Determination

	1	2	3
Direct effect: $p^2_{y\cdot i}$	.3625	.0910	.0492
Indirect effect: $p_{y\cdot i}p_{y\cdot j}r_{ij}$	.0197	.0147	−.0421
Net effect:	.3823	.1052	.0071

FIGURE 5. Research and Development Departments
Straight lines refer to paths of influence, in direction of arrow; respective path coefficients are indicated on each. Curved lines and associated numbers refer to correlations between variables. Size of respective coefficients of determination included in accompanying table.

their departments. It is suggested that other judges of performance, having little or no experience with nonfinancial measures and experiencing difficulty in evaluating the tasks performed by R&D departments, resort to financial data as the means of evaluation. Note that the independent judges of performance in this study were controllers.[6]

To avoid forcing their responses in particular directions, the controllers in the study were not questioned about the bases upon which they made their evaluations. The explanation advanced is thus essentially an hypothesis generated from further examination of the

[6]Controllers were selected for pragmatic reasons. It was necessary to obtain responses from independent judges with positions high enough in the organizational hierarchy that they would have sufficient knowledge of the departments involved in the study. As different titles usually accompany similar executive levels in different firms, it appeared that only controllers and presidents could be reached in each firm to assure some consistency across judges. It was felt that there would be a greater chance of obtaining responses from controllers, so they were utilized.

data. It should be noted that its tenor is not such as to deny that financial information on R&D departments is important; such information may serve as a useful signal-generating device for managers. The hypothesis is an empirical question worthy of investigation, for empirical support would aid in the search for alternative assessment methods.

Both the interdependence and environmental dimensions were represented in the analysis of R&D performance. The negative path coefficient ($P_{y.2} = -.3017$) on cooperation with marketing suggests an inverse relationship with effectiveness, implying some difficulty in cooperative activities. Perhaps differences in perceptions as to the urgency of particular tasks, which lead to fruitless meetings, may explain this result. Lawrence and Lorsch [1969] found a number of differences in the personalities of marketing and R&D personnel, among which was a difference in time horizons.

Implicit in the development of the proposition on R&D departments was the assumption that innovative pressures from the environment would be channeled via marketing departments. The environmental variable present concerns innovation; to some extent it can be interpreted as relating to interdependence.

Indications of the importance of the interdependence dimension of the model in assessing R&D effectiveness are provided by the results. The primary conclusion, however, must be that further exploration is required on the proposition advanced. Given the hypothetical explanation of the financial data variable, it is suggested that refutation is not warranted at this stage.

Marketing Departments

Approximately equal contributions to the explanation of marketing department effectiveness were expected from interdependency and environmental variables. Limited explanation was expected from internal variables.

Examination of the coefficients of determination of the respective variables (Figure 6) shows that environmental variables had by far the greatest impact. The sum of net effects of the two environmental variables (4 and 5) is approximately 35 percent; the direct effects are even greater. The interdependent relationship with production is evidenced by the inclusion of variables 2 and 3, the summary judgment and pressure variables. However, the values of the path and determination coefficients are quite low. The total direct effect of the two variables is less than 9 percent, lower than that of the summary internal variable (.094). It would appear that interdependence is less important than proposed. However, the major environmental variable, concern with product quality, has some implications for the production/marketing relationship. Its relative size and impact in explaining variation in effectiveness implies that marketing personnel may be able to exercise some control over product quality by the provision of feedback from the environment. The correlations ($r_{24} = -.2843$) with the summary judgment variable and the felt pressure variable ($r_{34} = .2655$) suggest this interpretation. The absolute values of the correlation r_{45} ($-.1565$) and r_{14} (.0824) are substantially less than those with the interdependency variables, indicating that it has a relatively closer relationship to the interdependency variables than the others.

Another important relationship to note is that between the internal summary variable (1) and concern with customers' future requirements (5); $r_{15} = .3622$. One aspect of this association is the departmental ability to perform its boundary-spanning role between the firm and the environment. It suggests that internal task-performance is associated with satisfying environmental requirements. As such, it provides supportive argument for the proposition and

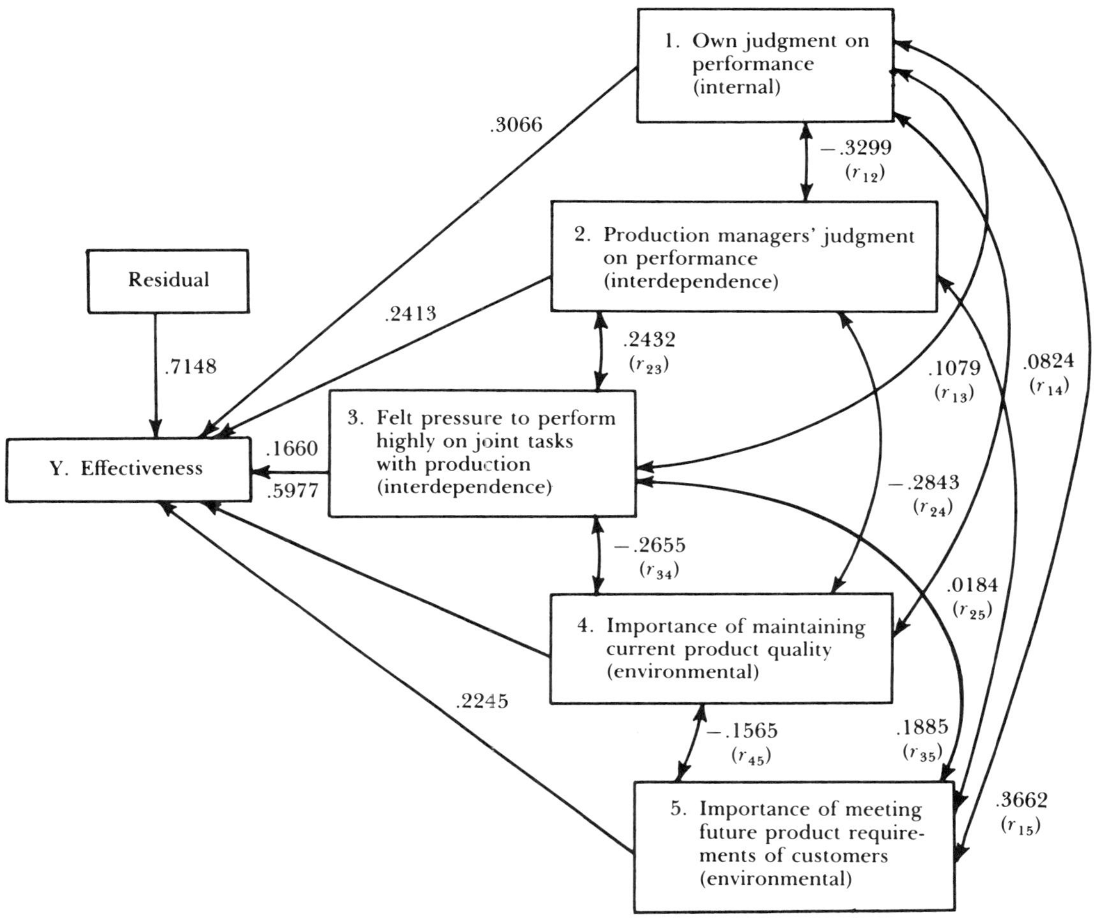

Coefficients of Determination

	1	2	3	4	5
Direct effect: $p^2_{y \cdot i}$	.0940	.0582	.0275	.3573	.0504
Indirect effect: $p_{y \cdot i} p_{y \cdot j} r_{ij}$	.0214	−.0547	−.0041	−.0733	.0122
Net effect:	.1154	.0036	.0235	.2840	.0626

FIGURE 6. Marketing Departments
Straight lines refer to paths of influence, in direction of arrow; respective path coefficients are indicated on each. Curved lines and associated numbers refer to correlations between variables. Size of respective coefficients of determination included in accompanying table.

its rationale as outlined in an earlier section of the paper.

Examination of the variables and their interrelationships indicates substantive support for the proposition advanced concerning marketing department effectiveness. However, environmental variables may contribute more to the explanation than interdependencies. Further refinement and empirical work are required to clarify the various interrelationships.

Evaluating the results for all three departments suggests strong support for the propositions on production and marketing departments, and indications of such support for research and development departments.

IMPLICATIONS

The research results reported here indicate that the traditional managerial accounting tools were relatively poor explanators of effectiveness. The following exploration of some implications of this finding is performed within the constraints on generalizability imposed by the obvious limitations of the study.

One of the problem areas of managerial accounting is that of budgeting and its behavioral ramifications. The standard research approach has been the exploration of factors such as the extent of participation in budget setting and the performance effects of tight and loose standards. The emphasis of this study has been on more fundamental issues, and these other aspects were intentionally excluded. What have been explored are the perceptions of managers with respect to the accuracy and importance of budgets and other financial data utilized in performance evaluation. The results indicate a general dissatisfaction with such measures, tending to reinforce the arguments from previous work that they are unsatisfactory assessment tools [Argyris, 1953, Lowe and Shaw, 1968]. In fact in most instances, environmental and interdependency factors were generally more important than financial data. The implication is that budgets, which are essentially surrogates for the entire set of factors which influence performance, do not perform the surrogation function well. By explicitly recognizing controllable and uncontrollable influences [Horngren, 1972, pp. 162–163] the link is formed to the concept of responsibility accounting.

Responsibility Accounting

The basic tenet of responsibility accounting is that subunit managers should only be held accountable for aspects of subunit performance over which they have control. As Caplan [1971, p. 19] argued, accountants usually mean by this responsibility for costs. However, the notion really is broader than costs for the extent of controllability of the factors cause certain costs to occur, and that really delimits the extent of responsibility. From the theoretical development and empirical results reported here, it is argued that these factors fall into three classes. Controllability and responsibility are differentials across the classes.

The personnel variables included in the internal dimension are of intuitive importance in determining the actual costs that a subunit will incur. Managers regard the variables in this manner, as demonstrated by their uniformly high responses to questions concerning the importance of each variable to the effective functioning of the subunit [Hayes, 1975]. Cost data are not good surrogates, especially in marketing and R&D departments. The path analyses showed that environmental influences had a substantial impact on the performance of departmental tasks. In many instances, the inferred ability of the department to deal with these influences was of primary importance in the explanation of the results. Another aspect of causation behind actual cost figures is the interdependent relationship among subunits.

To the extent that this relationship is more complex, the influence on the performance of a particular subunit and the costs incurred therein, too, would be greater. With each class of items which influence and lay behind the cost data, the question to be addressed (as far as responsibility accounting and budgeting are concerned) is the extent of controllability.

Personnel factors are controllable to a large degree by various levels of the management hierarchy. The abilities or skills of the workforce may not be controllable by immediate supervisors, but they are controllable by those performing the personnel function in the firm. The way in which such skills are utilized, inter- and intra-group relationships, and other aspects are under the influence of subunit management.[7]

With respect to control over the environment, Thompson [1967, pp. 20–22] outlined a number of strategies an organization may employ. For example, organizations attempt to protect their technical cores by buffering them from environmental fluctuations. In cases where this is not completely possible, they either will try to smooth input and output transactions or try to anticipate and adapt to environmental fluctuations. Depending on the strategy employed, the ability of units that are interdependent with production to decrease the influence of the environment on the production department could be evaluated readily. The number of short lead-time orders or unplanned product specification changes requested are examples of such measures. The path analysis of production departments indicated that the protection offered them from environmental influence was not optimal in that some environmental effects on performance were disclosed. As such factors behind cost figures are controllable to some extent, they could be assessed in overall subunit evaluation.

A number of environmental control strategies can be employed by the organization as a whole [Thompson, 1967, pp. 35–36]. Contracting entails obtaining agreement on the undertaking of future activities with task environment elements. A more restrictive means of attempting to gain some environmental control is cooptation, whereby elements of the task environment are absorbed into the leadership of the organization; e.g., the inclusion of external directors on the board. Finally, joint ventures may be undertaken with other organizations; this is referred to as a coalescing strategy.

Although such strategies refer to a broader spectrum than that addressed in this study, the extent to which an organization undertakes them will directly influence departmental functioning. Responsibility for adoption of some of these strategies may rest with marketing departments and could provide an assessment alternative to simply costs, both for marketing and production subunits.

Direct evaluation of interdependence is an explicit part of such environmental impact measures. However, there are other controllable aspects of interdependence, such as the performance of the integrating function as explored by Lawrence and Lorsch [1969], which imply further evaluation approaches. Depending on the hierarchical level of those charged with performing the integration, responsibility could be assessed directly.

The overall implications of the study for managerial accounting are severe, for they suggest a major reorientation from the narrow examination of surrogates to the evaluation of the underlying causal variables. This implies not only employing methods and techniques which are not necessarily universally applicable but also having a major reorientation in the approach to assessment. Indeed, the primary im-

[7]This provides a slightly different rationale for "human asset accounting" than that generally advocated [Flamholtz, 1972]; i.e., accountants should measure personnel factors (*not* in financial terms) because the current cost data obtained are poor surrogates for this causal influence behind costs.

plication is that a contingency approach be taken to managerial accounting, the relevant assessment methods being determined by subunit type, subunit interrelationships and the extent of environmental influence on subunit functioning.

REFERENCES

Aldrich, Howard E., "Technology and Organization Structure: A Re-examination of the Findings of the Aston Group," *Administrative Science Quarterly*, Vol. 17, No. 1 (March 1972), pp. 26–43.

Argyris, Chris, "Human Problems with Budgets," *Harvard Business Review* (January-February 1953), pp. 97–110.

Boudon, Raymond, "A New Look at Correlation Analysis," in Hubert M. Blalock and Ann B. Blalock, eds., *Methodology in Social Research* (McGraw-Hill, 1968), pp. 199–235.

Caplan, Edwin H., *Management Accounting and Behavioral Science* (Addison-Wesley, 1971).

Demski, Joel S., "Optimal Performance Measurement," *Journal of Accounting Research*, Vol. 10, No. 2 (Spring 1972), pp. 243–258.

——— and Gerald A. Feltham, *A Conceptual Approach to Cost Determination* (Iowa State University Press, 1976).

Duncan, Otis D., "Path Analysis: Sociological Examples," *American Journal of Sociology*, Vol. 72, No. 1 (July 1966), pp. 1–16.

Feltham, Gerald A., "Information Evaluation," *Studies in Accounting Research #5* (American Accounting Association, 1972).

Flamholtz, Eric G., "Towards a Theory of Human Resource Value in Formal Organizations," THE ACCOUNTING REVIEW (October 1972), pp. 666–678.

Friedlander, Frank and Hal Pickle, "Components of Effectiveness in Small Organizations," *Administrative Science Quarterly* (September 1968), pp. 289–304.

Georgopoulos, Basil S. and Arnold S. Tannenbaum, "A Study of Organizational Effectiveness," *American Sociological Review*, Vol. 22 (October 1957), pp. 534–540.

Hayes, David C., "The Contingency Theory of Managerial Accounting: An Empirical Test of an Assessment Model" (Ph.D. diss., The Ohio State University, 1975).

Hopwood, Anthony G., "Leadership Climate and the Use of Accounting Data in Performance Evaluation," THE ACCOUNTING REVIEW (July 1974), pp. 485–495.

Horngren, Charles T., *Cost Accounting: A Managerial Emphasis*, 4th ed. (Prentice-Hall, 1972).

Kinney, William R., Jr., "An Environmental Model for Performance Measurement in Multi-Outlet Businesses," *Journal of Accounting Research* (Spring 1969), pp. 46–52.

Klammer, Thomas, "The Association of Capital Budgeting Techniques with Firm Performance," THE ACCOUNTING REVIEW (April 1973), pp. 353–364.

Land, Kenneth C., "Principles of Path Analysis," in E. F. Borgatta, ed., *Sociological Methodology* (Jossey-Bass, 1969).

Lawrence, Paul R. and Jay W. Lorsch, *Organization and Environment* (Irwin, 1969).

Lowe, E. A. and R. W. Shaw, "An Analysis of Managerial Biasing: Evidence from a Company's Budgeting Process," *The Journal of Management Studies* (October 1968), pp. 304–315.

Mahoney, Thomas A., "Managerial Perceptions of Organizational Effectiveness," *Management Science*, Vol. 14, No. 2 (October 1967), pp. B76–91.

——— and William Weitzel, "Managerial Models of Organizational Effectiveness," *Administrative Science Quarterly*, 14(3) (1969), pp. 357–365.

——— and Peter J. Frost, "The Role of Technology in Models of Organizational Effectiveness," *Organizational Behavior and Human Performance*, Vol. 11 (February 1974), pp. 122–138.

March, James J. and Herbert A. Simon, *Organizations* (Wiley, 1958).

Oppenheim, A. N., *Questionnaire Design and Attitude Measurement* (Basic Books, 1966).

Pugh, Derek S., David J. Hickson, C. R. Hinings and C. Turner, "Dimensions of Organization Structure," *Administrative Science Quarterly*, Vol. 13 (1968), pp. 65–105.

Seashore, Stanley E. and Ephraim Yuchtman, "Factorial Analysis of Organizational Performance," *Administrative Science Quarterly* (December 1967), pp. 377–395.

Simon, Herbert A., Harold Guetzkow, George Kozmetsky and Gordon Tyndall, *Centralization Vs. Decentralization in Organizing the Controller's Department* (Controllership Foundation, 1954).

Solomons, David, *Divisional Performance: Measurement and Control* (Irwin, 1965).

Thompson, James D., *Organizations in Action* (McGraw-Hill, 1967).

Torgerson, Warren S., *Theory and Methods of Scaling* (Wiley, 1958).

Wahba, Mahmoud A. and Harris J. Shapiro, "Managerial Assessment of Organizational Components," *Academy of Management Journal,* Vol. 16, No. 2 (June 1973), pp. 277–284.

Wright, Sewall, "Correlation and Causation," *Journal of Agricultural Research,* Vol. 20, No. 7 (January 1921), pp. 557–585.

———, "The Method of Path Coefficients," *Annals of Mathematical Statistics,* Vol. 15 (September 1934), pp. 161–215.

Transfer Pricing: A Behavioral Context

David J. H. Watson

John V. Baumler

The accounting, management science, and economics literature contains numerous models addressing the resource allocation and transfer pricing problems. Some of the earliest statements on the transfer pricing problem are recorded by Hirshleifer (1956 & 1957), Dean (1955), and Cook (1955). These authors suggest solutions to the transfer pricing problem which reflect the analogy of the internal price problem to the determination of the (Competitive) market price of traditional economics. The advent of mathematical programming produced another stream of articles addressing the transfer price problem, especially after the relation between a decentralized firm and the Dantzig and Wolfe (1960) decomposition principle was stated by Whinston (1964) and Baumol and Fabian (1964).[1]

This paper represents an attempt to place the solutions proposed by the mathematical programming models as well as other traditional solutions in an appropriate context. Since the transfer pricing problem only arises within a recognizable social system (be it an organization or a socialist economy) the paper considers the solutions in a social system context.[2] The paradigm developed can then be used to evaluate the usefulness and limitations of the various proposed solutions.

DECENTRALIZATION AND DIFFERENTIATION

Decentralization is one approach to organizational design. Implicit in this approach is the segmentation of the organization into various specialities. Numerous reasons are provided in the transfer price literature for decentralization. For example, Dean (1955) suggests, ". . . the modern integrated multiple product firm functions best if it is made into a miniature of the competitive free enterprise system." Dopuch and Drake (1964) suggest that the division managers are in a better position to process information concerning resource allocation. Along a similar vein Ronen and McKinney (1970) argue that the division manager's nearness to the market place provides relevant information regarding changes in prices of inputs and outputs and that more effective coordination of production factors should be obtained at the divisional level. Reasons such as size and diversity of modern corporations and the pro-

From *The Accounting Review,* Vol. 50, No. 3 (July 1975), pp. 466–474.

David J. H. Watson is Assistant Professor of Accountancy, University of Illinois at Urbana-Champaign and John V. Baumler is Associate Professor of Accounting at Ohio State University.

[1]As examples of this see the articles by Dopuch and Drake (1964); Godfrey (1971); Gordon (1970); Hass (1968); Ruefli (1971 a&b).

[2]In this paper we only consider an organizational context, but there seems to be a direct analogy to a planned (or socialist) economy.

motion of morale (because of the decision-making autonomy of managers) are also offered in support of decentralization (Godfrey, 1971). While each of these reasons may be true, none of the authors has offered a coherent theory of decentralization. Consequently, the implications that the authors see of decentralization for transfer pricing are fairly restricted and pragmatic.

We consider the central problem facing complex organizations is one of coping with uncertainty. This is the view many current organizational theorists propose. Similarly, we identify the two major sources of uncertainty for a complex organization as its technology and its environment. An organization's design, then, represents a response to these sources of uncertainty.[3] Specifically, an organization may create parts to deal with the uncertainty and thereby leave other parts to operate under conditions of near certainty, i.e., the organization will departmentalize and decentralize.[4] Decentralization is a response to uncertainty.

Decentralization, however, does not quite explain the process involved. A consequence of the segmentation of the organization into parts (departments, divisions, etc.) is that the behavior of organizational members will be influenced by the segmentation. Because of the differences in the nature of the task and in the environmental uncertainty facing various segments, the organizational members will develop different mental processes and working styles, adopt different decision criteria, and may have varying perceptions of reality. A well-known example of this differentiation at the perceptual level is the research report of Dearborn and Simon (1958) which demonstrated that different executives can interpret differently the same organizational problem. The differences in interpretation reflect the departmental identification of the executives.

Therefore, we use the term *differentiation* to include not only the segmentation of the organization into specialized parts, but also to include the consequent differences in attitudes and behavior of organizational members. Requisite differentiation is a requirement for organizational success. That is, each organizational unit must be designed so as to cope effectively with the demands of its technology and environment. Later we will discuss the role of management accounting and transfer pricing in achieving the requisite degree of differentiation between organizational units.

ORGANIZATIONAL INTEGRATION

The Concept

Differentiation is only one design problem facing the organization. The other side of the same coin, and another design problem, is integration: the process of insuring that efforts of the several organizational units, now appropriately differentiated, do collectively attain the goals of the total organization.

Lawrence and Lorsch (1967) in their research demonstrated that the most successful firms (in terms of the traditional measures of profitability) in the various industries studied were the firms that achieved the required differentiation and were then able to integrate the diverse units. Further, the research indicates that only firms that achieve these dual requirements can be successful. However, a basic organizational dilemma is that the more successful an organization is in achieving the requisite differentiation (especially those organizations requiring significant differentiation) the more

[3]The exact roles technology and environment play in determining organizational design is still the subject of research: see Burns and Stalker (1961); Lawrence and Lorsch (1967); Mohr (1971); Thompson (1967); Woodward (1965).

[4]Even in the most dynamic industries manufacturing operations are often sufficiently buffered to allow the effective use of standard cost systems to control manufacturing processes.

difficulty the organization has in achieving the necessary integration. But, of course, the difficulties in achieving the required degree of differentiation and then integrating the total organizational effort is not uniformly distributed over all firms and industries. Rather, the more diverse and dynamic (uncertain) the subenvironments faced by organizational units, the more differentiated they must be. The greater the degree of differentiation, the more difficult is integration.

We stated, originally, that the central problem facing organizational designers is one of coping with uncertainty. This problem has now been restated in terms of achieving requisite differentiation of organizational components while simultaneously coordinating (or integrating) their collective efforts. The magnitude of the differentiation problem is basically determined by uncertainty in technological and environmental factors. However, the magnitude of the integration problem is partly determined by uncertainty factors and partly by the state of interdependence between organizational components.[5] To summarize, the most challenging problems to those seeking integration arise when organizational components are strongly differentiated and highly interdependent. At the opposite extreme, mildly differentiated subunits which exhibit only minimal interdependencies do not pose significant integration problems.

[5](i) We are considering interdependence basically from a technological (the actual technical processes employed) and resource allocation viewpoints, although interdependence may also arise through the environment (e.g., from operating in common input and output markets). Environmental interdependence is not excluded, although we believe the most important aspect of the environment is the uncertainty dimension.

(ii) We are using the term "interdependence" in the Thompson (1967) sense. He identifies pooled, sequential, and reciprocal interdependence. Pooled interdependence is a situation in which each part of the organization renders a discrete contribution to the whole and each is supported by the whole. The parts do not interact directly with one another. This is basically the situation where the only major common organizational link among subunits is some scarce organizational resource, e.g., capital. Sequential interdependence is a situation in which, in addition to the pooled aspect, direct interaction between the units can be pinpointed and the order of that interdependence specified. Reciprocal interdependence refers to the situation in which the outputs of two units become inputs for each other. The three types of interdependence are, in the order indicated, increasingly difficult to coordinate.

Integrating Mechanisms

Integration is achieved by the use of integrating mechanisms of which there are obviously many. One list of such mechanisms is indicated below. This list is adapted from an article by Galbraith (1972).[6]

- Rules, Routines, Standardization
- Organization Hierarchy
- Planning
- Direct Contact
- Liaison Roles
- Temporary Committees (task forces or teams)
- Integrators (personnel specializing in the role of coordinating inter-subunit activities)
- Integrating Departments (departments of integrators)
- Matrix Organization (an organization that is completely committed to joint problem solving and *shared* responsibility)

The list is ordered from the least elaborate to the most sophisticated integrative mechanisms. All organizations employ the first several mechanisms on the list. These mechanisms are sufficient for integrating many organizational functions and are probably all that is needed by

[6](i) Galbraith actually expands this list somewhat especially with regard to organizational planning.

(ii) Thompson (1967) has provided a somewhat different list. He suggests three mechanisms for achieving integration, coordination by standardization, coordination by planning, and coordination by mutual adjustment. The first two mechanisms we present correspond to Thompson's No. 1, while mechanisms 4 to 9 (lateral mechanisms in Galbraith's terminology) correspond to Thompsons No. 3.

organizations facing minimal environmental and technological demands. However, when environmental and technological demands become more complex, organizations become more differentiated and this increases the problem of integration. Consequently, more sophisticated integrating mechanisms (the latter ones listed), in addition to the simpler mechanisms, are required.

DIFFERENTIATION, INTEGRATION, AND MANAGEMENT ACCOUNTING

The amount of differentiation required is determined primarily by technological and environmental demands, and an organization's adaptation to these demands is reflected in the first instance by the organizational design. The accountant, in designing the management accounting system, needs to consider the requisite degree of differentiation as a constraint. That is, the accountant cannot create or demand differentiation when behavioral factors dictate otherwise.

This is not to say that the management accounting system has no part to play in organizational design. In fact, the accounting system can be designed to facilitate or enhance the differentiation achieved. For example, each of the concepts—expense center, profit center, and investment center—may be employed, depending upon the differentiation required by the technological and environmental demands. When the appropriate accounting techniques are used in conjunction with required organizational design we expect the claimed benefits of decentralization to be realized.[7]

We are now in the position to consider the role of the accounting system in integration. An accounting system is a well-defined, formal information system within an organization. Basically, it is a set of rules and standard procedures. The accounting system can thus be classified as an integrating mechanism primarily of the first type listed above.[8] In more complicated integrating situations, although the accounting system (or, more precisely, the costs and prices generating by the accounting system) may be helpful in obtaining integration, this will only be *one* input to the integrating process.

DIFFERENTIATION, INTEGRATION, AND TRANSFER PRICING

Essentially we have argued that the requisite differentiation has to be taken as given by the accountant when he designs an organization's formal control and reporting subsystems. In some cases there will be a one-to-one mapping between the differentiated units and the accountant's responsibility centers, i.e., the expense, profit, and investment centers. However, when there is not this convenient mapping we would argue that the behavioral factors dominate, and that the accountant should not try to impose differentiation through the creation of artificial responsibility centers. Organizational design is a complete task. Numerous variables must be simultaneously considered. The accountant must accept the organizational structure as given. Restructuring the organization merely to facilitate the management accounting system is not recommended.

---

[7]For one listing of these claimed benefits "automatically" arising from decentralization see Horngren (1972), p. 693.

[8]Budgeting and planning are also usually considered part of the management accounting system. Notice, however, that planning has also been classed as a fairly simple or routine integrating mechanism.

What then is the role of transfer pricing? Obviously, once responsibility centers are established, goods and services transferred among these units need to be priced. This helps separate and pinpoint responsibility for different aspects of the firms functioning. In other words, to some extent, the transfer pricing mechanism *enhances* differentiation. But, we have also demonstrated above that differentiation is only one part of the problem. Integration is another facet of this problem. Can the transfer pricing mechanism be used to help achieve the required integration? Again the answer is obviously "yes." In many cases the pricing mechanism is a routine or standardized process, a formula like, for example, standard cost, cost plus, marginal cost, a fixed price, etc. This type of transfer pricing is at least applicable in simple integrating situations, although in more complicated integrating situations it may be only one input to the integrating process.

MATHEMATICAL PROGRAMMING SOLUTIONS TO THE TRANSFER PRICING PROBLEM

As stated in the introduction to this paper many of the papers proposing programming solutions to the transfer price problem rely on the interpretation of the decomposition principle as a model of decision making in a decentralized firm. While the analogy is undoubtedly useful for analyzing some situations, the methodology appears to have some limitations.

The first limitation of these approaches is that they maintain only the facade of decentralized decision making. The last phase of the process is usually dictated by central management. For example, in the Baumol and Fabian (1964) model, although the optimal divisional plan will be a weighted average of the plans submitted by the division, the weights are entirely determined by central management. Godfrey (1971, pp. 289–90) in evaluating the Baumol and Fabian article and the more recent refinements to their model says:

> Despite the appeal of the decomposition technique, in our opinion, it is still a highly centralized decision making procedure. The divisions are at the mercy of central headquarters and would probably not agree that they enjoy the autonomy of decision making that is intended.[9]

There seems to be two explanations for this problem. The first is that many authors of the programming solutions are primarily interested in the mathematical properties (or elegance) of their solutions and only secondarily in the model's organizational implications. The second is that most authors in the transfer price literature are asking the question, "What transfer price will result in the decentralized firm maximizing joint (or corporate) profits?" Since the emphasis is on the maximization of joint profits whenever conflict arises between this goal and the decentralization philosophy, the latter tends to be sacrificed. The solution is always centralized decision making whether this is through some stated price rule, a wishful appeal to competitive market prices and their surrogates, or to mathematical programming solutions. The result is predictable since none of these authors has offered a coherent theory for decentralization. On the other hand, we have offered a theory for explaining decentralization, and under this theory it is not clear that decentralization should be sacrificed or that sacrificing decentralization will optimize decision making.

A second limitation of this approach is that they concentrate on the behaviorally simple integration problems.[10] The environments

[9]Godfrey also uses the decomposition approach in his short-run planning model but freely admits it is a centralized decision making model.

[10](i) We are using mathematical programming models as the example. However, the same argument could be

are stable and the interdependencies are of the simplest kinds. This is true even of recent articles in the area. Ruefli (1971a), for example, develops a decomposition model which can be interpreted as a representation of decision making in a three-level hierarchial organization. Ruelfi greatly restricts the degree and incidence of interdependent relationships within his tri-level hierarchy.[11]

THE CASE AGAINST NEGOTIATED PRICES

The use of negotiated prices has rarely been seriously entertained by those writing in the transfer price literature. Joel Dean (1955) pressed for negotiated prices, but in such a way that they simulated a competitive market. The foundation for his recommendations really lay in the availability of markets outside the decentralized firm. Cook (1955) also discussed the use of "free negotiation" but proceeds to point out two disadvantages: (1) the amount of executive time it is likely to take, and (2) negotiated prices may distort the profit center's financial reports.[12] However, Cook (1955, p. 93) does suggest, ". . . if managers are sophisticated and equipped with good accounting data on their operations, such a free negotiation system could satisfy the basic criteria outline above; that is, a transfer price that will not lead to transfers which will reduce the company's profit but will permit and encourage any transfer which increases the company's profit."[13] Dopuch and Drake (1964, p. 13) also seem to be concerned about Cook's second point above when they state:

> In evaluating the resulting performance of the divisional managers, however, the central management may be evaluating their ability to negotiate rather than their ability to control economic variables. Accordingly, the information economies of decentralization may be more apparent than real.

Later, in their paper, when discussing the decomposition procedure solutions Dopuch and Drake (1964, p. 18) suggest:

> The relevant point is that, if this method can be applied in practice, it will provide a basis for negotiation between the departmental and central management levels. In this respect it would not be necessary for the divisional managers to negotiate with each other. This in itself may be an advantage since situations of negotiation between divisional managers may degenerate into personal conflicts.

Although there is undoubtedly some truth to each of these observations, that is, at times negotiated transfer prices may have these dysfunctional effects, we believe a very strong case can be made for the use of negotiated

made against the economic solutions and against the traditional accounting solutions.

(ii) We are not arguing against the future development of programming models. Even the development of more efficient algorithms for handling solved problems is undoubtedly important.

[11](i) Ruefli's model, as he notes, is easily generalized to an *n*-level hierarchial model.

(ii) In a second article Ruefli (1971b) does mention, with regard to behavioral externalities, the question of bidirectional effects (reciprocal interdependence) for operational units within a management unit. However, he does not propose any solution. Ruefli even proposes an integrating mechanism (a behavioral center) which he says could be a liaison arrangement, a joint planning committee, etc. However, this behavioral center seems to act very similarly to the central management unit and consequently be subject to the same "centralization" criticism.

[12]One, often mentioned, example of this is when one division occupies a monopoly position.

[13]Unfortunately, (technically) sophisticated managers and good accounting data are probably not sufficient conditions for insuring proper integration. Dean (1955) also suggests the position of "price mediator" for a company when *initially* installing his system. These ideas are similar to the concepts of an integrator which we will discuss later.

transfer prices. In presenting this case we will also be suggesting a way for obtaining suitable transfer prices for the complicated integrating situations.

TRANSFER PRICES AND CONFLICT RESOLUTION

Lawrence and Lorsch (1967) in their research were able to isolate three conflict resolution mechanisms in the firms they studied. One of their most interesting results was that the successful firms facing uncertain environments were able to resolve effectively interdepartmental conflict, and the most important means of resolving this conflict was confrontation, i.e., negotiation.[14] This effective resolution of interdepartmental conflict seemed to be an important reason why these successful firms could achieve a high degree of integration as well as the high degree of differentiation demanded by their uncertain environment.

A second point worth noting is that within a complex organization conflict is going to be multidimensional. In a highly differentiated organization this will at times involve the transfer and pricing of goods and services within the organization. But it may also include design and engineering changes, production and delivery schedules, and quality control. Seen in this light, the transfer pricing question becomes one facet of a multidimensional conflict resolution process.[15] If the appropriate conflict resolution process is negotiatation, then it appears the transfer price should be one arrived at through negotiation.[16] Specifically, determination of transfer prices could be part of the integrative process. Note that this is not a wholesale endorsement of negotiated transfer prices in all cases. There are undoubtedly instances in which unalterable formulas could be employed (e.g., the least difficult integration situations). Such formulas may be necessary to guard against obvious diseconomies or, more importantly, to enhance requisite differentiation. But if the requisite degree of differentiation is achievable and the problem is to obtain adequate integration, one of the integrative tools available might well be negotiating intrafirm prices. If organizational subunits seek to resolve conflict by confrontation—possibly with the aid of an integrator—and negotiate their differences, negotiated transfer prices might well be the desired result.

IMPLICATIONS FOR RESEARCH ON TRANSFER PRICING

The obvious implication is that we need to know something about the conflict resolution processes. In particular, we would like to know how accounting data are, or can be, used in a conflict situation. It may be, for example, that accounting data are completely irrelevant or unimportant in the more difficult integrating

[14]Forcing was also an important back-up means. Smoothing was the third method and generally was the least effective.

[15]Hence, it makes little sense to be concerned about a possible monopoly position by one department. It is unlikely, if at all possible, in uncertain environments or reciprocally interdependent situations (or both) that one department will have a monopoly position on all dimensions of the conflict.

[16]This general argument for negotiated prices could probably be extended into the simpler integrating situations. Resolving conflict in part depends upon how close the protagonists' expectations of a suitable solution point are (see Schelling for a clearly stated exposition of this point). The similarity of expectations is also a function of the complexity of the situation. Thus, it could be argued that, when environmental demands or organizational interdependencies or their interaction are least complex, expectations of a mutually agreeable solution point are closest and so the conflict is easily resolved. This seems to be, for example, the conditions when a competitive market transfer price can be established. In other words, the market-based transfer price is a limiting (or simple) case of negotiated prices. See Schelling (1960).

situations. Alternatively we may find some accounting data useful and other accounting data less useful. It may even be that we need to develop new kinds of data for these tougher areas.

Let us for the moment consider a difficult integrating situation—one that requires a formal integrator to integrate successfully the differentiated units. What can we say about this situation? First, although the protagonists may have somewhat different working styles, time horizons, decision criteria, and perceptions of reality (because they are part of a differentiated firm facing different subparts of the organizational environment), they are still members of the one organization and consequently have some attributes in common. There is some basis therefore for believing agreement can always be attained. Second, successful integration will depend largely on the skill of the integrator and how the personnel in the differentiated units perceive him.[17] Third, from a strict accounting viewpoint, instead of giving point estimates to all the parties on the "correct" transfer price (as, for example, the output of a mathematical program) we may wish to provide guides to simply bound the solution area.[18] These bounds could then reflect other accounting restraints on the transfer price (e.g., the fact that the transfer price may be used in the evaluation of the economic performance of the units). However, within the guides set, the final transfer price is a result of the confrontation process.

[17]Again notice Dean (1955) argues along a similar line when discussing his successful price mediator. He suggests the prime role of the mediator is not to dictate a price but to keep the negotiations flowing until that is a settlement.

[18](i) For example, the variable costs of the input units may represent a lower bound, and the selling price less the variable costs of the output units may represent an upper bound. We may also give the integrator various other combinations of cost data to facilitate his integrating role (e.g., full costs (plus a markup), the mathematical programming solutions, etc.)

(ii) These behavioral questions obviously require future empirical verification or falsification.

If we move to a more complicated integrating situation requiring an integrating department, some members of this department may need to be experts in internal financial matters. The implications of this and the wider implications of a matrix organization, for management accounting practice, are still very open questions. We are saying that at times the management accounting process must perform more than a mere scorekeeping or attention-directing function. The integrator has one of the most crucial roles within the organization. Certain aspects of the managerial accounting system—specifically, resolving transfer price disputes—must perhaps be merged within the integrator's total activities.

Further, little empirical evidence has been gathered on how transfer prices are established in various organizations. In gathering such evidence in the future, it is suggested that assessments of the states of differentiation and integration between buyer and seller subunits, the degree of interdependence between them, and the mode of conflict resolution utilized be made. This will allow the transfer pricing techniques to be viewed in terms of the relevant organizational and behavioral variances. Finally, it might be worth while to investigate the relative trade-offs between nonoptimal transfer prices and the dysfunctional consequences of removing this subject from the integrator's purview.

CONCLUSION

We have attempted to place the transfer pricing question in a relevant behavioral setting. Briefly, we have suggested the management accountant needs to consider organizational differentiation a constraint in designing the management accounting system. Working within this constraint we suggested the management accounting system can be designed to enhance the organizational differentiation achieved or to facilitate organizational integration. The transfer pricing mechanism, being part of the management accounting system, can be used to enhance organizational differentiation and to facilitate organizational integration. The transfer pricing mechanisms will probably play the role of enhancing differentiation in those instances in which integration is easily attained. This may well be achieved by the use of formula pricing mechanisms. In other cases, integration will be a major organizational problem. Consequently, the transfer pricing mechanism could be utilized to facilitate integration. An appropriate transfer price mechanism in this case seems to be negotiated pricing. Further areas of research suggested by this conclusion were discussed.

REFERENCES

Baumol, W. J. and Fabian, T., "Decomposition, Pricing for Decentralization and External Economics," *Management Science* (September 1964), pp. 1–32.

Burns, T. and Stalker, G. M., *The Management of Innovation* (London: Tavistock Institute, 1961).

Cook, P. W., "Decentralization and the Transfer Price Problem," *Journal of Business* (April 1955), pp. 87–94.

Dantzig, G. B. and Wolfe, P., "Decomposition Principles for Linear Programs," *Operations Research* (February 1960), pp. 101–11.

Dean, J., "Decentralization and Intracompany Pricing," *Harvard Business Review* (July-August 1955), pp. 65–74.

Dopuch, N. and Drake, D. F., "Accounting Implications of a Mathematical Programming Approach to the Transfer Pricing Problem," *Journal of Accounting Research* (Spring 1964), pp. 10–24.

Galbraith, J. R., "Organization Design: An Information Processing View," in J. W. Lorsch and P. R. Lawrence, eds., *Organizational Planning: Cases and Concepts* (Georgetown, Ontario: Irwin-Dorsey Limited, 1972).

Godfrey, J. T., "Short-Run Planning in a Decentralized Firm," THE ACCOUNTING REVIEW (April 1971), pp. 282–97.

Gordon, M. J., "A Method of Pricing for a Socialist Economy," THE ACCOUNTING REVIEW (July 1970), pp. 427–43.

Hass, J. E. "Transfer Pricing in a Decentralized Firm," *Management Science* (February 1968), pp. B-310–B-331.

Hirshleifer, J., "On the Economics of Transfer Pricing," *Journal of Business* (July 1956), pp. 172–84.

———, "Economics of the Divisionalized Firm," *Journal of Business* (April 1957), pp. 96–108.

Lawrence, P. R. and Lorsch, J. W., *Organization and Environment* (Irwin, 1967).

Mohr, L. B., "Organizational Technology and Organizational Structure," *Administrative Science Quarterly* (December 1971), pp. 444–59.

Ronen, J. and McKinney, G., "Transfer Pricing for Divisional Autonomy," *Journal of Accounting Research* (Spring 1970), pp. 99–112.

Ruefli, T. W., "A Generalized Goal Decomposition Model," *Management Science* (April 1971), pp. B-505–B-518.

———, "Behavioral Externalities in Decentralized Organizations," *Management Science* (June 1971), pp. B-649–B-657.

Schelling, T. C., *The Strategy of Conflict* (Oxford University Press, 1963).

Thompson, J. D., *Organizations in Action* (McGraw-Hill, 1967).

Whinston, "Pricing Guides in Decentralized Organization," in W. W. Cooper et al., eds., *New Perspectives in Organizational Research* (Wiley, 1964).

Woodward, J., *Industrial Organizations: Theory and Practice* (Oxford University Press, 1965).

*An Integrated Approach To Control System Design**

Shahid L. Ansari

Graduate School of Management, University of California, Los Angeles

Existing approaches to the problem of designing management control systems may be described as primarily structural *or* behavioral. *The first approach is characteristic of the accounting literature. It takes a rational and mechanistic view of control and treats the control system design problem as one of designing an effective information structure. The behavioral approach, exemplified by the socio-psychological literature on performance, views control as a problem of designing social relationships which lead to high performance.*

This paper presents evidence which shows that there is a close interaction between the information structure and the human and social relationships. Using an open systems approach, it argues for the adoption of a view of management control in which the two elements are considered jointly. The minimization of perceptual differences between managers and subordinates is proposed as an operational criterion which designers can use as a guide. Finally, some propositions for further research which emerge from this proposed perspective are also presented.

Researchers interested in the problem of management control system design have focused on it from two different perspectives. The first one, adopted by researchers in cybernetics, accounting, and management information systems (MIS) concentrates mainly on the information and communication aspects of a control system. It may be described as a *structural* view. The other, based upon studies of human behavior in organizations, regards control as a problem of getting subordinates to achieve performance goals. Because of its emphasis on the human and social aspects of control, this may be described as a *behavioral* view.

These perspectives have resulted in a fragmented approach in which designers attempt to optimize the structural or behavioral variables alone. In this paper I will argue that designing control systems requires a consideration of both these variables. With the help of existing evidence, it will be shown that information and human-social variables are really interacting subsystems. An operational criterion by which a designer can more effectively

From *Accounting, Organizations and Society,* Vol. 2, No. 2 (1977), pp. 101–112.

*I am grateful to my colleagues Jack McDonough, Dick Mason, Burt Swanson and Jim Taylor and two unknown reviewers for their useful comments and criticisms on earlier drafts of this paper.

integrate these components will also be proposed.

The presentation is divided into five parts. The first part introduces the terminology and assumptions used in the analyses. This is followed by a discussion of the two existing approaches to control system design. The next part of the paper argues that the present sole emphasis on information or behavior is inappropriate because of the interrelationships between these components. A framework which recognizes their interaction and suggests an operational way to combine them in a control system is proposed in the subsequent part. The final section is devoted to a consideration of the research implications of the proposed framework.

SOME KEY ASSUMPTIONS

The term management control has been used in a variety of ways in the literature.[1] To avoid confusion, this paper will restrict its usage to only those situations in which the controlled variable is human performance. Thus inventory control systems, using operational research models, are excluded. No distinction, however, will be made between controlling performance of first line supervisors as opposed to higher managers. The design problems are assumed to be generic and common to all echelons of an organization.

The working of a control system will be assumed to require a set of *structural* arrangements which allows the human behavioral *process* to function. While this will facilitate earlier discussion it will later be shown that this assumption, which is similar to a socio-technical systems view, is the proper perspective for a designer.[2]

Given these assumptions, a control system, as used here, may be simply described as "those organizational *arrangements* and *actions* designed to facilitate its members to achieve higher performance with least unintended consequences".

EXISTING VIEWS ON MANAGEMENT CONTROL

Most writers agree that a management control system consists of two elements. The first one is an information network which prescribes the rules for the measurement, collection, processing and transmission of information. It facilitates communication of information about performance goals, actual outputs and deviations from plans to managers and subordinates. The network may be regarded as the structure of a control system.

The other element is the set of social relationships through which such systems achieve their goals. It may be regarded as the control process. It is convenient to group existing research into these two categories according to the emphasis they place on the structural or human-social variables.

The Structural Approach

This view is best exemplified by the early work in cybernetics which has been strictly and narrowly interpreted in the control literature. It is a closed systems, highly mechanistic view, which defines control as a problem of designing optimal information networks. For example,

[1]For example, Anthony & Dearden (1976) distinguish between management control and operational control. The former they define as control managers exercise over other managers. The latter is control over lower echelon supervisors for the performance of specific tasks. No such distinction is made in this paper.

[2]Readers interested in getting a better understanding of the theoretical underpinnings of the socio-technical view of organizations should see Emery & Trist (1960).

Beer (1964, p. 23) states that control systems to be effective should be designed as cybernetic systems, which he defines as "a tightly knit network of information". Control is defined as "a homeostatic machine for regulating itself".

The cybernetics approach treats control as synonymous with communication of information. Therefore, it analyzes the control problem in terms of communication theory concepts. For instance, Ashby (1965) states that control consists essentially of blocking information about disturbances from reaching controlled variables by interjecting a regulatory mechanism. For effective control, the regulator must have so-called "requisite variety" and "channel capacity", concepts based upon Shannon's work on the mathematical theory of information communication.[3]

In the extreme cybernetics view there is no difference between a mechanical regulator, such as a thermostat, and a human regulator or manager. The model treats the response of the regulator as flowing automatically from the nature of communicated information. It fails to recognize that managers do not respond mechanically since they process information based on their *personal* goals and not the organizational goals imbedded in a control system.

The cybernetic closed systems perspective has been incorporated in recent years in the research in management information systems (MIS). Discussions about the design of MIS are conducted in much the same terminology and with many of the same assumptions. Behavioral effects, such as differences in information perception and reaction between people, if recognized, are sometimes regarded as nuisances. For example, Davis (1974, p. 97) states: "In much the same way that a closed system is insulated from disturbances in the environment, a closed feedback loop is insulated from disturbances in the control loop. An open control loop is one with *random disturbances,* such as those associated with *human control elements".* (Emphasis added.)

Again, to regard human behavior as a random disturbance, as the above quotation does, is to deny a great part of purposeful goal-oriented behavior of people in control systems. It is incorrect to deny this, and to assume that the problem of control can somehow be solved by providing management with "right" information. The fact that the behavioral climate within which this information is perceived may reduce its usefulness, or even distort it, should be recognized.

Much of the same perspective, with few exceptions, is also evident in discussions of control in the accounting literature. Anthony & Dearden (1976) suggest that this greater emphasis on information as compared to social variables, may be because the former are more amenable to a systematic description. Even while recognizing the importance of social interactions, they describe management control structure in terms of financial responsibility centers (cost, revenue, profit and investment), and the control process in terms of financial reporting activities (programming, budgeting, reporting and appraisal).

If a designer approaches control with a structural perspective, the following questions are likely to be the ones he will emphasize in his task.

1. What are the controlled variables and how are they to be broken down and measured at different levels? This question focuses on the goals or performance standards setting within a system. It deals with how large heirarchical organizations break down controlled variables into smaller components to be controlled separately. For example, breakdown of profit into divisional profit, departmental revenues or costs, etc., and assignment to a managerial responsibility

[3]For a detailed description of these concepts see Ashby (1956, p. 201).

center. This process of disaggregating goals into subgoals serves to: (a) coordinate activities of organizational units; and (b) evaluate performance of the various managers involved.

2. What disturbances should be recognized and measured? There are many causes which can reduce a system's effectiveness. Not all of these are worth tracking, however. Only those that reflect the presence of a problem need be identified. The choice of disturbances, therefore, reflects the criteria laid down for distinguishing between a system's stable and out-of-control behaviors.
3. When and how often to communicate information on deviations to management? The first issue (when) deals with the interval between performance and the preparation of reports. At the one extreme are *feedback* systems which wait for performance to occur before reporting deviations. At the other are *feedforward* systems which anticipate disturbances and enable corrective action to be taken before performance is affected. The second issue (how often) deals with the appropriate frequency of reporting.
4. What and how many transformations are to be performed on the information as it moves through a network? That is, at what point does the information enter the network, and how many times is it summarized, integrated or changed?
5. What and how often feedback reports should be provided to subordinates? This factor relates the choice available to designers with respect to the type and frequency of feedback reports to use in performance evaluation.[4]

[4]An important type of feedback system is what Ashby calls the *error controlled* regulator. This system allows room for errors, learns from them, and then takes corrective action. Most management control systems, such as budgetary systems, are designed as error controlled regulators.

The Behavioral Approach

This approach emphasizes the human and social process by which an organization achieves its goals. Its perspective is well stated by Tannenbaum (1964, p. 229), who describes control in a social organization as, "any process in which a person (or group of persons or organization of persons) determines or intentionally affects what another person or group or organization will do".

In most organizational situations, the above description refers to the process of affecting subordinate behavior. Research in how best to do this has gone through three evolutionary phases. Because of lack of space, only the most salient aspects are discussed here.

1. Traditional Management Phase. This first phase coincides with the scientific management and traditional organization theory period. Here the problem of control was analyzed in terms of power, authority relations and sanctions.[5] Management had power over subordinates because they controlled their economic rewards and could terminate their membership in an organization. The main problem of control was to provide direction by dividing tasks, responsibilities, etc. Compliance could be obtained by offering appropriate economic incentives and the threat to use sanctions.

Formal power and economic sanctions were the most important source of influence in this phase. The former was treated as a finite quantity (Tannenbaum, 1964). Delegation of authority, which allowed subordinates more freedom to control their actions, was regarded as a reduction in the power of the superiors. The key for management was to find how much authority to delegate without impairing its own power. In short, it regarded superiors as directive and subordinates as passive.

[5]This view of control is exemplified by the works of Taylor (1911), Urwick (1944) and Weber (1947).

*2. **Human Relations Phase.*** The second phase of research on the influence process coincides with the birth of the human relations movement.[6] It began by recognizing that subordinates have social needs which are sometimes more important than economic needs in determining their performance. What workers sought from organizations were not merely economic rewards, but also a sense of psychological satisfaction. A manager could, therefore, increase his influence by providing rewards that increased worker satisfaction.

The reduced role of economic rewards was accompanied by a concurrent deemphasis on the use of formal power. Researchers, such as Blau (1974) and Simon (1957), pointed out that compliance obtained by power can ensure a minimum effort but cannot guarantee a maximum effort by subordinates. To obtain high performance, a manager has to seek the cooperation of his workers. Techniques of persuasion were thus added to sources of influence.

The role of formal power was not only reduced, it was no longer viewed as a fixed quantity. On the basis of his own and other people's research, Tannenbaum (1964) concluded that "the total amount of control . . . can increase, and the various participants can each acquire a share of this augmented power". He noted that an individual's performance and satisfaction were likely to be affected by his perception of the amount of control exercised by him and over him. Such effects would differ across individuals due to personality differences.

The major impact of this phase may be summarized as a change in focus of the managerial function from direction to *leadership.* It was no longer sufficient for a manager to rely on the formal organizational relations to get the work done. He had to become a leader and provide the impetus necessary for increasing the performance and satisfaction of his subordinates.

3. Contingency Theory Phase. Both the first and second phases described above had one thing in common. They attempted to isolate a one best way. In the first phase it was the best management style, and in the second phase it was the one best leadership style. The third, and current, phase in the thinking on control is characterized by a move away from the search for a one best way suitable for all circumstances, to a search for circumstances under which certain combinations of variables work best.

This new emphasis results from the application of the general systems paradigm to the organizational design problem. As Kast & Rosensweig (1973, p. 307) note: "Systems concepts emphasize that organizations are composed of many subsystems whose interrelationships have to be recognized . . . There are so many relevant variables that it is impossible for a simplistic model to depict reality". The effort, therefore, is on discovering what works best in a given situation.

Contingency theory of organizations is one concrete expression of this philosophy.[7] Its approach to the problem of influencing subordinate behavior is to focus on those organizational variables and relationships whose combination results in high performance. A good example is Fiedler's (1967) work on leadership styles. His theory of leadership effectiveness is based on a study of the match between different

[6]The beginning of this movement is generally ascribed to the Hawthorne studies done by Homans and others at Harvard. A description of this approach, with later research findings, is contained in Homans (1950).

[7]A slightly different application of this philosophy is in the literature on socio-technical systems. While both socio-technical systems theory and contingency theory are applications of the general systems theory to organizational problems, the former, unlike the latter, is concerned with both technical and behavioral variables in a work situation. This concern has been translated into a broader emphasis on improving the quality of working life through organizational redesign.

supervision styles, worker personalities, and types of tasks. Results showed that autocratic leaders are more effective in some task environments and employee-oriented leaders are more effective in others.

The most comprehensive model of performance in organizations, based on the contingency philosophy, is the so-called *expectancy model.*[8] It includes, not only Fiedler's variables, but also considers the match between a subordinate's needs and goals and the rewards offered by an organization.

The model states that an individual is motivated to perform because he has certain goals which an organization can satisfy by providing extrinsic and intrinsic rewards. An individual, therefore, computes two "expectancies" which indicate to him the likelihood of a given level of (a) effort resulting in high performance; and (b) performance providing him with the desired rewards. The higher those likelihoods, the more he will be motivated to perform at a high level.

A designer's job is to make sure that a control system maximizes these expectancies for subordinates. He can do this by designing task structures, leadership styles and reward structures which strengthen linkages between effort, performance, and rewards.

This current phase of research, therefore, is more situational based. Also, unlike preceding phases, it focuses more on the broader issue of improving subordinate performance instead of a narrow conception of constraining their behavior. It is also a phase on which research continues and new ideas and evidence will be forthcoming.

To recapitulate, the three phases described above represent the so-called behavioral view of control systems. The difference between this and the structural approach is best stated by Drucker (1964, p. 287): "Instead of a mechanical system, the control system in a human social situation is a volitional system". It requires motivating people to make choices favorable to an organization.

[8]An excellent description and summary of the research on the expectancy model is contained in Cummings & Schwab (1973).

Need for a Broader View of Control Systems

The problem with these approaches is that they emphasize a single perspective—one which ignores the existence of the other. Existing evidence suggests that information and human social variables interact with each other in a way which necessitates their joint consideration. The nature of this interaction and the supporting evidence is described below.

The problem with the structural approach is that it treats information collection and communication as an abstract and rational decision-oriented process in which emotional and psychological variables play a limited role. The fact is that an information structure essentially represents a designer's perceptions of the control process. These perceptions reflect his *assumptions*—explicit or implicit—about the behavior of those using it, his *knowledge* and *skills*, and his *values.* All of these may be influenced by prior experiences and cultural factors.

This thesis is supported by Lawler & Rhode (1976, p. 129) who, after examining relevant evidence, conclude that "the financial control system of a corporation is demonstrably not isolated from the personality of the CPAs or financial officers who design, maintain and use the system". In discussing his experiences at General Motors, Sloan (1964) also concurs by stating that the decentralized reporting system of the company was a reflection of top management philosophy.

Caplan's (1968) field study of the assumptions underlying management accounting systems in organizations is one of the very few empirical studies on this subject. Some indirect support is provided by Reedy (1970) and

Schlesinger (1974). In discussing the decision-making system of U.S. presidents, they point out that Presidential use of information sources largely reflects personal attitudes and beliefs about how best to exercise control over the federal government.

Finally, at a more abstract level, Mason & Mitroff (1972) point out that most information structures contain an assumption about a decision maker's cognitive style. Present systems, according to them, are designed for so-called "thinking-sensation" types of information processors. They suggest more varied assumptions so that information systems can be better matched with cognitive styles.

While structuralists fail to recognize the impact of people on information structures, behavioral writers tend to ignore the effects of information on people. They assume that information is neutral, and that, only the way it is used matters. For example, a typical statement is like the one by Cammann & Nadler (1976, p. 66), who state: "If managers use information well, the system works. If they use it poorly, the system may produce unintended consequences".

Such a position, however, is unrealistic on two counts. First, studies in human cognition show that information must first be *perceived* before it can be used. One important factor which can alter a person's perception is the characteristics of the perceived object—in this case information. Hence managerial use of information depends upon the characteristics of the information structure.

Second, besides managers, subordinates also use information for self guidance and self-evaluation of performance. This process is independent of supervisory evaluation and its results may differ with those of the supervisor. How information is measured and communicated is thus likely to alter subordinate perceptions of such information also.

An examination of this literature shows that the following characteristics of information structures are particularly relevant for a designer: (1) Nature of measures; (2) source and order of presentation; (3) timing; (4) route for transmission; and (5) extent of shared information.

1. Nature of Measures. Lawler & Rhode (1976) point out that subordinate motivation is affected by three characteristics of performance measures. The first is *completeness* and refers to the extent to which all behaviors necessary for good performance are measured. The second is *objectivity* which determines the impartiality of a measure and thus affects the trust subordinates place in it. The last one is the extent to which a subordinate's behavior can *influence* a measure (e.g. profits do not respond to performance of lower echelon workers). According to them, the more complete, objective and influencable a measure, the more likely it is to motivate subordinates.

2. Source and Order of Presentation. This characteristic was one of the earliest to be studied. In a series of experiments, Hovland *et al.* (1953) showed that the order in which information is communicated, and the source attributed to such communications, can change a recipient's perception of a message. Credible sources tend to be used more often and have a greater influence on a user. Because of the conflicting research evidence, the influence of order is somewhat less clear.[9] A variant of order, placement, may explain why people get different signals when transactions are disclosed in footnotes as opposed to the body of a financial statement.

3. Timing. There are two aspects of information timing—*speed* and *frequency* of communication. Bruner *et al.* (1956) cite several studies

[9]Research studies have reported two types of order effects—primacy and recency—making it difficult to resolve which is more prevalent and when. For a review see Hovland *et al.* (1957).

which show that speed can change information processing strategies of recipients. Because information comes faster, users may be forced to respond quickly. To do so, however, they may have to abandon slow but safe information processing strategies in favor of quicker but riskier strategies. The resulting perceptions may well be different. Frequency, on the other hand, refers to the reporting interval. Too long an interval may mean a loss of interest and usefulness of information to a user. Too short an interval may not measure all the things that should be included in a measure.

*4. **Route.*** The communication network or route that information takes from a sender to a receiver can also influence the latter's perceptions. Ference (1970) shows that network features such as, point of entry of information, and the steps at which it is summarized, can alter the character of information. The sender and the receiver, therefore, may not be sharing the same information.

*5. **Shared Information.*** Information structures differ on the extent to which they have opened widely shared communications. For example, Lawler & Rhode (1976) point out that some systems keep pay and performance of workers secret from their co-workers. Also, in decentralized companies, divisions are known not to share information in order to increase their trading advantages with other divisions. The more open the communications, the more information a subordinate has to assess his own performance and the fairness of superior evaluation of his performance.

Based upon the prior discussion, it is now possible to offer a summary of the interaction between information and people in a control system. This is shown in Fig. 1. It shows that information structures reflect what a designer perceives to be the needs and goals of subordinates and managers. The designer, in essence, anticipates the type of information desired at the next stage in this system—self and supervisory evaluation of performance. These evaluations provide subordinates with most of their desired extrinsic and intrinsic rewards. Their satisfaction with such rewards determines their aspiration and motivation to perform in future.[10]

The above is a very brief overview of complex organizational relationships. It does make clear that it is inappropriate to talk of information for control without considering how people behave, or to talk of motivating behavior in control systems without considering the impact of information on it. This interaction is important not only from the practical standpoint of subordinate performance, but also provides a new conceptual way of analyzing control system problems.

A PROPOSED FRAMEWORK FOR CONTROL SYSTEM DESIGN

The need for a new way of thinking is especially important since even those who recognize the relationships between information and behavior still tend to treat control in a closed systems context. That is, they create closure or certainty by assuming one-way dependence relationships between these variables. For example, at one extreme, structuralists, including many who are aware of behavioral effects of information, treat technology and people as independent variables and information as dependent variable.[11]

---

[10]For a comprehensive discussion of these relationships see Cummings & Schwab (1973). The expectancy model describes this process in terms of the impact of information on "effort-performance" and "performance-reward" probabilities.

[11]A good example of this is Lawler & Rhode (1976, Chapter 10). Even though they recognize the behavioral implications of information, their suggestions for designing control systems are one-way. That is, they recommend changes in information structures that are likely to produce better results for control purpose. What this approach ig-

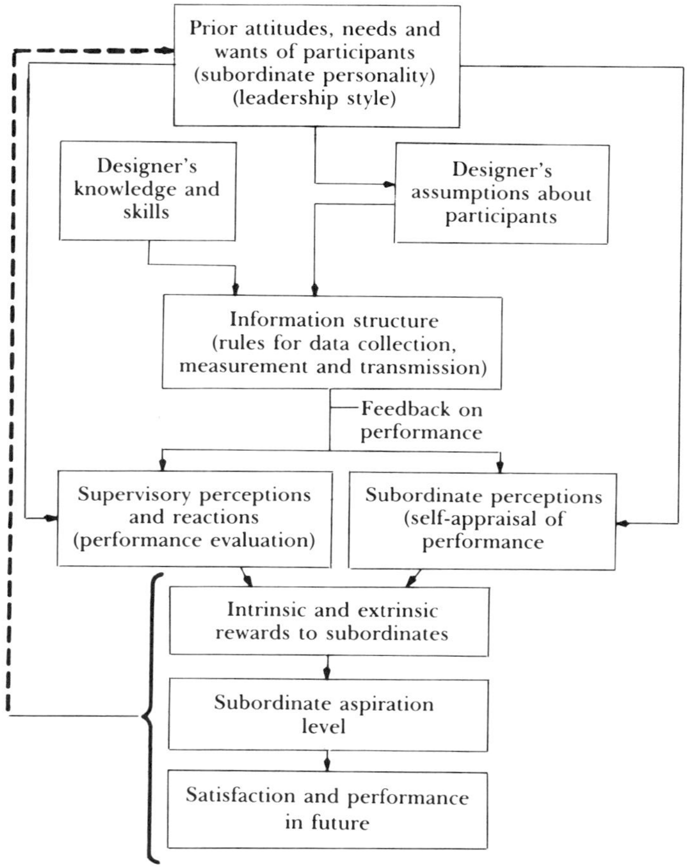

FIGURE 1. Relationship between information and behavioral variables in a control system.

What is needed, therefore, is a new paradigm which treats information, people and technology as *both* independent and dependent variables. This is a necessary precondition for a designer if he is to successfully address key design issues.

The *open systems concept* is proposed as a paradigm which is suitable for this purpose. It is consistent with the interactions shown in Fig. 1, and provides insights which allow dealing with design issues in a way which overcomes existing weaknesses.

The power of the open systems concept is best illustrated by socio-technical systems theory. Its use enabled those interested in the design of work systems to realize that: (1) technology was important in determining a system's efforts to achieve a steady state and, therefore, must be included in a system's boundaries along with the social system; and (2) technological and social systems were highly interactive components of a control system.

---

nores is that it may not be feasible or economical to change information alone. Old information habits die hard, and it may be easier to change social factors in some situations.

The concept of interaction, in particular, allowed designers to appreciate the relationship between these two components in a new way. They understood that technology dictates certain social inter-relations, and, in the absence of a one-to-one relationship between technological requirements and social systems, allows the use of alternative social systems with a given technology (see Emery & Trist, 1960). Interaction thus gave rise to the ideas of mutual influence and choice of technology and social systems.

In a similar way, the open systems view provides a conceptualization of control systems that allows designers to understand the unique relationships between its parts. The following four insights are especially noteworthy. First, in an open system, all components which enable it to achieve a steady state or self-regulation in the face of environmental changes are included within its boundaries. Since both information and social relationships enable control systems to achieve regulation, they should be included as parts of this system. Second, interaction of information and human-social variables is not a superficial one-way impact. Rather, it means that there are (i) socially induced information structures; and (ii) informationally induced human-social interrelations. Third, a designer may combine alternative information structures and human-social variables. The one he chooses to treat as a given will reflect the constraining variable in a given situation.[12] Finally, the self-regulating view of control views the job of the regulatory mechanisms as elimination of disturbances. This means that managers as regulators exercise control over disturbances and not over people. A designer, therefore, should focus on those disturbance sources or interactions that are likely to affect system performance more than others.[13]

Given this perspective, it is now possible to answer the two key issues facing a control system designer. First, what are the components and how are they related? Second, how to combine these components effectively?

Components of a Control System (Boundaries)

Figure 2 shows the four major components of a control system. They center around a controlled variable or objective of the system. The controlled variable is sometimes very difficult to pin down as one moves to higher management levels. For example, while it is relatively easy to define task performance as the objective of control at lower levels, the controlled variable is more difficult to identify at higher management levels. Nevertheless, some sort of working definition is usually adopted. It should be noted that task performance, particularly at lower echelons, requires the consideration of technology as a mediating variable. This requirement is less applicable to budgetary and profit oriented control systems.

These four components may be classed into three categories: Structural, Social and Support.

The *Structure* of the system is embodied in the information network. Measurement and communication of information are carried on through this network.

The *Social* side of the system revolves around the manager-subordinate interaction needed for goal accomplishment. It envisages two sets of psychological variables: (a) subordinate personality, which together with their

[12] In many organizations, especially bureaucracies, the available information, technology, rules and procedures of behavior, existing modes of thinking, etc. may actually make certain existing information as a constraint to be dealt with by a designer.

[13] This is similar to the concept of "key variances" used in socio-technical systems theory. It refers to the control of factors that are more significant in terms of affecting the outputs of a system than others.

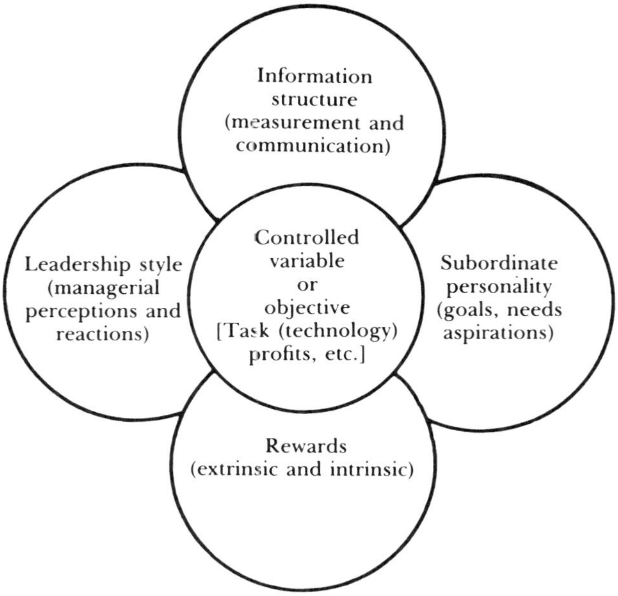

FIGURE 2. Components of a control system.

needs, wants, and attitudes governs how they perceive and react to a control system; and (b) leadership style which essentially represents the personality and attitudes of managers and determines how they interact with subordinates.[14]

Support refers to the extrinsic and intrinsic rewards available to a subordinate. Only some of these rewards are controlled by an organization which uses them to facilitate the social interactions for goal achievement.

The overlap in these components, shown in Fig. 2, represents their interaction—that is, their mutual influence upon each other. Changes in any one component are thus likely to have system wide effects. Also, the choice of any one component cannot be made without considering its impact upon the others.

[14]It should be noted that the terms manager and leader are used to refer to both individual as well as collective styles. For example, university faculties are usually evaluated by a committee of peers rather than any one person.

Criterion for Effective Integration

An effective combination of the components shown in Fig. 2 is one in which they are supportive of each other. In other words, there is a good match between them. The operational definition of a good match suggested here is the minimization of perceptual differences between managers and subordinates. That is, *a designer should choose those system elements which lower the possibility of cognitive conflict between the two.* The ultimate test of any design, of course, is the system's performance. It is, however, a post-design measure. What is needed is a predesign criterion because many components, once chosen, are difficult to change.

The above criterion is based on the concept of identifying the interactions critical to the success of a system (see page 168). In this case, the manager-subordinate interaction is viewed as the key to the effectiveness of a control system. Successful control requires leaders who can create conditions which motivate workers toward desired goals. For this to happen, subordinates must share, or at least must not reject, their manager's perceptions of what the goals are (ends), how they are to be met (means) and how well they were met (evaluation).

While managers and subordinates are likely to have different perceptions of all three —means, ends and evaluation—the greatest and potentially most harmful differences are likely to be at the evaluation stage. In fact, different perceptions of means and ends may well affect a subordinate's performance and thus show up in evaluation also. What turns their perceptual differences at this stage into a potentially disruptive conflict is that the outcomes (rewards) valued by subordinates are contingent on a favorable evaluation.

A brief digression on the nature of cognitive processes is needed to better understand the usefulness of the proposed criterion. Cognitive "consistency theories"—specially as set forth by Heider (1946), Osgood & Tannenbaum (1955), and Festinger (1957)—are particularly helpful. These theories predict that people as perceivers tend to organize their cognitions so as to achieve consonance (balance or congruity) between them. They find dissonant cognitions psychologically uncomfortable and undertake behaviors which remove them with least rearrangement of their existing beliefs.

The present problem can be analyzed with the help of Heider's (1946) "balance" framework which is the original formulation of the consistency theory. Figure 3 shows the cognitive systems of a subordinate and his supervisor. Figure 3a, in which the subordinate is the perceiver, has two cognitive units—his perception of his performance and his perception of his manager. The relations between these cognitions may be positive or negative. For example, if a subordinate feels positively about his manager, and he has a favorable self-appraisal of performance, then the arrows linking these cognitions are positive.

It should be noted that the sign of the manager-subordinate bond does not necessarily represent an affective like-dislike relationship. Rather, it represents an evaluation of the perceived fairness of a manager in his evaluative role. It thus depends on how he responds

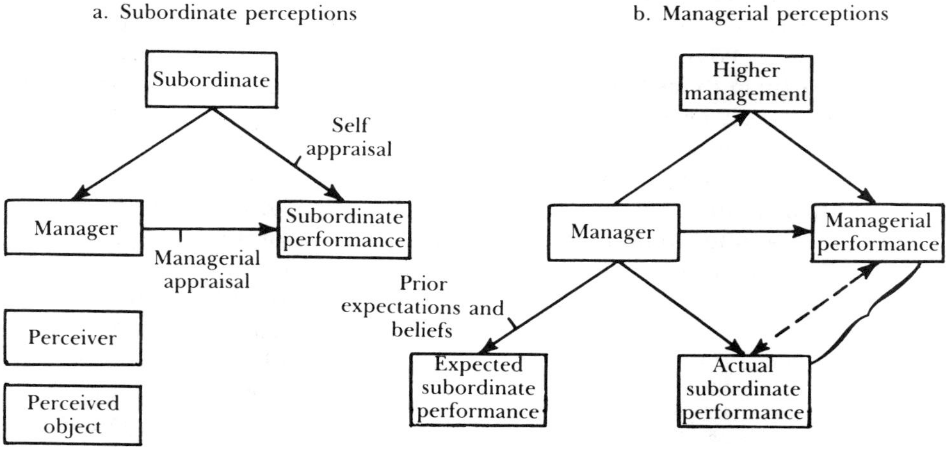

FIGURE 3. *Manager-subordinate perceptions in performance evaluation.*

to subordinate performance. This last relationship, shown as the manager-performance bond, completes the triad shown in Fig. 3a. According to Heider, the three cognitions are in balance when the product of their relationship signs (+/−) is positive. Such a result is possible only if all relationships are positive or two are negative and one is positive. As summarized below, of the eight possible states for the triad, only half are balanced states.

Subordinate to Performance	Manager to Performance	Subordinate to Manager	Resulting Product
+	+	+	+ Balanced
+	+	−	−
+	−	+	−
+	−	−	+ Balanced
−	+	+	−
−	+	−	+ Balanced
−	−	+	+ Balanced
−	−	−	−

How a manager reacts to subordinate performance in Fig. 3a, depends upon how he organizes his own cognitions. Figure 3b shows that he has two sets of cognitions. In the first set, consisting of two units, he has to reconcile his prior expectations of subordinates with their actual performance. Again, these will be in balance when both are either positive or negative. In other words, a supervisor experiences no dissonance when a subordinate's performance confirms his expectations.

The second set, consisting of three units, relates a manager to his own superiors in a triadic relationship similar to Fig. 3a. It emphasizes that, like the subordinate, he too has to go through an evaluation process. His performance, however, may depend on the performance of his subordinates. This means that his perception of the latter may be influenced by his judgment of how his evaluation is affected by it.

This linkage between the higher and lower level performance evaluations is shown by the braces in Fig. 3b. The strength of this association will depend upon the measurement rules used by an organization. For example, in production situations it is not uncommon to use a simple additive rule in which a manager's performance is simply the sum of subordinate productivities. In others, a manager may be evaluated not so much on how well his subordinates perform, but rather, on how he *evaluates* them.[15] In both cases, managerial appraisal of subordinate performance is linked to his own appraisal in ways which increase the subjectivity of the evaluation process.

Returning to the design theme, the nature of the determinants of organizational performance suggests that a control system's regulatory effectiveness may be affected by the behaviors resulting from its participants efforts to deal with cognitive conflict. Since regulation depends upon subordinates willingly aspiring to perform, and leaders being able to motivate them to do so, behaviors which alter determinants such as aspiration levels and motivation are especially undesirable.

For example, a subordinate can reduce dissonance caused by differing self and managerial appraisals of performance by either agreeing or disagreeing with the manager. If agreeing means revising his own assessment downward, it is likely to reduce his satisfaction and aspiration. Findings which support this are reported in research on the expectancy model (see Cummings & Schwab, 1973). They show that self-appraisal is related to many intrinsic rewards such as a sense of accomplishment. These rewards determine how satisfied a subordinate is, and, how high he aspires in future. Reductions in aspiration level, tied to low past performance, causes subsequent reductions in performance.

If he chooses to disagree with his manager, it will have an impact on their relation-

[15]For example, in small public accounting firms, senior accountants are evaluated on how they evaluate a junior's performance on an audit.

ship. The latter's ability to lead and motivate depends on acceptance by subordinates. If they feel that he is unfair in providing performance related rewards, they are likely to question his leadership. This may force managers to rely more on sanctions and less on persuasion—an outcome likely to reduce performance over time.

It is of course possible for the two to find a compromise alternative which is consistent with their differing views. For example, they can discount the information (e.g. student ratings do not reflect teaching ability), or assign a special interpretation (e.g. this was just a bad week). The willingness to compromise will depend not only on a subordinate, but also on how uncomfortable it is for a manager to revise his prior expectations about subordinates, and how much pressure he faces from his own superiors.

In summary, a designer should combine components in a way which: (1) minimizes cognitive conflict; or (2) encourages behavior which can resolve such conflict with positive results for systems performance.

CONCLUDING REMARKS

The proposed framework presented here is potentially superior to existing approaches both conceptually and operationally. Conceptually, the use of the open systems logic allows a designer to deal with variables and relationships not considered previously. The most important contribution here is the appreciation for the key role cognitive processes play in a control system's efforts to achieve regulation. This latter, in turn, leads to an operational criterion which can serve as a design guide.

Because it is based on previously tested consistency models, the proposed criterion lends itself well to further research and testing. Clearly, the most important research issue is whether control system designs which lead to lower cognitive conflict (and/or encourage positive modes of conflict resolution), also lead to higher performance. It may be difficult to test this since there are many factors in an actual situation which affect performance. Separating their effects may be difficult.

A more feasible research strategy is to study the effects of supportive or non-supportive combinations of the various components of a control system. It is similar to the contingency theory approach which searches for good "fits" by *a priori* hypothesizing of the effects of certain combinations. A good example is Fiedler's work on leadership effectiveness in different task situations.

In the case of a control system, a number of interesting issues arise out of the information-human interaction. One of the primary ones is the notion of the kind of information structure which is best suited for a given type of behavioral climate. This latter being the social factors such as leadership and subordinate personality. There is some evidence to suggest that optimal information does not necessarily mean more and free communication. Ackoff (1970) cites a case in which free communication of information between parts of an organization actually led to greater disruption in the organization. Similarly, Ansari (1976) shows that autocratic leaders are able to function better when their subordinates have limited access to information. Clearly, one issue for further research is the amount of information which best supports a given leadership style.

A closely related research question is the quality of information needed to sustain certain social relationships. For instance, it is important to examine whether quality dimensions such as precision, objectivity, and completeness are always desirable no matter what the behavioral situation in a control system. The answer is not obvious since less controversy about information measures also reduces the likelihood of a compromise in which managers and subordinates can blame information instead of each other.[16]

The design of information structures usually follows the responsibility division outlined in an organization chart and is constrained only by available economic resources. This, in turn, impacts on the choice of structural characteristics such as the number of points at which information is transformed before reaching its destination, and the way in which information measures are integrated at various organization levels. Little research has been done on how these characteristics, which determine the amount of shared information between managers and subordinates about a given event, affect their relationship.

Finally, another important design issue that has been largely ignored is the relationship between reward and information structures. If rewards are too highly contingent on the outputs of an information structure, the greater is the likelihood that it (information) will become controversial. For instance, Hopwood (1972) found that the concern for and acceptance of accounting data by cost center heads is related to the emphasis placed upon it, as compared to other criteria, in performance evaluation. The research issue, therefore, is which rewards, and how closely, to tie them to the information structure.

The availability of computers has begun to revolutionize information structures used by organizations. Before these newer structures are implemented, it is imperative that control system designers consider the changes that will be necessary in the behavioral variables to fully reap their benefits. The proposal here, it is hoped, provides a beginning towards that goal.

---

[16]One effort designed to foster greater agreement between participants is the management-by-objectives (MBO) effort. It would be interesting to see if the amount and patterns of resolving cognitive conflict differ in MBO systems as compared to other managerial systems.

BIBLIOGRAPHY

Ackoff, R. L., *A Concept of Corporate Planning* (New York: Wiley, 1970).

Ansari, S. L., Behavioral Factors in Variance Control, *Journal of Accounting Research* (Fall, 1976).

Anthony, R. N. & Dearden, J., *Management Control Systems* (Homewood, Ill.: Irwin, 1976).

Ashby, W. R., *An Introduction to Cybernetics* (London: Chapman & Hall, 1956).

Beer, S., *Cybernetics and Management* (New York: Wiley, 1964).

Blau, P. M., *On the Nature of Organization* (New York: Wiley, 1974).

Bruner, J. S., Goodnow, J. J. & Austin, G. A., *A Study of Thinking* (New York: Wiley, 1956).

Cammann, C. & Nadler, D. A., Fit Your Control System To Your Managerial Style, *Harvard Business Review* (Jan.-Feb., 1976), pp. 65–72.

Caplan, E. H., Behavioral Assumptions of Management Accounting—Report of a Field Study, *Accounting Review* (April, 1968), pp. 342–352.

Davis, G. B., *Management Information Systems* (New York: McGraw-Hill, 1974).

Drucker, P. M., Controls, Control and Management, in *Management Controls: New Directions In Basic Research,* C. P. Bonini, R. K. Jaedicke & H. M. Wagner, eds. (New York: McGraw-Hill, 1964).

Emery, F. E. & Trist, E. L., Socio-Technical Systems, in *Systems Thinking,* F. E. Emery, ed. (Harmondsworth, Middlesex: Penguin, 1969).

Ference, T. P., Organizational Communication System and the Decision Process, *Management Science* (Oct., 1970), pp. B285–293.

Festinger, L., *A Theory of Cognitive Dissonance* (Evanston, Ill.: Row, Petersen, 1957).

Fiedler, F. E., *A Theory of Leadership Effectiveness* (New York: McGraw-Hill, 1967).

Heider, F., Attitudes and Cognitive Organization, *Journal of Psychology,* 21, pp. 107–112.

Homans, G. C., *The Human Group* (New York: Harper & Row, 1950).

Hopwood, A. G., An Empirical Study of The Role of Accounting Data In Performance Evaluation, *Journal of Accounting Research, Empirical Studies* (1972), pp. 156–182.

Hovland, C. I., Janis, I. & Kelley, H. H., *Communication and Persuasion* (New Haven: Yale University Press, 1953).

Hovland, C. I., Mandell, W., Campbell, E. H., Brock, C., Luchins, A. S., Cohen, A. R., McGuire, W. J., Janis, I. L., Feierabend, R. L. & Anderson, N. H., *The Order of Presentation in Persuasion* (New Haven: Yale University Press, 1957).

Kast, F. E. & Rosensweig, J. E., *Contingency Views of Organization and Management* (Chicago: Scientific Research Associates, 1973).

Lawler, E. E. III & Rhode, J. R., *Information and Control in Organizations* (Pacific Palisades, Ca.: Goodyear Publ., 1976).

Lawrence, P. R. & Lorsch, J. W., *Organization and Environment* (Boston: Division of Research, Graduate School of Business Administration, Harvard University, 1967).

Mason, R. O. & Mitroff, I. I., A Program for Research on Management Information Systems, *Management Science* (Jan., 1973), pp. 457–487.

Morse, J. J., Organizational Characteristics and Individual Motivation, in F. E. Kast & R. E. Rosenzweig, eds., *Contingency Views of Organization and Management* (Chicago: Scientific Research Associates, 1973).

Osgood, C. E. & Tannenbaum, P. H., The Principle of Congruity in the Prediction of Attitude Change, *Psychological Review,* 62, (1955), pp. 42–55.

Reedy, G. E., *The Twilight of the Presidency* (New York: New American Library, 1970).

Simon, H. A., *Administrative Behavior* (New York: Free Press, 1957).

Sloan, A. P., *My Years with General Motors* (New York: Doubleday, 1964).

Schlesinger, A., M., Jr., *The Imperial Presidency* (Boston: Houghton Mifflin, 1973).

Tannenbaum, A. S., Control in Organizations: Individual Adjustment and Organizational Performance, in C. P. Bonini *et al.,* eds. *Management Controls* (New York: McGraw-Hill, 1964).

Taylor, F. W., *The Principle and Methods of Scientific Management* (New York: Harper & Row, 1911).

Urwick, L., *The Elements of Administration* (New York: Harper & Row, 1944).

Weber, M., *The Theory of Social and Economic Organization* (Glencoe, Ill.: Free Press, 1947).

Leadership Climate and the Use of Accounting Data in Performance Evaluation

Anthony G. Hopwood

The final effectiveness of any management accounting system is dependent not only upon its design and technical characteristics, but also upon the precise manner in which the resulting data are used. In the extreme, of course, a system contributes little or nothing to the efficiency of an organization's operations if the data are ignored. More generally, however, despite any amount of thought and consideration which may have gone into its design, no management accounting system ever achieves a perfect representation of the underlying structure of economic events. A careful use of the data is always essential to compensate for their many unavoidable inadequacies.

But it remains so much easier naively to acknowledge that the data should be used carefully than to specify what this entails in terms of managerial actions. Yet such an understanding is an essential prerequisite for the intelligent management of change and improvement. The present study was accordingly designed to investigate empirically some of the managerial factors which influence an accounting system's organizational and personal impacts. Particular consideration is given to the relationship between wider managerial behaviors and the use which is made of accounting data in performance evaluation.

From *The Accounting Review,* Vol. 49, No. 3 (July 1974), pp. 485–495.

Anthony G. Hopwood is at the Administrative Staff College, Henley-on-Thames, England.

The author wishes to acknowledge the helpful comments and advice of Professor L. Richard Hoffman of the University of Chicago.

DIFFERENT WAYS OF USING ACCOUNTING DATA IN PERFORMANCE EVALUATION

The investigation is based upon an analysis of the managerial determinants of the following three distinct styles of using budgeted and actual cost information in performance evaluation.

1. *A Budget Constrained Style.* Despite the many unavoidable problems in using accounting data as comprehensive measures of managerial performance, the manager's performance is primarily evaluated on the basis of his ability continually to meet the short-term budget.
2. *A Profit Conscious Style.* The manager's performance is evaluated on the basis of his ability to increase the long-term effectiveness of his unit in relation to the goals of the organization. The accounting data, although indicating whether the budget has been met, do not necessarily indicate

whether long-term effectiveness is being attained. Therefore, while important, they are used with some care in a flexible and creative manner, and where necessary, supplemented by alternative sources of information.

3. *A Nonaccounting Style.* Accounting data play a relatively unimportant part in the evaluation of the manager's performance.

Previous empirical research has demonstrated that these three ways of using accounting data have significantly different organizational and personal effects.[1] Although both the Budget Constrained and Profit Conscious styles resulted in a higher degree of involvement with costs than the Nonaccounting style, only the Profit Conscious style succeeded in attaining this without resulting in either emotional costs for managers or defensive behavior which was dysfunctional for the organization. The Budget Constrained style resulted in a belief that the evaluation was unjust, in widespread tension and worry on the job, and in feelings of distrust and dissatisfaction with the supervisor. Not only were the managers who were evaluated in this way found to manipulate the accounting data and make decisions which resulted in higher long-term processing costs for the company as a whole, but the consequent conflict and rivalry between colleagues impeded the cooperation which was so essential for controlling their interdependent activities. In contrast, the Profit Conscious style, while seen as very demanding, was accepted. It resulted in levels of tension and in satisfaction with the supervisor and colleague supportiveness similar to those which prevailed under a Nonaccounting evaluation.

[1]A. G. Hopwood, "An Empirical Study of the Role of Accounting Data in Performance Evaluation," *Empirical Research in Accounting: Selected Studies, 1972,* Supplement to Vol. X, *Journal of Accounting Research.*

FACTORS INFLUENCING THE USE MADE OF ACCOUNTING DATA

As Argyris noted in this study of the personal impact of budgets in four industrial organizations, the way in which a manager uses budgetary data is only one aspect of his more general approach to the job.

> . . . It became obvious that the way people expressed their interest in budgets, and the way in which they described and used them, were directly related to the pattern of leadership in their daily industrial life.[2]

Many recent studies have made a distinction between the instrumental or task aspects and the socio-emotional aspects of managerial behavior. In this study, these two aspects of behavior are characterized in terms of the two dimensions of the Ohio State University Leadership Behavior Description Questionnaire (LBDQ), namely, Initiation of Structure and Consideration.[3] The Initiation of Structure dimension reflects the extent to which a manager defines both his own work role and those of his subordinates. A high score is indicative of clearly delineated roles and attempts to establish clear channels of communication, patterns of organization, and detailed job instructions. The Consideration dimension reflects the extent to which a manager is friendly, trusting, and respectful of his subordinates. A high score is indicative of a manager who is willing to explain his actions and who tries to maintain warm and personal relationships with his subordinates.

[2]C. Argyris, *The Impact of Budgets on People* (School of Business and Public Administration, Cornell University, 1952), p. 24.

[3]E. A. Fleishman, "A Leader Behavior Description for Industry," in *Leader Behavior: Its Description and Measurement,* edited by R. M. Stogdill and A. E. Coons (Bureau of Business Research, Ohio State University, 1957), pp. 120–33.

A manager who is seen as using a Budget Constrained style of evaluation is expected to have a leadership style characterized by a high score on the Initiation of Structure dimension of the LBDQ and a low score on the Consideration dimension. Because accounting data have an aura of objectivity and clarity, their use in a rather direct manner should appeal to a manager who is concerned with establishing well-defined work procedures and means for evaluation.[4] To use the data in such a manner, however, the manager must also be relatively insensitive in his interpersonal relations, being more concerned with the task and goal attainment than with the maintenance of cordial and trusting relations with people. A more considerate supervisor is more likely to have that degree of empathy, and perhaps the open communications with his subordinates, which allow him to see the threat and the subsequent defenses which a rigid concern with the accounting data is capable of creating.[5]

It is, however, impossible to provide any adequate understanding of managerial evaluative behaviors without also considering the complex nature of the interrelationships between different levels of an organizational hierarchy. Since a manager himself is subject to an evaluation which may take on a similar form to those already described, it is necessary to look at the ways in which the demands and pressures are passed down from one level in the hierarchy to the next. In his simulation study of a firm's information and decision systems, Bonini[6] called such a process a "contagion effect," a term which is used in the present context to refer to any tendency for managers to evaluate their subordinates as they themselves are evaluated.

The contagion effect is particularly pertinent for a Budget Constrained style of evaluation because of the additive nature of accounting data. If a manager's superior pays attention to the extent to which the budget is met, the manager can satisfy this objective only by similarly paying attention to the budget variances of his own subordinates.

The above arguments can be summarized in terms of the following hypotheses which are discussed in this paper:

> A manager is more likely to be seen as using a Budget Constrained style of evaluation if (a) he has a leadership style which is characterized by low Consideration and high Initiation of Structure; (b) he is himself evaluated on the basis of a Budget Constrained style.

RESEARCH SITE

The manufacturing division of a Chicago-based company which served as the site for the study had a labor force in excess of 20,000 persons and an annual revenue of several hundred million dollars. The division's management accounting system had been in operation for over a decade and it was based on flexible budgets, standard costing techniques, and the allocation of certain overhead costs. All levels of management received monthly reports comparing their actual and budgeted costs; these were supplemented by daily and and weekly reports on such matters as production, labor, and supplies.

---

[4] P. Weissenberg and L. Grunefeld, "Relationships Among Leadership Dimensions and Cognitive Style," *Journal of Applied Psychology* (October 1966), pp. 392–5.

[5] See E. A. Fleishman and J. A. Slater, "Humanizing Relationships in a Small Business: the Relationship Between the Leader's Behavior and His Empathy Toward Subordinates," *Advanced Management* (March 1961), pp. 18–20.

[6] C. P. Bonini, *Simulation of Information and Decision Systems in the Firm* (Prentice-Hall, 1963). Mann and Baumgartel provided some evidence that a manager's general attitude towards costs influenced his subordinates' concern with them: F. Mann and H. Baumgartel, *The Supervisor's Concern with Costs in an Electric Power Company* (Survey Research Center, Institute for Social Research, University of Michigan, 1953).

The division was organized on the basis of a series of areas, departments, and cost centers. Each area included several departments; and each department, a series of cost centers. A simplified organization chart is shown in Figure 1. The cost centers were usually under the responsibility of a general foreman, although some foremen and assistant departmental supervisors also had responsibilities at this level. One person could also be in charge of several cost centers. At the time the study was conducted, there were over 350 cost centers under the responsibility of 193 cost center heads.

Questionnaires were sent to 27 departmental supervisors and the 193 cost center heads. When a respondent failed to return the questionnaire two follow-up letters were sent to him. The final response rate was very high: 96% (26 out of 27) for the supervisors and 87% (167 out of 193) for the cost center heads.

MEASUREMENT OF THE VARIABLES

It was preferable to test for the presence of a contagion effect on the basis of independent reports from at least two levels in the organizational hierarchy so as to avoid any tendency for persons at just one level to report in a consistent manner. Therefore, the departmental supervisors were asked to report on the evaluative styles of the area managers and the cost center heads on the supervisors' styles.

The Area Manager's Style of Evaluation

The major methodological problem confronting the investigation concerned the means for empirically distinguishing among the different styles of using accounting data in performance evaluation. Although a broad set of behaviors had been isolated for each style, their operational definition necessitated an understanding of the meanings which the managers attached to these behaviors and the language which they used to describe them.

During a series of exploratory interviews, it was found that all levels of management referred to patterns of evaluative behaviors which were in agreement with the distinctions described above. In particular, a Budget Constrained orientation was referred to in terms of "meeting the budget" and a Profit Conscious orientation in terms of "con-

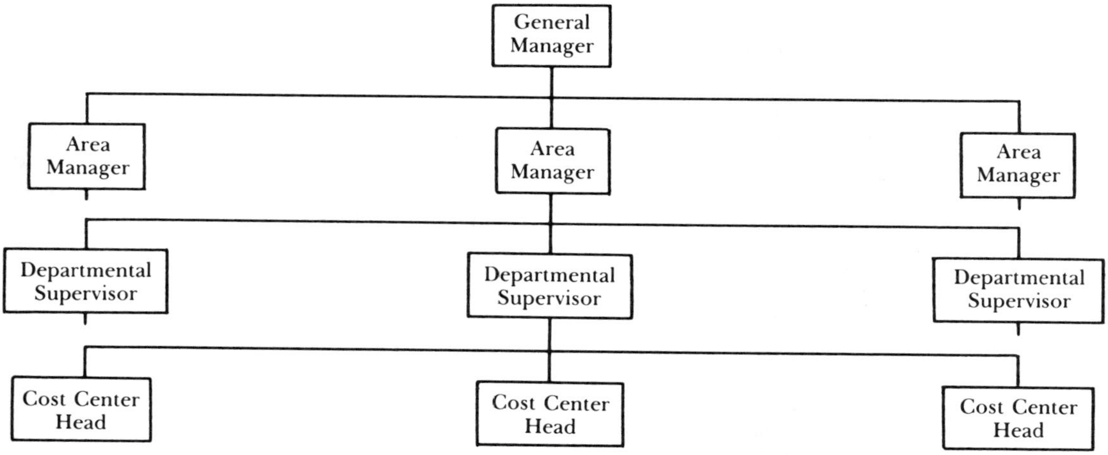

FIGURE 1. Organization Chart for Subject Company

cern with costs." These two phrases had distinct meanings which were known to all the managers interviewed, and therefore they were used as the basis for operationally defining the three styles of evaluation.

Each departmental supervisor was presented with a list of eight performance criteria which included both meeting the budget and concern with costs, as well as cooperation with colleagues, getting along with the boss, effort put into the job, concern with quality, attitude towards the work and company, and ability to handle the men. He was asked to rank-order the three factors which he saw as being most important in his own evaluation, and the following operational definitions of the evaluative styles were then defined on the basis of the rankings.[7] The number of respondents in each group is shown in parentheses.

1. *Budget Constrained Style* (BC): meeting the budget ranked among the top three criteria (6).[8]
2. *Profit Conscious Style* (PC): concern with costs, but not meeting the budget, ranked among the top three criteria (10).
3. *Nonaccounting Style* (NA): neither meeting the budget nor concern with costs ranked among the top three criteria (10).[9]

The Departmental Supervisors' Style of Evaluation

Although the 167 cost center heads completed an identical series of questions on their supervisors' styles of evaluation, the same operational definitions could obviously not be used because several subordinate cost center heads reported on the style of each of the 27 supervisors. Furthermore, in some departments, as is discussed subsequently, the cost center heads' perceptions were not in agreement. Some means of characterizing the *dominant* style reported by the cost center heads in each department was therefore required.

The following operational definitions of the supervisors' styles of evaluation are used in the study. The number of supervisors assigned to each style is shown in parentheses.

1. *Budget Constrained Style:* at least 40% of the cost center heads in a department reported that meeting the budget was one of the three most important criteria in their evaluation (12).
2. *Profit Conscious Style:* at least 40% of the cost center heads reported that concern with costs was one of the three most important criteria used in their evaluation, but less than 40% reported that meeting the budget was similarly important (7).
3. *Nonaccounting Style:* less than 40% of the cost center heads in a department reported that meeting the budget and concern with costs were amongst the three most important criteria in their evaluation (8).

Forty percent was selected since it was the median percentage for the relative importance of concern with costs, and although slightly above the median for the relative importance of meeting the budget, it took advantage of a break in the series.

[7]A discussion of the evidence on the validity of the operational procedures is given in Hopwood, "An Empirical Study of the Role of Accounting Data in Performance Evaluation."

[8]In an analysis of the cost center heads' perceptions of the departmental supervisors' styles of evaluation which was reported in the previous paper, a distinction was made between a Budget Constrained (BC) and a Budget-Profit (BP) style. The BC style referred to cases where meeting the budget, but not concern with costs, was ranked among the three most important criteria, and the BP style to cases where both the accounting-related criteria were in the top three. Subsequent analysis showed that the BC orientation dominated in the BP situation. There were no significant differences between the effects of the two styles, although the BP style did result in significantly different consequences than the pure PC style. In view of this evidence and the small size of the sample, the pure BC and BP styles are combined into a single Budget Constrained style in this analysis.

[9]The operational definition of the Nonaccounting style should be interpreted as implying a low *relative* importance to the accounting related criteria. It neither precludes some importance being attached to them nor their use for nonevaluative purposes.

The Departmental Supervisors' Leadership Style

The 48 items of the Ohio State Leadership Behavior Description Questionnaire were included in the questionnaire sent to the cost center heads. The responses were coded to provide scores for the Consideration and Initiation of Structure dimensions of leadership behavior. The totals for all responding cost center heads under a departmental supervisor were then averaged to arrive at values of the dimensions for each supervisor. The range of the values of the Consideration dimension was found to be 50 to 92 (the possible range was 0–112); the mean value, 75.6; and the standard deviation, 10.6. The range for the Initiation of Structure scores was 30 to 58 (with a possible range of 0–80); the mean value, 46.9; and the standard deviation, 7.0. The two dimensions were found to be independent (Kendall's Tau= −0.04).[10]

SELECTIVE USE OF A BUDGET CONSTRAINED STYLE

The cost center heads in some departments were not in agreement over whether or not their supervisors used a Budget Constrained style of evaluation. While at least two-thirds of the responding cost center heads in 19 of the 27 departments agreed that their supervisors either did or did not use this style, only 40% to 57% of the cost center heads in the remaining 8 departments reported that he did. Before proceeding with the main analysis, it was important first to investigate whether these differences in opinions were due to inaccurate perceptions or the insensitivity of the measurement procedures or a real selective use of this style by some supervisors. An analysis was therefore made of the factors influencing the style of evaluation reported by the 54 cost center heads employed in the 8 departments where there was substantial disagreement.

The analysis indicated that the cost center heads reporting a Budget Constrained style in these 8 departments tended to have been less successful in meeting their budget. In Table 1 the 54 cost center heads are divided on the basis of (1) whether or not they reported a Budget Constrained evaluation and (2) whether or not they had, on average, met their budget over the 6-month period prior to the receipt of the questionnaire. There is a difference between the two criterion groups, but the difference is only significant at the 11% level.[11]

[10]A review of the relationships between the two dimensions of the LBDQ is given by P. Weissenberg and M. J. Kavanagh in "The Independence of Initiating Structure and Consideration: A Review of the Evidence," *Personnel Psychology* (Spring 1972), pp. 119–30.

[11]There was no significant difference between these two criterion groups when the analysis was based on the average performance in the 9-month period prior to the receipt of the questionnaire. For the remaining 19 departments where there was substantial agreement over whether

TABLE 1. Relationship Between the Reported Style of Evaluation and the Extent to Which the Cost Center Heads Met the Budget for Departments with Disagreement

Relationship Between Actual Costs and the Budget for 6-Month Period Prior to Receipt of Questionnaire	Cost Center Head Reports a Budget Constrained Style of Evaluation	Cost Center Head Does Not Report a Budget Constrained Style of Evaluation	N
On average at least met the budget	9	17	26
On average did not meet the budget	16	12	28
N	25	29	54

$x^2 = 2.69$; 1 d.f.; $P < 0.11$.

Prevention might, however, have been seen as being preferable to cure. An analysis was therefore made to see whether the supervisors of these 8 departments focused their Budget Constrained approach on the large cost centers which had the greatest potential to influence the overall departmental results. The cost center heads were divided on the basis of whether or not they were responsible for a cost center or a series of cost centers which dealt with total annual costs above, equal to, or less than the departmental median. From Table 2 it can be seen that these supervisors were more likely to be seen as using a Budget Constrained style by persons in charge of the *relatively* large cost centers in a department.[12]

The findings suggest that the supervisors of the 8 departments where there was substantial disagreement over their style of evaluation used the Budget Constrained style with discretion, emphasizing it where it was seen as likely to have the greatest impact on the departmental results. As such, the evidence is in agreement with other studies which have shown that managers do not necessarily use one personal style of management irrespective of their circumstances and subordinates.[13]

LEADERSHIP STYLE AND THE USE OF ACCOUNTING DATA

As can be seen from an examination of Table 3, both the Budget Constrained and Profit Conscious supervisors were seen as creating a structured job environment geared to the attainment of their perceptions of the organization's goals. The Budget Constrained supervisors, however, were seen as showing significantly less consideration for the feelings and opinions of their cost center heads than either their Profit Conscious or Nonaccounting colleagues. Yet without the maintenance of such a considerate managerial climate, the structured concern with the financial aspects of performance was seen in terms of a threatening emphasis on the accounting data in isolation of their organizational context. The findings are therefore supportive of hypothesis (a).

or not the supervisor used a Budget Constrained style, there was no relationship between the reported style and performance in either the 6- or 9-month period.

[12]There was no relationship between the reported style and the *absolute* size of the cost centers. Also no significant relationship was found between the reported style and either relative or absolute size in the nineteen departments with substantial agreement.

[13]See E. Kay and R. Hastman, *An Evaluation of Work Planning and Goal Setting Discussions* (General Electric Behavioral Research Service, 1966), and A. Lowin and J. R. Craig, "The Influence of Level of Performance on Managerial Style: An Experimental Object Lesson in the Ambiguity of Correlation Data," *Organizational Behavior and Human Performance* (November 1968), pp. 440–58.

TABLE 2. Relationship Between the Reported Style of Evaluation and the Relative Size of the Cost Centers for Departments with Disagreement

The Total Annual Costs of the Cost Center(s) in Relation to the Median Cost for Its Department	Cost Center Head Reports a Budget Constrained Style of Evaluation	Cost Center Head Does Not Report a Budget Constrained Style of Evaluation	N
Above the departmental median	16	10	26
Equal to or less than the departmental median	9	19	28
N	25	29	54

$x^2 = 5.23$; 1 d.f.; $P < 0.05$.

THE CONTAGION EFFECT

The contagion effect was very strong for the Budget Constrained style of evaluation. With supervisors divided on the basis of whether or not their perceptions of the area managers' styles of evaluation were in agreement with their cost center heads' perceptions of their own dominant style, it can be seen in Table 4 that only one of the 6 supervisors who reported a Budget Constrained evaluation did not pass down the same style to his cost center heads.[14] In contrast, there was no evidence of a contagion effect for either the Profit Conscious or Nonaccounting styles. For the Profit Conscious style, however, many of the supervisors maintained a concern with the accounting data, although the concern was just as likely to be rigidly tied to the short-term budget variances as it was to longer-term cost effectiveness. Four of the 10 supervisors who were evaluated on this basis evaluated their cost center heads in a Budget Constrained manner compared with the 3 who maintained the Profit Conscious style.

[14]While the Budget Constrained style might have been easier to resist if the departmental variances had been consistently favorable, the single supervisor who was the exception to the rule resisted the contagion effect despite having had unfavorable departmental variances for most of the fifteen months prior to the receipt of the questionnaire. His cost center heads saw him as having an average concern with a structured job environment (his Initiation of Structure score of 47 equals the median for the sample of supervisors), but an exceptionally high consideration for their feelings and opinions. His Consideration score of 89 was the second highest in the sample, and compared with the median of 79.

TABLE 4. Relationship Between the Area Managers' and the Departmental Supervisors' Styles of Evaluation

Relationship between the Cost Center Heads' Perception of the Supervisor's Dominant Style of Evaluation and the Supervisor's Perception of the Area Manager's Style	Supervisor's Perception of the Area Manager's Style of Evaluation			
	BC	PC	NA	N
Agreement	5	3	4	12
Disagreement	1	7	6	14
N	6	10	10	26

Supervisors were seen as passing on a Budget Constrained style even though they *intended* to do otherwise. All the departmental supervisors were asked to report how they thought that they evaluated their cost center heads, the responses being referred to as the supervisor's intended style of evaluation. It can be seen in Table 5 that only 2 of the 6

TABLE 3. Relationship Between Leadership Style and the Supervisors' Style of Evaluation

Leadership Style	The Cost Center Heads' Perception of the Supervisors' Dominant Style of Evaluation			Significance of Paired Comparison[a]
	BC	PC	NA	
Mean Initiation of Structure	48.0	51.3	41.9	*BCvNA*: $p < 0.01$ *PCvNA*: $p < 0.05$
Mean Consideration	70.6	80.9	79.4	*BCvPC*: $p < 0.05$ *BCvNA*: $p < 0.05$
N	12	7	8	

[a]Significance of paired comparisons is based on the Mann-Whitney *U* Test. Unless otherwise stated, a paired comparison is not significant at the 5% level.

TABLE 5. Relationship Between the Area Managers' Style of Evaluation and the Departmental Supervisors' Intended Style of Evaluation

Relationship Between the Supervisor's Perception of the Area Manager's Style and the Supervisor's Intended Style	Supervisor's Perception of the Area Manager's Style of Evaluation			
	BC	PC	NA	N
Agreement	2	7	7	16
Disagreement	4	3	3	10
N	6	10	10	26

supervisors who reported being evaluated on the basis of a Budget Constrained style intended to evaluate their cost center heads in the same way. The other 4 supervisors intended to use a Profit Conscious style. In comparison, a majority of the supervisors who were evaluated on the basis of either a Profit Conscious or a Nonaccounting style intended to evaluate their cost center heads in the same manner, although they did not necessarily possess the requisite managerial abilities to put this into effect.[15]

The supervisors whose performance was evaluated upon the basis of their departments' short-term budget variances were in a conflict situation. It was easy for them to feel that it was necessary to evaluate similarly their cost center heads in order to obtain the desired results. Yet from their own experience they knew that this was an unfair evaluation which was likely to result in excessive tension and worry. One of them described his own experiences in the following way:

> "When I'm in the red [the Area Manager] will always blame you. I'll get a black eye. Even if I'm not to blame, I'll still get a black eye. I like a good budget to shoot at but when you have obvious discrepancies in the budget, then it's difficult to show what you are doing. A good budget is a good thing, but a bad budget is a bad thing."

Yet he felt that he had to pass on the Budget Constrained style since his own superiors "will generally criticize me if I'm unfavorable, regardless of reason." So for some of his cost center heads, "if they're in the red, I'll probably know why, but I'll ask *them* why and I'll tarpoon [sic] a few things with them." He was, however, aware of the anxiety and undesirable behaviors which this could cause.

> "The accounting numbers are a big thing for most of [the cost center heads]. It gets down to personalities; it's bound to. Generally [a cost center head] has to get a reasonable product to get a reasonable result. Well, he may want good relations with those who supply him with [his material], but then he wants to make himself look good, and to do that he makes others look poor."

With such problems in mind, he tried not to evaluate two of his cost center heads on the basis of their short-term budget variances because he thought that their highly skilled subordinates would react to the subsequent pressure by leaving the company. Since the two cost centers were also "low in real dollars," he was prepared to use a different style of evaluation.

All 5 of the superviors who were seen as passing down their own Budget Constrained evaluation used a similar means of resolving the conflict with which they were confronted. They were, in fact, responsible for 5 of the 8 departments where there was disagreement over this aspect of the supervisor's style of evaluation and in which, as we have already seen, the more rigid style was used for

[15]Recent evidence relating self-reported leadership behavior to subordinate descriptions of behavior has also found that the two are not necessarily equivalent. See M. G. Evans, "Leadership Behavior: Demographic Factors and Agreement Between Subordinate and Self-Descriptions," *Personnel Psychology* (Winter 1972), pp. 649–53, and W. K. Graham and T. Olena, "Perceptions of Leader Behavior and Evaluation of Leaders Across Organizational Levels," *Experimental Publications System* (February 1970), p. 144A.

the larger cost centers and possibly those with a poor budget record.[16]

DISCUSSION

In supporting the hypotheses, the evidence allows the initial distinctions which were made among the three styles of using accounting data in performance evaluation to be placed in a wider managerial perspective. For the final impact of an accounting system on managerial behavior has been shown to depend on its interaction with the forms of social- and self-controls which are reflected within the various leadership climates and the personal motives and defenses which they activate.

In being responsive to the feelings and opinions of their cost center heads, the Profit Conscious supervisors recognized and responded to the threat which the financial concerns and structured job environment were capable of creating. But, in addition, the supportive organizational climate encouraged the cost center heads to discuss openly their budgetary problems with the supervisor.[17] This might, of course, be viewed as a means of avoiding responsibility, although this would be an inappropriate description of the situation in these departments. The Profit Conscious supervisors, while listening to explanations, certainly did not readily accept them. In the words of one cost center head:

> "[A Budget Constrained supervisor] takes the budget to heart, while what [a Profit Conscious supervisor] does is to accept it upon himself and if he doesn't agree with it, then he'll reject the budget. He's a real tough guy and it's difficult to argue with him. You have got to have some good arguments, but if he agrees with you, then out goes the budget. [The Budget Constrained supervisor] can be stubborn. He aims to stay right on his budget and that's it."

The budgetary pressures associated with the Profit Conscious style of evaluation were seen, in the words of another cost center head, as being applied "where they [were] appropriate." The cost center heads were aware of both the supervisors' willingness to listen and, in turn, explain the reasons for accepting and rejecting explanations. As a result, the supervisors were provided with the alternative sources of information which enabled them to test continually the validity of the accounting data and keep the job environment devoid of the rigidities of the Budget Constrained approach. In contrast, the cost center heads subject to a Budget Constrained evaluation hardly felt free to offer realistic explanations. One such cost center head described his supervisor's attitude in terms of "just don't do it, rather than asking for explanations."

Unfortunately the study did not directly investigate the relationship among the three styles of using accounting data and the overall effectiveness of operations.[18] The observed leadership style configurations are, however, of interest in this respect since studies using the LBDQ dimensions have found that, although the Initiation of Structure and Consideration scores were designed to be independent,

---

[16]The percentage of cost center heads in the 5 departments reporting a Budget Constrained style were: 40%, 50%, 50%, 50% and 57%.

[17]In a field study conducted in three major industrial organizations Read found that trust in the supervisor resulted in accurate upward communications. See W. H. Read, "Upward Communication in Industrial Hierarchies," *Human Relations* (February 1962), pp. 3–15.

[18]A review of the evidence on the differential effects of the various styles did provide some basis for concluding that the Profit Conscious style was likely to be more effective than the Budget Constrained style in situations which required a careful consideration of a wide variety of information, a high degree of interunit coordination, a long time horizon, and an ability to respond in a flexible manner to unexpected circumstances: see the discussion in Hopwood, *op. cit.*

supervisors who are rated high on both dimensions are considered to be more effective by their superiors, as well as favorably influencing their subordinates' morale and improving indices of productivity and labor turnover. Fleishman and Harris,[19] for instance, found that for production supervisors scoring high on both dimensions, the structured job environment was seen as less threatening and had little or no effect on grievances and turnover. That a number of other studies have come to similar conclusions[20] provides some indirect evidence on the potential benefits of the Profit Conscious style, although it should be stressed that such findings are no more than suggestive in the present context.

However, while recognizing the need for further research on the overall effects of the various styles, the findings do point to a number of implications for both accounting practice and the study of the behavioral impact of accounting data. At the very least, they serve to emphasize the importance of the accountant's educational function. With the increasing complexity of management accounting procedures, it is unrealistic to expect managers to use the data in an appropriate manner without adequate preparation and training. But they need to be informed not only of the objectives and advantages of the accounting system, real though they may be, but also of the inadequacies of the data and the consequences of attaching too much importance to the short-term reports—a far more difficult task.

The different ways of using the data were not, however, simply based on ignorance. They were associated with much more widespread differences in managerial attitudes and behaviors, and for the Budget Constrained style, with the evaluative style of the superiors. Even the most carefully designed educational program is unlikely to provide an easy solution to the problem, and it would certainly require the active cooperation of specialists in organizational development. Hence, consideration needs to be given to how the use which is made of the data can be explicitly recognized as a factor in the design of accounting systems. This does not mean that accountants should immediately strive to stifle the undesirable responses by filling the obvious loopholes in their systems. Rather, there is a need for system designs to take account of the constraints and opportunities of their managerial environment in the manner that Wildavsky has contrived to design federal budgeting procedures which are congruent with the political process.[21]

Such a task requires both practical experimentation and systematic research. But, so far, many of the studies of the effects of accounting data on decision behavior have ignored their managerial context. They have all too often merely presented reports based on different accounting methods to samples of financial analysts, managers, and students, and observed whether their decision behaviors were dependent upon the type of data received. The present findings suggest, however, that the relationship between accounting data and decision behavior is moderated by the leadership style and social context of the decision maker.

---

[19] E. A. Fleishman and E. F. Harris, "Patterns of Leadership Behavior Related to Employee Grievances and Turnover," *Personnel Psychology* (Spring 1962), pp. 43–56.

[20] E. A. Fleishman and J. Simmons, "Relationship Between Leadership Patterns and Effectiveness Ratings Among Israeli Foremen," *Personnel Psychology* (Summer 1970), pp. 169–72; A. W. Halpin, "The Leader Behavior and Effectiveness of Aircraft Commanders," in Stodgill and Coons; H. Oaklander and E. A. Fleishman, "Patterns of Leadership Related to Organizational Stress in Hospital Settings," *Administrative Science Quarterly* (March 1964), pp. 520–32. A survey of the relationship between the two dimensions of the LBQD and various criteria of organizational effectiveness is given in A. K. Korman, " 'Consideration,' 'Initiating Structure' and Organizational Criteria—A Review," *Personnel Psychology* (Winter 1966), pp. 349–61.

[21] A. Wildavsky, *The Politics of the Budgetary Process* (Little, Brown, 1964) and *Toward a Radical Incrementalism: A Proposal to Aid Congress in Reform of the Budgetary Process* (American Institute for Public Policy Research, 1965).

Much greater explicit consideration needs to be given to these factors in further research, although, in so doing, there may be a need to rely less on the abstractions of laboratory experimentation and more on the complexities of field research.[22]

[22]This is not to deny that some aspects of the problem can be studied in controlled experiments. Lowin and Craig showed the potential for simulating different leadership styles in the laboratory, and among others, Mock *et al.* have recently reported experiments on the effects of cognitive style on decision behavior: See T. J. Mock, T. L. Estrin, and M. A. Vasarhelyi, "Learning Patterns, Decision Approach, and Value of Information," *Journal of Accounting Research* (Spring 1972), pp. 129–53. Nevertheless, there are formidable difficulties in trying to simulate hierarchical patterns and organizational contexts within the analytical and time constraints of the experimental method.

PART 3

Individual and Group Behaviour: Foundations of Behavioural Accounting

It is noted in Part 2 that the internal context of management accounting systems (MAS) encompasses both the organization's formal structure and its individuals. Part 2 deals with the organization's formal structure. The readings in this part of the book narrow the scope of the organizational context of management accounting to the individual level. At this level, the behaviour of the members of the organization, as individuals or in groups, becomes significant to the design and use of accounting information and control systems.

The importance of human behaviour, motivations and values to management accounting is highlighted in the introduction to the book, and is exemplified in Caplan's (1966) assumptions about individual and group behaviour. Given this importance, variables and mechanisms which are relevant to individual and group behaviour and motivation have been drawn from the basic behavioural disciplines of psychology, social psychology and sociology, and incorporated into management accounting research.

Psychology, the study of the human mind and its processes, is concerned with the nature of human behaviour at the individual level. It deals with concepts such as motivation, perception and cognition, and is potentially relevant to the management accountant in answering questions about the kinds of motivation and behaviours which are produced by accounting systems and reports; how individuals in the organization perceive the accounting system, its reports and information; and whether or not their perceptions of that information differ from those of the accountant.

Although concepts from individual psychology form the basis of our knowledge of behaviour in organizations, the contingency approach of this book indicates that this behaviour cannot be studied in isolation from organizational contextual variables, such as the internal administrative processes of the organization, and its environment. Social psychology is the study of the individual in a social context. This branch of psychology is also concerned with concepts such as motivation, behaviour and perception. However, social psychology is distinguished from other branches in that it concentrates on how these concepts are affected by social and organizational factors. Individual behaviour and attitudes can be influenced by social interactions to result in significantly different group behaviour and group attitudes. For management accounting, social psychology provides a theoretical framework for approaching problems such as how an individual's behaviour is influenced by the informational and control environments, and the organizational situation in which he functions; and whether or not his response to the information and control system differs if he acts as an individual or as a member of a group.

By contrast with psychology, which deals with the unique characteristics and behaviour of individuals, and social psychology, which examines the influence of social settings and group interactions on individual behaviour, sociology deals with the assumed aggregate behaviour of individuals and groups based on sociological characteristics. Sociology is concerned with the broad classification of organizational members by status or class, for example, and with the consequent interactions of people across classifications, particularly cooperation, mobility and conflict interactions. Sociological research is relevant to the management accountant in that it provides insight into how the information and control system may affect behaviour and whether it will contribute to or reduce conflict at different hierarchical (status) or functional (occupational) levels.

FRAMEWORK FOR ANALYSIS

Figure 3.1 provides a framework for examining the interdependence between MAS and concepts of individual and group behaviour. The behavioural assumptions underlying the design of management accounting systems are based upon theories of individual behaviour and motivation, moderating and intervening variables which may influence that behaviour, and the environment and context within which the behaviour occurs. Theories of individual behaviour include such aspects as individual needs and expectations; intervening variables include individuals' perceptual, information processing, and response limitations; and environmental and contextual influences include organizational characteristics such as organizational structure, reward systems and performance evaluation measures.

Of ultimate concern is the design of information and control systems. The linkage between our knowledge of individual behaviour and the design of such systems is the nature of the interactions between the individual and the system. Lawler and Rhode (1976) provide a useful description of this interaction by considering the organizational positions of the individual in relation to MAS, and by developing a series of systems characteristics which are based on those positions. The organizational positions include the individual as decision maker or as being subject to measurement or control by the management accounting system. Systems characteristics include such aspects as the nature

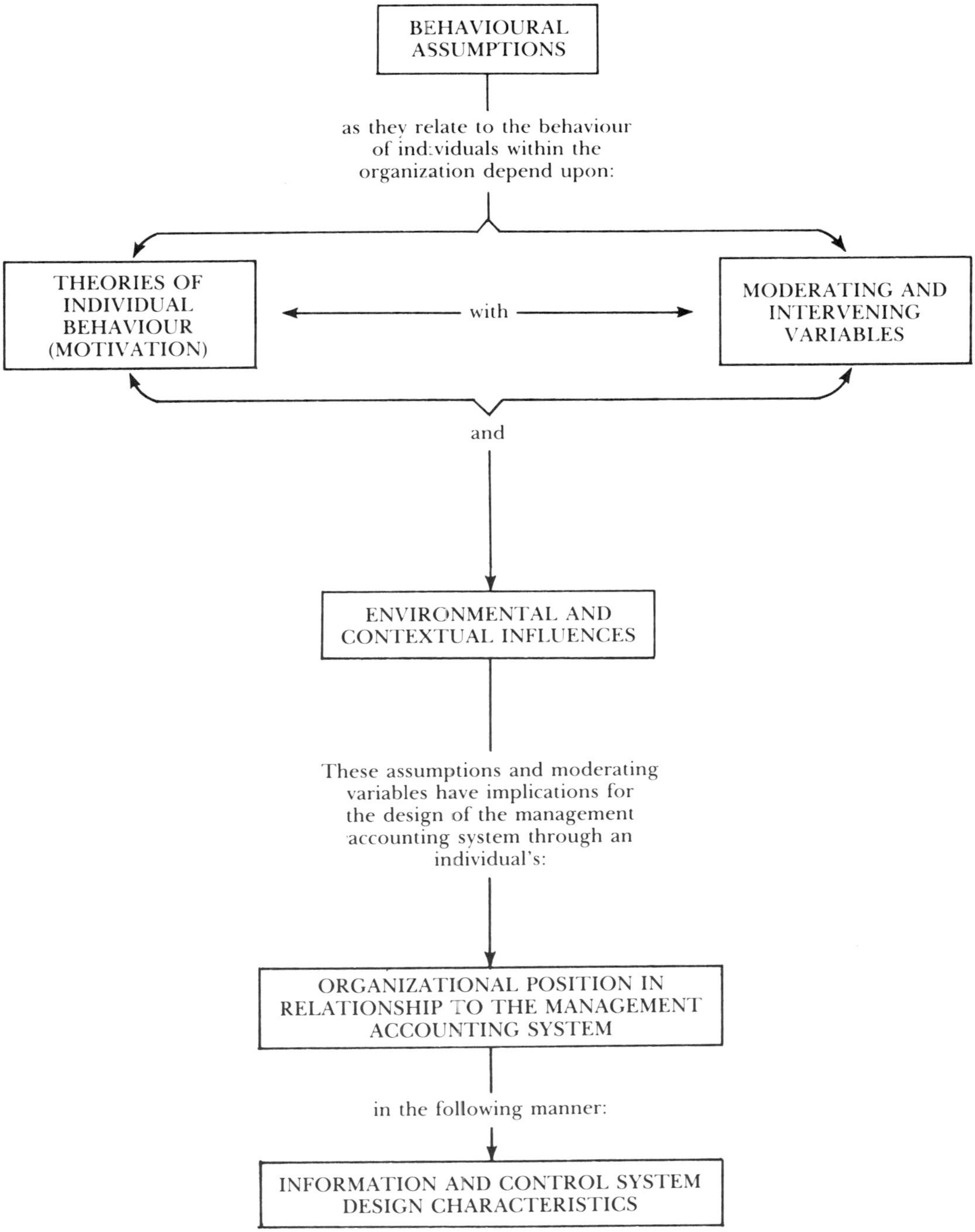

FIGURE 3.1 Behavioral Assumptions of MAS Design—A Framework for Analysis

of the standards which are used in the control system and the speed, frequency, pattern and form of the communication of information.

The readings in this part of the book are concerned with the specific relationship between MAS and individual and group behaviour. In this introduction to the readings, we will examine the bases for developing the behavioural assumptions underlying MAS: relevant theories of individual behaviour from the disciplines of psychology, social psychology and sociology, the moderating and intervening variables, and the environmental and contextual influences on individual behaviour. Although the individual is only one part of the internal context of MAS, the behavioural science literature accessible to the MAS designer at this level is extremely comprehensive and extensive. Consequently, the introduction to this part of the book is relatively larger than the introductions to previous parts.

THEORIES OF INDIVIDUAL BEHAVIOUR

We will consider first those theories of individual behaviour and motivation which are premised on the satisfaction of individual needs, and which formed the basis of much research in management accounting.

Need Satisfaction Theories

Need satisfaction theories of motivation, particularly those formulated by Maslow (1943, 1970) and Herzberg (1959), dominated research in individual and organizational psychology during the 1950s and 1960s. In essence, Maslow's "need hierarchy theory" proposes that motivation is the result of an individual's attempt to satisfy his needs. The theory maintains that these needs are inherent in human beings, are relatively universal, and can be classified and structured in a hierarchy of prepotency or influence over the individual's behaviour. The hierarchy he originally proposed is shown in Figure 3.2, with the needs at the base of the pyramid having the highest degree of prepotency.

The existence of needs activates behaviour through what Maslow called the "deprivation-gratification" cycle. The absence of satisfaction (deprivation of a more potent need such as physiological) results in the domination of that need over the personality and behaviour of the individual. Subsequent gratification of the need leads to the activation of the next higher, but relatively less potent, need within the hierarchical structure. Once a growth-oriented individual has reached the apex of the pyramid, gratification of the self-actualization need then causes an increase in its influence on behaviour, rather than a decrease.

Several modifications of Maslow's hierarchy of human needs have been proposed. One uses a two group classification of needs instead of five, condensing the physiological and safety needs into a "lower level" group, and affiliation, esteem and self-actualization needs into a "higher level" group (Lawler, 1973). Another approach refines Maslow's need structure into three categories: existence, relatedness and growth (Alderfer, 1969, 1972).

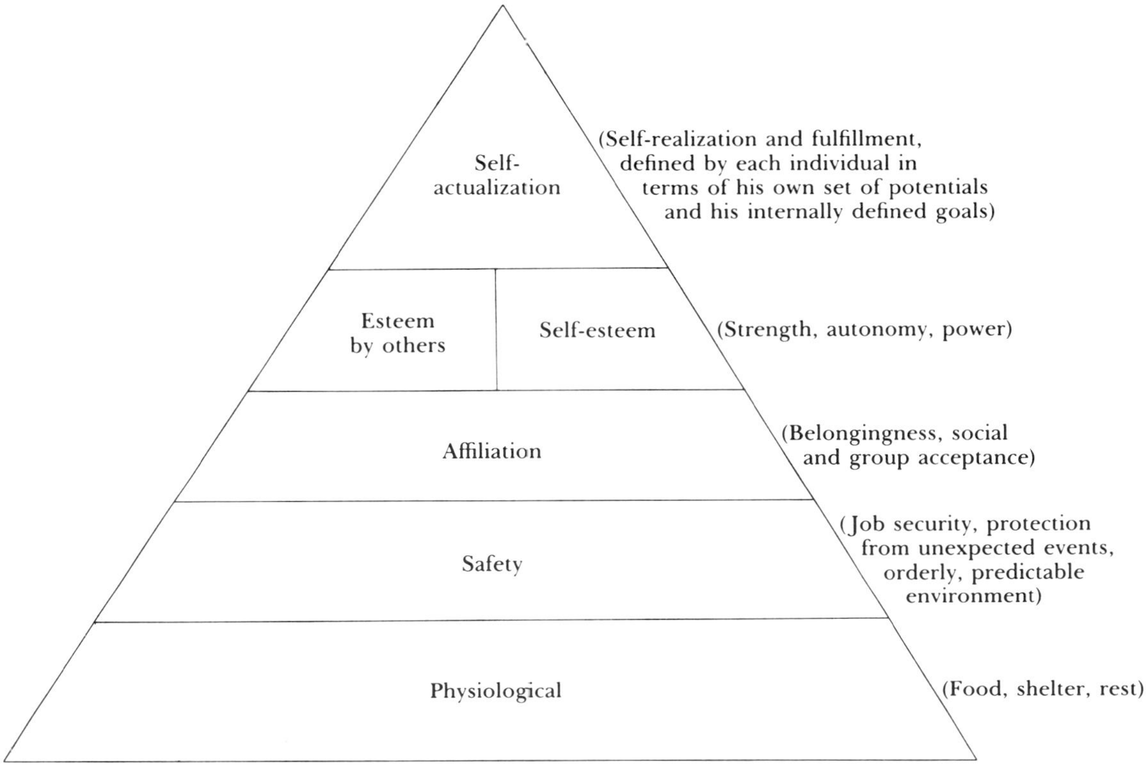

FIGURE 3.2 Maslow's Hierarchy of Needs

A second popular need satisfaction model is Herzberg's (1959) "two-factor theory" (sometimes referred to as "motivation-hygiene theory"), so named because it makes distinct two classes of factors which are relevant to individual satisfaction in a work situation. The first class of factors, "motivators", are related to the content of the job itself, or to the intrinsic dimensions of the job as they are seen by the individuals concerned, e.g., the nature of the work, recognition, responsibility and advancement. The second class, "hygiene" factors, are related to the context, or environmental setting of the job, e.g., salary, working conditions, company policies and superior/subordinate relationships.

Herzberg's theory contends that job content and job context factors have different effects on individual satisfaction and motivation. While the presence of job content factors may contribute to an individual's satisfaction with his job, the absence of those factors is unlikely to contribute to job dissatisfaction. Conversely, the absence of job context ("hygiene") factors has the potential to cause job dissatisfaction, while their presence is unlikely to result in job satisfaction. "Two-factor theory" postulates that attempts to increase work motivation should concentrate on facilitating the satisfaction of an individual's need for achievement, recognition, responsibility (i.e. the job content factors), rather than concentrating on the job context ("hygiene") factors.

Because of their popularity in organizational psychology, behavioural research into accounting information and control systems has drawn heavily on the need satisfaction theories of motivation and behaviour. The most important research has concerned the impact of budgetary planning and control systems on employee motivation. For example, Buckley and McKenna (1972) and Hofstede (1967) used Maslow's theory in suggesting that budgetary systems should attempt to facilitate satisfaction of individuals' higher level needs, through participation for example, as these were the needs most likely to be operative in modern organizations. In their important contributions to the development and dissemination of behavioural science applications in accounting, Schiff and Lewin (1974), Bruns and DeCoster (1969) and Caplan (1971) all emphasized need satisfaction models.

Contemporary State of Need Satisfaction Theories. In the psychology literature, need satisfaction theories have been conceptualized as "content" theories of motivation, and have been contrasted with "process" theories. Content theories are concerned with the essential nature of the variables that affect motivation, while process theories consider how those variables produce different behaviour and result in different levels of productive effort. Table 3.1 summarizes the major motivational theories using the content/process dichotomy.

TABLE 3.1

Content Theories	Process Theories	
Need Satisfaction Models	Reinforcement Models	Cognitive Models
Maslow (1943, 1954, 1970)	Skinner (1938, 1969)	Expectancy:
Herzberg et al (1959)		Vroom (1964)
McClelland (1961)		Porter & Lawler (1968)
Alderfer (1972)		Graen (1969)
		Lawler (1973)
		Goal Setting:
		Locke (1968, 1978)
		Yukl & Latham (1978)
		Equity:
		Adams (1965)
		Attitude:
		Fishbein (1967)
		Attribution:
		Jones & Thebault (1958)
		Heider (1944, 1958)

Mitchell (1979, p. 252) has illustrated the difference between process and content theories of individual motivation:

> . . . given a number of rewards (e.g. pay, promotion, recognition) a process theorist might be concerned with how frequently the rewards were administered (e.g. expectancy) and in what pattern they were administered (e.g. reinforcement schedules), while a content theorist might be concerned with how important these three rewards were and the specific needs which they satisfied.

Despite their wide acceptance within management, organizational, and management accounting literature, the general conclusion from the empirical evidence is that the most popular need based theories of motivation, notably those of Maslow and Herzberg, have accumulated sufficient disconfirmatory instances to make their validity suspect (Filley, House and Kerr, 1976, p. 195). Certainly, the concept of the universality of human needs has been largely disconfirmed (Salancik and Pfeffer, 1977, p. 436), as has the ability to classify potentially relevant needs into unambiguous and independent categories (Wanous and Zwany, 1977, p. 94). As a consequence of this, there has been a shift away from need satisfaction theories in current research in psychology and social psychology. The corresponding trend has been toward the major process theories of motivation.

However, before we examine process theories, we should summarize the potential relevance of need satisfaction models to MAS design and research. Although in retrospect it is possible to be critical of management accounting research based on need satisfaction theories on the grounds that this research may have adopted theories which were fashionable in behavioural research and used them in an over-simplistic manner in accounting applications, it may be equally imprudent to dispense with such theories entirely. Need theory has been proven to have limited usefulness for day-to-day management decisions; however, the needs concept itself still has significance for behavioural understanding. It remains relevant in examining major changes in behaviour, why individuals join or withdraw from organizations for example, even though it has reduced relevance in application to behavioural influence situations such as budgetary planning and control (Wanous & Zwany, 1977, pp. 95–96).

Need theories can also be used to provide a basis of broad differentiation between groups of people, although not at the highly disaggregated level proposed by Maslow, and not by themselves in isolation from such aspects as perceptions, expectations, and environmental and structural factors. The less disaggregated models, for example, based on two (Lawler, 1973; Lawler & Suttle, 1972) or three need categories (Alderfer, 1972), have received greater empirical support than Maslow's five category model (Wahba & House, 1974).

Finally, although the process models of individual behaviour have received far more current support than need theories, many process models themselves use the concept of needs, and integrate such concepts into explanations of changes in motivation, behaviour and performance.

Process Models of Motivation

By contrast with content models of motivation, process models purport to explain shifts in the level of individual performance. Most of the motivational research in psychology and social psychology during the 1970s has concentrated on process models, particularly expectancy theory models.

Expectancy Theory. Expectancy theory has received considerable support as a model of individual behaviour in organizations during the 1970s. Good descriptions of expectancy theory are given by Mitchell (1979) and Lawler (1973), and below we summarize, from Lawler's description, the theory's main propositions.

1. People have expectancies about the likelihood that certain outcomes will follow their behaviour; they form expectations that performance (P) will result in a certain outcome (O). These are designated (P → O) expectancies in Lawler's model.
2. People have preferences for the various outcomes that are potentially available to them; the preference for an outcome is referred to as its valence. Consequently, the valence of any particular outcome may be positive or negative for an individual and there may be more than one perceived outcome for any action.
3. People have expectancies about the likelihood that an action which they take will lead to the behaviour or performance needed to produce the outcomes. People not only have (P → O) expectancies, they also have (E → P) expectancies about whether or not their personal effort (E) will yield the level of performance (P) needed to produce the desired outcomes. A person may expect performance to produce the desired outcomes or valences [(P → O)(V)], but not be motivated to act because he does not believe that his effort can achieve that performance.

Summarizing these propositions into an operative model, expectancy theory maintains that an individual's motivation is a multiplicative function of the sum of the (E → P) expectancies (the expectancy that the individual's personal effort can result in the required performance), and the sum of the [(P → O)(V)] products (the expectancy that the required performance will result in perceived outcomes multiplied by the valence or attractiveness of these outcomes).

$$\text{Motivation to act} = \Sigma(E \rightarrow P) \times \Sigma[(P \rightarrow O)(V)]$$

There are many variations of expectancy theory. For example, one variation explicitly recognizes the forms of rewards flowing from individual performance (House, 1971), and another formally separates different types of outcomes (Fishbein, 1967).

Expectancy Theory Research in Management Accounting. Several attempts have been made during the last five years to use expectancy theories of motivation in the examination of management accounting systems.

In the article which is reprinted in this section, Ronen and Livingstone (1975) demonstrate how the budgetary planning and control system may affect the parameters of the expectancy model, particularly through the ability of a budget to influence an individual's perception of the effort–performance (E → P) link. They also use expectancy theory to provide a theoretical test for several assumptions underlying the budgeting process. In another study, Ferris (1977) tested the capability of expectancy theory to predict the performance and job satisfaction of audit staff accountants. He found that expectancy models were weak predictors of performance in this setting, but significant predictors of job satisfaction. Ferris concluded that the explanatory and predictive power of expectancy models is contingent upon boundary conditions such as the type of organizational environment and the hierarchical level within the organization. These findings reinforce and add a dimension to the contingency approach to MAS design which is taken in this book. They demonstrate that the management accountant must take account not only of first order interactions between MAS and the individual, but of the more complex interactions which are influenced by organizational contextual factors as well.

Expectancy theory has received significant support in psychological research. Consequently, its application to, and examination in management accounting settings are legitimate and necessary pursuits of accounting researchers. However, just as the attempt to apply need satisfaction models to accounting situations may be judged in retrospect to have been over-simplistic, caution should also be taken in the conclusions with respect to expectancy theories. The theoretical construct of the major concepts underlying expectancy theory is by no means universally accepted (Wahba and House, 1974), and the research evidence with respect to the explanatory and predictive power of the theory is not unambiguously supportive (Filley, House and Kerr, 1976).

Research in psychology and social psychology has pointed out the limitations, boundary conditions and perspectives of expectancy models. The application of these models in accounting situations should similarly incorporate such conditions and perspectives. For example, expectancy theory is formulated on the premise that perceptions of expectations and valences differ among individuals. However, it is only in recent psychological research that attempts are being made to examine these differences at the individual or group level. One area of research that should be of particular value to management accounting is the investigation into the causes of individual expectancies; that is, research aimed at determining the extent to which expectancies depend upon specific reward contingencies (Peters, 1977), personality variables, and group or organizational characteristics (Oldham, 1976). Peters (1977) found that expectancies (P → O), and valences (V) are all dependent on the determination of rewards and the method of performance evaluation. This research is important for management accounting to the extent that the accounting control system is tied to the administration of rewards and forms a major part of the performance evaluation process.

The other major limitation which affects the capability of expectancy theory to explain and predict individual behaviour is that, like other expected utility models, it is a normative theory. Mitchell notes the significance of this (1979, p. 255):

> Expected value approaches argue that if people (a) knew all the alternatives, (b) knew all the outcomes, (c) knew all the action → outcome relationships, and (d) knew how they felt about these outcomes, that they would use a rather complex formula to come up with an estimate of the best choice of action. It is obvious that people don't have all of the above information, nor do they use a complex formula in determining their actions. . . . Rather, expected value should be seen as a general approximation of people's behaviour. It points out the factors of importance (i.e. expectancies, instrumentalities, and valences) and it suggests ways in which these variables alone and in combination influence behaviour. In that perspective, it has made a valuable contribution to the field.

Goal Setting. One of the most promising motivational theories, in terms of providing empirically testable propositions for the design of information and control systems in organizations, is goal setting theory. This theory was originally examined for its organizational relevance by Locke (1968). Good summaries of the theory are provided by Steers and Porter (1974) and Mitchell (1979). Goal setting theory is based on the premise that the behaviour of individuals in the organization is consciously and purposefully directed toward the attainment of specific goals. Research in organizational psychology has developed a series of propositions in respect to the area of goal setting which are particularly relevant for the management accountant. The most fundamental of these propositions is that the setting of clear job goals for an individual results in a higher performance than if he were provided with only broad descriptions of his job responsibility.

This basic proposition is significant for the management accountant because it reinforces the value of formal budgetary planning systems. However, it is from the associated research into the effects of task–goal attributes on performance through the goal setting premise, that management accounting may derive the most benefit. Steers and Porter (1974) developed six task–goal attributes which affect goal setting propositions: goal specificity, goal difficulty, participation in goal setting, feedback, peer competition for goal attainment, and goal acceptance. The first four of these have been the subject of considerable management accounting research in the areas of budgeting and standard costing.

Goal Specificity. Sufficient evidence exists to indicate that increased goal clarity and specificity generally result in increased performance (Steers & Porter, 1974, p. 437). This is consistent with the central proposition of goal setting theory. However, some studies suggest that there are boundary conditions which affect this relationship. Frost and Mahoney (1976), for example, demonstrated that the nature of the task constitutes one such condition; they found that the existence of goals for highly structured tasks is less important than for highly unstructured tasks.

Goal Difficulty. The evidence that is available provides reasonable though not unequivocal support for the goal difficulty proposition, i.e. difficult goals result in better performance than easy goals when task difficulty is kept constant. Studies relevant to this proposition are summarized in Mitchell (1979) and Steers and Porter (1974).

This finding is of considerable significance to management accounting because such aspects of MAS as budgets and standard costs comprise and communicate targets of varying levels of difficulty or attainability. Stedry (1960), in his classic study, was concerned with the relationship between goal difficulty and performance and the relevance of that relationship for budgetary systems. Although the transferability of the results from Stedry's laboratory experiment to the organizational budget context has been questioned (Birnberg & Nath, 1968), these results have been frequently cited in the budgetary literature.

Stedry found that experimenter-assigned difficult goals produced better performance than assigned easy goals. However, this result held only when such goals were determined by the experimenter prior to the subjects' setting their own goals for the task. When subjects set their own goals first, they tended to reject the assigned goals as being too difficult. Stedry's conclusions are relevant not only for the examination of attainability and difficulty levels in goal and standard formulation, but also for the design of participative decision making programs of budget formulation.

Participation in Goal Setting. Considerable research in organizational behaviour has been done on the effect of participation in the decision making process. Participation may be described as a "process of joint decision making by two or more parties in which the decisions have future effects on those making them" (Vroom, 1960). Vroom (1964) argued that increased participation in the decision making process results in improved performance because such participation satisfies an individual's higher level needs. Participation, it was hypothesized, causes the individual to internalize the budget, and accept it as his own standard of performance. Similar arguments have been developed in budget context research to support the effectiveness of participative budgets in generating personal motivation (Becker & Green, 1962; Dunbar, 1971; Hofstede, 1968; Schiff & Lewin, 1970).

The results of management accounting research into the effects of participation on performance are very ambiguous however. Irvine (1970) pointed out the contradictory findings in the accounting literature, and Milani (1975) found only weak support for the relationship between participation and performance. Many studies have found relationships between participation and dependent variables such as morale and attitude, yet failed to find a positive relationship between participation and performance. It may be argued that the only real link to performance is that participation may influence an individual to increase the level of difficulty of his set goals, and if this occurs, higher performance may also result due to the goal difficulty effect.

Utilizing the contingency model presented in this book, we can suggest that the resolution of the contradictory research findings on the participation–performance link may lie in the modifying effects of intervening variables. These variables may have individual, structural or environmental origins. Individual variables, such as differential personalities and need strengths, may affect the influence of participation; so too may the organization structure. Autocratic, centralized organizations may yield different results than less autocratic, decentralized organizations with respect to the effectiveness of participative decision making. As an example of environmental influence, the conflicting findings of the classic Coch and French (1948) and French, Israel and As (1960) studies showed that different cultural and national settings may affect the benefits of participation. Given the potential significance of participation in the budget setting process, additional management accounting research to determine the effects of these contextual and environmental variables appear to be critical.

Feedback. As in the psychological research into the affect of participation on motivation and performance, research into the influence of feedback, or knowledge of results, on performance also provides inconsistent findings (Mitchell, 1979, pp. 256–57). In the accounting literature it has been argued (Becker and Green, 1962; Benston, 1963; Cook, 1967; Miles and Vergin, 1966) that feedback to employees of the results of their performance against the budget is essential to improved performance in the future. This argument is premised on the psychology based concept of "aspiration level", which may be defined as "the level of future performance in a familiar task which an individual, knowing his level of past performance in that task, explicitly undertakes to reach" (Lewin et al, 1944). An individual's level of aspiration, when just barely achieved, produces subjective feelings of success; when the level is not achieved, subjective feelings of failure result. Becker and Green argued that feedback is necessary in order that a feeling of success or failure may be produced in the individual, and consequently, that the aspiration level effect may occur.

Sufficient research exists which has found no relationship between feedback and performance to suggest that the feedback–performance link is a complex one which is dependent again upon boundary variables such as the personality traits and the organizational location of the people and activity concerned. At present, little research in management accounting has been carried out to identify and investigate the potential effects of such modifying variables on the feedback–performance relationship. One such attempt (Sorensen and Franks, 1972) examined the relative influence of ability, self-esteem and the style of feedback on performance in a goal setting framework.

In summarizing goal setting theories, we should recognize that goal setting approaches may not represent completely alternative models of behaviour when compared with, for example, expectancy theories; rather, they may be complementary to, or part of other theories. Most of the major motivation theories utilize, and in some cases, integrate goal setting concepts (Steers and Porter, 1974). Goal setting research does however provide important propositions for an understanding of human behaviour in organizations, particularly with respect to those contextual and environmental variables which may influence such behaviour. Management accounting research into the effect of participation, goal difficulty and feedback on motivation and performance must take account of these contingent variables.

OTHER THEORIES OF INDIVIDUAL BEHAVIOUR

Although expectancy and goal setting models are more prominent contemporary influences in motivational research, other theories also provide insight into individual behaviour in organizations. For example, although equity theory is shown to be limited as a motivational model in its own right (Goodman & Friedman, 1971), it provides propositions potentially relevant to MAS design.

Equity theorists argue that motivation is essentially a social comparison process. If an individual's perceived relationship between his inputs (effort) and outcomes (rewards) is at variance with the people with whom he compares, he will act to make the relationships comparable. He may do this by increasing performance (efforts) if he feels over-compensated in rewards by comparison with other individuals, or by decreasing efforts if he feels relatively under-compensated (Mitchell, 1979, pp. 258–59).

Perceptions of equity may be formed by individuals partly on the basis of the organization's systems of compensation, performance evaluation and reward allocation (Carrell & Dittrich, 1978). To the extent that the management accounting system forms an integral part of the performance evaluation process, the management accountant needs to consider any perceived equity imbalance which may result from the system. For example, return on investment comparison data, which is calculated using differentially valued asset bases, may contribute to perceived inequities among divisions, or other sub-units, and may in turn influence motivation dysfunctionally.

Although not given an equity justification, Lawler and Rhode (1976, Chs. 4 & 5) considered the success of performance evaluation systems to be critically dependent on the way in which the systems were perceived by individuals. Despite its potential relevance, equity theory has received no direct attention in management accounting research.

Achievement theory, developed by McClelland (1951) and Atkinson (1958) and summarized by Filley, House and Kerr (1976) provides another approach to examining individual behaviour in organizations. Achievement theory is concerned with explaining why some people have a higher need for achievement than others, under what conditions the achievement need is aroused, and the relationship between the need for achievement and performance. Buckley and McKenna (1972) noted that the theory signifies that the designers of budgetary planning and control systems need to identify high and low achievers, in order that the system may allow each to derive positive motivation. Additionally, they pointed out the need for timely feedback so that the high achiever particularly may formulate and adjust his level of aspiration. Again however, very little research has been carried out into the significance of achievement–motivation theory for management accounting.

Reinforcement Theories

The process models of individual behaviour which we have described so far all assume that behaviour results from conscious psychological or mental processes on the part of the individual. Consequently, they are called "cognitive" theories. By contrast, "reinforcement" theory denies the intervention of psychological constructs such as expectations and valences, and maintains that environmental conditions and processes are the determinants of behaviour (Skinner, 1938, 1969). Under this theory, behaviour is controlled by "reinforcers" where a reinforcer is any consequence which, when it follows an action, increases the likelihood that the behaviour will be repeated. In organizations, rewards such as salary, promotion and praise may act as reinforcers.

Very few attempts have been made to apply reinforcement theory to management accounting situations. Bodnar and Lusk (1977) used an operant conditioning reinforcement model in attempting to demonstrate how an accounting system of cost allocation may be used to influence individual motivation. Cherrington and Cherrington (1973) argued from a laboratory experiment that reinforcement theory principles can be applied to budgeting systems to predict and control attitudes and behaviour. These studies have been subjected to methodological criticism (Becker, 1973; Hofstede, 1973), as well as the more general criticism of reinforcement models that such models attempt to explain highly complex behavioural processes using a limited number of unrealistically simple variables (Mitchell, 1979).

Intrinsic and Extrinsic Motivation

Significant recent behavioural research has focused on the differential affects of intrinsic and extrinsic rewards on motivation. Intrinsic motivation "refers to an internal state resulting from knowledge of having accomplished something by individual effort", and extrinsic motivation "refers to an internal state brought about by the occurrence of external (reinforcing) events" (Scott, 1975, p. 118). Intrinsic motivation may result from the accomplishment of a task to the satisfaction of the individual concerned, with no requirement of an external reward; extrinsic motivation may result if the individual perceives and values a relationship between performance and administered rewards such as pay and promotion.

One of the major applications of intrinsic and extrinsic motivation concepts to the information and control system was made by Lawler and Rhode (1976, Chs. 4 and 5). They examined several rewards, including pay, promotion, praise from superiors and interesting work, for their ability to influence motivation through intrinsic and extrinsic dimensions. More importantly, they evaluated the critical aspects of the information and control system (including the nature of the standards contained in the system, and the pattern, speed and frequency of communication) for their potential impact on motivation through the rewards examined. This enabled them to develop a series of proposed characteristics of information and control systems which have the potential to produce high intrinsic and/or high extrinsic motivation.

Environmental and contextual factors also influence the potential of intrinsic and extrinsic rewards to affect individual behaviour. These include organizational structural factors such as size and the extent of decentralization, the kind of product and its technology (Lawler and Rhode, 1976, pp. 61–62), and individual variables such as age, class, and type of work and occupation (Andrisani and Miljus, 1977).

An aspect of psychological and organizational behaviour research that is still the subject of controversy is the relationship between intrinsic and extrinsic rewards. It is questioned whether the use of extrinsic and intrinsic rewards in a given situation will be compatible (will reinforce motivation) or conflicting (will actually reduce motivation below the level achievable with only one form of reward). Deci (1975), for example, argues that the addition of an extrinsic reward (e.g. an incentive payment) to a situation which the people involved already find intrinsically satisfying, will result in a decrease, rather than an increase, in motivation. Little attempt has been made to examine this latter dimension of intrinsic and extrinsic motivation in the management accounting literature. However, given the potential of the information and control system to reflect and influence individual behaviour, future behavioural research in this area should be of considerable relevance to the management accountant.

MODERATING AND INTERVENING VARIABLES

Important variables which influence behaviour through the models we have described include the ability of the individual to perceive, process, and respond to stimuli from his environment, and the affects of group interactions on individual behaviour. The information and control systems are major stimuli within the organizational environment, and consequently the moderating variables become relevant to the design of these systems.

In relation to an individual's ability to perceive and process information generated by the information and control system, much of the initial development in management accounting tended to accept traditional economic theory assumptions, which did not allow for perceptual difficulties or distortions arising from individual, social, or organizational contextual factors. By contrast, contemporary psychological literature provides strong evidence to indicate not only that such perceptual complexities exist and affect individual decision making, but also that these factors are systematic and ordered, and can be studied formally for their relevance to specific decision making situations. Zimbardo and Ruch (1975) provide a comprehensive description of the psychological process of perception, and Filley, House and Kerr (1976, pp. 56–71) elaborate on this description by identifying several important components of perception.

> The perceptual system acts like a computer, taking in multiple sources of information, selecting, abstracting, comparing, testing, sorting, outputting, and then repeating all these again and again. Each perceptual act is a construction or a creation of reality based on all of the relevant past and current information available to the organism. Far from being a direct experience of "things as they are", perception is thus a mediated process of organized conclusion drawing about the real world of time, space, objects and events based on much more than simply the stimulus input. (Zimbardo and Ruch, 1975, p. 238).

The inference from the work on perception is that the management accountant cannot expect the reports which he prepares as part of the information system to be viewed and interpreted objectively by their recipients. He cannot necessarily expect two recipients of the report to interpret it in the same manner, or to place the same meaning on it that he intended.

The way in which individuals perceive objects and events may be affected by personality variables, such as individual needs and values (Jones and Gerard, 1967), functional or occupational position (Dearborn and Simon, 1958; Hayes, 1977), and the context within which the object or event appears (Filley, House and Kerr, 1976, pp. 65–69). The MAS designer can rarely control the influence of personality or functional variables on the way in which individuals are likely to perceive the informational outputs of his systems; consequently, his requirement is to be aware of the affect of these variables and allow for them wherever possible.

By contrast, the accountant is often able to control the context within which the information appears. For example, the order in which items of information are presented may determine the relative importance which people attach to the items. In many cases, information which is received first is given highest importance (the primacy effect), in others, the most recent information is seen as most important (recency effect). Second, exception reporting may be used as a means of overcoming the perceptual problem of sensory adaptation, i.e. reduced sensitivity to a stimulus given continued exposure to it. Variation of the format of a regular report would be another means of approaching this problem.

Although the need to consider perceptual difficulties and distortions has been recognized for several years (American Accounting Association, 1971; Caplan, 1971), little attention has been given to this aspect of individual behaviour in management accounting research.

As for perception, limited accounting research has been carried out into other cognitive and personality variables which affect individual behaviour. Yet, such variables are of major relevance to management information systems design. Managers have different cognitive and emotional characteristics and different decision styles; these characteristics affect not only managers' perceptions of what information is important, but may also determine how the information and control systems influence managers' behaviour. Consequently, one area of research in accounting has concentrated on managers' personalities and cognitive characteristics, and the affects of such characteristics on their information processing behaviour (Dermer, 1973; Driver & Mock, 1975). Good summaries of the human information processing literature are provided by Driver and Mock (1975) and Libby and Lewis (1977).

McGhee, Shields and Birnberg (1978) suggest that personality alone has little affect on decision making behaviour, and that human information processing models need to consider not only the human processor himself, but also the nature of the task and the interaction between the processor and the task. Their research supports our contingency approach to the design of MAS, in that it recognizes the ability of the organizational context to influence the relationship between the system and the individual. A good analysis of the environmental variables which interact with the cognitive characteristics of the information processor is given by San Miguel (1976).

Another variable which is capable of affecting an individual's behaviour is his interaction with other members of the organization in group situations. Organizations are not simply collections of individuals acting in isolation from others; consequently, we cannot approach a study of behaviour solely from theories of individual motivation. Individual behaviour is influenced by the norms of the group with which the individual interacts, i.e., by the group's concensus of approved and expected behaviour. If the study of individual behaviour is relevant to the design of management accounting systems, then the potential of group variables to influence that behaviour is similarly relevant.

A group may be defined as "a collection of individuals among whom a set of interdependent relationships exists" (Bobbit et al, 1974), and may be formed in several ways. A group with task interdependencies may arise as a result of the formal structural design of the organization, or informal groups may develop paralleling or overlapping formal groups.

It is important to the management accountant that group norms not only modify the behaviour of individuals, but in addition, that those norms are influenced by the information and control system. As one example, San Miguel (1977), in his article which is reprinted in this section, notes the inconsistency between the budgetary planning system, which typically arises from group decision processes between marketing, production and finance functions, and subsequent performance evaluation and control systems which are usually designed around individual behaviour.

Although some earlier accounting literature (Becker and Green, 1962; Benston, 1963; DeCoster and Fertakis, 1968) referred to the importance of group membership on behaviour, little specific management accounting research has been directed towards the potential two-way interaction between information and control systems and group behaviour. Most notable in this area is the article by Flamholtz (1976), which is also reprinted in this section. Flamholtz develops a model of group dynamics and task performance, including aspects such as the nature of the group, its size and its cohesiveness, and proposes some implications of these aspects for the design of the budgeting system.

THE READINGS

The introduction to this part of the book has provided a basis for examining the potential interactions between the management accounting system and individual and group behaviour. These interactions are premised upon theories of individual behaviour and motivation, and are influenced by organizational contextual factors. The readings develop some specific dimensions of these interactions.

San Miguel (1977) examines the complex interrelations between behavioural research on the individual and small groups, and the management accounting process. Additionally, he establishes the critical interdependence of individual and group behaviour with the organizational structure and context. Consequently, this article serves both as a framework on which subsequent readings in this section depend, and a linkage with preceding sections of the book.

The article by Bariff and Galbraith (1978) discusses the importance of accounting information systems in organizational design and in facilitating adaptive organizational behaviour. In particular, the article is concerned with the potential capability of the information system to modify and redistribute power within the organization both vertically (from superior to subordinate within the hierarchy), and horizontally (across sub-units at similar organizational levels).

The third article in this section, by Moskowitz, Schaefer and Borcherding (1976), illustrates the information and decision making dimension of behavioural accounting. The authors concentrate on the behavioural characteristics and capabilities of the managerial users of information, and suggest that information and control systems produce systematic biases on the part of decision makers. The article argues the need for better understanding by accountants and information systems designers of the psychological and sociological dimensions of the human information processing mechanism.

Driver and Mock (1975) also examine the implications of the cognitive capabilities of the potential users of information for the design of MAS. They support their interpretative framework with a limited empirical exposition of the relationship between one aspect of a user's cognitive make-up, decision style, and his preference for and use of accounting feedback.

Ronen and Livingstone (1975) furnish an instance of the budgeting and leadership dimension of behavioural accounting at both the individual and group decision making levels. Specifically, their article evaluates the impact of budgets on motivation and behaviour within the context of psychology's expectancy theory, and suggests how a clearer appreciation of the behavioural ramifications of the budgetary process can be used to minimize its potentially undesirable effects.

Although the readings by Moskowitz et al, and Ronen and Livingstone considered the behaviour of groups as well as individuals, the final reading in this section, by Flamholtz (1976), is concerned especially with a formal model of group dynamics and task performance that is relevant to management accounting. Flamholtz's article explains the relevance of group dynamics for accounting, presents a model that attempts to integrate the behavioural science research on group dynamics, and identifies factors in a situation which suggest individual or group based systems for decision making and control.

DISCUSSION QUESTIONS

1. In his article in Part 1 of this book, Amigoni proposes an open systems/contingency approach to management control systems design that takes account of two relevant independent variables: the organization's structure and its environment. By contrast, Ansari (in Part 2) argues for a broader approach to management control systems design which considers the behavioural, i.e. human and social, factors which affect organizational functioning. Examine: how the behaviour of individuals and groups may influence organizational functioning; and whether or not such behaviour should be included as an independent variable in management control system design.
2. Individuals' perceptual, cognitive and information processing capabilities are dependent on personality variables, functional and occupational position, and the context within which an object or event appears. Given the

"uniqueness" of individual personalities, is it feasible for the management accounting systems designer to incorporate such individual variations in MAS design?

3. All individuals in organizations are members of groups, whether these groups are formally or informally constituted. How is the affect of group membership on individual behaviour relevant to the designer of management accounting systems?
4. It has been argued that expectancy theories of individual behaviour are normative and make unrealistic assumptions about individuals' cognitive abilities. Discuss the relevance of expectancy theory to management accounting systems design in light of this criticism.
5. Participation in the budget setting process has been the subject of much management accounting research; however, the results of such research into the benefits of participation, particularly on subsequent performance, have been inconsistent and contradictory. Using a contingency approach, examine some potential explanations for the ambiguous research findings.
6. Bariff and Galbraith contend that accountants and management information systems staff have the ability to effect shifts in the distribution of power within the organization, and to acquire additional power for themselves. Explain how this capability arises, and examine its implications for the management accountant.
7. The behavioural sciences provide numerous theories, and variations of theories, which attempt to explain individual behaviour and motivation. Often these theories are based on different premises and emphasize different behavioural variables and processes. Examine: how theories of individual behaviour, in general, are relevant to the management accounting systems designer; and how the MAS designer may take account of the different premises and emphases of different theories.

*The Behavioral Sciences and Concepts and Standards for Management Planning and Control**

Joseph G. San Miguel
Harvard University Graduate School of Business Administration

This article reviews behavioral research on the individual, small groups and organizations and the implications of this research for management accounting. Also, opportunities for accounting research are identified and, where appropriate, extant accounting research is discussed. The conclusion is that studies of individual and group behavior are inseparable from studies of complex organizations and vice versa. Furthermore, fundamental research into personal, organizational, and environmental variables and their impact on effective management planning and control systems is urgently needed.

Technological developments in recent years have greatly increased our capacity to design planning and control devices in modern organizations. The emergence of applications of logical and mathematical tools and the advent of the computer are two primary sources of these technological developments (Churchman, 1961; Simon, 1959). The important question is how do these techniques and tools benefit organizational planning and control in a real sense? One test of these developments must rest in how they improve management control systems (Arrow, 1964). The techniques are only a means to an end. The end is a system that enables managers to make sound decisions as to the efficient and effective allocation of human, physical, and financial resources to attain the objectives of the organization. This is the essence of modern planning and control (Anthony, 1965; Barnard, 1938).

Since human resources are an integral part of planning and control systems, a comprehensive understanding of the behavior of managers and those they seek to manage, or more properly motivate (Roethlisberger & Dickson, 1939), is necessary to the development of standards for planning and control. However, we are discovering that behavioral implications of management control systems are extremely complex (Argyris, 1952; Bruns, 1968; Burns, 1969). And as if the behavior of human resources were not complex enough we

From *Accounting, Organizations and Society,* Vol. 2, No. 3 (1977), pp. 177–186.

*The idea for this paper was conceived while the author was a member of the American Accounting Association's Committee on Concepts and Standards for Management Planning and Control. The comments of William J. Bruns, John K. Shank, Andrew C. Stedry, an anonymous referee, and especially Anthony G. Hopwood are gratefully acknowledged. Also, the financial support of The Associates of the Harvard Graduate School of Business Administration is acknowledged.

must also contend with the effects of uncertainty on behavior (Edwards, 1954; Simon, 1959).

Quantitative and economic decision tools attempt to deal with uncertainty and its concomitant effects on human decision makers in an impersonal, objective way (Marschak & Radnor, 1972; Simon, 1956; von Neumann & Morgenstern, 1953). However, the assumptions underlying the specified decision models are simplistic. The richness of decision situations actually encountered in large-scale organizations defy these simple notions of behavior (Bonini, 1963; Churchman, 1961). The interaction of human behavior and uncertainty in even simple decision situations reminds us of the little knowledge we have about human information processing and decision making.

Because of this lack of knowledge of human behavior in organizations, intensive research is needed to establish the constraints or requirements for designing planning, reporting and control systems. To provide an overview and possibly encourage fresh approaches to research as it concerns managerial accounting, several areas of relevant behavioral science literature will be examined. The contributions come from various disciplines and the literature review is by no means exhaustive. One of the difficulties in gaining an understanding (for student and instructor alike) of this subject area is the dispersion of publications across the various disciplines.

Behavioral research on information processing and decision making can be examined at three levels: research on the individual, on small groups, and on large, complex organizations. This does not imply that the levels of research are distinct or independent. Rather they are very interrelated and hierarchical. This follows the chronological development of behavioral research from individual transactions to transactions within and between large organizations. Research on individual behavior has helped to formulate theories and conduct research on small groups. The research on individuals and small groups in turn has had an influence on our understanding of behavior in larger organizations.

RESEARCH ON THE INDIVIDUAL

Individual information processing and decision making are strongly rooted in theories of personality, learning, perception and cognition. The success of individuals in managerial positions and risk taking has been explained by personality theorists such as McClelland, Atkinson, Clark & Lowell (1953) in terms of their motive to achieve. Also, Maslow (1954) has broken down motivation into five hierarchical levels. These theories bear directly on how management control systems affect behavior. For example, Lawler (1973) and Lawler & Rhode (1976) have related these and other motivation theories to information and control systems in organizations. They emphasize that information and control systems have a significant impact on individual behavior. The understanding of this impact on behavior is important to anyone concerned with organizational effectiveness, those concerned with designing and implementing information and control systems, and to managers who must understand the effects on subordinates' motivation and performance.

Whether the individual participates in goal setting and decision making is often cited as a critical factor in motivating performance. There have been numerous, and often controversial, research efforts on the effects of participation. Stedry (1960) and Becker & Green (1962) have provided a forum for the discussion of the motivational effects of cost standards and budgets and more recently research has started to investigate the relationship between managers' attitudes and participation (Tosi, 1975). In one study, Onsi (1973) investigated managers' attitudes toward budgets, budget pressure, and budget slack and concluded that "positive participation" could lessen managers' perceived need for budgetary slack. In addition, Swieringa & Moncur (1975) used organizational, personality, and interpersonal variables to explore the effects of participation on managerial attitudes. They found that personality and attitudinal data were relatively less important than organizational data in explaining managerial attitudes. However, they reported that participation in budgeting was related to the individual's self-actualization.

Vroom (1960) first attempted to relate personality traits to the effects of participation in budgeting. Recently, Heller (1971) and Vroom & Yetton (1973) have extended this research into motivation by taking a contingency view of participation. This incorporates not only managers' personal characteristics but also includes situational factors such as organizational structure and context. Heller (1971) studied the effects of influence and power sharing on managers' attitudes and found that perception of skill, experience, span of control, job function, importance of the decision, and proximity of decision are important factors that determine the location of influence and power. Vroom and Yetton (1973) examined the effects of styles of leadership on participative decision making and found that situational variables were relatively more useful than personal variables in explaining managers' participative decision making. This is consistent with the findings of Swieringa & Moncur (1975).

One hypothesis that has emerged from this research on motivation is that extrinsic rewards, such as money, do not continue to motivate performance. Furthermore, intrinsic factors, such as participation, that lead to self-actualization are important variables to consider (Lawler & Rhode, 1976). Extrinsic motivation of individuals is influenced by the organization's reward and punishment system. Intrinsic motivation is not visible nor so readily controllable by the organization. Thus, the organization through its information and control system must provide an environment in which the individual can relate intrinsic rewards to performance (Lawler & Rhode, 1976; Porter & Lawler, 1968).

Learning theorists have contributed to our understanding of concept formulation and mental development (Bruner, Goodnow & Austin, 1956; Piaget, 1950; Skinner, 1953). There then followed an interest in perceptual research (Brunswick, 1956; Harvey, Hunt & Schroder, 1961) and cognitive research (Neisser, 1967; Zazonc, 1969) which appears to be influencing the direction and scope of behavioral research on accounting information and control systems (Burns, 1969, 1972; Fertakis, 1970).

For example, an individual's perception of information is receiving more attention from behavioral researchers than the amount of information transmitted in an information theoretic sense (Rapoport, 1956). This research recognizes that simply providing more and more data to individual decision makers does not necessarily lead to better performance if the decision maker does not attach importance to the information. In this regard, perception plays an important role in communication (the flow of information) because if information is not perceived in the manner intended, then communication does not occur (Cherry, 1966). Research in information processing has recognized that factors such as intelligence, motivation, and experience influence perception in different ways (Harvey, Hunt & Schroder, 1961). Dearborn & Simon (1958), for instance, have shown that we perceive only those things that are congruent with our predispositions and beliefs (selective perception). These personal characteristics of the user of information are thus important considerations in the design of information systems.

Psychological research on individual differences in information processing (Irwin & Smith, 1957; Schroder, Driver & Streufert, 1967), risk taking (Kogan & Wallach, 1964) and decision making (Simon, 1959) has particular promise in our need to understand the behavior of participants in organizations. For example, Revsine (1970) has emphasized the importance of research into questions of information overload and data disaggregation. Although he addressed human information processing and decision making in the external reporting environment, his recommendations are equally applicable to internal reporting and control systems. Cravens (1970) studied individual information processors in an industrial research organization and discovered that risk-taking propensity and information processing efficiency were related. This exploratory study serves to emphasize the importance of relationships between the decision maker, the task, and information processing behavior.

Cognitive theorists have advanced our knowledge concerning decision-making behavior (Zazonc, 1969). Festinger (1957) provided an impetus to this area with his theory of cognitive dissonance. Zimbardo (1969), Simon (1957), and Driver & Streufert (1969) have hypothesized the usefulness of these theories in explaining management behavior. In a management accounting setting, Dermer (1973) investigated how users' cognitive characteristics affect the perceived importance of information. He found that individuals who are intolerant of ambiguity (conceptually concrete processors) seek out more information than those who are more tolerant of ambiguity (conceptually abstract processors) and that the utility of information cannot be determined separately from the user of that information. In a laboratory experiment, Huysmans (1970) tested the effects of two cognitive styles (analytical vs heuristic) on the implementation of operations research recommendations and discovered that matching the method of recommendation with the subject's cognitive style is an important factor in achieving manager's implementation of the recommendations.

Other perceptual and cognitive research in accounting has focused on the human information processing and decision-making interface. Ashton (1974a, 1974b), for example, examined internal control judgments of independent auditors and generally found high levels of group consistency. He also pointed out the need for additional research into individual inconsistencies. Driver & Mock (1975) used decision styles in a laboratory experiment to study the effects on information purchasing behavior. They found that "complex" decision makers purchase more information and that "decisive" decision makers become quickly overloaded and cannot function effectively in complex decision tasks. Libby (1975a, 1975b) found a strong relationship between perceived usefulness of financial accounting ratios to bank loan officers and their predictive accuracy and individual behavior. In a laboratory setting, San Miguel (1976) found strong relationships between levels of information purchasing behavior and psychological characteristics but only a moderate relationship between information purchasing behavior and levels of integrative complexity. Not surprisingly, all of the above research studies point to the need to explicitly consider individual behavior in accounting research on information processing and decision making.

Communication of accounting measurements is at the heart of management control systems (Ackoff, 1958; Anton, 1964; Fertakis, 1970). Consider the discussions in the management accounting literature of "perceived fairness", "responsibility centers", and "goal congruence". Since performance is linked to these concepts, individual behavior plays an important role in successful management control systems. Argyris (1952) first pointed out the importance of interpersonal relationships and the humanistic approach to communicating profit budgets to managers. On the other hand, Schiff & Lewin (1970) have shown how misunderstanding and improper communication can lead managers to manipulate budgetary data to their advantage. Also, Hofstede (1967) has found that the motivational impact of goals and standards can be influenced by managers' perceived goal difficulty. Neither too high nor too low goal difficulty motivates good performance. Thus, communication between the manager, top management, and the managerial accountant are vital to the successful use of budgets and cost controls. Effects of budgets on personal characteristics are also important. For example, DeCoster & Fertakis (1968) have found evidence of a relationship between budget induced pressure and managers' leadership styles.

What can we learn from the above and what are the implications for managerial accounting research and methods? First, behavioral science theories concerning individual behavior have evolved from painstaking research on individuals in different settings. Second, rarely, if ever, have behavioral scientists studied individuals in settings where accounting information comprised the stimuli (Burns, 1972; Fertakis, 1970). As a result we lack first-hand knowledge of the implications of behavioral science theories for explaining the behavior of individuals in cost accounting and management control systems (Miles & Vergin, 1966; Ridgway, 1956). However, we can distill this knowledge from laboratory research in which existing and new theories can be tested and from field research in which laboratory findings or research hypotheses are submitted to tests. Since the purpose of managerial planning and control systems is to motivate performance, we need fundamental research on individual behavior. Research areas include how decision makers handle uncertainty (Irwin & Smith, 1957), the needs and preferences for information (Lanzetta & Kanareff, 1962), the effects of information overload (G. Miller, 1956; J. Miller, 1962), and the motivational impact of management planning and control systems on users and their decisions (Lawler & Rhode, 1976).

RESEARCH ON BEHAVIOR IN SMALL GROUPS

The study of small group behavior has helped behavioral scientists bridge the gap between understanding individual behavior and the behavior of complex organizations. It is understood that to speak of the "behavior" of organizations really means the collective behavior of individuals and groups of individuals in a social institution that has a defined mission (Homans, 1950; Zaleznik & Moment, 1964). Since large, complex organizations evolve from small groups, research on the latter provides valuable insight in understanding the former (Cartwright & Zander, 1953; Guetzkow, 1951; Schein, 1965). For example, much of the current thinking concerning bargaining and labor negotiation processes stems from the experimental research on small groups by Siegel & Fouraker (1960).

Each individual in a group brings to it his own personal experience, attributes, and values. The major distinction is that the individual is now studied in a social setting in which he must interact with others to accomplish some task. This was emphasized in Roethlisberger & Dickson's (1939) early research on informal organizations. Subsequent research has focused on how leadership is established in group behavior (Fiedler, 1967), how role differentiation and expectations affect the group (Etzioni, 1961), how authority is distributed and accepted (Homans, 1950), and how communication takes place (Bavelas, 1950). The development of group norms and rules are of particular interest to some researchers in this area. March

& Simon (1958) in particular have extended Barnard's (1938) pioneering work on group participation and rewards to larger organizations.

As with research on individual behavior, research on small group behavior considers personal characteristics of the members of the group, environmental variables and task variables. However, accounting researchers have not explicitly studied these factors as they relate to the effectiveness of group risk taking, resource utilization, and decision making. This is unfortunate, because group processes exist in organizations and influence, or are influenced by, information and control systems. For example, production line groups frequently set up norms against which performance is judged. This obviously impacts the setting of productivity standards. Budgeting decisions also frequently result from group processes between marketing, production, and finance functions, but performance evaluation systems are usually designed around individual behavior. There are no existing management control systems for considering group performance. The negotiation of transfer prices between managers is also a group process that impacts the effectiveness of management control systems.

Another example which is illustrative of the information processing and decision-making behavior of groups is the research and development project team. Here individuals are assigned responsibility for certain tasks in the overall project. To succeed as a group these tasks require cooperation and communication between group members. The research committee responsible for the research efforts is also a group worthy of investigation. The effectiveness of this group's information processing and decision making is vital to the success of the company's products and processes. Group cohesiveness, group size, group structure, and communication networks are important factors to consider in group motivation and performance. These factors should be receiving more attention from accounting researchers examining management planning and control systems.

BEHAVIORAL RESEARCH OF ORGANIZATIONAL BEHAVIOR

Modern organizations range from very large, multinational and conglomerate corporations to extremely large multi-service institutions such as hospitals and universities. These organizations have emerged from relatively small organizations during the past half century. In a world of scarce resources, the way we plan and control these organizations can have a serious socio-economic impact (Churchman, 1961; Drucker, 1954; Etzioni, 1961).

The primary purpose of behavioral research at the organization level is to improve internal decision-making processes such as resource allocation, innovation, and change (Likert, 1961, 1967). These are human decisions. Information is received, processed and acted upon by internal decision makers. The information may be internally generated in the organization or gathered from external sources.

As a result of behavioral research on the individual and groups of individuals, the economic theory of the firm and the assumptions of the behavior of participants in the firm have been questioned. Cyert & March (1963) and March & Simon (1958) have given us new concepts of decision making and information processing in the firm such as satisfying behavior, bounded rationality, and the effects of organizational structure on goals. Extensions by Charnes & Stedry (1964) to multiple objectives and Williamson (1964) to discretionary managerial control and utility functions combine theories of individual behavior discussed earlier (i.e. Maslow & McClelland) with these theories of organizational behavior.

During the period that these new theories of managerial behavior in organizations have been developed, there has been no discernible impact on the design of cost accounting and reporting systems (Rosen & Schenck, 1967). Too often, cost standards and budgets are based on idealized models of economic behavior that conflict with the complex realities of behavior in large organizations. For example, cost standards and budgets require efficient, machine-like compliance of workers and managers. This assumes that workers and managers as physiological machines can be controlled through basic drives and emotions. Performance evaluation based on profit targets and return on investment also reflects this technical view of managerial accounting. A broader framework is needed for examining the impact of organizations and organizational design on management planning and control systems (Hopwood, 1974).

Recognizing the rather limited and outmoded assumptions of traditional internal accounting, Caplan (1966) developed a list of behavioral assumptions that reflect modern organization theory. His work was based primarily on the recommendations of Drucker (1954) and McGregor (1960) concerning management by objectives and self-control. By studying the effects of various styles of performance evaluation on job-related tension, interpersonal relations and manipulation of accounting information, Hopwood (1973) sought explanations of the actual behavior of individuals. Although not a broad enough field study for drawing conclusions, his findings are suggestive of the significant impact that actual, rather than presumed, managerial attitudes can have on management control systems.

Recent research on formal organizations has been extremely useful to the formulation of new organizational theories, and understanding the behavior of individuals and groups has been important to this research (Katz and Kahn, 1966). Research on organizations, like research on individuals, has incorporated situational factors such as the organizational setting—its structure, technology, and environment (Sathe, 1975). Among others, Woodward (1965) identified technology (routine vs non-routine production) as a determinant of organizational structure and the distribution of authority for maintaining internal control and coordination. Thompson (1967) proposed a theoretical framework for organizational structures which treats both technology and environment. In turbulent environments characterized by uncertainty, he argued that organizations structure themselves around their primary technologies to reduce uncertainty and best maintain control and coordination among the organization's subunits.

The field work of Lawrence & Lorsch (1967) on organizations and their environment is probably the most influential organizational research in recent years. Their contingency theory views the organization as an information processing system that must adapt to its external environment by internally manipulating states of differentiation and integration between the various subunits. They found that financially successful firms had organization structures that were consistent with the demands of the environment confronting the firm. These organizations used differentiated structures to cope with different environments faced by different subunits. In addition, successful organizations required a high level of integration among the subunits. Among other things, the findings suggest that there is no one optimal structure for all organizations.

Reflecting the influence of the works of Cyert, March and Simon, Galbraith (1973) has taken a similar approach to organizational information processing as Lawrence & Lorsch (1967) except that he uses task uncertainty to specify the need for processing information for decision making. The higher the task uncertainty the greater the amount of information that must be processed among decision makers in order for the organization to succeed. Thus, the information requirements of the task must be matched by the information processing capacity of the organization.

The implication of the above research on contingency theories of organization structure is that the internal reporting and control system should match the organization structure. This is particularly stressed in Galbraith's (1973) research. The accounting information system is the major means by which production, marketing, and finance subunits effectively communicate their plans, budgets, and decisions to achieve overall coordination and control. The information flows and decision making are largely determined by the structuring of responsibility and authority across and within each of the organization's subunits. Devices used within organizations to fix financial responsibility are cost centers, revenue centers, profit centers and investment centers. Therefore, questions of divisionalization, decentralization, and related issues such as transfer prices are usually resolved in the design of the organization's structure and management control system. And these designs are a function of the environment and key social and economic characteristics faced by the individual firm.

There is evidence that accounting researchers are beginning to use contingency theory in their research. In the section on individual behavior we discussed recent works that have concluded that situational factors, in addition to personal characteristics, are important variables to consider when examining managers' attitudes toward budgets and participation (Heller, 1971; Swieringa & Moncur, 1975; Vroom & Yetton, 1973). In addition, recent work by Sathe (1975) and Watson (1975) has stressed the importance of contingency theory to management planning and control. In a related study, Bruns & Waterhouse (1975) have investigated the relationship between formal properties of organization structure and budgetary control in twenty-five firms. Several findings have emerged from their research that bear upon the importance of contingency theory to management control systems. First, high participation and perceived budgetary control were related to organization structure. Second, organization variables such as size and technology were related to structure which is consistent with organizational research findings (Lawrence & Lorsch, 1967; Woodward, 1965). Thus, organization structure variables should be a requisite part of future studies of budget-related behavior and managerial performance. Similar to the recommendation that no one structure is optimal for all organizations, Bruns and Waterhouse advise against a universal policy about budget preparation.

Although still relatively young, the research on contingency theories of organization structure suggests the need to examine organizational, environmental, and personal variables as multidimensional systems with complex interrelationships among the variables. This requires the study of large numbers of organizations and an increase in sample size as more variables are studied (Sathe, 1975).

We have seen in this section that behavioral research has come full circle—from an emphasis on individual behavior to an emphasis on complex organizations and then back to an emphasis on the individual as an active participant in large, complex organizations. Before the rise of large organizations, behavioral scientists were concerned with individual's motives, personality, and cognitive processes. This research dealt with relatively simple problems such as entrepreneurial behavior and relationships between the worker and manager where the owner was usually the manager. The problems became more complex as ownership and stewardship separated and owners sought control over managers who in turn sought control over subordinates. Thus, as organizations grew, interpersonal relations and communication between individuals and groups of individuals became more and more important. At the same time the complexity of the technology and environment increased. The emergence of large, complex organizations initially inspired research that viewed organizations as information processing entities that structured themselves according to technological and environmental demands. There is evidence that recent research in behavioral science and management accounting has begun to include the study of individual behavior along with organizational structure and environmental variables.

One of the primary reasons for this reemphasis on individual behavior stems from the way organizations have structured their activities. Organizations have coped with dynamic environments and technologies by assigning responsibility for information processing and decisions to fairly autonomous subunits. This movement to decentralization and divisionalization of lines of business and functions has placed a great deal of pressure on management control systems to provide accurate and timely information to individuals or groups of individuals who are responsible for efficient and effective performance of the organization. Thus it is not the information processing capacity of the organization *per se* that determines the success of the organization, but the collective information processing capacity of the organization's individual decision makers. Different individuals have different needs, preferences, and attitudes which influence their information processing and decision-making behavior. Environmental factors also influence this behavior. In this regard there is a striking similarity between human information processing theories and contingency theories of organization. Human information processing relates the structuring of information processing activities in terms of differentiation and integration to efficient performance in the same way that contingency theory explains organization structure and performance. Therefore, it is extremely difficult to avoid including personal characteristics of the individual in research studies of effective organizations and vice versa.

CONCLUSION

The purpose of this review of behavioral science and management accounting was to provide a concise introduction into the literature for those interested in this area. To accomplish this we organized the literature into three interrelated categories: research on individual behavior, research on small group processes, and research on complex organizations. We have traced behavioral research from its early focus on individual behavior to its emphasis on individual behavior in small groups and large organizations. We have also traced behavioral research in management accounting along the same three levels of behavioral systems. Except in the area of small group processes, accountants have indicated an interest in transferring behavioral science theories and concepts to research designs on the effectiveness of management planning and control systems. Although the research is relatively young and fragmented, we have at least gained vital, foothold knowledge. But a great deal of fundamental research remains.

Measurement and communication are at the heart of internal planning, reporting, and control systems. There is general agreement that how measurement and communication systems affect the behavior of individuals in organizations and how individual behavior affects measurement and communication systems are legitimate concerns for those responsible for their design and implementation. Because very few behavioral scientists have taken an active role in this area, it is incumbent on accountants to take responsibility for transferring behavioral science knowledge to the design and implementation of effective management control systems.

BIBLIOGRAPHY

Ackoff, R. L., Towards a Behavioral Theory of Communication, *Management Science* (April, 1958), pp. 218–234.

Anthony, R. N., *Planning and Control Systems: A Framework for Analysis* (Division of Research, Harvard Graduate School of Business Administration, 1965).

Anton, H. R., Some Aspects of Measurement and Accounting, *Journal of Accounting Research* (Spring, 1964), pp. 1–9.

Argyris, C., *The Impact of Budgets on People* (The Controllership Foundation, 1952).

Arrow, K. J., Control in Large Organizations, *Management Science* (April, 1964), pp. 397–406.

Arrow, K. J., *The Limits of Organization* (New York: W. W. Norton, 1974).

Ashton, R. H., An Experimental Study of Internal Control Judgments, *Journal of Accounting Research* (Spring, 1974), pp. 144–157.

Ashton, R. H., Cue Utilization and Expert Judgment: A Comparison of Independent Auditors with Other Judges, *Journal of Applied Psychology* (August, 1974), pp. 437–444.

Barnard, C. I., *The Functions of the Executive* (Cambridge: Harvard University Press, 1938).

Bavelas, A., Communication Patterns in Task-Oriented Groups, *Journal of the Acoustical Society of America* (1950), pp. 725–730.

Becker, S. & Green, D., Jr., Budgeting and Employee Behavior, *Journal of Business* (October, 1962), pp. 392–402.

Bonini, C. P., *Simulation of Information and Decision Systems in the Firm* (Englewood Cliffs, N.J.: Prentice-Hall, 1963).

Bruner, J. S., Goodnow, J. & Austin, G., *A Study of Thinking* (New York: Wiley, 1956).

Bruns, W. J., Accounting Information and Decision Making: Some Behavioral Hypotheses, *The Accounting Review* (July, 1968), pp. 469–480.

Bruns, W. J. & Waterhouse, J.H., Budgetary Control and Organization Structure, *Journal of Accounting Research* (Autumn, 1975), pp. 177–203.

Brunswik, E., *Perception and the Representative Design of Experiments* (Berkeley: University of California Press, 1956).

Burns, T. J., ed., *The Behavioral Aspects of Accounting Data for Performance Evaluation* (Columbus: College of Administrative Science, The Ohio State University, 1969).

Burns, T. J., ed., *Behavioral Experiments in Accounting* (Columbus: College of Administrative Science, The Ohio State University, 1972).

Caplan, E. H., Behavioral Assumptions of Management Accounting, *The Accounting Review* (July, 1966), pp. 496–509.

Cartwright, D. & Zander, A., eds., *Group Dynamics* (Evanston, Illinois: Row Peterson, 1953).

Charnes, A. & Stedry, A.C. Investigations in the Theory of Multiple Budgeted Goals, in *Management Controls*, ed. C. P. Bonini *et al.* (New York: McGraw-Hill, 1964), pp. 186–202.

Cherry, C., *On Human Communication* (Cambridge, Massachusetts: MIT Press, 1966).

Churchman, C. W., *Prediction and Optimal Decision* (Englewood Cliffs, N.J.: Prentice-Hall, 1961).

Cook, D. M., The Effect of Frequency of Feedback on Attitudes and Performance, Supplement to Vol. 5 of *Journal of Accounting Research* (1968), pp. 213–224.

Cravens, D. W., An Exploratory Analysis of Individual Information Processing, *Management Science* (June, 1970), pp. B656–670.

Cyert, R. M. & March, J. G., *A Behavioral Theory of the Firm* (Englewood Cliffs, N.J.: Prentice-Hall, 1963).

Dearborn, D. C. & Simon, H. A., Selective Perception: A Note on the Departmental Identifications of Executives, *Sociometry* (June, 1958).

DeCoster, D. T. & Fertakis, J. P., Budget-Induced Pressure and Its Relationship to Supervisory Behavior, *Journal of Accounting Research* (Autumn, 1968), pp. 237–246.

Dermer, J. D., Cognitive Characteristics and the Perceived Importance of Information, *The Accounting Review* (July, 1973), pp. 511–519.

Driver, M. J., & Mock, T. J., Human Information Processing, Decision Style Theory, and Accounting Information Systems, *The Accounting Review* (July, 1975), pp. 490–508.

Driver, M. J., & Streufert, S., Integrative Complexity: An Approach to Individuals and Groups as Information Processing Systems, *Administrative Science Quarterly* (June, 1969).

Drucker, P. F., *The Practice of Management* (New York: Harper, 1954).

Edwards, W., The Theory of Decision Making, *Psychological Bulletin* (April, 1954), pp. 380–417.

Etzioni, A., *Complex Organizations* (New York: Holt, Rinehart & Winston, 1961).

Fertakis, J. P., On Communication, Understanding, and Relevance in Accounting Reports, *The Accounting Review* (October, 1970), pp. 623–640.

Festinger, L., *A Theory of Cognitive Dissonance* (Palo Alto: Stanford University Press, 1957).

Fiedler, F. E., *A Theory of Leadership Effectiveness* (New York: McGraw-Hill, 1967).

Galbraith, J., *Designing Complex Organizations* (Reading, Massachusetts: Addison-Wesley, 1973).

Guetzkow, H., ed., *Groups, Leadership, and Men: Research in Human Relations* (Pittsburgh: Carnegie Institute of Technology Press, 1951).

Harvey, O. J., Hunt, D. E. & Schroder, H. M., *Conceptual Systems and Personality Organization* (New York: J. Wiley, 1961).

Heller, F. A., *Managerial Decision-Making: A Study of Leadership Styles and Power Sharing Among Senior Managers* (Assen: Van Gorcum, 1971).

Hofstede, G. H., *The Game of Budget Control* (New York: Van Nostrand, 1967).

Homans, G. C., *The Human Group* (New York: Harcourt, Brace & World, 1950).

Hopwood, A. G., *An Accounting System and Managerial Behavior* (Lexington, Massachusetts: Lexington Books, 1973).

Hopwood, A. G., *Accounting and Human Behavior* (London: Haymarket Publ., 1974).

Huysmans, J. H. B. M., The Effectiveness of the Cognitive-Style Constraint in Implementing Operations Research Proposals, *Management Science* (September, 1970), pp. 92–104.

Irwin, F. W. & Smith, W. A., Value, Cost and Information as Determiners of Decision, *Journal of Experimental Psychology* (September, 1957), pp. 229–232.

Katz, D. & Kahn, R. L., *The Social Psychology of Organizations* (New York: J. Wiley, 1966).

Kogan, N. & Wallach, M. A., *Risk Taking: A Study in Cognition and Personality* (New York: Holt, Rinehart & Winston, 1964).

Lanzetta, J. T. & Kanareff, V. T., Information Cost, Amount of Payoff, and Level of Aspiration as Determinants of Information Seeking in Decision Making, *Behavioral Science* (October, 1962), pp. 459–473.

Lawler, E. E., *Motivation in Work Organizations* (Monterey, California: Brooks/Cole, 1973).

Lawler, E. E. & Rhode, J. G., *Information and Control in Organizations* (Pacific Palisades, California: Goodyear, 1976).

Lawrence, P. R. & Lorsch, J. W., *Organization and Environment* (Boston: Division of Research, Harvard Graduate School of Business, 1967).

Libby, R., The Use of Simulated Decision Makers in Information Evaluation, *The Accounting Review* (July, 1975), pp. 475–489.

Libby, R., Accounting Ratios and the Prediction of Failure: Some Behavioral Evidence, *Journal of Accounting Research* (Spring, 1975), pp. 150–161.

Likert, R., *The Human Organization* (New York: McGraw-Hill, 1967).

Likert, R., *New Patterns of Management* (New York: McGraw-Hill, 1961).

March, J. G. & Simon, H. A., *Organizations* (New York: Wiley, 1958).

Marschak, J. & Radner, R., *Economic Theory of Teams* (Yale University Press, 1972).

Maslow, A. H., *Motivation and Personality* (New York: Harper & Row, 1954).

McClelland, D., Atkinson, J. W., Clark, R. A. & Lowell, E. L., *The Achievement Motive* (New York: Appleton-Century-Crofts, 1953).

McGregor, D., *The Human Side of Enterprise* (New York: McGraw-Hill, 1960).

Miles, R. E. & Vergin, R. C., Behavioral Properties of Variance Control, *California Management Review* (Spring, 1966), pp. 57–65.

Miller, G. A., The Magical Number Seven, Plus or Minus Two, *Psychological Review* (March, 1956), pp. 81–97.

Miller, J. G., Information Input Overload, in *Self-Organizing Systems,* ed. Marschall C. Yovits *et al.* (Washington: Spartan Books, 1962), pp. 61–78.

Neisser, U., *Cognitive Psychology* (New York: Appleton-Century-Crofts, 1967).

Onsi, M., Factor Analysis of Behavioral Variables Affecting Budgetary Slack, *The Accounting Review* (July, 1973), pp. 535–548.

Piaget, J., *The Psychology of Intelligence* (London: Routledge & Kegan Paul, 1950).

Porter, L. W. & Lawler, E. E., *Managerial Attitudes and Performance* (Homewood, Illinois: Irwin, 1968).

Rapoport, A., The Promise and Pitfalls of Information Theory, *Behavioral Science* (October, 1956), pp. 303–309.

Revsine, L., Data Expansion and Conceptual Structure, *The Accounting Review* (October, 1970), pp. 704–711.

Ridgway, V. F., Dysfunctional Consequences of Performance Measurements, *Administrative Science Quarterly* (September, 1956), pp. 240–247.

Roethlisberger, F. J. & Dickson, W. J., *Management and the Worker* (Cambridge: Harvard University Press, 1939).

Rosen, L. S. & Schenck, R. E., Some Behavioral Consequences of Accounting Measurement Systems, *Cost and Management* (October, 1967), pp. 6–16.

San Miguel, J. G., Human Information Processing and Its Relevance to Accounting: A Laboratory Study, *Accounting, Organizations and Society* (forthcoming).

Sathe, V., Contingency Theory of Organizational Structure, J. L. Livingstone, ed., *Managerial Accounting: The Behavioral Foundations* (Columbus, Ohio: Grid, 1975), pp. 51–63.

Schein, E. H., *Organizational Psychology* (Englewood Cliffs, N.J.: Prentice-Hall, 1965).

Schiff, M. & Lewin, A. Y., The Impact of People on Budgets, *The Accounting Review* (April, 1970), pp. 259–268.

Schroder, H. M., Driver M. J. & Streufert, S., *Human Information Processing* (New York: Holt, Rinehart & Winston, 1967).

Siegel, S. & Fouraker, L. E., *Bargaining and Group Decision Making* (New York: McGraw-Hill, 1960).

Simon, H. A., *Models of Man: Social and Rational* (New York: Wiley, 1957).

Simon, H. A., Theories of Decision-Making in Economics and Behavioral Science, *The American Economic Review* (June, 1959), pp. 253–283.

Skinner, B. F., *Science and Human Behavior* (New York: Macmillan, 1953).

Stedry, A. C., *Budget Control and Cost Behavior* (Englewood Cliffs, N.J.: Prentice-Hall, 1960).

Swieringa, R. J. & Moncur, R. H., *Some Effects of Participative Budgeting on Managerial Behavior* (New York: National Association of Accountants, 1975).

Thompson, J. D., *Organizations in Action* (New York: McGraw-Hill, 1967).

Tosi, H., The Human Effects of Managerial Budgeting Systems, J. L. Livingstone, ed., *Managerial Accounting: The Behavioral Foundations* (Columbus, Ohio: Grid, 1975), pp. 139–156.

Von Neumann, J. & Morgenstern, O., *Theory of Games and Economic Behavior* (Princeton University Press, 1953).

Vroom, V. H., *Some Personality Determinants of the Effects of Participation* (Englewood Cliffs, N.J.: Prentice-Hall, 1960).

Vroom, V. H. & Yetton, P. W., *Leadership and Decision-Making* (University of Pittsburgh Press, 1973).

Watson, D. J. H., Contingency Formulations of Organizational Structure: Implications for Managerial Accounting, J. L. Livingstone, ed., *Managerial Accounting: The Behavioral Foundations* (Columbus, Ohio: Grid, 1975), pp. 65–80.

Williamson, O. E., *Economics of Discretionary Behavior* (Englewood Cliffs, N.J.: Prentice-Hall, 1964).

Woodward, J., *Industrial Organization: Theory and Practice* (New York: Oxford University Press, 1965).

Zaleznik, A. & Moment, D., *The Dynamics of Interpersonal Behavior* (New York: Wiley, 1964).

Zazonc, R. B., Cognitive Theories in Social Psychology, in *The Handbook of Social Psychology,* ed., G. Lindzey and E. Aronson (New York: Addison-Wesley, 1969), Vol. I, pp. 320–411.

Zimbardo, P. G., *The Cognitive Control of Motivation* (New York: Scott-Foresman, 1969).

Intraorganizational Power Considerations for Designing Information Systems

Martin L. Bariff

Jay R. Galbraith
The Wharton School, University of Pennsylvania

Organizations may be viewed as shifting political coalitions competing for organizational resources. Control over the administration and distribution of information is one means for influencing the distribution of intraorganizational power. Both accountants and MIS staff share this ability to acquire power for themselves and affect a redistribution of power among their users. In this paper the vertical, horizontal and information services perspectives of power are discussed. Propositions for redistributing power are suggested and impacts from changing information services technology are evaluated.

Organizations may be viewed as groups of functionally differentiated or self-contained subunits which require some integrative mechanism to achieve organizational objectives. Typically, individuals within these subunits and hierarchical control positions will compete for scarce resources within an organization. Successful resource acquisition will be highly dependent upon political rather than rational-economic decision-making. One important influence mechanism is the degree of a group's intraorganizational power, i.e. an individual's or group's ability to influence the task behavior of another organizational member (Dahl, 1957; Hickson *et al.,* 1971). Sources of intraorganizational power are generally represented by formal authority and influence associated with the capability of an individual's or group's comparative advantage for providing information, materials or other services to support other individuals' or groups' tasks. Thus, the design and operation of an organization's information system (IS) will affect the distribution of intraorganizational power, i.e. availability, accuracy, and sharing of information. These information systems (including accounting) support operations, control activities and planning for organizational change.

Task performance in organizations is dependent upon information system output which becomes task input signals with varying degrees of "ambiguity, uncertainty and equivocality" (Weick, 1969). Less information uncertainty permits activities to be coordinated through rules, hierarchical relationships and goal setting (Galbraith, 1977). As uncertainty increases and these mechanisms are unable to support the information processing demands, additional strategies should be considered. In-

From *Accounting, Organizations and Society,* Vol. 3, No. 1 (1978), pp. 15–27.

formation processing demands can be reduced through the creation of slack resources or self-contained tasks. Likewise, information processing capabilities can be increased by investments in vertical information systems or the creation of lateral relations. Although this paper will specifically discuss the role of information systems for organizational design, other design alternatives, e.g. changes in organizational structure, tasks and technology, reward systems and decision processes, will be considered when appropriate.

The initial implementation and subsequent modifications of an IS may result in a functional or dysfunctional redistribution of intraorganizational power. The purpose of this paper is to examine potential power impacts derived from IS modifications. Implications from previous research will be related to IS design.

The politics of organizational decision-making has three important implications for providers of information services. First, the objective of an information system project may be successful implementation with minimal effect upon the current social structure. Thus, knowledge of existing political relationships is required. Second, an information system modification may be used to effect a planned change in the social structure. Finally, information system modifications may be used to enhance the relative power of the information systems group. In this paper, information services will include both the accounting function and the computer support function. Much of the discussion will apply equally to both groups. Where appropriate, distinctions will be stated.

The first section of the paper will discuss the characterization of information as a valuable resource and its importance for adaptive organizations. The second section will relate the concept of intraorganizational power to both information and the information services activity. The following three sections will discuss IS design considerations and power implications from three perspectives: both (1) vertical and (2) horizontal relationships between organizational members (Zald, 1970), and (3) the relationship between the IS group and other groups in the organization.[1] Accounting information system illustrations will be included and the role of IS to facilitate adaptive behavior will be discussed. The final section will provide some prescriptions for IS design and comments on the impact of technological trends upon the design of organizations.

VALUE OF INFORMATION

Organizations may be characterized as a set of purposeful systems which select and modify objectives and the means for their attainment (Ackoff, 1971). Most organizations and their members operate within infrastructures and environments exhibiting varying degrees of uncertainty. Thus, the choice of objectives and the performance of tasks require information processing activities which obtain additional information necessary for the planning and execution of tasks (Galbraith, 1977).

The sources of this information may reside within the firm or external to the firm. Furthermore, transmission of the information may occur through formal communication channels (human or machine) or informal channels (Sutton & Porter, 1968). Information systems are designed to facilitate these types and modes of communication. The intriguing aspect, however, is the redistribution of power caused by the choice of information mechanism, e.g. a change from a human to a computer-based reporting system with automatic source data entry.

---

[1]Formal propositions for the effect of information systems changes on the distribution of power are found in Table 1 and referenced in the text as: V = vertical, H = horizontal, and IS = information services.

Information is contained in many forms (Weick, 1969; 40), and is generally recognized as a valuable resource. Although many measures of information value have been proposed, e.g. changes in expected value of information, increased revenue, decreased costs, decreased decision time and dissonance reduction, information is not formally recognized and recorded as an asset within an organization's financial reports. Surrogate measures of information value are represented by an organization's investment in data base administrators, data base management systems and data security mechanisms. The information resource, however, is necessary for the performance of daily activities. Moreover, the complexity and uncertainty of organizational environments require intelligence information for shaping the environment or adapting to uncontrollable events (Hedberg *et al.*, 1976). The next section discusses control over information resources and amount of organizational power.

INTRAORGANIZATIONAL POWER

Various concepts of power have been proposed (e.g. Cartwright, 1959; Dahl, 1957; Emerson, 1962; Hamilton, 1977; Hickson *et al.*, 1971; Kornberg & Perry, 1966; March, 1955, and Simon, 1953). Dahl (1957) suggested that power is the ability of one individual to influence the actions of another person. Dimensions of power included source, means, amount and scope (Dahl, 1957). Various sources of power, e.g. expert, reward and legitimate, have been proposed and studied (French & Raven, 1959, and Raven, 1974). Traditionally, the impact of IS on intraorganizational power has not been a research focus, especially for accountants. Most studies of the effects of IS on organizations (e.g. Withington, 1969, and Whisler, 1970) have been limited to structural characteristics which are somewhat easier to measure. Although accounting information systems research has not directly addressed the distribution of power, some budget and resource allocation studies have considered this issue (e.g. Birnberg *et al.*, 1970; Bower, 1970; Hopwood, 1972; Simon *et al.*, 1954; Swieringa & Moncur, 1975, and Wildavsky, 1974). Recent emphasis upon the political processes affecting decision-making in organizations provides a new impetus for studying power. The concept of power has two applications for this paper.

The first relates to the power of individuals who provide sources of information which are necessary for task performance and evaluation. A number of studies (e.g. Crozier, 1964; Mechanic, 1962; Mumford & Pettigrew, 1975; and Pettigrew, 1972, 1973) indicate that the ability of individuals to control information provides perceived power over other individuals. Strategies for information control include procurement, interpretation (uncertainty absorption [March & Simon, 1958]), misspecification, delay, overload and suppression. For this paper, a question of interest is: How might alternative IS designs influence the access, objectivity and speed of information and thus effect a vertical or horizontal redistribution of power?

The second application relates to the process of producing information—the IS function. Hickson *et al.* (1971) proposed that the services provided by organizational subunits affect their power in relation to other organizational subunits. Perrow (1970) found that the Marketing Department was a more powerful subunit due to its uncertainty reduction activities. Hinings *et al.* (1974) found that perceived subunit power was correlated with measures suggested by their strategic contingencies theory (e.g. workflow pervasiveness, immediacy and substitution). Although information processing was not directly studied, the perceived power of the accounting subunit was highest for financial tasks. In this paper we will examine the changes in the intraorganizational power (hereafter denoted as "power") of the IS subunit as caused by modifications to the IS (Hedberg *et al.*, 1975).

The ultimate interest in the redistribution of power is the impact upon the effectiveness and efficiency of task performance. Few studies of these potentially functional and dysfunctional consequences have been conducted. Usually the end result or dependent variable is the redistribution of power. Objective measures of power for an organizational subunit include budget dollars, number of personnel, and committee appointments. In contrast, subjective measures include workflow pervasiveness, immediacy and substitutability (Hickson, 1971), ability to prevent or absorb uncertainty and control over information. When appropriate in this paper, implications for consequences on task performance will be proposed. The next section examines the vertical redistribution of power.

VERTICAL DISTRIBUTION OF POWER

The vertical distribution of intraorganizational power may be viewed from both macro and micro perspectives. The former relates to structural variables, e.g. specialization, hierarchy, and span of control. The latter addresses the contacts between superiors and subordinates at any pair of contiguous hierarchical levels. The impact of IS design on power at both levels of analysis will be discussed.

At the macro level, Leavitt & Whisler (1958) predicted the absorption of middle management into the ranks of their superiors and subordinates, the upward shift of planning, and a trend toward recentralization. These organizational changes would tend to shift the locus of power upward. Whisler (1970) found a decrease in the number of organizational levels and in the span of control in insurance companies (V.1.1). Burlingame (1961), however, had predicted that the computer would aid the control tasks of middle management and foster decentralization. Some support is offered by Hofer (1970) who found no changes in span of control and size of subunits (V.1.3). Mumford & Banks (1967) discovered a reduction in hierarchical level and an increase in span of control. However Blau *et al.* (1976) found that the number of levels increased, for the direct computer information channel reduced the dependency of superiors on the manual upward flow of written reports. A trend toward centralization existed for geographically dispersed subunits with remote computing facilities linked to corporate headquarters. Likewise, decentralization was characteristic of subunits with inhouse computing facilities. However, this distinction may be confounded with the cost versus profit center roles, respectively, for the organizations studied.

Withington (1969) suggests that computers may lead to centralized data processing, but will also lead to decentralization of responsibilities. Primarily, it reduces the monopoly on companywide data that top managers previously held. Withington's interpretation of his consulting experience is consistent with recent findings in organization research. Both Child (1972) and Blau *et al.* (1976) find a greater degree of decentralization in organizations having greater proportions of staff specialists and a more extensive use of formal systems and procedures (V.1.2). Similarly, Bruns & Waterhouse (1975) have found that more sophisticated control systems are related to decentralization and greater perceived control on the part of managers.

Thus, there is no consistent set of findings concerning the extent of computer use or of formalized systems' use and centralization. There are several reasons for this. In part, this is due to different measures of centralization. When similar measures are used (Child, 1972; Blau *et al.*, 1976; Bruns & Waterhouse, 1975), similar results are obtained. Second, the effect of formal systems may vary with stage of implementation. Whisler suggests that middle level roles are first more influential, then less influential as the system passes from design to operational use. Third, none of the studies control for the divisional structure or the control system prevailing (cost center, profit center, investment center). Whisler suggests that his organizations moved back to functional organizations after computer installation. The Blau *et al.* (1976) study suggests that greater centralization results when computers are used in functional organizations and less centralization when they are used in divisionalized structures. These results suggest that it is not useful to view the effect of formal information independent of other structural properties, such as the basis of divisions, in attempting macro studies. The results also suggest that if management wants to use computers to decentralize, they can. If they want to centralize, they can. There is an important element of choice that gets eliminated when an overly deterministic view is taken.

At the macro level of analysis, a number of implications for power redistribution exist. Formalization and increased access to "objectively" captured data relating to subordinates' tasks may modify the utilization of informal information channels and reliance on reported performance information (V.3.1). Increased reliability of upward information flows may be obtained by two methods: (1) a computer may directly capture input, or (2) accountants, acting as agents for top management, can capture source data at operating subunits (Simon *et al.*, 1954). Furthermore, expansion of the formally captured data, e.g. report decision assumptions, provides additional insight into the subordinate's performance (V.3.2). These types of IS modifications tend to upwardly redistribute power. It should be pointed out that there is a great deal of confounding in many of the case studies that lead to this conclusion. There is an effect due to a redesign of work which may or may not be linked to the computer. There is also an information effect. It is the information effect that we are interested in. In order to make statements about information effects, the system change must be defined more specifically.

A key variable is the percentage of human-mediated input to a formal system (V.5). Previous studies have documented the degree to which superiors are dependent on subordinates for input on performance (Pettigrew, 1972; Mechanic, 1962). There are also studies that show that upward information is systematically biased by subordinates. The installation of a system that includes an "objective" redundant information channel which captures source data and reports it without going through subordinates should eliminate this dependence on subordinates. This is precisely the result obtained by Galbraith (1976). Figure 1 depicts the system. Two departments had ac-

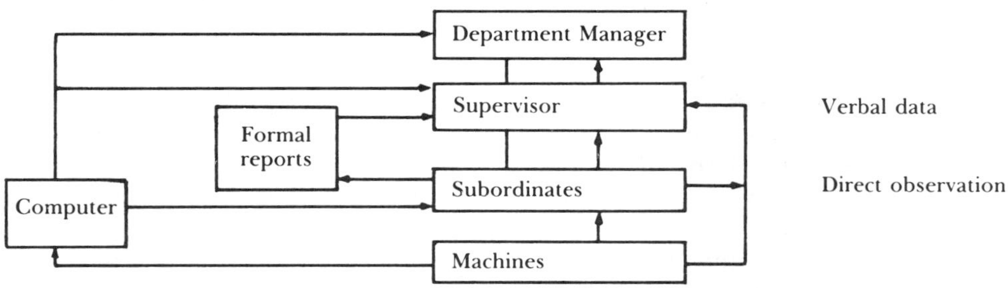

FIGURE 1. Information channels relaying performance data (direct observation, verbal, formal reports and computers).

cess to a computer system as shown, while two comparable departments did not. In both departments for both supervisors and managers, the result was less reliance on the verbal channel as measured by the proportion of verbal contacts with subordinates. Interview data with the managers suggest that they no longer rely exclusively on subordinate input or when they do, they get the straight story (V.2). Before, they had to probe and question several people to get the same data. They claim the redundant channel eliminates disputes and improves superior subordinate contacts.

The output from the computer was available every two hours. In times of crisis, this was too infrequent. When machines broke down, supervisors relied exclusively on verbal data and direct observation (V.4). Also, the managers relied more on verbal data. These results suggest that the more uncertain the task, the greater the reliance on verbal data.

What was the effect on power? First, there is the power equalizing effect of everyone having access to the same data. The second effect depended on the manager. One was a 25-year veteran and his behavior was no different than that of the department manager's without a computer. The other used the computer extensively as an exception reporter, delegated more activities to others and spent much less time on matters within his department. He spent more time on long-run activities (experimenting with an energy conservation program), with his superior and with colleagues in other departments. Thus, the access to valid performance data permitted greater delegation and freed the manager of the necessity of direct supervision. The time made available was used for longer-run activities and interdepartmental coordination. It could have been used to expand the span of control. Again, a design choice is available to the organization. Some may choose span adjustment, while others may redefine the manager's role. A macro study would miss this difference and conclude no relation between computer use and decentralization, and span of control. The relation depends on the organization's choice and whether the formal system uses human-mediated input.

If the unit of analysis is extended from contiguous superior-subordinate relationships to include those contacts with more intervening levels, additional factors, e.g. data expansion and mechanical data capture, can be suggested. The formal recording of decision assumptions or adequate data to infer the assumptions will provide more power to superiors (V.2). In one continuous process, manufacturing organizations, Bariff discovered that a computer-based budget system was installed to provide better insight to budgets submitted by subunits to the central administration. Members of the central administration could fit mathematical models to the data base to develop budget assumptions of subunits. Thus, the budget assumptions could be inductively derived by the central administration.

The expansion of a reporting system to include all quantitative performance criteria enabled superiors to more quickly affect subordinate behavior (Blau, 1963). This context also provided a more objective basis for performance evaluation which had previously been perceived as a subjective process by subordinates. Likewise, the introduction of a computer-based information system by a health care funding agency to collect standardized operations data from health centers provided for increased agency control (Quinn, 1976) (V.3.3). Pfeffer (1976) found that the existence of satisfactory objective criteria minimized the impact of social influences on the allocation of research grants by a government agency. Nadler *et al.* (1976) reported that the joint formulation and review of performance criteria (in contrast to solely a management determination) significantly reduced employee turnover.

A similar effect may arise from automated, rather than human-mediated, data capture. The inability of subordinates to "smooth" data inputs for formal reports may upwardly shift power to performance evaluators (Mechanic, 1962).

Some choices of accounting systems affect the relative power between managers at various levels in an organization. For example, incremental budgeting requires the justification for additional projects, thus favoring the subordinates. Zero-base budgeting, however, favors the superordinate (or tends to equalize power), for existing programs also need to be justified. This "gaming the system" attitude is also represented by the subunits' treatment of discretionary expenditures. Unfavorable budget overruns can be "masked" by reducing these discretionary expenditures. Unless an IS reports disaggregated budget data, the subordinate's strategy may be successful.

This review of previous studies indicates that formalization of information flows and machine-based data captured at the source can promote vertical power equalization. Other IS policies, however, could have continued to foster asymmetrical relationships. Thus, top management needs to specify the intended, resultant power distribution. The next section discusses a lateral, rather than a hierarchical, distribution of power.

HORIZONTAL POWER DISTRIBUTION

The horizontal distribution of intraorganizational power has been studied in a variety of organizations (e.g. Perrow, 1970; Pfeffer & Salancik, 1974; Salancik & Pfeffer, 1974, 1977). From this perspective, the focus is the potential redistribution of power across subunits at comparable, organizational levels. Some of the design factors for consideration include: mechanization and location of data capture, degree of information sharing, numbers and types of applications embedded in the IS, and the complexity of IS models.

Interdepartmental conflict (Walton & Dutton, 1969) is often attributed to mistrust, insufficient information sharing for planning and type of performance measures. To achieve better firmwide utilization of resources (decrease in slack), shared access (subject to privacy laws) to planning and operating data for sequentially-linked subunits (Thompson, 1967) should minimize potentially dysfunctional gaming strategies and tend to equalize power. As the level of trust between subunits increases, the need to gather more objective data may decrease in order to achieve joint success (Lawler, 1976) (H.2). A complementary, yet essential, element is the use of cooperative, rather than competitive, performance criteria. Information system designers can influence the degree of data sharing and thus the equalization of subunit power (H.4). In a similar manner, the formalization of planning models and data in the IS will tend to equalize power.

Dutton & Walton (1966) studied subunit relations in two plants. One exhibited a cooperative climate; the other exhibited a competitive climate. In the former firm, which displayed a high degree of shared information between sales and production, performance for a range of activities surpassed the other plant. For example, in the competitive plant, the lack of shared information resulted in the acceptance of unprofitable orders as production had implemented, but did not communicate technological innovations. In a laboratory experiment, London (1975) found that groups with homogeneous, rather than heterogeneous, information displayed a more equal distribution of influence. Knowledge of other subunits' activities (perhaps jointly determined performance measures also) appears to reduce subunit bias (Dearborn & Simon, 1958).

The introduction of autonomous work groups at the Volvo plant (Hedberg, 1975) also introduced information sharing across functional subunits. Prior to this process innovation, minimal information concerning workflows between work units often resulted in unanticipated taskloads downstream in the assembly line. After the introduction of CRT consoles for each work unit, anticipated work demands could be determined. The reduction of this task uncertainty was a factor in reducing employee turnover and absenteeism.

Mirvis & Macy (1976) in a hospital context, proposed joint planning by admissions and ward staffs to anticipate and balance patient inflows across ward. Prior to the engagement, nurses were frequently transferred between wards to satisfy unanticipated demands and were unhappy with this scheduling procedure which resulted in unacceptable staff turnover. The implementation of the joint planning effort significantly reduced turnover.

In contrast to power equalization, as more applications per task set are incorporated into the IS, relative power tends to shift to the IS personnel who maintain the applications (H.3.2). This example of expert power (French & Raven, 1959) will be pervasive across subunits who utilize IS services. Furthermore, additional tasks within a subunit may become computer-based.

Planning, as one such example, has been and continues to be an important function for sustained organizational growth and adaptation to complex dynamic environments (Emergy & Trist, 1965). In addition to corporate planning, functional subunits, e.g. inventory control, manpower planning, financial analysis, require feedforward data (Koontz & Bradspies, 1972) to cope with changing conditions (H.3.3). In the past, purchasing agents have infiltrated other subunits by placing one of their staff in client subunits (Strauss, 1962). The action was justified (rationalized) on the basis that these subunits needed purchasing advice prior to submitting formal requests which may not be completely satisfied or incur penalty charges—excess transportation and expedition costs. The purchasing subunit was thus successful in shifting some power to their unit. Likewise, Simon *et al.* (1954) found members of the controller's department involved in most policy-making committees. In a computerized environment, the IS personnel can convert this feedforward monitoring function into an IS application and thus redistribute power to their subunit. Most input data are automatically captured. Some inputs, e.g. sales estimates and manpower projections, require human mediation. This control aspect over entry data introduces a sequential dependence of the IS upon some aspects of other subunits' tasks. In this situation, power tends to shift from the IS to other subunits.

For more appropriate control monitoring, organization designers may choose functional, program or matrix configurations (Galbraith, 1971) (H.6). The first two choices provide some cost allocation problems for the accounting IS personnel; however, matrix organizations produce the most complex allocation process. They also facilitate formal and informal communication (Knight, 1976). An example of a matrix IS is a program budget with complementary line item disclosure. Based upon technical expertise, accounting IS personnel would gain power from performing a more sophisticated allocation task (H.5). The implementation of a decision support system (DSS) for financial planning, however, permitted line management to develop cost allocation procedures (McLean & Riesing, 1977). Thus, the DSS shifted power from accountants to managers and the computer support group.

The degree of subunit differentiation may affect the design of an accounting system in two additional ways. First, the formal specification of responsibility centers will affect the allocation of resources among managers. Second, the choice of a transfer pricing scheme, e.g. full costs, marginal costs, market prices or negotiation, will contribute to the distribution of power (Watson, 1975) among subunits.

The lateral distribution of power is also sensitive to a subunit's ability to secure critical resources from the environment (Lawrence & Lorsch, 1967; Salancik & Pfeffer, 1974) and support internal critical activities.

Prior to discussing IS subunit power, a brief example (Conrath & de Roure, 1977) of the implementation effects of a computer-based logistics system will be presented. A U.S. military command has the responsibility for controlling flows of material for certain facilities from inception through field usage. Both status information and control of materials are administered by the unit. Prior to computer support, geographically dispersed junior staff would upwardly pass information to senior officers for decision-making. The centralized computer storage of these data and a model for specifying optimal coordination of material flows permitted junior staff to respond directly to information inquiries. Since senior officers adopted material allocation recommendations by the computer model, junior staff informally communicated model outputs to affected parties. Thus, decision-making and power was effectively shifted from senior officers to junior staff. The impact on the horizontal distribution of power among the junior staff was not reported. The use of computer, rather than manual, data bases may have reduced gaming among junior staff.

In response to the loss of power, the senior officers demanded that the old manual system remain in operation. Their rationale was that the computer system was unreliable. Manual system input was allocated more resources and, thus, the computer system data contained less reliable data—a self-fulfilling prophecy. The final solution required an additional installation of a computer-based monitoring system (and removal of the manual system) for senior officers which maintained their "feelings" of participation and control. Thus, IS designers need to consider both actual and apparent power implications for system implementation. The next section specifically discusses power consequences for the IS subunit.

INFORMATION SYSTEM SUBUNIT POWER

Hickson *et al.* (1971) proposed three measures of subunit power—workflow pervasiveness, immediacy and substitutability. Pervasiveness represents the number of tasks dependent upon the source activity (IS.1). The IS has numerous applications across a wide range of activities within a firm. Immediacy represents (1) the severity of the loss of the subunit's activities, and (2) speed at which the lost IS services impact other subunits. Data driven organizations, e.g. financial institutions, are good examples. Substitutability of subunit services is critical unless all the software can easily be run at an adjacent field site. This option, however, is not usually readily available. Although this measurement methodology has not been directed at the IS subunit, it is reasonable to expect results comparable to other technology-rich subunits.

As new or existing applications become computer-based, dependency upon the IS subunit increases. The stage hypothesis of IS function growth (Nolan, 1973) provides some empirical support for a positive relationship between increased IS budgets and a proliferation of IS applications. Although some dispute over the shape of the budget growth exists (Lucas, 1977), it is clear that emerging IS technology with data bases, communication networks and word processing will continue to maintain the criticality of IS activities.

Recently, organizations have formally recognized the administration of a data base as a critical role. Data base administrators create and maintain information for users; some of this data is shared among users. Thus, the data base administrator accrues power through the granting of access to data, the development of data standards, and the mediation of conflicts between users (DeBlasis & Johnson, 1976).

The design and implementation stages of the system development life cycle create a psychological contract; the IS analysts define user information requirements (Bariff, 1977), and the maintenance stage perpetuates this dependency. IS departments normally invite users to serve as systems analysts for limited "tours of duty". This action tends to increase IS power upon their return to operating subunits. Furthermore, the natural tendency for IS staff to move into line positions legitimizes the presence of IS in "client" subunits. Even the current trend toward distributed computing and, thus, local user control still fosters this dependency for IS staff conduct repairs, and can provide access to computing resources at another installation if the local unit should fail.

As these applications increase, structural differentiation within the IS subunit will occur. Accounting departments also display specializations, e.g. financial transactions, budget analysis, and internal audit. Most likely, some unequal distribution of power will result.

To facilitate flexible access and manipulation of stored data, natural language processors can retrieve information from a relational data base. For implementation, however, the aggregation level of the data must be rather detailed, e.g. events approach (Sorter, 1969), to facilitate meaningful retrievals. This type of flexibility increases the IS staff "technological" power, but also facilitates an adaptive planning style.

The increasing use of corporate models and rolling forecasts for business planning places IS personnel into the strategic policy function. Even financial (DRI, NBER) and nonfinancial *(New York Times)* data bases from external vendors are administered through the IS function. At lower organizational levels, more "turnkey" applications are being procured from vendors. Again, however, it is IS staff which install and maintain the packages.

If the IS subunit charges user subunits with real budget dollars for the services, the development of the transfer price algorithm will impact user subunit performance. Moreover, accountants typically define financial control measures, e.g. variance analyses and report the results upward to top management (Simon *et al.,* 1954). This activity often requires operating management to provide accountants with explanations for the variances and increases user dependency. The continuing complexity of regulatory accounting policies also enhances accountants' expert power.

As co-ordination within an organization becomes increasingly complex, investments in IS may occur (Galbraith, 1977) (IS.4). Since these investments are more permanent than those in human resource reallocation, further investments to cope with lagged fine tuning of the IS may be predicted from dissonance theory. Thus, the IS subunit will gain increasing power. For organizations in dynamic environments, however, this may be dysfunctional, for adaptive strategy mechanisms may be unable to operate within a relatively, fixed IS (Hedberg *et al.,* 1976).

Furthermore, it is not evident that investments in IS improve organizational performance. Grinyer & Norburn (1976) found no significant relationship between the number and types of information channels and financial performance. Lorsch & Allen (1973) studied high and medium performing conglomerates. The existence of more complex control mechanisms, e.g. monthly budgets and revisions facilitated upward information flows, but not downward flows. Lower performing firms exhibited limited downward flows. In both studies, bidirectional verbal vertical information flows appeared to be associated with more favorable financial performance. Thus, alternatives to formal written information systems should be considered. In a hospital study,

Mirvis & Macy (1976) recommended a joint planning effort (a liaison mechanism) which was adopted, rather than the computer-based patient admitting system proposed by the hospital administration.

Formal verbal channels (Mintzberg, 1973) and informal verbal and document channels will continue to facilitate information flows. However, formal document channels (manual or computer-based) offer well-defined decision models or decision support systems for users. Recent applications move toward the unstructured-strategic variety (Gorry & Scott Morton, 1971). Although computer-based information systems (CBIS) have been given greater scrutiny for cost-benefit analyses, the increasing utilization of computer-supported activities indicates a continuing expansionist era. In parallel, the intraorganizational power of the IS subunit should also be enhanced.

SUMMARY

The importance of power for predicting and explaining interpersonal behavior is generally recognized within organizational behavior research. The effectiveness of management control systems is highly dependent upon the functional use of power. In this paper, information systems have been characterized as one means for redistributing influence within an organization. They may be used either to perpetuate or modify decision-making processes and social structures. Both accountants and MIS staff design and administer information systems. Yet power has not been an important research focus. One objective of this paper is to foster a greater interest in the political impacts of information systems.

Organizational behavior researchers have studied the vertical and horizontal distribution of power at both individual and subunit levels of analysis. These perspectives are also useful for research into the impact of information systems on the distribution of power. A number of propositions concerning information systems and power have been suggested in this paper (Table 1).

For the vertical distribution of power, two perspectives were discussed. A macro-perspective focused upon the impact of CBIS on structural attributes of organizations, e.g. number of hierarchical levels, span of control and level of decision-making. Previous research indicates that CBIS support both centralization and decentralization. This is not surprising, for both centralized and decentralized data processing can be used to support either centralized or decentralized management decision-making. Thus, CBIS may effect an upward or downward redistribution of power. Future research studies need to introduce additional mediating variables to better define the research area. The micro-perspective relates to superior-subordinate relationships at contiguous organizational levels. The use of CBIS to: (1) reduce human-mediated data capture, (2) provide a faster and a redundant upward information flow, and (3) reveal subordinate decision-making assumptions to superiors promotes an upward shift of power.

The horizontal distribution of power is an index of the relative influence of functional subunits. Information which is machine captured or shared will effect an equalization of subunit power. Replacement of computer-based applications for human decision-making will reduce political influence and thus equalize power. A third and final perspective is the specific study of information system subunit influence.

Two perspectives of power are of interest. The first is the increase in the relative horizontal and vertical redistribution of power as a proliferation and criticality of computer-based applications increase. A similar effect for accountants is due to increasing external reporting regulations. The second perspective relates

TABLE 1. Intraorganizational Power Propositions

Area of Interest	Variables	Power Impact
Vertical distribution		
V.1 Centralization	1. Hierarchical levels 2. Specialization 3. Span of control 4. Level of decision-making (and number of CBIS applications)	Shift up (some findings to contrary)
V.2 Superior-subordinate relationship	Leadership behavior	Shift up
V.3 Formalization and sharing	1. Speed and accuracy 2. Decision-maker's assumptions 3. Basis for decision-maker's criteria	Shift up Shift up
V.4 Normal/crisis conditions	Formal versus informal channel utilization	Shift up
V.5 Information capture at source	Percentage of human mediated inputs (smoothing, etc.)	Shift up
Horizontal distribution		
H.1 Information input	Percentage of human mediated inputs	Pooled—sequential distribution or equalize
H.2 Sharing	Presence/absence of access, degree of trust, and objectivity	Equalize
H.3 Formalization	1. Objectivity of data 2. Number of computerized applications per task set 3. Number of computerized task sets per subunit	Equalize Shift to IS
H.4 Type of performance measures	Competitive versus cooperative	Equalize
H.5 Type of cost allocation	Simple-complex (matrix)	Shift to IS
H.6 Type of financial control system	Functional or program to matrix	Shift to IS
Magnitude of IS Power		
IS.1 Pervasiveness	1. Number of applications per task set	Shift to IS

TABLE 1. (Continued)

Area of Interest	Variables	Power Impact
	2. Number of computer applications per task set 3. Number of subunits with computer applications 4. Number of subunit links	
IS.2 IS Structure	Differentiation in IS	Unequal within IS
IS.3 Matrix organization	Cost Allocation Complexity	Shift to IS
IS.4 Coordination by IS	1. Investments in IS 2. Cognitive dissonance 3. Reduction by continuing IS investments	Shift to IS

to the task and structural differentiation which occurs within information services as the scope and magnitude of activities increase. This introduction of specialization will effect an unequal distribution of power within the information services subunit. Accountants also represent heterogeneous groups of financial, budget, cost, tax and audit specialists. These three major perspectives on the distribution of power offer challenging research areas since the politics of organizations often dominate organizational decision-making and resource allocation.

Since the introduction of computers for organizational information processing, a number of predictions about their impacts have been made. Leavitt & Whisler (1958) predicted that the adoption of computer technology would produce centralized decision-making with centralized computing facilities. The former still remains as an idiosyncratic choice of top management. Although the cost of mass memory systems has dramatically decreased, the advent of mini-computers, micro-processors and networks has provided an attractive alternative to centralized computing facilities. Furthermore, the current trend toward distributed computing appears to continue in the near term. This type of computer configuration facilitates the creation of autonomous subunits rather than large, central complexes.

By 1980, middle management was to disappear (Leavitt & Whisler, 1958). Any remaining individuals would be clerks performing routine tasks. Whisler (1974) still prophesizes reduced middle management, more centralized control of operations, and a shift in the basis of departmentalization. However, Vergin (1967) and Hunt & Newell (1971) all indicate that the ranks of middle management have not been materially affected. The more routine tasks have been delegated to the computer, but new free time is devoted to new managerial analyses.

The current variety of computing equipment provides for the development of information processing structures which support symmetrical or asymmetrical individual and subunit interrelationships. Current and future computer technology, e.g. data bases, mini-computers and word processing, indicates higher visibility and criticality for information system activities. Decision support systems and end user application programming facilitate the expansion of IS influence. Although accountants lose some influence to users and computer support groups, increasing governmental regulation provides for a net gain in power. IS designers can use the design process as a means to reinforce or modify management policies. To better understand this process and its consequences, additional research on intra-organizational power and its socio-economic consequences is necessary for organizations to actively influence or cope with their uncertain environments.

REFERENCES

Ackoff, R. L., Towards a System of Systems Concepts, *Management Science* (July 1971), pp. 661–71.

Bariff, M. L., Information Requirement Analysis: A Methodological Review, Decisions Sciences Department, W.P. 76-08-02, University of Pennsylvania, 1977.

Birnberg, J., Pondy, L. & Davis, L., Effect of Three Voting Rules on Resource Allocation Decisions, *Management Science* (February 1970), pp. B356–72.

Blau, P., Statistical Records of Performance, in *The Dynamics of Bureaucracy* (2nd ed.) (University of Chicago, 1963), pp. 36–49.

Blau, P., Falbe, C. H., McKinley, W. & Tracy, P., Technology and Organization in Manufacturing, *Administrative Science Quarterly* (March 1976), pp. 20–40.

Bower, J., *The Resource Allocation Process* (Irwin, 1970).

Bruns, W. J., Jr. & Waterhouse, J. H., Budgetary Control and Organizational Structure, *Journal of Accounting Research* (Autumn 1975), pp. 177–203.

Burlingame, J. F., Information Technology and Decentralization, *Harvard Business Review* (November–December 1961), pp. 121–26.

Cartwright, D., A Field Theoretical Conception of Power, in D. Cartwright, ed., *Studies in Social Power* (Institute for Social Research, 1959), pp. 183–220.

Child, J., Organization Structure and Strategies of Control: A Replication of the Aston Study, *Administrative Science Quarterly* (June 1972), pp. 163–77.

Conrath, D. W. & du Roure, G., Organizational Implications of Comprehensive Communication-Information Systems, Some Conjectures, Working Paper, University of Waterloo, 1977.

Crozier, M., *The Bureaucratic Phenomenon* (University of Chicago Press, 1964).

Dahl, R. A., The Concept of Power, *Behavioral Science* (July 1957), pp. 201–15.

Davis, K., Success of Chain-of-Command Oral Communication in a Manufacturing Management Group, *Academy of Management Journal* (December 1968), pp. 379–87.

DeBlasis, J. P. & Johnson, T. H., Data Base Administration—Review of Current Recommendations, Decision Sciences Department, W.P. 76-03-03, University of Pennsylvania, 1976.

Emerson, R. M., Power-Dependence Relations, *American Sociological Review* (February 1962), pp. 282–98.

French, J., Jr. & Raven, B., The Bases of Social Power, in D. Cartwright, ed., *Studies in Social Power* (Institute for Social Research, 1959), pp. 150–67.

Galbraith, J. R., Matrix Organizational Designs, *Business Horizons* (February 1971), pp. 29–40.

Galbraith, J. R., A Change Process for the Introduction of MIS—A Successful Case, Decision Sciences Department, W.P. 76-10-04, University of Pennsylvania, 1976.

Galbraith, J. R., *Organizational Design* (Addison-Wesley, 1977).

Grinyer, P. H. & Norburn, D., Planning for Existing Markets—Perceptions of Executives and Financial Performance, *Journal of the Royal Statistical Society,* Series A (January 1975), pp. 70–95.

Gundelach, P. & Tetzschner, Measurement of Influence in Organization—Critique of the Control Graph Method, *Acta Sociologica* (January 1976), pp. 49–63.

Hamilton, M., An Analysis & Typology of Social Power—H, *Philosophy of Social Science* (March 1977), pp. 51–65.

Hedberg, B., Computer Systems to Support Industrial Democracy, in E. Mumford & H. Sackman, eds., *Human Choice and Computers* (North-Holland, 1975), pp. 211–30.

Hedberg, B., Edstrom, A., Muller, W. & Wilpert, S. B., The Impact of Computer Technology on Organizational Power Structures, in E. Grochla &

N. Szyperski, eds., *Information Systems and Organization Structure* (New York, 1975), pp. 131–48.

Hedberg, B. L. T., Nystrom, P. C. & Starbuck, W. H., Camping on Seesaws—Prescriptions for a Self-Designing Organization; *Administrative Science Quarterly* (June 1971), pp. 216–29.

Hinings, C. R., Hickson, D. J., Pennings, J. M. & Schneck, R. E., Structural Conditions of Intraorganizational Power, *Administrative Science Quarterly* (March 1974), pp. 22–44.

Hofer, C. W., Emerging EDP Pattern, *Harvard Business Review* (April 1970), pp. 162–70.

Hofstede, G. H., *The Game of Budget Control* (Van Gorcum & Co., 1967).

Hopwood, A., An Empirical Study of the Role of Accounting Data in Performance Evaluation, Empirical Research in Accounting—Selected Studies, *Journal of Accounting Research* (Suppl., 1972), pp. 156–82.

Hunt, J. G. & Newell, P. F., Management in the 1980's Revisited, *Personnel Journal* (January 1971), pp. 35–43, 71.

Knight, Kenneth, Matrix Organizations—A Review, *The Journal of Management Studies* (May 1976), pp. 110–30.

Koontz, H. & Bradspies, R. W., Managing Through Feedforward Control, *Business Horizons* (June 1972), pp. 25–36.

Kornberg, A. & Perry, S., Conceptual Models of Power and Their Applicability to Empirical Research in Politics, *Political Science* (March 1966), pp. 52–70.

Lawrence, P. R. & Lorsch, J. W., *Organization and Environment* (Harvard University, 1967).

Lawler, E. E. III., Control Systems in Organizations, in M. D. Dunnette, ed., *Handbook of Individual and Organizational Psychology* (Rand McNally, 1976), pp. 1247–91.

Leavitt, H. J. & Whisler, T. L., Management in the 1980's, *Harvard Business Review* (November-December, 1958), pp. 41–48.

London, M., Effects of Shared Information and Participation on Group Process and Outcome, *Journal of Applied Psychology* (October 1975), pp. 537–43.

Lorsch, J. & Allen, S. III., *Managing Diversity and Independence* (Division of Research, Graduate School of Business, Harvard University, 1973).

Lucas, H., Jr. & Sutton, J., The Stage Hypothesis and the S-Curve—Some Contradictory Evidence, *Communications of ACM* (April 1977), pp. 254–59.

March, J. G., An Introduction to the Theory and Measurement of Influence, *American Political Science Review* (June 1955), pp. 431–51.

March, J. G. & Simon, H. A., *Organizations* (Wiley, 1958).

McLean, E. R. & Riesing, T. F., MAPP: A DSS for Financial Planning, *Database* (Winter, 1977), pp. 9–14.

Mechanic, D., Sources of Power of Lower Participants in Complex Organizations, *Administrative Science Quarterly* (December 1962), pp. 349–64.

Mintzberg, H., *The Nature of Managerial Work* (Harper & Row, 1973).

Mintzberg, H., *Impediments to the Use of Management Information* (NAA, 1975).

Mirvis, P. H. & Macy, B. A., Changing Organizations with Financial Information, Survey Research Center (Institute for Social Research, University of Michigan, 1976).

Mulder, M., van Eck, J. R. Ritsenna & deJong, R. D., An Organization in Crisis and Non-crisis Situations, *Human Relations* (February 1971), pp. 19–41.

Mumford, E. & Banks, O., *The Computer and the Clerk* (London: Routledge & Kegan Paul, 1967).

Mumford, E. & Pettigrew, A., *Implementing Strategic Decisions* (New York: Longman, 1975).

Nadler, D. A., Mirvis, P. H. & Camman, C., The Ongoing Feedback System: Experimenting with a New Managerial Tool, *Organizational Dynamics* (Spring 1976), pp. 63–80.

Nolan, R., Thoughts About the Fifth Stage, *Data Base* (Summer 1975), pp. 4–10.

Perrow, C., Departmental Power and Perspective in Industrial Firms, in M. N. Zald, ed., *Power in Organizations* (Vanderbilt, 1970), pp. 59–89.

Pettigrew, A. M., Information Control as a Power Resource, *Sociology* (May 1972), pp. 187–204.

Pettigrew, A. M., *The Politics of Organizational Decision-making* (Tavistock, 1973).

Pfeffer, J. & Salancik, G. R., Organizational Decision-making as a Political Process: The Case of a University Budget, *Administrative Science Quarterly* (June 1974), pp. 135–50.

Pfeffer, J., Salancik, G. R. & Leblebici, H., The Effect of Uncertainty on the Use of Social Influence on

Organizational Decision-making, *Administrative Science Quarterly* (June 1976), pp. 227–45.

Quinn, R. E., The Impacts of a Computerized Information System on the Integration and Coordination of Human Services, *Public Administration Review* (March–April 1976), pp. 166–74.

Raven, B., The Comparative Analysis of Power and Power Preference, in J. Tedeschi, ed., *Perspectives on Social Power* (Aldine, 1974), pp. 172–98.

Salancik, G. R. & Pfeffer, J., The Bases and Use of Power in Organizational Decision-making—The Case of a University, *Administrative Science Quarterly* (December 1974), pp. 453–73.

Salancik, G. R. & Pfeffer, J., Who Gets Power—and How They Hold on to It: A Strategic Contingency Model, *Organizational Dynamics* (Winter 1977), pp. 3–21.

Schoderbek, P. P. & Babcock, J. D., The Proper Placement of Computers and Management Involvement in EDP, *Business Horizons* (October 1969), pp. 35–42.

Simon, H., Notes on the Observation and Measurement of Power, *Journal of Politics* (November 1953), pp. 515–16.

Simon, H. A. *et al., Centralization versus Decentralization in Organizing the Controllers Department* (Controllership Foundation, 1954).

Simon, H. A., Applying Information Technology to Organizational Design, *Public Administration Review* (May-June 1973), pp. 268–77.

Sorter, G., An Events Approach to Accounting, *Accounting Review* (January 1969), pp. 12–19.

Starbuck, W. H., Organizations and Their Environment, in M. Dunnette, ed., *Handbook of Industrial and Organizational Psychology* (Rand McNally, 1976), pp. 1069–1123.

Strauss, G., Tactics of Lateral Relationship—The Purchasing Agent, *Administrative Science Quarterly* (September 1962), pp. 161–86.

Sutton, H. & Porter, L. W., A Study of the Grapevine in a Governmental Organization, *Personnel Psychology* (Summer 1968), pp. 223–30.

Swieringa, R. & Moncur, R., *Some Effects of Participative Budgeting on Managerial Behavior* (NAA, 1975).

Tannenbaum, A. S., *Control in Organization* (McGraw-Hill, 1968).

Vergin, R. C., Computer-Induced Organizational Changes, *MSU Business Topics* (Summer 1967), pp. 61–68.

Walton, R. E. & Dutton, J. M., The Management of Interdepartmental Conflict—A Model and Review, *Administrative Science Quarterly* (March 1969), pp. 73–84.

Walton, R. E., Theory of Conflict in Lateral Organizational Relationships, in Lawrence, J. R., ed., *Operational Research and the Social Sciences* (Tavistock, 1966), pp. 409–26.

Watson, D. J. H., Contingency Formulations of Organizational Structure: Implications for Managerial Accounting, in J. L. Livingstone, ed., *Managerial Accounting—The Behavioral Foundations* (Grid, Inc., 1975).

Weick, K., *The Social Psychology of Organizing* (Addison-Wesley, 1969).

Whisler, T. L., *The Impact of Computers on Organizations* (Praeger Publ., 1970).

Whisler, T. L., The Business Organization of the Future, in H. Leavitt, L. Pinfield & E. Welds, eds., *Organizations of the Future—Interaction with the External Environment* (Praeger, 1974), pp. 78–91.

Wildavsky, A., *The Politics of the Budgetary Process* (2nd ed.) (Little Brown & Co., 1974).

Withington, F. W., *The Real Computer—Its Influences, Uses and Effects* (Addison-Wesley, 1969).

Zald, M., Political Economy: A Framework for Comparative Analysis, in M. Zald, ed., *Power in Organizations* (Vanderbilt University Press, 1970), pp. 221–61.

'Irrationality' of Managerial Judgments: Implications for Information Systems[1]

Herbert Moskowitz[2]

Ralf E. Schaefer[3]

Katrin Borcherding[3]

Four principal factors affecting rational information processing behavior in organizations are discussed. These are: (1) the nature and attributes of the messages received from the Management Information and Decision System (MIDS); (2) The personal qualities and attitudes of the manager himself; (3) the degree of social interaction; and (4) if a collective is involved, the format and group decision function used in arriving at a group position. Ways in which information specialists and operations researchers can counter, ameliorate, and exploit managers' judgmental biases and inconsistencies are then proposed. Areas for further research are suggested.

An area of neglect and ever increasing concern in the design of management information and decision systems (MIDS) is the psychology of the manager *qua* judge and decision maker. This consideration has become specially relevant and important to operations researchers and management scientists as they increasingly turn their energies toward building MIDSs for solving the 'wicked', unstructured problems in organizations [11], [25]. A key characteristic of such problems is uncertainty. Most of the models developed for these problems require subjective inputs, often expressed as probabilities or probability distributions. The *sine qua non* of such models' value rests on the quality of these subjective inputs. Good probability assessments become especially critical when the output from one model in the form of a prediction or decision serves as input data for higher level and/or other organizational decisions. Here errors can become dangerously amplified throughout the organizational hierarchy [5]. A familiar example of the state of affairs that poor subjective inputs can create is seen in research and development (R&D). In most cases, project

From *Omega,* Vol. 4, No. 2 (1976), pp. 125–140.

(Received August 1975; in revised form November 1975)

[1]This is a slightly abridged version of the original paper. The unabridged version, which contains a comprehensive list of references, can be obtained by writing to Herbert Moskowitz at Purdue.

[2]Krannert School of Industrial Administration, Purdue University, U.S.A.; Guest Professor at the Sonderforschungsbereich (SFB) 24 'Sozial-und Wirtschaftspsychologische Entscheidungsforschung', at the University of Mannheim.

[3]Sonderforschungsbereich (SFB) 24 'Sozial-und Wirtschaftspsychologische Entscheidungsforschung', at the University of Mannheim, Germany.

management models like PERT have not prevented or even mitigated the large cost and schedule overruns usually experienced. Nor have any of the many stochastic R&D decision models been implemented in practice, either due to the lack of a historical data base or 'poor' subjective inputs [3].

Design Shortcomings of MIDS

Recognizing the pivotal role that managers play as integrators or processors of information for decision making, modern technology has been mobilized to help increase their ability to judge and decide by supplying them with a proliferation of data in the most timely and efficient manner. The underlying premise has been, "The *more, quicker,* and *higher quality* the information, the better the judgments and decisions." Manifestations of these efforts in organizations are seen in the growth of computerized MIDSs and the pervasive use of groups and experts. Unfortunately, instances abound where the provision of more timely, complete, and reliable information has not improved decision making. There are at least three basic reasons for this:

1. MIDS designers are ignorant of the needs and capabilities of the manager, the recipient and user of the information [1].
2. Operations research models are all too frequently developed with no consideration given to information system requirements and capabilities (i.e. the information and decision systems are treated independently rather than as a unified whole) [11]. Nor is any consideration really given to the behavioral characteristics and capabilities of the managers who provide the subjective inputs and who perform as an integral component of the MIDS [25].
3. Management control systems in organizations generally discourage rather than encourage accurate assessment of uncertain events. For example, Woods [28] and Souder [21] found that firms' control systems produced systematic biases in the form of underestimation and undue optimism.

Need for Behavioral Research

The foregoing underscores the need to understand better, both *psychologically* and *sociologically,* the relationship between man and information if MIDSs are to be improved. We must thus ask, "What are man's limitations as an information processor and how is his behavior affected by the informational environment and social situation in which he functions?" Surprisingly, much of this area has received little attention and has been virtually ignored in MIDS design.

One purpose of this paper is to summarize some effects of various informational characteristics, social factors, and personal attributes of the manager or human information processing behavior and to discuss their implications with respect to MIDS design. Many of the results derive from a series of studies which examined human information processing behavior in a simulated financial MIDS environment. The studies were also designed, in part, to determine whether certain behavior observed in the psychological laboratory was representative of behavior in the 'real world'.

A second purpose is to suggest several options open to MIDS designers and operations researchers to improve MIDSs by incorporating, countervailing, attenuating, and exploiting human foibles and limitations and tendencies to subvert such systems.

RESEARCH PERSPECTIVE

A MIDS can be broadly defined in terms of the following principal components (Fig. 1): (1) An

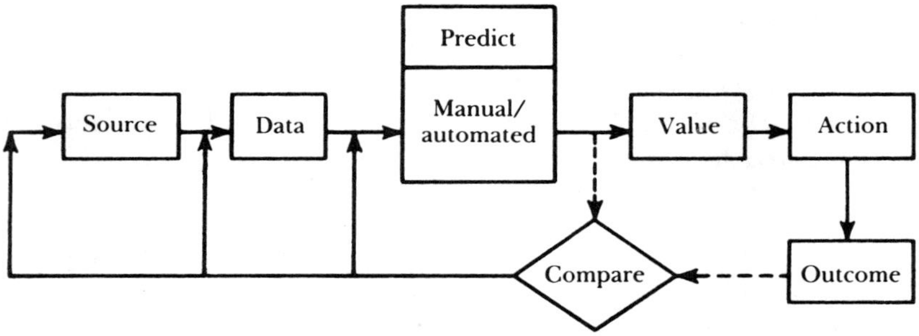

FIGURE 1. Management information system (MIDS).

information source—the organization for which decisions are to be made and from which information is collected. (2) *Data*—the process of observing, measuring, and recording information about the source. (3) *Prediction*—the process of estimating and drawing inferences. (4) *Values*—the evaluation of these predictions with regard to the objectives or goals of the organizations. (5) *Action*—the choice of a course of action. (6) *Outcome*—the consequences of the action which was taken. The major focus of the research concerned the third MIDS component—prediction. However, the implications of the results cannot be decoupled from the other MIDS components.

A model for organizing research on the prediction component is depicted in Fig. 2. Briefly, a message characterized by a vector of

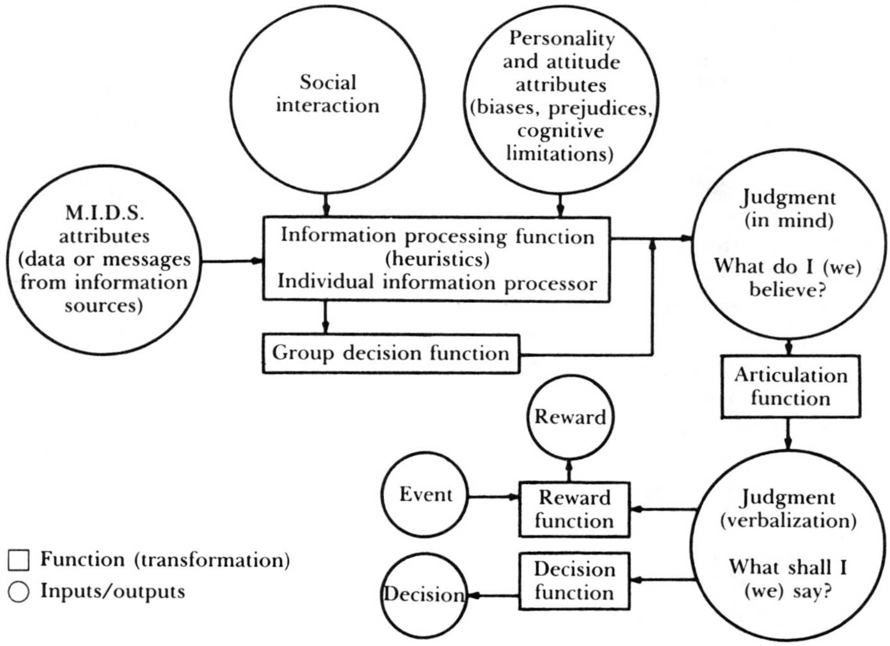

FIGURE 2. Some motivational and cognitive factors impinging on information processing behavior.

attributes (such as informativeness, complexity, timeliness, etc.) is received by an information processor from an information source. This message along with the processor's accumulated knowledge is then processed into a judgment. Additional inputs impinging on the information processor include his inherent motivations, biases, perceptions, and cognitive limitations as well as external social interaction forces (e.g. isolation or presence of others, feedback or no feedback on previous judgments, discussion or no discussion of judgment to be made with others, etc.). All these factors bear on *how* and *how well* the messages received are processed into a judgment. In the case of groups, a group decision function for amalgamating individual member beliefs into a common position is also involved in arriving at the ultimate judgment. Moreover, in both individual and group circumstances, the correspondence between the cognitive judgment and the articulated judgment depends on the reward function. Unfortunately, there is no way of knowing whether the verbalization and the belief are isomorphic. Through the use of a proper reward structure (e.g. scoring rules [26]), however, one can hopefully achieve isomorphism.

BEHAVIORAL LITERATURE

Although there was little research in the area of human information processing prior to 1960, since then much has been done, and the annual volume of research has been increasing exponentially, stimulated by the growing awareness of the problem's significance and the aid of the omnipresent computer. An excellent summary of this research up to 1971 is found in Slovic and Lichtenstein [20]. Much of the recent work has been accomplished within the 'Bayesian' school by psychologists, where Bayes' Theorem has served as the baseline paradigm for opinion revision upon receipt of new information. The modern impetus for what we are calling the Bayesian paradigm is rooted in the work of von Neumann and Morgenstern [24] who revived interest in maximization of expected utility as a core tenet of rational decision making, and to Savage [15], whose *Foundations of Statistics* fused the concepts of utility and subjective probability into an axiomatic theory of decision making under uncertainty. One aspect of this rapidly emerging school of thought called 'Decision Theory' asserts that we ought to cast our opinions (beliefs) about the world in probabilistic terms. When we translate our opinions into probabilities, a mathematical formula, Bayes' Theorem, dictates the optimal way that our estimates should change upon receipt of new information.

This line of inquiry has turned up a number of consistent tendencies associated with human information processing behavior. One such tendency is described by the notion of *conservatism.* Conservatism denotes that upon receipt of new information, humans revise their beliefs in the same direction as Bayes' Theorem prescribes, but that the revision is typically too small. Much of the Bayesian research has been motivated by a desire to discover the determinants of conservatism.

Unfortunately, the work in this area, until recently, has been largely confined to the psychological laboratory where introductory psychology students served as subjects, and the tasks employed have had little relevance to real world decision problems. For example, most Bayesian experiments have been based on statistical data-generating paradigms employing such devices as book bags and poker chips, etc. [20]. Whether other groups of people behave similarly in more realistic decision settings remains an important empirical question, which is now receiving increasing attention [20], [27]. Moreover, little systematic attention has been paid to the effect of such organizational factors as the nature and characteristics of the information system, social environment, and social interaction on information processing behavior.

As a result, there is a pressing need to replicate and extend the various types of studies performed in the laboratory to specific organizational settings. If the results of such research confirm the findings in the psychological laboratory, then such persistent tendencies may have sufficient generality to qualify as propositions or laws. These could then serve as guidelines for integrating behavioral factors in MIDS design and for training managers as information processors or to provide reasonable inputs for information processing by a formal model. Such studies would also provide further insights into the nature of man's cognitive processes.

MIDS ENVIRONMENT

The decision context in our investigation, from which much of the evidence in this paper is drawn, involved the evaluation of applicants for personal loans by a bank lending officer. One of the fundamental judgments that a loan officer (or loan committee) must make in processing loan applications is an assessment of the likelihood that an applicant will either default or be delinquent in repaying his loan. Lending officers arrive at this judgment on the basis of the data that they receive about the applicant. The loan officer has several different sources upon which to base his judgment. For this particular task setting four of these sources were used: (1) the prospective borrower's application form, (2) the bank's internal records, (3) a credit scoring system based on the borrower's attributes, and (4) an independent retail credit evaluation. Reports from each of these sources were provided in the form of objective (relative frequency) conditional probabilities relating the possible messages to past delinquencies and nondelinquencies of previous borrowers. These sources and messages were basically the same as those available to and used by many bank lending officers.

In the experiments, each subject acting as a bank loan officer or loan committee member assessed the probability that a loan applicant requesting a $5000, unsecured, vacation loan would become delinquent in his payments during the coming year. His assessments were based on the background information obtained from the loan application and data on the applicant from the three conditionally independent, binary information sources mentioned. Illustrations of the information sources are shown in Table 1. Further details on the experimental tasks and the development of the normative Bayesian proba-

TABLE 1.

Data / Hypothesis	Credit Data Service (retail information)		Bank's Internal Records		Borrower's Attributes	
	X	X′	Y	Y′	Z	Z′
H (delinquent)	0.20	0.80	0.10	0.90	0.30	0.70
H′ (not delinquent)	0.80	0.20	0.90	0.10	0.70	0.30

X Good rating
X′ Bad rating
Y Never delinquent in past 5 years on loans, etc.
Y′ Delinquent at least once on loans, etc.
Z Score of greater than 75 points
Z′ Score of equal to or less than 75 points

bility revision model are found in [10] and [12].

OVERVIEW OF RESULTS

The findings of these bank lending studies, to be briefly summarized and contrasted to existing literature, concern the effects on information processing behavior of: (1) the message attributes of the MIDS information sources, (2) an individual's characteristics and attitudes, (3) the social environment and degree of social interaction, and when groups are involved (4) the group decision function for aggregating individual member judgments into a group judgment. The subjects used in these studies varied, but mainly included upper level undergraduate business and engineering students, and graduate industrial management students. Most had some prior work experience; some had actually worked in financial institutions and were former bank loan officers. All groups were limited to three members.

Before discussing the effects and implications of the above factors it is worth pointing out that the results from these studies in general confirmed the conservatism findings in the psychological laboratory for both individuals and groups [10], [12]. This phenomenon thus appears to have considerable generality. It is of further interest to note that interacting consensus groups (a common group format), were found to be more conservative than individuals or artifactual groups (randomly selected individuals whose responses were averaged to obtain a group response). This finding, too, has been supported in the psychological laboratory [6].

Message Attributes

The MIDS designer has considerable control over the messages sent to a decision maker, and thus can influence as well as compensate for their psychological effects through his design. To do this, he must understand the relationship between the attributes of his system and human biases in processing the messages received into judgments.

1. Informativeness. As found in many psychological experiments [20, pp. 701–703], conservatism increased with increased message informativeness with individuals as well as groups [12]. The numerous replications of this finding would seem to qualify it as a generally consistent human tendency.

2. Order Effects. As in most psychological studies, individuals exhibited primacy effects, i.e. gave earlier received messages more salience than later received messages [10]. Moreover, the order in which both positive (confirming evidence with respect to the hypothesis in question) and negative information (disconfirming evidence) was received, influenced the magnitude of this effect. Similar order effects were found with artifactual groups, but order effects were vitiated with interacting consensus groups.

While it is clear that the sequence in which messages are received can influence individual beliefs, the nature of its effect is less clear, as recency effects (later received messages are given more salience) have also been observed in several experiments [20, p. 704]. It is even more difficult, however, to generalize on sequence effects for groups because of the dearth of such experimentation. It has been found that the group format and group decision function used to amalgamate individual member judgments into a group position influence the nature of the order effect and can vitiate it. Order effects, however, have a much weaker influence on conservatism than does message informativeness [12].

3. Sequential Versus Simultaneous Presentation. Often in a MIDS, a choice exists as to whether to transmit information all at once or item by item (e.g. the use of a single aggregated report versus a set of individual reports). Our results indicate that significant differences in processing behavior occur when messages are received and processed simultaneously as opposed to sequentially with both individuals and groups. In some cases sequential information is processed more conservatively than simultaneous information and vice versa. The nature of these differences seems to depend in part on the perceived conditionality of the information sources, the specificity of the task, and the diagnostic element of the messages. Psychological experiments have similarly found that sequentially received and processed messages result in different judgments from simultaneously received and processed messages, partly due to an 'inertia effect' [20, pp. 704–706].

4. Favorability. Messages are generally either favorable or unfavorable. If favorable messages are processed differently from unfavorable ones, then messages might be worded such that unfavorable messages sound more favorable, or vice versa, depending on which wording results in more nearly optimal processing behavior. The bank lending experiments found that unfavorable messages (e.g. bad credit rating) tended to be weighted somewhat more than favorable ones (e.g. good credit rating) by individuals and artifactual groups [12]. Interacting consensus groups, however, seemed to treat unfavorable messages as being significantly more informative than favorable messages.

Several behavioral and marketing studies suggest contradictions and extensions of the above findings. Hughes [7], in a series of marketing experiments using executives surmised that the nature of the behavior is dependent upon message reinforcement (i.e. when a hypothesis about an object is favorable, a favorable message induces a greater positive change in attitude than an unfavorable message will induce a negative change, and vice versa).

5. Objective Versus Subjective Sources. Information sources can be classified as being either objective or subjective, depending on the nature of the *data* and its source. Objective sources, for example, would be conditional probabilities known by the decision maker to be based on relative frequency data obtained from historical records and outputted from a computer. Subjective sources are known by the decision maker to have no historical data base; the conditional probabilities are subjectively determined and provided by another decision maker.

Messages received from subjective sources seem to be processed more conservatively than those from objective sources. This difference in behavior might be related to the difference in perceived credibility between these two types of sources. While these results have some psychological support, Hughes [7] found that the subjectivity of the messages was not considered by businessmen when acting on messages.

6. Source Complexity. The complexity of an information source can be defined by: (a) the number of possible messages emanating from it, and (b) the degree of asymmetry of the conditional probabilities relating the messages to the hypotheses. Examples of symmetry, for a given diagnostic element, are provided in Table 2. Symmetry, in a binary information source, for example, can be defined as the difference between the likelihood ratios of the two data states, and can vary from 0 (perfectly symmetric) to ∞ (maximally asymmetric).

Information sources in real MIDSs are characteristically 'complex'; that is, there are many possible messages, and the likelihood functions relating the messages to the hypotheses are generally asymmetric. How complex or to what degree of accuracy and

TABLE 2.

	D_X	$D_{X'}$		D_X	$D_{X'}$		D_X	$D_{X'}$
H	90%	10%	H	63%	37%	H	45%	55%
H′	10%	90%	H′	7%	93%	H′	5%	95%
	$L_X = 9$			$L_X = 9$			$L_X = 9$	
	$L_{X'} = 9$			$L_{X'} = 2.5$			$L_{X'} = 1.7$	
	$S = 0$			$S = 6.5$			$S = 7.3$	

detail ('fineness') should an information source be specified to? Stated another way, should the data be made symmetrical and condensed or 'coarsened'? Normatively speaking, the more accurate and detailed the information the better, but realistically, 'symmetrizing' and 'coarsening' could result in improved assessments and information processing behavior.

In the bank lending experiments, messages from more complex information sources were processed more conservatively by individuals and there was less variance among the responses than with messages from simpler information sources (groups were not tested). Two explanations have been offered for this phenomena: (1) Symmetric sources were perceived as being more credible or trustworthy than asymmetric sources; (2) the behavior evinced was an artifact of the heuristics which decision makers employed in processing the information. That is, most individuals in attempting to intuitively weight the informativeness of an information source in revising their judgments do not consider the likelihood ratio associated with a given message in a manner similar to Bayes' Theorem. Instead they appear to focus on a single conditional probability, the one relating the message with the hypotheses in question.

7. Format of Presentation. The format used to specify the informativeness of an information source can affect information processing behavior. To illustrate, consider the different ways in which the data from the information sources in the bank lending experiment could be presented (Tables 1 and 3). Only two conditional probabilities are needed, one associating any given message to each hypothesis. Thus, there exist four such possible presentations:

1. $P(D|H)$, $P(D|H')$ (likelihood ratio of message);
2. $P(D'|H)$, $P(D'|H')$ (likelihood ratio of alternate message);
3. $P(D|H)$, $P(D'|H')$ (conditional probabilities of 'correct' messages associated with each hypothesis); and
4. $P(D'|H)$, $P(D|H')$ (type I and II errors respectively).

Theoretically there should be no difference in the way messages from each of these presentations are processed; but this is not necessarily so, psychologically. Consider, for example, the

TABLE 3.

	D_X	$D_{X'}$		D_X	$D_{X'}$		D_X	$D_{X'}$		D_X	$D_{X'}$
H	X		H		X	H		X	H	X	
H′	X		H′		X	H′	X		H′		X

processing of message *D*. By using representation (1), the predictor (manager) receives the likelihood ratio directly, presumably facilitating intuitive processing of information more nearly in accordance with Bayes' Theorem. The other presentation formats provide different 'anchor points' which, if used directly, would result in suboptimal probability revisions, or require additional manipulations to obtain the likelihood ratio.

In the bank lending situation the various formats have been studied using both simple and complex information sources. Only slight to moderate differences in behavior occurred among the different formats. Training in the use of likelihood ratios for revising beliefs, as in Bayes' Theorem might, however, facilitate optimal behavior, especially in cases where binary hypotheses are involved.

Individual Attributes and Attitudes

1. Perceived Source Credibility. Although an individual may have verbalized his degree of belief in a hypothesis by means of a subjective probability, it makes sense to talk about his degree of belief or confidence concerning the accuracy of its numerical value.

Research in communication and persuasion indicates that one possible factor influencing the confidence associated with a probability judgment is an individual's perception of the credibility of the message he receives. Conservatism may derive then, in part, from an individual's disbelief in the datum itself or the source from which it came.

The results from the bank lending experiments showed that subject's perceived truthworthiness of the messages and sources (which were objective) did not influence the observed tendencies towards conservatism in either individuals or groups [10]. Other researchers [16], however, have shown a direct relationship between an individual's revised probabilities and the extent to which he questions the trustworthiness of the information source. In fact, it has been observed that when source credibility is very low, people tend to become overly radical rather than conservative in their probability revisions [17]. The lack of significance in the bank lending experiments may have been due to the measurement instrument. Further research is suggested.

2. Risk Attitude. One partial explanation of conservatism may stem from an individual's or a group's risk-taking proclivity. That is, conservatism may be a function of risk-taking, and consequently individuals with high risk-taking propensities tend to be less conservative than those with low risk-taking tendencies. Using the standard Kogan and Wallach 'Choice Dilemma Instrument' (CDI) [8] as a measure of risk attitude, it was found that information processing behavior was not affected by the risk attitudes of individuals or of groups. These results should be interpreted cautiously on two counts: First, the CDI is an increasingly questionable measure of risk-taking propensity [9]. Second, the majority of evidence in the psychological literature argues against the existence of risk-taking propensity as a generalized characteristic of people. A person's previous learning experiences in specific risk-taking settings seem much more important than his general personality characteristics [19].

3. Problem Familiarity. In making joint decisions, executives generally are or have an opportunity to become familiar with the problem beforehand, but in some cases do not. Without prior familiarization or experience a decision maker might not want to commit himself to a judgment until he had ample time to ponder it. This is especially so if the problem were either complex or important. With a complicated problem, the decision maker might feel he wanted an opportunity to weigh up all the evidence. With an important problem, even a simple one, he might be reluctant to make a hasty decision. In both cases he might feel inclined to give an initially cautious response, meaning "Don't know" or "Not yet ready to decide". After he had time to study the problem, however, his initial caution may vanish. In psychological studies of risk attitude further familiarization with the risk-taking problem led to an increase in riskiness [4]. Such an effect might conceivably occur when processing information and thus could counterveil the conservatism phenomenon. Our findings show, however, that individuals and groups with prior problem familiarization do not process information significantly differently from unfamiliarized individuals and groups. Strub [22], however, found that highly experienced decision makers in the military sphere, were clearly more nearly optimal than inexperienced decision makers. But Slovic's observations of investment analysts indicate that experienced and familiarized decision makers may be less accurate than those with less experience and familiarization [18].

Social Interaction

The decision maker in an organization processes information in a wide variety of social situations including virtual isolation, conference telephone calls, committee meetings, and numerous others. The characteristics of the information processed (e.g. its diagnosticity, complexity, etc.) are similarly diverse. The question arises as to whether the decision unit (viz, an individual or group) processes the various forms of information similarly in the numerous social situations encountered. If the social situations and the nature of the information evoke a change in processing behavior (ultimately reflected in the final judgment), it may then be desirable to adapt the social situation to the information which is to be processed, or, conversely, adapt the form in which (or the media through which) the information is presented to the nature of the decision unit. It is thus important to examine systematically the effects of social interaction on information processing behavior in individuals and groups. Such a study was performed using the bank lending situation [13]. In this study social interaction was defined in terms of social exchange and social environment. Social exchange refers to the degree of communication exchange or feedback from person to person, while social environment is concerned with the isolation or presence of others. The results found were: (1) Individuals, artifactual groups, and interacting consensus groups were not affected by social interaction in the processing of messages of medium and high informativeness. (2) However, with messages of low informativeness both individual and group responses were affected by social interaction. At this level of informativeness individuals working alone without discussion and groups who functioned in visual isolation were the best information processors.

The implications inherent in these findings are in certain respects contrary to the typical assumptions which underlie certain management practices. Committees are usually organized for judgmental and decision making purposes for those situations in which uncertainty is high and the consequences are great. The rationale, for such action, at least in part, is based on the "two heads are better than one" adage. In government, for example, judgments and decisions involving matters of national security are usually entrusted only to committees, as the conditions under which such judgments and decisions are made are generally highly charged and fluid, and can have catastrophic consequences. These findings question the assumption upon which this practice is based, as individuals acting alone, made better and less extreme judgments with highly uncertain information. The results also question the value of visual communication devices for probabilistic judgments (e.g. such as the newly developed picture phone) in lieu of verbal or written communication which require no visual contact. Operationally, then, the very same message through different media (such as written media, a telephone, T.V.) may indeed have a significantly different impact on the audience (in our case, decision maker), partially as a result of social interaction.

It would be well to mention that there is no evidence in the psychological literature regarding the effects of social factors on the type of human judgmental behavior that we are concerned with. A fuller understanding of the processes involved in the interaction of social factors and information characteristics warrants further study.

Group Decision Function

When a group judgment is required, some rule or "group decision function" must be used to amalgamate individual members' judgments into a consolidated group position. There exists a number of such rules, which can be conveniently categorized into four types: (1) informal, (2) Delphi, (3) mathematical, and (4) voting rules. Informal techniques (letting the group arrive at a consensus via discussion) while admittedly *ad hoc,* are nevertheless the most common in practice. The Delphi technique is probably the most widely known formal method for eliciting and refining the judgments of a group of people. Delphi does not permit any direct contact among the people involved. It is usually done operationally through an interactive questionnaire in which each person, on a given cycle, purveys his judgment based on a summary of the judgments of each person from the previous cycle.

There exists a variety of mathematical aggregation techniques [2]. However, only a few such rules were examined in the bank lending experiments. One *ad hoc* rule is to average the individual group member's likelihood ratios implied by his judgments. Another mathematical rule is a Bayesian amalgamation procedure proposed by Roberts [14]. In brief, the group posterior distribution is determined by taking a weighted average of each individual member's posterior distribution. The weights are formally revised after each message according to each individual's assessment. Numerous voting rules also exist as a means of aggregation. Only majority rule was examined. For three member groups this is the median probability response value.

Results show that the rules result in different judgments (no one rule being clearly superior to any other) and that only the judgments resulting from a few of the rules tested were affected by order of message presentation, favorability of the message, etc. Much work needs to be done in this area. Paralleling our efforts here is a large body of work now being done on this topic by social psychologists and behavioral decision theorists.

RELATIONSHIP OF FINDINGS TO REAL WORLD

The results of these and other experiments, while not conclusive, indeed, show that man has difficulty both individually and collectively in processing probabilistic information. Many factors appear to affect his performance in various ways, some more predictable than others. Moreover, much of man's biases and fallibilities found in the bank lending studies replicate and extend those found in psychological studies. To generalize beyond this, however, is risky. Our experiments, although more realistic than the psychological experiments, were not reality. Some obvious potential differences that often exist in real-world situations and not found in the bank lending studies are: (1) conditional dependence among information sources, (2) nonstationarity of the environment (e.g. the hypotheses change, the messages change, or the conditional probabilities relating the messages to the hypotheses change, etc.), (3) relative undiagnosticity of the real information sources, and (4) unreliability or cascaded inference structures (inferences involving a hierarchy of several levels) [27].

Nevertheless, there exists an abundance of evidence in the real-world indicating that the above biases and difficulties in processing information observed in the bank lending studies and the psychological laboratory persist outside the laboratory in business, military, and societal decision making situations [12]. Consider order effects: note its relationship to the adage, "First impressions are most lasting". How many times have we been in the miserable position of attempting to overcome a first bad impression (primacy effect); or, being unfairly judged for a merit increase or promotion based on events and performance over the past few weeks rather than over the entire review period (recency effect). Consider conservatism: this is the fundamental principle of the accounting profession! In marketing, salesmen's sales forecasts usually, if not virtually always, underestimate actual sales; in R&D, project completion time is almost always severely underestimated.

OPTIONS OPEN TO MIDS DESIGNER

Humans need help in making sound judgments. While training will mitigate errors and biases to some extent, it will not eliminate them entirely, either because of the complexity of the many different situations encountered, fatigue, or just the sheer infeasibility or impossibility of developing a training program that will achieve errorless results. Managers, information specialists, and operations researchers must therefore identify and account for human biases and deficiencies in order to design better MIDSs. What are some of the options open to them?

1. Incorporate in the System Counter-Biases or Eliminate Conditions which Create Human Biases and Inconsistencies. For example, with respect to order effects: (1) Control the timeliness with which data is presented to the information processor. For instance, the information system specialist can analyze the delay time patterns (i.e. elapsed time from the original data to its presentation to the decision maker) to determine any bias that would cause one kind of data to be systematically presented before another and to analyze forms and reporting structures for any obvious sequence biases. Here attempts could be made to synchronize data delay patterns and to reorganize forms and reports. (2) Alert information processors to the possible impact of order effects on behavior and suggest they re-evaluate all relevant data in that light prior to making a judgment (of course, here, one runs the risk of imparting new biases).

2. Exploit Human Biases and Irrationalities. Consider, for example, the societal decision problem of vehicle accident prevention. The actual (objective) probability of detection of a speeding violation is exceedingly small; in fact, it is a rare event. Yet people's beliefs regarding the probability of detection might be surreptitiously inflated by withholding information (keeping such data confidential), providing misinformation (propaganda), repeated or redundant information, or by simply dramatizing the consequences (resulting in a violation of Savage's independence of beliefs and tastes axioms of decision theory [5] which humans tend to violate). Similar strategies could be advantageously employed for problems in pollution detection, nuclear reactor safety, etc.

3. Decision Aids. Automate the information aggregation process (let a mathematical model and machine do it). Bayesian Probabilistic Information Processing (PIP) systems and regression models already have been proposed and successfully used in a variety of real decision making contexts [20]. Such models eliminate an individual's inconsistency, hence seem appropriate for stationary environments and perhaps for nonstationary environments as well.

Another approach is to incorporate human fallibilities directly into the decision model. For example, inspector errors have been incorporated directly into mathematical models for determining optimal sampling plans.

4. Incorporate Flexible and Adaptable Control Systems. Most judgments and decisions will continue to be made subjectively by humans. To assure better judgments and more efficient use of the organization's resources, imbed in the planning and control function (a) a 'proper' reward function to assure honest judgments, and (b) a feedback system to foster rationality and optimality through learning [26].

CONCLUSIONS

Considerably more research must be done on human information processing behavior particularly in realistic environments with emphasis on understanding the heuristics people use in arriving at a judgment both individually and collectively. It is only recently that any effort at all has been made in trying to determine what rules people use in forming and revising their beliefs [23]. No longer can the psychologist remain in his laboratory and no longer can the information specialist and operations researcher ignore human behavior if MIDSs are to be more than marginally successful.

REFERENCES

1. Ackoff RA (1967) Management misinformation systems. *Mgmt Sci.* 14 (4), 147–156.
2. DeGroot MH (1974) Reaching a consensus. *J. Am. Statis. Ass.* 69, 118–121.
3. Ebert RJ (1970) Methodology for improving subjective R&D estimates. *IEEE Trans. Engng Mgmt* 17, 108–116.
4. Flanders JP and Thistlethwaite DL (1967) Effects of familiarization and group discussion upon risk taking. *J. Personality & Soc. Psychol.* 5, 91–97.
5. Forrester J (1961) *Industrial Dynamics.* MIT Press, Cambridge.
6. Goodman BC (1972) Action selection and likelihood ratio estimates by individuals and groups, *Organ. Behav. & Hum. Perform.*, 7, 121–141.
7. Hughes GD (1971) *Cognitive models and individual determinants of changes in subjective probability.* Delivered at the International Meeting of the Institute of Management Science, Washington, D.C.
8. Kogan N and Wallach MA (1964) *Risk Taking: A Study in Cognition and Personality,* Holt, Rinehart and Winston, New York.
9. Mackenzie KD (1971) An analysis of risky shift experiments. *Organ. Behav. & Hum. Perform.* 6, 283–303.
10. Mason RO and Moskowitz H (1972) Conservatism in information processing—implications for management information systems. *Decision Sci.,* 3(4), 35–55.
11. Mjosund A (1972) The synergy of operations research and computers. *Ops. Res.* 20 (5), 1057–1064.
12. Moskowitz H & Mason RO (1973) Accounting for the man/information interface in management information systems. *Omega,* 1 (6), 679–694.
13. Moskowitz H and Silva WT (1973) *Effects of social interaction on human probabilistic inference.* Krannert Institute Paper No. 397, Purdue University.
14. Roberts HV (1965) Probabilistic prediction. *J. Am. Statis. Ass.* 60, 50–62.
15. Savage LJ (1954) *The Foundations of Statistics.* Wiley, New York.
16. Schaefer RE and Borcherding K (1973) A note on the consistency of two approaches to incorporate data from unreliable sources in bayesian analysis. *Organ. Behav. & Hum. Perform.* 9 (3), 504–507.

17. Schum DA, Du Charme WM and DePitts KE (1973) Research on human multistage probabilistic inference processes. *Organ. Behav. & Hum. Perform.* 10 (3), 318–348.
18. Slovic P (1972) Psychological study of human judgment: implications for investment decision making. *J. Fin.* 27, 779–799.
19. Slovic P, Fleissner D and Bauman WS (1972) Analyzing the use of information in investment decision making: a methodological proposal. *J. Bus.*, 45, 283–301.
20. Slovic P and Lichenstein S (1971) Comparison of bayesian and regression approaches to the study of information processing in judgment. *Organ. Behav. & Hum. Perform.*, 6, 649–744.
21. Souder WE (1969) The validity of subjective probability of success forecast by R&D project managers. *IEEE Trans. Engng Mgmt,* 16, 35–49.
22. Strub MH (1969) Experience and prior probability in a complex decision task. *J. Appl. Psychol.*, 53, 112–117.
23. Tversky A and Kahneman D (1973) *Judgment under uncertainty: heuristics and biases.* Proceedings of the Fourth Research Conference on Subjective Probability, Utility, and Decision Making. Rome.
24. von Neumann J and Morgenstern O (1947) *Theory of Games and Economic Behavior.* 2nd ed. Princeton University Press, Princeton.
25. Wagner HM (1971) The ABC's of OR. *Ops Res.* 19 (6), 1271–1281.
26. Winkler RL (1969) Scoring rules and the evaluation of probability assessors. *J. Am. Statis. Ass.* 64, 1073–1078.
27. Winkler RL and Murphy AH (1973) Experiments in the Laboratory and the Real World. *Organ. Behav. and Hum. Perform.*, 10, 252–270.
28. Woods DH (1966) Improving estimates that involve uncertainty. *Harv. Business Rev.* 44, 91–98.

Human Information Processing, Decision Style Theory, and Accounting Information Systems

Michael J. Driver

Theodore J. Mock*

Within the past ten years, literature concerned with accounting information system design has increased significantly. More importantly, perhaps, the number of distinct approaches or methodologies to information systems research and design has also multiplied. For instance, a recent American Accounting Association (1971) committee report identified statistical decision theory, information economics, cybernetics, communication theory, measurement theory, and behavioral theories as providing both research methodologies and a body of knowledge which underly information theory and ultimately accounting.

This paper explores one important aspect of information system design—human information processing systems.[1] Although the receiver or user has long been recognized as an important variable to consider, only recently have research results and methods led to useful insights. In a recent empirical study, Dermer (1973, p. 518) states the basic problem when referencing his own behavioral study.[2]

> These results also indicate that the utility of a particular type of information cannot be effectively evaluated apart from the users of that information. There may be little point in providing financial forecast data or human resource accounting data to administrators whose *cognitive makeup* is such that they ignore it. This does not mean that the information may not be of use to others, however, just that it may not be of use to these particular individuals. It is to the accountant's advantage to be able to recognize this before he designs an information system.

More specifically, this research considers extensions of the original information processing models of Schroder, Driver and Streufert (1967) which facilitate the accounting system designer's consideration of cognitive make-up. In presenting this augmented model, we shall attempt both to clarify some misconceptions which have appeared in the literature concerning human information processing and to discuss some limited experimental research which

From *The Accounting Review*, Vol. 50, No. 3 (July 1975), pp. 490–508.

*Michael J. Driver and Theodore J. Mock are, respectively, Professor and Associate Professor, Graduate School of Business Administration, University of Southern California.

This paper was presented at seminars at The Ohio State University and The University of Florida and benefited from the resulting discussions. In addition, we would like to acknowledge the critique of many of our colleagues and of the editorial reviewers of this article.

[1]In the general case, a human information processing system refers to both individuals and groups although the single decision maker is the system most frequently considered. See M. J. Driver and S. Streufert (1969).

[2]For a similar viewpoint see T. R. Dyckman, T. R. Hofstedt and R. Murdock (1972).

relates one construct of a user's cognitive make-up (decision style) to his preference for and use of accounting feedback.

This paper is organized as follows. First a review of accounting research into human information processing is presented. The main studies considered include both those that speculate as to the implications of human information processing upon alternative financial accounting systems (Revsine, 1970; Miller, 1972) and several empirical studies (Dermer, 1973; Mock, Estrin and Vasarhelyi, 1972; Barefield, 1972) that have investigated the impact of behavioral variables including "decision style" upon accounting information use and value. Then our discussion turns to a review of the psychological literature on human information processing where we identify several distinct approaches (normative, descriptive, general, differential, and unique) which have not previously been discussed within the accounting literature. Recent research findings are then presented including an improved information processing model and related scaling techniques. We conclude with some exploratory empirical results obtained in an accounting gaming experiment.

REVIEW OF ACCOUNTING LITERATURE ON HUMAN INFORMATION PROCESSING

The premise that behavioral factors are important in accounting seems to be generally accepted and much research has been conducted. In fact, entire accounting conferences have been devoted to this topic (Burns, 1972). In this review, the discussion is limited to accounting studies concerned directly with human information processing systems (HIPS) in the fashion of Schroder, Driver and Streufert (1967) and studies concerned with decision style.

Our general analytical model exhibited in Figure 1 is that found in information eco-

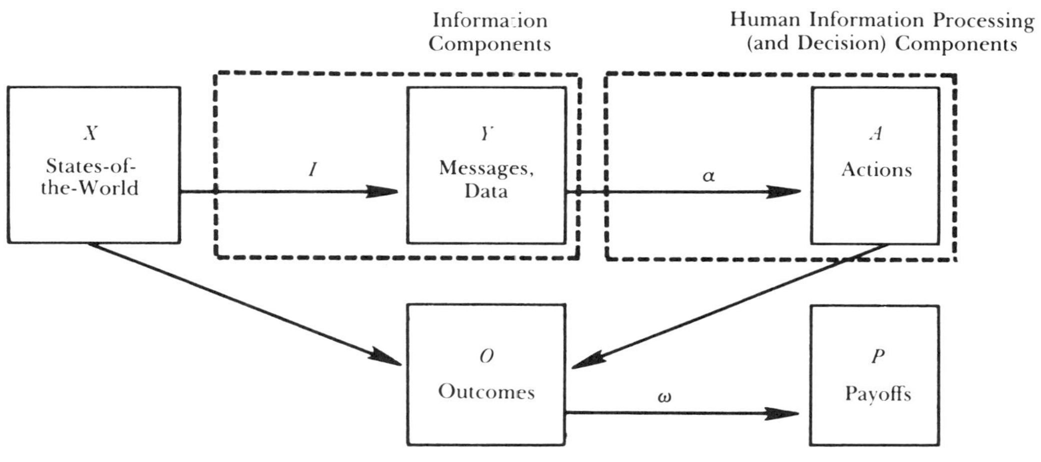

Notation:

X = Set of relevant states-of-the-world.
Y = Set of messages (information) about X.
A = Set of possible actions.
O = Set of outcomes (one outcome for each X, A pair).
P = Set of payoffs (associated with each outcome).
I = An information relation relating states and messages.
α = A decision function (rule) such that $a = \alpha(Y, I)$.
ω = A utility or preference function such that $p = \omega(O)$.

FIGURE 1. An Information Economics Model of Information, Information Processing, Decision, and Payoff See T. J. Mock (1971) for a more complete development of this model.

nomics. Here the accountant is depicted as being concerned with the ex ante evaluation and selection of an information system *I* given his best understanding of the other model elements. For reasons of simplification and emphasis, attention may be directed to the information and human information processing components depicted in this model.

As is characterized in Table 1, the information component, which is partially controllable by the accountant, consists mainly of a set of information procedures and a data base. Those concerned with the interrelations among the information and human information processing components have considered data expansion, data aggregation, and timing as important design variables. Such variables have also been investigated in nonaccounting studies.

The uniqueness of the research considered is the explicit considerations of the decision maker as an information processing system. In particular, conceptual structure, degree of environmental complexity, and personality variables have been shown to be potentially important design constraints.

The original articles in the accounting literature (Revsine, 1970; Miller, 1972), which

TABLE 1. The Information and HIPS Components and Aspects Discussed in the Accounting Literature

Information Components	HIPS Components
1. An information system or set of procedures to develop available data and messages 2. Data base, messages, stimuli	1. Decision rules, strategies 2. Alternative actions 3. An implicit human information processing system
Aspects Considered in Reviewed Research: 1. Data expansion (Revsine, 1970) 2. Aggregation of data (Barefield, 1972) 3. Timing/Accuracy (Mock, Estrin & Vasarhelyi, 1972)	Aspects Considered in Reviewed Research: 1. Conceptual Structure (Revsine, 1970)—Concrete/Abstract Differentiation, Integration 2. Decision Style (Mock et al., 1972) —Analytic/Heuristic 3. Information Processing Model (Barefield, 1972)—Bayesian, Regression (Additive) 4. Behavioral Processing Effects (Barefield, 1972; Revsine, 1970)—Conservatism, Primacy, Recency, Overload, Confirmation Effects, Source Redundancy, Source Predictability 5. Personality Variables (Dermer, 1973)—Tolerance to Ambiguity, Dogmatism 6. Information Search Behavior (Dermer, 1973) 7. Environmental Complexity (Revsine, 1970; H. Miller, 1972)

are more speculative than empirical in nature, are concerned with the constraint that conceptual structure places upon proposed data expansion in financial reports. Revsine hypothesized that the inclusion of forecasted and multidimensional statements may increase complexity to a point beyond the range of optimum information processing (see Figure 4). Empirical data for this proposition were not provided in his original article although such studies were called for by the author.

A subsequent article by Miller (1972) argues that further data expansion is likely to bring us closer to the range of optimal information processing for certain users. As evidence, Miller cites surveys of financial investors which indicate that they would prefer more accounting data. Unfortunately, psychological and HIPS research (Streufert, Suedfeld and Driver, 1965) has shown that users invariably prefer more data even past the point of maximum level of information processing and conceptual abstraction. Thus users' capacity for and preference for information do not seem to coincide.

Three other empirical studies within the accounting literature are tangentially relevant to HIPS as developed by Schroder, Driver and Streufert. In a laboratory experiment, Dermer (1973) has found that subjects intolerant to ambiguity prefer a greater amount of information and more readily interpretable signals. This, he concludes, is consistent with Schroder, Driver and Streufert.

In their business game study, Mock, Estrin and Vasarhelyi (1972) have investigated decision style and found this construct to explain variance in learning patterns and information value. As will be seen, their construct is directly related to cognitive structure dimensions within HIPS.

Lastly, Barefield (1972) has studied data aggregation and (implicitly) information processing models of the decision maker. Note that his research is concerned with a different aspect of human information processing—e.g., whether information is processed according to a Bayesian probability revision or some alternative model.

CURRENT RESEARCH IN HUMAN INFORMATION PROCESSING

Given the growth of interest in human information processing in accounting, a brief review of the varieties of approaches to this area (see Figure 2) may provide clarity for future research. The study of cognition or thinking processes is one of the earliest developments in scientific psychology. In its inception, cognitive psychol-

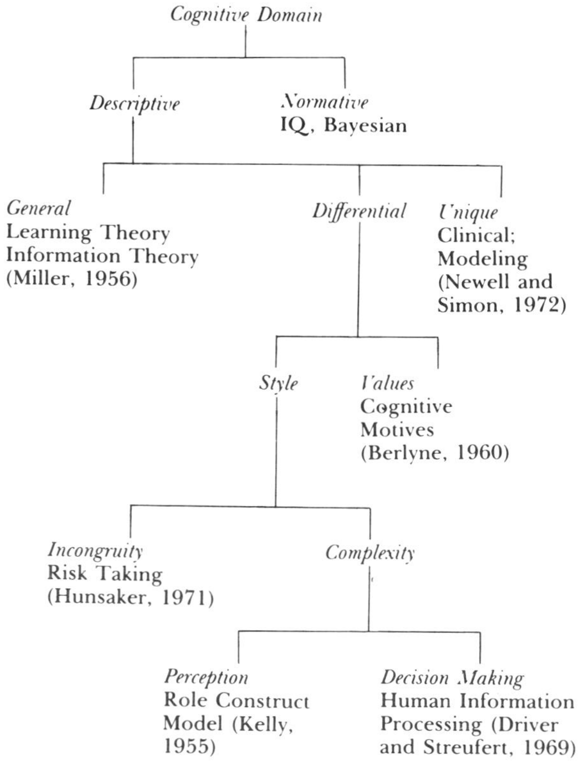

FIGURE 2. A Conceptual Map of Some Approaches to Cognitive Psychology and Human Information Processing Systems

ogy divided into normative and descriptive approaches.

The normative approach is concerned with measuring and understanding the quality of information processing—with trying to determine how well people think or how well people make decisions. An example in the accounting literature is Barefield's use of the Bayesian and multiple regression models of information processing. The most familiar aspects of the normative approach are the realms of intelligence testing or ability measurement. In recent years, this approach has come under heavy fire not only because of cultural bias issues, but also because supposedly innate capabilities in information processing seem to be subject to change given differential training. We will not pursue the normative approach here, but rather will examine the descriptive approach to information processing.

The descriptive approach is not concerned with assessing thinking quality against some absolute criterion. On the contrary, it is concerned with understanding and measuring how people make decisions and process information. It is concerned with issues such as how much information is used in a decision, rather than whether the decision is good or bad. Importantly for accounting, the descriptive approach assumes that criteria for effectiveness vary, e.g., that high data use and low data use both can lead to good decisions in the right context.

Within the descriptive approach, there are several distinct schools of thought. Figure 3 shows this graphically. At one end we encounter the "generalist" school, largely identified with experimental psychology. The assumption here is that men are basically the same; that any random sample of people can be used to generalize to the whole human species. Individual differences are ascribed to meaningless "error." The generalist approach has the advantage of great simplicity. It has led to many useful insights into general human information processing. For instance, the application of Shannon's statistical communication theory to information processing has been pursued by generalists. G. A. Miller (1956) has found that the number of bits or distinct information units (as measured by discreet levels of physical stimuli) man can track simultaneously is seven plus or minus two. Other studies have found that most people seem to have a similar moderate level of information input which optimizes their information use (Streufert, Suedfeld and Driver, 1965). In the accounting literature the generalist approach is best illustrated by Revsine (1970) who emphasizes the impact of the environment on the "general user" of financial statements.

The basic problem with this generalist view is pragmatic. Whereas generalization may be sufficient for science, it often fails in organizations. Although an experimental psychologist may dismiss individuals who differ in information use from the average as "error," a designer of an accounting information system cannot. If generalized information handling theories were adequate, we would have long ago settled on a single optimal mode of summarizing and presenting information. But it is in-

GENERAL	DIFFERENTIAL	UNIQUE
Studies of human information processing using random subjects, e.g. G. A. Miller's (1956) Information Theory	Studies of differences between types of people in information processing, e.g., Schroder, Driver and Streufert (1967)	Computer Modeling of a person's decision process, e.g., Newell and Simon's (1972) research on music composers or chess

FIGURE 3. Basic Schools in Descriptive Human Information Processing Research

creasingly clear that generalized systems breed problems (Ackoff, 1967).

At the opposite end of this spectrum is the "unique" school of thought. The assumption here is that each person represents a unique case with respect to his mode of information processing. This approach has the advantage of great precision. With careful analysis, a man's information processing can be modeled so well that a computer program can duplicate it. Newell and Simon (1972) and their associates epitomize this approach with their programs for playing chess or solving problems.

However, the "unique" school has at least one serious flaw. One cannot form "general" laws of thought or cognition if each person is seen as unique. Hopefully this approach will ultimately generate the empirical substance out of which more general theories may emerge.

A third school (Figure 3) is termed "differential." The assumption here is that people differ in cognition but that categories of people can be identified with similar thought processes. The approach here would be similar to the "contingency theory" school in organization theory. In accounting literature this point of view is seen in the Mock, Estrin and Vasarhelyi (1972) study of differences in decision approach, in Dermer's (1973) analysis of high and low tolerance for ambiguity, and in Miller's (1972) view on varied conceptual structures in information processing. The advantage of this approach is that one can generalize yet be concerned with individual differences. An optimum trade-off between precision and simplicity is sought. This approach will be reviewed in more depth. In classifying people in regard to cognition, two different methods have emerged. One focuses on *values;* the other on the actual mode or *style* of information processing in individuals.

The values approach asks people how much they value or like different modes of information processing; i.e., how much they like maintaining an open or flexible stance toward new information or how much they like ambiguous versus clear information. The values approach often uses self-description questionnaires or tests (Rokeach, 1960). A variant is the use of visual stimuli of varying information content (Berlyne, 1960; Barron, 1953). Within either approach it is found that people do differ consistently in how much they value aspects of information. For instance, some people like great complexity; others do not.

The second approach focuses on how people actually use information, not on what they say they like. The two approaches do not always agree—for instance, it is found that people who use high amounts of data often do not actually like high amounts of data. Use of information has been examined in a variety of ways (Warr, 1970). Some investigations are concerned with how people perceive and seek data, some with how they use data in analysis or decision, and some with how they implement decisions.

In each of the above areas of activity, investigations have isolated many dimensions of difference (see Figure 2). *Incongruity* and *complexity* seem to be the most common dimensions of individual difference. Many studies reveal that ambiguity, novelty, incongruity, and uncertainty produce very different responses in men. Some people seek uncertainty and manipulate ambiguity or risk with ease. Others shy away from uncertainty and even distort data to avoid risk or ambiguity. These differences in ambiguity tolerance are beginning to be applied to the understanding of organization development (Driver and Streufert, 1965; Hunsaker, 1971) and to the design of accounting information systems (Dermer, 1973).

Information complexity also generates differential responses. Some models focus on how finely people discriminate information or to what extent they differentiate data (Warr, 1970). Other models are concerned with how people put data together in making decisions. Among the latter, one seems to be of growing interest. It is called the Human Information Processing System (HIPS) model. Its origin is in the formulation that individuals and groups, as systems, develop different tendencies to process information. Some systems use high amounts of data; some, little data. These tendencies seem to be due primarily to learning, not heredity (Harvey, Hunt and Schroder, 1961).

The HIPS model was further developed to include reactivity to current environments (Schroder, Driver and Streufert, 1967). It is argued that each person or group information processing system responds in a typical curvilinear manner to current variation in environmental input (see Figure 4). Environmental input or load is defined as the aggregate effect of subjective information complexity, noxity, and eucity. Subjective information complexity is defined as the amount of change produced by input in a person's internal concepts or values (Driver and Streufert, 1969). In rough terms, the greater the amount of nonredundant input a person is given, the more *internal* change (i.e., subjective information) he is expected to have experienced. Noxity is defined as the degree of increase in negative feeling due to an input. Noxious inputs include inputs reflecting threat or failure such as significant "unfavorable" budget variances. Eucity is defined as the degree of increase in positive feeling due to an input (e..g., rewards produce eucity). As seen in Figure 4, as environmental load increases, the amount of information actually *used* in decisions or problem solving increases to "optimum load" and then information use declines. It is important to distinguish information used, i.e., related to solution choices, from information sought or purchased but not used in the decision.

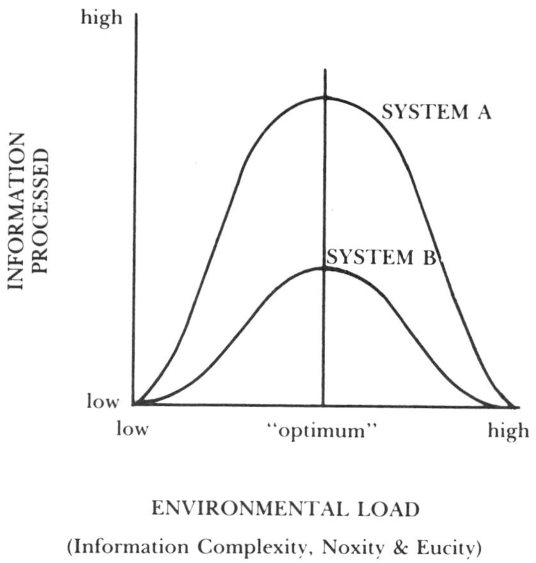

FIGURE 4. Relation of Information Used to Environmental Load

Experiments in laboratory settings and field studies in organizations have confirmed the basic model (Driver and Streufert, 1969; Alawi, 1973). Individuals and groups use more information in decisions with increasing load, up to a point; then they begin to process less as they move into "overload." Within the general trend, differences occur. High data-using systems (A in Figure 4) consistently use more data than low data-using systems (B in Figure 4). Only at extremes of overload or lack of input do the two systems resemble each other in data use.

After this initial formulation, a more elaborate model has been emerging. It had been noted that all high data-using systems were not alike. In some high data-using persons, the data were organized to support one overriding point of view; in other high data-users, the information was scattered among many simultaneously held points of view (sometimes the same data was seen as serving several conflicting points of view). These differences in focus led to the development of Decision Style Theory (Driver and Lintott, 1973).

Decision Style Theory is best illustrated

by Figure 5. Two dimensions of information processing are postulated; amount of information used and degree of focus. A minimal data user is seen as a person who uses just enough data to make an adequate decision and then moves on. In a real sense, he satisfices on information use in order to gain time or results. In financial terms, the "satisficer" will settle for less than maximum profit to save time; he will process just enough data to "break even" or obtain a "reasonable" profit and then move on to the next problem. On the other hand, a maximal data-user is not satisfied until all data perceived to be relevant are examined. He will massage data until one or more "excellent" solutions are apparent, often ignoring time. In financial terms, he seeks to maximize profit by maximizing use of data and implicitly valuing time at a low cost.

The second dimension of Decision Style Theory concerns focusing. At one extreme lies the person who sees all data leading to one conclusion; at the other extreme is the person who sees information having varied meanings. Where the former style can be accused of being rigid, it is also consistent; where the latter can be accused of being wishy-washy, it is also flexible.

Combining these two dimensions, we derive four basic decision styles which are labeled in Figure 5. Figure 6 summarizes some attributes of each style. The *Decisive Style* is one

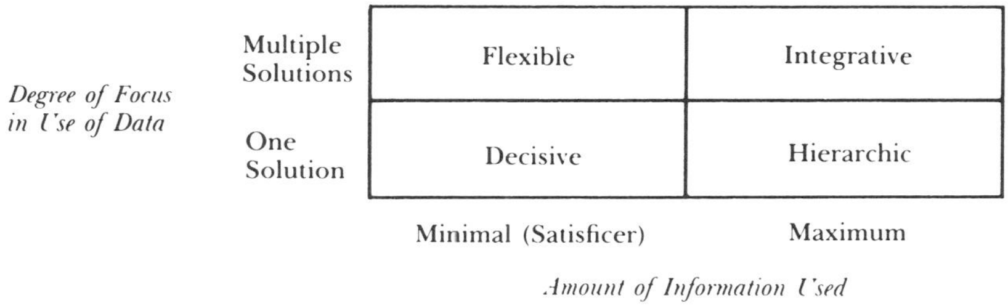

FIGURE 5. Decision Style Model

	Decisive	Flexible	Hierarchic	Integrative
Values	Efficiency Speed Consistency	Adaptability Speed Variety	Quality Rigorous Method System	Information Creativity
Planning	Low data base Short-range Tight control for results	Low data base Intuitive	High data base Long-range Tight control of method and results	High data base Long-range Adaptive
Goals	Few; organization focus	Many; self-focus	Few; self-focus	Many; self- and organization-focus
Organization	Short span of control Rules Classic organization	Control by confusion Loose	Wide span of control Elaborate procedures Automation	Team process Matrix organization
Communication	Short summary format Results focus one solution	Short, summary format Variety several solutions	Long, elaborate reports Problem, methods, data, give "Best Conclusion"	Long, elaborate Problem analysis from many views; Multiple solution

FIGURE 6. Summary Decision Style Chart

in which a person habitually uses a minimal amount of data to generate one firm opinion. It is a style characterized by a concern for speed, efficiency, and consistency. In planning, the Decisive Style uses a minimal data base to develop tightly controlled and scheduled short-range plans. Deadlines are critical since time is of the essence. Only a few goals are set in keeping with a single focus. Goals are usually those of the organization since they reduce conflict and personal complexity. In organization, the Decisive Style prefers a classic, simple, hierarchic organization with a short, clear span of control and clearcut rules. The Decisive likes to communicate briefly and to the point. In reports he prefers summaries focusing on results and action. He likes to see one solution. Long, detailed reports are "turned off."

A decision maker using the *Flexible Style* also uses minimal data, but sees it having different meaning at different times. A Flexible decision maker can confront the same data and give it one interpretation one day, another interpretation the next day. It is a style associated with speed, adaptability, and intuition. Planning is not liked since this style prefers to play it by ear and use intuition. Many self-oriented goals are pursued, one after another, since only reliance on personal goals can provide requisite freedom to maneuver. Reliance on organizational goals limits the Flexible Style—it therefore is often associated with so-called "loners." Clearcut organization is shunned; rather a loose, fluid pattern is used. Confusion among subordinates generates creativity and ultimate control by a Flexible manager. Like the Decisive, the Flexible likes short, to-the-point communication. Unlike the Decisive, he likes variety and many briefly stated solutions (alternatives).

In sharp contrast, the *Hierarchic Style* uses masses of carefully analyzed data to arrive at the one best conclusion. It is associated with great thoroughness, precision, and perfectionism. Planning is a favored high data-using activity and is long range. Control over both method and results is sought since the one "best method" is to be enforced. Goals tend to be personal and few, with elaborate strategies for goal attainment. The classic organization with broad span of control and elaborate procedure is favored. Communication is characterized by long, formal, and thorough reports which state problem, method, and data and generate one "best" conclusion. Brief or inconsistent reports are viewed as inadequate.

The *Integrative Style* also uses masses of data, but will generate a multitude of possible solutions. Unlike the Flexible, the Integrative system will produce these varied interpretations not at successive appraisals, but at the same time. It is a highly experimental, information-loving style—often very creative. Planning is used and is based on much data, but plans are constantly being altered. There is an affinity for simulation and gaming in this style. Multiple goals are sought which integrate personal and organizational objectives. The Integrative style works well in nonautocratic teams and in nonhierarchic organizations of the matrix type. Communication is complex and fluid. The preference is for long, involved discussion rather than unrelated reports or brevity.

One last development of decision style theory concerns mixed styles. Research (Driver, 1974) has shown that some persons use one style predominately whereas others employ one style as often as another. One very common mixed style is the Integrative/Hierarchic mix. This type of person mixes both styles in a complex approach to data. This mixed style is so common it has been given a specific title—the *Complex Style.*

In keeping with the research on environmental load (Figure 4), Decision Style Theory proposes that each person or system has one (or two) dominant style(s), learned over time. However, when load is very low or high, most systems shift to Decisive or Flexible styles of functioning.

Research on Decision Style has been extensive. Two psychometric measures have been used most frequently. One is called the APSE (Administrative Problem Solving Exercise) or IST (Integration Style Test). It consists of a business problem which a person solves. He then indicates on the test how he used the data in the problem. It has proven reliable, but should not be used if people are under extreme pressure, since nondominant styles will emerge. The APSE has been validated in laboratory and field settings. In the lab, it predicts decision speed, use of data, use of contingencies, amount of creativity, and type of group process, among many information processing variables (Driver, 1972; Raynolds, 1972). In field studies, it has related to level of management, area of business specialization, use of information search and screening, longevity with companies, and even age and education (Alawi, 1973; Boulgarides, 1973).

The other widely used measurement scale is the CXSD, a self-description questionnaire which assesses both style and values. It reveals a person's self-concept regarding his use of information. It is somewhat more reliable than the APSE yet less valid as a predictor since self-concepts are often somewhat distorted. The CXSD does serve well, however, and in both laboratory and field studies the results parallel those of the APSE (Driver, 1970). When possible, the two instruments taken together offer the best analysis.

With respect to accounting and information systems, Decision Style Theory has many implications. It postulates that each style has an optimal pattern for information search and use (Alawi, 1973). Furthermore, environmental load can alter the utility of information systems, if styles shift under extreme environmental load. Ideally, one would want to design information systems which are reactive both to decision maker styles and environmental load. The experiment reported here is a preliminary exploratory assessment of the direct relevance of Decision Style Theory—derived from Human Information Processing Theory—to Accounting.

INFORMATION PROCESSING WITHIN THE INFORMATION STRUCTURE EXPERIMENTS

In order to begin testing Decision Style and Human Information Processing Theories within the accounting domain, a set of prior information structure experiments (Mock, 1969, 1973A) was redesigned. Within this context, one can consider behavior with respect to information search, information purchase, decision speed, decision quality, and several other variables. The results reported in this paper are limited to *information purchase* and *decision speed.* From an information system design point of view, the focus of the analysis is tailoring the system with respect to input load, level of detail, etc., in relation to decision style. The key to this approach is the assumption that varying information structures (e.g., input loads) are optimal for various decision styles. In addition, further empirical data are provided which permit the examination of construct and predictive validity of the referenced information processing and decision style theories.

Hypotheses

Because many of the HIPS notions have not been extensively tested in business decisions, especially within an economic decision making context, many of our preexperiment expectations were more of the nature of "priors" than well-developed hypotheses. Most importantly, such priors are derived from psychological settings with quite different experimental tasks. For example, the purchase hypotheses are based on a Stock Market Game (Driver, 1960) and a Tactical Military Game (Streufert et al.,

1965). In these two experiments, it was found that:

1. Complex (Integrative, Hierarchic) subjects requested less *simple* input than less complex subjects (Decisive, Flexible) especially under overload conditions.
2. Complex subjects requested more *complex* input than less complex subjects under overload conditions in the Streufert et al. study and under all conditions in the Driver study.
3. Information seeking of all types in all conditions declined from very high levels under low environment load to very low levels under high load.

To transfer from this data to hypotheses for the present business game is attended by several problems:

1. Measurement of styles is via different psychometric tests. Sentence Completion and Situation Interpretation Tests were used in early studies; the IST was used here.
2. In the earlier work, only high and low information users were measured (i.e., Integratives and Hierarchics were not distinguished).
3. The type of decision is very different. Earlier sites were largely verbal, nonquantitative settings, whereas the present site involves a fairly quantitative framework.
4. Requests for information and information purchase are not necessarily the same variable, although information costs in the present site are minimal, perhaps even negligible.
5. Level of environmental load is not known in the present site. If it were low to moderate, little style difference is expected, especially for simple information requests.
6. Type of information—simple or complex—is not clear in the present site. In previous studies, simple information meant data obtained by merely asking an authority for advice (e.g., stock analyst, intelligence). Complex information resulted from subject's actions on the environment (e.g., trial purchases, probes). The accounting data in this experiment probably most resembles *complex* (subject generated) data.

Given all these problems, prior research can only *suggest* that: (a) if Driver (1960) is right, Complex subjects (i.e., Integrative and Hierarchic) will purchase more data than less complex subjects (i.e., Decisive and Flexible; or (b) if Streufert et al. (1965) are right, Complex subjects will purchase more data only under overload.

Based therefore upon these previous experiments, the following hypothesis may be offered:

I. INFORMATION PURCHASE BEHAVIOR VERSUS DECISION STYLE

The Integrative, Hierarchic and Complex (I/H) decision styles are expected to prefer more complex information input. Experimentally, this will result in greater frequency of information purchase. In contrast, the Decisive and Flexible decision styles are expected to exhibit the opposite behavior.

Our second area of interest is a gross measure of information use, namely, decision time. In past research Driver (1972) has found an inverse relationship between information use in decisions and decision time. However, Streufert et al. (1965) found that information use did not parallel information requests, although (1) both use and requests for information declined under overload and (2) with underload conditions request for information was high while use was low.

In a more recent study specifically on decision time, Driver (1972) found that the Decisive Style was significantly faster than Complex and Integrative Styles and the Integrative Style tended to be faster than the Complex Style. (No useful data on Hierarchic and Flexible Styles were previously available.)

Again, when considering expected decision speed behavior in the present experiments, several cautions are needed:

1. The task in the Driver (1972) study was the Luna I moon colony (Driver and Hunsaker, 1972). In this task, nonquantitative, heuristic decision making prevailed in regards to the choice of scientific studies. Luna I is a loose, yet complex decision environment, whereas the present site is quantitative and "tight." A related study by Pollay (1970A and B) has shown that decision tasks, and more specifically the complexity of decision alternatives, will have significant effects on decision time.
2. Teams were the bases of analysis in Driver (1972), not individuals as in the present study.

II. Thus, based upon the previous evidence we would hypothesize (1) that Integrative and Complex decision styles would utilize more decision time in contrast to Decisives and (2) that Complex Styles will take more decision time than Integrative Styles. Also, although no previous data exist on the Flexible style, if decision time is affected significantly by the amount of information processed, this style should be relatively faster than the Integratives, Hierarchics, or Complex decision styles. Similarly, one can theoretically expect that the Hierarchic Style should be faster than the Complex Style, not different from the Integrative Style, and slower than the Flexibles and Decisives.

Experimental Tasks

The information structure experiments were based on a business game modeled upon a manufacturing concern. The experiment required production and marketing decisions over a number of decision periods. After each period, performance and other feedback were received (see Figure 7). Background information provided to subjects included both a complete description of the firm's underlying cost, production and market functions, and a ten-year period history of firm performance.[3] These experiments differed from previous tests as follows:

1. Subjects were able to purchase additional accounting feedback reports:

Report	Purchase Designation	Cost Per Period
a. None	0	0
b. Operating Cost Detail	1	3 Percent of sales
c. Unit Cost Detail	2	2 Percent of sales
d. Both	3	5 Percent of sales

Figure 7 shows the additional information that was received if one purchased either operating cost or unit cost detail (or both). If one postulates that this kind of information would be valuable in the learning (attention direction) sense (Mock, 1971), then it would be used by certain decision styles and its use presumably would require additional decision time. Thus our subsequent statistical tests consider decision style theory with respect to frequency of information purchase, presuming use, and then with respect to decision speed.

2. Subjects submitted Period Budgets with respect to Total Revenues, Expenses, and Profits.
3. Subjects were asked to specify brief rationales for their budgets, including data and decision rules used.
4. The experiment's length was specified to

[3]Details are available upon request or see Mock (1969).

be three hours' maximum with an unknown number of decision periods. Pilot and subsequent tests resulted in the vast majority of subjects completing five or more periods; thus our analysis uses five decisions per subject.

The subjects consisted of 54 first-year MBA students, a significant number of which had previous business or military experience. In prior testing, the students had been given the Integration Style Test (IST) to determine decision style.[4] Subjects were classified as follows:

Decision Style	Number of Subjects
Decisive	8
Flexible	15
Integrative	14
Hierarchic	6
Complex (*I/H* Combined)	11
	54

EXPERIMENTAL RESULTS

As stated earlier, differences in decision style are expected to result in differences in subject information purchase behavior and decision speed. For example, the cognitively more complex integrative decision style, as indicated by high data use and multiple focus, is expected to exhibit a relative preference for additional accounting feedback. This would be measured in terms of additional information purchase.

Information Purchase Behavior

Consider the data displayed in Table 2 which presents the percentage of each decision style which purchased the various kinds of feedback in each decision period. Figure 8 presents a plot of frequencies for those who purchased complete or partial feedback. Clearly a period effect is evident as all subjects purchased less feedback in the later decision periods.[5] Also the possibility of significant differences among decision styles is evident. Note, for example, that the Decisives exhibited almost no preference for partial feedback. Thus, they either purchased all special reports or none.

An overall test of significant difference in information purchase behavior is provided by Friedman's two-way analysis of variance on the period frequency rankings. The resulting Xr^2 statistics with four degrees of freedom were:

	Decision Style (Row) Effects		Period/Learning (Column) Effects	
Purchase Decision	Xr^2	Significance	Xr^2	Significance
No feedback (0)	6.88	n.s.	13.2	0.05
Partial feedback (1 or 2)	9.08	n.s.	6.56	n.s.
Complete feedback (3)	1.06	n.s.	14.32	0.05

In each case the null hypothesis cannot be rejected for differences attributed to decision style; thus significant overall differences in purchase behavior are not evident. Of course, the learning or period effects which are apparent in the graph are significant for no and complete feedback.

In order to consider whether significant purchase differences existed among particular decision styles, the data were transformed to a matrix of differences in the percentage of subjects that purchased some feedback (1, 2, or 3)

[4]The test-retest reliability of this classification instrument has proven satisfactory, with x^2 better than $p = .01$ for all four categories. See Driver (1974) for further reliability and validity data.

[5]Decreasing marginal value of information which is oriented toward model building and strategy evaluation has been postulated. See Mock (1971) and C. C. Ying (1967).

Income Statement for the Year 1974

		Actual (X)	Budgeted (Y)
Sales		465,815.18	500,000.00
Less Operating Cost			
Operating Cost Detail (purchased)	Production	152,752.36	
	Fixed	76,100.00	
	Information	23,290.76	
	Advertising	154,000.00	
Total Cost		406,143.12	400,000.00
Net Profit		59,672.06	100,000.00
Unit Cost Detail (purchased)	STD Cost of Unit	965.38	

The Environmental Factors for the Year 1974 were:

Unit Cost of Material 1,170	Unit Cost of Labor 796
Fixed Cost 76,100	Demand Index 1,223

Figure 7. Example of Financial Performance Feedback and Purchased Items

TABLE 2. Frequency of Information Purchase Decision Classified by Decision Style

Purchase Decision	Decision Style	Decision Period 1	2	3	4	5
1. no feedback	Decisive	0.25	0.625	0.5	0.5	0.75
	Flexible	.4	.2	.533	.533	.533
	Hierarchic	.167	.5	.333	.667	.833
	Integrative	.357	.429	.571	.429	.929
	I/H	.0909	.273	.455	.364	.455
2. partial feedback	Decisive	0	0	0.125	0.125	0
	Flexible	.0667	.4	.333	.2	.2
	Hierarchic	.167	0	.333	0	.167
	Integrative	.0714	.214	.357	.286	0
	I/H	.273	.364	.273	.364	.182
3. complete feedback	Decisive	.75	.375	.375	.375	.25
	Flexible	.533	.4	.133	.267	.267
	Hierarchic	.667	.5	.333	.333	0
	Integrative	.571	.357	.0714	.286	.0714
	I/H	.636	.364	.273	.273	.364

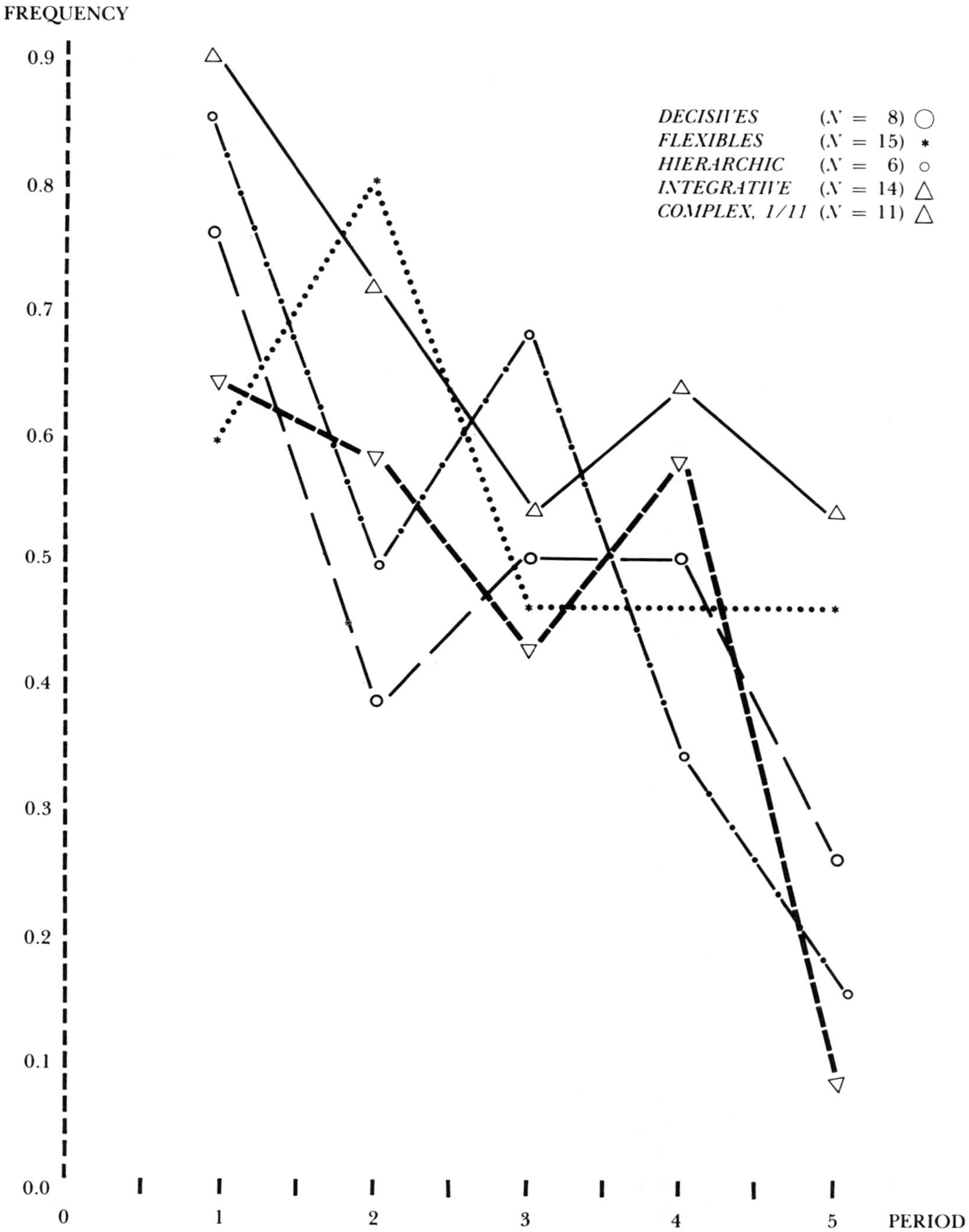

FIGURE 8. Plot of Frequency of Purchase of Any (Partial or Complete) Feedback by Decision Style

less those that purchased none. The Wilcoxen Matched-Pairs Test was then applied to each style pair as follows:

Decision Style Pair	Wilcoxen T	Significance
1. *I/H* vs. Decisive	0	0.05
2. Integrative	0	.05
3. Hierarchic	1	.05
4. Flexible	3.5	n.s.
5. Flexible vs. Decisive	1.5	.05
6. Integrative	4.5	n.s.
7. Hierarchic	8.5	n.s.
8. Hierarchic vs. Decisive	1.5	.05
9. Integrative	5.5	n.s.
10. Integrative vs. Decisive	7	n.s.

In all cases except number 10, these results are consistent with previous findings. (Recall that no previous results are available on the Flexible Style.) As expected, the Complex *I/H* Style exhibited a preference to purchase more information than other previously studied styles. Also, the Integratives failed to show significant differences in data purchase and the Hierarchic Style purchased more information than the Decisive Style as was predicted from theory. Lastly, the Flexible Style conformed to theory in purchasing more information than the Decisive Style, but showed no significant differences with any other style.

The strategy of information purchases shows some interesting patterns, generally consistent with Decision Style Theory. For example, the Decisives initially were high information purchasers,[6] but rapidly settled into a low information posture. In contrast, each period the Flexible seems to assess the situation differently and to use a different information purchase strategy. The Hierarchic sample (although small) shows a steady gradual shift towards less information as opposed to the abrupt shift of the Decisive. The Integrative used various strategies, but overall purchased surprisingly little data. Finally, the combined *I/H* Style was consistent in their high purchase of data.

Decision Time Behavior

Also as hypothesized earlier, decision style differences in terms of information search and processing are expected to result in varying decision times for subjects. In order to test for overall differences in decision speed, the Friedman χ_r^2 was calculated for the average decision times presented in Table 3. For this sample, χ_r^2 is 13.44, which is significant at the 0.05 level. Thus, decision style does explain significant variance in required decision times.

Similar to our previous analysis, an attempt was made to consider paired comparisons among decision styles. For instance, as hypothesized earlier, Decisives should experience economies in decision speed when com-

[6]As Driver and Streufert (1969) note: our culture has a norm for using high information; but the Decisive Style, as it gets into overload quickly abandons this norm.

TABLE 3. Average Decision Time (Min.) Per Period for Each Decision Style

Decision Style	Decision Period 1	2	3	4	5
Decisive	51.69	30.51	21.67	16.82	17.53
Hierarchic	63.38	20.88	15.66	11.62	10.85
Integrative	64.59	24.28	18.53	16.25	12.31
Flexible	67.26	23.93	16.77	13.37	11.5
I/H	53.48	28.02	19.71	16.54	15.61
Overall average	61.02	25.49	18.43	15.08	13.37

pared to, say, Integratives. This question may be tested using the Mann-Whitney *U* as applied to each pair of decision style samples. The results (Mann-Whitney *U*'s) are as shown below.

These data show that, in the early periods, significant differences in decision speed do not exist. Yet in the later two periods, differences do begin to appear with Decisives becoming *slower* than other decision styles and with Hierarchics tending to react most quickly.

In overall speed the rank order (slow to fast) of styles is:

1. Decisive
2. *I/H*
3. Integrative
4. Flexible
5. Hierarchic

The expected sequence was:

1. *I/H*
2. Integrative
3. Hierarchic
4. Flexible
5. Decisive

Clearly the relatively slow decision making of the *I/H* and Integrative Styles fits both theory and prior data. Also, the relatively quick time of the Flexible Style is a new finding which fits theoretical expectation. The very fast time of the Hierarchic is also a new finding, but is counter to theory. Their fast time does not indicate low data use (see purchase data) and suggests that a re-examination of theory may be needed on this style.

The real surprise was the extremely slow pace of the Decisive Style. Does this pace imply high data use? Probably not, since the Decisives are not high data purchasers. In a prior nonquantitative setting the Decisives moved very quickly. Why the slowdown in this site?

As noted above, task strongly affects decision time. It is our surmise that this very structured complex task produced a state of overload in the Decisive player not produced in the less structured Lunar Colony Game. In this overload condition the Decisives lost their normal speed and moved slowly with little data.

This interpretation is furthered by examining the performance (profit) data in this site (Mock and Driver, 1974). Here, the Decisives were clearly least capable of success, although in some ways the Integratives also did poorly. The performance data show that after

Decision Style	Sample Size	Decision Period				
		1	2	3	4	5
Decisive vs. Flexible	8, 15	36	42	37	32*	22*
Hierarchic	8, 6	18	12*	15	12*	6*
Integrative	8, 14	48	41	38	54	20*
I/H	8, 11	41	41	29	40	36
Flexible vs. Hierarchic	15, 6	41	32	40	34	42
Integrative	15, 14	87	103	93	66†	104
I/H	15, 11	52	63	66	62	56
Hierarchic vs. Integrative	6, 14	40	38	35	20†	39
I/H	6, 11	26	20	27	11†	21
Integrative vs. *I/H*	14, 11	60	55	73	74	55

*Significantly slower at 0.05 level.
†Significantly faster at 0.05 level.

an initial success, the Decisives collapse and show no further learning. The hypothesis that the Decisives went into overload in this game seems substantiated. Further research will be needed to verify this suggestion that the normally fast Decisive: (a) is more easily overloaded by a complex structured game than other styles; and (b) when overloaded becomes quite deliberate—i.e. slow and low data using.

Turning back to the other unanticipated result—the fast Hierarchic—we further verify that speed is not at the price of good data use since the Hierarchic is just about the most successful style in this game (along with the much slower Complex *I/H* Style).

Given these data the theory could be modified as follows:

In very structured tasks, the Hierarchic Style will be a high data user but will process data at very high speed compared to I/H or Integrative Styles.

Presumably this high speed is due to the early formulation of decision rules which allow rapid analysis in a stable environment. One would assume that in less-structured environments (e.g., Lunar Colony) the Hierarchic speed would be less noticeable since rules would not continue to work and would have to be reformulated.

The Integrative Style was predictably slow but showed little data purchase. Their performance was poor until the later periods where they showed significant improvement. One therefore cannot infer that their low data purchase meant low data use. Apparently they were using limited data to develop a complex strategy which put them in good shape at game's end. The Integrative in a highly structured task and heavy load decreases data purchase (and requests), but maintains use as found in earlier experiments.

The Complex *I/H* Style shows little overload effect. They purchase much data, go slowly, and generally were high performers. A point for further analysis is why the Complex, Hierarchic, and Flexible Styles seemed less overloaded, whereas the Decisive, and to a lesser extent, the Integrative Styles were probably overloaded.

The Flexibles functioned as expected in overall performance. They purchased data and moved faster than the *I/H* Style and did relatively poorer. This suggests moderate data use as expected.

Given the data generated by these first exploratory studies of human information processing and Decision Style Theory within Accounting, several research questions and tentative conclusions seem worthy of mention. Specifically, our future research is being designed to examine the following issues:

1. What is the effect of perceived load?
2. What is the impact of structure versus looseness of task?
3. What is the impact of interest in task?

Given the complex structured task of these experiments, several tentative conclusions seem warranted:

1. Complex decision makers prefer (re their purchase behavior) and effectively use more complete feedback.
2. Integrative decision makers prefer less complete feedback but use moderate initial data to formulate effective long-range plans. (In more unstructured tasks, the Integrative seemed to prefer more constant data input.)
3. Hierarchic decision makers prefer and effectively use moderately complete feedback.
4. Flexible decision makers prefer but are somewhat less able to use effectively moderately complex feedback.
5. Decisive decision makers become rapidly overloaded in complex structured tasks and hence cannot effectively use complex feedback.

REFERENCES

American Accounting Association, Report of the Committee on Accounting and Information Systems, THE ACCOUNTING REVIEW (1971 Supplement to Vol. XLVI), pp. 287–350.

Ackoff, R., "Management Misinformation Systems," *Management Science* (December 1967), pp. B147–B156.

Alawi, H., "Cognitive, Task and Organizational Complexities in Relation to Information Processing Behavior of Business Managers," Ph.D. Dissertation, G.S.B.A., USC (1973).

Barefield, R. M., "The Effect of Aggregation on Decision Making Success: A Laboratory Study," *Journal of Accounting Research*, Vol. 10, No. 2 (1972), pp. 229–42.

Barron, F., "Complexity—Simplicity As A Personality Dimension," *Journal of Abnormal and Social Psychology* (1953), pp. 163–72.

Beishon, R. J., "Information Flow and Manager's Decisions," *Management Accounting* (November 1970), Vol. 48, No. 11, pp. 385–90.

Berlyne, D. E., *Conflict, Arousal, and Curiosity,* (McGraw-Hill, 1960).

Boulgarides, J. D., "Decision Style, Values and Biographical Factors in Relation to Satisfaction and Performance of Supervisors in a Government Agency," Ph.D. Dissertation, GSBA, USC (1973).

Burns, T.J. (Ed.), *Behavioral Experiments in Accounting,* The Ohio State University (1972).

Dermer, J. D., "Cognitive Characteristics and the Perceived Importance of Information," THE ACCOUNTING REVIEW (July 1973), pp. 511–19.

Doktor, R. and W. F. Hamilton, "Cognitive Style and the Acceptance of Management Science Recommendations," *Management Science* (April 1973), Vol. 19, No. 8, pp. 884–94.

Driver, M. J., "Decision Style, Self Concepts and Decision Making Behavior," (unpublished manuscript), Graduate School of Business Administration, University of Southern California (1970).

———, "Decision Style and Decision Speed," (unpublished manuscript), Graduate School of Business Administration, University of Southern California (1972).

———, "Decision Style and Its Measurement," (unpublished manuscript) Graduate School of Business Administration, University of Southern California (1974).

——— and Phillip L. Hunsaker, "The Luna I Moon Colony: A Programmed Simulation for the Analysis of Individual and Group Decision Making," *Psychological Reports* (1972).

——— and J. T. Lintott, *Managerial Decision Diagnostics,* Graduate School of Business Administration, University of Southern California (1972, in progress).

——— and S. Streufert, "The General Incongruity Adaptation Level (GIAL) Hypotheses: An Analysis and Integration of Cognitive Approaches to Motivation," Krannert School of Industrial Administration, Purdue University, Paper No. 114 (1965).

——— "Integrative Complexity: An Approach to Individuals and Groups as Information-Processing Systems," *Administrative Science Quarterly,* Vol. 14, No. 2. (June 1969), pp. 272–85.

Dyckman, T. R., T. R. Hofstedt and R. Murdock, "Information, Data Aggregation and the Effects of Ambiguity: A Preliminary Experiment," *Behavioral Experiments in Accounting* (T. J. Burns, Ed.) The Ohio State University (1972), pp. 485–513.

Estrin, T. L., "The Relationship Between Brain Hemispheric Activity Differences and the Use of Management Information," Research Proposal, Simon Frazier University (January 1974).

Hamilton, R. E., "The Effect of Aggregation on Decision-Making Success: A Laboratory Study —A Reply," (mimeographed) University of California, Berkeley (1974).

Harvey, O.J., D. Hunt and H. Schroder, *Conceptual Systems and Personality Organization* (Wiley, 1961).

Hoffman, P. J. and W. A. Blanchard, "A Study of the Effect of Varying Amounts of Predictor Information on Judgment," *Oregon Research Institute Bulletin* (1961).

Hofstedt, T. R., "The Processing of Accounting Information: Perceptual Biases," *Behavioral Experiments in Accounting* (T. J. Burns, Ed.), The Ohio State University (1972), pp. 285–315.

Hunsaker, P., "Some Cognitive and Environmental Determinants of Risk Taking Behavior in Individual and Group Decision Making," Ph.D. Dissertation, Graduate School of Business Administration, University of Southern California (1971).

——— "Incongruity Adaptation Capability and Risk Preference in Turbulent Decision Making Environments," *Organizational Behavior and Human Performance* (1974, in press).

Huysmans, H. H. B. M., "The Effectiveness of the Cognitive Style Constraint in Implementing Operations Research Proposals," *Management Science* (September 1970), pp. 92–104.

Kelly, G., *The Psychology of Personal Constructs* (Norton, 1955).

McKenney, J. L. and P. G. W. Keen, "How Managers' Minds Work," *Harvard Business Review* (May–June, 1974).

Miller, G. A., "The Magic Number Seven Plus or Minus Two: Some Limits on Our Capacity for Processing Information," *Psychological Review* (1956), pp. 81–97.

Miller, H., "Environmental Complexity and Financial Reports," THE ACCOUNTING REVIEW (January 1972), pp. 31–7.

Mock, T. J., "Comparative Values of Information Structures," *Journal of Accounting Research* (Supplement, 1969).

——— "Concepts of Information Value and Accounting," THE ACCOUNTING REVIEW (October 1971).

——— "The Value of Budget Information," THE ACCOUNTING REVIEW (July 1973A).

——— "A Longitudinal Study of Some Information Structure Alternatives," *Data Base* (Winter 1973B).

——— and M. J. Driver, "Decision Style, Value of Complete Variance Feedback and MIS Design," Working Paper, Graduate School of Business Administration, University of Southern California (October 1974).

——— T. L. Estrin and M. A. Vasarhelyi, "Learning Patterns, Decision Style and Value of Information," *The Journal of Accounting Research* (Spring 1972).

Newell, A., H. A. Simon, *Human Problem Solving* (Prentice-Hall 1972).

Pollay, R. W., "A Model of Decision Times in Difficult Decision Situations," *Psychological Review* (1970A), pp. 274–81.

——— "The Structure of Executive Decisions and Decision Times," *Administrative Science Quarterly*, (December 1970B), pp. 459–71.

Raynolds, P., "Cognitive Style, Self Perceptions and Effective Creativity Training," paper given in symposium, American Psychological Association Meeting, Honolulu (1972).

Revsine, L., "Data Expansion and Conceptual Structure," THE ACCOUNTING REVIEW (October 1970), pp. 704–11.

Rokeach, M., *The Open and Closed Mind* (Basic Books, 1960).

Ronen, Joshua, "Some Effects of Sequential Aggregation in Accounting on Decision-Making," *Journal of Accounting Research,* No. 2 (1971), pp. 307–32.

San Miguel, J. G., "Goals, Information and Psychological Variables in Decision-Making," Unpublished Ph.D. Thesis, University of Texas (1972).

Schroder, H. M., M. J. Driver and S. Streufert, *Human Information Processing* (Holt, Rinehart and Winston, 1967).

Streufert, S., P. Suedfeld and M. J. Driver, "Conceptual Structure, Information Search and Information Utilization," *Journal of Personality and Social Psychology* (1965), pp. 736–40.

Warr, P., *Thought and Personality* (Penguin Books, 1970).

Ying, C. C., "Learning by Doing—An Adaptive Approach to Multiperiod Decisions," *Operations Research* (September–October 1967), pp. 797–812.

An Expectancy Theory Approach to the Motivational Impacts of Budgets

J. Ronen

J. L. Livingstone*

In this paper we discuss the implications of budgets for motivation and behavior in the context of expectancy theory as developed in the psychology of motivation. We argue that propositions from expectancy theory can be used to integrate and accommodate the fragmented research findings on budget and behavior in the accounting literature. We discuss how the expectancy model reconciles what might appear to be contradictory findings from prior studies.

THE FUNCTIONS OF BUDGETS

Budgets serve three decision-making functions: planning, control, and motivation. Budgets aid planning in that they incorporate forecasts which reflect the anticipated consequences of different combinations of plans (actions) made by management and the relevant uncontrollable events that may occur in the environment. Budgets also serve the planning function through being utilized as a tool for sensitivity analysis which includes the examination of how slight changes in management plans affect the consequences (budgets). Many budgets could be thus generated as a result of alternative plans so that the most desirable plan could then be chosen.

The control function is typically a feedback process whereby information about past performance (both anticipated and actual) is provided to those who "control," to be utilized by them for making decisions. As a motivational tool, the budget conveys information to the subordinate about expectations of superiors regarding what constitutes successful task performance and the consequent reinforcement contingencies. These characterizations of the control and motivation processes probably apply whether the budget is imposed on subordinates, whether developed through the participation of the "controlled," or whether they result from a dynamic, interlevel bargaining process over goals and resource allocations (Schiff and Lewin, 1970).

The three functions of budgets are interdependent. The motivational effect must be explicitly considered in planning and control. Similarly, knowledge by subordinates of superiors' plans and control styles have motivational effects. Furthermore, the budgeting process is likely to cause subordinates to bargain for increases in the resources they command. This

From *The Accounting Review,* Vol. 50, No. 4 (October 1975), pp. 671–685.

*J. Ronen is Associate Professor of Accounting, New York University; and J. L. Livingstone is Callaway Professor of Industrial Management, Georgia Institute of Technology.

We gratefully acknowledge the comments and helpful suggestions of Arie Y. Lewin.

may result in dysfunctional budgetary slack (Schiff and Lewin, 1970; and Williamson, 1964).

THE DYSFUNCTIONAL ASPECTS OF BUDGETS

Budgetary slack is not the only potential dysfunctional aspect of budgets. The literature is filled with exhortations to consider the behavioral effects of standards and budgets on motivation and consequently on performance (Argyris, 1952; Benston, 1963; Becker and Green, 1962; and Usry, 1968). These effects could be either dysfunctional or positive. Many articles deal specifically with the behavioral impacts of budgets on employees; some base their conclusions on generalizations from the psychological literature, and others show findings from empirical experiments (Cherrington and Cherrington, 1973; Stedry, 1960; Stedry and Kay, 1966). Mostly, these discussions were launched in terms of specific principles taken from various areas of psychology such as aspiration level, participation, and attitude change.

To gain better understanding and insight into how these behavioral effects are created, we propose the expectancy model as a unifying framework within which the effects could be analyzed. While the universal usage of budgets implies that their benefits are perceived to exceed the possible dysfunctional effects, the latter can be minimized if the budget's behavioral impacts are better understood.

By choosing the expectancy model (a description of the model appears below) as a framework, we do not wish to imply that it accurately describes behavior even though some recent progress has been made.[1] Rather, we view it as a framework that facilitates the generation of hypotheses about the behavioral effects of budgets. The testing of these hypotheses would indicate whether subordinates' behavior is consistent with the model.

In the following section we describe the expectancy model. After that, we reinterpret the budget's behavioral implications discussed in the literature within the expectancy framework.

THE EXPECTANCY MODEL

The expectancy model is viewed as underlying the superior-subordinate budget relationship in two respects: (1) as the model according to which the subordinate's motivation to perform the task is influenced via the budget; and (2) as the model which the superior regards as determining the subordinate's motivation. (It is assumed that the superior can and may affect the subordinate's motivation via the budget in accordance with the expectancy model.)[2]

The particular expectancy model version that we use in this paper is the one advanced by House (1971) which in turn is derived from the Path-Goal hypotheses advanced by Georgopoulos, Mahoney, and Jones (1957) and from previous research supporting the class of expectancy models of motivation (Atkinson, 1958; Galbraith and Cummings, 1967; Graen, 1969; Lawler, 1968, 1971, 1973; Porter and Lawler, 1967; Vroom, 1964b). The basic tenet of expectancy theory is that an individual chooses his behavior on the basis of (1) his expectations that the behavior will result in

[1]Indeed, the model has been found wanting with respect to its description power. (See, e.g., Kerr, Klimoski, Tolliver and Von Glinow, 1974.) But there is some recent evidence of progress (see footnote 4).

[2]Clearly, motivation is only one variable that is likely to affect performance. Others are the subordinate's general ability, as well as specific skills. To improve the subordinate's performance, the superior may choose to initiate training programs or take other actions to enhance the subordinate's skill, in addition to affecting his motivation.

a specific outcome and (2) the sum of the valences, i.e., personal utilities or satisfaction that he derives from the outcome. A distinction is made (Galbraith and Cummings, 1967) between valences that are intrinsic to behavior itself (such as feelings of competence) and those that are the extrinsic consequences of behavior (such as pay). Behavior that is intrinsically valent is also intrinsically motivational because the behavior leads directly to satisfaction, whereas extrinsic valences are contingent on external rewards.

House's formulation can be expressed as follows:

$$M = IV_b + P_1\left(IV_a + \sum_{i=1}^{n} P_{2i}EV_i\right), \quad i = 1, 2, \cdots, n$$

where

M = motivation to work

IV_a = intrinsic valence associated with successful performance of the task

IV_b = intrinsic valence associated with goal-directed behavior

EV_i = extrinsic valences associated with the ith extrinsic reward contingent on work-goal accomplishment

P_1 = the expectancy that goal-directed behavior will accomplish the work-goal (a given level of specified performance); the measure's range is $(-1, +1)$

P_{2i} = the expectancy that work-goal accomplishment will lead to the ith extrinsic reward; the measure's range is $(-1, +1)$.

The individual estimates the expectancy, P_1, of accomplishing a work-goal given his behavior. For the estimate he considers factors such as (1) his ability to behave in an appropriate and effective manner and (2) the barriers and support for work-goal accomplishment in the environment. Also, he estimates the expectancy, P_2, that work-goal accomplishment will result in attaining extrinsic rewards that have valences for him such as the recognition of his superiors of his goal accomplishment. He also places subjective values on the intrinsic valence associated with the behavior required to achieve the work-goal IV_b, the intrinsic valence associated with the achievement of the work-goal IV_a, and the extrinsic valences associated with the personal outcomes that accrue to him as a result of achieving the work-goal, EV_i.

The superior can affect the independent variables of this model:

1. He partially determines what extrinsic rewards (EV_i) follow work-goal accomplishment, since he influences the extent to which work-goal accomplishment will be recognized as a contribution and the nature of the reward (financial increases, promotion, assignment of more interesting tasks or personal goals and development).
2. Through interaction, he can increase the subordinate's expectancy (P_2) that rewards ensue work-goal accomplishment.
3. He can, through his own behavior, support the subordinate's efforts and thus influence the expectancy (P_1) that the effort will result in work-goal achievement.
4. He may influence the intrinsic valences associated with goal accomplishment *(IV_a)* by determining factors such as the amount of influence the subordinate has in goal setting and the amount of control he is allowed in the task-directed effort. Presumably, the greater the subordinate's opportunity to influence the goal and exercise control, the more intrinsically valent is the work-goal accomplishment.
5. The superior can increase the net intrinsic valences associated with goal-directed behavior *(IV_b)* by reducing frustrating barriers, by being supportive in times of stress, and by permitting involvement in a wide

variety of tasks and being considerate of the subordinate's needs (House, 1971).

Three classes of situational variables that determine which particular superior behaviors are instrumental in increasing work motivation were hypothesized by House (1973):

The Needs of the Subordinate. The subordinate views the superior's behavior as legitimate only to the extent that he perceives it either as an immediate source of satisfaction or as instrumental to his future satisfaction. For example, subordinates with high needs for social approval find warm, interpersonal superior behavior immediately satisfying and therefore legitimate. On the other hand, subordinates with high need for achievement desire clarification of path-goal relationships and goal-oriented feedback from superiors. The perceived legitimacy of the superior's behavior is thus partially determined by the subordinate's characteristics.

Environmental Demands. When the task is routine and well defined, attempts by the superior to clarify path-goal relationships are redundant and are likely to be viewed as superfluous, externally imposed control, thus resulting in decreased satisfaction. Also, the more dissatisfying the task, the more the subordinate resents behavior by the superior directed at increasing productivity and enforcing compliance with organizational procedures.

The Task Demands of Subordinates. The superior's behavior is assumed to be motivational to the extent that it helps subordinates cope with environmental uncertainties, threat from others, or sources of frustration. Such behavior is predicted to increase the subordinate's satisfaction with the job content, and to be motivational to the extent that it increases the subordinate's perceived expectancies that effort will lead to valued rewards.

THE RELATION BETWEEN THE EXPECTANCY MODEL AND THE ACCOUNTING BUDGETING PROCESS

Budgets have long been recognized as a managerial tool of communication between superiors and subordinates with respect to the parameters of the task. As a tool of communication, the budgets are perceived by subordinates as an aspect of their superior's attitudes toward them, the task, and the work environment.

First, the budgets reflect management's expectations about what constitutes successful task performance; implicit in this is the promise of extrinsic rewards for the subordinates if the budget is accomplished. The imposition by management of a particular budget implies that its accomplishment will be recognized by management since it is in accordance with what management views as desirable goal attainment. To the extent that subordinates value the superior's recognition of their accomplishment, the budget communication constitutes a specification of the potential level of some of the extrinsic valences associated with work-goal accomplishment, (EV_i). The budgeting process, when coupled with subordinate knowledge of the external reinforcement contingencies (i.e., the set of rewards contingent on effective performance), clarifies the set of external valences associated with work-goal accomplishment or at least helps the subordinate to assess subjectively these valences.

Second, the perceived difficulty of the budget affects the expectancy of the subordinate that his effort would lead to budget achievement. Thus, the content of the budget also serves as an input for the subordinates to formulate their P_1 expectancies. Comparison of past levels of performance with past budgets generates a record of deviations which clearly influences P_1.

Third, the degree to which superiors were consistent or inconsistent in delivering the contingent rewards following budget accomplishment may induce the subordinates to revise their estimates of P_{2i}. Also, the degree to which superiors show recognition of past accomplishments will affect the subordinate's expectation of the level of future extrinsic valences (EV_i) associated with work-goal accomplishment.

The budget may also fulfill the role of providing structure to an ambiguous task as well as of coordinating activities so that merely working toward accomplishment of the budget provides satisfaction. To the extent that the budget content facilitates the derivation of this satisfaction, the budget also affects the intrinsic valence associated with the goal-directed behavior (IV_b).

Thus the budgeting process can crucially affect the parameters of the expectancy model. Consequently, we can gain insights into the effect on motivation—the dependent variable in this model—by examining the effects of the budgets on the independent variables of the model, such as the subordinate's expectations, perceived valences, etc. Such an examination should increase the likelihood of identifying the psychological mechanisms underlying the effects of budgets on work motivation. Among the psychological states of subordinates that deserve exploration are the subordinate's intrinsic job satisfaction, his expectancies that effort leads to effective performance, and his expectancies that performance leads to reward.

In the next section, it is shown that reinterpretation of previous experimental and other empirical investigations regarding the effects of budget on behavior makes it possible to integrate and reconcile the otherwise fragmented findings cited in the literature within the expectancy model framework.[3]

INTEGRATION OF PRIOR STUDIES WITHIN THE EXPECTANCY FRAMEWORK

It is useful to reconcile prior findings and assumptions regarding impacts of budgets by focusing on the underlying behavioral assumptions assumed (although not necessarily valid) by accountants in the budgetary process:

A. The budget should be set at a reasonably attainable level.
B. Managers should participate in the development of budgets for their own functions in the organization.
C. Managers should operate on the principle of management by exception.
D. Personnel should be charged or credited only for items within their control.
E. Dimensions of performance that cannot be conveniently measured in monetary terms are outside the budgetary domain.

The possible invalidity of these assumptions has been extensively discussed in the accounting literature. The generalizations offered can be summarized as follows.

Achievement of budgeted performance may not satisfy the needs of the subordinates, who thus need not be motivated by the budget. Also, the individual's goals and the organiza-

[3]Cherrington and Cherrington (1973) tested experimentally the effect of various conditions of budget participation and reinforcement contingencies on performance and on psychological states of subordinates such as satisfaction with job and perceived superior consideration. However, they did not test an expectancy model per se but merely investigated the effects of their manipulated conditions in the context of reinforcement and operant conditioning theory.

tion's goals may not be identical. For an individual to internalize or accept the budget, he must believe that achieving it will satisfy his needs better than not achieving it. A goal that an individual has internalized is known as his aspiration level—the performance level that he undertakes to reach (see, e.g., Becker and Green, 1962). The probability that an individual will internalize the budget is influenced by his expectations of what he is able to achieve (Costello and Zelking, 1963), his past experience of success in reaching budgeted goals, and the priority that he assigns to the need for a sense of personal achievement.

These assumptions are now closely examined in an attempt to show how the expectancy model can be used to integrate findings and assertions related to them within a cohesive framework.

A. The Assumption That Standards Should Be Reasonably Attainable

Summary of Existing Studies. The assumption implies that as long as the standards do not exceed what is reasonably attainable, the subordinate will internalize them. If too tight, presumably the subordinate will regard the budget as unrealistic and either cease to be motivated or be negatively motivated by it. Thus, while loose standards (as opposed to reasonably attainable standards) will lead to slackening of effort, tight standards could be perceived as unrealistic and therefore fail to motivate personnel, except perhaps in a negative direction (National Association of Accountants, 1948). For example, Stedry (1960) suggested that, under certain conditions, performance could be improved if management will impose unattainable standards on subordinates. Under laboratory conditions, he found that his measurements of the subjects' aspiration levels were influenced by the level at which the imposed standards were set. He also found that performance that was significantly different from the aspiration level led to an adjustment of the aspiration level in the direction of the performance level that was actually achieved. Thus, he suggested that standards be changed from period to period so that they are met some of the time and are slightly above the attainable level the rest of the time. Hofstede (1967) also found that motivation is highest when standards are difficult to reach but are not regarded as impossible.

Other discussions and evidence in the literature support these findings. When an individual barely achieves the level of aspiration, he is said to have subjective feelings of success; subjective feelings of failure follow nonachievement of the level of aspiration (Lewin, Dembo, Festinger and Sears, 1944). In particular, Child and Whiting (1954) argue that (a) success generally raises the level of aspiration, failure lowers it; (b) the probability of rise in level of aspiration is positively correlated with the strength of success or failure; (c) changes in the level of aspiration partially depend on changes in the subject's confidence in his ability to attain goals; and (d) failure is more likely than success to lead to avoidance of setting a level of aspiration.

From their review of the literature, Becker and Green (1962) conclude that "level of aspiration not only describes a goal for future attainment but also it partially insures that an individual will expend a more than minimal amount of energy, if necessary, to perform at or above the level." Indeed, although not in a business budgeting setting, Bayton (1943) found that higher performance followed higher level of aspiration in testing the performance of 300 subjects on seven arithmetic problems. Also, Cherrington and Cherrington (1973) experimentally found that, when supervisors imposed either a minimum or a specific standard of performance, the subordinate's estimate of their performance (level of aspiration) was higher than when supervisors imposed either lenient minimum standards of performance or imposed none at all. They also found that the higher estimates of performance also were followed by higher actual performance. Cherrington and Cherrington's findings seem somewhat to contradict some of Stedry's (1960) results. In Stedry's study, one group was first given the standard and then asked to indicate its own goal for performance in the subsequent period. The second group was asked to indicate its goals *before* it knew what the experimental manager's goals were. The group setting its personal goals first set higher goals and performed better than the group which was informed of management's goals first, although it must be noted that, in Cherrington and Cherrington's study, high estimates and performance were achieved when the group also formulated its estimates before knowledge of the supervisor's imposed minimums. Thus, in a sense, the situation is not unsimilar to Stedry's except that revision of the estimate after knowledge of the supervisor's higher standards proved to be beneficial.

Reconciliation with the Expectancy Model. In terms of the expectancy model, the conclusion that standards regarded as impossible are not motivational or negatively motivational can simply be explained by the fact that P_1, the expectancy that goal-directed behavior would lead to work-goal accomplishment, was low or even negative and, to show this more clearly, Stedry's conclusions are examined in light of the expectancy model.

As indicated, Stedry found that his measurements of the subject's aspiration levels were influenced by the level at which the imposed standards were set. The results of the Cherringtons' study partially confirm Stedry's results in that the experimental group's estimate of their performance was highest under nonparticipation conditions, i.e., when high minimum standards were imposed. If the aspiration level is taken to reflect the level which the subordinate sets out to achieve, then it is understandable that (within limits) the higher the imposed standards by superiors, the higher would be the aspiration level. In comparison with other levels of attainment, P_{2i}, the expectancies that work-goal accomplishment will lead to extrinsic valences would be higher the nearer the performance level is to the imposed standard. Thus, if the subordinate's task is viewed as a selection among different aspiration levels, it is only natural that he will choose the aspiration level that maximizes the dependent variable M in the model.

However, if the imposed standards are too high, the aspiration level will lag behind since, although P_{2i} will increase, P_1, the expectancy that goal-directed behavior will lead to work-goal accomplishment, is likely to be negatively correlated with the perceived difficulty of attaining the standard.

The assessment of P_1 is also likely to be affected by feedback on past performance; P_1 will tend to be positively correlated with prior levels of performance and consequently the dependent variable and the aspiration level will tend to move in the same direction as performance. This "Expectancy Model" induced observation could explain Stedry's other finding that performance which differed significantly from the aspiration level led to the latter's adjustment in the direction of the performance level actually achieved.

It is particularly important and interesting to relate the level of aspiration conceptualization of the budgeting process with the expectancy approach. The expectancy model's dependent variable—motivation to exert effort in the task—is a direct function of the expected valences. The model's underlying assumption is that the higher the expectation of valences, the greater the effort the subordinate is likely to exert and, thus, the higher the performance level. In other words, the subordinate's effort exerted in task performance is assumed to change along a continuum as a function of the expectation of valences.

Level of aspiration, on the other hand, is operationally defined as "the goal one explicitly undertakes to reach," where "maximum effort will be exerted to just reach an aspiration goal" (Becker and Green, 1962). According to this view, effort is seen not as a continuum but as changing discretely where the level of aspiration goal of performance is that for which a maximum—a specifically defined amount of effort—is spent in order to derive the subjective feeling of success. If we attempt to interpret the meaning of the level of aspiration within the expectancy framework, it seems that it corresponds to the performance level consciously chosen by the subordinate (among alternative performance levels) so as to maximize the expectation of valences—the value of the expectancy equation. That is, the subordinate behaves as if he computes the expected values associated with different performance levels, which clearly depend on the model's parameters (P_1, P_2, IV_b, IV_a, and EV_i) and selects the one that maximizes M as the level of aspiration. The implications of this relationship between the level of aspiration and the expectancy model's dependent variable to the specification of desirable attributes of the budgetary process could be far-reaching.

B. Participation

Summary of Existing Studies. Participation means that decisions affecting a manager's operations are, to some extent, jointly made by the manager and his superior. As such, it is more than mere consultation by which the superior informs himself of the manager's views but makes the decisions himself. The participation of subordinates in budget setting is usually regarded as effective in getting subordinates to internalize the standards embodied in the budgets and thus in achieving goal congruence (Welsch, 1971).

The role of participation can perhaps be best understood in the context of group dynamics. Aspiration levels are said partially to depend on the levels of aspiration prevailing in the groups that the individual belongs to (Lewin, 1964). The amount of influence that group members are said to have on the individual's aspiration level depends on the group's cohesiveness, i.e., the degree to which individual members value their group membership.

The value of group membership to an individual derives from the degree to which the individual believes that group membership will help him attain his own goals (Caplan, 1966 and Vroom, 1964a). Perceived value of membership seems to be correlated with the likelihood that different members in the group will have similar goals—thus the individual's likelihood of continued membership in the group. The relationship between the two appears to be reciprocal. Similarity of goals among the group's members will make membership in the group more attractive. On the other hand, if membership in the group is highly valued, the individual will tend to assimilate the group's goal to be able to maintain the valued membership. As a result of valuing his own membership and his desire to maintain it, the individual will tend to reject goals that he believes conflict with those prevailing in the group and accept those that appear to be consistent with the group's goals (Caplan, 1966 and Vroom, 1964a).

Thus, participation does not seem automatically to produce congruence between the group's goal and that of the firm. Conditions may be such that a more authoritarian managerial style will be more effective in raising the aspiration levels of subordinates. Becker and Green (1962) describe these conditions in greater specificity. Their position could be summarized as follows: if greater interaction of individuals leads to greater group cohesiveness, and if this cohesiveness plus some incentive to produce either at higher or lower levels are positively correlated, then participation can be an inducement for higher or lower levels of performance. Also, if participation at an upper level generates positive attitudes on the part of supervisors, then they will try to induce higher individual and group aspirations in the subgroup which will hopefully lead to higher rather than lower levels of performance.

There is also some evidence that participation improves morale. Coch and French (1948) found a much lower turnover rate, fewer grievances about piece rates, and less aggression against the supervisor as individual participation in planning job changes increased. Vroom (1960) argues that participation makes employees feel more a part of the activities and less dominated by a superior, more independent, and thus improves their attitude toward the job. But while participation enhanced satisfaction, it did not necessarily increase productivity. Or at least the results are ambiguous. Literature to date shows no direct correlation between participation and improved productivity (e.g., Cherrington and Cherrington, 1973; Coch and French, 1948; and French, Kay, and Meyer, 1962).

Personality variables can also affect the relation between participation and performance. For example, Vroom emphasizes the affective consequences of the degree of consistency between a person's performance and his self-concept: persons were found to perform better on tasks perceived to require highly valued ability or intelligence which they believed themselves to possess (Vroom, 1960).

Reconciliation with the Expectancy Model. It was indicated that participation tends to increase performance if interaction of individuals leads to greater group cohesiveness and if the group norms are such that they are conducive to higher levels of production. These particular effects of participation can be accommodated within the expectancy model. A group is cohesive when the individual members value their acceptance within the group. Participation in the context of a cohesive group would be a process of reaching consensus within the group on the desirable standards of performance within the group. Once such a consensus has been reached as a result of the group's participation, it would be viewed by the individual as reflecting the group's own norm. Striving to attain that goal would, therefore, increase the individual's likelihood of maintaining his acceptance in the group. In terms of the expectancy model, the existence of a cohesive group of which the subordinate is a member enhances the extrinsic valence associated with work-goal accomplishment. With the attainment of the goal, the individual achieves not only the extrinsic and intrinsic valences that exist in the absence of a group context, but in addition, he maintains his acceptance in a cohesive group which can be regarded as an extrinsic valence associated with goal-accomplishment.

In addition, participation may create intrinsic valences that are absent in nonparticipative environments. These intrinsic valences may be due to a tendency for individuals to become "ego-involved" in decisions to which they have contributed, as would be the case in participative decision-making. A similar process is suggested by evidence that participation by a single person in decision-making with a superior affects the subsequent performance of that person (Vroom, 1970).

Thus, only when groups are cohesive and their norms support the organization would participation be likely to increase motivation and hence the aspiration level and hence performance. When groups are not cohesive, no additional valence is introduced and therefore motivation is not likely to be increased, although participation may increase group cohesiveness, as stated above. In fact, participation in certain environments can lead to negative results as related, for example, by Shillinglaw (1972). The introduction of participative budgeting in a large electrical equipment factory years ago was received coldly by most of the first level supervisors. The reason offered was that foremen were reluctant to accept the risk of censure for failure to achieve targets that they had set themselves (Stedry and Kay, 1966). In terms of this expectancy model, this phenomenon can be explained in terms of the effect of undesired participation on IV_b. Since participation under this environment induced anxiety and thus a decrement in the intrinsic valence associated with goal-directed behavior, motivation and performance were likely to decline.

C. Management by Exception

Summary of Existing Studies. The fact that accountants and managers emphasize deviations (we use this term instead of variances) in accounting reports implies that, by and large, attention is merited when significant deviations are observed and not when standards are met. Such a system, however, may be perceived as emphasizing failure with only exceptional success attracting management attention. The response to favorable deviations not requiring corrective actions often seems to be weaker than that to unfavorable deviations. As a result, subordinates may be led to view the system as punitive rather than as informative. This may lead to defensiveness, overcautious behavior, and other dysfunctional effects (Sayles and Chandler, 1971). This suggests that effort should be made to emphasize positive as well as negative aspects of performance to provide "positive reinforcement" (Birnberg and Nath, 1967).

Reconciliation with the Expectancy Model. In terms of the expectancy model, it is easy to predict the effect of these practices. Nonreinforcement or mere attainment of the budget will tend to decrease P_{2i}, the expectancy goal that accomplishment leads to extrinsic valences. The same effect would be produced by relative nonreinforcement of performance that is superior to the budget. On the other hand, punitive response to unfavorable deviations, while it may accomplish some results since subordinates have no alternatives, may also result in resistance, sabotage, and other kinds of conflict. Punishment is known to have generally negative effects (Vroom, 1964a). The Cheringtons' (1973) finding that only appropriate reinforcement contingencies (i.e., when subordinates can control the performance on which rewards are contingent) were motivational can also be explained in terms of the effect on P_{2i}.

D. The Controllability Criterion

Summary of Existing Studies. Controllability refers to the ability of the subordinate to make decisions and execute them in his attempt to accomplish specified goals or a budget. A distinction must be made between *actual* control and *perceived* control. The motivational variable of interest is perceived control, which may differ from the actual degree of control that the subordinate can apply to a task. Personality as well as sociological factors can affect the degree of deviation between perceived control and actual control (Feather, 1967).

It is generally asserted that only controllable activities in the budget should constitute the basis for evaluation and reinforcement of the subordinate. For example, according to Vroom (1970, p. 213):

> the effectiveness of any system in which rewards and punishments are contingent on specified performance outcomes appears to be dependent on the degree of control which the individual has over these performance outcomes. The increment in performance to be expected from an increase in the extent to which the individual

> is rewarded for favorable results and/or punished for unfavorable results is directly related to the extent to which the individual can control the results of his performance.

Several sources can contribute to the lack of control over results which appears from existing evidence to reduce the effectiveness of organizationally administered reward-punishment contingencies. The first source is the existence of interpersonal and interdepartmental interdependencies within the formal organization. The jointness of the inputs in terms of subordinate's effort makes it extremely difficult to measure and assess a particular subordinate's contribution to the results. In such an interdependence set-up, only the effort of a group as a whole can be adequately evaluated and each person has but partial control over the group's outcome.

The second source for lack of control is the operation of "chance" events that perturb the otherwise one-to-one relationship between the subordinate's efforts and his accomplishments. States of nature that are beyond his control affect the results of his effort. The existence of these "chance" events is partially a function of the nature of the task itself. Shooting at a fast-moving target, for example, is subject to far more external and uncontrollable events than performing a standard manufacturing operation.

The degree of skill of a subordinate to perform a job constitutes a third source of lack of control over results. While the degree of skill tends to be inversely related to the incidence of "chance" events, the two variables (skill and chance) are usefully viewed as distinct from each other (Feather, 1967). The degree to which "chance" factors affect performance depends on the skill of the performer as well as on the nature of the task. Thus, a very competent and skillful performer may still fail because the task is subject to many external perturbances, and, at the same time, an unskilled worker may fail to perform effectively even if his task is highly structured and subject to no external disturbances.

As indicated above, the perceived and not the actual degree of control is the variable of interest from the standpoint of predicting motivation and performance. And, as suggested, perceived control may differ from actual control, and the difference can depend on personality variables such as degree of achievement motivation, risk-taking behavior, as well as on cultural variables such as blacks vs. whites, etc. (Lefcourt, 1965; Rotter, Liverant, and Crowne, 1961; and Sutcliffe, 1956).

Reconciliation with the Expectancy Model. Using the expectancy model, it can be explained why only activities in the budget that are perceived as controllable by the subordinate should constitute the basis for evaluation and reinforcement. Only activities that are perceived as controllable are likely to be associated with a relatively high P_1. In addition, performing tasks that are perceived as controllable could be associated with higher intrinsic valences (Ronen, 1973).

Unfortunately, since it is difficult to discriminate finely between controllable and noncontrollable activities, dysfunctional decisions may result:

(1) Excluding from the evaluation basis activities that are partially controllable but classified as uncontrollable will direct the subordinate not to exert effort in those activities and eventually to jeopardize the accomplishment of the organization's goals. When basically controllable activities are excluded from the evaluation basis, the dependent variable, M, of the expectancy model operates on only some of the activities that are instrumental to the firm's over-all goal attainment and it by-passes other beneficial activities.

(2) Including in the evaluation basis activities

that are perceived by the subordinate as noncontrollable can result in lowering his expectancy that effort will lead to work accomplishment, i.e., P_1.

Also, the intrinsic valence associated with goal-accomplishment may decrease if the task is perceived as partially beyond the subordinate's control. Under both cases, the subordinate's motivation to exert effort in his performance will tend to decrease.

E. The Exclusion of Criteria That Are Not Easily Measured in Monetary Terms

Summary of Existing Studies. Because of the difficulty of measuring nonmonetary dimensions of performance, the accounting structure usually restricts itself to reporting financial performance. As a result, managers may be motivated to emphasize the things that are measured to the neglect of those that are not. One suggested solution to this problem is the development of a composite measure of performance, with each dimension assigned a weight in proportion to top management's perceived priority. But this solution is deficient because the weighting schemes are implicit, difficult to translate into numerical form, and possibly nonstable over time. However, a useful step is said to be to identify the major dimensions of performance, whether measurable or not, so that they could be incorporated into the performance review process. The motivational problem involved is that the subordinates lack knowledge of the precise managerial reward structure and the weighting schemes implicit in the evaluation system.

Reconciliation with the Expectancy Model. The exclusion of nonmonetary criteria from the evaluation basis can be interpreted in terms of the expectancy model as motivating subordinates on the basis of only one dimension. In other words, the dependent variable, M, is characterized by only one dimension—the maximization of monetary profits. Since the work-goal accomplishment that is expected to secure extrinsic rewards EV_i, is only defined by the criterion of maximizing monetary profits, the kinds of effort spent by the subordinate in the task will be only directed to that, and other objectives will be neglected.

Using the expectancy model, the subordinate can be motivated to spend effort to accomplish nonmonetary objectives if these are formally introduced into the control system by: (1) making extrinsic rewards contingent on their accomplishment, (2) by facilitating their accomplishment through task clarification, (i.e., through increasing P_1), and (3) also by attempting to make the accomplishment of the nonmonetary criteria intrinsically valent to the subordinate.

As suggested by Vroom, one of the conditions needed to improve productivity by making effective performance on a task instrumental to the attainment of organizationally mediated rewards or the avoidance of punishments is that:

> There is no conflict, either actual or perceived, between those behaviors necessary to attain a short term reward (for example, higher wages this week) and those required to avoid a longer term punishment (for example, a tightening of standards) (Vroom, 1970).

However, merely introducing the nonmonetary criteria into the expectancy model through the explicit specification of effective performance via the budget does not in itself facilitate the attainment of goal congruence, unless the importance attached by top management to the attainment of various criteria is also made explicit to subordinates and internalized by them. If the weights to be attached to the criteria that are implicit in management's preference function are not made explicit to the subordinate, he may impose his own preference ordering on the criteria. That may not coincide with the management's preference ranking. In this case, goal congruence will not be attained in spite of the incorporation of the nonmonetary criteria into the model.

SUMMARY AND CONCLUSIONS

The literature on the effects of budgets on behavior is quite fragmentary and draws upon many diverse and partial areas of behavioral science. We have shown that this is the case for five general assumptions made in accounting with respect to budgets and behavior. These assumptions are:

(A) that standards should be reasonably attainable,
(B) that participation in the budgeting process leads to better performance,
(C) that management by exception is effective,
(D) that noncontrollable items should be excluded from budget reports, and
(E) that budgetary accounting should be restricted to criteria measurable in monetary terms.

We then introduced an expectancy model of task motivation within which, with some refinement, it was possible both to reconcile the fragmentary and contradictory past research findings and to explain the five assumptions in a consistent manner. To summarize, the following relations between the assumptions and variables in the expectancy model were discussed:

Standards:	P_1, P_2 (expectancies of performance and of reward)
Participation:	IV_a, IV_b, EV_i (intrinsic and extrinsic valences)
Exception Management:	P_2
Controllability:	P_1, IV_a
Monetary Criteria:	P_1, EV_i

We examined not only the budget's impact on behavior per se, but also the effects of the superiors' responses contingent on given levels of budget achievement on the part of the subordinate. Thus, the administration of extrinsic rewards contingent on successful budget achievement and the facilitation of intrinsic values are both related to the budgeting process and affect the subordinates' performance. As a result, the expectancy model could be also used as a framework for evaluating the effect of the accounting reports that compare actual performance with the budget on the subordinates' future performance.

Of course, there is a wealth of other relations which fall outside the immediate scope of this paper. The literature of expectancy theory is large, rich in empirical research, and fast-growing. We recognize that the expectancy theory and its assumptions have come under criticism and that tests of the model's predictive ability have produced ambiguous results (see footnote 1). Nonetheless, recent progress in the testing and the operationalization of the model has apparently been made.[4]

Future research should be concerned with the derivation of testable hypotheses that

[4]Reviews of recent empirical studies in nonbudget context, which were designed either to test directly the expectancy model or to provide an inferential basis for assessing the model's validity indicate some empirical support for the relationships stipulated by the expectancy theory (Dessler, 1973; House and Dessler, 1973; House and Wahba, 1972; Kopelman, 1974). In fact, Kopelman (1974) observed coefficients of correlation between the model's independent variables and performance indicators as high as 0.53. Furthermore, operational tools for measuring the model's parameters are available and are in the process of being continually improved and refined (House, 1972).

apply the expectancy framework to the budgeting process as well as with further improving the predictive validity of the model through better operationalization of its variables. Also, the moderating effects of situational variables that are part of the working environment on the relation between budgets and motivation should be explored and tested. These situational aspects include variables such as the needs of subordinates, the environmental pressures and demands that subordinates must cope with to accomplish work goals and satisfy their needs, and the task demands of subordinates. Another particularly promising avenue for future research is the rigorous formulation of an expectancy model version which ties in with the SEU (Subjections Expected Utility) model, and with the level of aspiration theory.

Motivation, the dependent variable in the expectancy model, can be used as an indication of the probability that the task will be performed, given the ability of the subordinate. In other words, the probability that a task will be performed is a function of motivation and ability. To the superior it is important to assess this ability in order both to evaluate the merit of competing activities and to allocate effectively people to tasks. Hypotheses generated and tested within an expectancy framework should be helpful toward that end.

REFERENCES

Argyris, C., *The Impact of Budgets on People* (Controllership Foundation, 1952).

Atkinson, J. W., "Toward Experimental Analysis of Human Motivation in Terms of Motives, Expectations and Incentives," in J. W. Atkinson, ed., *Motives in Fantasy, Action and Society* (Van Nostrand, 1958).

Bayton, J. A., "Inter-relations Between Levels of Aspiration, Performance, and Estimates of Past Performance," *Journal of Experimental Psychology* (1943), *33*, p. 1–21.

Becker, S. and Green, D., "Budgeting and Employee Behavior," *Journal of Business* (October 1962), pp. 392–402.

Benston, G., "The Role of the Firm's Accounting System for Motivation," THE ACCOUNTING REVIEW (April 1963), pp. 351–3.

Birnberg, J. G. and Nath, R., "Implications of Behavioral Science for Managerial Accounting," THE ACCOUNTING REVIEW (July 1967), p. 478.

Caplan, E., "Behavioral Assumptions of Management Accounting," THE ACCOUNTING REVIEW (July 1966), pp. 476–509.

Cherrington, D. J., and Cherrington, J. O., "Appropriate Reinforcement Contingencies in the Budgeting Process," presented at the *Accounting Empirical Research Conference*, University of Chicago (May 1973).

Child, J. L. and Whiting, J. W. M., "Determinants of Level of Aspiration: Evidence from Everyday Life," in H. Branch, ed., *The Study of Personality* (Wiley, 1954), pp. 145–58.

Coch, L. and French, J. R. P., "Overcoming Resistance to Change," *Human Relations* (1948), *1*, pp. 512–32.

Costello, T. and Zelking, S., *Psychology in Administration: A Research Orientation* (Prentice-Hall, 1963).

Dessler, G., "A Test of the Path-Goal Theory of Leadership," Doctoral Dissertation, Bernard M. Baruch College, City University of New York, 1973.

Feather, N. T., "Valence of Outcome and Expectation of Success in Relation to Task Difficulty and Perceived Locus of Control," *Journal of Personality and Social Psychology* (1967), 7, pp. 372–86.

French, J. R. P., Kay, E., and Meyer, H. H., *A Study of Threat and Participation in a Performance Appraisal Situation* (General Electric Co., 1962).

Galbraith, J., and Cummings, L. L., "An Empirical Investigation of the Motivational Determinants of Past Performance: Interactive Effects Between Instrumentality, Valence, Motivation and Ability," *Organizational Behavior and Human Performance* (1967), pp. 237–57.

Georgopoulos, B. S., Mahoney, G. M., and Jones, N. W., "A Path Goal Approach to Productivity,"

Journal of Applied Psychology (1957), *41*, pp. 345–53.

Graen, G., "Instrumental Theory of Work Motivation: Some Empirical Results and Suggested Modifications," *Journal of Applied Psychology* (1969), *53*, pp. 1–25.

Hofstede, G. H., *The Game of Budget Control* (Assen, The Netherlands, Koninklijke Van Corcum and Comp. N. V., 1967), pp. 152–6.

House, R. J., "Some Preliminary Findings Concerning a Test of the Path Goal Theory of Leadership," (unpublished manuscript, University of Toronto, April 1972).

———, *Notes on Questionnaires Frequently Used by or Developed by R. J. House*, Faculty of Management Studies, University of Toronto, July 1972.

———, "A Path-Goal Theory of Leader Effectiveness," *Administrative Science Quarterly* (September 1971), *16, 3*, pp. 321–38.

——— and Dessler, G., "The Path-Goal Theory of Leadership: Some Post Hoc and A Priori Tests," paper presented at the Second Leadership Symposium: Contingency Approaches to Leadership; Southern Illinois University, Carbondale, Ill., April 1973.

——— and Wahba, M. A., "Expectancy Theory as a Predictor of Job Performance, Satisfaction and Motivation: An Integrative Model and a Review of the Literature," paper presented at the American Psychological Association Meeting, Hawaii, August, 1972; Working Paper 72–21, Faculty of Management Studies, University of Toronto, 1972.

Kerr, S., Klimoski, R. J., Tolliver, J., and Von Glinow, M. A., "Human Information Processing and Problem Solving," paper presented at the Workshop in Behavioral Accounting: Annual Meeting of the American Institute for Decision Sciences, Atlanta, Ga., Oct. 30, 1974.

Kopelman, R., "Factors Complicating Expectancy Theory Prediction of Work Motivation and Job Performance," paper presented at the meeting of the American Psychological Association, 1974.

Lawler, E. E., "A Correlation Causal Analysis of the Relationship Between Expectancy Attitudes and Job Performance," *Journal of Applied Psychology* (1968), *52*, pp. 462–8.

Lawler, E. E., *Pay and Organizational Effectiveness: A Psychological Perspective* (Wiley, 1971).

——— and Suttle, J. K., "Expectancy Theory and Job Behavior," *Organizational Behavior and Human Performance* (1973), *9*, pp. 482–503.

Lefcourt, H. M., "Risk Taking in Negro and White Adults," *Journal of Personality and Social Psychology* (1965), *2*, pp. 765–70.

Lewin, K., "The Psychology of a Successful Figure," in *Readings in Managerial Psychology*, H. S. Leavitt and L. R. Pondy, eds. (University of Chicago Press, 1964), pp. 25–31.

——— Dembo, T., Festinger, L., and Sears, P., "Level of Aspiration," in J. McV. Hunt, ed., *Personality and Behavior Disorder* (Ronald Press, 1944), *1*, pp. 338–78.

Porter, L, and Lawler, E. E., *Managerial Attitudes and Performance* (Irwin-Dorsey, 1967).

National Association of Accountants, *How Standard Costs Are Used Currently* (New York, 1948), pp. 8–9.

Ronen, J., "Involvement in Tasks and Choice Behavior," *Organizational Behavior and Human Performance* (February 1974), *2*, pp. 28–43.

Rotter, J. B., Liverant, S., and Crowne, D. P., "Growth and Extinction of Expectancies in Chance Controlled and Skill Tasks," *Journal of Psychology*, (1961), *52*, pp. 151–77.

Sayles, L. R. and Chandler, M. K., *Managing Large Systems: Organizations for the Future* (Harper & Row, 1971).

Schiff, M. and Lewin, A. Y., "The Impact of People on Budgets," THE ACCOUNTING REVIEW (April 1970), pp. 259–68.

Shillinglaw, G., *Cost Accounting, Analysis and Control*, 3rd ed. (Irwin, 1972).

Stedry, A., *Budgetary Control and Cost Behavior* (Prentice-Hall, 1960).

——— and Kay, E., "The Effects of Goal Difficulty on Performance: A Field Experiment," *Behavioral Science, II* (1966), pp. 459–70.

Sutcliffe, J. P., "Random Effects as a Function of Belief in Control," *Australian Journal of Psychology* (1956), *8*, pp. 128–39.

Usry, M., "Solving the Problem of Human Relations in Budgeting," *Budgeting* (Nov.–Dec. 1968), pp. 4–6.

Vroom, V. H., "Industrial Social Psychology," in

Handbook of Social Psychology (Addison-Wesley, 1970)
———, "Some Psychological Aspects of Organizational Control," in Cooper, Leavitt & Shelly, eds., *New Perspectives in Organizational Research* (Wiley, 1964a).
———, *Work and Motivation* (Wiley, 1964b).
———, *Some Personality Determinants of the Effect of Participation* (Prentice-Hall, 1960).
Welsch, G. A., *Budgeting: Profit Planning and Control*, 3rd ed. (Prentice-Hall, 1971), pp. 17, 22–23.
Williamson, O.E., *The Economics of Discretionary Behavior: Managerial Objectives in a Theory of the Firm* (Prentice-Hall, 1964), pp. 28–37.

Toward a Formal Model of Group Dynamics in Task Performance Relevant to Accounting

Eric Flamholtz*

Recently there has been an increasing interest in the behavioural aspects of accounting. This has involved attempts to apply concepts, models, research findings and theories drawn from behavioural science to accounting problems. The result has been the emergence of a field labelled "behavioural accounting".

A basic premise of behavioural accounting is that the raison d'etre *of accounting is ultimately to influence human behaviour. This means that accounting information is intended to influence the decisions of people (investors or managers) or to motivate certain behaviours and prevent others. As Caplan (1966) has aptly stated: "It also seems clear that the entire management accounting process can be viewed from the standpoint of attempting to influence the behaviour of others". Similarly, Hofstedt (1972) has shown that the behavioural effects of accounting are important not only in management accounting but also in external reporting.*

This paper deals with the implications of group dynamics and in task performance for accounting. This is an area of behavioural accounting that has been recognised as important (Becker and Green, 1962, 1964; Stedry, 1964; Benston, 1963; Wallace, 1966) but has received little systematic investigation.

THE STUDY'S OBJECTIVES

The study is intended to take some initial steps toward the development of a formal model of group dynamics and task performance that is relevant to management accounting systems. The paper first examines the relevance of group dynamics for accounting and discusses the need for a formal model. Next, the paper presents a model that attempts to integrate and synthesize a large body of behavioural science research on group dynamics in task performance. Finally, the paper draws upon this model in order to develop a set of propositions about relationships between group-task variables in the context of budgeting.

From *Journal of Business Finance and Accounting,* Vol. 3, No. 4 (Winter 1976), pp. 3–25.

*The author is Associate Professor and Director of the Accounting and Information Systems Research Program, at the University of California, Los Angeles. (Paper received May 1975)

IMPORTANCE OF GROUP DYNAMICS TO ACCOUNTING

Groups are ubiquitous. They exist irrespective of personal or organisational desires. Groups even form groups within themselves (called cliques or subgroups). The existence of groups is relevant to accountants as information-control system designers for at least three major reasons:

1. Accounting is designed to influence individual and group behaviour, and groups, too, can influence such behaviour. Thus, there may be either a congruence or conflict between the motivation caused by the accounting system and the group. The result may be unintended, suboptimal decisions and behaviour.
2. Groups are not merely the sum of a collection of individuals, and may behave differently as a group than as a mere set of individuals.
3. In some contexts, accounting control systems should be designed with the individual as the basic unit of control, while in others the group should be the basic unit of control.

First, given the objective of accounting to influence behaviour, group dynamics is important to accounting because groups also influence individual behaviour. As Festinger *et. al.* have stated: "There is no question any longer that individuals and groups do exert influences on others which can and do result in uniform opinions and behaviour patterns. There have been many studies which demonstrated the existence and importance of this phenomenon". Groups can influence individual perception (Sherif, 1936; Asch, 1955); motivation (Bonner, 1959; Whyte, 1951; Coch and French, 1948); attitudes (Newcomb, 1943); and decisions and judgements (Stoner, 1968; Asch, 1955). Since accounting systems are intended to influence individual behaviour, and since groups can influence individual behaviour, it is necessary to understand the effects of small groups on individuals for the purpose of designing accounting control systems.

Second, group dynamics has implications for accounting because groups are not merely the sum of a collection of individuals. Groups have properties which may differ from the individuals comprising them. Thus accounting control systems designed with the individual as the basic unit of analysis will not necessarily be appropriate for a group. Presently, accounting systems are typically based, either explicitly or implicitly, upon assumptions about individual-to-formal-organisation relations. There are no existing theories for the design of group-based managerial accounting systems. Yet, the use of individual-based systems in a context where a group-based system would be appropriate may lead to unintended dysfunctional results. For example, the use of an accounting control system which is based on techniques for motivating individuals in a situation where cohesive groups exist may result in a lack of congruence between individual, group, and total organisational goals.

Third, just as individual-based accounting control systems are not always appropriate, the same is true of group-based systems. For example, Demski and Swieringa (1974) have examined the audit choice problem and presented a cooperative (group) model as a solution. They state (p. 513) that "under appropriate conditions" their approach ". . . leads to group-level surrogate utility and probability functions such that the audit program chosen should maximise expected surrogate utility" for the auditee and auditor as a group rather than as individuals. Thus research is required to identify the factors or conditions in a situation which require either individual or group-based systems for decision making and control.

NEED FOR A FORMAL MODEL

In their 1974 report, the American Accounting Association's Committee on the Relationship of Behavioural Science and Accounting stated that (p. 135) "unfortunately, too much of behavioural accounting research has consisted of hunting and tracking something without knowing what it was. Perhaps the greatest deficiency in behavioural accounting research is the lack of formal models. By formal models, here, we simply mean systematic attempts to formulate sets of principles, postulates, and hypotheses about relationships among variables which can then be tested empirically".

Drawing upon the Committee's report (1974), a formal model of group dynamics in task performance is an essential prerequisite for understanding the implications of groups on accounting. First, the model would identify the variables which influence group task performance such as budgetary decisions. This means that it would suggest the specific group dynamics factors which need to be considered in developing accounting planning and control systems. Second, the model would suggest hypothesised relations among the variables, which, in turn, might help provide the basis for a set of statements or propositions about the effects of accounting systems on groups. Finally, these propositions or generalisations about the implications of group dynamics for accounting would provide the basis for future empirical tests. In brief, the model is viewed as a necessary step toward understanding group dynamics in accounting.

TOWARD A MODEL OF GROUP DYNAMICS AND TASK PERFORMANCE

The purpose of this section is to take some initial steps toward developing a model of group dynamics and task performance that will be useful in accounting. The rationale for presenting the model may be summarised briefly: in order to reach our ultimate objective of deriving a set of propositions about group dynamics relevant to accounting, we must first develop an understanding of group interaction and task performance per se. Ideally, we would like to examine the findings in behavioural science on group dynamics and attempt to apply them to accounting. This means we would like to identify the relevant variables and propositions about group dynamics, and then apply them to accounting. Unfortunately, at present, there is a great body of research on group dynamics, but there have been only a few attempts to integrate or synthesise this literature (Golembiewski, 1965; Kelley and Thibaut, 1968). As Kelley and Thibaut (1968, p. 61) and Herold (1974) point out, there is an absence of a coherent body of generalisations from small group research about group process. Therefore we found it necessary to examine the behavioural science literature and develop a conceptual scheme to guide thinking in this area. This model consists of three parts: (1) a list of major variables which explain group dynamics and task performance and seem potentially relevant to accounting, (2) statements about hypothesised relations among the variables, and (3) a set of propositions about the behaviour of groups in the context of task performance.

The model of group dynamics and task performance presented in this paper is shown schematically in Figure 1. It is a complex model, consisting of 17 variables and hypothesised interrelationships. The model's variables are discussed below, and their definitions are summarised in Table 1 for the reader's convenience.

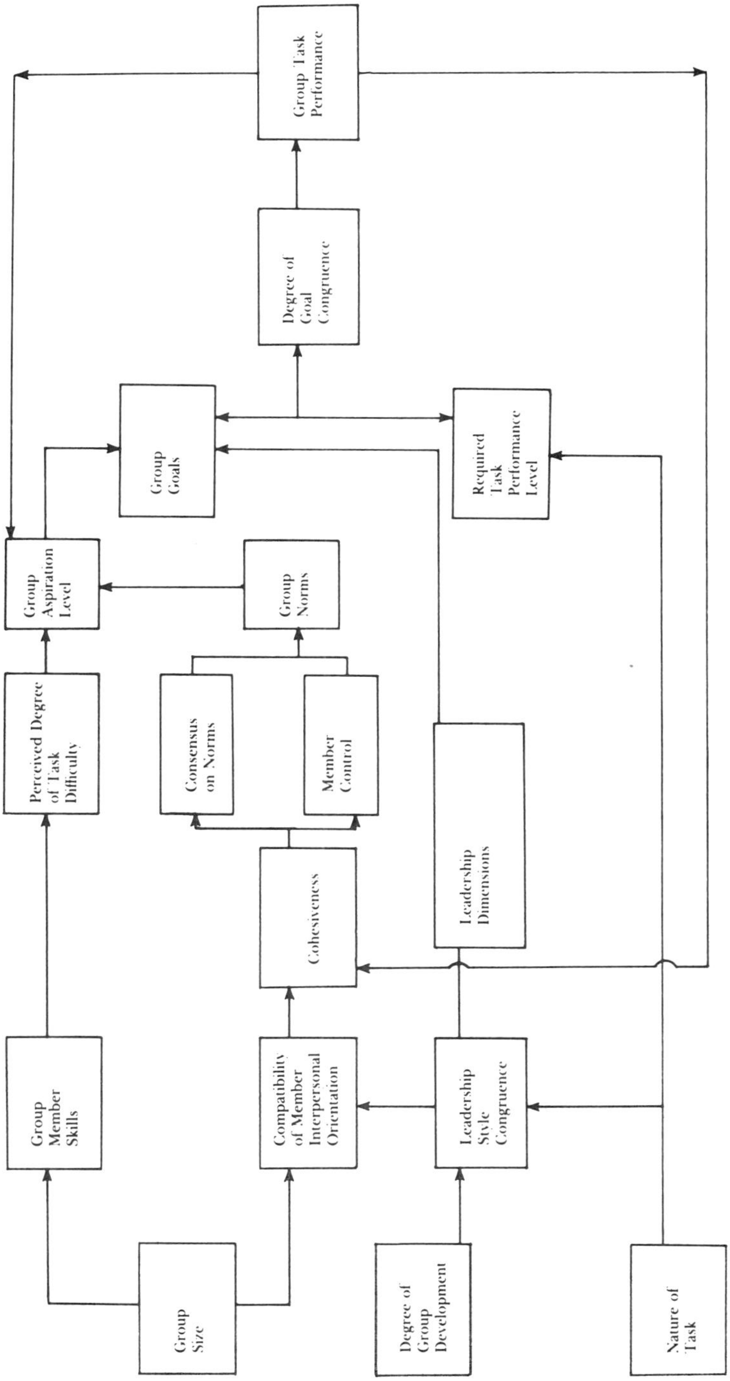

FIGURE 1. A Model of Small Group Interaction and Task Performance

THE MODEL'S VARIABLES AND HYPOTHESISED RELATIONS

A Group. The term "group" is the most fundamental idea underlying the model. There are two primary notions of a group which are of concern to us. As Lorge et. al. (1958, p. 338) points out, "The social psychologist tends to think of the "group" as having a "tradition", i.e., a cooperative association of individuals whose members have progressed through the states of coming together in physical proximity, of organising for common goals, and of accepting commitment for the group's purposes". Lorge et. al. (1958, p. 338) refer to this type of group as a "traditioned group". The other no-

TABLE 1. Definitions of Key Variables Relevant to Accounting from Small Group-Task Theory

1. TRADITIONAL GROUP. A group whose members have progressed through the states of coming together in physical priority, of organising for common goals, and of accepting commitment for the group's purposes (Lorge et. al., 1958, p. 338).
2. AD HOC GROUP. Any collection of assembled individuals (Lorge et. al., 1958, p. 338).
3. DEGREE OF GROUP DEVELOPMENT. The degree of which groups have passed through the different stages required to become a group.
4. GROUP SIZE. The number of people comprising a group.
5. GROUP MEMBER SKILLS. The technical, administrative, and interpersonal skills possessed by group members.
6. PERCEIVED DEGREE OF TASK DIFFICULTY. The degree of which a group perceives a task as "easy", "challenging", "impossible", etc.
7. GROUP ASPIRATION LEVEL. The "score" a group desires (or expects) to achieve on a given task.
8. COMPATIBILITY OF MEMBER INTERPERSONAL ORIENTATION. The ability of group members to get along with one another.
9. COHESIVENESS. Two definitions: (1) the morale or spirit of a group; (2) the attractiveness of the group for its members.
10. MEMBER CONTROL. The power of a group to create and maintain group norms or standards of behaviour.
11. CONSENSUS ON NORMS AND NORMS. Norms are group standards of attitudes or behaviour.
12. LEADERSHIP STYLE CONGRUENCE. The extent to which the leadership style used in a group is consistent with group norms of appropriate leadership behaviour.
13. LEADERSHIP DIMENSIONS. These are support, interaction facilitation, work facilitation, and goal emphasis.
14. NATURE OF TASK. The dimensions of a task's structure (programmability, required interdependence, etc.).
15. GROUP GOALS. The performance goals of a group facing a specified task.
16. REQUIRED TASK PERFORMANCE LEVEL. The level of performance prescribed by the formal organisation for a given task.
17. DEGREE OF GOAL CONGRUENCE. The degree of congruence between the required task performance and group goals.
18. GROUP TASK PERFORMANCE. The output of small group interaction to perform tasks.

tion of a group refers to any collection of assembled individuals, or what Lorge and his colleagues term an "ad hoc group". In a sense, the traditioned group is a real group while the ad hoc group is a nominal group.

In this paper, except as noted, the model developed is intended to explain behaviour in real or traditioned rather than nominal or ad hoc groups. For as Lorge et. al. suggest (1958, p. 338): "A common and dangerous practice is to generalise the principles valid for ad hoc groups to traditioned groups".

Degree of Group Development. As suggested by the concept of a traditioned group, "groups require organisation and time to develop it" (Kelley and Thibaut, 1968, p. 76). This simply means that group members require time to pass through the different stages required to become a group. As a result, there can be different degrees of group development.

This variable, as seen in Figure 1, relates closely to leadership style congruence. The degree of group development will determine, at least in part, the style of supervision which is perceived as legitimate. However, there is insufficient evidence to make a prediction about the specific style which will be preferred at each stage of development.

Group Size. This variable refers to the number of members comprising a group. Thomas and Fink (1963) have reviewed studies in which the major independent variable was group size. They concluded (p. 405) that "on the basis of this review it is apparent that group size has significant effects on aspects of individual and group performance, on the nature of interaction and distribution of participation of group members, on group organisation, on conformity and consensus, and on members' satisfaction. This appraisal suggests that the variable of group size should be included in theories of group behaviour . . ."

Thomas and Fink (1963, p. 403) suggest that size may be an important variable in determining a group's input to problem solving. "Two types of input may be assumed to increase with group size. The first is resource input, such as interaction skills, knowledge, capacities, and physical strength". The second type of input is the heterogeneity of group members. As the size of the group increases, the group tends to include more variables from the extremes in the population. This increases the likelihood that there will be more varied skills, knowledge, and abilities required for specialised tasks.

Studies of size have also shown that as group size increases there is a decrease in group cohesiveness. Its relation to cohesiveness, as shown in this model, is probably indirect. It probably influences cohesiveness through the intervening variable of compatibility of member interpersonal orientations. This means that the larger the group, the more diverse its component personalities, and the less the degree of compatibility of member interpersonal orientation. For example, the larger the group, the more likely there will be competition for leadership, and, in turn, the greater the probability of the group developing factions, etc.

Group Member Skills. This variable refers to the technical, administrative, and interpersonal skills possessed by members of a group. These skills play a major role in task performance because they determine, at least in part, the nature of tasks which can be performed as well as the level of achievement possible for those tasks.

As seen in Figure 1, group skills interact indirectly with the nature of the task through the chain of variables leading to "degree of goal congruence". The variable also is hypothesised to influence the perceived degree of task difficulty. The greater the degree of member skills on a given task, the less the perceived level of difficulty.

Perceived Degree of Task Difficulty. Stedry and Kay (1966) have studied the effects of different degrees of perceived difficulty of tasks on productivity. They found that performance was greater when goals perceived as challenging or easy were used as motivators rather than as goals perceived as impossible. Thus the greater the perceived degree of task difficulty, the lower a group's level of aspiration, and vice versa.

This hypothesis and Stedry and Kay's (1966) findings seem to contradict the popular notion that "people will try harder" to achieve impossible goals and, in turn, produce more. This notion fails to take into account the feedback effects of success and failure on successive levels of aspiration.

The variable group skills is likely to relate to the perceived degree of task difficulty, as skills provide the basis for task performance.

Group Aspiration Levels. The term "level of aspiration" (with respect to individuals) has been defined as the "score" a person expects to achieve on a given task (Zander and Medow, 1963, p. 127). It might also be defined as the score a person desires (as opposed to expects) to achieve. This concept may be extended to groups, for groups, like individuals, also may have expectations about future "scores" on a given task. As Zander and Medow state (1963, p. 127): "Often a collection of people engage in deciding upon a desired score for their group".

According to Zander and Medow (1963, p. 127), a group's level of aspiration, like an individual's level of aspiration, can influence task performance. "There can be little doubt that such decisions have demonstrable effects of the performance of the group, that is, on the score of the group".

There have been a variety of studies of a group's level of aspiration. Lewin et. al. (1944, p. 241) noted that: "It has been shown, by a series of independent studies (references deleted), that people's aspirations and goal-seeking behaviour are strongly influenced by information they possess about how others behave and their relationship to these others". Zander and Medow (1963) studied the effects of success and failure on group levels of aspirations as compared with individuals. They found that both individuals and groups raise their level of aspiration after success and lower it after failure (p. 132). They also found a stronger tendency to raise the level of aspiration after success than to lower it after failure common to both groups. However, Zander and Medow (1963) found a major difference between individuals and groups in their reaction to failure. After failure, individuals were more likely than groups to maintain their aspiration levels (p. 132). Stedry and Kay (1966), as noted previously, found that groups who perceived their productivity goals as easy or challenging, significantly out-performed groups who perceived their goals to be impossible. This suggests that groups who perceive goals as impossible did not internalise them, did not accept them as their level of aspiration.

In brief, this variable has a dependent relationship with task difficulty and group norms. It is a subset of the variable "group goals", and influences group performance through a chain of iterative relationships.

It is not possible to hypothesise a simple, positive relationship between aspiration level and performance. First, the aspiration level—task performance curve may follow the inverted "U" shaped pattern common for arousal—performance in individuals (Scott, 1966). Thus, at too high levels of aspiration, group performance may actually decline as a result of stress caused by over-motivation.

Level of aspiration may operate in a more subtle manner through the degree of congruence of group goals and required task performance—that is, goal congruence. Since level of aspiration is a subset of group goals, it is influenced by those goals. Thus we hypothesise that the greater a group's level of aspiration, the greater a group's goals, with goals referring to desired future states of affairs and being only partially measurable. In a sense, level of aspiration might be used as a surrogate for group goals.

Compatibility of Member Interpersonal Orientation. This variable refers to the compatibility of group members or their ability to get along together. Schutz (1955; 1958; 1961) has argued that the degree of "compatibility" is a "subtle but amazingly large contributor" to the effectiveness of a group. Drawing upon Schutz's work, Golembiewski (1965) has included this variable in his model of small group properties. Golembiewski (1965, p. 91) suggests that it is an intervening variable between leadership and group norms. This model presented in Figure 1 shows it to operate in the following chain: leadership style congruence influences "compatibility", which influences cohesiveness, which, in turn, influences group norms. The reasoning is that if there is not high compatibility of members there will not be high group cohesiveness, etc. Thus we hypothesise: the greater the degree of "compatibility" the greater the degree of cohesiveness. The greater the degree of cohesiveness, the greater the consensus on group norms (Golembiewski, 1965, p. 98). If we consider informal group leadership, then the greater the leadership style congruence, the greater the compatibility.

Cohesiveness. This variable is one of the most complex and closely studied in small group theory. It has been defined in several ways. Golembiewski (1965, p. 90) has also noted that this concept of cohesiveness may be measured by answers to such questions as: "How much do you want to remain a member of this group?" According to Cartwright and Zander (1969, p. 14) "the cohesiveness of a group is the resultant of all the forces acting on all the members to remain in the group".

Both of these notions of cohesiveness relate to the attraction of members to the group. However, as Schacter et. al. (1951) point out, cohesiveness has been defined as referring to morale, togetherness, productivity, power, feelings of belongingness, and good team work. They argue that there are essentially two basic notions of cohesiveness: One equates cohesiveness with the "morale" or "spirit" of a group. The other is concerned with the attractiveness of the group for its members, as is the Golembiewski (1965) and Cartwright and Zander (1960) concepts.

Schacter et. al. (1951) suggest that these two notions lead to different concepts of the relationship between cohesiveness and productivity. "The cohesiveness-morale formulation suggests that since a cohesive group is marked by good morale and since the members of such a group like one another and get on well together, it should follow that the more cohesive the group, the greater should be its 'productivity' " (Schacter et. al., 1951), (as cited in Cartwright and Zander, 1960, pp. 152–153). This study has been tested by R. L. French (1951), and in Darnley, Gross, and Martin (1952). Neither study has supported the anticipated relationship. The cohesiveness—attraction theory suggests that ". . . the greater the cohesiveness the greater the power of the group to influence its members. The power of the group will be equal to the magnitude of the force on the members to remain in the group" (Schacter et. al., 1951, as cited in Cartwright and Zander, 1960, p. 153). This latter theory does not suggest that high cohesiveness will lead to high productivity; rather, it suggests that cohesiveness can influence productivity. "Whether cohesiveness will increase or decrease productivity, however, is determined largely by the direction of group induction. If the group attempts to influence its members to increase production, high cohesive groups should be more productive than low cohesive groups. If the group attempts to decrease production, low cohesive groups should be more productive than high". Schacter et. al., (1951, as cited in Cartwright and Zander, 1960, p. 153). In an empirical test of these hypotheses, Schacter et. al., found that: (a) there is no necessary relationship between cohesiveness and high productivity (group members in cohesive groups will accept norms of either high or low productivity) and (b) when the norm is to lower productivity, high cohesive groups are more likely to accept the norm than low cohesive groups.

Cohesiveness is also related, as shown in Figure 1, to member control. As Cartwright and Zander (1960, p. 175) state: "The power of a group over its members is directly proportional to the cohesiveness of that group". Thus we hypothesise that the greater the degree of cohesiveness, the greater the control of group members. Similarly, the greater the cohesiveness of a group, the greater the degree of consensus of group norms. Consensus on group norms will follow cohesiveness and be reinforced by member control (Golembiewski, 1965, p. 100).

Member Control. This variable refers to the power of a group over its members, i.e., its ability to create and maintain group norms or standards of behaviour. Festinger et. al., (1950) have suggested that the ability to control members can be measured by the group's cohesiveness: "the power of a group may be measured by the attractiveness of the group for the members" (cited in Cartwright and Zander, 1960, p. 25). This suggests that cohesiveness may be a surrogate measure for member control, but the two concepts should not be thought of as identical.

Consensus of Norms and Norms Per Se. In his model of small groups, Golembiewski (1965, p. 90) cites a definition of the concept of "group norms" by Naess (1948): "Reflections of social pressures which apply either to all group members or to performers of specific roles". Golembiewski (1965, p. 90) also suggests that norms may be measured by "asking group members to report on the norms influencing them in various situations, the consensus of group members on such reports being a crucial datum".

There has been considerable research on norms. In laboratory experiements, Sherif (1936) studied the origin of social norms and how such norms influence human behaviour, using the "autokinetic effect"[1] Sherif (1936) found that individual judgements tended to converge to a group range that was peculiar to the specified group. Sherif (1936) also found that when individuals first established a range before being placed in a situation with individuals who also came into the situation with their own ranges, the ranges for the group tended to converge. In addition, when an individual has first been part of a group where a group norm is established and later is placed alone, he tends to perceive the situation in terms of the norm previously established in the group. Newcomb (1943) also studied the operation of social norms, but he chose a field rather than a laboratory setting. According to Cartwright and Zander (1960, p. 26), Newcomb's study "showed that the attitudes of individuals are strongly rooted in the groups to which people belong, that the influence of a group upon an individual's attitudes depends upon the nature of the relationship between the individual and the group, and that groups evaluate members, partially at least, on the basis of conformity to group norms".

In summary, previous research has shown not only that consensus on group norms is an important variable in understanding group processes, but also that group norms are able to exert strong influences on individual behaviour. For example, "workers may agree on an acceptable speed of production, and exert pressures on those who differ from this rate so that they will return to the standard of

[1]The autokinetic effect refers to a perceptual phenomenon that occurs if a person looks at a stationary point of light in an otherwise dark room; he will soon perceive it to be moving (Cartwright and Zander, 1960, p. 24).

the group. This group standard is often seen by management as an unwarranted restriction of output which they find difficult to overcome". (Cartwright and Zander, 1960, p. 165).

Consensus also correlates positively with cohesiveness. In addition, consensus is influenced by member control. Thus we hypothesise that the greater the degree of member control, the greater the degree of consensus on group norms.

In addition to its dependent relationship with consensus on norms and member control, the group norms variable influences the variable "group aspiration level". Thus the greater the degree of high productivity norms, the greater the group's level of aspiration.

Leadership Style Congruence. This variable refers to the extent to which the leadership style used in a group (or to manage a group) is consistent with group norms of appropriate leadership role behaviour. Leadership is one of the most studied of group variables, and has been defined in many ways (Golembiewski, 1965, p. 89; Cartwright and Zander, 1960, pp. 488–489). As Cartwright and Zander (1960, p. 488–489) concisely and aptly state: "To some, leadership is a property of a group while to others it is a characteristic of an individual. To those who emphasise the group, leadership may be synonymous with prestige, with the holding of a particular office, with the performance of activities important to the group, or with an emotional relationship between the leader and the group. To those who stress the individual, leadership may mean the possession of certain personality characteristics such as dominance, ego-control, aggressiveness, or freedom from paranoid tendencies. The variety of notions contained in these alternative conceptions makes it plain that a single meaning for the term, leader, which would be acceptable to all those interested in leadership cannot readily be chosen".

An exhaustive discussion of this variable is well beyond the scope of this paper. It is, however, an important and complex variable that must be reflected in any model of group-task performance. The model presented in this paper accepts contingency theory (Fiedler, 1971) as the most plausible explanation of leadership style congruence. In brief, the contingency model of leadership effectiveness is based upon the idea that ". . . the performance of interacting groups is contingent upon the interaction of leadership style and situational favourableness", that is upon the interaction of the leader and the situation (Fiedler, 1971, p. 128).

This suggests that the variable depends upon the degree of group development and the nature of the task as suggested under contingency theory. It influences compatibility of member interpersonal orientation. Thus the greater the degree of leadership style congruence, the greater the degree of compatibility.

Leadership Dimensions. In addition to the variable "leadership style congruence", the dimensions of leadership per se must also be considered. This variable refers to the elements or factors which constitute leadership in group situations. Again, this is an extremely complex area, but Bowers and Seashore's four factor theory seems promising (1966). Their four factors are: (1) support, (2) interaction facilitation, (3) goal emphasis, and (4) work facilitation (Bowers and Seashore, 1966, p. 247).

The leadership dimensions variable influences cohesiveness and member control. Drawing upon the four factor theory (Bowers and Seashore, 1966), leadership "support" and "interaction facilitation" will influence cohesiveness and group member control. "Goal emphasis" will influence group goals. Thus the greater the degree of leadership support (or interaction facilitation) the greater the degree of cohesiveness (or member control). Similarly, the greater the degree of goal emphasis, the greater group goals (or levels of aspiration).

Nature of Task. As Herold (1974, p. 4) states, "That which the group is asked to do can be a major factor in determining group process (references deleted), group structure, as well as the final group product. The Hackman study demonstrated that close to 50% of the variance in certain group performance measures can be accounted for by the type of task performed by the group".

There are various dimensions of the nature of tasks which are relevant to small group process. Herold (1974) presents a typology of tasks based upon two dimensions: technical and social. An alternative view of the dimensions of tasks is suggested by Dalton (1971, p. 22), who identified three elements: (1) the programmability of the task, (2) the amount of required interdependence, and (3) the time span of the performance cycle. "Programmability" of a task refers to the degree to which the behaviour required to perform a task can be specified. "Interdependence" of a task refers to the degree to which a task requires cooperative effort by group members. "Time span of performance cycle" refers to the length of time needed to perform a task.

In addition to these dimensions of tasks, the degree of operationalisation of task goals is another factor which may influence group process. This is the degree to which it can be determined whether and to what extent a goal has been accomplished by a group's activities. It essentially is the measurability of task goals. This dimension is clearly related to the notion of "group goals" as well as to "nature of task".

Group Goals. This variable refers to the goal of a group facing a specified task. As Hinton and Reitz (1971, p. 125) state: "A group goal is most accurately defined, then, as a desired state of future affairs for the group which is held by a sufficient number of group members to ensure movement toward that state".

According to Cartwright and Zander (1960, p. 365): ". . . when the members of a group accept a group goal they experience satisfaction or frustration, depending upon what happens to the group as an entity. This common dependence on the fate of the group tends to make members interdependent, for if one member performs an activity which helps the group reach its goal, he thereby improves the probability for each other member that he will gain satisfaction".

"Goals which are clear rather than fuzzy, operational rather than unworkable, quantifiable rather than unmeasurable, challenging rather than unrealistic will greatly facilitate group performance and enhance the group's cohesiveness". (Hinton and Reitz, 1971, p. 125).

The very fact that a goal exists can influence both individual and group behaviour. "The term 'zeigartnik effect' describes the phenomenon whereby the establishment of a goal creates in an individual an arousal (manifested by heightened recall of the goal) which is extinguished by task completion by the group or part of the group, or by a group decision not to complete the task" (Hinton and Reitz, 1971, p. 125).

As noted above, goals (like tasks) can differ in the degree to which they are operational. The distinction between operational and nonoperational goals has been discussed by March and Simon (1958), as noted in Cartwright and Zander (1960, p. 352): "If there is some way of determining whether and to what extent a goal will be realised by a particular sequence of group activities, then the goal is operational; otherwise it is not". According to Cartwright and Zander (1960, p. 362), "March and Simon (reference deleted) have advanced the hypothesis that when a group has an accepted, operational superordinate goal, differences of opinion about subgoals will be resolved by predominately analytical processes, i.e., by the analysis of expected consequences of courses of action directed toward each subgoal. On the other hand, when superordinate goals are nonoperational, the decision will be reached by predominately bargaining processes".

It should also be noted that the concepts of group goals and group level of aspiration are closely related. A goal has been defined as a desired future state of affairs, and level of aspiration has been defined as an expected (or desired) score on a specified task. Thus a level of aspiration may be viewed as the measurable portion of a goal, or as the subset of goals which are operational (and, in turn, measurable).

Required Task Performance Level. This variable is simply the required level of performance by a group on a specified task. It is the level imposed, requested, or specified by the formal organisation. This required level may or may not correspond to the group's aspiration level.

Group goals interact with the required task performance level to produce the degree of goal congruence. Thus the greater the correspondence of group goals and task performance, the greater the degree of goal congruence.

Degree of Goal Congruence. This variable refers to the degree of Congruence of Required Task Performance and Group Goals. It is a resultant variable from group processes and task requirements. It is the degree of congruence between group goals and total formal organisational goals.

Group Task Performance. This variable is the output of small group interaction and task requirements. It is the ultimate variable in the model. The preceding variables represent input and transformation factors to bring about group performance. It is, in other words, the end-result of the group's task input—process—output sequence (see Herold, 1974).

The variable is primarily dependent upon the degree of goal congruence, which is, in turn, determined by the chain of relations described above. Thus the greater the degree of goal congruence, the greater the degree to which actual performance will correspond to both group goals and required task performance.

The Model as a Whole. The model includes seventeen variables in addition to the variable "group". These seventeen variables may be viewed as comprising five independent clusters. In brief, these clusters are: (1) group properties —group size, group development, and group member skills; (2) group process variables—compatibility of member interpersonal orientations, cohesiveness, consensus on norms, member control, group norms, perceived degree of task difficulty, group aspiration level, and group goals; (3) leadership variables—leadership style congruence, and leadership dimensions; (4) task variables—nature of task, and required task performance level; and (5) end-result variables—degree of goal congruence (a penultimate variable) and group task performance (the ultimate variable). Figure 2 shows these clusters of variables in schematic terms.

THE MODEL'S ACCOUNTING IMPLICATIONS

The development of the model described above to explain group dynamics in task performance is the first step toward deriving implications for accounting. The next step required is to formulate a set of basic propositions about group dynamics which are potentially applicable to accounting. Specifically, we need a set of generalisations about group interaction and task performance. Once such statements have been developed, we may assess their applicability to accounting, formulate specific hypotheses, and test them empirically.

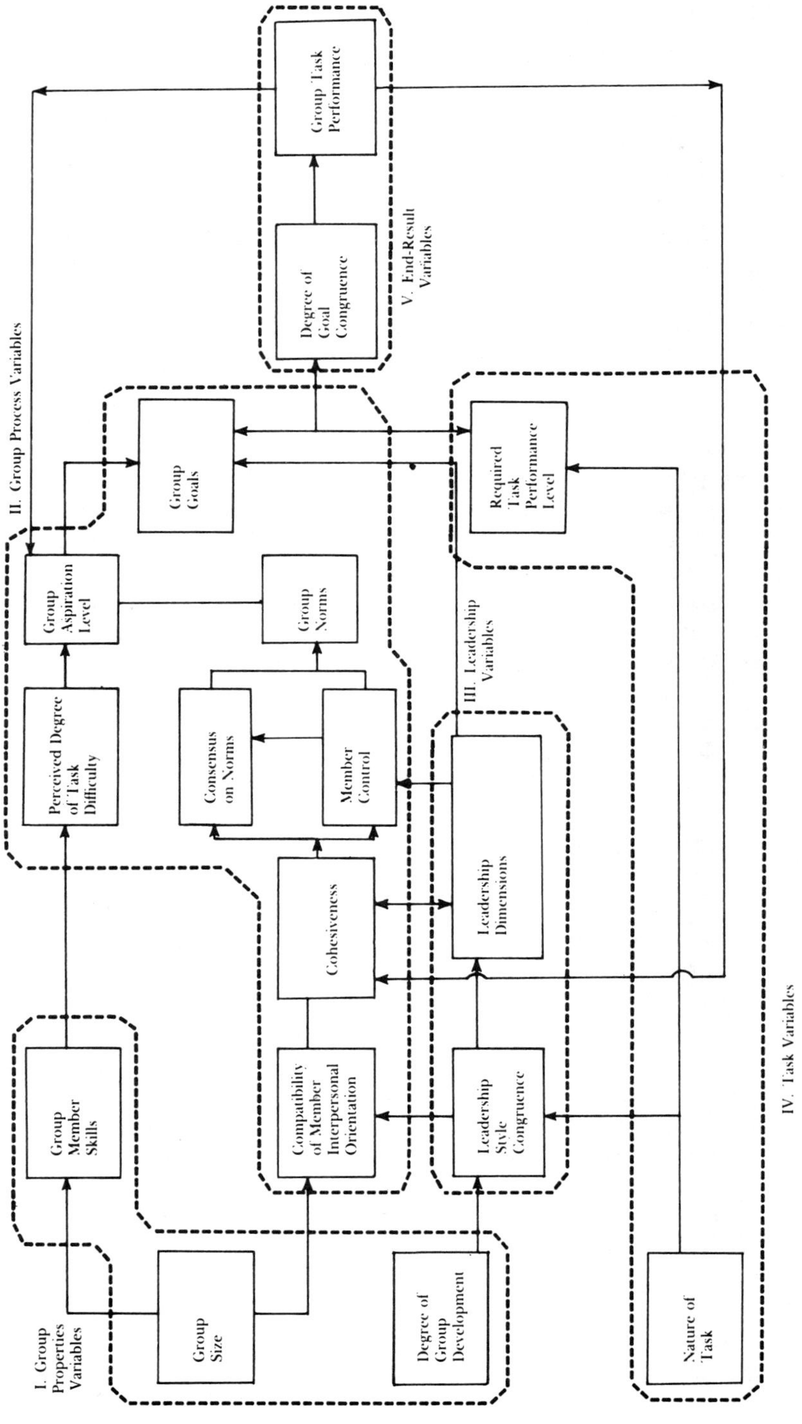

FIGURE 2. Model of Small Group Interaction and Task Performance: Clusters of Variables

A set of propositions about group dynamics in task performance is presented in Table 2. These propositions have been derived from the model, and represent summary statements about the key relations among the model's variables. An exhaustive examination of the model's accounting implications is beyond the scope of this paper; indeed, it is an

TABLE 2. Summary of Propositions about Small Group Interaction and Task Performance

1. NATURE OF GROUPS. A group is not a group is not a group: There are nominal as well as real groups.
2. EFFECT OF GROUP MEMBERSHIP. Members of real (as opposed to nominal) groups share a common dependence on the fate of a group.
3. GROUP DEVELOPMENT. Groups require organisation and time to develop it.
4. GROUP SIZE. Group size has significant effects on aspects of group and individual performance, on the nature of interaction and distribution of participation of group members, on group organisation, on conformity and consensus in groups. It influences the resources available to the group. It also influences the cohesiveness of groups.
5. GROUP EFFECTS ON INDIVIDUALS. Groups can influence individual behaviour in many significant ways. Groups can influence individual perception, motivation, decisions, and attitudes.
6. GROUP INFLUENCE ON INDIVIDUALS. The personality traits of individuals determine their propensity to be influenced by a group. Thus individuals differ in the extent to which groups can influence their behaviour.
7. GROUP LEVEL OF ASPIRATION. Group levels of aspiration are influenced by the perceived degree of task difficulty.
8. EFFECTS OF SUCCESS AND FAILURE ON LEVEL OF ASPIRATION. Groups may differ from individuals in terms of the effects of success and failure on their level of aspiration. Groups, like individuals, raise their level of aspiration after success and lower it after failure. Groups are less likely than individuals to maintain their level of aspiration after failure.
9. COMPATIBILITY OF GROUP MEMBERS. Group task performance is influenced by the degree of compatibility of members' interpersonal orientation.
10. GROUP COHESIVENESS. Cohesive groups have more power to control members' behaviour (and make them conform to group norms) than noncohesive groups. High cohesiveness may be correlated with either high or low group task performance, depending upon group norms.
11. GROUP NORMS. Group norms are important influences on both individual and group behaviour. Once established, norms influence individuals even when they are not in a group situation.
12. LEADERSHIP STYLE CONGRUENCE. Groups may develop norms of appropriate leadership behaviour or style.
13. NATURE OF TASK. Group performance depends upon the nature of the task.
14. GROUP GOALS. Group goals can influence both individual and group behaviour by their very existence.
15. REQUIRED TASK PERFORMANCE. Groups may not simply accept required task performance levels (as specified by the formal organisation) as their aspiration levels. Individual group members will accept required task performance only if they are consistent with group norms.

appropriate subject for extensive future research. However, the subsequent discussion will illustrate some of the possible implications which may be derived from the model.

IMPLICATIONS FOR BUDGETING

The model suggests that a group is not a group is not a group. This means that "groups" are not identical. Traditioned groups may behave differently from ad hoc (nominal) groups during the budgeting process. If future behavioural accounting research uses ad hoc groups in laboratory experiments, researchers will face serious difficulties in generalising the results to traditioned groups in organisations.

Group size is another variable with implications for budgeting. It will influence the nature and pattern of interaction during budgetary decision making. The larger the group the more diverse its component personalities, and, in turn, the less the degree of compatibility of members' interpersonal orientations. The less the degree of compatibility, the greater the degree of grup conflict in budgetary decision making and resource allocation.

Another aspect of group size is its impact upon the ability of the group to influence individuals to conform to a group consensus. As Asch (1953) has shown, individuals holding opinions differing from the majority opinion in a group may perceive strong social pressures to change their position even when the group does not exert any overt pressure. Asch (1953) studied the effect of peer group disagreement on individual judgements under conditions of a relatively unambiguous physical stimulus. When not confronted with unanimous peer group disagreement, individuals made judgement errors about the stimulus less than 1% of the time. However, under perceived group pressure the subjects' judgements became incorrect 36.8% of the time. Asch's (1953) study also has other implications for budgeting. He found not only that many individuals would tend to bow to unanimous peer group disagreement, but also that if there is some peer support for the individual, the probability that the subject would yield to the opposition decreased.

This latter finding by Asch (1953) together with the finding by Thomas and Fink (1963) that as group size increases there is decreasing cohesiveness and increasing diversity of people suggests the need for careful consideration of the size and composition of budgeting groups. It suggests the need for heterogeneity of group composition to increase the likelihood that minority viewpoints will have at least some peer support and will not face unanimous opposition. It also suggests the need of group leaders to encourage a group norm that disagreement is to be encouraged.

Another variable in the model with implications for budgeting is "group goals". First, the very fact that groups reach a decision about a group goal during the budgetary process may create a "zeigartnik effect" which motivates groups behaviour to achieve the goal. Second, the existence of subgroups or cliques within a budgetary group or committee may cause suboptimal decisions. Specifically, the existence of subgroups may create subgroup loyalties which conflict with overall group or organisational goals.

The variable "cohesiveness" also has potential implications for budgeting. Cohesive groups will tend to be more committed to group decisions and goals than noncohesive groups. Thus cohesive groups are more likely to be committed to achieving budgetary goals set by the group than noncohesive groups.

The degree of consensus on group norms and the nature of norms per se will also influence budgeting. Based on the model, we would predict that decisions of individual members will be influenced by group norms just as in Sherif's (1936) demonstration of the autokinetic effect. For example, group attitudes or norms toward the personnel function in organisations will influence the budgetary allocation decisions.

Another of the model's variables of importance in budgeting is a group's level of aspiration. The budgeted level set by a group will not necessarily be the same as the level that management would have set. Group participation in budgeting may lead the group to internalise the budgeted level as their aspiration level. The greater the degree of cohesiveness, the more the group will try to achieve the level they set, if it is perceived to be reasonably attainable or challenging. "Impossible" goals will not be internalised.

If the group is successful in achieving its budgeted aspirational level in period t–1, it will tend to raise its level in period t. If the group is unsuccessful in t–1, it will lower its aspiration level in t.

The nature of the task is another of the model's variables that has implications for budgeting. The nature of the budgetary task determines the nature of the budgetary process. If the task is nonprogrammable (for example in budgeting discretionary costs), bargaining as opposed to analytical budgeting processes will be used.

The variable "leadership style congruence" also has implications for budgeting. Directive leadership styles may be used in programmable budgetary processes, while nonprogrammable budgeting tasks require a nondirective (participative) style.

Finally, the end result variable "degree of goal congruence" influences budgeting. For example, in nonprogrammable (discretionary cost) budgeting, the existence of subgroups with local subunit goals and loyalties will tend toward suboptimal decisions from the total system's perspective.

The implications derived from the model for budgeting are, of course, tentative, and require empirical testing. They are presented to illustrate the role of the model in generating potential behavioural accounting theory. The model also has potential implications for other areas of accounting, such as standard cost variance control systems and responsibility accounting. These should be the subject of future research.

CONCLUSION

The model presented in this paper is intended as a first step toward a formal model of group dynamics in task performance relevant to accounting. Such models are prerequisites to future empirical research in behavioural accounting, as noted by the American Accounting Association Committee on the Relationship of Behavioural Science and Accounting (1974). The next step is to assess the model's potential implications for other areas of accounting. Then these generalisations should be studied and tested empirically. It is hoped that this paper will provide a stimulus to future research in this area.

REFERENCES

1. American Accounting Association Committee on Behavioural Science Content of the Accounting Curriculum, "Report of the Committee on Behavioral Science Content of the Accounting Curriculum", THE ACCOUNTING REVIEW SUPPLEMENT to Vol. XLVI, 1971, pp. 247–285.
2. Asch, S.E., "Effects of Group Pressure upon the Modification and Distortion of Judgements", SCIENTIFIC AMERICAN, Nov., 1955, pp. 31–34.
3. Becker, S. and Green, D., "Budgeting and Employee Behavior", THE JOURNAL OF BUSINESS, XXXV (October, 1962), pp. 392–402.
4. Becker, S. And Green, D., "Budgeting and Em-

ployee Behavior: A Rejoinder to A 'Reply'," THE JOURNAL OF BUSINESS, XXXVII (April, 1964), pp. 203–205.

5. Benston, G.J., "The Role of the Firm's Accounting System for Motivation", THE ACCOUNTING REVIEW, XXXVIII (April, 1963), pp. 347–354.
6. Birnberg, J. and Nath, R., "Implications of Behavioral Science for Managerial Accounting", THE ACCOUNTING REVIEW, Vol. 42, No. 3, pp. 468–479.
7. Bonner, H., GROUP DYNAMICS: PRINCIPLES AND APPLICATIONS, New York: Ronald Press, 1959.
8. Bowers, D.G. and Seashore, S., "Predicting Organisational Effectiveness With a Four Factor Theory of Leadership", ADMINISTRATIVE SCIENCE QUARTERLY, Vol. 11, No. 2, 1966, pp. 238–263.
9. Bruns, W.J. and De Coster, D.T., ACCOUNTING AND ITS BEHAVORIAL IMPLICATIONS, New York: McGraw-Hill Book Company, 1969.
10. Burns, T.J., BEHAVIORAL EXPERIMENTS IN ACCOUNTING, Columbus, Ohio: College of Administrative Science, The Ohio State University, 1972.
11. Caplan, E.H., "Behavioral Assumptions of Management Accounting", THE ACCOUNTING REVIEW, Vol. 41, No. 3, pp. 496–509.
12. Cartwright, D. and Zander, A., GROUP DYNAMICS, Second Edition, Evanston, Illinois: Row, Peterson and Company, 1960.
13. Clark, R.D., "Group-Induced Shift toward Risk: A Critical Appraisal", PSYCHOLOGICAL BULLETIN, Vol. 76, No. 4, 1971, pp. 251–270.
14. Coch, L. and French, J.R.P., "Overcoming Resistance to Change", HUMAN RELATIONS, 1948, I, pp. 512–532.
15. Dalton, G., "Motivation and Control in Organizations", in Dalton, G. and Lawrence, P. (Editors), MOTIVATION AND CONTROL IN ORGANIZATIONS, Irwin, 1971, pp. 20–35.
16. Darnley, J., Gross, M. and Martin, W., "Studies of Group Behavior: Factors Associated with the Productivity of Groups", JOURNAL OF APPLIED PSYCHOLOGY, 1952, 36, pp. 396–403.
17. Festinger, L., Schacter, S. and Back, K., "The Operation of Group Standards", in Cartwright and Zander, 1960, pp. 241–259.
18. Fiedler, F.E., "Validation and Extension of the Contingency Model of Leadership Effectiveness: A Review of Empirical Findings", PSYCHOLOGY BULLETIN, Vol. 76, No. 2, 1971, pp. 128–148.
19. French, R.L., "Sociometric Status and Individual Adjustment among Naval Recruits", JOURNAL OF ABNORMAL AND SOCIAL PSYCHOLOGY, 1951, 46, pp. 64–71.
20. French, J.R.P., Israel, J.I. and As, D., "An Experiment on Participation in a Norwegian Factory", HUMAN RELATIONS, XIII, 1960.
21. Golembiewski, R.T., "Small Groups and Large Organizations", in J.G. March (Editor) HANDBOOK OR ORGANIZATIONS, Chicago: Rand McNally & Company, 1965, pp. 87–141.
22. Herold, D.M., "Group Effectiveness As A Function of Task-Appropriate Interaction Processes", unpublished paper, 1974.
23. Hinton, B. and Reitz, H.J., GROUPS AND ORGANIZATIONS, Belmont, California: Wadsworth Publishing Company, Inc., 1971.
24. Kelley, H.H. and Thibaut, J.W., "Experimental Sketches of Group Problem Solving and Process", in G. Lindzey (Editor), HANDBOOK OF SOCIAL PSYCHOLOGY, Cambridge, Mass.: Addison-Wesley, 1959, pp. 735–785.
25. Lewin, K. et al., "Level of Aspiration", in J. McV. Hunt (Editor), PERSONALITY AND THE BEHAVIOUR DISORDERS, Vol. I, New York: Ronald, 1944.
26. Lorge, I. and Solomon, H., "Group and Individual Performance in Problem Solving related to Previous Exposure to Problem, Level of Aspiration, and Group Size", BEHAVIORAL SCIENCE, 1960, 5, pp. 28–39.
27. March, J.G., and Simon, H.A., ORGANIZATIONS, New York: Wiley, 1958.
28. McDavid, J., "Personality and Situational Determinants of Conformity", JOURNAL OF ABNORMAL AND SOCIAL PSYCHOLOGY, 1959, 58, pp. 241–246.
29. Naess, A., OBJECTIVITY OF NORMS, Oslo: Univeritetes Student-Kontor, 1948.
30. Newcomb, T.M., PERSONALITY AND SOCIAL CHANGE, New York: Dryden, 1943.

31. Pondy, L.R., "Budgeting and Intergroup Conflict in Organizations", PITTSBURGH BUSINESS REVIEW, April, 1964.
32. Schacter, S., Ellertson, N., McBride, D., and Gregory, D., "An Experimental Study of Cohesiveness and Productivity," HUMAN RELATIONS, 1951, 4, pp. 229–238.
33. Schutz, W.C., "What Makes Groups Productive?" HUMAN RELATIONS, 1955, 8, pp. 429–466.
34. Schutz, W.C., FIRO: A THREE-DIMENSIONAL THEORY OF INTERPERSONAL BEHAVIOR, New York: Rinehart, 1958.
35. Scott, W.E., "Activation Theory and Task Design", THE AMERICAN SCHOLAR, Vol. 35, No. 2, Spring, 1966, pp. 275–276, as reprinted in Scott, W.E. and Cummings, L.L., READINGS IN ORGANIZATION BEHAVIOR AND HUMAN PERFORMANCE, Irwin, 1973, pp. 188–202.
36. Sherif, M., THE PSYCHOLOGY OF SOCIAL NORMS, Harper, 1936.
37. Stedry, A.C., "Budgeting and Employee Behavior: A Reply", THE JOURNAL OF BUSINESS, XXXVII, April, 1964, pp. 195–202.
38. Stedry, A.C. and Kay, E., "The Effects of Goal Difficulty on Performance: A Field Experiment", BEHAVIORAL SCIENCE, 1966, 11, pp. 459–470.
39. Stoner, J.A.F., "Risky and Cautious Shifts in Group Decisions: The Influence of Widely Held Values", JOURNAL OF EXPERIMENTAL SOCIAL PSYCHOLOGY, 1968, 4, pp. 442–459.
40. Thomas, E.J. and Fink, C.F., "Effects of Group Size", PSYCHOLOGICAL BULLETIN, Vol. 60, No. 4, 1963, pp. 371–384.
41. Whyte, W.F., PATTERNS FOR INDUSTRIAL PEACE, New York: Harper, 1951.
42. Zander, A. and Medow, H., "Individual and Group Levels of Aspiration", HUMAN RELATIONS, 1963, 16, pp. 89–105.

PART 4

Social and Human Resource Accounting as Management Tools: Implications for Management Accounting

The final aspect of management accounting systems (MAS) which is considered in this book is social and human resource accounting. The purpose of social and human resource accounting is to provide information on factors which are related to social issues, such as the firm's environmental impact (industrial pollution is a much-quoted example), and to individual organizational members, for example, human resource development programs.

There are two reasons why designers of MAS need to be aware of the issues related to social and human resource accounting; both reasons are concerned with the inclusion of social and human resource dimensions in the firm's goal structure. First, if managers identify social goals as an element of the firm's goals (either as a result of their own volition, or community or government pressure), the accounting system will need to provide information which reflects the impact of corporate activities on society. This will enable both society and the firm to evaluate the firm's performance on socially relevant activities. Additionally, it will enable managers to plan resource allocation decisions that incorporate social goals (Epstein, Flamholtz & McDonough, 1976). A particular example of social goals is the managers' perceived responsibility to provide individuals in the organization with opportunities for personal development, and for improved "quality of working life" through human resource development programs (Mills, 1975). Human resource accounting systems may be implemented with this objective in mind (Mirvis & Macy, 1976). However, human resource accounting systems may also facilitate the achievement of the organization's traditional economic (non-social) goals, by providing information to assist the human resource allocation decision (Flamholtz, 1976).

A final aspect of human resource accounting is the valuation of human assets for external reporting purposes (Elias, 1973; Hendricks, 1976; Schwan, 1976). The objective is the provision of information to enable external users such as shareholders to allocate their capital funds to different firms. Because the focus of this book is the management accounting system and its role in assisting internal decision making and control, the external reporting dimension of human resource accounting will not be examined.

SOCIAL ACCOUNTING

The area of social accounting is relevant to this book in that it makes explicit the importance of the social context within which organizations operate, and the relationships between elements of the social context and managers' decisions. The dimensions of the social context are considerable and extend over a wide range of groups in contemporary society which may be affected by managers' decisions.

Some society groups, such as employees, may be encompassed within the firm; managers' decisions with respect to work settings and task assignment, for example, may affect employees' personality development opportunities. Other groups will exist outside the traditionally recognized boundaries of the organization; managers' decisions which alter environmental pollution levels, for example, may affect social groups which are characterized by physical or geographical similarities.

The potentially relevant social context also extends beyond members of contemporary society to members of future society. Managers' decisions which determine the consumption rates and patterns of scarce resources is one example; the potential of current organizational activities to affect the health of future generations through genetically transferable disease is another.

The social responsibility of business firms has been a matter of increasing concern to individuals, governments and organizational managers during the 1970s (Birnberg, 1978; Gröjer & Stark, 1977; Ullman, 1979). If it continues to be a matter of importance, as is predicted (Dierkes & Preston, 1977), and remains a part of managers' goal structures, management accounting systems will need to provide information on socially relevant activities in order that managers can plan and evaluate these activities.

The accounting profession has in fact recognized the need for the provision of information on the social costs and benefits of managers' decisions. Although very little research in the area of social accounting was carried out prior to 1970, considerable progress has been made since then, both in terms of corporate programs (American Accounting Association, 1975, 1976), and accounting research (Churchill & Toan, 1978; Dierkes & Preston, 1977; Estes, 1976; Ramanathan, 1976; Spicer, 1978).

The complexity of the time and spatial dimensions of organizations' activities and their affects on society produce considerable difficulties for the

MAS designer. These problems are classified by Spicer (1978) as identification and specification problems, measurement problems, and accountability problems. Although these categories are interdependent, we will be concerned with the first two only, as the third is related to the purposes of external reporting and third-party evaluation of organizations' social programs.

Resolving the identification and specification problem involves the determination of the social constituents which are affected by managers' decisions and the nature of the impact of the decision on those constituents. Different approaches to this problem may be found in the literature. Spicer (1978) discusses a normative approach, which relies on *a priori* specification of the components of a firm's social performance, and a descriptive approach which traces the impact of managers' decisions through social channels.

Normative and descriptive approaches have led to the development of several taxonomies of socially relevant activities, examples of which are given in Table 4.1. Another taxonomy which is directed at the identification of areas for social accounting research for internal management decision making and evaluation was developed by the National Association of Accountants (NAA,

TABLE 4.1

Normative Approach	Descriptive Approach
Taxonomy Developed by Corson & Steiner (1974)	Taxonomy Developed by Beresford (1973)
Economic growth and efficiency	Environmental controls
Education	—Equipment to abate pollution and reduce operating costs
Employment and training	—Improvement of products to reduce their pollutive effects
Civil rights and equal opportunity	—Recycling of waste materials
Urban renewal and development	Minority employment
Pollution abatement	—Hard core minorities employment
Conservation and recreation	—Training minorities for advancement
Culture and the arts	Responsibility to Personnel
Medical care	—Personnel counselling
Government	—Assist displaced employees in locating new employment
	—Employee training
	Community activities
	—Donations of cash or employee services to community welfare
	—Public health projects
	—Aid to education and the arts
	Product improvement
	—Safety
	—Quality (e.g. nutritional value)

1974). Activities were included under four headings: community involvement, human resources, physical resources and environmental contributions, and product or service contributions.

Measurement of social cost and benefit problems have occupied considerable social accounting research effort in the 1970s. An American Accounting Association committee (AAA, 1975) identified a major difficulty in measuring social costs and benefits to be the complex series of contingent events following a particular management decision.

> For example, suppose coal is strip mined and the surface land is not restored. This degradation ultimately may be an opportunity loss to society in terms of erosion, scenic loss, timber loss, food crop loss, water contamination, wildlife loss, etc. But measuring such opportunity losses requires looking into the future through a maze of contingent events which might "take" or "have taken" place on the land and products of the land. Similarly, there may be social benefits from not having coal users bear the cost of strip-land restoration. Measuring such benefits forces analysts to examine the maze of ultimate effects on possibly millions or billions of products which at some point utilized or were affected by coal prices (AAA, 1975, pp. 56–57).

The AAA committee nominated four possible measurement levels with which organizations' social activities could be planned and evaluated: an "inventory" level which consists of determining qualitatively what activities have social impact; an "input" level, which examines the resources used in social activities; a level which evaluates the immediate "outputs" of an action; and a higher level, which attempts to value the "worth" of the results of the activities. "This is more than an enumeration of the immediate results and often requires consideration of second and third order effects, foregone alternatives, and displaced activities" (AAA, 1975, p. 65). Social measurement ideally requires the last of these measurement levels (the value of the results of social impact actions), but the development of measures at this level is, practically, very problematic.

Also at the abstract measurement level, Churchill and Toan (1978) discuss the single unit approach to social measurement (using either monetary or non-monetary units) and an eclectic system based on the development of different units which may arise naturally, or are uniquely appropriate to particular social activities.

At the specific measurement level, attempts have been made to measure the costs of industrial pollution (Beams & Fertig, 1971), the community impact of plant closure (AAA, 1975), and other physical environmental impacts such as energy usage, despoliation of landscape, and noise (Dierkes & Preston, 1977).

The future for social accounting research is unclear. Attempts to achieve higher order measures of the social impact of managers' decisions have not been satisfying (AICPA, 1977). Although measurement concepts from other disciplines (such as the "quality of life" indicators) may provide new avenues for development, these too are unlikely to provide effective measures for many organizational social activities (Spicer, 1978, p. 164).

HUMAN RESOURCE ACCOUNTING

As one of the earliest and most consistent researchers in human resource accounting, Flamholtz has noted the purposes of human asset valuation for internal management purposes. These include manpower planning and control, covering such decisions as manpower acquisition, assignment to tasks and functions, and replacement, and the ability of management to predict the potential impact of its decisions on the value of human resources as reflected in individual attitudes, motivation and satisfaction (Flamholtz, 1972, p. 666). These aspects of human resource accounting (HRA) are designed to improve managers' resource allocation decisions and the operating effectiveness of the organization.

To the extent that managers accept responsibility for contributing to the development of individual members of the organization through, for example, changes in the nature of jobs and work settings or task re-assignment, human resource accounting has the purpose of providing cost/benefit data on such development programs (Cheek, 1973; Mills, 1975; Mirvis & Macy, 1976). This aspect of HRA is intended to permit improvement in the "quality of organizational life" of the individual.

Although some human asset valuation research and practice pre-dates 1965 (Hermanson, 1964; Schultz, 1959), the majority of accounting research has taken place in the late 1960s and in the 1970s. The perceived importance of HRA was evidenced by the significant quantity of literature available in the ten years from 1965, and by the well-documented applications of HRA by the R.G. Barry Corporation and other organizations (Flamholtz, 1974). A good tabular summary of the more prominent contributors to human resource valuation research is given in Puett and Roman (1976), and a comprehensive bibliography of the human resource accounting literature is provided in *Accounting, Organizations and Society* (1976).

Despite this interest in HRA, considerable problems remain in measuring the cost and value of an organization's human resources, and in implementing a system of HRA. At the implementation stage individual cognitive limitations and behavioural responses become relevant. The measurement and implementation problems have received attention from accounting researchers.

Human Resource Measurement

The problems of human resource measurement have constituted a major obstacle to the development of an effective model of HRA. Lawler & Rhode (1976, pp. 154–168) demonstrate, in their model of organizational effectiveness, a number of different human system variables that impact effectiveness, and which could form the basis of human resource measurement. These include the characteristics of the individuals themselves, such as personality, ability, intelligence, skills; the characteristics of the organization which influence the effectiveness of the human system (for example the nature of jobs, and the organization's communication channels); and behavioural outcomes purporting to reflect the human system, such as turnover and absenteeism rates. There is also the problem of whether measurement systems should focus on the individual or on the value of the group of which the individual is a member (Lawler & Rhode, 1976, p. 159). A final general instance of the difficulties of human resource measurement is the ability of the individual to leave the organization at will; the organization has no assurances about the length of time that the individual will contribute his services.

Additional difficulties in human asset measurement arise when we consider the various valuation approaches which have developed over the last ten to fifteen years, most of which have focused on the individual. A good analysis of these approaches is given by Grove, Mock & Ehrenreich (1977), and their summary is reproduced as Table 4.2.

Those approaches, which have been based on input attribute measurement (measurement of the costs of hiring, training and maintaining individuals in the organization), may be criticized on the grounds that there is only a tenuous link between the cost of an individual, reflected in salary payments, and his value to the organization, reflected in relevant outputs.

Within input attribute measurement systems additional difficulties exist. Approaches based on historical cost do not allow for differences in the value

TABLE 4.2

Measurement System	Major References
Input:	
Acquisition cost	Brummet, Flamholtz & Pyle (1968) Caplan & Landekich (1974)
Replacement cost	Flamholtz (1973, 1975)
Discounted wage flows	Lev & Schwartz (1971) Friedman & Lev (1974)
Dollarized attitudes	Myers & Flowers (1974)
Output:	
Opportunity cost	Hekimian & Jones (1967)
Market value	Hermanson (1964)
Discounted earnings flows	Brummet, Flamholtz & Pyle (1968)
Economic value:	
Service states	Flamholtz (1971a) Flamholtz & Lundy (1975c)
Individual value model probabilities	Jaggi & Lau (1974) Sadan & Auerback (1974) Flamholtz (1972b; 1972c; 1974) Gambling (1974) Ogan (1976) Dermer & Siegel (1974)
Group value model	Likert (1967)

of individuals as their skills and abilities change over time; and discounted future wage flow methods suffer from the forecasting and discount rate estimation problems which are present in all discounted cash flow analysis (Grove, Mock & Ehrenreich, 1977, p. 224).

Replacement cost methods overcome the additivity and relevance constraints of historical cost systems, and although they are still input measurement systems, some evidence exists to suggest that the input measures developed in replacement cost systems, particularly that of Flamholtz (1973), are valid surrogates for relevant human value output characteristics (Carper & Posey, 1976; Flamholtz, 1975).

Grove, Mock & Ehrenreich also summarize several approaches to human resource valuation based on human value output characteristics. These include opportunity cost and market value systems which may be criticized because they rely on tenuous, unexamined links to human value, and models which attempt to identify and measure the determinants of human value. One such approach is the model proposed by Flamholtz (1972) which is reprinted in this section of the book. This model seeks to specify the elements that constitute the expected value of the individual to the organization. Although Flamholtz's model did not, at the time, attempt to quantify these elements, it has received some empirical support (Grove, Mock & Ehrenreich, 1977, pp. 228–9) and provides a useful framework for continued research.

Implementation of Human Resource Accounting

Another obstacle to human resource systems application is the problem of implementation. Van Der Bergh & Fischer (1976) point out the difficulties of communicating human resource accounting concepts within a commercial organization, and of obtaining and developing the trust of organizational participants.

> It may, however, be that the real problem is the managers' perception of the likely effects of this (HRA) research. They may see it as the creation of a system which would lead to a change in their established authority and therefore to jeopardise their future. This is quite a natural reaction to a system which is still full of unknowns and in which various aspects directly concern particular management functions (Van Der Bergh & Fischer, 1976, p. 226).

Tomassini (1976), in an article which is reprinted in this section, is similarly concerned with the behavioural effects of HRA implementation. He identifies three categories of variables which may impact the extent to which a system of HRA is accepted and is effective. These categories include attributes of the information in the system, organizational attributes such as the task environment, the management control system, and organizational goals and rewards, and individual attributes which cover aspects such as the individual's cognitive information processing and overt behaviour. Tomassini develops a series of propositions which purport to explain how an HRA system is dependent upon these variables. Incorporating Flamholtz's "hierarchy of information measurement" concept, Tomassini provides a significant impetus to direct future research in an area of HRA that has seen little research attention. His "contingency" approach also reinforces the theme of this book, and demonstrates the critical dependence of the information and control system (in this case the HRA system) on internal organizational and individual characteristics.

Impact on Management Decision Making

Before introducing the readings in this section, we should re-emphasize our purpose in discussing HRA. Our objective in this book is to provide an analysis of information and control system (management accounting system) issues within the context of modern organizational and behavioural theory. To the extent that information on the organization's human resources is relevant to managers' resource allocation decisions, the management accounting system may be seen to include, as a subset, the human resource valuation system.

The evidence that such information is relevant to managers' decisions is not strong. Lawler & Rhode (1976, pp. 169–170) noted that none of the HRA research at that time produced any empirical support for improved managerial decision making.

> This means that a decision to put measures of individuals in Human Resource Accounting terms must be made on the basis of faith in the hope that it will improve decision making rather than on the basis of factual evidence (Lawler & Rhode, 1976, p. 170).

Flamholtz (1976) supported this in respect of monetary human resource values when, in a laboratory study, he was unable to establish a relationship between such values and managers' decisions. By contrast, Flamholtz suggested from the results of his study that non-monetary valuations of human resource assets may influence managers' decisions. If these results are corroborated, human resource accounting research may have to be directed towards non-monetary methods. The need to incorporate non-financial externalities in human asset valuation is also argued by Mirvis & Macy (1976) in their article which is reprinted in this section.

THE READINGS

The article by Ramanathan (1976) is a pioneering attempt to develop a theoretical foundation for social accounting. Starting from the empirical evidence that progress in the implementation and evaluation of firms' social activities has been spasmodic, Ramanathan contends that part of the cause of this situation is the lack of an adequate foundational and operational framework for the role of the firm in its broadening social environment. He proposes such a framework comprising three major objectives of social accounting: the identification and measurement of a firm's social contribution, the consistency of a firm's strategies and practices with shared social priorities, and the availability of relevant company information to social constituents.

Spicer (1978) reviews the problems faced by accountants in providing information on the social consequences of corporate activities. He considers two main problems in this area: identifying or specifying the components of corporate social performance, and measuring and reporting on such performance.

The remaining readings deal with the valuation of human resources within the organization with the objectives of promoting optimal decision making generally, and specifically in the area of manpower planning and control.

As a milestone in the development of a theory of HRA, Flamholtz (1972) proposes a model of the nature and determinants of an individual's value to an organization. The model is based on two main interacting variables: the individual's "conditional value" to the firm, and the probability that the individual will maintain membership in the firm. Analysis of these variables discloses that each has major behavioural and organizational dimensions.

In contrast with the considerable amount of research into the problem of human resource measurement, Tomassini's (1976) article is one of the few attempts to identify and analyze the behavioural problems which are associated with implementation of a system of HRA. Tomassini develops a "contingency framework", incorporating information, organizational and individual characteristics, and proposes hypotheses demonstrating the impact of these variables on HRA implementation.

The article by Mirvis & Macy (1976) is concerned with organizations' human resource development programs. They examine the ability of HRA to measure the costs and benefits of these programs, and relate HRA to other interdisciplinary measures of development programs.

DISCUSSION QUESTIONS

1. Factors related to social issues constitute part of an organization's general environment. Discuss how this has implications for the design of management accounting systems.
2. Examine the difficulties faced by the management accounting systems designer in providing information on the firm's social performance.
3. Approaches to the valuation of firms' human assets have been classified into those which rely on input attribute measurement and those which attempt to measure human resource output characteristics. Compare and contrast these two approaches to human resource valuation.
4. Some of the problems of human resource accounting systems appear to lie in the potential behavioural consequences of their implementation. Identify the problems and discuss ways in which they may be overcome.
5. Discuss some potential uses of human resource cost and value measures in the management planning and control processes.

Toward A Theory of Corporate Social Accounting

Kavasseri V. Ramanathan*

A contemporary problem of concern to all technology-rich industrialized societies is that of continuing to provide a high level of motivation for private enterprise while ensuring that its aggregate impact upon society is consistent with social goals and aspirations. This is an exceedingly complex problem for several reasons. Traditional performance criteria for private enterprise have emphasized results which may be in conflict with societal priorities. There are many divergent views as to the most desired social goals and aspirations. The qualitative dimensions of social goal formulation and evaluation add further to the complexity. Yet, the problem is of such significance that there is a pressing need to explore its many dimensions and find ways of formulating solutions.

The nature of the problem can be related further to performance as it is typically viewed from a management perspective. A corporate management's attention, decisions and actions are focused more on those components of the firm's performance which are included in the firm's formal measurement system. To the extent that a firm's social impacts are not subjected to formal measurement process, these aspects are not likely to enter into the firm's planning decisions or performance evaluation.

The traditional view of corporate performance is idealized in the quest to maximize profits. It also is widely acclaimed that a firm's only social responsibility in a free market system is to maximize its profits, for in so doing, it is presumed to maximize its contribution to society. Under this notion, the profits of a firm which operates within the society's legal framework would provide the all-inclusive criterion for evaluating its social performance. However, the economic depression phenomenon of arriving at full equilibrium with substantial unemployment; the relentless disparities in income and employment opportunities among different social groups; and the serious erosion in the quality of environment caused by productive activities have led to sharp criticisms of the use of profits as an all-inclusive criterion of corporate social performance.[1]

A comprehensive analysis of the social impact of private enterprise suffers, at the present time, from a general absence of reliable data on aggregate social costs and benefits of business and on how these are shared among various social groups. However, some progress has been reached in recent years toward gathering and reporting data on corporate social performance, both as a result of internal initiatives of progressive corporations and in response to external influences. Thus, Beresford's [1973] annual survey reports that 298 of the Fortune 500 industrial firms disclosed some type of so-

From *The Accounting Review*, Vol. 51, No. 3 (July 1976), pp. 516–528.

*Kavasseri V. Ramanathan is Associate Professor of Accounting at the University of Washington.

[1]The literature on this debate is voluminous. Sethi [1974] contains discussions on most of the pertinent issues.

cial performance data in their 1973 annual reports. The majority of these disclosures were in the environmental control category. Other broad categories used in the Beresford survey were minority employment, responsibility to employees, community activities and product improvement. Disclosure practices varied considerably as regard to scope, format, use of quantitative and financial measures and the significance of items disclosed. The trend appears to be toward greater disclosure. Apparently, this follows from firms' increasing concern with their social responsibility and their attempts to institute some form of social audit [Ackerman, 1973; Dierks and Bauer, 1973].

There have been several other attempts to gather data on corporate social performance from firms on an ad hoc or routine basis by private research groups such as the Council of Economic Priorities [American Accounting Association, 1975; pp. 57–63). Further, several statutory agencies, such as the Federal Trade Commission, Environmental Protection Agency, Occupational Safety and Hazards Agency and the Office of Equal Employment Opportunity, are requiring data from firms in specific aspects of social concern. Recently, the Securities and Exchange Commission has proposed increased disclosure of corporate environmental policy, plans and performance.

The challenges involved in accounting for corporate social performance has engaged the particular attention of the major accounting institutions in the United States. The Study Group on Objectives of Financial Statements [1973, pp. 53–55 and 66] proposed as an objective of financial statements the reporting on those activities of the firm which have major social impacts. An American Institute of Public Accountants' committee is studying the problems of developing measurement systems for corporate social accounting. The National Association of Accountants' Committee on Accounting for Corporate Social Performance published its report in the February 1974 issue of *Management Accounting*. Several American Accounting Association Committees have been concerned with the broad area of social accounting [1971, 1972, 1973, 1974, 1975, 1976]. The Association also has sponsored a major research study on social cost measurement problems.

Despite such widespread and growing concern and support for accounting for corporate social performance, progress has been slow and sporadic. "Apparently, no corporation has yet designed or implemented anything approaching a systematic information system for its socially relevant actions" [American Accounting Association, 1975, p. 64]. Historically, the theory and practice of accounting has evolved in four interrelated areas—a framework of objectives, valuation concepts, measurement methodology and reporting standards. There is no reason to believe that evolution in social accounting will not follow the same course. This paper will concentrate on developing a theoretical framework consisting of a proposed set of social accounting objectives and concepts in the belief that an acceptable framework of objectives is fundamental to the development of social accounting theory in the areas of valuation, measurement methods and reporting standards.

BASIC PREMISES

Although there is considerable debate about which corporate actions constitute socially responsible corporate behavior, there appears to be a general acceptance of two assumptions.

1. The solutions to many of the current social problems require the active and willing involvement of private business organizations; and
2. To the extent that measured corporate profits are an inadequate guide to policy, a

broader scheme of corporate performance measurement is necessary.

The absence of a broader scheme of corporate social performance measurement is partly due to the recency of the public's concern over corporate social impact. But in a large measure it also is due to the failure to arrive at an operational definition of the role of a corporation in its broader social context [Preston, 1975; Bell, 1971, Ch. 6]. The elements of such a definition and the philosophical justification for a broader scheme of corporate social performance measurement is to be found in the notion of a social contract whereby a firm agrees to perform certain socially desirable functions in return for certain rewards. This notion of a social contract, which is of fundamental importance to this paper, is explained well by Shocker and Sethi [1974, p. 67]:

> Any social institution—and business is no exception—operates in society via a social contract, expressed or implied, whereby its survival and growth are based on:
>
> (1) the delivery of some socially desirable ends to society in general, and
> (2) the distribution of economic, social, or political benefits to groups from which it derives its power.
>
> In a dynamic society, neither the sources of institutional power nor the needs for its services are permanent. Therefore, an institution must constantly meet the twin tests of legitimacy and relevance by demonstrating that society requires its services and that the groups benefiting from its rewards have society's approval.

Social Performance Criteria—the Macro Context

The development of a set of social performance criteria is essential for bringing the notion of social contract from the level of ideas to the realm of operationality and to provide answers to the following types of questions:

1. What are the performance dimensions implied by the social contract?
2. What is socially responsible performance?
3. How is it to be measured and evaluated in the aggregate social context?

The task of developing social performance criteria, particularly at the macro-level, is unlikely to be the exclusive province of any one group of specialists or of any one discipline. There is ample evidence to suggest that such criteria will result from the combined efforts of philosophers, historians, sociologists, psychologists, political scientists, measurement theorists and others. [See footnote 4].

Social Performance Criteria—the Micro Context

Once such macro-level dimensions and criteria for social performance measurement become generally available and accepted, the unique tasks of the accountant are (1) to develop corresponding micro-level criteria applicable to specific firms and (2) to design and operate internal accounting systems which will make the resulting corporate social performance measures routinely available. Several difficult issues must be resolved before these tasks can be completed. Chief among these are the choice of performance dimensions to be included in the corporate measurement system, the selection of measures and measurement procedures and the development of methods for independent verification of reported data. The firm-level measurement system developed ultimately must be such that reported social performance data would be useful not only for internal decision making, but also for external evaluation of the firm's performance within the framework of macro-level social performance criteria.

Definition of Social Accounting

The purpose of social accounting is to help evaluate how well a firm is fulfilling its social contract. It would accomplish this purpose by providing visibility to the impact of a firm's activity upon society. While the micro-level measurement system provides the information regarding the corporation's social performance, the macro-level performance criteria provide the evaluative framework. In light of this background, social accounting is:

> the process of selecting firm-level social performance variables, measures, and measurement procedures; systematically developing information useful for evaluating the firm's social performance; and communicating such information to concerned social groups, both within and outside the firm.

PROPOSED OBJECTIVES FOR SOCIAL ACCOUNTING

The notion of a social contract offers crucial assistance in objectives formulation by recognizing as two unique roles of a firm (1) the delivery of some socially useful goods and services and (2) the distribution of economic, social or political rewards to social groups from which the firm derives its power. The nature of these two roles warrants further examination.

As a deliverer of socially desirable goods, the firm is cast in the role of an agent of production. In this role, the ultimate test of a firm's success is whether its aggregate contribution to the society is more than its aggregate consumption of the society's resources. Under the traditional classical economics view, a firm's contribution and consumption are presumed to be completely valued in the market place—profits are presumed to be the all-inclusive measure of a firm's net contribution to society.

However, certain types of decisions of an individual firm may affect the actions of other firms or social groups or individuals in ways which are not reflected in the market process. For example, a major bank's decision to close down its branch in the ghetto area may prompt similar actions by other banks operating branches there and, thus, accentuate the economic and social decline of that neighborhood. The adversity caused to this social segment may not be reflected in the bank's net profits. Indeed, the bank's profits presumably will increase as a result of closing down the ghetto area branch. Many such instances are conceivable where the pursuit of private benefits may not result in the optimization of social benefits. Consideration of such external costs and benefits arising from an individual firm's action are necessary for the attainment of a socially optimal allocation of a society's resources. Whether such optimization is arrived through internalization of externalities or through direct government intervention, a common prerequisite to policy making within and outside the firm is information on, and separate consideration of, the externalities which give rise to social costs and benefits [Ronen, 1974].

Objective 1

An objective of corporate social accounting is to identify and measure the periodic net social contribution of an individual firm, which includes not only the costs and benefits internalized to the firm but also those arising from externalities affecting different social segments.

While the first role of a firm under the notion of social contract is that of an agent of production, its second unique role is that of an agent in the resource sharing and benefit distribution processes in society. The resource sharing and benefit policies (e.g., hiring, training, retention and promotion policies; plant location strategies; political philosophies; ethical norms) which a firm adopts have a direct impact upon how the aggregate benefits and sacrifices generated in the society are shared among individuals, communities, social segments and generations. The complexities of making tradeoff decisions among these competing groups are overwhelming, and the absence of theories which deal with interpersonal preferences and aggregate social utility functions are well recognized. Hence, in this second role, the the firm's decision process is concerned more with notions of fairness, equity and consistency with social goals than with considerations of optimality.

The social monitoring of individual firm performance in this second role is less direct and more complex than the market-mechanism-based social monitoring of its economic performance. Indeed, the successful attainment of social welfare goals and priorities depends, in a large measure, upon how well embedded they are in the strategies and performance of individual firms—one of the largest organized sectors in modern socities. This relationship between individual firm performance and social welfare is the basis for a second major objective for corporate social accounting.

Objective 2

An objective of corporate social accounting is to help determine whether an individual firm's strategies and practices which directly affect the relative resource and power status of individuals, communities, social segments and generations are consistent with widely shared social priorities on the one hand and individuals' legitimate aspirations on the other.

The foregoing two unique roles—a production agent and a distribution agent—of individual firms in modern society, together with the two corresponding objectives of corporate social accounting, indicate the basic directions, dimensions and challenges involved in measuring corporate social performance. Attainment of these two social accounting objectives is necessary for systematically evaluating how well a firm is fulfilling its social contract.

The two preceding objectives may be viewed as *measurement objectives* of social accounting. Implementing these measurement objectives would ensure that a data base relevant to appraising corporate social performance would be available. However, there remains the task of providing relevant information from this data base to the users of social accounting information. For internal reporting purposes, the firm's management presumably will develop specific reporting objectives consistent with the unique features of the firm's technology, the strategies the firm adopts for fulfilling its social contract and its internal management structure. Obviously, this is not a public policy issue.

However, from the external reporting standpoint, there is need for a public policy on corporate social reporting. The purpose of such a policy is to ensure that social reporting by individual firms would be adequate and relevant for aiding public accountability, evaluation, coordination and monitoring of corporate contributions toward social goals attainment. A further purpose of such a public policy would be to insure that external reporting required of individual firms is cost/benefit-effective from the aggregate social standpoint. In the absence of such a policy, different user groups—the different social constituents of firms—will have different degrees of access to corporate social performance data. Further, an overabundance of data on some aspects of social performance and a paucity of information on other relevant aspects could result. Still further, potentials for biased reporting also exist, e.g., as when a firm reports only favorable aspects of its social performance. Finally, there exists the problem of resolving, without adverse social consequences, conflicts of interest in information needs of the various social constituents. There is thus a compelling need for an explicitly stated *reporting objective* of social accounting:

Objective 3

An objective of corporate social accounting is to make available in an optimal manner, to all social constituents, relevant information on a firm's goals, policies, programs, performance and contributions to social goals. Relevant information is that which provides for public accountability and also facilitates public decision making regarding social choices and social resource allocation. Optimality implies a cost/benefit-effective reporting strategy which also optimally balances potential information conflicts among the various social constituents of a firm.

Of the three proposed social accounting objectives, two relate to the measurement process and the third to the reporting process. All three follow from the notion of a social contract under which the firm has both a productive role and a distributive role in society. While these social accounting objectives provide the basic theoretical framework, implementing these objectives would be facilitated by a set of social accounting concepts discussed in the following section.

PROPOSED CONCEPTS FOR SOCIAL ACCOUNTING

The central notion in the first measurement objective proposed is that of a firm's periodic net contribution to social goals. Traditional accounting income provides only a partial measure of this contribution because its computation is based only on an analysis of historical transactions in the market place. Many of the "transactions" between a firm and the society, e.g., positive and negative externalities, are not handled presently through the market place.

The earlier example of a bank branch withdrawing from a ghetto area provides one example of the nature of such nonmarket transactions between a firm and the society. In this case, the local community is deprived of easily accessible banking services and also perhaps of some employment opportunities. Further, the community would incur additional transportation costs due to more distant commuting for both banking facilities and jobs. Another adverse consequence might be the decline in the value of real estate upon withdrawal of prominent business units from a neighborhood. All of these results may be characterized as the consequences of a nonmarket transaction between the bank and the local community.

Nonmarket transactions also could lead to social benefits—e.g., when a bank decides to open a new branch in a ghetto. Furthermore, nonmarket transactions may involve shifting costs or benefits from one social segment to another. This may not affect the firm's contribution to society as a production agent, but could do so in its distributive role. Affirmative action programs by firms represent transactions whose main direct impact upon society is in the redistribution of income and growth opportunities among different social segments. Social accounting requires recognition of such nonmarket transactions in addition to the traditional market-based financial transactions. Thus, a fundamental concept in social accounting is that of a *social transaction.*

1. A *social transaction* represents a firm's utilization or delivery of a socioenvironmental resource which affects the absolute or relative interests of the firm's various social constituents and which is not processed through the market place.

The significance of recognizing social transactions lies in the fact that their net cumulative effect, along with traditionally determined financial net income, provides the proper measure of a firm's aggregate social impact. For the purpose of bridging the measurement gap between a firm's aggregate social impact and its financial net income, two more concepts are necessary:

2. *Social overheads (returns)* represent the sacrifice (benefit) to society from those resources consumed (added) by a firm as a result of its social transactions. In other words, social overheads is the measured value of a firm's negative externalities, and social returns is the measured value of its positive externalities.
3. *Social income* represents the periodic net social contribution of a firm. It is computed as the algebraic sum of the firm's traditionally measured net income, its aggregate social overheads and its aggregate social returns.

These two concepts are bound to receive considerable attention from both theoreticians and practitioners in social accounting because of the variety of alternative descriptions and measures applicable for these purposes. A proper evaluation of social overheads/returns would require, in the first instance, an identification of the different externalities and social segments affected by each social transaction. A complete enumeration of these would require an impractically elaborate input-output model. Considerable experimentation will be necessary before practical solutions are found in this area.

Secondly, each consequence needs to be "priced" using rates or prices or opportunity costs derived from an appropriate macro-level framework. The problem of developing rates and pricing social transactions of a firm is roughly analogous to, but incredibly more complex than, the problem of developing overhead rates and transfer prices in multidivision organizations [Ronen, 1974].

The problem of developing social overhead/return rates is a derivative of, and is coterminous with, the problem of developing an operational definition of social income. The definition proposed above is admittedly vague. As in financial accounting, one approach would be to accept a definition of social income based on a matching of identifiable social costs and identifiable social benefits. While such an approach might be a necessary first step, a more comprehensive and precise definition of social income should be the subject of further research by social scientists.

The next concept, although not yet formally introduced, was used in stating the reporting objective of social accounting. Also, the central notion in the second objective relates to the impact of a firm's activity upon different social groups, with reference for whom the firm is presumed to be a distributive agent. These are the groups with whom the firm has an expressed or implied social contract.

Traditional accounting does not provide formal recognition to these groups. Only the claims of financial equity-holders and the periodic changes in their equity in the firm are measured in conventional accounting. In order to implement the second objective of social accounting, it is necessary to recognize formally in the accounting system all concerned groups. Thus:

4. *Social constituents* are the different distinct social groups (implied in the second objective and expressed in the third objective of social accounting) with whom a firm is presumed to have a social contract.

Formal recognition of social constituents in the accounting system is facilitated through social equity accounts where:

5. *Social equity* is a measure of the aggregate changes in the claims which each social constituent is presumed to have in the firm.

Obviously, social equity claims may not be enforceable under the existing legal system. But measures of social equity would serve as a useful basis for social decision making and for evaluating corporate social performance.

Finally, as a firm's social transactions enhance social well being or consume social resources, formal recognition of these nonmarket events in the firm's accounting system is facilitated by means of a social assets account. A positive externality of the firm (e.g., a decrease in neighborhood crime) would increase the value of its social assets. A negative externality (e.g., pollution) would deplete the firm's social assets. Thus:

6. *Net social asset* of a firm is a measure of its aggregate nonmarket contribution to the society's well being less its nonmarket depletion of the society's resources during the life of the firm.

The net social asset of a firm obviously is not recognizable under the current legal system and does not represent legal title to any future benefits to the firm. However, measures of net social assets would serve as a useful basis for social decision making and for evaluating corporate social performance.

METHODOLOGICAL IMPLICATIONS

Considerable experimentation will be necessary before the objectives and concepts proposed can be translated into a methodology of social accounting. The basic approach implied by the proposed concepts is described below, however, and major problems of implementation are discussed in the next section.

A fundamental step in social accounting would be to identify a firm's social transactions. All decisions and activities of a firm, whether or not they involve a market exchange, would be examined to identify the associated externalities. Such externalities then would be formulated as social transactions.

The process of formulating a social transaction involves identifying three elements. The first element is the *social constituent(s)* affected by the externality being considered.[2] Examples of social constituents are consumer groups, employees, minorities, the local community, investors groups, the general public, groups representing environmental aspects, youth groups and senior citizen groups.

The second element in formulating a social transaction is the specific nature of the *impact* of a firm's action upon the social constituent. In general, such impacts might be either technology-derived or management policy-derived. Thus, product safety and improved service efficiency are illustrative of technology-derived impacts upon consumers. Truth in advertising and sensitivity to customer service needs are illustrative of policy-related variables impacting upon consumers. Other examples of social transactions relevant to various social constituents are pollution-caused damage to health and environment, quality of human resource management, degree of commitment to affirmative action and concern for quality of life and welfare of the local community.

The final, and perhaps most difficult, element is the determination of the relevant social overhead/return *rates* to be used for pricing each social transaction. Since social transactions are not subject to market tests, no automatic process reveals the rates relevant for pricing such transactions. Instead, the rates would have to be developed within a macro social framework. In principle, this issue would be similar to the problem of developing cost and credit transfer rates in integrated multiplant operations. However, the practical problems would pose a serious challenge to any group of experts working on the problem. An interim solution might be to develop social overhead/return rates at specific industry levels which could be used by individual firms in that industry.

[2]It is possible that more than one social constituent might be affected by one externality, thus giving rise to multiple social transactions.

The proposed methodology would require each firm to undertake an audit of its externalities in order to develop a reasonably complete set of social transactions reflecting the firm's ongoing impact upon society which are not subject to the market process. The methodology also requires the valuation of each social transaction using social overhead/return rates. The formal accounting for social transactions then would require determination of a social asset effect on the one hand and social income and social equity effects on the other. Certain transactions may involve an exact tradeoff between one type of social benefit (or cost) and another—both affecting the same social constituent. The accounting for such transactions might not involve a social equity effect. On the other hand, certain other social transactions might involve shifting benefits (or costs) from one social constituent to another, e.g., affirmative action. Accounting for this type of transaction might not involve any social income effect.[3]

To illustrate the approach further, consider the case of a bank. Based on the nature of a bank's function and its operating characteristics, the following social constituents and transactions are plausible.

Illustrative Social Constituents	Illustrative Social Transactions
1. Clients	1. Quality of services which affect thriftiness, savings habits, etc., of clients
	2. Client satisfaction with services
2. Employees	1. Job satisfaction
	2. Opportunities for personal development and professional growth
3. Local community	1. Effect on neighborhood economic development
	2. Effect on education, training, crime prevention, etc., in the neighborhood
	3. Effect on commuter traffic, congestion, pollution, etc.
4. Minority groups	1. Minority hiring, training and utilization
	2. Financial services designed especially to meet minority needs

[3]This may not be true if affirmative action programs lead not only to reduced disparities in income and opportunities among social segments, but also to other secondary benefits like greater political stability, fewer crimes, etc.

Clients. The financial earnings of the bank usually are a major indicator of a bank's contribution to its clientele. However, the bank's impact upon them may go beyond that. Through aggressive campaign and management policies, the bank may influence its clientele to achieve greater thrift and more responsible personal fiscal management. Part of the resulting benefits may accrue to the bank in terms of greater client loyalty and business, but the aggregate benefit to the client group may exceed that realized by the bank.

Employees. Payroll costs and employee productivity may be reflected by traditional accounting. However, if the job situation leads to personal or professional enrichment, for instance, this positive benefit should be recognized through a social transaction.

Local Community. Traditional accounting recognizes only local taxes, utility payments and other such market transaction effects on the community. But the bank's impact upon the community may include greater stability of, and fillip to, the local economy and employment potential. These, in turn, could help lessen crime, enhance educational and training opportunities and, generally, improve the quality of life. On the other hand, the bank's presence might also contribute to traffic problems, congestion and pollution. In all these cases, of course, there is a problem of identifying how much of each effect is attributable to the bank under study.

Minority Groups. These may be employees, clients or other social segments. Efforts to reduce disparities in income and employment opportunities are examples of an employee-related social transaction. Client-related social transactions are illustrated by special programs to promote minority enterprises and minority capital formation. In all such cases, those evaluating the social transactions would attempt to recognize the social costs and benefits which are not reflected in the bank's market transactions and, hence, are not recognized by traditional accounting.

PROBLEMS OF IMPLEMENTATION

The objectives, concepts and methodology proposed here hopefully provide a tentative framework for developing pilot empirical applications of corporate social accounting. However several complex problems at the macro and micro levels must be resolved before a comprehensive and generally acceptable approach to social accounting can be developed. These include, at the macro level, the development of generally accepted social goals and social indicators to provide the normative framework within which firm-level performance dimensions and measurement criteria must be developed.[4] It is not the accountant's task to prescribe social goals, programs, or structure, just as it is not his or her task to prescribe a firm's goals, policies or management structure. The accounting theorist would necessarily look to sociologists, political scientists, economists and philosophers, among others, to interpret what is socially desirable and to formulate an operational set of goals—just as he or she relies on economists, behavioral scientists and others to interpret and operationalize a firm's goals and decision/performance system. It is essential that the accountant be familiar with the logic and content of the operationalized social goal set, as he or she is to be guided by it in designing appropriate firm-level social accounting systems. Indeed, he or she might be expected to contribute to the macro-level social goal operationalization process by commenting upon the relative merits and problems of measurement implied by alternative operationalization approaches.

The problem of developing relevant social performance measures is particularly challenging at the micro level. On the one hand, they must follow logically from the firm's strategies and technological realities. At the same time, they must be technically congruent with the macrolevel social indicators such that firm-level performance scored as positive using these measures also would imply positive contribution toward social goals. One solution might be to develop a social input/output model in which the coefficients capture all the interrelationships between a given set of firm-level social performance criteria and the macro-level social goal dimensions.[5] However, considerable research will be necessary before data for such models become available.

Another major micro-level problem relates to social overhead/return rates. This is a fertile field for research aimed at better understanding the economics of externalities and the

[4]Milestones in the "social goals" literature include *Goals for Americans* [The American Assembly, 1960]; *Agenda for the Nation* [Gordon, 1968]; *Toward Balanced Growth: Quantity with Quality* [National Goals Research Staff, 1970); and *Setting National Priorities* [Schultze, et al.]. Milestones in the "social indicators" literature include *Indicators of Social Change* [Sheldon and Moore, 1968]; *Toward a Social Report* [U.S. Dept. of H.E.W., 1969] which is the first attempt to implement the social indicators concepts; and *Social Indicators 1973* [Office of Management and Budget] which provides a substantial volume of relevant social and behavioral information.

[5]Knowledge of this type is assumed in the input/output model presented by Charnes, Colantoni, Cooper and Kortanek [1972].

behavioral impact of alternative rates upon firm managements and social constituents. Empirical research testing the feasibility and usefulness of alternative approaches to developing rates in selected performance dimensions would be of immediate benefit to the refinement of social accounting methodology.

CONCLUDING COMMENTS

The proposals in this paper are based on the premise that accounting for a firm's social performance requires a broader definition of a firm's role in society than is reflected in the legal entity notion underlying current accounting practices. Accordingly, the notion of a social contract was introduced which led to the three objectives and five concepts of social accounting proposed earlier. Table 1 summarizes these objectives and concepts. They provide a general framework within which several refinements are possible. More important, they suggest useful directions for further research into the various aspects of social accounting, some of which have been noted earlier. In particular, the concepts of social constituents and social transactions require further debate and empirical testing, and methods appropriate for determining social overheads/returns need to be developed. Alternative versions of the concept of social income are bound to emerge with corresponding implications for measuring social overheads/returns and social equity. In the absence of supporting legal sanctions, the notion of social equity and the determination of its shares attributable to various social constituents will have to be resolved through socio-political reasoning. Choices of measures and measurement procedures will have to be resolved based on which alternatives best help meet social accounting objectives. The usefulness and problems of integrating financial accounting and social accounting in one combined system need to be explored. Research into questions of materiality, verifiability and bias will receive fresh impetus as corporate accounting systems are broadened to include social performance data. This paper will have served its purpose if it helps to organize the emerging debate on such issues within a logical framework of objectives and concepts.

REFERENCES

Ackerman, R., "How Companies Respond to Social Demands," *Harvard Business Review* (July–August 1973), pp. 88–98.

American Accounting Association, Committee on Nonfinancial Measures of Effectiveness, "Report of the Committee on Nonfinancial Measures of Effectiveness," THE ACCOUNTING REVIEW, Supplement to Vol. XLVI (1971), pp. 164–211.

———, Committee on Measures of Effectiveness for Social Programs, "Report of the Committee on Measures of Effectiveness for Social Programs," THE ACCOUNTING REVIEW, Supplement to Vol. XLVII (1972), pp. 336–396.

———, Committee on Environment Effects of Organizational Behavior, "Report of Committee on Environmental Effects of Organizational Behavior," THE ACCOUNTING REVIEW, Supplement to Vol. XLVIII (1973), pp. 73–119.

———, Committee on Measurement of Social Costs, "Report of the Committee on Measurement of Social Costs," THE ACCOUNTING REVIEW, Supplement to Vol. XLIX (1974), pp. 98–113.

———, Committee on Social Costs, "Report of the Committee on Social Costs," THE ACCOUNTING REVIEW, Supplement to Vol. XLX (1975), pp. 50–89.

———, Committee on Accounting for Social Performance, "Report of the Committee on Accounting for Social Performance," THE ACCOUNTING REVIEW, Supplement to Vol. LI (1976).

Bauer, R. A. and D. H. Fenn, Jr., *The Corporate Social Audit* (Russell Sage Foundation, 1972).

TABLE 1. Proposed Objectives and Concepts for Social Accounting

Objective 1

An objective of corporate social accounting is to identify and measure the periodic net social contribution of an individual firm, which includes not only the costs and benefits internalized to the firm, but also those arising from externalities affecting different social segments.

Objective 2

An objective of corporate social accounting is to help determine whether an individual firm's strategies and practices which directly affect the relative resource and power status of individuals, communities, social segments and generations are consistent with widely shared social priorities, on the one hand, and individuals' legitimate aspirations, on the other.

Objective 3

An objective of corporate social accounting is to make available in an optimal manner, to all social constituents, relevant information on a firm's goals, policies, programs, performance and contributions to social goals. Relevant information is that which provides for public accountability and also facilitates public decision making regarding social choices and social resource allocation. Optimality implies a cost/benefit-effective reporting strategy which also optimally balances potential information conflicts among the various social constituents of a firm.

Concept 1

A *social transaction* represents a firm's utilization or delivery of a socioenvironmental resource which affects the absolute or relative interests of the firm's various social constituents and which is not processed through the market place.

Concept 2

Social overheads (returns) represent the sacrifice (benefit) to society from those resources consumed (added) by a firm as a result of its social transactions. In other words, social overheads is the measured value of a firm's negative externalities, and social returns is the measured value of its positive externalities.

Concept 3

Social income represents the periodic net social contribution of a firm. It is computed as the algebraic sum of the firm's traditionally measured net income, its aggregate social overheads and its aggregate social returns.

Concept 4

Social constituents are the different distinct social groups (implied in the second objective and expressed in the third objective of social accounting) with whom a firm is presumed to have a social contract.

Concept 5

Social equity is a measure of the aggregate changes in the claims which each social constituent is presumed to have in the firm.

Concept 6

Net social asset of a firm is a measure of its aggregate nonmarket contribution to the society's well being less its nonmarket depletion of the society's resources during the life of the firm.

Bell, D., *The Coming of Post-Industrial Society* (Basic Books, 1971).

Beresford, D., *Compilation of Social Measurement Disclosures in Fortune 500 Annual Reports—1973* (Ernst & Ernst, 1973).

Charnes, A., C. Colantoni, W. W. Cooper, and K. O. Kortanek, "Economic, Social and Enterprise Accounting and Mathematical Models," THE ACCOUNTING REVIEW (January 1972), pp. 85–108.

Dierkes, M. and R. A. Bauer, eds. *Corporate Social Accounting* (Prager Publishers, 1973).

Gordon, K., ed., *Agenda for the Nation* (The Brookings Institution, 1968).

National Goals Research Staff, *Toward Balanced Growth: Quantity with Quality* (U.S. Government Printing Office, 1970).

Office of Management and Budget, Executive Office of the President, *Social Indicators 1973* (U.S. Department of Commerce, Social and Economic Statistics Administration).

Preston, L. E., "Corporation and Society: The Search for a Paradigm," *Journal of Economic Literature* (July 1975), pp. 434–453.

Report of the Study Group on *Objectives of Financial Statements* (American Institute of Certified Public Accountants, October 1973).

Ronen, J., "Accounting for Social Costs and Benefits," in J. J. Cramer, Jr. and G. H. Sorter, eds., *Objectives of Financial Statements* (American Institute of Certified Public Accountants, May 1974), pp. 317–340.

Schultze, C. L., et al., *Setting National Priorities* (The Brookings Institution, annually issued.)

Sethi, S. P., ed., *The Unstable Ground: Corporate Social Policy in a Dynamic Society* (Melville Publishing Company, 1974).

Sheldon, E. and W. E. Moore, eds. *Indicators of Social Change: Concepts and Measurements* (Russell Sage Foundation, 1968).

Shocker, A. D., and S. P. Sethi, "An Approach to Incorporating Social Preferences in Developing Corporate Action Strategies," in S. P. Sethi, ed., *The Unstable Ground: Corporate Social Policy in a Dynamic Society* (Melville Publishing Company, 1974), pp. 67–80.

The American Assembly, *Goals for Americans,* The Report of the President's Commission on National Goals (Prentice-Hall, 1960).

U.S. Department of Health, Education and Welfare, *Toward a Social Report* (U.S. Government Printing Office, 1969).

Accounting for Corporate Social Performance: Some Problems and Issues

Barry H. Spicer
University of Oregon

Measures used to assess effects of corporate social activities should be expanded and new ones developed.

Several factors account for the developing interest of the accounting profession in social—as distinct from economic—measurement of corporate performance. Perhaps the most important of these has been the growing awareness of the far reaching social change taking place in society. Concern over the impact of this change on social well being and the quality of life has resulted in an ongoing debate over the past, current, and future roles of the primary institutions in promoting social change. This debate has led to demands for social information that would help to describe and monitor the social changes taking place and which, hopefully, would also provide a basis for the development and application of better methods of evaluating and controlling social change. As Liu[1] puts it:

> People have come to realize that Quality of Life is not necessarily directly related to material wealth, nor is their positive association totally considered desirable. The generally accepted economic health indicator, Gross National Product (GNP), which has served as a means of establishing goals and measuring achievement of the goals at the policy-making level, has already been questioned in connection with its definition and measurement. Growing attention to the social, economic, political and environmental health of the nation has led to the quest for indicators which will more adequately reflect the overall health of the nation and its citizens' well being.

Similarly, Seashore[2] notes that:

> Social commentary in many countries of late has included the notion that the continuous monitoring of the quality of life in a society must be enlarged from the familiar base of economic system surveillance to include other important aspects of the social system and individual lives of its members.

Current proposals in the accounting literature to measure and report on the social performance of large corporations may be viewed as an outgrowth of the above concerns.

From *Journal of Contemporary Business,* Vol. 7, No. 1 (Winter 1978), pp. 151–170.

[1]Ben-Chieh Liu, "Quality of Life Indicators: A Preliminary Investigation," *Social Indicators Research* (September, 1974) p. 187.

[2]Stanley E. Seashore, "Job Satisfaction as an Indicator of the Quality of Employment," *Social Indicators Research* (September, 1974) p. 135.

There is concomitant pressure on corporations to pay greater attention to issues of social concern. Some examples are environmental protection, discrimination in hiring and promotion, occupational health and safety, product safety, and consumer policies. These proposals raise a number of questions for the future development of accounting. They foreshadow both a fundamental change in disclosure philosophy and a significant expansion in subject matter.

Even though progress is currently being made in this developing field of social accounting,[3] major problems remain. The purpose of this paper is to comment on a number of these problems and to offer some suggestions as to how they might be handled. These problems include:

1. *A problem of identification or specification;* how are the effects of corporate activities that are to be considered component parts of a corporation's social performance to be identified or specified?
2. *A measurement problem;* how are the effects of corporate activities considered part of social performance to be measured?
3. *An accountability problem;* to whom should the corporation have a responsibility to report measures of its social performance?

These problems are interrelated. The severity of the measurement problems faced will depend on which effects of corporate activities are considered. On the other hand, difficulties encountered in measurement will tend to severely limit the final output of any corporate social accounting model. Most of the comments made here are directed at the problems of identification and measurement, putting aside for the moment the accountability question. However, all three problems pose theoretical and practical difficulties. As Corson and Steiner[4] write:

> There is substantial evidence that 'the public wants business to contribute a good deal more to achieving the goals of a good society' and that individuals and groups (for example, minorities, consumers, investors) alike want evidence with which to measure the contribution of business—positive or negative—to the well-being of society.
>
> There agreement ends. There is no consensus on what is meant by the social actions of business, what social responsibility it will be expected to bear, how its performance in discharging them is to be made or to whom the findings will be reported.

The accountability question will not be addressed in this paper. Whether corporate accountability should run beyond accountability to investors to also include an accountability to consumers, employees, suppliers, local communities and the public at large is an involved question. It requires a careful consideration of (1) the interests and rights, both legal and otherwise, of investors and other constituencies in those activities of the corporation that affect its

[3]While there is still some controversy over whether this is an appropriate subject for accountants to address, several serious attempts have been made towards developing a normative theory of accounting for corporate social performance (Churchill, 1974: Estes, 1975; Ramanathan, 1976), and the form and content of corporate disclosures has been (1) the subject of recent public hearings and pronouncements by the SEC (see SEC Releases 5386, April 1973; 5627, October 15, 1975; and 5704, May 6, 1976); the topic of committee deliberations and reports by the three major accounting associations in the U.S.A. (American Accounting Association 1973, 1974, 1975, 1976; National Association of Accountants, 1974; American Institute of Certified Public Accountants, 1972, 1977); and (3) the subject of numerous articles, monographs and books (a computerized search of the Accountant's Index for the last three years alone turned up 396 references with the words "social responsibility" in their titles). For summaries of the current state of the art in social accounting see Jensen (1976), Estes (1976) or Epstein, Flamholtz and McDough (1976).

[4]J.J. Corson and G.A. Steiner, *Measuring Business's Social Performance: The Corporate Social Audit* (Committee for Economic Development, 1974) p. 21.

social performance, and (2) the relevance of information regarding these activities to investors and other constituencies. On this general issue of accountability it is simply noted that the American Institute of Certified Public Accountants' Study Group on the Objectives of Financial Statements concluded in 1973 that:

> Whoever has a responsibility to others for his actions and their consequences is accountable for them. That responsibility may derive from law, contract, organization policy or moral obligation.
>
> The enterprise itself is accountable to those who furnish resources, that is, to its creditors and its owner. Society may impose broad and at times unspecified, but nevertheless implicit, responsibilities. And an enterprise may voluntarily assume certain social responsibilities. The enterprise is accountable for its actions, or inactions, in discharging a wide range of responsibilities.

The Study Group accepts the proposition that the corporation has a reporting responsibility with respect to its social performance. This is further evidenced by their inclusion among the recommended objectives of financial statements the following objective:

> An objective of financial statements is to report on those activities of the enterprise affecting society which can be determined and described or measured and which are important to the role of the enterprise in the social environment.

COMPONENTS OF CORPORATE SOCIAL PERFORMANCE

There are two distinct approaches to the specification or identification of the components of corporate social performance. The first is normative, relying on individual notions of socially responsible behavior to specify the components of corporate social performance. The second is positively oriented, relying on descriptive analysis to identify significant social effects of corporate activities.

Normative approaches to specification of the components of corporate social performance have resulted in disputes as to what should be included, because they rely on individual notions of what constitutes socially responsible behavior. This is not surprising given the considerable divergence of opinion expressed on this topic. Opinions range from the classical view that the sole responsibility of business in a free market economy is to make profits to more or less expansive conceptions of corporations bearing a number of social responsibilities.

Which of those views one holds is clearly relevant, as value judgments, based on these views, will determine the components of corporate social performance. This determination will strongly influence the type and comprehensiveness of conceptual corporate social accounting models and schemes that are developed.

The Classical View

If the purely classical view is accepted, the sole responsibility of business is to make profits for shareholders provided it stays within the rules of the game.[5] In this view, problems arising from side effects or externalities of business activities, such as the social benefits of hiring and training the disadvantaged or the social costs of environmental pollution, are considered to be the responsibility of government. Where private bargains between the affected parties are impractical because, for example, of the dispersed nature of the external effects, the classical view is that it is a governmental responsibility to intervene and assess appropriate

[5]Milton Friedman, *Capitalism and Freedom* (University of Chicago Press, 1962) p. 133.

costs and benefits to the affected parties. Similarly, the attainment of social goals other than economic efficiency, growth and technological progress is considered to be the responsibility of government and not of individual business firms.

In the classical view direct corporate action on social issues is considered to violate management's responsibility to shareholders and results in an underspecialization of business management.[6]

In the classical view the criteria for judging performance of a business firm are strictly economic. It follows that the set of components of corporate social performance is empty. Hence, no social measurement problems arise nor is there a question of accountability for corporate social performance.

The Managerial View

In the managerial view of corporate social responsibility, the large corporation is regarded as having responsibilities to a number of constituencies—including, but not limited to shareholders—who are affected by corporate activities. Large corporations are viewed as permanent and prominent institutions having lives and purposes of their own. They are run by professional managers who consider themselves trustees with responsibilities to employees, customers, suppliers and other parties having rights in the organization that are not merely contractual claims.[7]

In the managerial view, managers are regarded as having sufficient discretionary control of corporate resources due to market power and dispersed shareholding[8] to introduce social responsibility objectives into corporate operations.[9] It also recognizes that there are limits on the extent to which managers can redirect corporate resources and energies for this purpose. These limits take the form of constraints built into the market system which act to protect shareholders against excessive diversions of corporate resources or energies to unprofitable—or marginally profitable—social responsibility objectives. They include managers' fears of stockholder dissatisfaction, competition for their positions from more profit-oriented managers, and adverse effects on their future earning.[10] At the same time managers will be constrained from completely neglecting

[6]Richard A. Posner, *Economic Analysis of Law* (Little, Brown and Company, 1972) pp. 187–188.

[7]James W. McKie, "The Issues" in *Social Responsibility and the Business Predicament,* edited by James W. McKie (The Brookings Institution, 1974), p.30.

[8]Market power refers to the ability of a firm to behave persistently in a manner different from the behavior a competitive market would force on a firm having similar cost and demand conditions (Kaysen and Turner, 1959, p. 75). Shepherd (1970, p. 246) indicates that at least 35 to 45 percent of market activity in the U.S.A. is conducted by firms with substantial market power. A firm with market power is insulated to a greater or lesser degree from the compulsions of the market and, therefore, has considerable discretion in choosing among alternative business policies. The effect of widely dispersed ownership has been to reduce managers' dependence on owners, making it possible for managers to pursue their own goals (within limits) by directing the firm away from the profit maximizing position assumed to represent the objective of shareholders.

[9]Will managers be motivated to introduce social responsibility objectives into business operations if they have the necessary discretion? McKie (1974, pp. 24–25) conjectures that one motive managers would have for voluntarily introducing social goals arises from psychological strains on managers. Following Sutton et al. (1965, p. 354) McKie notes that these strains arise from the fact that while self-interested profit-seeking is tolerated in law and approved in social mores, self-interest is considered to be an unworthy goal of action which conflicts with ethical norms to which society attaches great importance. Therefore, it may be expected that managers may exercise their discretion (in part) to have the corporation pursue social objectives which are not entirely motivated by profitability considerations. Moore (1974, p.336) provides a more cynical view of manager motivation for introducing social goals when he argues that external pressures for corporate social responsibility provide managers with the opportunity to actually increase their discretionary power by playing one claimant off against the other. Moore writes that "Casual perusal of statements of corporate executives is consistent with this thesis. It should not be surprising if managers welcome this trend since it provides opportunities for them as well."

[10]See Furubotn and Pejovich (1974) for an excellent discussion of these constraints.

social issues because of pressures from their constituencies and influential power blocks such as labor unions, consumers and environmentalists. There is also the threat of government intervention.

In contrast to the classical view, acceptance of the managerial view would result in an expansion of the elements of the set of components of corporate social performance. In addition to economic efficiency and profitability, other socially oriented criteria might be introduced to evaluate corporate social performance. Unfortunately, the managerial view does not explicitly define what these responsibilities should be; nor does it seem possible to do so. Chamberlein[11] argues that there can be no universal creed or responsibility doctrine for business managers. Like public office holders it depends on the point of view of their multiple constituencies and circumstances of the times. Chamberlein writes:

> . . . the social responsibility of a corporate executive runs to the numerous groups which he affects and with whom he interacts, some of which (the stockholders perhaps) are more important than others, but all of which must be recognized. Not all corporations have identical constituencies or face similar circumstances. Their social responsibilities cannot be subsumed under some common catalog of desirable behavior but measured only in terms of satisfactory political performance.

The Activist View

The activist view of corporate social responsibility is much broader in conception than either the classical or managerial views. In the activist view the large corporation is considered to be the repository of massive economic and political power with concomitantly broad social responsibilities. The large corporation is believed to have a moral obligation to directly promote social objectives and to aid in the solution of society's ills, such as hard-core unemployment, environmental deterioration, inadequate educational systems, substandard housing and outmoded transportation systems. This view should be distinguished from those of more radical critics who believe that satisfactory performance cannot be expected from private enterprise and that a wide-ranging restructuring of society is required to achieve social goals. In contrast, the activist sees the solution to current social ill within the context of society as presently structured. If only large corporations would recognize their social responsibilities and use their power and energies for the solution of the ills of society, the activists believe, social revolution and the dramatic restructurings of society promoted by more radical critics may be avoided.

The activists' list of demands for corporate social responsibility is lengthy. For example, Corson and Steiner[12] identify 58 activities in ten fields. Their list includes: economic growth and efficiency, education, employment and training, civil rights and equal opportunity, urban renewal and development, pollution abatement, conservation and recreation, culture and the arts, medical, and government. Extensive as this list is, Corson and Steiner note that it still does not encompass the complete range of activities for which some would hold the corporation accountable. Recent hearings held by the Securities and Exchange Commission on corporate disclosures of social information resulted in submission of over 100 matters for disclosure consideration by "ethical investors" and other interested parties.[13]

If an activist view is adopted, the set of elements specified as components of corporate social performance would be greatly expanded,

[11]Neil W. Chamberlein, *The Limits of Corporate Responsibility* (Basic Books, Inc., 1973), p. 204.

[12]Corson and Steiner, pp.27–29.

[13]Securities and Exchange Commission *Release No. 5627* (Oct. 14, 1975).

as would criteria needed to measure and evaluate that performance. The problem lies in reaching reasonable agreement about what to include or exclude and on what grounds.

To conclude, the prospect for reaching agreement on corporate social responsibility seems remote given the considerable divergence of opinion on this topic. Even with respect to the three major viewpoints reviewed it was noted (at least with respect to the latter two) that there was a problem of reaching agreement among the proponents of a particular view. Under such conditions, it is unlikely that normative approaches to specification will result in the development of useful corporate social accounting models and schemas. It seems more likely that the endless dialogue and disagreement over corporate social responsibility will continue and will frustrate attempts to make progress in the measurement of corporate social performance. Many of the efforts that have been made to date, for example, by Linowes and Estes, have been based on normative approaches.

A Positive Approach

Pressure for improved social measurement and monitoring systems is due to widespread concern with the effects of social change on the state of well being or the Quality of Life. Since large corporations are such prominent institutions in society and their activities may significantly affect the Quality of Life of large segments of the population, they may be viewed as a driving force of social changes.[14]

A positive approach to the specification of the components of corporate social performance would require a specific, case by case analysis to identify those aspects of social well being or Quality of Life of subsegments that are affected by the corporation's activities. Instead of addressing the value-laden normative question, "What ought to be the social responsibilities of a corporation?" a positive approach to specification would simply attempt to identify the wider social consequences of corporate activities. Individual notions of corporate social responsibility would not be included. This is likely to be a difficult task. An attempt to identify all positive and negative impacts of corporate activities on the Quality of Life of all affected parties would be complicated, time consuming and costly. Each corporation's activities will simultaneously affect a multitude of Quality of Life or social issues. For this reason, attention should be concentrated initially on identifying the most significant social or Quality of Life effects of corporate activities.

To accomplish this, a methodical descriptive study and analysis of each corporation's activities and its environmental setting is necessary. In broad outline such a study would include:

1. *A general review of the major social or Quality of Life issues* currently facing society and business. The purpose of this review would be to develop a general background understanding of social issues and their issue-attention cycles. An understanding of how the issue-attention cycle operates provides insight into how long public attention is likely to remain focused upon a given social issue.[15]
2. *A more specific industry level study* aimed at identifying major social or Quality of Life issues currently confronting the industry of which the corporation is a member or likely to be confronting the industry in the future.

[14]Andrew Hacker *The Corporate Take-Over* (Doubleday, 1965) p.9.

[15]The term issue-attention cycle is attributable to Downes (1972, p. 38) who argues that "a systematic 'issue-attention cycle' seems strongly to influence public attitudes and behavior concerning most key domestic problems."

These issues are likely to vary in both kind and importance from industry to industry. For example, issues facing firms in the tobacco industry are likely to differ from those which face firms in the steel or pulp and paper industry.

3. *A detailed firm level study,* based partly on the succeeding parts of the study and aimed at identifying significant social or Quality of Life effect of corporate activities and the parties affected.

From the viewpoint of a social accountant concerned with problems of objectivity, this approach is a desirable one. Through descriptive empirical studies of this sort, controversial value judgments over the brands of corporate social responsibility can be avoided. However, some judgments on the part of the social accountant would still be needed to distinguish between significant and trivial effects of corporate activities a priori. What constitutes a significant effect may not be immediately obvious without measurement and the establishment of discriminating criteria. Because the identification of significant effects and their measurement are so closely intertwined, it may be appropriate to view identification and measurement as a cyclical process with successive rounds of identification and measurement, rather than as a two-stage process.

CLASSIFYING THE COMPONENTS OF SOCIAL PERFORMANCE

Whatever components of corporate social performance are specified through identification of significant social effects of corporate activities, it is desirable to classify them in a way that facilitates measurement and inter-firm comparisons. One classification scheme that may facilitate this has been suggested by Ackerman.[16] It is based on a consideration of whether or not corporate responses to major social issues directly affect the normal operating activities of the corporation. The rationale is that there is an important difference between corporate responses to social issues that involve mainline operating functions and those which are essentially nonoperating matters. As he puts it:

> Efforts to curtail pollution clearly entail expenditures in manufacturing facilities; hiring and advancing minorities involve alterations in the employee profile, and so forth. On the other hand, contributions to the arts or higher education or investments in small business in the ghetto do not ordinarily disturb the ongoing affairs of the corporation.

Using Ackerman's suggested classification scheme the structure of a report on a corporation's social responsiveness would be broken into two sections: (1) responsive activities directly affecting normal operations and (2) responsive activities having no significant effect on normal operations.

Depending on the purpose, more detailed subclassifications can be added to this basic structure. For the purpose of internal management of corporate responsiveness to major social issues Ackerman[17] draws a further distinction between socially responsive activities that are the responsibility of operating managers and those which are corporate level concerns. The former might include pollution control, employment practices, occupational health and safety, and product safety. Decisions to enter fields of social interest such as mass transit or low-cost housing or to withdraw from lines of business due to social pressure are generally made at the corporate level. Corporate policy with respect to such issues as pollution

---

[16]Robert W. Ackerman, *The Social Challenge to Business.* (Harvard University Press, 1975) p.13.

[17]Ibid., p. 12.

control, employment practices, etc., must ultimately be integrated into management practices at operating levels. This integration may pose an organizational challenge to the large firm requiring changes in organization structure and incentives to overcome resistance at operating levels. For example, Bendix Corp. under the management of W. Michael Blumenthal, now Secretary of the Treasury, is reported to have instituted hiring of minorities for its high-technology operations by trimming executives' bonuses if they failed to meet affirmative action goals.[18]

For external reporting, Ackerman's basic structure could be further refined using a classification scheme such as that suggested by the National Accounting Association's Committee on Accounting for Corporate Social Performance, 1974. The major categories suggested by the committee include: community involvement, human resources, physical resources and environment, and products and service. Community involvement would be subclassified under activities having no significant effect on normal operations, and others subclassified under activities directly affecting normal operations. However, if concern is with the significant social or Quality of Life effects of corporate activities, in addition to corporate responsiveness to social issues, a modified version of Ackerman's basic classification could be used. In this version a corporation's social report would be broken into two sections (1) social impacts due to normal operating activities and (2) social impacts due to non-operating activities. These basic classifications may then be subclassified further using the NAA Committee's classification scheme. Of course, the items actually included for a particular corporation will depend on the significant social or Quality of Life effects identified as resulting from its activities.

[18]"The Furor Over Reverse Discrimination," *Newsweek,* September 26, 1977, p. 55.

MEASURING SOCIAL PERFORMANCE

Having identified *a priori* areas of potentially significant social or Quality of Life impact of corporate activities and the parties affected, the next problem is measurement. In keeping with the descriptive analysis I have recommended for identification of significant effects, it will be assumed that the purpose of measurement is primarily descriptive rather than evaluative. It is aimed at describing, monitoring and understanding the wider social consequences of corporate activities, rather than evaluating how well the corporation is performing in the social dimension. Evaluation requires criteria about which there is great difficulty obtaining agreement. Those who wish to make evaluations, however, are not precluded from doing so. They can utilize the reported descriptive measures in conjunction with their own individual notions of what constitutes adequate social performance.

Common Units of Measure

One popular proposal in the literature (see, for example, Seidler, 1975; Estes, 1976; Abt, 1972;[19] Sater, 1972;[20] Brummett, 1973) is to measure all of the diverse social effects of corporate activities not presently captured in corporate accounts in terms of a single common unit. This can be accomplished either by translating nonmonetary measures into dollar terms or by the use of some type of weighing procedure. The rationale for this approach apparently lies in a desire to arrive at a single "bottom line" with respect to overall corporate performance. For example,

[19]Past annual reports (1971, 1972, 1973) of Abt Associates, Inc. attempt to measure in dollars the social assets, social liabilities, social benefits, and social cost of the entire business firm.

[20]Sater's proposal is described in Bauer and Fenn (1972, pp. 18–20).

Estes'[21] normatively based corporate social accounting model relies on cost/benefit measurement techniques to convert individual nonmonetary effects of corporate activities into dollar terms. He explains:

> A major advantage of the proposed model is that the socially responsible company would look better on the "bottom line" than its irresponsible competitor—a result exactly the opposite of that produced by the traditional financial income statement.

There are, however, many problems with the use of a common unit of measure in situations where social measurement is called for. Above all there is the danger of bias entering the measurement process through the introduction of value judgments of the measurer and the conscious or unconscious suppression of more relevant but non-commensurable measures. Hoos[22], Hatry[23] and Quade[24] among others have all commented on the dangers of using common units of measure to describe and analyze the effects of social programs publicly administered.[25] Their criticism is also applicable to attempts to combine all of the individual social effects of corporate activities using a single common unit of measure. The use of dollars or other weighing techniques incorporate the value judgments they involve of the measures rather than those measurers using the resulting information. Value judgments on such controversial issues as what weights should be assigned the individual effects of social programs or corporate activities accruing to different groups or affected parties may get buried in the measures and key value concerns may get completely ignored. To illustrate, Estes[26] has proposed using the change in present value of the future estimated earnings of affected minorities as a measure of the effect of discrimination in hiring (external discrimination) and in placement, advancement and training (internal discrimination). If the underlying concern is with an increase in national output, such a measure may be appropriate; however, if the underlying concern is with the enhancement of the Quality of Life of minorities, then other measures and considerations are called for as well. The argument is not that dollar measures of individual effects (or measures based on other weighing schemes) should not be used. The point is that these common unit measures should only be used to provide additional information, to be reported along with the unweighed, unconverted effects measured in whatever units are most meaningful. The following subsections discuss some other ways to make measurements of the wider social consequences of corporate activities.

Measures of Impact on Quality of Life

A *promising development* in the search for measures of social consequences of corporate activities is the recent work of social scientists on the meaning and measurement of the Quality

---

[21]Ralph W. Estes, "A Comprehensive Corporate Social Reporting Model," *Social Accounting: Theory, Issues and Cases,* edited by Lee J. Seidler and Lynn L. Seidler, Melville Publishing Company, 1975, p. 106.

[22]Ida R. Hoos, *Systems Analysis in Public Policy: A Critique* (University of California Press, 1972), pp. 75–76.

[23]Harry P. Hatry, "Criteria for Evaluation in Planning State and Local Programs," *Planning, Programming, Budgeting,* edited by Fremont J. Lyden and Ernest G. Miller (Markham Publishing Company, 1972,) pp. 199–200.

[24]E.S. Quade, *Analysis for Public Decisions* (American Elseviar Publishing Co., Inc., 1975) p. 100.

[25]Use of a common unit of measure has also been criticized at more macro levels. Gross (1966, p.167) argues that current national economic accounting with its emphasis on the monetary value of goods and services and lack of concern with nonmonetary values and social measures ". . . has promoted a 'new Philistinism'—an approach to life based on the principle of using monetary units as the common denominator of all that is important in human life." A similar criticism might be leveled at those who promote the use of monetary values as the exclusive measure of corporate social performance.

[26]Estes, p. 102.

of Life.[27] The possibility of drawing on this work and to use the Quality of Life indicators that have been developed to measure the social effects of corporate activities should be explored.

The Quality of Life literature recognizes two major dimensions of the unobservable Quality of Life: an objective dimension and a subjective dimension. Sheldon and Land[28], note that Quality of Life is generally thought of as being comprised of two dimensions. They are: (1) objective conditions of society, such as the levels and extent of pollution, and the availability of housing and natural resources, and some attributes of persons such as health, educational achievement and family stability and (2) subjective perceptions of life experiences such as frustrations, satisfactions, aspirations and perceptions. Thus, the Quality of Life is seen as a function not only of the objective characteristics of a person's situation but also his expectations and aspirations. As Rodgers and Converse[29] conclude: "the perceived quality of life is evidently the consequence of a complex set both of objective conditions faced by individuals and of personal characteristics of those individuals."

Monitoring the Quality of Life, therefore, is a difficult task requiring the development of sets of both objective and subjective indicators that have the ability to provide information about the unobservable. Bunge[30] describes an indicator as a token or symptom of some condition, "an observable trait of a thing (physical, biological, social or other) that is rightly or wrongly assumed to point to the value of some other trait, usually an unobservable one, of either the same or a different thing." A Quality of Life indicator is an indicator of the physical, psychological, social, or cultural well-being of the individual members of some human community. Bunge writes:[31]

> The quality of the air people breathe and the water they drink, the value and quantity of food they eat, the size and quality of their shelter, the satisfaction they derive from their family life and their jobs, the degree of their participation in the affairs of their community, indices of work and safety, the numbers of books read and theatrical performances attended—all these qualify as Quality of Life indicators.

More specifically, he recognizes the following kinds of Quality of Life indicators: (1) physical, e.g., water quality, access to natural resources; (2) biosocial, e.g., health and housing conditions; (3) psychological, e.g., marriage and job satisfaction; (4) technical, e.g., percentage of skilled workers, numbers of people per washing machine; (5) economic, e.g., income and wealth distribution; (6) social, e.g., welfare services and public safety; (7) political, e.g., participation in community decision making; and (8) cultural, e.g., opportunity for intellectual or artistic creation and continuing education.[32]

While work on the development of indicators of both objective conditions of society and subjective perceptions of life experiences is continuing, most indicators proposed have been of the objective kind. Apparently this is because so-called objective indicators tend to

---

[27]See, for example, Bauer (1966), Sheldon and Moore (1968), and Campbell and Converse (1972). For reviews of the work being done on the definition and measurement of the Quality of Life see Sheldon and Land (1972) and Sheldon and Parke (1975). Much of the contemporary work on the Quality of Life is published in the journal *Social Indicators Research.*

[28]Eleanor B. Sheldon and Kenneth C. Land, "Social Reporting for the 1970s: A Review and Programmatic Statement," *Policy Sciences* (July, 1972) p. 140.

[29]Willard L. Rogers and Phillip E. Converse, "Measures of the Perceived Overall Quality of Life," *Social Indicators Research* (September, 1975) p. 147.

[30]Mario Bunge, "What is a Quality of Life Indicator?" *Social Indicators Research* June, 1975) p. 66.

[31]Bunge (1975) also discusses validity and reliability requirements for indicators and offers a set of formal definitions.

[32]Bunge, p. 75.

be more readily available, and also because of a feeling subjective indicators are likely to be less reliable and valid than objective indicators. This latter conclusion is now being challenged by a number of social scientists including Rodgers and Converse[33] who argue that "both types of indicators are important inputs to a veridical perspective on the quality of life, and that neither type can be properly interpreted in the absence of the other." In the context of monitoring the quality of employment, objective measures would include time series measurement of such indicators as pay, hours of work, duration of vacations, occurrence of job injuries, rate of promotion and the like. Subjective measures, on the other hand, would include satisfaction with pay preference for more or fewer hours of work, need for a vacation, perception of hazard and expectation of promotion. Seashore[34] argues that both types of indicators are needed to monitor the quality of employment:

> They are distinctly different kinds of information and complimentary to one another, one cannot be substituted for the other, each illuminates the other. Each is particularly pertinent in its own way to the task of understanding the quality of employment; and each feeds a somewhat different system of social action towards the maintenance and improvement of the quality of employment. The 'hard' indicators appear to be more often useful in the technical design of public programs and associated legislation; the 'soft' indicators appear to be particularly useful in policy and goal formation, in setting priorities, and in evaluating the success of action programs.

Objective measures of environmental quality would include time series measurement of indicators of the natural and physical environment, physical environment of the dwelling, activity environments and characteristics of the community.[35] Subjective indicators would deal with the perceptions of persons of the various elements of the environment. Milbrath and Sahr[36] argue that high scores on objective measures of environmental conditions do not lead *(ipso facto)* to a high quality environment. "Quality, rather, lies in the eyes of the beholder." Like Seashore, Milbrath and Sahr argue that both types of indicators have their uses. Even though they believe that environmental quality is inherently subjective (if a person believes his water is clean then it is for him of high quality) they recognize that objective indicators of environmental conditions are extremely useful for "detective purposes"—for example, for the detection and measurement of pollutants that are not readily detectable by our normal senses, yet cause injury to persons or flora and fauna.

A final point is that the definition and measurement of well-being or the Quality of Life requires a comparative perspective. To be meaningful, indicators of objective conditions and subjective perceptions should be considered in relation to one or a number of reference points. These are in relation to earlier points, some standard or goal, to other population subgroups, or other geographical locations.

What are the implications of this work on the definition and measurement of corporate performance? Perhaps the most important contribution of this work will be to provide both a useful frame of reference for those interested in the measurement of corporate social performance. It is also a fertile source of ideas and new directions. Close attention should be given to the applicability of the objective and subjective indicators being developed for the measurement of corporate social performance.

[33]Rogers and Converse, p.127.
[34]Seashore, p. 151.

[35]Lester W. Milbrath and Robert C. Sahr, "Perceptions of Environmental Quality," *Social Indicators Research* (March, 1975), p. 397.
[36]Ibid, p. 399.

One interesting possibility is to draw on the work being done on definition and measurement of the quality of employment to describe and measure the effect of the activities of the large corporation on the quality of working life of its employees. Seashore presents an insightful look at the work being done by social scientists in this area.

However, while some Quality of Life indicators may be pressed into service to describe and measure effects of corporate activities, not all indicators will be applicable. To illustrate, many objective and subjective indicators of environmental quality (air, water and land)[37] have been developed.

However, because of the complexity of the causal chain running from the waste disposal activities of a corporation to the impact on the receiving environmental medium, it is usually not possible to attribute changes in indicators directly to the waste disposal activities of a particular corporation. The mixing of waste discharge from a firm's production processes with discharges from other sources produces synergistic and antagonistic effects.

In addition, the assimilative capacity of the receiving environmental medium will vary, depending on the stochastic nature of such things as air currents, stream flow, temperature and sunlight. This makes it virtually impossible to measure changes in the environmental quality due to the activities of a particular discharger.

Other Measures

While it will not always be possible to directly measure the effects of corporate activities on Quality of Life, it should still be possible to (1) describe significant corporate responses to social or Quality of Life issues, and (2) describe the immediately observable impacts of corporate activities.

Corporate actions and responses, immediately observable impacts of corporate activities, and indicators of the Quality of Life of affected parties are all related. For instance, a decision by an electric utility to install a stack scrubber to reduce its emissions of air pollutants (corporate response), will result in a future reduction in the utility's emissions of air pollutants (immediate impact). This may also result in an improvement in indicators of atmospheric quality, although the cause-effect relationship is likely to be obscure.

Corporate responses to Quality of Life issues can be split into two parts: general responses and specific responses. General responses would include such things as changes in policy or organizational structure aimed at institutionalizing and managing corporate responses. Specific responses would include goal setting in particular areas of concern and specific actions taken by a corporation to meet those goals, e.g., institution of a minority hiring and training program with clearly specified goal. Other examples could include making plans to install pollution control equipment or the redesign of a product for safety reasons. Descriptions of corporate responses will tend to be non-quantitative and confined to a simple narrative of actions taken or contemplated. In many cases it will be possible to indicate the dollar amount of resources committed to, or expended on, a particular response. Ackerman, however, has suggested a formal assessment of a corporation's general response to social issues. It is based on observations of over 25 companies by a research team at Harvard Business School, and supported by discussions with the representatives of several dozen other firms. Ackerman has developed a "Corporate Social Issues Profile" aimed at answering questions about how, and how well, corporate responses to social issues are being managed.

[37]Objective indicators of the quality of an environmental medium include physical, chemical and biological indicators of quality. Subjective indicators utilize individuals' subjective perceptions of the quality of environmental mediums.

The profile is specifically designed to provide information to top management for assessing and managing the response process. However, the descriptive information provided by such a profile may also prove useful for purposes of external reporting on the general organizational response of the corporation to social or Quality of Life issues.

In addition to describing corporate responses to social or Quality of Life issues, immediately observable impacts of corporate activities productive employment, the level of employment, pay rates and career may also be measured and described. For example, one effect of the production activities of many firms is to discharge pollutants into the environment. Measures of these emissions may be relevant for descriptive purposes, provided that they are in a form which can be related to the underlying parameters of interest, in this case indicators of environmental quality. That is, measures made of the quantity, concentration, type, location and timing of emissions of major pollutants can be related forward to indicators of environmental quality, as well as backwards to the corporate activities giving rise to the emissions. In this context, it is proposed that measures of immediately observable effects should meet the following criteria.

1. *The measures employed should be clearly relevant* to the social or Quality of Life issues thought to be significantly affected by corporate activities.
2. *As many measures as are necessary* to adequately describe the significant effect of corporate activities on affected parties should be employed. While parsimony in measurement is desirable, multiple measures of impact may be needed to avoid excluding or obscuring major impacts. Confining measures of the effect of a minority hiring and training program to numbers hired and trained, for example, would not adequately describe the effect of such a program on minorities. Additional information on numbers subsequently finding productive employment, the level of employment, pay rates and career opportunities are also relevant.
3. *Where possible, measurements should be* made in units meaningful to those population subgroups affected by particular corporate activities. Cooper and Ijiri[38] suggest the use of units or metrics which are natural to those groups having major interests.
4. *Each measure employed* should be capable of meaningful qualification. In certain cases, with proper controls, it may be possible to utilize rankings, rating, judgments or opinions.
5. *Each measure employed should be capable* of being employed consistently over time and should be capable of verification. How are measures of impact of corporate activities to be reported? Given the multiple measures involved, a scorecard presentation structured along the lines suggested in the earlier section on classification seems most appropriate. The advantages of such a presentation are commented on by Quade[39] in the related context of presenting the impact and consequences of social programs:

> A scorecard is not only an acceptable method of handling the criterion problem when no clearly dominant single measure can be agreed upon, but is also a way to protect against or counter the biases of the analyst which are possibly unconscious. The biases cannot be countered completely, of course, for the analyst still largely decides what impacts to present,

---

[38]W. W. Cooper and Yuji Ijiri, "From Accounting to Accountability: Some Steps to Corporate Social Reporting," in *Accounting in the 1980s—Some Issues: Proceedings of the Arthur Young Professors' Roundtable,* edited by Norton Bedford (The Council of Arthur Young Professors, 1977) p.106.

[39]Quade, p. 101.

and his is the point of view that classes them as favorable or unfavorable.

Regardless of the types of measures used, or the format used to present them, it is important that they be presented in a comparative framework. They may be presented (1) in relation to earlier points; (2) in relation to a reference group, e.g., companies in the same industry; or (3) in relation to some goal or standard set internally, or externally, through legal requirements or public pressures.

Summary

The purpose of this paper was to review a number of problems faced by academics and accounting practitioners in devising means of measuring and reporting on the social consequences of corporate activities. Two major problems were discussed in some detail: the problem of identifying or specifying the component of corporate social performance, and the related problem of measurement. Some suggestions were made as to how each of these problems might be addressed in specific instances: however, it is clear that much remains to be done. In particular, there is a real need to expand the range of measures being used to measure the social or Quality of Life effects of corporate activities, either by adapting existing measures from other fields or by developing new ones. There is also a need to explore the validity and reliability of each of these measures over a long enough period to establish their usefulness and practicality. As Morgenstern[40] has pointed out:

> It is through constant expansion of measurement where there was none, better measurement where it was poor, that we extend our knowledge. Where we have measurement we do not need intuition to determine the characteristics of what was measured. Our intuitive efforts can then be better concentrated on the areas that still remain inaccessible for measurement.

[40]Oskar Morgenstern, *On the Accuracy of Economic Observations* (Princeton University Press, 1963) p. 122.

REFERENCES

Abt, Clark, "Managing Money by Doing Good," *Innovation* (January, 1972).

American Accounting Association, "Report of the Committee on Environmental Effects of Organization Behavior," *The Accounting Review,* Supplement to Vol. XLVIIII, 1973.

———, "Report of the Committee on Measurement of Social Costs," *The Accounting Review,* Supplement to Vol. XLIX, 1974.

———, "Report of the Committee on Accounting for Corporate Social Performance," *The Accounting Review,* Supplement to Vol. XLXL, 1976.

———, "Report of the Committee on Social Costs," *The Accounting Review,* Supplement to Vol. XLX, 1975.

American Institute of Certified Public Accountants, Social Measurement (American Institute of Certified Public Accountants, Inc., 1972).

———, Study Group on the Objective of Financial Statements, *Objectives of Financial Statements,* (American Institute of Certified Public Accountants, 1973).

———, Committee on Social Measurement, *The Measurement of Corporate Social Performance* (American Institute of Certified Public Accountants, Inc., 1977).

Bauer, Raymond A., ed., *Social Indicators,* (M.I.T. Press, 1966).

———, and Fenn, Dan H., Jr., *The Corporate Social Audit,* (The Russell Sage Foundation, 1972).

Brummet, Lee, "Total Performance Measurement," *Management Accounting* (November, 1973).

Campbell, A. and Converse, P.E. *The Human Meaning of Social Change* (Russell Sage Foundation, 1972).

Churchill, Neil C., "Toward a Theory for Social Accounting," *Sloan Management Review* (Spring, 1974).

Downes, Anthony, "Up and Down with Ecology:

'The Issue-Attention Cycle,' " *The Public Interest* (Summer, 1972).

Epstein, M., E. Flamholtz and McDonough, J.J., "Corporate Social Accounting in the United States. State of the Art and Future Prospects," *Accounting Organizations and Society* (June, 1976).

Estes, Ralph W., Corporate Social Accounting (John Wiley and Sons, 1976).

Furubotn, E., and Pejovich, S., "Property Rights and Economic Theory: A Survey of Recent Literature," *Journal of Economic Literature* (December, 1972).

Gross, Bertram M., "The State of the Nation: Social Systems Accounting" in *Social Indicators,* edited by Raymond A. Bauer (M.I.T. Press, 1966).

Hacker, Andrew, ed., *The Corporate Take-Over* (Doubleday, 1965).

Jensen, Robert, *Phantasmagoric Accounting: Research and Analysis of Economic, Social and Environmental Impact of Corporate Business,* Studies in Accounting Research No. 14 (American Accounting Association, 1976).

Kaysen, Carol and Turner, Donald F., *Antitrust Policy* (Harvard University Press, 1959).

Linowes, David, "Socio-Economic Accounting," *The Journal of Accountancy,* November, 1968).

———, Strategies for Survival (AMACOM, 1973).

Moore, J., "Managerial Behavior in the Theory of Comparative Economic Systems," in *The Economics of Property Rights,* edited by E.G. Furubotn and S. Pejovich, (Ballinger Publishing Company, 1974).

National Association of Accountants, "Report of the Committee on Accounting for Corporate Social Performance," *Management Accounting* (February, 1974).

Ramanathan, Kavasseri V., "Toward a Theory of Corporate Social Accounting," *The Accounting Review* (July, 1976).

Seidler, Lee J., "Dollar Values in the Social Income Statement," in *Social Accounting: Theory, Issues and Cases,* edited by Lee J. Seidler and Lynn L. Seidler, (Melville Publishing Company, 1975).

———, and Moore, W.E., eds, *Indicators of Social Change: Concepts and Measurements* (Russell Sage Foundation, 1968).

———, Parke, Robert, "Social Indicators," *Science* (May 16, 1975).

Toward a Theory of Human Resource Value in Formal Organizations

Eric Flamholtz*

This paper deals with the problem of measuring the value of people as organizational resources. This problem is important to management, investors and accountants as well as to others for two basic reasons.

First, there is evidence that the present failure to measure and report the value of human resources to management can conceal suboptimal decision-making in organizations. Specifically, the failure to measure the economic value of people may cause managers to ignore the effects of their decisions upon the value of human resources. The problem is a tendency for management to base decisions only on variables which can be quantified. Thus, so-called intangibles such as human resources tend to be ignored. Consequently, a decision or policy that *seems* beneficial may actually harm an organization by unintentionally depleting human resources. For example, decisions to undertake cost-control programs are typically based upon expected cost savings without consideration of the effects of such programs upon employee attitudes, motivation and satisfaction. Yet these programs may cause deterioration in employee motivation and satisfaction which is equivalent to a liquidation of human asset value. Thus, decision makers considering such programs should take into account the expected opportunity cost of lost human resources as well as the expected benefits of cost-savings.

Second, measurements of human resource value are also anticipated to be useful in several aspects of manpower planning and control. For example, they are expected to be useful in manpower acquisition, development, allocation, replacement and compensation decisions. They are also expected to be useful in evaluating the effectiveness of management's maintenance and utilization of human assets.[1]

THE ACCOUNTANT'S ROLE

Given their managerial importance, the accountant's role as an information-supplier is to

From *The Accounting Review,* Vol. 47, No. 4 (October 1972), pp. 666–678.

*Eric Flamholtz is Professor of Accounting at U.C.L.A.

An earlier version of this paper was selected for "Honorable Mention" in the 1971 Call for Papers of The Academy of Management and presented at the Annual Meeting at Atlanta, Georgia in August, 1971. Research for this paper was supported, in part, by a grant from the Accounting-Information Systems Research Program of the Graduate School of Management at the University of California, Los Angeles. I am grateful to Gordon Shillinglaw for many helpful comments on a previous version of this paper.

[1]For further discussion of the importance of measures of human resource value, see Rensis Likert, *The Human Organization: Its Management and Value* (McGraw-Hill Book Co., 1967); James Hekimian and Curtis Jones, "Put People on Your Balance Sheet," *Harvard Business Review* (Jan.–Feb. 1967), pp. 105–13; and Eric Flamholtz, "Should Your Organization Attempt to Value Its Human Resources?" *California Management Review* (Winter 1971), pp. 40–45.

develop the required methods of quantifying human resource value. It may be necessary for the accounting information system to provide not only monetary measurements of human resource value but also nonmonetary measurements.

PRIOR RESEARCH

Recently, some theoretical and empirical research has been focused upon the problem of developing monetary measures of human resource value.[2] However, no attempt has been made to understand or explain the nature and determinants of a person's value to a formal organization. In other words, there has been no attempt to develop a theory of human resource value.

NEED FOR THEORY OF HUMAN RESOURCE VALUE

A theory of the value of people to organizations is an essential prerequisite for the problem of developing methods of measuring of human resource value. First, the theory would, by definition, identify the variables which determine a person's value to an organization. This means that it would suggest the specific variables which need to be considered in developing valid and reliable monetary measures of human value. Second, by identifying the variables comprising a person's value, the theory would facilitate the development of nonmonetary surrogate measures of human value. In other words, since it identifies the determinants of the value of people, measures of these determinants might be used as nonmonetary indicators of human resource value, which would serve as a proxy for monetary measures of human value.

THE STUDY'S OBJECTIVES

This paper attempts to formulate a model of the nature and determinants of a person's value to an organization. The model represents a first step toward the development of a theory of human resource value.

The model is shown schematically in Figure 1. It draws upon a variety of behavioral (social and psychological) as well as economic variables.

This model attempts to synthesize or integrate these variables in order to explain the nature and determinants of an individual's economic worth to an organization. Its main purposes are: (1) to identify a set of variables which purport to explain a person's value to a firm, and (2) to discuss the variables' interrelationships. Since the model is quite complex, it may be helpful for the reader to refer to this schematic model in order to visualize the relations among the variables.

THE CONCEPT OF HUMAN RESOURCE VALUE

All economic theories of value are based explicitly or implicitly upon the premise that the attribute determining whether and to what extent an "object" possesses value is the perceived ability to render future economic "utility," "benefits," or "services." Thus, Von Mises once wrote that "whoever wants to construct an elementary theory of value and price

[2]For discussions of human resource valuation, see for example Baruch Lev and Aba Schwartz, "On the Use of the Economic Concept of Human Capital in Financial Statements," THE ACCOUNTING REVIEW (January 1971), pp. 103–18; and Eric Flamholtz, "A Model for Human Resource Valuation: A Stochastic Process with Service Rewards," THE ACCOUNTING REVIEW (April 1971), pp. 253–67.

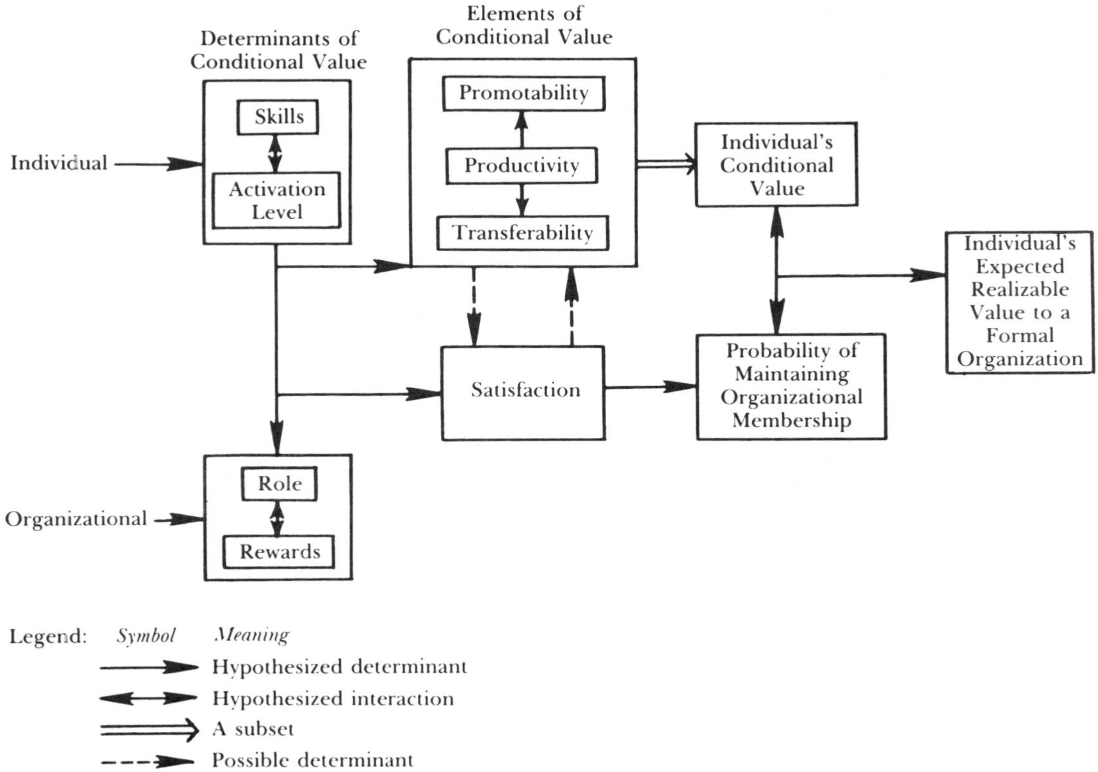

FIGURE 1. Model of the Determinants of an Individual's Value to a Formal Organization

must first think of utility."[3] Similarly, Fisher said that:

> . . . no one will dispute that the buyer of any article of capital will value it for its expected services to him, and that "at the margin" of his purchases, the price he will pay is the equivalent to him of these expected services, or, in other words, is their "present worth," their "discounted value," or "capitalized value."[4]

If an object is not capable of rendering future economic services, it has no value. In these terms, an object's value is typically constitutively defined as the present worth of the services it is anticipated to render in the future.[5] Thus, a "resource" may be defined as an object that possesses expected future services; objects which do not possess expected future benefits can not, by definition, be "resources."

The concept of "human value" is derived from general economic value theory. Like all resources, people possess value because they are capable of rendering future services. In principle, then, the value of people, like that of other resources, can be defined as the present worth of their expected future services.

From a macroeconomic viewpoint, the

[3]Von Mises, *Human Action* (Yale University Press, 1963), p. 121.

[4]Irving Fisher, *The Nature of Capital and Income* (MacMillan and Company, Ltd., 1927), p. 189.

[5]This notion of value is attributable to Fisher. See *Ibid.*, pp. 188, 202.

services people can potentially provide constitute a form of capital.[6] Similarly, from the viewpoint of a specified firm or other organization, the expected services of employees are a form of asset.[7] In either case, people are resources because they possess expected future service potential.

The concept of an individual's value to an organization is derived from the generic concept of human value. Thus, an individual's value to an organization can be defined as the present worth of the set of future service he is expected to provide during the period he is anticipated to remain in the organization.

Unlike other resources, however, human beings are not owned by organizations, and hence they are relatively free either to supply or to withhold their services. From an organization's viewpoint, this means that the probability of realizing an individual's services is typically less than certainty. This also suggests that there is a dual aspect to an individual's value: (1) the amount the organization could potentially realize from a person's services if he maintains organizational membership during the period of his productive service life and (2) the amount actually expected to be derived, taking into account the person's likelihood of turnover.

DETERMINANTS OF AN INDIVIDUAL'S VALUE

An individual's value to an organization is thus multidimensional. It is comprised of two interacting variables: (1) the individual's "conditional value" and (2) the probability that the individual will maintain membership in the organization. An individual's "conditional value" is the present worth of the potential services that could be rendered to the organization, if the individual maintained organizational membership throughout his expected service life. The probability that the individual will maintain membership in the organization is the complement of the probability of turnover or exit. It determines the extent to which the organization will realize the individual's potential services or conditional value. The product of these two variables is thus the individual's "expected realizable value"—the present worth of services actually expected to be derived during the individual's anticipated tenure in the organization, as shown in Figure 2.

Conditional Value

An individual's conditional value is a multidimensioned variable, and is comprised of three factors: productivity, transferability and promotability. "Productivity" refers to the set of services an individual is expected to provide while occupying his present position. A synonym for productivity is performance. "Transferability" is the set of services an individual is expected to provide if and when he transfers to other positions at the same posi-

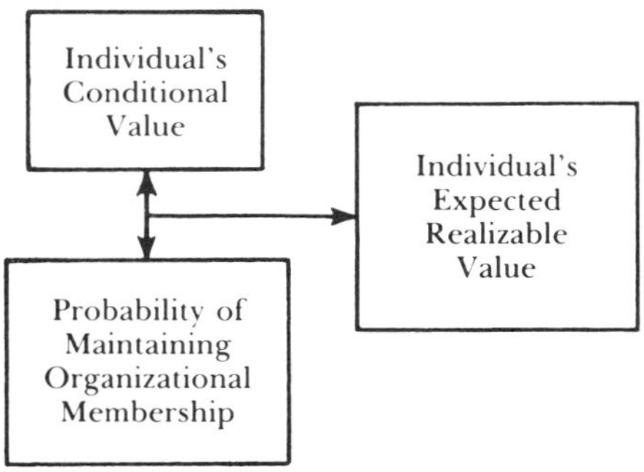

FIGURE 2. Variables Interacting to Produce An Individual's Expected Realizable Value

[6]Theodore Schultz, "Investments in Human Capital," *American Economic Review* (March 1961), pp. 1–17.

[7]Although relatively few writers have considered the question of whether people are a form of asset, Chambers has argued that human beings are not "assets" in the traditional accounting sense. See Raymond J. Chambers, *Accounting, Evaluation, and Economic Behavior* (Prentice-Hall, Inc., 1966), p. 104.

tion level in a different promotion channel. "Promotability" represents the set of services the individual is expected to provide if and when he occupies higher level positions in his present or different promotion channels. Productivity, transferability and promotability are, in other words, subsets of the set of "services" which the person is expected to render, and which are the elements of conditional value, as shown in Figure 3.

The hypothesized relations among the elements of conditional value are also indicated in Figure 3. In this model, productivity is the central or causal variable. It is hypothesized to influence both promotability and transferability. Productivity influences promotability—or, more accurately, *perceived* promotability—because it affects an individual's elegibility for promotion. In other words, since promotion practices in formal organizations are at least in part a function of past performance or prior services rendered, an individual's promotability is affected by evaluations of his past and expected productivity. Similarly, transferability is influenced by productivity, which may affect the likelihood that the organization will consider the individual for a possible transfer. In some cases, transfer may also indicate promotion elegibility. For example, the rotation of "high potential" MBAs through various jobs, functional areas, and geographical locations may indicate grooming for future promotion.

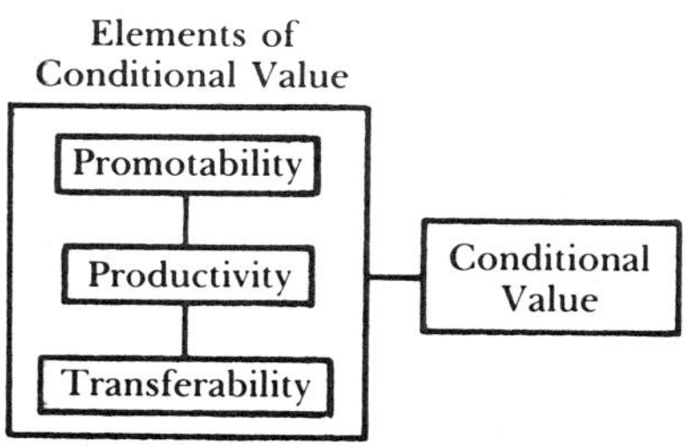

FIGURE 3. Elements of Conditional Value and Their Interrelationships

Determinants of Elements of Conditional Value

The elements of an individual's conditional value are the product of certain attributes of the individual and certain dimensions of the organization. The major "individual determinants" of conditional value are the individual's skills and activation level. The major "organizational determinants" of conditional value are the individual's role and the nature of organizational rewards. Each of these variables will be discussed below.

Individual Determinants of Conditional Value: Skills and Activational Level. The individual's "skills" represent his currently developed potential to provide services to an organization. Drawing upon Floyd Mann, we are primarily concerned with a trilogy of technical, administrative and human interaction skills.[8] These general skills are relatively stable and enduring. However, they can be changed by various forms of training. In principle, the set of skills a person possesses sets limits on the nature and magnitude of the services he can render to an organization. At a more elementary level, such skills are the product of cognitive abilities and personality traits.

The individual's "activation level" is another determinant of his conditional value. The term "activation level" can be defined ". . . as the extent of release of the stored energy of the organism through metabolic activity in the tissues."[9] In other words, it is the neuropsychological counterpart of the notion of "motiva-

[8]Floyd C. Mann, "Toward an Understanding of the Leadership Role in Formal Organization," in R. Dubin, G. C. Homans, F. C. Mann, and D. C. Miller, *Leadership and Productivity* (Chandler Publishing Co., 1965), as cited in D. Bowers and S. Seashore, "Predicting Organizational Effectiveness with a Four-Factor Theory of Leadership," *Administrative Science Quarterly* (September 1966), p. 245.

[9]Elizabeth Duffy, *Activation and Behavior* (John Wiley & Sons, 1962), as cited in William E. Scott, Jr., "Activation Theory and Task Design," *Organization Behavior and Human Performance* (Sept. 1966), p. 11.

tion." The level of activation is a major variable influencing human behavior. An individual's activation level is not constant and may vary as a result of changes in physiological and psychological determinants.

It is hypothesized that an individual's skills and activation level (motivation) interact to determine the person's potential for rendering services to an organization.[10] Although an individual's skills set a theoretical limit upon the services that can be rendered, in practice his activation level is very probably also a crucial determinant of the potential services to be realized by an organization.[11] Thus, while an engineer may be limited in his ability to solve technical problems by his intelligence, and a manager may be limited in his ability to cope with interpersonal problems by his personality, individuals can also compensate to a great extent for a lack of specific skills by increasing their activation level. On the contrary, even an individual possessing a high degree of technical, administrative, and interpersonal skill may provide less service to an organization than warranted by his potential because of a relatively low activation level. The relationships between skills and activation level in producing productivity is quite complex. The hypothesized relations among these determinants and conditional value is shown in Figure 4.

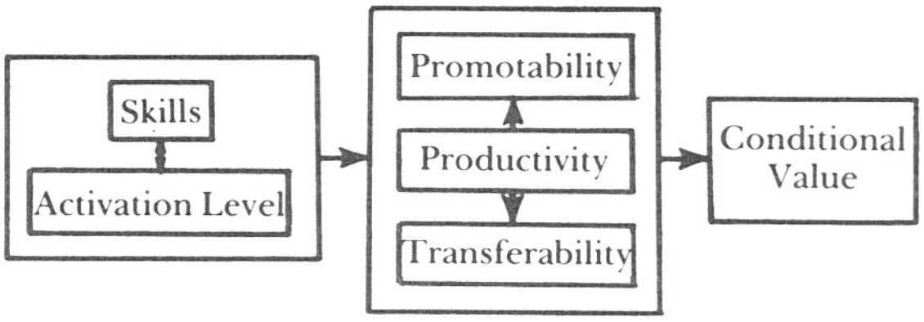

FIGURE 4. Relation of Individual Determinants To Conditional Value

Organizational Determinants of Conditional Value: Role and Rewards. The individual determinants of conditional value also interact with certain organizational determinants. Although an individual may possess a set of skills and the motivation to apply them, the organizational role he occupies influences the extent to which he is offered the opportunity to render his potential services. In this context a "role" refers to the set of behaviors expected from all persons occupying a specified position in an organization. For example, a person with a high degree of administrative skill may occupy the role of engineer, or the individual with great skill in solving mathematical problems may occupy the role of salesman. In either case, the individuals' conditional value to the organization is determined, in part, by the interaction between his skill and his organizational role. In other words, the individual is included in his role on only a partial or segmental basis. This occurrence is very probably quite typical in organizations, for, as Katz and Kahn observe: "Unlike the inclusion of a given organ in the body in the biological system, not all of the individual is included in his organizational membership. The organization neither requires nor wants the whole person."[12]

To clarify the nature of the interaction between the individual and his organizational role as a determinant of a person's conditional value, their relationship is shown schematically in Figures 5, 6, and 7. Figure 5 shows two subsets, P and R, with P representing a person and R a role. From the diagram it can be seen that $P \cap R = E$, where E denotes the empty set. That is, there is no overlap or intersection between

[10]Some of the evidence for this hypothesis has been reviewed by Lawler and Vroom. See E. E. Lawler, "Ability as a Moderator of the Relationship between Job Attitudes and Job Performance," *Personnel Psychology* (Summer 1966), pp. 153–64, and V. H. Vroom, *Work and Motivation* (John Wiley & Sons, 1964).

[11]See E. A. Fleishman, "A Relationship Between Incentive Motivation and Ability Level in Psychomotor Performance," *Journal of Experimental Psychology*, 1958, 56, No. 1, pp. 78–81.

[12]Daniel Katz and Robert L. Kahn, *The Social Psychology of Organizations* (John Wiley & Sons, 1966), p. 50.

$P \cap R = E$

FIGURE 5.

the person and his role. The skills available are simply not required by the role to which the person has been allocated.

In Figure 6, the situation can be expressed as $P \cap R \neq E$; the intersection of the person and the role is not empty. The individual is partially included in the role.

When the individual is totally included in his role—that is, when the set of behavior required by the role exactly match those exhibited by the individual—then $P = R$. Figure 7 diagrams this situation.

The relation between the individual and the role is not merely a question of fit or matching. Both the role and the individual interact with one another. Considered abstractly, there is a set of role requirements, which refer to the formal or prescribed behaviors expected from all occupants of a specified role, position or office. For example, the role of manager generally connotes certain universal expectations, and, in a particular organization these expectations are made even more precise by systemic values, traditions and norms. However, the perceptions of the role incumbent also affect the role. The set of attributes of the role perceived by the incumbent may or may not correspond

$P \cap R \neq E$

FIGURE 6.

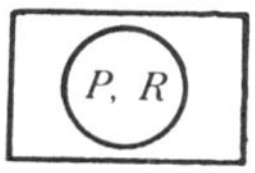

$P = R$

FIGURE 7.

closely to the role's formal requirements. For example, a newly promoted manager may "bring with him" a set of activities which were typically associated with his previous position.

The role and the individual also interact in other ways. Role prescriptions, as mechanisms specifying the tasks and jobs which people are to perform, are important influences upon an individual's activation level. Scott has reviewed several neuropsychological studies on the determinants of activation, and has noted their implications for a better understanding of the relation between the structure of tasks and the degree of activation of an individual. He cites studies which give some evidence that there are several aspects of a task's structure which may be determinants of activation level, including such variables as stimulus variation, intensity, complexity, uncertainty and meaningfulness.[13]

Another organizational determinant of an individual's conditional value is the "rewards" which people expect to derive from different aspects of their membership in an organization. As Katz has pointed out, "it is important to distinguish between rewards which are administered in relation to individual effort and performance and the system rewards which accrue to people by virtue of their membership in the system."[14] "Instrumental individual rewards"—rewards which are administered in relation to individual effort—are intended to motivate optimal role performance. "Instrumental system rewards"—rewards which accrue by virtue of membership in the system—are more effective for holding members within the orga-

[13]Scott, pp. 3–30. For a discussion of the mechanisms through which the dimensions of tasks interact with the characteristics of individuals to influence role performance, see J. Richard Hackman, "Nature of the Task As a Determiner of Job Behavior," *Personnel Psychology* (Winter 1969), pp. 435–44.

[14]Daniel Katz, "The Motivational Basis of Organizational Behavior," *Behavioral Science* (April 1964), p. 137.

nization, but they will not necessarily lead to higher productivity.

In terms of the proposed model, it is hypothesized that instrumental individual rewards influence the individual's conditional value by affecting the degree of activation. The rewards associated with behaviors required by an individual's role influence the extent to which there is a fit between the person and the role. That is, the extent to which task-performance will be instrumental in satisfying an individual's needs will determine the likelihood that he will fulfill role requirements. This is the essence of the so-called "path-goal hypothesis" presented by Georgopoulos, Mahoney and Jones.[15] Thus, it is hypothesized that the more likely it is that the behaviors required by a given role will lead to rewards perceived to be instrumental in satisfying an individual's needs, then the greater the inclusion of the person in the role, and, therefore, the greater the individual's conditional value to an organization. The hypothesized relations among the variables which determine an individual's conditional value are shown schematically in Figure 8.

[15]B. S. Georgopoulos, G. M. Mahoney and H. W. Jones, "A Path-goal Approach to Productivity," *Journal of Applied Psychology,* 1957, Vol. 41, pp. 345–53.

Probability of Maintaining Organizational Membership

Since people can leave an organization, it is necessary to consider not only the determinants of conditional value but also the determinants of the probability that an individual will maintain membership in an organizational system. Research on causes of turnover have suggested that there is an inverse relationship between need satisfaction and the likelihood of existing. For example, Ross and Zander found that ". . . the degree of satisfaction of certain personal needs supplied by an individual's place of employment has a significant direct relationship to his continuing to work for that company." They concluded that ". . . workers whose personal needs are satisfied on the job are more likely to remain in the organization."[16] Similarly, in reviewing the findings of research on the relation between job satisfaction and turnover, Fournet, Distefano and Pryer concluded that the findings consistently show turnover negatively related to job satisfaction.[17] Thus, there seems to be evidence to

[16]Ian C. Ross and Alvin Zander, "Need Satisfactions and Employee Turnover," *Personnel Psychology* (Autumn 1957), pp. 327–38.

[17]G. P. Fournet, M. K. Distefano and M. W. Pryer, "Job Satisfaction: Issues and Problems," *Personnel Psychology* (Summer 1966), p. 176.

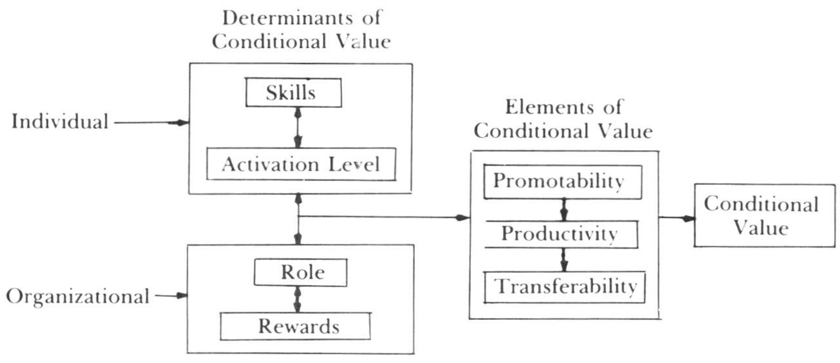

FIGURE 8. Relations Among Variables Determining an Individual's Conditional Value

support the generality of the relation between these variables, as depicted in Figure 9.

To the extent that satisfaction with organizational membership is related to the perceived opportunity to satisfy individual needs, then it is hypothesized that satisfaction is the product of the interaction between the individual and organizational determinants of an individual's value. This means, in other words, that satisfaction is presumed to be caused by the same *process* that produces an individual's conditional value—the interaction between and among the individual's skills, activation level, role, and the organizational reward structure. These hypothesized relations are shown schematically in Figure 10.

It should be noted that "satisfaction" is a global construct. Thus the variable "satisfaction" is really a composite of several separate variables such as satisfaction with pay, satisfaction with working conditions and satisfaction with supervision.

In addition to the relation between satisfaction and the probability of remaining in the organization, there is also a possible relation

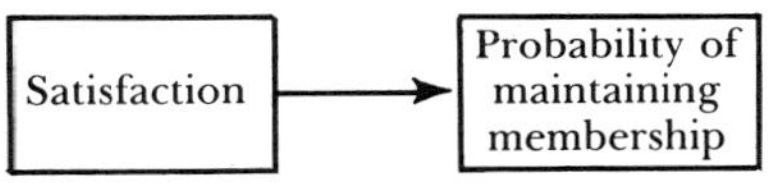

FIGURE 9. Determinants of the Probability of Maintaining Organizational Membership

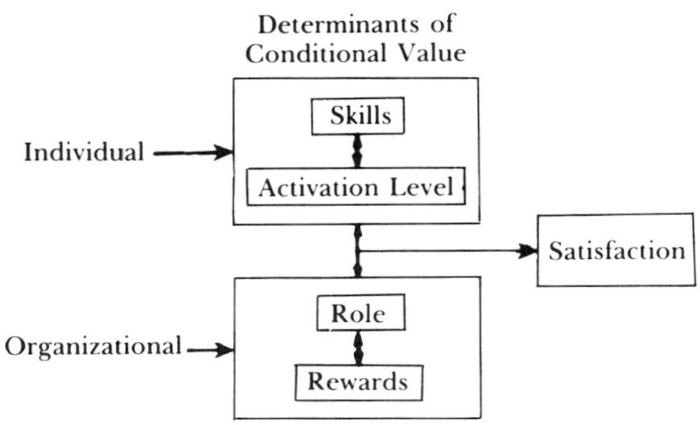

FIGURE 10. Relations Among Variables Determining an Individual's Satisfaction

between satisfaction and one of the elements of an individual's conditional value, i.e., productivity. Research findings have generally tested the hypothesized relation between productivity (performance) and satisfaction from the viewpoint that the latter is determinant of the former. Unfortunately, in reviewing and analyzing the results of such studies, Brayfield and Crockett argued that ". . . we expect the relation between satisfaction and job performance to be one of concomitant variation rather than cause and effect." In addition, they concluded that ". . . satisfaction with one's position in a network of relationships need not imply strong motivation to outstanding performance within that system. . . ."[18]

Although many researchers expected to find a positive relationship between satisfaction and productivity, some have found a negative relationship. Obviously the relationship between these variables is quite complex, and it is likely that there are other variables which moderate their effect upon each other. Accordingly, there is presently insufficient evidence to fully support a hypothesis on the nature of the relation between these variables.[19] It may be just as likely that satisfaction is caused by productivity as it is that productivity is determined by satisfaction.[20]

[18]A. H. Brayfield and W. H. Crockett, "Employee Attitudes and Employee Performance," *Psychological Bulletin* (Sept. 1955), pp. 416, 421.

[19]This argument is supported by the conclusion of Schwab and Cummings, who reviewed the various theories of the relation between performance and satisfaction. They stated that: "We are frankly pessimistic about the value of additional satisfaction-performance theorizing at this time. The theoretically inclined might do better to work on a theory of satisfaction *or* a theory of performance. Such concepts are clearly complex enough to justify their own theories." See Donald P. Schwab and Larry L. Cummings, "Theories of Performance and Satisfaction: A Review," *Industrial Relations* (October 1970), p. 420.

[20]Indeed, Porter and Lawler have developed a model of the relationship between managerial attitudes and performance in which there is circularity in the relationship between performance and satisfaction. See Lyman W. Porter and Edward E. Lawler, III, *Managerial Attitudes and Performance* (Homewood, Illinois: Richard D. Irwin, Inc., 1968), especially Chapters 2 and 8.

The Model As A Whole
The model of the nature and determinants of an individual's value developed in this paper was shown schematically in Figure 1. Taken as a whole, it represents a framework for understanding the factors comprising and influencing an individual's value to an organization.

IMPLICATIONS OF THE MODEL FOR ACCOUNTING

According to the Committee to Prepare a Statement of Basic Accounting Theory, the objectives of accounting are to provide information for the following purposes: (1) Making decisions concerning the use of limited resources, including the identification of crucial decision areas, and determination of objectives and goals; (2) effectively directing and controlling an organization's human and material resources; (3) maintaining and reporting on the custodianship of resources; and (4) facilitating social functions and controls.[21] The model developed in this paper can help accounting achieve all of these objectives.

Decision Making
This theory will increase the effectiveness of decision-making concerning resource utilization because it will assist accountants in developing methods of measuring human resource value. As noted previously, measurements of human resource value are required to facilitate decisions involving a mix of human and other resources so that managers will not overlook the effects of such decisions upon the value of human assets. In addition, measurements of human resource value are required to facilitate a variety of manpower management decisions, including human resource acquisition, development, allocation, compensation and replacement.

The theory will help to develop such measurements in two ways. First, the model's constructs indicate the kinds of variables which must be considered in developing a monetary measure of an individual's worth to an organization. For example, the model suggests that the ultimate measure of a person's worth is his expected realizable value. It also suggests that the penultimate measure of a person's worth is his conditional value. The differential, if any, between these two measures represents the opportunity cost of the anticipated probability of turnover. Thus, it represents the amount a firm ought to be willing to spend to reduce the probability of turnover to zero.

Another example of the model's implications for the measurement of human value is suggested by the kinds of variables it includes. To illustrate, suppose we were to ask managers or accountants or organizational psychologists: "What factors determine the value of people to an organization?" One might reasonably expect a sample of respondents to mention such things as a person's skills, personality traits and intelligence. These variables are all individual determinants—attributes associated with the individual per se. However, it is doubtful that many people would mention the organizational determinants of a person's value such as the role a person occupies. It is even possible that satisfaction might not be mentioned as a determinant of the person's value.

There is a rather deceptively simple explanation for the probable failure to cite organizational determinants. For a variety of reasons, we tend to assess the value of human resources by using a different framework than for other resources. With respect to material resources, we are aware that it is a fallacy to value the agent rather than the services provided by the agent. Not so for people. Here it is common practice to value the agent rather than its ser-

[21]American Accounting Association, Committee to Prepare a Statement of Basic Accounting Theory, *A Statement of Basic Accounting Theory* (American Accounting Association, 1966), p. 4.

vices. Thus, the model contributes an important insight: a person's value to an organization is not merely a function of personal attributes; rather, it is the product of a set of interacting human and organizational determinants.

The second major way in which the model will help develop measures of human resource value is by identifying the variables which might be used as nonmonetary measurements of a person's value. In other words, the variables simultaneously provide a theoretical foundation for developing monetary representations of the value of people; they also constitute a set of possible quantitative but nonmonetary accounting measurements. This recommendation is consistent with the Committee to Prepare a Statement of Basic Accounting Theory's conclusion that "while the measurement process currently focuses on economic dollar-valued data and relates the performance of the organization to either profitability or to the extent of budgeted expenditure, accounting in the future can well consider several aspects of a transaction or event simultaneously."[22] Thus, this model may be used by accountants to determine user information needs with respect to the value of human resources, and the future accounting information system may well include measures of these determinants of human resource value, where each variable possesses its own unit of measurement.

Effective Management of Resources

According to the Committee, the second objective of providing accounting information is to facilitate the effective management of an organization's human and material resources. The proposed theory can play an important role in helping achieve this objective. Specifically, the proposed theory provides the basis for a new paradigm for the management of human resources.

[22] *Ibid.*, p. 65.

At present, the management of human resources in organizations is less effective than it might be because it lacks a unifying framework to guide it. Managers have neither a valid criterion to guide decisions affecting people nor a methodology for assessing the anticipated or actual consequences of such decisions. Clearly the criteria of productivity and satisfaction which frequently underlie strategies of human resource management have not been entirely helpful in coping with the problems of managing people. Similarly, since it is exceedingly difficult to measure productivity and satisfaction, or to assess the tradeoffs a manager should rationally be willing to make to increase one by decreasing the other, it is not frequently possible to predict the economic consequences of alternative actions with respect to people.

The notion of "human resource value" seems to provide one possible solution to these problems. It can serve as the *raison d'être* of human resource management: it can simultaneously provide the goal and the criterion for the management of human resources. More specifically, the aim of human resource management can be viewed as the need to contribute to the value of the organization as a whole by optimizing the value of its human assets; the effectiveness criterion can be the measured change in the value of the organization's human resources.

If the aim of human resource management is seen as the optimization of human resource value, then task design, selection, role assignment, development, performance appraisal and compensation are not merely a set of service functions to be performed; rather, they are a set of available strategies that can be adopted to change the value of human assets, and, in turn, the value of the organization as a whole.

Thus, the theory provides the basis for a new paradigm because it establishes an ultimate criterion of effective human resource management. Accounting can help to operationalize this paradigm by providing measurements of management's effectiveness in utilizing human resources, as described above.

Reporting on Custodianship of Resources

One aspect of the present failure of organizations to account for human resources is the resulting lack of information about the extent to which a firm's human resources are being appreciated, maintained, or depleted. One measure of human resource liquidation is, of course, turnover. However, there are other, more subtle ways for a firm's human resources to be depleted without management being aware of it. For example, the model clearly shows that a decrease in employee satisfaction is actually equivalent to depletion of an organization's human resources. We know that turnover is inversely related to satisfaction, and that, therefore, an increase in a person's dissatisfaction with an organization is likely to increase the probability that he will exit. This, of course, means that there has been a decrease in the probability that the organization will actually realize an individual's expected future service potential. This is equivalent to a decrease in the person's expected realizable value, which, as previously noted, is the measure of an individual's ultimate worth to a firm.

Accountants should report changes in such variables as employee satisfaction and motivation to management. The expected effects of such observed changes upon personnel turnover and the opportunity cost of unrealized human resource value should also be reported. This information will enable management to evaluate the extent to which the organization has effectively maintained stewardship over human resources. It will also provide an indicator of the need to take corrective action prior to the time that decreases in satisfaction are translated into increased turnover or decreases in motivation are translated into decreased productivity.

Facilitation of Social Controls

The proposed theory also has possible implications for accounting's role in facilitating social functions and social controls over organizations. For example, many firms are currently engaged in hiring and developing the so-called "hard core unemployed." One measure of a firm's social contribution in this case might be the observed increase in the value of the underdeveloped human resources. This information might be reported in the president's letter of a corporate annual report.

Another illustration of the social aspect of this theory concerns the current trend toward a greater concern with the "quality of life." As a product of a changing social ethos, we can anticipate a greater emphasis upon the satisfactions people derive from their work. It is possible that organizations of the future may be required to account for the satisfaction of employees as an end in itself. Government may, for instance, decide to assess a tax upon so-called Theory X organizations, or provide investment credit incentives to organizations to motivate them to undertake organizational change programs in order to increase opportunities for employee satisfaction.

CONCLUDING COMMENTS

The model presented in this paper is intended as a first step toward a theory of human resource value in formal organizations. This theory seems to have relevance to accounting's objectives of measuring and reporting information for decision-making, management of human resources, custodianship of human resources and social controls over the utilization of people. Thus, the model can potentially help enlarge the scope of accounting in accordance with the recommendations in *A Statement of Basic Accounting Theory*.

There are, of course, some limitations involved in the model. First, the model's scope is restricted to the nature and determinants of an individual's value to an organization. Thus it should not be inferred that the model purports to explain the value of groups of people in formal organizations. Similarly, it should not be inferred that the model purports to fully explain the nature of an individual's value. Future research may find that other variables should be included or that present variables are unnecessary. Similarly, the validity of the hypothesized relations among the variables needs to be assessed. These are empirical questions.[23]

The model treats an individual's value as an independent or marginal phenomenon. The validity of this treatment depends upon several variables including the nature of the organization and the degree of interdependence of organizational roles. Accordingly, this model does not fully take into account the dynamic aspects of organizational phenomena. For example, an individual's promotability may be determined not only by his own skills, activation level and expected service potential but also by the promotability of others.

These limitations suggest the need for further research on this complex problem. In the meantime, it is hoped that the model provides a useful preliminary framework for analyzing and understanding the nature and determinants of a person's value to an organization, and that it makes a contribution toward the development of a very necessary theory of the value of an organization's human resources.

[23]For some preliminary results on these issues, see Eric Flamholtz, "Assessing the Validity of a Theory of Human Resource Value: A Field Study," *Empirical Research in Accounting: Selected Studies 1972* (forthcoming).

*Behavioral Research on Human Resource Accounting: A Contingency Framework**

Lawrence A. Tomassini
The University of Texas at Austin

Developments in human resource accounting (HRA) have prospered in recent years. Research on HRA's behavioral dimensions, however, has been notably deficient. This paper proposes a framework, based upon contingency theory, to facilitate such research. Specific information, organizational, and individual attributes are described and related to HRA research. In addition, specific research hypotheses are suggested to demonstrate the framework's applicability and significance.

During the past decade, accountants have expanded the scope of their activities and responsibilities to provide more useful information to decision-makers. One of the more controversial aspects of this expansion is generally known as "human resource accounting" (HRA). Primarily aimed at the measurement and reporting of human resource costs and values to management, HRA has been debated on grounds of measurement feasibility and reliability, ethics of disclosure, and behavioral effects of implementation. Unfortunately the last matter, while critical to the widespread acceptance of HRA, has been considered primarily by speculative rather than by scientific means.[1]

PURPOSE OF THIS PAPER

The American Accounting Association's Committee on Accounting for Human Resources (1974) specified that behavioral research on HRA is necessary if HRA is to sustain itself as a viable sub-discipline. Two foci for such research may prove necessary: (1) the effects of HRA on employee attitudes and performance, and (2) the impact of HRA on management decision-making. This paper is principally directed toward the latter topic, although the concepts considered may be partially applicable to the former as well.

Specifically, the purpose of this paper is to foster behavioral HRA research by providing a structural framework within which critical issues may be identified and related, and by suggesting certain research hypotheses through which the framework may be applied.

With this purpose in mind, the paper is organized into two parts. First, the relevant dimensions of the framework are described; second, specific hypotheses are suggested with respect to each dimension.

From *Accounting, Organizations and Society,* Vol. 1, No. 2–3 (1976), pp. 239–250.

*The author is grateful to Professor Eric Flamholtz of the University of California, Los Angeles, and to Professor Kermit Larson of the University of Texas at Austin for their helpful comments on an earlier draft of this paper.

[1]A few experimental studies stand out as exceptions. See, for example, Elias (1972), Tomassini (1974) and Tomassini (1975).

CONTINGENCY FRAMEWORK

To conduct research on the behavioral effects of HRA, we propose a framework based upon recent contingency theories of organization to identify the variables (contingencies) upon which the effects of HRA are dependent.[2] The framework developed in this paper includes three categories of attributes which, when combined in certain ways, represent contingencies for the behavioral assessment of HRA. While the framework may not fully exhaust relevant attributes, it should provide direction and structure for future behavioral HRA research.

The three categories which form our contingency framework are the following:

(1) Information Attributes. Characteristics of the information (data) to which the user or decision-maker has access, including content or type, format, and quantity;

(2) Organizational Attributes. Characteristics of organizational systems or sub-systems regarding their structure, task environment, and goals;

(3) Individual Attributes. Characteristics of the user or decision-maker relating to his or her cognitive processing of information and overt behavior.

Each of these categories is examined in detail in the following sections of the paper.

INFORMATION ATTRIBUTES

Three information attributes appear to be relevant for assessing the behavioral impact of HRA: the type and format of HRA data (cues) and the quantity of decision cues. Components of these attributes are discussed below.

Type of HRA Data

HRA data are no more uniform in character than are any other accounting messages communicated to decision-makers. Rather, HRA consists of various types of cost and value measures, including historical (outlay), replacement and opportunity costs, and economic (discounted present) value.[3] Many authors have discussed the need to provide accounting information which fits the decision context of its user.[4] The implication of this purposive orientation, which applies equally well to HRA, is that different types of data will be more or less useful and effective depending upon the decision set for which the data are prepared. For example, estimated replacement costs may be useful in determining an individual's value to a firm and his or her compensation for such, while opportunity cost data may be useful in assessing the impact of employee turnover.

Furthermore, one might expect that various types of HRA measures would provoke different user credibility responses. For example, the pioneering work at the R. G. Barry Corporation focused upon human resource investment (HRI) or outlay cost measures.[5] This type of HRA is less subjective and controversial than the measurement of human resource value (HRV), advocated by Flamholtz and applied at Lester Witte & Co.[6] One might expect, therefore, that the more complex and subjective HRV measures would, at least initially, be considered less credible than HRA measures by

---

[2]For a concise, interesting presentation of the basic tenets of a contingency theory, see Luthans (1973).

[3]See Flamholtz (1974) for a thorough discussion of these alternative measurement methods.

[4]See, for example, Davidson & Trueblood (1961) for an early proposal of this kind.

[5]For a thorough discussion of the R. G. Barry experience with HRA, see Pyle (1970) and Woodruff (1970).

[6]The HRA work at Lester Witte is described in Flamholtz (1974, pp. 249–267) and Flamholtz & Lundy (1975).

management decision-makers. This credibility difference due to measurement subjectivity is, of course, only one factor of concern in assessing the behavioral impact of HRA measures. For example, decision-makers may very well perceive HRV data to have greater utility in spite of the aforementioned subjectivity. If this were the case, accountants and managers would want to recognize the credibility-utility tradeoff in assessing various types of HRA measures.

Format of HRA Data

The format of HRA data may be another significant variable for behavioral research. One basis for considering this variable is the "hierarchy of (information) measurement" concept, recently described by Flamholtz (1975). Flamholtz hypothesized that five levels of information measurement exist, including the following:

(1) profit,
(2) monetary (other than profit),
(3) quantitative (excluding monetary),
(4) qualitative statements about measurements, and
(5) qualitative information without measurement.

Furthermore, Flamholtz speculated that, when two or more competing information alternatives (decision inputs or arguments) are based upon different levels of measurements, the information (argument) with the highest level of measurement is likely to be most influential. For example, if two managers present arguments about the effects of a cost control program, one using monetary arguments about the program's effects and the other using qualitative arguments about the same matter, the hierarchy concept would predict that the former's arguments would likely prevail.

Since proposals for HRA measurements have been made which include both monetary and non-monetary formats, we might expect differences in the impact of HRA to be dependent, in part, upon such format variations. The hierarchy of information measurement notion would hypothesize the argumentative superiority of monetary HRA measures. One limitation of this reasoning is that variations in the purpose and format of decision *responses* are not considered explicitly.

Another basis for considering HRA data format is the compatibility between the data provided and the response required. The superiority of data (cues) provided in a format which is compatible with the required response (action) has been demonstrated and examined in a variety of psychological research settings. For example, Slovic & Lichtenstein (1968) found probability and payoff cue utilization in a gambling setting to vary with response formats. Since HRA data can be provided in different formats (as can measures which HRA augments), this variable is likely to be influential on management decision behavior.

Quantity of Data

The third attribute considered in our contingency framework is the quantity of data (HRA and other) provided to a decision-maker. Since humans are limited in their ability to process effectively large quantities of information or data about many variables (Miller, 1956), the impact of HRA on decision behavior is contingent upon the total amount of data (or the number of cues) confronting an individual.

This contingency is particularly relevant in external reporting contexts where *both* conventional financial statements and financial statements with HRA data are presented to decision-makers. In addition, this quantity contingency may be important in managerial reporting, particularly when firms are making the transition between conventional accounting and HRA systems.

ORGANIZATIONAL ATTRIBUTES

Three organizational attributes appear relevant for assessing the impact of HRA: nature of the task environment, management control system, and organizational goals and rewards. The relevant components of these attributes for HRA research are described below.

Task Environment

One of the primary considerations in organizational contingency theory has been the nature of a firm's task environment.[7] By *task environment,* we mean the context in which a firm attempts to achieve its objectives. Included in this context are factors affecting information clarity, identifiability of cause and effect relationships, and the time span of the performance-evaluation-feedback cycle. Two relevant elements of a firm's task environment for behavioral HRA research are: (1) the extent of labor (i.e. human capital) intensity in the system; and (2) the degree of task structuring.

Organizations that are very labor intensive, relying primarily upon the effective and efficient use of *human* resources for success, such as professional service organizations, are likely to find HRA data most relevant to their decision-making. We are not implying that such data are unimportant to very physical capital intensive firms, such as steel manufacturers. The point is merely that, *ceteris paribus,* HRA data will better satisfy the needs of management decision-making in labor intensive organizations.

Highly structured task environments are those in which the objectives of the system, its operating methods, and its performance (output) measures can be clearly, and in some cases, precisely defined. This type of structure is often referred to as "programmable" because of its clear definition and routine character. An example of a highly structured task environment is a production assembly operation. Unstructured task environments, referred to as "nonprogrammable", have objectives, operating methods, and performance measures which are much less certain and precise. An example of an unstructured task environment is that of a research and development project team.

Morse & Lorsch (1970) have identified the appropriateness of task environment structure as a contingent variable in organizational design. Watson (1975) has attempted to demonstrate the relevance of this contingency theory to managerial accounting. These studies recognize that prescriptions about organizations and accounting information systems, presumably including HRA systems, should be tailored to circumstantial factors.

Management Control System

The prevalent system through which management organizes and controls a firm's activities may influence the effectiveness of HRA. Two relevant components of this attribute are: (1) the philosophy underlying the organization's management, and (2) the extent to which management is concerned about human organizational factors in its decision-making and control activities.

Organizations tend to structure their activities according to a prevalent management philosophy or set of values. Logically, management decision-making, including cognitive information processing, should be consistent with these values.

Of the many organizational theorists who have studied these philosophical issues, probably Rensis Likert most closely affiliated with HRA. Likert (1967) developed a classification scheme (Systems 1–4) for organizations based upon employee perceptions of certain variables (e.g. communication methods, interaction-influence patterns, and goal setting

[7]This approach is usually associated with Lawrence & Lorsch (1967).

procedures). This classification approximates a range of management control structures from autocratic to democratic (participative), the latter representing Likert's preference. Since Likert's work on participative management was a major impetus for the pioneering HRA work at the R. G. Barry Corporation, we would expect his (or similar) classification(s) of management philosophy and organizational structure to be relevant for assessing the impact of HRA on internal decision-making.

Likert & Seashore (1963) noted that dysfunctional consequences result from certain cost control efforts by management. They suggested that these consequences might go unheeded because of the chronological separation between causal factors (e.g. a cost control program) and end results (e.g. additional costs due to decreased productivity of organizational personnel). Additionally, they proposed that, by monitoring intervening variables (e.g. maintenance of employee morale and technical competence), management could better recognize these cause-effect relationships and take more timely corrective action, where necessary.

Organizations vary in their concern about human organizational factors, such as those discussed by Likert and Seashore. Since much of HRA formalizes the type of intervening variables they proposed, we would expect the extent of an organization's concern to be a relevant contingency for behavioral HRA research. For example, firms which are concerned about depletion of human resource potential would be receptive to the use of HRV measures.

Organizational Goals and Rewards

The goals of an organization and the rewards offered as incentives to achieve them are likely to affect the decision behavior of most managers. To the extent that managers are influenced by their perceptions of goals and rewards, HRA data effectiveness should vary among organizations. For example, the effectiveness of HRA data should depend, in part, upon the degree to which human resource development is encouraged by management and reinforced through the reward system. Additionally, HRA may be used as a basis for rewards administration in such systems.

INDIVIDUAL ATTRIBUTES

Three attributes of the decision-maker appear relevant for assessing HRA's impact upon his or her behavior: cognitive style, leadership style, and managerial experience. Various components of these attributes are discussed and related to HRA research below.

Cognitive Style

A great deal of the psychological literature indicates that individuals differ in their manner of converting information stimuli into overt behavior. In the management field, studies have indicated that differences in decision behavior can be attributed to an individual's cognitive process and, further, that differences in these processes can be meaningfully classified.[8] We shall label such classifications *cognitive styles.* Many dimensions of an individual's cognitive style are discussed in the literature; two which seem appropriate for HRA research are: (1) cognitive complexity and its related concepts in decision style theory; and (2) tolerance for ambiguity.

"Cognitive complexity", as we employ the term, refers to the extent to which individuals process different types and amounts of information stimuli prior to taking some action, such as making a decision. The primary notions

[8]For examples of work in this area, see Hall, O'Leary, & Williams (1964), Driver & Streufert (1969), and Driver & Lintott (1972).

about individuals' tendencies to process different amounts of data under certain environmental conditions were developed by Schroder, Driver & Streufert (1967). More specific and elaborate models of information processing among types of individuals have led to the development of decision style theory (Driver & Lintott, 1972). This theory categorizes individuals according to various dimensions of information processing, including the amount of information usage and the method of communication preference. Recently Driver & Mock (1975) have attempted to relate decision style theory to the evaluation of accounting information systems. These decision style characteristics relate to behavioral research on HRA, since decision-makers should have different preferences for HRA data as they do for other accounting information. For example, individuals with a strong need to make timely decisions may not utilize all aspects of an HRA system.

By "tolerance for ambiguity" we refer to an individual's willingness to cope with uncertainty and to accept risks in his information seeking and decision behavior. According to Budner (1962), individuals differ in their ambiguity tolerance and will demonstrate these differences as they do other personality factors. Dermer (1973) has applied the concept of ambiguity tolerance to the perceived importance of accounting information. One aspect of this ambiguity tolerance is the willingness (or lack thereof) to accept subjective or incomplete information in decision-making. This tolerance is a relevant contingency for HRA research, since different aspects of HRA affect information subjectivity and uncertainty.

Leadership Style

The manner in which a decision-maker manages people and tasks may be relevant for HRA research. We refer to the philosophical values and *modus operandi* which characterize individuals in this regard as *leadership styles.* While the literature about leadership styles concentrates heavily on attitudinal constructs,[9] we expect that these styles can also be useful indicators of information processing and decision behavior in HRA research. Our primary reason for this expectation is that HRA embraces specific management concepts (e.g. Likert's participative approach[10]) which are more in concert with certain human values (styles) than with others. Two major leadership style dichotomies which seem appropriate for HRA research are: (1) the distinction between autocratic and democratic management philosophies; and (2) the distinction between task and interpersonal orientations.

The distinction between autocratic and democratic styles of management has been discussed by several management theorists. Most prominent among these is McGregor (1960), who created the Theory X and Theory Y classification scheme. Haire, Ghiselli & Porter (1966) later studied the prevalence of these styles in an international study of more than 3600 managers. Caplan used a similar classification scheme to study the behavioral assumptions of managerial accounting.[11]

Perhaps the most pronounced contributions to a contingency theory of leadership have been made by Fiedler. In his work, Fiedler (1971) has postulated that the performance of an organization depends upon the interaction of leadership style and certain situational factors. Fiedler's basis for discriminating leadership styles is his "least preferred co-worker" (LPC) questionnaire, which purportedly identified an individual as primarily task-oriented or primarily interpersonal relationship-oriented.

[9]For a discussion of the various leadership style models, see Shetty (1970).

[10]The first major exposition of this approach can be found in Likert (1961).

[11]Caplan expressed this dichotomous classification within the context of classical and modern organization theories. For details of his analysis and the results of a subsequent field study, see Caplan (1966) and Caplan (1968).

Although the LPC and the contingency model have been challenged by other researchers,[12] Fiedler has provided evidence indicating that the LPC can be interpreted in this fashion when applied to stressful, anxiety-arousing situations (Fiedler, 1967). This leadership variable should be relevant for HRA research since its characteristics parallel those of certain HRA data (e.g. non-monetary HRV measures). This point is explicated later in the section on research hypotheses.

Managerial Experience

Decision-makers' familiarity with situations and analytical methods may affect their processing of HRA data. This familiarity overlaps with the previously-mentioned individual attributes in that such experience shapes the manner by which individuals perceive problems and make value judgments about appropriate courses of action. In addition, however, one's degree of managerial experience may influence the extent to which one is expert in utilizing intuition (as opposed to formalized data) to reduce uncertainty in decision-making.

[12]One such study critiquing Fiedler's work can be found in Graen, Alvares, Orris & Martella (1970).

SUMMARY OF THE FRAMEWORK

The contingency framework's major categories, including their attributes and components, are summarized in Table 1 below.

THE FRAMEWORK APPLIED: RESEARCH HYPOTHESES

Having identified the specific components of our contingency framework for behavioral HRA research, we will attempt to demonstrate its significance by presenting a series of research hypotheses with our rationale. The stated hypotheses do not fully exhaust the framework's potential, nor are they necessarily the most crucial questions of interest for HRA researchers. They are, rather, illustrative of

TABLE 1. Contingency Framework Summary

Categories	Attributes	Components
A. Information	1. Type of HRA data	
	2. Format of HRA data	a. Hierarchy of information measurement b. Compatibility of cues and rdsponses
	3. Quantity of data	
B. Organizational	1. Task environment	a. Extent of labor intensity b. Degree of task structure
	2. Management control system	a. Management's philosophy b. Concern for human organizational factors
	3. Organizational goals and rewards	
C. Individual	1. Cognitive style	a. Cognitive complexity/decision styles b. Tolerance for ambiguity
	2. Leadership style	a. Autocratic vs democratic b. Task vs interpersonal relationship orientation
	3. Managerial experience	

some key issues which we believe to be significant for future study.

Some of these hypotheses concern attitudes toward HRA (e.g. manager's *acceptance, receptivity,* etc.) rather than overt decision behavior. In this regard, we are assuming that, generally, such attitudes will be highly correlated with decision behavior. However, where we state or imply an effect of HRA *on* decision behavior, we do not necessarily assume the same effect *of* decision behavior. Consideration of such effects *of* decision behavior (i.e. outcomes or payoffs) is outside the scope of this paper. Furthermore, normative statements or value judgments about the hypothesized relationships are excluded from the following discussion.

Information Attributes

The first set of hypotheses relates to the general research question: How is the effect of HRA on managerial decision behavior dependent upon the type and format of HRA data and the total quantity of decision cues and information? Three such hypotheses are advanced, each of which is followed by a brief discussion of its theoretical rationale.

H_1: The information content of HRV measurements will be greater than that of HRI measurements to a managerial decision-maker.

The premise underlying this hypothesis is that managers, particularly knowledgeable ones, are more capable of estimating HRI measurements from conventionally reported data (i.e. noncapitalized outlay costs) than they are capable of estimating HRV measurements from conventional data (e.g. psychological test scores). Consequently, managers' judgment (prediction) errors would be decreased more by the HRV than by the HRI measurements. This hypothesized effect would be evidence of greater information content in the HRV measurements.

H_2: Monetary measures of HRV will be preferred to non-monetary measures of HRV in making compensation decisions.

As a general rule, we would expect formal measurement and reporting of HRV to benefit compensation decisions, since this process gives the decision-maker a more complete cost-benefit calculus (Flamholtz, 1974, p. 16) upon which to make judgments. The compatibility of cues and responses, previously discussed, would further support this hypothesis, since decision-makers would find monetary HRV measures more compatible with the format of response required in the compensation decision.

The hypothesis does not imply any general superiority or utility of monetary, as opposed to non-monetary, HRV measures. On the contrary, the inclusion of data format as a contingent variable recognizes that the preference for one or the other will vary among decision contexts. For example, non-monetary HRV data may be preferable in personnel selection decisions where the matching of people to role profiles is desired by the personnel manager.

H_3: HRA data will be utilized most effectively by decision-makers who are slightly below their optimal level of environmental complexity and information processing.

Much of the accounting literature that attempts to provide greater disclosure and better data for decision-makers neglects to consider circumstances which favor or inhibit the ability of an individual to cognitively process such data. The hypothesis, listed above, is addressed to one aspect of that processing—the state of mind where information can be "optimally" processed (as opposed to a stage of "information overload").

Schroder, Driver & Streufert (1967, p. 37) have argued that the decision-maker processes information in a typical curvilinear manner associated with the variation in current environmental parameters (complexity, noxity and eucity).

As is illustrated in Fig. 1, information usage in decision-making increases up to a point; thereafter, information overload occurs. Similar to this general schema, as HRA data are presented to decision-makers, the amount of information complexity (and, therefore, environmental load) should increase. We would expect to find most effective use of HRA data where these decision-makers are near, but slightly below, their optimal usage level.

Organizational Attributes

The second set of hypotheses relate to the general research question: How is the effect of HRA on decision behavior dependent upon an organization's task environment, management control system, or goals and rewards? Five such hypotheses are advanced.

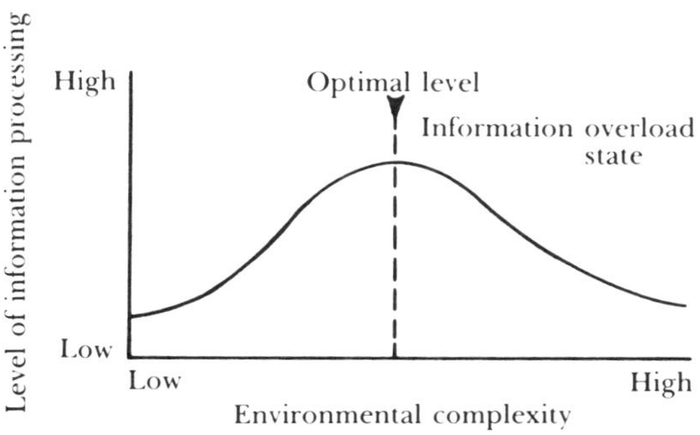

FIGURE 1. General relationship between environmental complexity and the level of human information processing.

H_4: The extent of HRA data utilization in performance evaluation will be positively associated with the degree of a firm's labor intensity.

Many physical capital intensive manufacturing firms should find certain aspects of HRA useful; the pioneering work at the R. G. Barry Corporation is a classic example of this fact. Notwithstanding this potential application, firms which are more labor intensive, such as C.P.A. firms and advertising agencies, should find HRA data intuitively more relevant. Particularly in the area of performance evaluation (based upon the efficient use of resources), labor intensive firms have more to gain from the systematic measurement and reporting of human resource cost and value than do physical capital intensive firms.

H_5: HRA replacement cost measures will be more important to decision-makers in structured than in unstructured task environments.

Some of the literature on contingency theory indicates that performance is improved when an organizational structure and philosophy is tailored to the task environment. For example, matching autocratic and participative managements with structured and unstructured task environments, respectively, tends to improve task performance.[13] Given the close association between the underlying tenets of HRA and the participative management school, one might expect HRA to be most beneficial in unstructured task environments.

[13]Results of this kind can be found in Lawrence & Lorsch (1967) and Morse & Lorsch (1970).

The hypothesis, above, which alludes to the contrary is based upon the expectation that human resource replacement costs are likely to be more reliably measured in a structured task environment where roles are well-defined and indicators of personnel output are more clearly identified. If this is the case, decision-makers in structured task environments will probably attach more importance to these replacement cost data.

H_6: System 4 (i.e. participative) organizations will be more receptive to HRA than will System 1 (i.e. hierarchic) organizations.

The system 1–4 classification is based upon Likert's (1967) work on structuring the human organization. The underlying premises and operational methods of System 4 are more consistent with the spirit of HRA concepts and measures than are those of System 1.

We would therefore expect that System 4 organizations would be more favorably inclined toward and more receptive to HRA than System 1 organizations. On the other hand, System 1 organizations may find certain aspects of HRA, such as its systematizing of that which is conventionally unstructured, to be appealing.

H_7: Utilization of HRV measures will be positively correlated with the emphasis on human organizational factors in management's control system.

Where management is concerned with developing and maintaining the potential of its human resources, we would expect that they would monitor changes in HRV measures and would, subsequently, incorporate such data in their control actions. This reasoning is based upon the arguments of Likert and Seashore, previously discussed.

H_8: Measures of HRV will be utilized more in firms which have "long-term" profit goals than in those with "short-term" profit goals.

Firms with "short-term" profit goals tend to place primary emphasis on current productivity and cost reduction. In contrast, firms with "long-term" profit goals tend to stress development of potential in addition to emphasizing current productivity.[14] Since measures of HRV are concerned with both the productivity and potential of individuals or groups, managerial decisions in organizations stressing "long-term" profit goals should be most responsive to such measures. Of course, HRA may cause a firm with "short-term" profit goals to redirect itself toward the "long-term". Flamholtz (1975) refers to this as the *paradigm function* of HRA.

Individual Attributes

The third, and final, set of hypotheses relate to the general research question: How is the effect of HRA on decision behavior dependent upon one's cognitive style, leadership style, or managerial experience? Five such hypotheses are advanced.

H_9: Individuals with less complex cognitive styles will be most receptive to the use of specific HRA data.

In the Driver & Mock (1975) framework, *decisive* individuals would be most receptive to HRA data. One might argue that those with more complex cognitive styles, such as the *integrative,* have personal values and organizational structure preferences that are more consistent with the philosophical spirit of HRA. However,

[14]Likert & Seashore (1963) describe the relative merits of the "long-term" approach and the dysfunctional consequences of the "short-term" approach.

receptivity to HRA data within the formal accounting information system (as opposed to receptivity to the less-structured information for which HRA is a supplement or a substitute) may be stronger for efficiency minded, limited data seekers such as the *decisives.*

H_{10}: Acceptance of HRV measures will be positively associated with individuals' tolerance for ambiguity.

The complexity and controversiality of HRV measures should make them more acceptable to certain types of individuals than to others. One might argue, for example, that HRV measures are less ambiguous cues than information provided by traditional personnel measurement techniques, such as psychological inventory scores. An intuitive extension of this argument would be that those who are intolerant of ambiguity can benefit, in terms of information processing ability, from the use of HRV measures. The hypothesis, above, which alludes to the contrary is based upon the premise that the subjective nature of HRV measurement will be a dominant factor in the acceptance or rejection of these data. In addition, those who are more tolerant of ambiguity tend to have personality traits, such as democratic management styles, which are more conducive to a human resource orientation.

H_{11}: In evaluating organizational performance, democratic style managers will make greater use of HRV information than will autocratic style managers.

The philosophical underpinnings of HRA concepts and measures, particularly those related to an individual's value to an organization, are closely linked with the modern school of organizational thought. In fact, it seems reasonable to argue that the conceptual origins of HRA can be traced back to Likert's work on participative management and the human organization.[15] We would expect, therefore, that democratic style managers would find the concept of HRV very appealing. In the McGregor tradition, this type of manager (Theory Y, in contradistinction to the autocratic Theory X manager) believes that subordinates can be motivated to accept responsibility for their work and that they are most effective when given an opportunity to influence their superiors' planning and decision-making. This thinking pattern seems directly antecedent to the more recent "human resources" school of thought, which prescribes the recognition of human knowledge, skills, and abilities as economic resources to be used for the achievement of organizational goals.[16] Recognizing the importance of these resources to organizational effectiveness, we would expect measures of HRV to be most relevant for individuals with a democratic management style.

H_{12}: Managers who are interpersonal relationship-oriented will be more attentive to non-monetary HRA data than will task-oriented managers.

As indicated previously, Fiedler (1967) has distinguished between managers who place primary emphasis on task accomplishment and those who place emphasis on maintaining strong superior-subordinate relations in the work environment. Underlying the latter relationship-oriented management style is a philosophy that the morale, satisfaction, and personal growth of subordinate employees are very important components of effective performance. Since nonmonetary HRA measures[17] are

[15]For an evolutionary perspective, see Brummet, Flamholtz & Pyle (1969, pp. 1–10).

[16]The philosophy of the human resources school is examined in Miles (1965).

[17]Three good discussions of this non-monetary, socio-psychological approach are contained in Likert & Bowers (1969), Likert & Pyle (1971), and Flamholtz (1974, pp. 151–163).

related directly to the assessment of morale and other sociopsychological variables, we expect that these data will be perceived as critical attention-direction[18] factors by interpersonal relationship-oriented managers.

H_{13}: The information content of HRA will be inversely related to the degree of a user's managerial experience.

This hypothesis stems from a study by Tomassini (1975) in which students (acting as managerial surrogates) made a personnel decision with HRA data as the experimental variable. Subjects without quantified HRA data apparently made erroneous subjective estimates of costs which an HRA system explicitly measures and reports. One might speculate, therefore, that HRA has the most information content, *ceteris paribus,* to inexperienced managers, while the more experienced individuals would be in a position to make more accurate estimates of non-quantified factors. If this were the case, the more experienced managers would gain less from the reporting of HRA data.

SUMMARY OF RESEARCH HYPOTHESES

The hypotheses suggested in previous sections of the paper are summarized in Table 2 below. Further, the hypotheses are classified to indicate their relation to our contingency framework.

[18]The term "attention-directing" is a middle-range problem solving process. For details, see Simon, Guetzkow, Kozmetsky & Tyndall (1954). A typical example of attention directing is standard cost variance reporting in managerial accounting systems.

LIMITATIONS OF THE FRAMEWORK

The contingency framework for behavioral HRA research presented in this paper has certain limitations, three of which seem worthy of comment here. First, the frame of reference assumed for this paper—an attempt to structure research about the effects of HRA on managerial decision behavior—may not be an optimal place from which to begin an empirical assessment of HRA. This approach merely represents the author's interests and the American Accounting Association Committee's mandate for research in this area.

Second, the scope of this framework (including its sets of attributes and their components) may not include all of the significant contingencies for behavioral HRA research. While the framework's elements appear to be relevant for the current state of the art, the importance of these and other factors should be continuously reassessed as a result of new research findings.

Third, the hypotheses utilized to illustrate the framework's potential application focused primarily on one attribute component at a time. This approach was used merely for simplicity. Where feasible, multivariate interactions should be examined in actual research projects. For example, an individual with a *decisive* cognitive style in a *structured* task environment may desire a different type or amount of HRA data than would an individual with an *integrative* cognitive style in an *unstructured* task environment. Another example of multiple contingency relationships is the likelihood that various types (e.g. cost and value) and formats (e.g. monetary and non-monetary) of HRA data will vary in usefulness with a particular decision's purpose and, possibly, with different cognitive and personality characteristics of the decision-maker.

What we are pointing out through these examples is that the *ceteris paribus* type of hy-

TABLE 2. Classified Summary of Hypotheses

Related to information attributes

H_1 : The information content of HRV measurements will be greater than that of HRI measurements to a managerial decision-maker.

H_2 : Monetary measures of HRV will be preferred to non-monetary measures of HRV in making compensation decisions.

H_3 : HRA data will be utilized most effectively by decision-makers who are slightly below their optimal level of environmental complexity and information processing.

Related to organizational attributes

H_4 : The extent of HRA data utilization in performance evaluation will be positively associated with the degree of a firm's labor intensity.

H_5 : HRA replacement cost measures will be more important to decision-makers in structured than in unstructured task environments.

H_6 : System 4 (i.e. participative) organizations will be more receptive to HRA than will System 1 (i.e. hierarchic) organizations.

H_7 : Utilization of HRV measures will be positively correlated with the emphasis on human organizational factors in management's control system.

H_8 : Measures of HRV will be utilized more by firms which have "long-term" profit goals than in those with "short-term" profit goals.

Related to individual attributes

H_9 : Individuals with less complex cognitive styles will be most receptive to the use of specific HRA data.

H_{10}: Acceptance of HRV measures will be positively associated with individual's tolerance for ambiguity.

H_{11}: In evaluating organizational performance, democratic style managers will make greater use of HRV information than will autocratic style managers.

H_{12}: Managers who are interpersonal relationship-oriented will be more attentive to non-monetary HRA data than will task-oriented managers.

H_{13}: The information content of HRA will be inversely related to the degree of a user's managerial experience.

potheses identified in this paper are not likely to generate sufficient explanatory evidence for behavioral assessments of HRA. Rather, more complex questions/hypotheses must be addressed if such research is to prove fruitful.

SUMMARY AND A CONCLUDING NOTE

We have presented a framework for behavioral HRA research, emphasizing the factors upon which HRA's impact may be contingent. Information, organizational, and individual attributes were identified and described. Thirteen hypotheses were proposed to demonstrate the framework's potential significance. While this framework provides an initial stimulus and structure for behavioral HRA research, the future of this line of inquiry depends greatly upon the persistence and communicative efforts of those attracted to HRA's concepts and methods. We hope that professional and industrial organizations will cooperate with new research endeavors so that many of the current uncertainties about HRA's behavioral impact may be resolved in the near future.

BIBLIOGRAPHY

American Accounting Association, Committee on Accounting for Human Resources, Report of the Committee on Accounting for Human Resources, *The Accounting Review, Supplement to Volume XLIX* (1974), pp. 115–126.

Brummet, R. L., Flamholtz, E. G. & Pyle, W. C., eds., *Human Resource Accounting: Development and Implementation in Industry* (Foundation for Research on Human Behavior, 1969).

Budner, S., Intolerance of Ambiguity as a Personality Variable, *Journal of Personality* (March, 1962), pp. 29–50.

Caplan, E. H., Behavioral Assumptions of Management Accounting, *The Accounting Review* (July, 1966), pp. 496–509.

———, Behavioral Assumptions of Management Accounting—Report of a Field Study, *The Accounting Review* (April, 1968), pp. 342–362.

Davidson, H. J. & Trueblood, R. M., Accounting for Decision-Making, *The Accounting Review* (October, 1961), pp. 577–582.

Dermer, J. D., Cognitive Characteristics and the Perceived Importance of Information, *The Accounting Review* (July, 1973), pp. 511–519.

Driver, M. J. & Lintott, J. T., *Managerial Decision Diagnostics,* unpublished paper, University of Southern California, 1972.

——— & Mock, T. J., Human Information Processing, Decision Style Theory, and Accounting Information Systems, *The Accounting Review* (July, 1975), pp. 490–508.

——— & Streufert, S., Integrative Complexity: An Approach to Individuals and Groups as Information-Processing Systems, *Administrative Science Quarterly* (June, 1969), pp. 272–285.

Elias, N. S., The Effects of Human Asset Statements on the Investment Decision, *Empirical Research in Accounting: Selected Studies, 1972,* pp. 215–233.

Fiedler, F. E., *A Theory of Leadership Effectiveness* (McGraw-Hill, 1967).

———, Validation and Extension of the Contingency Model of Leadership Effectiveness: A Review of Empirical Findings, *Psychological Bulletin,* Volume 76 (1971), pp. 123–148.

Flamholtz, E., *Human Resource Accounting* (Dickenson, 1974).

———, The Metaphysics of Human Resource Accounting and Its Implications for Managerial Accounting, *The Accounting Forum* (December, 1975), pp. 51–61.

——— & Lundy, T. S., Human Resource Accounting for C.P.A. Firms, *The CPA* (October, 1975), pp. 45–51.

Graen, G., Alvares, K., Orris, J. B. & Martella, J. A., Contingency Model of Leadership Effectiveness: Antecedent and Evidential Results, *Psychological Bulletin* (1970), pp. 285–296.

Haire, M., Ghiselli, E. E. & Porter, L. W., *Managerial Thinking—An International Study* (Wiley, 1966).

Hall, J., O'Leary, V. & Williams, M., The Decision-Making Grid: A Model of Decision-Making Styles, *California Management Review* (Winter, 1964), pp. 43–54.

Lawrence, P. R. & Lorsch, J. W., *Organization and Environment* (Harvard Business School, 1967).

Likert, R., *New Patterns of Management* (McGraw-Hill, 1961).

———, *The Human Organization: Its Management and Value* (McGraw-Hill, 1967).

——— & Bowers, D. G., Organization Theory and Human Resource Accounting, *American Psychologist* (June, 1969), pp. 585–592.

——— & Pyle, W. C., Human Resource Accounting: A Human Organizational Measurement Approach, *Financial Analysts Journal* (Jan/Feb, 1971), pp. 75–84.

——— & Seashore, S. E., Making Cost Control Work, *Harvard Business Review* (Nov/Dec, 1963), pp. 96–108.

Luthans, F., The Contingency Theory of Management: A Path Out of the Jungle, *Business Horizons* (June, 1973), pp. 75–84.

McGregor, D., *The Human Side of Enterprise* (McGraw-Hill, 1960).

Miles, R. E., Human Relations or Human Resources? *Harvard Business Review* (July/Aug, 1965), pp. 148–163.

Miller, G. A., The Magic Number Seven, Plus or Minus Two: Some Limits on Our Capacity for Processing Information, *Psychological Review* (1956), pp. 81–97.

Morse, J. J. & Lorsch, J. W., Beyond Theory Y, *Harvard Business Review* (May/June, 1970), pp. 61–68.

Pyle, W. C., Monitoring Human Resources "On

Line", *Michigan Business Review* (July, 1970), pp. 19–32.

Schroder, H. M., Driver, M. J. & Streufert, S., *Human Information Processing* (Holt, Rinehart & Winston, 1967).

Shetty, Y. K., Leadership and Organizational Character, *Personnel Administration* (July/Aug, 1970), pp. 14–20.

Simon, H. A., Guetzkow, H., Kozmetsky, G. & Tyndall, G., *Centralization vs Decentralization in Organizing the Controller's Department* (The Controllership Foundation, 1954).

Slovic, P. & Lichtenstein, S. C., The Relative Importance of Probabilities and Payoffs in Risk Taking, *Journal of Experimental Psychology Monograph Supplement* (1968).

Tomassini, L. A., *Human Resource Accounting and Managerial Decision Behavior: An Experimental Study.* Unpublished doctoral dissertation, University of California, Los Angeles, 1974.

———, Assessing the Impact of Human Resource Accounting: An Experimental Study of Managerial Decision Preferences, Working Paper 75–50, Bureau of Business Research, The University of Texas at Austin, July, 1975.

Watson, D. J. H., Contingency Formulations of Organizational Structure: Implications for Managerial Accounting, in *Managerial Accounting: The Behavioral Foundations,* J. L. Livingston, ed. (Grid Inc., 1975).

Woodruff, R. L., Human Resource Accounting, *Canadian Chartered Accountant* (September, 1970), pp. 2–7.

*Accounting for the Costs and Benefits of Human Resource Development Programs: An Interdisciplinary Approach**

Philip H. Mirvis

Barry A. Macy
University of Michigan

An interdisciplinary approach to measuring the costs and social and financial benefits of human resource development is presented. The approach includes three distinct components: a cost model, an effectiveness model, and a cost-benefit comparison. The diverse interdisciplinary measures of development programs are presented. A critical discussion of the role of human resource accounting and other accounting measures in evaluation is included. Examples from two organizations illustrate the measurement approach. An examination of program evaluation criteria highlights the effect of cost-benefit analyses on the human resource development movement.

Even the casual reader of the organizational literature has noted that working people have come to be regarded as human resources. This transition is not simply a shift in terminology or a rephrasing of traditional managerial values, rather a semantic reflection of the heightened awareness of employees' importance to the firm. Bakke (1961; p. 24) captured this philosophy by characterizing the human resource function as a distinct series of managerial responsibilities and practices designed to

> achieve productive work and arrange for the maximum opportunity for expression of the full range of people's abilities and capacities in that productive work.

Most recently, Mills (1975) employs human resource development, HRD, as an acronym for a wide range of behavioral science and management technologies intended to improve both the operating effectiveness of the firm and the quality of working life experienced by its employees.

Behavioral scientists have been the most active in this movement, designing tools for stimulating and effecting organizational

From *Accounting, Organizations and Society,* Vol. 1, No. 2–3 (1976), pp. 179–193.

*This paper was prepared in connection with research being conducted in the Quality of Work Program, Survey Research Center, Institute for Social Research, University of Michigan and supported by the Ford Foundation (Grant No. 740–0430) and the United States Development Administration (Grant No. 99-06-009377) and the National Commission on Productivity.

changes consistent with those aims. They have experimented with job enrichment, interpersonal training programs, participative management, and autonomous work groups in a variety of organizations (see reviews in *Work in America*, 1972; Davis & Cherns, 1975). Yet, as two recent reviews of the field report, there is a paucity of well documented assessments of these projects (Katzell *et al.*, 1975; Srivastva *et al.*, 1975). Instead, there are a series of case studies, characterizing the experimental technologies and their implementation, but offering only a minimal evaluation of their effects.

Kahn (1974) and others have noted that, as a result, there is little comparative evidence by which to evaluate the strength and generalizability of these various technologies. Moreover, practicing managers and decision makers, unguided by systematic evaluations of past experiments, remain uninformed as to the cost and benefits of various development programs when contemplating experimentation in their own organizations. Consequently, Ash (1973) and others have questioned the current enthusiasm for human resource development and quality of work.

Accounting techniques are presently being developed which will test the merits of HRD. Alexander (1971) has proposed cost-benefit analyses of these programs. Pyle (1970) suggests using human resource accounting to compute a return-on-investment in human resources. Cheek (1973) reports on cost-effectiveness evaluations of personnel programs. This paper will examine these techniques and the more general role of accounting in HRD research. Admittedly, accounting has a circumscribed role, for assessment of these projects has an interdisciplinary flavor, attracting the services of psychologists, sociologists, and engineers, too. Nevertheless, some distinct accounting contributions can be identified, and this paper will report on the successes and limitations of the first applications.

A FRAMEWORK FOR HRD RESEARCH

Human resource development efforts produce multiple effects: work settings may be altered, attitudes may be improved, behavior may be changed, and financial benefits may accrue. The research function is to measure and report these effects. Yet, Steele (1973) and others have criticized research limited to program evaluation. They argue for research designed to generate and validate theory and principles. As such, the researchers' responsibilities include not only identifying program effects, but tracing their causal lineage. Further, the researchers must assess the costs and gains of these programs to guide future HRD decision making. This requires:

1. An underlying theory of human resource development which specifies the social and financial effects of HRD;
2. Broad measurement of the development program and a research design suited for causal inference; and
3. A model of financial assessment for determining the costs and benefits of HRD.

A Theory of Human Resource Development

The HRD research effort should not be left to a particular researcher's whim or convenience. It must be guided by an underlying theory of program effectiveness and employee development. This enables the researcher to: (1) identify variables likely to be influenced by the HRD efforts, and (2) formulate and test hypotheses regarding the intervening processes that produce the effects. As such, assessment incorporates not only the outcomes, but the process of HRD.

HRD programs can concentrate on individuals and their work setting. Resources may be allocated to produce structural changes in the nature of employees' jobs, work assignments, supervision, and so on, creating a more challenging and stimulating work environment. These changes are sometimes coordinated with interpersonally oriented programs, designed to facilitate employees' integration into the new working environment. Both these activities are intended to alter employees' perceptions of their jobs and their experienced work environment. They manifest themselves through individual growth, self-direction, satisfaction, physical and mental well-being. While this is a normative expectation, ignoring the quality and appropriateness of the development efforts and individual reactions to particular programs, it underscores the contention that HRD can effect socially-oriented objectives.

HRD can produce financial results, too. Employees' behavior may be conceptualized as a decision making process. Employees make choices about being available to work (March & Simon, 1958) and choices about how to perform at work (Lawler, 1973). Research indicates that employees will be more likely to come to work, rather than be absent or quit, if they obtain satisfaction from their jobs (Porter & Steers, 1973). They are likely to give more effort and better utilize new working methods if they expect to be rewarded for their efforts (Vroom, 1964). Thus, as HRD programs alter working environments and influence employees' perceptions of their jobs and their satisfaction, they should also effect employees' decisions with respect to job-related behavior. Resulting changes in absenteeism, turnover, accidents, and performance, in turn, will effect the operating effectiveness of the firm. Again, this is a normative view, but illustrates how HRD can impact financial objectives.

The purpose of HRD assessment is to measure the accomplishment of these social and financial aims. By incorporating and validating the underlying theory, however, researchers can come to document how these effects are produced and under what conditions. Toward this end, longitudinal assessment must be undertaken within the context of a research design and expansive measurement approach.

HRD Research Design and Measurement

To document that changes in intervening processes and outcomes are due to HRD activities, behavioral scientists have begun utilizing quasi-experimental designs in the field. Frequently, they employ comparison groups to assess the relative effects of the projects (see discussion by Sherwood, Morris & Sherwood, 1975). In practice, however, a myriad of exogenous events often cloud parallels between experimental and comparison groups and it becomes difficult to trace changes in employees' attitudes and behavior to particular development activities (see discussion by Weiss & Rein, 1970).

In response, Lawler (1975) calls for interdisciplinary assessment of these HRD projects over time. By evaluating these projects using measures from different disciplines, the researchers seek convergent validity between multiple measures of program effects (see discussion by Edwards, Guttentag & Snapper, 1975). This argues for formation of an interdisciplinary research team to document both the process and outcomes of HRD. The immediate effects of the human resource development project can be captured via on-site observation. Sociologists can assess changes in the formal structures of the organization such as decision making and communication patterns. Engineers can evaluate improved work methods and estimate their effects on the costs of goods and services. Psychologists can document changes in employees' attitudes and behavior. The accountant's function, where possible, is to assess the project in financial terms.

A Model of Financial Assessment

Ideally, the accountant can report the costs and benefits of these projects. Figure 1 presents a cost-benefit approach for assessing HRD projects. The figure depicts several different development programs, $x_1 - x_5$. There are three distinct accounting activities (King, 1970) necessary for evaluating these programs: (1) a *cost model* needed for identifying the firm's direct costs and losses in productive time traced to the development effort; (2) an *effectiveness model* used for measuring and validating the effects of a project on the work environment and employees' attitudes, behaviors, and performance and expressing these effects in financial terms; and (3) a *synthesizing model* needed to compare the costs and benefits of a program. Both social and financial goals can be contrasted with project costs. The synthesizing model is used to identify either the most cost-effective or most cost-beneficial HRD program. Both criteria can be used when evaluating a number of HRD efforts.

Armed with a theory of employee development, a broad array of measures, and a model of financial assessment, researchers are prepared to evaluate a HRD program. The remainder of this paper will consider the accounting tasks in this endeavor, noting the particular measurement methods and strategies and providing some illustrative examples.

THE ACCOUNTING FUNCTIONS

Identifying the Costs of an HRD Program

It would seem evident that organizations would want to know what they spend on human resource development. Yet, in many organizations their expenditures are scattered in the budgetary accounts of various cost centers. Following the introduction of human resource accounting dissaggregation guidelines (Brummet, Flamholtz & Pyle, 1968), however, an organization's expense-per-employee can be computed.

Human resource accounting, as envisioned by Likert (1961), treats these expenditures as an investment in employees, indicative of their value to the firm (Woodruff, 1970). The logic behind this is straightforward, arguing that development costs produce benefits beyond the current accounting period. However, a number of researchers have challenged the accuracy and utility of human asset valuation.

Specifically, Lawler (1974) and others have questioned the legal and ethical implications of human asset valuation. In rejoinder, Flamholtz (1974) contends that employees' services are the appropriate asset, and offers a stochastic model valuing predicted service time, a process analogous to valuation of capital investments. Mirvis & Macy (1976) note the absence of convergence between different valua-

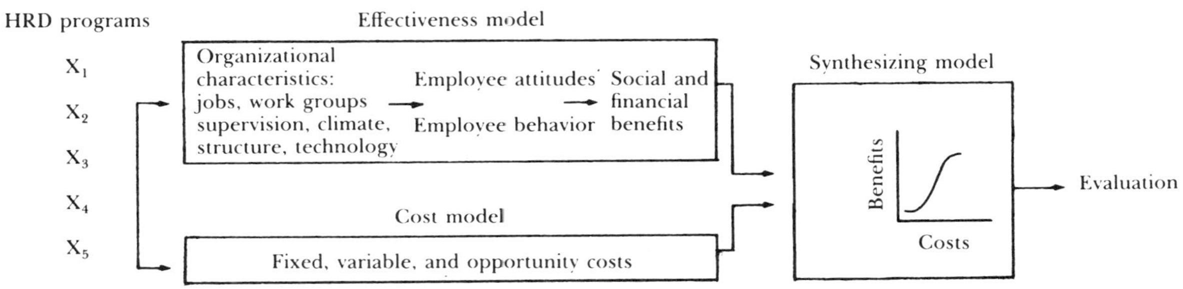

FIGURE 1. Cost-benefit model for HRD programs.

tion models. Flamholtz (1972) argues instead for surrogate measures of value and reports finding convergent validity between measures of replacement costs, performance, and compensation and discriminant validity vs other valuation methods. Nevertheless, these surrogate measures are hardly inviolate, failing to contend with a non-interval salary structure and differences between wages and marginal productivity.

This is not to say that human resource accounting is not useful for HRD. Indeed, if employer's expenses in these projects can be capitalized, it may help to stimulate future expenditures. Rather, it is the assignment of value to individual's services that raises problems for HRD research. To evaluate a specific HRD program, the researcher must distinguish the investment value-per-employee. If gross or net book value is used, Rhode & Lawler (1973) note there is no accounting for individual differences in skill acquisition and development. Beyond these individual differences, there is also the potential for group or situational variability. If economic value is used, there is a danger of circularity when comparing the investment with the financial return, for anticipated benefits are incorporated in the initial valuation (see discussion by Dearden, 1969). Given these troubling measurement issues, Macy & Mirvis (1976) argue that for research and assessment purposes, these expenditures should be treated as costs. As such, they can be contrasted with future benefits using the cost-benefit calculus.

Notwithstanding these objections, many of the tools developed by human resource accountants can be utilized in assessing the costs of human resource development. Human resource accountants have distinguished the fixed, variable, and opportunity costs of HRD efforts. Variable costs include the consultants' fees and expenses associated with their activities. These costs vary depending on the type of program and the intensity and duration of the development activities, and should be reported in deflated dollar terms. The site incurs variable costs, too, in the form of lost worker productivity and overtime. The project's fixed costs include salaries, wages, and benefits associated with employees' lost time, and the resulting unabsorbed burden. Opportunity costs reflect the profit contribution of employees' lost time. In addition, there is an estimable opportunity cost, the "opportunities foregone" (Rothenberg, 1975) which might have been realized had the HRD resources been directed toward other organizational ends.

Measuring the Benefits of an HRD Program

As an HRD program takes effect, changes should be observed in the work environment. Consequently, attitudes and behaviors may be altered and, as HRD theory proposes, social and financial benefits should result. Recently, several accounting methods have been advanced to measure these benefits in monetary terms.

Financial Benefits. Following an HRD program, major financial benefits could be realized in increased productivity and cost savings associated with reduced absenteeism and turnover. Herrick (1975), recognizing this possibility, proposed a group of nonproductive behaviors likely to be influenced by human resource development programs. He further suggested reporting the cost savings associated with reductions in these behaviors.

The expression of behavior in financial terms is not a novel idea. A classic article by Brogden & Taylor (1950) addressed the potential for developing on-the-job performance criteria in cost accounting terms. Rather, it is the intention to systematically identify, define, measure, and financially quantify the behavioral and performance outcomes of employees that represents a new undertaking. This shifts the emphasis from assigning a value to employees, to assessing the economic consequences of their behavior.

Macy & Mirvis (1976) developed the behavioral-economic methodology for defining, measuring, and costing the behaviors likely to be influenced by human resource development efforts. They provide three criteria for inclusion of a behavior:

1. It had to be defined so that it was significantly affected by the work structure;
2. It had to be measurable and convertible to significant costs to the organization;
3. The measures and costs of the behaviors had to be mutually exclusive.

Consistent with these criteria, behavioral definitions were devised, distinguishing behaviors such as absence because of jury duty, funerals, maternity, and so on from those related to the work environment. Behaviors like alcohol consumption were omitted, for though potentially related to working conditions, they manifest themselves in the costly behaviors of absenteeism and tardiness.

The research identified ten behavioral variables in two broad categories:

- *Participation - Membership.* Absenteeism — Turnover—Strikes—Tardiness.
- *Performance-on-the-Job.* Production under standard—Quality under standard—Grievances—Accidents—Unscheduled downtime and machine repair—Material utilization and inventory shrinkage.

Coupling behavioral definitions with standard measures developed from governmental reporting requirements and accepted organizational and accounting practices provided the behavioral indices from which to allocate the costs to a firm. The costs were conceptualized in two fashions. The first provided a distinction between outlay and time costs, the second between fixed, variable, and opportunity costs. These reflect direct and indirect costs and lost profit potential. An example of a variable cost would be paid overtime traced to absenteeism; a fixed cost would be salaries plus benefits of personnel involved in replacing the absent worker, while an opportunity cost would be the profit lost during the replacement process. These distinctions are important as only variable costs are directly related to incidents of nonproductive behavior. Fixed and opportunity costs will probably vary only with incremental changes in those incidence levels.

Using this methodology, a researcher can identify the financial outcomes of a human resource development project. Variable savings might include improved marginal productivity through increased product quality and quantity, limited overtime, reduced supply and material consumption, and less unscheduled maintenance. Further, wages and other expenses due to absenteeism, accidents, and grievances could be decreased. These would include the expense of maintaining a replacement work force. Potential fixed savings could be realized if some of the service demands placed on the personnel, industrial relations, safety, and quality control departments were reduced. Opportunity savings might be realized if supervisor's time, formerly spent in replacing absent employees or turnovers, could be put to more productive use. Behavioral-economic measurement provides the methods for highlighting these cost savings.

However, this approach, like human asset accounting, has inherent measurement difficulties. While the return-on-employee-investment is limited to assessing changes in the expected service life of personnel, the behavioral-economic measures include a more complete accounting of financial results. Moreover, while individual and situational differences in skill acquisition and development following a project cannot be accurately assessed using a singular return-on-investment measure, a series of benefit measures can reflect that development through behavioral changes. Nevertheless, like asset models, this method incorporates estimations of lost productivity, learning curve costs, supervisory training time, etc. While the accuracy of these costs can be checked through time-sampled observation, some estimation is always included. Further, some of the dollar components are averaged across persons or incidents of behavior, blurring some of the uniqueness of individual actions. While this methodology can be used for identifying the financial effects of HRD, social benefits can be produced, too. Accounting methods have recently been proposed to estimate the financial gain associated with these social benefits.

Social Benefits. The effects of an HRD program can be assessed using traditional psychological and social indicators. For example, improvements in the working environment can be assessed using job observations (Jenkins *et al.*, 1975). Some firms have conducted medical examinations to assess the effects of HRD on employees' health. Most often, however, these social effects are measured using attitude questionnaires. Myers & Flowers (1974) propose to financially assess employees' attitudes by multiplying salary dollar times a weighted attitude score to measure the potential dollar value increases that would be expected from improved attitudes. However, no mention is made of the relationship of these attitudes to the firm's development programs or to resulting behavioral changes. Further, whether the marginal productivity associated with attitude and behavior changes will equal the estimated value improvement is ignored. This work, at best, provides a way for organizations to estimate the impact of organizational salaries on employee morale. It offers little guidance on relating financial improvements to human resource development.

An alternative approach is advanced by Mirvis & Lawler (in press). Building on the work of Likert & Bowers (1973), they propose to correlate relevant job attitudes and perceptions with employees' behavior, and using the cost methodology presented earlier, determine the cost-per-employee associated with existing levels of job satisfaction, motivation, etc. When the human resource programs produce attitude changes, future behavioral changes are predicted and a new cost-per-employee level estimated. The degree of estimated behavioral and cost change is predicted on the amount of behavioral variance accounted for in the attitude-behavior relationships. As the projects influence attitudes, behaviors and costs, these estimates are validated against cost reductions.

For example, these authors found the correlation between bank tellers' intrinsic motivation and balancing shortages was $-.23$ in a midwestern bank employing 160 tellers. The average shortage per teller was $25.27 per month. It was estimated that an improvement in intrinsic motivation of $.145\sigma$ would reduce shortages per teller to $23.25 per month. Similar estimates were made incorporating the costs of absenteeism and turnover. Using this approach, gains in intrinsic motivation could be reflected in estimated cost savings.

Following change activities in the bank, it was found that intrinsic motivation increased $.145\sigma$ and that shortages per teller were reduced to $21.71. As such, the actual cost savings only approached the estimate. This model assumes a constant attitude-behavior relationship. Over the course of the project, however, the magnitude of this relationship can change, invalidating the previous estimates. Further, this model assumes a direct relationship. Again, the relationship might be linear or curvilinear. While these factors complicate the calculations, they are easily accommodated into future estimates. This approach provides a means for estimating changes in employee's perceptions and attitudes in financial terms.

Merely reporting social and financial gains does not guarantee that the improvements resulted from the human resource development program. Reduced turnover, for example, may be indicative of employment market conditions, rather than effective employee development. Therefore, it is important for the research team to validate the effectiveness model and underlying theory of HRD. This can be accomplished by observing concomitant improvements in behavioral and attitudinal measures in experimental as opposed to control groups. Further, multivariate analyses should indicate a correlation between the behavioral and attitudinal increases (cf. Azzi, 1973). By validating the effectiveness model, researchers analytically relate financial and social gains to the HRD program. In addition, by estimating the financial impact of employee attitudes, researchers can provide estimates of future financial improvements. These estimates can serve to justify resource expenditures to otherwise skeptical organizational decision makers. These analyses, however, will account for only a percentage of the variance in resulting benefits. The remaining variance is unrelated to measured variables in the effectiveness model. As this variance becomes large, confidence that HRD produced the benefits is reduced. It remains for the researchers to compare the costs and benefits of an HRD program.

Cost-Benefit Comparisons

For illustrative purposes, two diverse examples of HRD cost-benefit comparisons are presented. In the first case, project costs are related with improvements in employee attitudes following an organizational development experiment. In the second case, project costs are contrasted with the financial results of another experiment.

Example 1. In this case, the costs of an organizational change effort in an engineering design division of a major United States utility company have been computed. Nearly 385 unionized employees, predominantly professional engineers and draftsmen responsible for preparing complex designs and technical drawings, were involved in an 18 month development effort. The major costs of the program include the fees and expenses of several consultants, $124,346, and the employees' time spent in project meetings, training activities, etc., involving 8,275 hr at a cost of $95,898. The total project's costs during this period were $220,224.

Table 1 reports the intercorrelations between the consulting expenses, manpower hours, manpower costs, and total costs for ten participating departments. It indicates significant relationships between the two cost components and both are related to the project's departmental manpower hours and, of course, total costs.

Table 2 shows the relationship of these cost components and manpower hours with changes in employees' job attitudes and self-reported attendance, measured at the begin-

TABLE 1. Inter-Relationships of Project's Cost and Manpower Hours in a U.S. Utility
$N=10$

Consultant's expense	1.0			
Manpower costs	.97**	1.0		
Manpower hours	.99**	.97**	1.0	
Total costs	.90**	.89**	.92**	1.0
	Consultant's Expense	Manpower Costs	Manpower Costs	Total Costs

**$p<0.01$

TABLE 2. Relationship of Project Costs to Attitude and Attendance Changes[1] in a U.S. Utility N=10

	Intrinsic Motivation	Absenteeism	Supervision	Effort to Performance
Consultant's expense	−.53	−.20	.02	.75**
Manpower costs	−.58*	−.22	.07	.72**
Manpower hours	−.52	−.19	.00	.77**
Total costs	−.31	−.16	−.20	.90**

[1]Reported as 'true' gain score
*$p < 0.05$
**$p < 0.01$

ning of the project and, again, after 10 months. The changes in attitudes and attendance are reported as "true" gain scores (Cronbach & Furby, 1970). This measure is calculated by partialling out, through regression, that portion of attitude or attendance change that would be predicted simply from the initial measure, irrespective of the level of development activities. Surprisingly, the table shows that the project's costs are negatively related to improvements in intrinsic motivation, that is, in those departments where consultants' and employees' expenses are the highest, employees' personal motivation for doing their jobs well has actually decreased. There is little relationship between the project's costs and improvements in supervision, but some correlation between the costs and reductions in employees' absenteeism. The most significant relationship is between the project's costs and employees' beliefs that effort leads to good performance. Over the course of the project, in those departments where the expenditures are highest, the belief that effort leads to good performance has solidified. Figures 2 and 3 show this effect graphically, depicting the relationship of total project costs and manpower hours with effort-to-performance improvements in each department of the utility.

While Table 2 provides some evidence of the HRD program's effects, it is subject to overinterpretation. First, analyzing the true gain scores with a comparison analysis of variance (Hays, 1973, p. 596) shows that none of the gain scores used in Table 2 were found to be significant. In essence, after 10 months of an HRD project in the U.S. utility, there was no significant attitudinal change. Second, the number of participating departments is only ten, calling into question the stability of the resulting relationships. Still, in larger organizations with more experimenting units, this problem is minimized and confidence levels can be computed to test the stability of the resulting correlations. Third, this approach assumes a

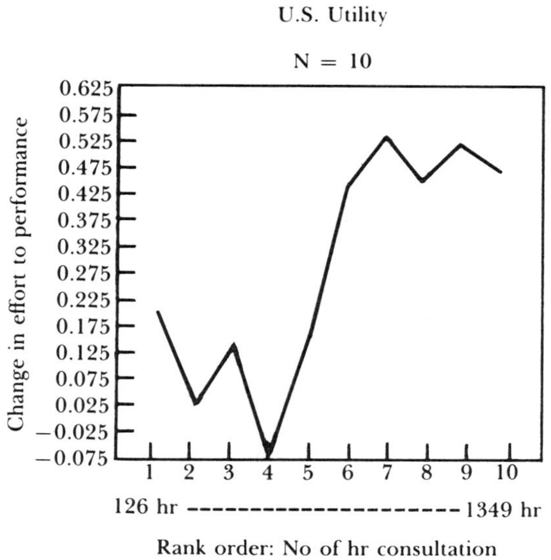

FIGURE 2. Total project hours and costs and changes in effort-to-performance beliefs.

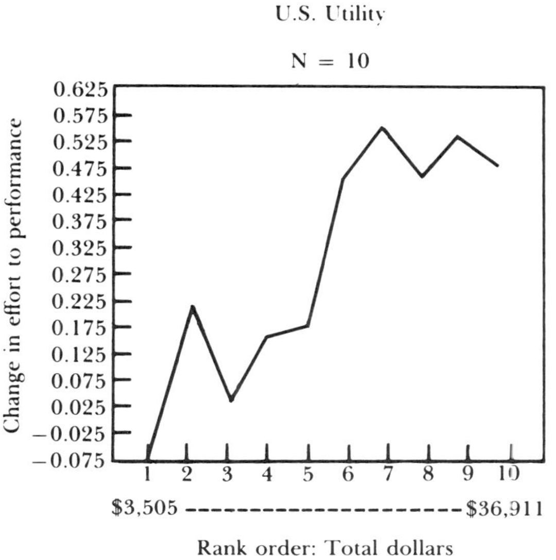

FIGURE 3. Total project costs and changes in effort-to-performance beliefs.

linear cost-attitude change relationship. This relationship might be curvilinear, but this, too, can be accommodated statistically.

This analysis compares projects with respect to the firm's expenditures, only. It says nothing about the quality of the project. To accomplish this, common qualitative characteristics of the development project can be measured. Questionnaires can ask employees to evaluate the quality of the consultant's work, their understanding of relevant theory, the clarity of their role expectations and the goals of the project, their beliefs about its efficacy, their commitment to the project, etc. These common descriptors can be related with employees' job perceptions, too. Combining these measures with the firm's expenditures provides a means to relate both the quality and quantity of human resource development activities to employees' perceptions of their work environment. This provides for a comparative assessment of these projects and their impact.

The advantage of this cost and social benefit comparison is that it can be used for ongoing project assessment. Researchers can gain insight into the early effects of HRD activities, noting areas of attitudinal improvement and the intervening time lags. If warranted, this can stimulate changes in the intensity or direction of HRD activities. Further, it can highlight for organizational decision makers the initial results of the project, albeit, the non-financial ones. The theory of HRD argues that these attitudinal improvements will influence financial results. A second example illustrates this cost and financial benefit comparison.

Example 2. In this case, the costs and benefits of HRD at another experimental site are reported. XYZ Corporation is a unionized manufacturing and supplying plant in a rural area of the United States. It is located in a small community of 8000 people. The plant's average hourly employment for study periods one, two, and three respectively was 652, 884, and 900 persons. The average hourly wage rates per hour during these periods were $2.67, $2.83, and $3.24 respectively. The average supervisory wage per hour for these same periods were $6.46, $8.08, and $8.50. The XYZ workforce was composed of approximately 53% minority employees; 66% of the personnel lacked a high school diploma. The firm's cost accounting system was a typical industrial product costing system which accumulates cost through direct labor cost centers.

The original social science team was composed of three third-party consultants from the disciplines of social and organizational psychology and productivity measurement. After the initial HRD action period, the social psychologist became the sole project director working with an on-site quality of work committee and an advisory committee. Both of these committees were comprised of union and management personnel from the company and their international union. In addition, the project director had two on-site participant-observers for assistance. The HRD project at XYZ has been on-going for 3 yr. Behavioral and financial data have been collected for 4 yr (i.e. baseline period from May, 1972–April, 1973; period 2 from May, 1973–April, 1974; period 3 from May, 1974–April, 1975; and period 4 from May, 1975–April, 1976.

Tables 3 and 4 present the behavioral and financial data for the baseline period and periods 2 and 3.

Table 3 reflects the incidence and rate of some of the participation membership and performance-on-the-job behaviors over three periods of time at the research site. Such reporting attests to the feasibility of computing measures over multi-year periods, providing the opportunity for change assessment. Table 4 reports the cost per incident and total estimated organizational costs for each behavior measurable at the research site during the baseline and the first two periods of the change activities. Costs for the last period represent data from only eight months, except for production and quality below standard, so for computational purposes, year-end projections were computed and are reported. Constant dollar comparisons indicate a significant cost increase in period 2

TABLE 3. Incidents and Rates of Behaviors at XYZ Corporation 1972–1975

Behaviors and Performance	Period 1 1972–1973		Period 2 1972–1973		Period 3* 1972–1973	
	Number of Incidents	Rate(%)	Number of Incidents	Rate(%)	Number of Incidents	Rate(%)
Absenteeism[1]						
Absences	4,420	3.3	9,604	5.19	6,905	3.76
Leave days	—	—	12,486	6.75	13,332	7.25
Accidents						
OSHA						
Hourly workforce	251	38.35	316	35.34	208	23.76
Salaried workforce	16	17.56	12	10.90	9	7.90
Minor[2]	3,181	421.80	6,713	706.08	5,559	635.26
Revisits[2]	1,806	216.99	2,455	258.22	2,028	231.74
Turnover						
Voluntary						
Hourly workforce	132	24.10	229	29.59	116	14.57
Salaried workforce	18	17.00	29	24.17	4	3.25
Involuntary						
Hourly workforce	118	21.40	161	20.80	120	16.08
Salaried workforce	—	—	5	4.17	4	3.25
Tardiness[3–4]	48	8.68	—	—	—	—
Grievances[4]	57	10.40	40	5.17	41	5.15

*Actual incidents and rates only for 8 month period; projection for the period is reported.
[1]Hourly workforce; leave days were instituted in periods 2 and 3 are measured and computed as absences.
[2]Hourly and salary employees combined.
[3]This is a daily rate; available only in period 1.
[4]Hourly workforce.

(Source: B. A. Macy & P. H. Mirvis, *ASQ*, in press)

TABLE 4. Estimated Costs of Behavior at XYZ Corporation 1972–1975

	Period 1 1972–1973		Period 2 1973–1974		Period 3 1974–1975*	
Behaviors and Performance	Estimated Cost Per Incident ($)	Estimated Total Cost ($)	Estimated Cost Per Incident ($)	Estimated Total Cost ($)	Estimated Cost Per Incident ($)	Estimated Total Cost ($)
Absenteeism[1]						
Absences	55.36	$ 286,360	53.15	$ 510,453	62.49	$ 431,494
Leave days	—	—	55.04	687,229	61.64	821,795
Accidents[1]						
OSHA	727.39	194,213	698.31	229,046	1,106.52	240,115
Minor	6.64	21,122	5.71	38,331	6.45	35,856
Revisits	6.64	11,992	5.71	14,018	6.45	13,081
Tardiness[1,2]	4.86	56,920	—	—	—	—
Turnover[1]						
Voluntary	120.59	18,089	131.68	33,973	150.69	18,083
Involuntary	120.59	14,230	131.68	21,859	150.69	18,686
Grievances	32.48	1,851	34.44	1,378	56.10	2,300
Quality below standard[3]	19,517	663,589	19,517	573,800	19,517	409,857
Production below standard[4]	22,236	266,838	22,236	335,764	22,236	255,714
Total costs[5,6]		$1,535,204		$2,445,851		$2,246,971

*Costs associated with absenteeism, leave days, accidents, turnover and grievances during the last 4 months of this period are projections. Product quality and production below standard are actual figures.

[1]Rates and costs for salaried personnel are assumed to be the same as those for hourly employees (Period 1: salaried absence costs—$41,669; salaried accident costs—$11,638; salaried tardiness costs—$9,641; salaried turnover costs—$1,829).

[2]Average tardiness time was 27 min.

[3]The costs of rejects and scrap was 3.4% of total sales for period 1. Each .1% reduction is valued at $19,517 per incident. Period 2 costs were 2.94% of total sales; period 3 costs were 2.1% of total sales. A constant dollar equivalency of $19,517 was used in periods 2 and 3 to discount inflation. Nondiscounted cost of quality below standard in period 2 was $667,015 ($23,028 per incident); in period 3, nondiscounted cost was $613,970 ($29,237 per incident).

[4]Plant productivity for period 1 was 88% of standard. The production below standard rate is 12%, thus, a reduction of 1% is valued at $22,236 per incident. Plant productivity in periods 2 and 3 was 84.9% and 88.5% of standard respectively. A constant dollar equivalency of $22,236 was used in periods 2 and 3 to discount inflation. Nondiscounted cost of production below standard in period 2 was $400,567 ($26,528 per incident); in period 3, nondiscounted cost was $405,938 ($25,299 per incident).

[5]The total cost in period 1 is $1,470,427 for hourly personnel; $64,777 for salaried personnel.

[6]The total cost is reflected in standard labor dollars. The estimated cost in real dollar equivalents in period 1: $1,688,724 or 10.4% of sales; in period 2: $2,690,436 or 8.45% of sales; in period 3: $2,471,668 or 10.61% of sales.

(Source: B. A. Macy & P. H. Mirvis, *ASQ*, in press)

and a moderate reduction, approximately $53,000 below the baseline figures, in period 3.

The cost-benefit analyses reported in Table 5 of the HRD project at XYZ Corporation reflect differences from the baseline attendance, turnover, and performance, etc. (see Table 4 for baseline figures). Table 5 indicates total costs have been $303,588 during periods 2 and 3. The total financial gains have been (−$227,240). From a financial viewpoint alone, the XYZ change experiment had a total net cost-benefit outcome of a (−$530,828).

After two complete years of an HRD project at XYZ Corporation that entailed over $300,000 of external and internal investment, the financial results have been disheartening.

TABLE 5. XYZ Corporation Human Resource Development Project Cost-Benefit Analysis

	Period 2 Initial Year HRD May, 1973–April, 1974 (Differences from base year)	Period 3—Second Year HRD May, 1974–April, 1975 (Differences from base year)	
Costs			
(1) Consultant fees, expenses, etc.[1]	$225,000	$ 61,000	
(2) Site employee time,[2,3] training activities, earned idle time, etc.	2,403	14,585	
Totals	$227,403	$ 76,185	$303,588
Benefits[4]			
Absenteeism	(224,093)	(145,134)	
Leave days	—	—	
Accidents			
OSHA	(34,833)	(45,902)	
Minor	(17,209)	(14,734)	
Revisits	(2,026)	(1,089)	
Tardiness	—	—	
Turnover			
Voluntary	(15,884)	6	
Non-voluntary	(7,629)	(4,456)	
Grievance	473	(449)	
Quality below standard	89,789	253,732	
Production under standard	(68,926)	11,124	
Totals[5–7]	($280,338)	$ 53,098	($227,240)

[1]Nine different organizations and funding agencies contributed action monies to the project. In addition, three organizations provided office space and services to project staff. These action monies do not include any assessment funds.

[2]Projected for 12 months from 5 months of data during period 2.

[3]Estimates of actual costs are low due to reporting of only hourly personnel.

[4]All estimate of benefits (costs) are indicated in relationship to Table 4.

[5]The HRD project has a negative effect of $280,338 in period 2 and a positive effect of $53,098 in period 3 compared to the baseline period.

[6]Assumes the benefits to be financial only.

[7]Comparing the total costs ($303,588) of the HRD project against the total estimated financial benefits (−$227,240) indicates the project has a net cost-benefit outcome of (−$530,828).

However, some social and non-work related benefits are just beginning to appear. Indeed, employees have been exposed to a variety of educational experiences, training opportunities, and health services, all important social aims. Moreover, the experiment is now proceeding into its fourth year with all participation indicating positive changes in labor-management relations at the site and some experimental groups reporting improvements in individual productivity.

This cost-benefit comparison assumes that all of the financial results are due to the HRD program. A more conservative cost-benefit analysis would compare the project's costs with only that percentage of the variation in financial results which could be traced to measured variables in the effectiveness model. Alternatively, as more comparable HRD experiments are undertaken, it will become possible to attach probabilities to achieving various financial gains. Confidence intervals could be established around the financial benefits and costs could be contrasted with gains weighted by the probability within the interval.

Both examples illustrate comparisons between the costs and benefits of HRD programs. They report only the early findings, but illustrate the use of cost-benefit comparisons in evaluating these undertakings. However, the organization uses distinct criteria in evaluating and interpreting these findings. Specifically, they may attempt to identify either the most cost-effective program or the most cost-beneficial one. Often these are not the same program. This determination can have a decided impact on the future of HRD within a firm.

THE PROBLEM OF EVALUATION

Cost-Effective HRD

Sometimes the organization will seek to find the most cost-effective human resource development program. These can be of two sorts: (1) the program that maximizes benefits, while keeping expenditures within an accepted range, and (2) the program that reaches an acceptable benefit level, while keeping expenditures to a minimum (both rely on suboptimization with Pareto criteria; see discussion in Merewitz & Sosnick, 1971). Utilization of either of these criteria can be a disservice to a HRD program.

In the first case, the organization has determined that the resources to be devoted to HRD are limited. Implicitly, the goals of the HRD program have been ordered against other organizational priorities and the available resources allocated accordingly. However, should market exigencies change, optimization of higher priority objectives may legitimate reductions in the HRD budget. Funds originally designed for employee development are often re-allocated as the market tightens. As a result, only those firms with the strongest philosophical commitment to HRD or those holding substantial uncommitted resources will be able to sustain a human resource development effort. The financially troubled firm, where HRD might have a substantial effect, may decide that a program is too expensive and drop it from consideration.

In the second case, the organization has determined that resources will be allocated until a pre-determined HRD goal is met. For example, an organization might consider employee challenge to be an important goal. The emphasis they place on challenge is determined by its merit or social good (see discussion by Musgrave, 1959). If merit criteria are used, the organization determines that consumers want goods or services produced by challenged workers, but that consumers are unwilling to pay for this challenge. Hence, the firm or the government is left to subsidize HRD. If social good criteria are employed, the increased cost of employee challenge is passed along to the consumers. In both circumstances, the firm and the market jointly establish an acceptable level of employee challenge. Thus, the most cost-effective program is the one that produces challenge within this accepted range, while minimizing expenditures to the firm. This, too, has consequences for HRD.

Specifically, cost-effectiveness evaluations discourage the full exploration of the potential of HRD. When resources are restricted, the productive possibilities of HRD are ignored. When goals are pre-determined, the potential associated with increased investment is untapped. Accordingly, cost-effectiveness comparisons may actually constrain a human resource development program within a firm. This argues for utilization of cost-beneficial evaluation criteria.

Cost-Beneficial HRD

Using cost-benefit criteria, a project would be judged successful if expenditures were outweighed by the present value of future benefits. It would be anticipated that challenged employees, for example, will compensate the firm through increased production and less absenteeism. The most beneficial program is the one that maximizes financial benefits while minimizing expenditures (suboptimization with Kaldor-Hicks criteria; see Merewitz & Sosnick, 1971). Cost-benefit criteria seem more suited to HRD than cost-effective criteria. They give full reign to the productive capacities of human resource development. They do not constrain investment or goal achievement, rather permit the firm to establish a balance between a project's costs and gains. Yet, it may be unreasonable to expect that the program which maximizes benefits will be the least expensive. Thus, the organization must identify the optimal investment point. Quirin (1967) argues for optimal determination based on the benefit/cost ratio. Merewitz & Sosnick (1971) argue that the resulting derivative may cause the firm to cease expenditures short of the point of maximal net benefit. Accordingly, they advocate optimization of the present value of net benefits (benefits-costs). This is the cost-benefit comparison reported in Example 2. Further, this comparison can be modified to incorporate resource limitation constraints where necessary. Nevertheless, cost-benefit comparisons should not be the sole criteria for evaluating HRD.

A FINAL NOTE

Traditional cost-benefits comparisons have relied solely on financial data. They do not incorporate externalities such as the non-financial costs or gains. While accounting methods are being developed to reflect social aims in financial terms, individual growth and well-being, organizational adaptability and goodwill cannot, and perhaps, should not be assigned an economic value. Consequently, decisions made solely to optimize financial gains are unguided by the effects of HRD on non-financial results.

Monsen & Downs (1968) argue that decision making in the firm is a process of maximizing individual decision maker's utilities. Banner & Baker (1973) contend that firms experimenting with HRD are committed to social ends. They note, "Employee satisfaction and growth is a legitimate corporate goal by itself, regardless of whether or not it contributes to profits" (p. 47). Consequently, for decision makers committed to the social goals of HRD, the net benefit point is merely one input into the decision process. Indeed, limiting program evaluation to a single financial indicator counterfeits the underlying philosophy of HRD. The goals of these programs are multifold; evaluation should follow suit. It seems imperative, then, to undertake interdisciplinary assessment of HRD.

The role of interdisciplinary assessment is to inform decision makers in the firm with respect to the full range of effects of HRD. This should not inhibit accountants and other researchers from participating with decision makers in evaluating a project (see discussion by Churchman & Schainblatt, 1969), rather, it simply argues that all costs and benefits be measured and reported. Otherwise, as Hatry (1970) notes, "Key value judgements that are rightfully the task of the political decision making process are instead made by analysts . . ." (p. 777).

Program evaluation must be guided by measurement, not impressions. Cost and benefit comparisons, under research conditions, provide one test of the merits of HRD. Further, validation of the effectiveness model determines a program's generalizability. The potential of cost-benefit comparisons of HRD is enormous. For example, the data reported here have helped to stimulate the consultants, the management, and the union of the aforementioned XYZ Corporation to reshape their development effort. They are beginning a cost savings program where employees and the management jointly share the financial benefits of increased output and reduced scrap, supply utilization, downtime, and rework. In addition, the management and the union are collaborating in establishing levels of plant efficiency and profitability. This experience suggests that those experimenting with HRD can utilize cost-benefit findings as well as other research information. The researcher's charge is to produce such data. It remains to refine the assessment methods, including the accounting activities, and incorporate them in interdisciplinary assessment in future HRD research.

BIBLIOGRAPHY

Alexander, M., Investments in People, *Canadian Chartered Accountant* (July, 1971), pp. 1–8.

Ash, P., Review of "Work in America," *Personnel Psychology* (1973), pp. 597–604.

Azzi, C. F., *Equity and Efficiency Effects from Manpower Programs* (Lexington, Mass.: Lexington Books, 1973).

Bakke, E. W., The Human Resources Function, *Management International Review* (1961), pp. 16–24.

Banner, D. & Baker, G., Human Resource Accounting: A Critical View, *MSU Business Topics* (Autumn, 1973), pp. 45–52.

Brogden, H. & Taylor, E., The Dollar Criterion-Applying the Cost Accounting Concept to Criterion Construction, *Personnel Psychology* (1950), pp. 133–154.

Brummet, R., Flamholtz, E. & Pyle, W., Human Resource Measurement—A Challenge for Accountants, *The Accounting Review* (1968), pp. 217–224.

Cheek, L. M., Cost Effectiveness Comes to the Personnel Function, *Harvard Business Review* (May–June, 1973), pp. 96–105.

Cronbach, L. J. & Furby, L., How We Should Measure 'Change'—or Should We? *Psychological Bulletin* (1970), pp. 68–80.

Churchman, C. W. & Schainblatt, A. H., PPB: How can it be Implemented? *Public Administration Review* (March–April, 1969), pp. 178–188.

Davis, L. E. & Cherns, A. B., eds., *The Quality of Working Life* (New York: The Free Press, 1975).

Dearden, J., The Case against ROI Control, *Harvard Business Review* (May–June, 1969).

Edwards, E., Guttentag, M. & Snapper, K., A Decision-Theoretic Approach to Evaluation Research. In E. Struening and M. Guttentag, eds., *Handbook of Evaluation Research* vol. 1 (Beverly Hills, Cal.: Sage Publications, 1975), pp. 139–182.

Flamholtz, E. G., Assessing the Validity of a Theory of Human Resource Accounting: A Field Study, *Journal of Accounting Research—Empirical Research in Accounting: Selected Studies,* 1972.

Flamholtz, E. G., *Human Resource Accounting* (Encino, Cal.: Dickenson Publ., 1974).

Hays, W. L., *Statistics for the Social Sciences* (New York: Holt, Reinhart & Winston, 1973).

Hatry, H., Measuring the Effectiveness of Nondefense Public Programs, *Operational Research Quarterly* (October, 1970), pp. 772–784.

Herrick, N., *The Quality of Work and its Outcomes: Estimating Potential Increases in Labor Productivity* (Columbus, Ohio: The Academy for Contemporary Problems, 1975).

Jenkins, G. D., Nadler, D. A., Lawler, E. E. & Cammann, C., Standardized Observations: An Approach to Measuring the Nature of Jobs, *Journal of Applied Psychology* (1975), pp. 171–181.

Kahn, R. L., Organizational Development: Some Problems and Proposals, *Journal of Applied Behavioral Science* (1974), pp. 485–502.

Katzell, R. A., Yankelovich, D., *et al., Work, Productivity, and Job Satisfaction* (New York: The Psychological Corporation, 1975).

King, B. G., Cost-Effectiveness Analysis: Implications for Accountants, *The Journal of Accountancy* (March, 1970), pp. 43–49.

Lawler, E. E., *Motivation in Work Organizations* (Monterey, Calif.: Brooks/Cole Pub. 1973).

Lawler, E. E., *Measuring the Human Organization.* Paper presented at Human Resource Accounting Seminar, Bonn, Federal Republic of Germany, 1974.

Lawler, E. E., *Evaluation Research: A Needed Emphasis in Organizational Behavior,* Paper presented at the Academy of Management Annual Convention, New Orleans, 1975.

Likert, R., *New Patterns of Management* (New York: McGraw-Hill, 1961).

Likert, R. & Bowers, D. G., Improving the Accuracy of P/L Reports by Estimating the Change in Dollar Value of the Human Organization, *Michigan Business Review* (1973), pp. 15–24.

Macy, B. A. & Mirvis, P. H., Measuring Quality of Work and Organizational Effectiveness in Behavioral-Economic Terms, *Administrative Science Quarterly* (in press, 1976).

March, J. & Simon, H., *Organizations* (New York: Wiley, 1958).

Merewitz, L. & Sosnick, S. H., *The Budget's New Clothes* (Chicago: Marham Publ., 1971).

Mills, T., Human Resources—Why the New Concern? *Harvard Business Review* (March–April, 1975), pp. 120–134.

Mirvis, P. H. & Macy, B. A., Human Resource Accounting: A Measurement Perspective, *Academy of Management Review* (in press, 1976).

Mirvis, P. H. & Lawler, E. E., Measuring the Financial Impact of Employee Attitudes, *Journal of Applied Psychology* (in press).

Monsen, R. J. & Downs, A., A Theory of Large Managerial Firms, in P. Lebreton, ed., *Comparative Administrative Theory* (Seattle: University of Washington Press, 1968), pp. 56–57.

Musgrave, R. A. *The Theory of Public Finance* (New York, McGraw-Hill, 1959).

Myers, M. S. & Flowers, V. S., A Framework For Measuring Human Assets, *California Management Review* (1974), pp. 5–16.

Porter, L. W. & Steers, R. M. Organization, Work, and Personal Factors in Employee Turnover and Absenteeism, *Psychological Bulletin* (1973), pp. 151–176.

Pyle, W. C., Monitoring Human Resources—'On Line', *Michigan Business Review* (July, 1970), pp. 19–32.

Quirin, D., *The Capital Expenditure Decision* (Homewood, Ill.: Irwin, 1967).

Rhode, J. & Lawler, E. E., Auditing Change: Human Resource Accounting. In M. D. Dunnette, ed., *Work and Nonwork in the Year 2001* (Monterey, Calif.: Brooks/Cole Publ., 1973), pp. 154–178.

Rothenberg, J., Cost-Benefit Analysis: A Methodological Exposition. In M. Guttentag and E. Struening, eds., *Handbook of Evaluation Research* vol. 2 (Beverly Hills, Cal.: Sage Pub., 1975), pp. 55–88.

Sherwood, C. D., Morris, J. N. & Sherwood, S., A Multivariate, Nonrandomized Matching Technique for Studying the Impact of Social Interventions. In E. Struening and M. Guttentag, eds., *Handbook of Evaluation Research* Vol. 1 (Beverly Hills, Cal.: Sage Publ., 1975), pp. 183–226.

Srivastva, S., Salipante, P. F., Jr., Cummings, T. G., Notz, W. W., Bigelow, J. D., Water, J. A., *et al., Job Satisfaction and Productivity* (Department of Organizational Behavior, Case Western Reserve University, Cleveland, Ohio, 1975).

Steele, S. M. *Contemporary Problems to Program Evaluation: Implications for Evaluating Programs for Disadvantaged Adults* (Syracuse, New York: Eric Clearinghouse on Education, 1973).

Vroom, V. H., *Work and Motivation* (New York: Wiley, 1964).

Weiss, R. S. & Rein, M., The Evaluation of Broad-Aim Programs: Experimental Design, Its Difficulties, and an Alternative, *Administrative Science Quarterly* (1970), pp. 97–109.

Woodruff, R., Human Resource Accounting, *Canadian Chartered Accountant* (1970), pp. 2–7.

Work in America. United States Department of Health, Education, and Welfare: Report of a Special Task Force to the Secretary, Washington, D.C., United States Government Printing Office, 1973.

Bibliography

Abdel-Khalik AR & EJ Lusk, "Transfer Pricing—A Synthesis", Accounting Review (January 1974), 8–23
Accounting, Organizations and Society, "Towards a Human Resource Accounting Bibliography", Bibli-oscene, Accounting, Organizations & Society (1976), 271–279
Adams JS, "Inequity in Social Exchange" Advanced Experiments in Social Psychology (1965), 2: 267–300
Alderfer CP, "An Empirical Test of a Need Theory of Human Needs", Organizational Behavior & Human Performance (1969), 142–175
Alderfer CP, Existence, Relatedness & Growth: Human Needs in Organizational Settings, (NY Free Press 1972)
American Accounting Association, Report of the Committee on Accounting & Information Systems, Supplement to Accounting Review (1971), 286–350
American Accounting Association, Report of the Committee on the Behavioral Science Content of the Accounting Curriculum, Supplement to Accounting Review (1971), 247–285
American Accounting Association, Report of the Committee on Social Costs, Supplement to Accounting Review (1975) 50–89
American Accounting Association, Report of the Committee on Accounting for Social Performance, Supplement to Accounting Review (1976), 38–69
American Institute of Certified Public Accountants, The Measurement of Corporate Social Performance (AICPA, 1977)
Amey LR, The Efficiency of Business Enterprises, (Allen & Unwin, 1969)
Amey LR, "Towards a New Perspective on Accounting Control", Accounting, Organizations & Society (1979), 247–258
Amey LR, Budget Planning and Control Systems, (Pitman, 1979)
Amey LR & DA Egginton, Management Accounting (Longman, 1973)
Andrisani PJ & RC Miljus, "Individual Differences in Preferences for Intrinsic Versus Extrinsic Aspects of Work" Journal of Vocational Behavior (1977), 14–30
Argyris C, Integrating the Individual & The Organization (Wiley, 1964)
Ashby WR, Design for a Brain: The Origin of Adaptive Behavior (Chapman & Hall, 1960)
Atkinson JW, "Towards Experimental Analysis of Human Motivation", in Atkinson (ed), Motives in Fantasy, Action and Society (Van Nostrand, 1958)
Baker F (ed), Organizational Systems (Irwin, 1973)
Barnard C, Functions of the Executive (Harvard University Press, 1938)
Becker SW & D Green, "Budgeting and Employee Behavior" Journal of Business (October, 1962), 392–402
Beer S, Decision and Control (Wiley, 1966)
Bennis WG et al, The Planning of Change (Holt, Rinehart & Winston, 1970)
Benston GJ, "The Role of the Firm's Accounting System for Motivation", Accounting Review (April 1963), 374–354

Berg N, "Strategic Planning in Conglomerate Companies", Harvard Business Review (May–June 1975), 79–92
Birnberg JG & R Nath, "Laboratory Experimentation in Accounting Research", Accounting Review (January 1968), 38–45
Blau P & R Schoenherr, The Structure of Organizations (NY Basic Books 1971)
Bobbitt HR et al, Organization Behavior (Prentice-Hall 1974)
Bodnar G & EJ Lusk, "Motivational Considerations in Cost Allocation Systems", Accounting Review (October 1977), 857–868
Boulding K, The Meaning of the Twentieth Century (Allen & Unwin 1965)
Bower J, Managing the Resource Allocation Process (Harvard University, Graduate School of Business Administration, Division of Research, 1970)
Bruns WJ & DT DeCoster, Accounting and Its Behavioral Implications (McGraw-Hill 1969)
Buckley A & E McKenna, "Budgetary Control and Business Behaviour", Accounting & Business Research (Spring 1972), 137–150
Burlingame JF, "Information Technology and Decentralization", Harvard Business Review (November–December 1961)
Burns T & GM Stalker, The Management of Innovation (Tavistock 1961)
Caplan EH, "Behavioral Assumptions of Management Accounting", Accounting Review (July 1966), 496–509
Caplan EH, Management Accounting & Behavioral Science (Addison-Wesley 1971)
Carper WB & JM Posey, "The Validity of Selected Surrogate Measures of Human Resource Value", Accounting, Organizations & Society (1976), 143–52
Carrell MR & JE Dittrich, "Equity Theory: The Recent Literature", Academy of Management Review (April 1978), 202–210
Chandler A, Strategy and Structure (MIT Press 1962)
Channon DF, The Strategy and Structure of British Enterprise (MacMillan 1973)
Chenhall RH, "Modelling/ Some Implications for Accountants", Australian Accountant (October 1974)
Cherrington DJ & JO Cherrington, "Appropriate Reinforcement Contingencies in the Budgeting Process", Journal of Accounting Research, Selected Studies (1973) 225–253
Child J, "Organizational Structure and Strategies of Control: A Replication of the Aston Study", Administrative Science Quarterly (1972) 163–177
Child J & R Mansfield, "Technology, Size, and Organization Structure", Sociology (1972) 368–393
Churchill NC & AB Toan, "Reporting on Corporate Social Responsibility", Journal of Contemporary Business (Winter 1978), 5–18
Coch L & J French, "Overcoming Resistance to Change", Human Relations (1948)
Cohen MD, JC March & JP Olsen, "A Garbage-Can Model of Organizational Choice", Administrative Science Quarterly (1972), 17: 1–25
Cook DM, "The Effect of Frequency of Feedback in Attitudes and Performance", Journal of Accounting Research, Selected Studies (1967)
Cyert RM & JG March, A Behavioral Theory of the Firm (Prentice-Hall 1963)
Dearborn DC & HA Simon, "Selective Perception: A Note on the Departmental Identification of Executives", Sociometry (June 1958), 140–144
Deci EL, Intrinsic Motivation (NY Plenum 1975)
DeCoster DT & JP Fertakis, "Budget Induced Pressure and Its Relationship to Supervisory Behavior", Journal of Accounting Research (1968), 237–246
Dermer JD, "Cognitive Characteristics and The Perceived Importance of Information", Accounting Review (July 1973), 511–519
Dessler G, Organization and Management (Prentice-Hall 1976)
Dierkes M & LE Preston, "Corporate Social Accounting—Reporting for The Physical Environment", Accounting, Organizations & Society (1977), 3–22

Dopuch N, JG Birnberg & J Demski, Cost Accounting for Management Decisions (Harcourt, Brace Jovanovich 1974)
Dunbar RLM, "Budgeting for Control", Administrative Science Quarterly (March 1971), 88–96
Dyas GP & HT Thanheiser, The Emerging European Enterprise (MacMillan 1976)
Emery FE, Systems Thinking: Selected Readings (Penguin 1969)
Emery FE & EL Trist, "Socio-Technical Systems", in C West Churchman & M Verhulst (eds), Management Sciences (Pergamon 1960)
Emery FE & EL Trist, "The Causal Texture of Organizational Environments", Human Relations (1965), 18: 21–31
Epstein M et al, "Corporate Social Accounting in the United States", Accounting, Organizations & Society (1976), 23–42
Estes RW, Corporate Social Accounting (Wiley 1976)
Fayol H, General and Industrial Management (Pitman 1949)
Ferris KR, "A Test of the Expectancy Theory of Motivation in an Accounting Environment", Accounting Review (July 1977), 605–615
Filley AC, RJ House & S Kerr, Managerial Process of Organizational Behavior (Scott, Foresman 1976)
Fishbein M, "Attitude and the Prediction of Behavior", in Fishbein (ed), Readings in Attitude Theory and Measurement (Wiley 1967)
Flamholtz EG, "Assessing the Validity of a Theory of Human Resource Accounting", Journal of Accounting Research, Selected Studies (1972)
Flamholtz EG, Human Resource Accounting (Dickinson 1974)
Flamholtz EG, "The Metaphysics of Human Resource Accounting and Its Implications for Managerial Accounting", The Accounting Forum (Dec. 1975)
Flamholtz EG, "The Impact of Human Resource Valuation on Management Decisions", Accounting, Organizations & Society (1976), 153–166
Follett MP, Creative Experience (Longmans, Green 1924)
Forrester JW, Industrial Dynamics (MIT Press 1961)
French J, J Israel & D As, "An Experiment on Participation in a Norwegian Factory", Human Relations (1960)
Frost PJ & RA Mahoney, "Goal Setting and the Task Process", Organizational Behaviour and Human Performance (1976), 17: 328–350
Galbraith JR, "Organizational Design: An Information Processing View", Interfaces (May 1974), 28–36
Golembiewski RT, "Accountancy as a Function of Organizational Theory", Accounting Review (April 1964)
Goodman PS & A Friedman, "An Examination of Adams' Theory of Inequity", Administrative Science Quarterly (September 1971), 271–288
Gordon MJ, "Toward a Theory of Responsibility Accounting Systems", N.A.A. Bulletin (December 1963) 3–9
Gouldner A, Patterns of Industrial Bureaucracy (Free Press 1954)
Graen G, "Instrumentality Theory of Work Motivation", Journal of Applied Psychology Monograph (1969), 53: 1–25
Grojer J-E & A Stark, "Social Accounting: A Swedish Attempt", Accounting, Organizations & Society (1977), 349–386
Grove HD et al, "A Review of the Human Resource Accounting Measurement Systems from a Measurement Theory Perspective", Accounting, Organizations & Society (1977), 219–236
Gulick L & F Urwick, Papers on the Science of Administration (NY: Institute of Public Administration, Columbia University 1937)
Hage J & M Aiken, Social Change in Complex Organizations (Random House 1970)
Hall RH, Organizations' Structure and Process (Prentice-Hall 1977)

Harvey E, "Technology and the Structure of Organizations", American Sociological Review (1968), 33: 247–259
Heflebower RB, "Observations on Decentralization in Large Enterprises", Journal of Industrial Economics (November 1960), 7–22
Heider F, The Psychology of Interpersonal Relations (Wiley 1958)
Hellriegel D & JW Slocum, Management: A Contingency Approach (Addison-Wesley 1979)
Herzberg F et al, The Motivation to Work (Wiley 1959)
Hofstede GH, The Game of Budget Control (Tavistock 1968)
Homans GC, The Human Group (Harcourt Brace Jovanovich 1950)
Hopwood AG, Accounting and Human Behavior (Haymarket Pub. 1974)
Horngren CT, Cost Accounting: A Managerial Emphasis (Prentice-Hall 1977)
House RJ, "A Path Goal Theory of Leader Effectiveness", Administrative Science Quarterly (September 1971), 321–338
Hunt JW, The Restless Organization (Wiley 1972)
Inkson JHK et al, "Organization Context and Structure: An Abbreviated Replication", Administrative Science Quarterly (1970), 318–329
Irvine VB, "Budgeting: Functional Analysis and Behavioral Implications", Cost and Management (March–April 1970), 6–16
Jackson JH & CP Morgan, Organization Theory (Prentice-Hall 1978)
Jones EE & HB Gerard, Foundations of Social Psychology (Wiley 1967)
Kast FE & JE Rosenzweig, Organization and Management (McGraw-Hill 1974)
Katz D & RL Kahn, The Social Psychology of Organizations (Wiley 1966)
Khandwalla PN, The Design of Organizations (Harcourt Brace Jovanovich 1977)
Kinnunen RM, "Hypotheses Related to Strategy Formulation in Large Diversified Companies", Academy of Management Review (1976)
Lawler EE, Motivation in Work Organizations (Brooks/Cole 1973)
Lawler EE & JG Rhode, Information and Control in Organizations (Goodyear 1976)
Lawler EE & JL Suttle, "A Causal Correlation Test of the Need Hierarchy Concept", Organizational Behavior & Human Performance (1972), 265–287
Lawrence P & J Lorsch, Organization and Its Environment (Harvard University Press 1967)
Lewin K, Field Theory in Social Science (Harper 1951)
Lewin K et al, "Level of Aspiration", in J McV Hunt (ed), Personality and the Behavior Disorder (Ronald Press 1974), 333–378
Libby R & BL Lewis, "Human Information Processing Research in Accounting", Accounting, Organizations & Society (1977), 245–268
Likert R, New Patterns of Management (McGraw-Hill 1961)
Lindblom C, "The Science of Muddling Through", Public Administration Review (Spring 1959) 79–88
Locke EA, "Toward a Theory of Task Motivation and Incentives", Organizational Behavior and Human Performance (1968), 3: 157–189
Locke EA, "The Ubiquity of the Technique of Goal Setting in Theories of and Approaches to Employee Motivation", Academy of Management Review (July 1978), 594–601
Lorsch JW, "Introduction to the Structural Design of Organizations", in Lorsch JW & PR Lawrence, Organizational Structure and Design (Irwin 1972)
Lorsch JW & SA Allen, Managing Diversity and Interdependence (Harvard University Graduate School of Business Administration 1973)
Lowe EA & JM McInnes, "Control of Socio-Economic Organizations", Journal of Management Studies (1971) 213–227
March J & HA Simon, Organizations (Wiley 1958)
Maslow A, Motivation and Personality (Harper 1954)

McClelland DC, Personality (Sloan 1951)
McClelland DC, The Achieving Society (Van Nostrand 1961)
McGhee W et al, "The Effects of Personality on a Subject's Information Processing" Accounting Review (July 1978), 681–697
McGregor D, The Human Side of Enterprise (McGraw-Hill 1960)
McNally GM, "Profit Centres and Transfer Prices—Are They Necessary?", Accounting & Business Research (Winter 1973), 13–22
McNally GM, "Responsibility Accounting and Organizational Control", Journal of Business Finance & Accounting (Summer 1980), 165–181
Milani K, "The Relationship of Participation in the Budget Setting Process to Industrial Supervisor Performance" Accounting Review (April 1975), 274–284
Miles RE & RC Vergin, "Behavioral Properties of Variance Controls", California Management Review (Summer 1966) 57–65
Mills T, "Human Resources—Why the New Concern?" Harvard Business Review (March–April 1975) 120–134
Mintzberg H, The Structuring of Organizations: A Synthesis of the Research (Prentice-Hall 1979)
Mitchell TR, "Organizational Behavior", Annual Review of Psychology (1979), 30: 243–281
Murdick RG & JE Ross, Information Systems for Modern Management (Prentice-Hall 1971)
National Association of Accountants, Report of the Committee on Accounting for Corporate Social Performance, Management Accounting (February 1974)
Oldham GR, "Organizational Choice and Some Correlates of Individual Expectancies", Decision Science (October 1976), 873–884
O'Shaughnessy J, Patterns of Business Organization (Allen & Unwin 1976)
Otley DT, "Budget Use and Managerial Performance", Journal of Accounting Research (Spring 1978), 122–149
Parsons T, Structure and Process in Modern Societies (Free Press 1960)
Perrow C, "A Framework for the Comparative Analysis of Organizations", American Sociological Review (1967), 32: 194–208
Perrow C, Organizational Analysis: A Sociological View (Wadsworth 1970)
Peters LH, "Cognitive Models of Motivation, Expectancy Theory and Effort", Organizational Behavior and Human Performance (1977), 20: 129–148
Pick J, "Is Responsibility Accounting Irresponsible?", New York Certified Public Accountant (July 1971), 487–494
Pollard S, The Genesis of Modern Management (Edward Arnold 1965)
Porter LW & EE Lawler, Managerial Attitudes and Performance (Dorsley 1968)
Puett JF & DD Roman, "The Human Resource Asset", Management International Review (1976), 47–60
Pugh DS, Writers on Organizations (Penguin 1971)
Pugh DS et al, "An Empirical Taxonomy of Structures of Work Organization", Administrative Science Quarterly (1969), 116–126
Pugh DS et al, "The Context of Organizational Structures", Administrative Science Quarterly (1969), 91–114
Rumelt RP, Strategy, Structure and Economic Performance (Harvard University, Graduate School of Business Administration, Division of Research 1974)
Salancik GR & J Pfeffer, "An Examination of Need Satisfaction Models of Job Attitudes", Administrative Science Quarterly (Sept. 1977), 427–454
San Miguel JG, "Human Information Processing and Its Relevance to Accounting", Accounting, Organizations & Society (1976), 357–373
Schwan ES, "The Effects of Human Resource Accounting Data on Financial Decisions", Accounting, Organizations & Society (1976), 219–238

Schiff M & AY Lewin, "The Impact of People on Budgets", Accounting Review (April 1970), 259–268
Schiff M & AY Lewin, Behavioral Aspects of Accounting (Prentice-Hall 1974)
Scott WE, "The Effects of Extrinsic Rewards on Intrinsic Motivation", Organizational Behavior and Human Performance (1975), 118
Selznick P, TVA and the Grass Roots (Univ. of California Press 1969)
Silverman D, The Theory of Organizations (Heinemann 1970)
Simon HA et al, Centralization Versus Decentralization in Organizing the Controller's Department (NY Controllership Foundation 1954)
Simon HA, Administrative Behavior (NY Free Press 1957)
Skinner BF, The Behavior of Organisms (Appleton Century Crofts 1938)
Solomons D, Divisional Performance: Measurement and Control (Irwin 1968)
Sorensen JE & DD Franks, "The Relative Contribution of Ability, Self-Esteem and Evaluative Feedback to Performance", Accounting Review (October 1972), 735–746
Stedry AC, Budget Control and Cost Behavior (Prentice-Hall 1960)
Steers RM, Organizational Effectiveness: A Behavioral View (Goodyear 1977)
Steers RM & LW Porter, "The Role of Task-Goal Attributes in Employee Performance", Psychological Bulletin (1974), 434–452
Taylor FW, Principles of Scientific Management (Harper & Row 1911)
Thompson JD, Organizations in Action (McGraw-Hill 1967)
Toffler A, Future Shock (Random House 1970)
Tomkins C, Financial Planning in Divisionalised Companies (Haymarket 1973)
Ullman A, "Corporate Social Reporting in the Federal Republic of Germany", Accounting, Organizations & Society (1979) 123–134
Van Der Bergh RJA & J Fischer, "Human Resource Accounting—Some Problems in Implementation", Accounting, Organizations & Society (1976), 265–270
Vroom VH, Some Personality Determinants of the Effects of Participation (Prentice-Hall 1960)
Vroom VH, Work and Motivation (Wiley 1964)
Wahba MA & RJ House, "Expectancy Theory in Work and Motivation", Human Relations (1974), 121–147
Wanous JP & A Zwany, "A Cross-Sectional Test of Need Hierarchy Theory", Organizational Behavior & Human Performance (1977), 18: 78–97
Watson DJH, Contingency Formulations of Organizational Structure, in Livingstone JL (ed), Managerial Accounting: The Behavioral Foundations (Grid 1975), 65–80
Weber M, The Theory of Social and Economic Organizations, Edited by Talcott Parsons (Oxford University Press 1947)
Woodward J, Industrial Organization (Oxford University Press 1965)
Yukl GA & GP Latham, "Interrelationships Among Employee Participation, Individual Differences, Goal Difficulty, Goal Acceptance, Instrumentality and Performance", Personnel Psychology (1978)
Zaltman G et al, Innovations and Organizations (Wiley 1973)
Zimbardo & Ruch, Psychology and Life (Scott, Foresman 1975)